China from the Opium Wars
to the 1911 Revolution

The Pantheon Asia Library

New Approaches to the New Asia

No part of the world has changed so much in recent years as Asia, or awakened such intense American interest. But much of our scholarship, like much of our public understanding, is based on a previous era. The Asia Library has been launched to provide the needed information on the new Asia, and in so doing to develop both the new methods and the new sympathies needed to understand it. Our purpose is not only to publish new work but to experiment with a wide variety of approaches which will reflect these new realities and their perception by those in Asia and the West.

Our books aim at different levels and audiences, from the popular to the more scholarly, from high schools to the universities, from pictorial to documentary presentations. All books will be available in paperback.

Suggestions for additions to the Asia Library are welcome.

Other Asia Library Titles

China from the Opium Wars to the 1911 Revolution

by Jean Chesneaux, Marianne Bastid, and Marie-Claire Bergère

Translated from the French by Anne Destenay

PANTHEON BOOKS, NEW YORK

First American Edition

English translation Copyright © 1976 by Random House, Inc.

China from the Opium Wars to the 1911 Revolution combines *Des guerres de l'opium à la guerre franco-chinoise, 1840–1885* by Jean Chesneaux and Marianne Bastid and the first three chapters of *De la guerre franco-chinoise à la fondation du parti communiste chinois, 1885–1921* by Jean Chesneaux, Marianne Bastid, and Marie-Claire Bergère. Chapters 1, 2, 3, 4, 6 of the English translation were written by Jean Chesneaux, chapters 5, 7, 8, 9 were written by Marianne Bastid, and chapter 10 by Marie-Claire Bergère. The authors of chapters 1–7 revised them together.

Library of Congress Cataloging in Publication Data

Main entry under title:

China from the Opium Wars to the 1911 Revolution.

(The Pantheon Asia Library)
    Translation of Des guerres de l'opium à la guerre franco-chinoise, 1840–1885, by J. Chesneaux and M. Bastid, v. 1 of Histoire de la Chine; and chapters 1–3 of De la guerre franco-chinoise à la fondation du parti communiste chinois, 1885–1921, by Chesneaux, Bastid, and M.-C. Bergère, v. 2 of the Histoire.
    Includes index.
    1. China—History—19th century. 2. China—History—Revolution, 1911–1912. I. Chesneaux, Jean. II. Bastid, Marianne. III. Bergère, Marie-Claire.
DS757.5.H5713 1976   951'.03   75-38111
ISBN 0–394–49213–7
ISBN 0–394–70934–9 pbk.

Manufactured in the United States of America

Grateful acknowledgment is made to the following for permission to reprint previously published material:

Cornell University Press: Excerpts from Harold Shadick (trans.), *The Travels of Lao Ts'an*, by Liu T'ieh-yun. Copyright © 1952 by Cornell University. Used by permission of Cornell University Press.

Stanford University Press, and George Allen & Unwin Ltd.: Excerpts from pp. 28–31 of *The Opium War Through Chinese Eyes* (from Lin Ze-xu's diary), translated by Arthur Waley, 1958.

Harvard University Press: Excerpts from *China's Response to the West*, translated by Ssu-yu Teng and John K. Fairbank, Cambridge, Harvard University Press. Copyright © 1954 by the President and Fellows of Harvard College. Reprinted by permission of the publishers.

Oxford University Press: Excerpts from pp. 39–41, 72, and 88–89 of *Chinese Sources for the Taiping Rebellion*, by J. C. Cheng. Copyright © 1963 by Oxford University Press.

Contents

Maps

China from the Opium Wars
to the 1911 Revolution

Chapter One

China in 1840: Foundations of Society

Both in area and in population, China around 1840 was the largest country in the world. Its territory extended well beyond the 9 million square kilometers now occupied by the People's Republic of China. During the first third of the nineteenth century, China still possessed land which would soon be taken over by Tsarist Russia: the region lying between the Amur and the Ussuri, yielded to Russia in 1858–1860, and some western territories (the Ili), yielded in 1878. In addition, Outer Mongolia (now the People's Republic of Mongolia) was part of the empire, and so were Tibet, Turkestan, and Inner Mongolia. As for China's population, according to official statistics it had reached 410 million by 1839.

This vast empire was profoundly different from the West, a fact which had already struck travelers like Marco Polo, and which had influenced the thinking of eighteenth-century philosophers such as Voltaire, Diderot, and the physiocratic school. The Chinese themselves were still more conscious of their uniqueness. They expressed it in the names they gave to their country: *Zhongguo* (Middle Kingdom) and *Zhonghua* (Central Civilization).[1]

One of China's remarkable aspects was the continuity of its civ-

---

[1] The transcription of Chinese that will be used in this book is Pinyin, adopted in the People's Republic of China in 1958 and gradually coming into favor among Western scholars. The only exceptions made here are a few proper names such as Peking, Nanking, Sun Yat-sen, and Mao Tsetung.

ilization, which had endured without interruption over several thousand years. Many characteristics of nineteenth-century China can be traced directly to traditions contemporary with the Pharaonic and Babylonian civilizations, which had disappeared centuries ago beneath the desert sands. The long history of Chinese civilization, and the Chinese sense of belonging to a dense historical continuum, make it essential to have an adequate knowledge of imperial China at the moment when the "modern" period began. Historians of the People's Republic of China define the eighty-odd years from the first Opium War (1840) to the May Fourth movement and the founding of the Chinese Communist Party (1919–1921) as the modern period, or *jindai*. (The contemporary period, or *xiandai*, begins at the second date.) The chief characteristic of the modern period was the injection of foreign elements into the body of Chinese society and into the "historical whole" that was China.

Principles of the Chinese Political System

The traditional political system was founded on a set of highly coherent philosophical and moral concepts formulated gradually over the centuries. For simplicity they are commonly referred to as Confucianism. This term, however, should not be considered synonymous with the personal contribution of Confucius himself, a minister of the kingdom of Lu who lived during the Warring States era in the fifth century B.C.

A unitary conception of nature and society

The Chinese conceptual system (termed "organic materialism" by Joseph Needham) was one in which the worlds of nature and of man formed an integrated whole governed by identical laws. The sense of cosmological unity was expressed in a system of complex correlations—for example, between the five elements (wood, fire, earth, metal, water), the points of the compass (north, south, east, and west, together with the center itself), colors, virtues, and flavors. It was also reflected in a taste for gardens, since miniatures are microcosmic projections of the macrocosm, and in the Chinese respect for geomancy or *fengshui* (rules of wind and water), since the human dwelling had to harmonize with the natural setting in accordance with clearly defined rules. The failure of Westerners, and particularly missionaries, to observe these rules bred endless conflict.

The essence of the Chinese view of the world was to be found in the relations between things, not in their individual being. Man himself was defined by the "five relationships" (*wu lun*)—between emperor and subject, father and son, husband and wife, elder brother and younger brother, friend and friend. These relationships embodied moral obligations which the individual was bound to assume, whatever his station in life.

The same organic approach was expressed in a reverence for calligraphy, because the Chinese made no distinction between the political value of a text and its graphic form. This approach is also seen in the importance given to a process called the "rectification of names" (*zheng ming*). The choice of a word is considered a matter of substance, not of form, and applying the appropriate term is the sign of harmony between a social element and its general context. In 1860 an international treaty was necessary before the Chinese would agree to stop putting Westerners into the political category of "barbarians" (*yi*). In 1967 China stopped opposing Soviet arms shipments to Vietnam after the Russian government had agreed to call them "Vietnamese arms" as soon as they crossed the Russian frontier.

Yin and *yang*

The Chinese conception of the world was neither monist nor creationist. It assumed that every phenomenon, whether natural or social, has two opposite, complimentary aspects. These are the *yin* and the *yang* (female and male, winter and summer, night and day, moon and sun, passive and active, for example), whose alternate and reciprocal action gives the world its movement—the *dao*, the "way." It has been suggested that the elementary dialectic of *yin* and *yang*, and the ancient sense of contradiction they express, provided favorable conceptual ground for Marxism.

The world—social and natural reality—is therefore neither immobile nor immutable. Things have their own dynamism; every situation evolves, and a person has to know how to wait for the favorable moment. This is the doctrine of *wu wei* (minimizing of action upon other things), which is sometimes poorly translated as "doing nothing." Actually *wu wei* is not a process of remaining passive but of refraining from distorting the natural course of events by clumsy or premature intervention. The Chinese style of politics has always been heavily influenced by the principle of *wu wei*. The same sense of interdependence among elements of a whole that are in motion is found in the Chinese preference for "action from a distance." Historians like Joseph Needham have pointed out that long before Europeans were capable of it, the Chinese arrived at the lunar theory of the origin of tides and the wave theory of light. The principle also governed social affairs; a good sovereign did not need to take direct action to make his country prosperous.

The Mandate of Heaven

All these moral and philosophical concepts were united in the definition of imperial power. The emperor, the Son of Heaven, was the mediator between nature and human society through the authority given him by the Mandate of Heaven (*tianming*). In the character *wang*, or king, which was the ancient title of Chinese sovereigns before the unification of the empire, a vertical stroke leaves heaven to join earth, cutting through man (the smallest of the three horizontal strokes) on the way and imprisoning him in his condition. In his role as mediator the emperor ritually plowed the first furrow in spring as a propitiatory gesture toward the biological forces of the world. The calendar was an affair of state for which the emperor was responsible; his reign provided the basis on which the years were calculated. The emperor was set apart from other human beings by a series of taboos: for example, it was forbidden to write certain characters designating his person.

The Mandate of Heaven was not irrevocable, however. Various omens indicated that it was being withdrawn—omens that were recognized as "signs preceding the fall of dynasties." Characteristically, they belonged simultaneously to the natural and social orders. They included celestial portents and meteors, droughts and floods, social agitation in the hinterlands, incompetence on the part of the mandarins, and corruption in the sovereign's entourage extending even to the sovereign himself.

Thus at a certain point, revolt was legitimate and beneficial to society. *Geming*, "discontinuance of the Mandate," was a traditional Confucian term that has been adopted by modern political movements to mean "revolution," which it does not. *Geming* aimed at restoring social order and reintegrating it with the cosmic order.

The leader of a rebellion often renewed the Mandate of Heaven in his own name, thereby becoming the head of a new dynasty (as in the cases of the Tang dynasty in the seventh century and the Ming dynasty in the fourteenth). As a result the Chinese political tradition was able to accommodate popular revolts. It incorporated them into the Confucian ideological system so that, paradoxically, they contributed to the long-term stability of the established order —the traditional "historical whole." This flexible political philosophy also allowed to a tottering dynasty the possibility of "restoring" itself (*zhongxing*), as the advisers of the Tongzhi Emperor did for the Qing dynasty in 1870.

Public office

From the philosophical foundations of Confucianism came a morally based approach to the duties of public office. A good civil servant followed the principle of *wu wei*; he abstained as much as possible from direct action, for his role was to supervise the natural workings of society. It was essential for him to have a thorough knowledge of good and evil, a good character, and the ability to draw inspiration from the experience of the past. The imperial examinations for civil servants, or mandarins, were based on knowledge of the Chinese classical tradition, not of contemporary government work. Civil servants were regarded not as specialists but as learned men who could be assigned different tasks by turns with no special technical preparation.

Public office was an extension of the imperial office. Like the emperor, the civil servant shared in the Mandate of Heaven—the responsibility to maintain order and harmony in the world. A mandarin had absolute authority over his staff and over all people in the territory he administered. But anyone who considered himself wronged by a civil servant had the right to take his grievance even up to the throne, for it was essential to restore the balance of society if an erring public official had disturbed it.

The mandarins reported to the sovereign through "memoirs addressed to the throne," which were sent to him with highly complicated rites and procedures. If the mandarins thought it necessary, they could draw his attention to problems and recommend courses of action. (The duty to give advice—"pure opinion," *qingyi*)—was adopted as a slogan in 1880 by a political faction in Peking.) The emperor could also decide to consult the mandarins, or at least the most prominent of them, on pressing questions. He did this by opening a "debate"—for example, the famous debate on government control of salt and iron under the Han dynasty in the first century B.C., and the debate on opium legislation around 1835.

The moral nature of civil service was particularly apparent in the case of the imperial censors, who might be described as impartial government investigators. Some of them were posted in Peking to supervise the various ministries; the others toured the provinces. In theory, at least, they were entirely independent, and their powers were discretionary; but they themselves could not enforce the law.

Generally speaking, power and knowledge were so closely linked that the civil service and literary culture were inseparable. The Western idea of the intellectual as a thinker remote from political responsibilities was foreign to the Chinese tradition; the few intellectuals who did avoid public service were regarded with disapproval. Because of the long-standing association of knowledge and power, many Chinese intellectuals became involved as a matter of course in the revolutionary movements of the twentieth century. After 1949, the authorities of the People's Republic of China were faced with awkward problems when the Chinese intellectuals still considered it normal to occupy a "special position" in public affairs.

Law and the penal system

Consistent with the Chinese conception of the organization of society, law was not an absolute principle but a practical arrangement rooted in concrete situations. The code of the Manchu dynasty was a collection of penal provisions illustrated by specific cases. Above all, it referred to offenses against public order and the imperial authority. Private law was merely a "formulation of morality," in the words of J. Escarra.

Each time a difference, whether civil or criminal, arose between private individuals, the question was how to restore social harmony, not how to sort out the abstract rights and wrongs of the case. The judge was an arbitrator, and the aim of the sentence was to propose a reasonable compromise acceptable to both parties. The penalties were more like social rites than individual punishments. The death penalty, for example, had several gradations according to the method by which the condemned was put to death. One degree less serious than the death penalty was exile, which could be for a certain period or for life. Perpetual exile, since it canceled a person's right to be buried on his ancestors' land, meant that his spirit after death was also condemned to exile.[2] Generally speaking, the Chinese penal system and penal procedures were organized to promote the social good, not individual rights. Torture, even of a suspect's family, was the accepted practice.

The custom-oriented, practical nature of the law was also apparent in the fact that no separate court system existed. Civil officials administered justice as one of their many functions. They intervened as seldom as possible, and a great deal of litigation was settled by village, clan, and guild authorities. Private individuals could bring suit at any time in criminal or civil matters.

The Chinese legal system was highly original and almost totally incomprehensible to the Westerners who settled in the "treaty ports" after the Opium Wars. As described in Chapter 3, they quickly assumed the privilege of extraterritoriality, which put them outside the reach of Chinese justice.

Foreign relations

Like the Chinese approach to law and to public office, relations with other countries were a logical outgrowth of China's political and philosophical system. The Chinese believed that the world is square, that heaven is round, and that heaven projects its circular shadow onto the center of the earth. This circle, the "zone beneath heaven" (*tianxia*), is the Chinese empire itself. The outer pieces formed by the four angles of the square (called the "four seas") do not receive the celestial emanations, and they have therefore become the domain of foreign barbarians (*yi*), demons, and sea monsters.

Clearly, the leaders of barbarians cannot enter on an equal footing into relations with the emperor, the Son of Heaven. In fact the very idea of foreign relations is meaningless. Thus as a matter of principle China had no foreign ministry, and "barbarian affairs" were handled by local officials. In compliance with the doctrines of indirect action and economy of means, these officials generally tried to "use one barbarian to control another barbarian," avoiding direct action themselves as much as possible. The relations which grew up between China and its neighbors were necessarily relations

[2] See the scale of punishments and crimes in the Qing dynasty, given in document 1 at the end of the chapter.

of inequality, symbolized by the tribute that other countries sent to Peking in exchange for China's guarantee of protection.

The sense of the past

China, pre-eminently an agricultural civilization, had been molded by the unchangeable course of the seasons and the immemorial calendar of agricultural work. Time was a closed dimension whose terms of reference lay always in the past. The criteria for moral conduct and political action were determined in relation to past experience alone.

The necessity for having a thorough knowledge of the past explains the importance of the Confucian and pre-Confucian canonical works, particularly the Five Classics (*Classic of Songs, Classic of Documents, Classic of Changes, Spring and Autumn Annals, Record of Rituals*) and the Four Books (*Analects, Mencius, The Great Learning, The Doctrine of the Mean*). It also explains the importance of history. Writing history was a political act that made the achievements of a dynasty available to future generations. One of the first duties of a new dynasty, together with repairing dikes and canals and revising the calendar, was to appoint a committee of official historians. The strongly cumulative nature of Chinese culture was further reinforced by the early adoption of the printing press.

Commentaries and encyclopedias were among the favorite literary forms of Chinese scholars. One of their greatest accomplishments, *The Complete Library of the Four Treasuries*, took twenty years (1773–1793) to compile and consisted of over 36,000 volumes. Seven manuscript sets existed.

Except in a few unorthodox systems of Chinese thought, the national sense of the past excluded any notion of progress. History was regarded as cyclic; each dynasty went through successive phases of ascension, apogee, and decline, at which stage rebellion became legitimate. The same cycle began again with the next dynasty.

Education and morality

The education of the individual man was considered extremely important. According to the teachings of the philosopher Mencius, man is naturally good; therefore he has the ability to respect the harmony of the world and adjust himself to his position in life. The Chinese education was designed to initiate man into his moral duties, which were to observe the proper rites, to submit to the established order, to respect political, social, and family authorities, and to accept the inequality that is the human condition.[3] The five relationships—between emperor and subject, father and son, husband and wife, elder brother and younger brother, friend and friend—had to be observed. So did others that were derived from these five: for example, the relationships between scholar and disciple and between artisan and apprentice. The essential Confucian virtues were filial piety, moral integrity, frugality, deference, self-control, loyalty to superiors, and kindness to inferiors.

This moral code was regarded as a universal one: it was founded on general philosophical considerations and not on an ethnocentric consciousness. Even barbarians could be educated, and it was the responsibility of the imperial authorities to extend the influence of civilization and its beneficial effects. This was, in fact, the substance of the Sinicizing process applied to the peoples of South China through the centuries. The duty to educate barbarians led to the concept of "tributary" countries. It also generated friction with Westerners when they began to cluster on the coasts of China.

Confucianism (a conventional term, it must be remembered) was a political and moral system, not a religion in the formal sense. It ignored the distinctions between natural and supernatural, human and divine, lay and ecclesiastic. It vaguely acknowledged a supreme being, "heaven," and the "lord on high," thereby creating complex problems for Western missionaries trying to formulate a theological vocabulary in Chinese. On various feast days of the calendar, the Confucian rites were celebrated by the emperor and the complete hierarchy of mandarins. In the seventeenth century these rites were much discussed by Western theologians during the "rites controversy" between Jesuits and Dominicans. The Confucian ceremonies, however, were acts of civil prestige, not true religious rituals. The old saying about the "three religions" in China (Confucianism, Taoism, and Buddhism) does not correspond to reality, for it bundles together a philosophical-political system, a set of esoteric and mystical individual practices, and a religion in the strict meaning of the term.

[3] The Kangxi Emperor's edict on political loyalty and social harmony is given in document 2 at the end of the chapter.

Taoism, Buddhism, and Islam

Taoism, one of the main currents of thought in ancient China, developed over the centuries into a collection of practices and recipes enabling men to identify with the universal principle (*dao*). By following various biological taboos, breathing techniques, laxative measures, and magic rites, a person could increase his energies and attain a natural state aspiring toward immortality. The Taoist claim that it could feed the individual's "vital principle" accounts for the success of the cult with the common people, who were always seeking an escape from their misery. Taoist priests were an influential social group among the lower classes and often became leaders of peasant revolts. Although they had prestige, they did not form a distinct clerical body with a formal structure.

On the other hand, Buddhism, which came from India at the beginning of the Christian era, was a formal religion founded on a church, scriptures, and a highly elaborated conception of the supernatural. In the early nineteenth century it was no longer as widespread in China as it had been under the Tang. Many Buddhist monastic communities of men and women still existed, but there were few orthodox Buddhists among the mass of the people. The religious themes of Buddhism survived in a diffuse way: in the sense of destiny (*karma*) and of renunciation, in the belief in the millennium and the coming of a messiah (*maitreya*), and in the theological vision of cosmic cycles, or *kalpa*. Buddhist divinities were included in the pantheon of the popular religion which, in the nineteenth century, was no doubt the only really living form of religious activity in China. Peasant cults, family cults with altars to the ancestors, and cults based on clan or guild divinities all combined Buddhist and Taoist elements in a syncretic mixture.

In addition, Islam still had a strong foothold in Southwest China. It was particularly well established in Yunnan (where it had spread during the Chinese Middle Age[4] from the Arab settlements in Canton), and in Shenxi, the Gansu corridor, and Turkestan (in other words, at the end of the Silk Road). By the nineteenth century Mohammedanism in China had lost some of its social identity through contact with Chinese institutions—especially with Chinese conceptions of law and of the family. But it retained its religious

---

[4] The Middle Age denotes the period following A.D. 200, when the empire was divided after the fall of the Han dynasty. It ended in the seventh century with the accession of the T'ang dynasty.

identity; Chinese Mohammedans read the Koran and made pilgrimages to Mecca as all Mohammedans did.

Organization of the State

Ministries and provinces

The Chinese bureaucratic machine was intricately wrought, fashioned by centuries of experience. Ideally the emperor governed in person, assisted by the Grand Secretariat (*Neige*) and the Grand Council (*Junjichu*). The dividing line between the powers allotted to the two bodies was not entirely clear. In general, the Council was responsible for drawing up general policy and preparing the texts of imperial edicts. The Secretariat coordinated the activities of the civil service, which was divided into six ministries.

Of these, the Ministry of Civil Affairs had charge of China's 40,000-odd mandarins, beginning with their examinations and continuing through their careers. The mandarins were divided into nine ranks, and each rank had two grades. The Ministry of Revenue was responsible for finance and for keeping records on land and population. The Ministry of Rites arranged state ceremonial sacrifices, court banquets, and music for state occasions. The Ministry of War ran the army, the navy, and the postal service. The Ministry of Punishments drew up legal codes and reviewed appeals. Lastly, the powerful Ministry of Public Works was responsible for imperial buildings and temples, imperial factories (which produced both civilian and military goods), the currency, and the upkeep of roads and dikes. Each ministry, as well as the Grand Council and Grand Secretariat, was under the control of a committee of senior officials.

The Ministry of Rites was also responsible for relations with the tributary countries which had become part of the Chinese world over the centuries. Some, like Vietnam and Korea, had adopted the Chinese ideographic script. Others, like the Ryukyu Islands, the Sulu Archipelago, Burma, Laos, Siam, and Nepal, were linked economically and politically with China. At varying intervals they all sent missions to Peking bearing tribute (Korea every year, Vietnam every three years, the others every ten years). Some missions came overland, some by way of the ports of Guangdong and Fujian.

Besides these "dependencies" inhabited by different peoples, the empire was divided into eighteen provinces which made up China proper. Each province was under the authority of a governor, except for Zhili, which was managed by the central government. Provinces were often grouped in clusters of two or three and administered by a governor-general. For example, Hubei and Hunan formed *Lianghu* (the Two Hu), also known as *Huguang*; Guangdong and Guangxi formed *Liangguang* (the Two Guang); Jiangsu, Jiangxi, and Anhui formed *Liangjiang* (the Two Jiang). Sharing jurisdiction with the governor of each province were special branches dealing with finance, justice, and so on. But in the local divisions—prefectures (*fu*), departments (*zhou*), and districts (*xian*)—the magistrate had total responsibility.

The examinations

Mandarins were recruited by a complicated system of competitive literary examinations which took place at the local level, at the provincial capitals, and at the capital annually or every three years, depending on the level. Successful examinations at the lower levels obtained the "bachelor" or "licentiate" degree; at higher levels a man could become a metropolitan graduate, or a member of the Hanlin Academy, the summit of the literary hierarchy. Although the examinations gave access to the different ranks of the mandarinate and the public service, not all scholars became officials. Many stayed in their country houses, leading an influential life of semileisure. Around 1840 there were about a million holders of degrees—twenty-five times the number of civil servants.

The examinations dealt with literary subjects (which included history, philology, and ethics). True to the Confucian conception of public office, they did not mention administrative responsibilities. They were highly formal, particularly the famous "eight-legged essay," which young modernist intellectuals in the twentieth century used as the symbol of a scholastic, arid culture.

The Confucian ranks (and consequently the access to public office) could also be bought, by means of special quotas allocated each year. Most of the purchasers were merchants eager for a place within the conventional channel of social advancement. In this way the social dynamism of Chinese business circles was absorbed by the established order.

In theory the examinations were open to all, and there are exam-

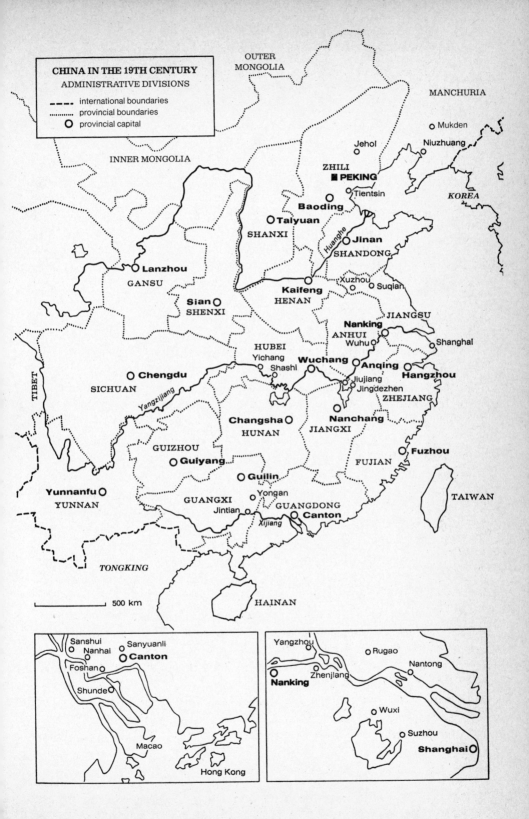

CHINA IN THE 19TH CENTURY
ADMINISTRATIVE DIVISIONS

- - - international boundaries
· · · provincial boundaries
○ provincial capital

OUTER MONGOLIA

MANCHURIA

INNER MONGOLIA

○ Mukden

Jehol ○

○ Niuzhuang

ZHILI
■ PEKING

KOREA

○ Baoding
○ Tientsin

○ Taiyuan

SHANXI

Huanghe

○ Jinan

SHANDONG

○ Lanzhou

GANSU

○ Sian
SHENXI

Kaifeng ○

HENAN

Xuzhou ○

○ Suqian

JIANGSU

Nanking ○

ANHUI
Wuhu ○

○ Shanghai

HUBEI
Yichang

○ Chengdu

SICHUAN

Shashi ○

Wuchang ○

○ Anqing

○ Hangzhou

Jiujiang ○
Jingdezhen ○

ZHEJIANG

Yangzijiang

TIBET

Changsha ○

HUNAN

Nanchang ○

JIANGXI

GUIZHOU

○ Guiyang

○ Fuzhou

FUJIAN

○ Guilin

GUANGXI

Yongan ○

Jintian ○

GUANGDONG
○ Canton

Xijiang

TAIWAN

○ Yunnanfu
YUNNAN

TONGKING

500 km

HAINAN

Sanshui ○
Nanhai ○

○ Sanyuanli

○ Canton

Foshan ○

Shunde ○

Macao

Hong Kong

Yangzhou ○

○ Rugao

○ Nantong

Zhenjiang ○

Nanking ○

○ Wuxi

○ Suzhou

Shanghai ○

ples of peasants who achieved the highest honors. Social mobility in classical China should not be exaggerated, however. Long years of study were required, and it was rare that a poor family could support one of its members for this period, even in the hope of profiting later from the high position he might gain. Moreover, the son of a well-to-do family had influential friends who could help him rise, or he could simply bribe the examiners. An ironical account of these abuses is given in *Ru Lin Wai Shi* (*The Scholars*), one of the great Chinese novels of the eighteenth century. The ideal of equal opportunity for all was more or less an illusion. The ruling class used the examinations to perpetuate itself and to consolidate its power by assimilating the most able people from the other classes.

Administrative practices

In theory, the Chinese administrative system was flexible, stable, and balanced in its distribution of power. All officials were appointed by the central government. They could not hold the same job for more than three years, and they could not be assigned to their native provinces. As a further deterrent to continuity of power, they had to observe three years' mourning on the death of a close relation. The distribution of tasks was ingenious and complicated, with an elaborate system of checks and balances for allocating responsibility. The provincial and local authorities were closely supervised by the imperial censors, but at the same time had considerable autonomy and retained a generous share of the taxes collected.

By its nature, however, this system engendered a tendency to irresponsibility, indifference, and procrastination. The good civil servant was often the one who "kept out of trouble." Fraud was common; so were inflated reports exaggerating local difficulties and overstating an official's need for troops and money. The mandarins' salaries were very low, and it was accepted practice for them to "live off the land" and off "presents" from officials below them in the hierarchy. In spite of all precautions, intrigue played a large part in the government. Private cliques based on family connections, school friendships, and provincial solidarity proliferated both at court and in the provinces. The mandarins, whose official title meant "father and mother of the people," were disliked and feared.

Local administration

The formal machinery of the local mandarin administration was slight. China contained about 1,500 districts, and each district official was responsible for a population of several hundred thousand. The only way to carry out his duties was to delegate authority to a large staff of clerks, private secretaries, messengers, and servants. As a rule the staff was thoroughly competent, particularly because the rule forbidding officials to work in their native province did not apply to staff assistants. But no matter how well they performed, they were considered social inferiors. They did not belong to the ruling class, and they vented their resentment by taking bribes and bullying the public.

The local seat of administration, the *yamen*, contained offices, the law court, the private residences of the mandarin and his assistants, the prison, the stores of grain and money, and the weapons of the village police force (*baojia*), which was recruited from the peasants. The *yamen* was the symbol and the nerve center of state power. It was the focus of attack during peasant rebellions and later during the revolutionary fighting.

The local mandarin could not govern without the cooperation of the local scholar-officials—the holders of Confucian ranks who lived in his area. They gave him voluntary help (which they made very profitable for themselves) with tax collecting, making arrangements for forced labor, constructing public works, organizing mass relief in times of famine, and holding "indoctrination meetings," at which they expounded the sacred edict of the Kangxi Emperor (document 2) to remind the peasants of their duties.

Finance and the tax system

Government finance reflected two main characteristics of Chinese national life: the diffuse administrative organization and the agricultural base of the economy. The principal tax was a land tax—the "single whip" tax, levied partly on individuals and partly on land according to a complicated system. It brought in three-quarters of the central government's revenue: 30 million taels (a unit of silver) out of 40 million. Added to this was the grain tribute (sometimes payable in cash) levied on the lower Yangzi rice-growing provinces in order to feed the court, the imperial clan, and the officials and troops living in the capital. Revenue in much smaller

3) Customs +
salt tax

amounts also came from the customs and from the salt tax (4 million and 6 million taels, respectively).

The land tax was subject to all sorts of abuses. In theory the rate had been determined at the beginning of the eighteenth century on the basis of a fixed price in silver for a bushel of rice. Thus a tax due in kind could be paid in cash—a sign of the evolution of a monetary economy. But by the nineteenth century the "substitution rate" fluctuated so much that the agents of the *yamen* often manipulated it as they pleased. Similar oscillations in the conversion rate between copper cash and silver also made it easy to cheat the peasants.

Tax collectors had countless other methods of extracting "presents" from the peasants and levying surtaxes (for such items as inspection costs, transportation expenses, the cost of torches, the cost of notices, and upkeep expenses for horses). They avoided levying taxes directly; in each group of ten families (*jia*) a collector appointed someone (a *jiazhang*) to see that the tax was paid on time. The *jiazhang* was punished in case of delay or default. Rich families were given more favorable terms (say, in the substitution rate, or through exemptions), depending on how influential they were.

It was reckoned that the total amount handed over to the central government represented only one-third to one-fifth of the sum paid by taxpayers. The rest was absorbed for provincial or local public budgets—and as private profits by the officials and their assistants. For the central government of a country as large as China, 40 million taels was a meager budget. In the nineteenth century the severe indemnities exacted from China by foreign powers (5 million taels after the first Opium War, 200 million after the Sino-Japanese War of 1894–1895, and 450 million after the Boxer Rising) threw Chinese public finances severely out of balance.

The army

like so much
removed from
land in
70k.

On one hand, Chinese military forces were composed of tribal units—the Manchu Banners, who had conquered China in the seventeenth century, and their allies the Mongolian Banners. With the possible exception of the Mongolian cavalry, these units had lost all fighting spirit by the nineteenth century.

On the other hand, there was the regular Chinese army, called the Army of the Green Standard. This body showed the same weaknesses as the rest of the machinery of state. The troops were scattered around the country in tiny units, since the main concern of the authorities was to avoid concentrations of military power. Whenever it was necessary to assemble a fighting force (say, to deal with peasant revolts), troops of very different localities were brought together. Inevitably their commanders were jealous of each other, and the units worked badly together. In general the army officers neglected discipline, allowed the soldiers to maraud, and grew rich by sending in false duty sheets. The army was completely unprepared to meet the wars and rebellions which occurred in the middle of the century.

The Sino-Manchu duality

Since the seventeenth century China had been ruled by the Manchu Qing dynasty, which had taken advantage of internal disturbances to overthrow the Ming. The government was thus a combination of Manchu and Chinese elements, though the conquerors seem to have been integrated to some extent into the Chinese political and ideological system. The Qing governed according to the same rules as the preceding dynasties, the imperial power was founded on the same principles, and the Confucian examinations were based on the same classical texts.

Manchu had become the second official language in Peking, however, along with classical Chinese. This necessitated an elaborate system of oral and written translations, made especially difficult because written Manchu used a semi-alphabetic system instead of Chinese ideograms. Manchu dignitaries and nobles belonging to the imperial clan were in the majority at court, and Manchus outnumbered Chinese proportionately in the leading state offices. It was easier for a Manchu to gain promotion, even though there were rules providing for an equal distribution of government posts among Manchus and Chinese. The privileged position enjoyed by the Manchus was also reflected in the fact that Manchuria, the cradle of the Qing dynasty, was closed to Chinese peasants, who would otherwise have flocked to farm its rich uncultivated land.

Manchu domination was felt throughout China. Manchu garrisons were stationed in the citadels of the chief towns. Every Manchu, whether he was an aristocrat or a plain soldier, was fed free of charge from an annual quota of rice. The privileges that enabled these people to lead a semiparasitic life irritated the Chinese. They were also bitter that the Qing made them wear the queue as a humiliating token of their dependence. Anti-Manchu national feeling was pervasive.

Ethnic minorities

The Manchus were not the only people in China who had ethnic backgrounds different from the Chinese. A fundamental distinction was made between the Chinese in the ethnic sense of the word, the Han (so called after the great dynasty at the beginning of the Christian era) and the other "Chinese" (*zhongguo ren*) who inhabited the empire. Some of the *zhongguo ren* lived in the eighteen provinces of China proper: the Zhuang of Guangxi, the Yi or "Lolos" (a scornful term) of Sichuan, the Miao of Guizhou, and the Dungans (or Hui) of Gansu. Such groups often retained their tribal chiefs and chiefdoms under the authority of the local officials.

Larger groups of *zhongguo ren* lived in the border regions and dependencies: Mongols in Inner and Outer Mongolia, Uighur Turks to the west, and Tibetans. These peoples retained their social and political institutions, and Chinese government control over them was fairly remote. The cultural distinctiveness of the Uighurs and the Hui was reinforced by their Moslem faith, and that of the Tibetans by their closed Lamaist theocracy. In contrast, relations between Manchus and Mongols were close, particularly between the aristocracies.

Social Hierarchies

The basic hierarchy of Chinese society consisted of the four occupational orders which reflected the political and moral values of Confucianism. Highest of all were the scholars (*shi*); next came the peasants (*nong*), then the artisans (*gong*), and last the merchants (*shang*). Excluded from the four orders were people in some occupations regarded as infamous: actors, prostitutes, servants, soldiers, *yamen* messengers, vagrants, and all sorts of down-and-outers.

The four orders were rounded out by intermediate structures, each with its own hierarchy, and every individual fitted snugly into an appointed place. The guild had its patrons, members, and apprentices, the village its local hierarchy, and the family its complex network of relationships based on authority.

Scholar-officials

The scholar-officials are sometimes called "gentry," although the term is misleading because of its connection with eighteenth-century England. They were the ruling class in the full sense of the term; they possessed power, knowledge, and land.

In practice, individual members of the gentry did not hold all three of these resources, or possess them in equal quantities. There were some educated people who failed the Confucian examinations and others who, in a spirit of independence, refused to take them. Moreover, only a small fraction of the gentry directly assumed po-litical duties. As for ownership of land, the relations between this asset and membership in the ruling class were complex. Land was the main source of economic power in ancient China. It was gener-ally possessed by men who held Confucian degrees and occupied public office—although there were landowners with no degrees, as well as impoverished scholars. But membership in the gentry of-fered many chances to grow rich. One was the opportunity to buy land; social status was as much the source as the result of land ownership. Although customs of inheritance, in which a man's land was generally divided among his children, tended to disperse landed fortunes, the children of a rich man were likely to become scholars or officials in their turn and to build up fortunes like their father's.

The situation of the ruling class was no doubt the result of an ancient "Asiatic" tradition in which economic power was conferred by office. (In contrast, political power in the Western feudal system was the reflection, not the foundation, of economic power.) Basi-cally, however, the scholar-official class was defined by all three aspects of its position—political, economic, and educational.

The members of the gentry enjoyed a large number of legal privileges. They were entitled to special treatment in the courts, and if they were found guilty of a crime, their punishment was lighter than the statutory penalty. They were entitled to wear honorific insignia and were admitted to official ceremonies from which the other orders were excluded. They were exempt from forced labor, because manual work would be unworthy of their learning.

Besides their official privileges, the gentry had many prerogatives granted by custom. They were allowed extra time to pay their taxes.

They could approach the local official directly, which meant that they could obtain special treatment for a petitioner, a taxpayer, or a lawbreaker. They had the immense power of access to the written culture—a power which is relatively exclusive in the case of Chinese script, composed as it is of tens of thousands of ideograms.

As already mentioned, the ruling class did many unpaid chores for society. Scholar-officials supervised public works, particularly irrigation projects, helped compile local encyclopedias, organized schools or taught in them, sponsored local academies, founded and endowed hospitals, orphanages, and other charitable institutions, and acted as unofficial arbitrators in disputes that people wished to settle out of court. This public service was an outward expression of the fact that the gentry were concerned with maintaining order— that it was in the interest of the ruling class to avoid crises. For the same reason the gentry worked with the local mandarin, giving talks to the peasants about their obligations to the state, helping the tax collectors, and organizing the militia in times of trouble. As required by law, the local mandarin came from outside the province and thus could not run the administrative machine without the support and advice of the local gentry. Even when the gentry went over his head to protest an abuse, it was a gesture arising from the basic solidarity uniting members of the ruling class.

Peasants

Agriculture had a privileged position in the Confucian economic ethic, and peasants came second in the hierarchy of the four orders. Yet Chinese peasants were basically in a state of dependence, whether they rented their farms or owned them. There were many tenant farmers in regions such as Guangdong or the lower Yangzi valley. They rented land at what was often a very high rate—sometimes fixed, sometimes variable—and paid in cash, produce, or some combination. Tenant farmers were also liable to many kinds of customary duties and forced labor. Peasants who worked their own land were probably in the majority, but they were not much better off than the tenants. They were in the power of the "big houses"—the wealthy landowners who acted as moneylenders. These landowners, who were gentry or near-gentry, stayed on the best of terms with the local mandarin. Peasants, whether they were tenants or farm owners, had to reckon with the landowners' influence with tax collectors, courts, and police.

Not enough research has been done to specify the exact connection between the scholar-officials as a statutory group and the landowners as a class founded on landholding. What is certain is that it was a feudal situation: the mass of the peasants were under the domination, both economic and extra-economic, of a minority. Joseph Needham has suggested the term "bureaucratic feudalism" to emphasize the unique combination of economic and political power.

More research is also needed to trace the links between these feudal relationships and the remains of the ancient village structures. The villages, under the leadership of "elders," were still strong units bound together by venerable customs. They had their temples, they cooperated in community projects (roads and dikes, for example), and they maintained their militia, whose ambivalent role has been highly significant in the modern political history of China. Sometimes the village militia was used by the central government (during the repression of the Taiping movement, for instance), and sometimes by peasant movements (for example, by the Nian). The militia also took part in the Boxer movement.

There was another large stratum in rural society made up of day laborers, the down-and-out, vagrants, and vagabonds (the last of whom included itinerant workers such as boatmen, peddlers, and porters). The entire group played a substantial role in secret societies and popular risings.

Artisans

The town-dwelling artisans, the third order of society, were organized into guilds which controlled production and marketing in each professional sector: weaving, shoemaking, bamboo handicrafts, goldworking, and so on. The guilds were also mutual insurance societies, religious fraternities, and unofficial arbitrators in trade disputes. Each guild had a patron saint or legendary founder, usually a divinity from the Taoist pantheon, whose annual feast day it celebrated.

Not all handicraft work was performed in towns under the supervision of guilds. Rural manufacturers, which provided work on the farms during the off-season, were an important part of each village economy.

Merchants

Manufacturing and trade were lively and profitable during this period, in spite of the fact that merchants were given the lowest position on the Confucian social scale. Essentially the inferior status assigned to them represented the defensive reaction of an agricultural society against economic forces that were threatening its equilibrium. (For the same reason Saint Thomas Aquinas condemned the charging of interest on loans as a mortal sin.) Chinese society accommodated its wealthy merchants by the back door, however, through the special quotas that enabled them to buy Confucian degrees. In this way they could bring their social status into harmony with their economic power.

Like the artisans, merchants had their guilds. Some were professional groups (such as the tea and silk guilds), though most were regional associations. Under the auspices of the regional guilds, merchants from the same town or the same locality could find backing, information, and many other kinds of help wherever they traveled in China.

Families and clans

The highly structured nature of the family hierarchy was seen in the precise and detailed kinship system. The Chinese vocabulary expressed all the nuances of family relationships. There were different terms for a paternal or a maternal uncle, for a first, second, or third cousin, for an elder or younger brother, for brothers-in-law on the husband's or wife's side. Ideally, five generations lived under the same roof in the extended family, and the authority of the oldest members was uncontested. The head of the family punished his children and grandchildren as he saw fit. He had a right to absolute obedience from them, and the family estate was under his exclusive control.

The position of any woman in the family was inferior to that of the newest male infant. The custom of foot binding was a symbol of the woman's complete submission. Marriages were arranged by professional intermediaries; the couple themselves were not consulted, and the young wife was abandoned, sometimes when she was still a child, to the bad temper of her mother-in-law. A husband was free to keep several concubines under his roof (the "second," "third," etc., wives), while a wife's adultery was severely punished.

It was essential for the head of the family to beget a male heir in order to perpetuate the cult of the ancestors and thereby ensure continuity with the past.

The family structure was based on authority; indeed, inequality among people was built into the general conceptions of Confucianism. Thus the groups which opposed the established order (such as the young intellectuals of the 1919 May Fourth movement, and before them the Taiping and the anti-Manchu secret societies) also traditionally opposed the authoritarian structure of the family and championed the cause of women.

Families which were regarded as being descended from a common ancestor formed a clan (*zu*). Clans were exogamous—meaning that a married woman automatically left the clan to which she belonged by birth and entered that of her husband. The clans were lively social units, particularly in South China. That region had been settled relatively late by the Chinese, and their feeling of strangeness in new surroundings led them to put great emphasis on their customary ties.

Clans owned land and used the income from it for their temples and tombs and for the ritual ceremonies held in them. Clans were administered by "elders," who were often the richest or most influential members. Like the guilds and the villages, the clans tried to settle disputes among their own members out of court. A clan was also a mutual aid society, giving help to the poorest of its members. In these ways clan solidarity tempered the economic antagonisms that were endemic in Chinese rural society.

Economic Development

The "historical whole" of traditional China, made up of an integrated political philosophy, system of government, and social hierarchy, was characterized by the primary emphasis it gave to agriculture. The old Confucian formula *Zhong nong bing shang* (Respect agriculture and despise trade) expressed a deep-seated reality.

Yet the Chinese economy was far more developed than this maxim would indicate. It was not simply a combination of subsistence-level production in the villages and a government perpetuating the "oriental" traditions of public administration. Handicrafts and proto-industrial production were important segments of the country's day-to-day economic life, and so were medium- and long-distance trade.

The political system, represented by the elaborate structure of the Chinese imperial government, had considerable direct economic power. Its indirect role was still more important, for it acted to maintain a rigid social structure that no longer corresponded to the dynamics of the Chinese economy.

Agriculture

In the nineteenth century China was the leading agricultural country in the world, owing to the size of the peasant population (four-fifths of all inhabitants) and the volume and variety of the crops grown. Farming techniques were advanced and involved considerable human investment: for example, in terraced hillsides, an intricate network of dikes, reservoirs, canals, and many types of farm equipment, such as norias (water wheels with buckets), sluices, plows, and winnowing machines.

Food crops included rice in South and Central China, millet, wheat, and kaoliang (a grain) in the North, as well as tea, corn, soybeans, and groundnuts. Industrial crops consisted of mulberry trees and silk, cotton, hemp, ramie (a fiber that can be woven into cloth), and various oil-bearing plants. Wild crops in the forests were also harvested to manufacture such products as varnish, medicine, and tong oil (a drying lubricant).

Contrary to accepted scholarly opinion, the agricultural and botanical resources of the Chinese were far from static, and they increased steadily over the centuries. Rice dates from the beginning of the Christian era. But the early-ripening variety, which can be harvested after 100 days instead of 180, was brought from Champa (the kingdom of South Indochina) in the eleventh century under the Song dynasty, and it did not come into widespread use until the Ming and Qing dynasties. With this strain of rice the difficult crop-less period in the spring is shorter, the zones where two crops can be grown in spite of winter weather are larger, and since it needs less water than the traditional variety, hillsides as well as plains can be planted to rice. It brought about a true agricultural revolution in China. Another such revolution occurred in the sixteenth to eighteenth centuries, when food crops of American origin were introduced by Spanish and Portuguese travelers. It was in this period that China acquired the sweet potato, groundnuts, tobacco, and most important, corn. All these crops could be grown in sandy soil or uneven ground that was unsuitable for growing rice.

In the West during the Middle Ages, agriculture was associated with environmental damage—injury to forests and grazing land. By that time, however, Chinese farmers had eliminated these resources completely. Forests had disappeared long ago, except in the mountains.

Beasts of burden were rare, since human labor was cheaper. Pigs and poultry were the only common farm animals, though enough sheep were raised in the semidesert fringes of the Northwest to supply the entire country with wool.

Whether the peasants owned their land or rented it, farms were small. Their form of agriculture, which resembled gardening, required meticulous, exhausting work; rice in particular is a labor-intensive crop. Yet the human labor on Chinese farms was not very productive. The country was self-sufficient as far as food was concerned, but what small surpluses did exist came about only because the majority of the people lived in wretched poverty. Agricultural yields were marginal in many regions plagued by floods and drought. In the country as a whole agricultural disasters and famines occurred frequently and contributed to the repeated outbreaks of rebellion among the peasants.

A substantial part of the farm population devoted some of each year to fishing, salting fish, working local quarries and small mines, and manufacturing rural handicrafts. These simple manufactures, which were distinct from the Chinese specialized handicraft and factory production, included such skills as weaving, brick and tile making, bamboo work, and paper making. They were important to the rural economy because they provided work and income during the off-season, utilized women's labor, and filled local needs.

Economic responsibilities of the state

The Chinese government developed as a result of its economic commitments, particularly in the field of hydraulic engineering. By the nineteenth century the government was directly operating many sectors of the economy.

The state was generally responsible for the upkeep of dikes and canals—a duty which was considered the paramount injunction of the Mandate of Heaven. Some dikes that served strictly local areas were maintained by the villages, but most were controlled by the district official, by the provincial governor, or (as in the case of the Yellow River) by an autonomous interprovincial administrative body.

The "reserve granaries," which were equally important for the agricultural economy, were managed by the district authorities with the help of the local gentry. The authorities bought grain at its lowest price just after the harvest and sold it for the same amount in the spring, enabling consumers to avoid the inflated rates charged by speculators. Other local granaries built up stores for use in times of famine. These should not be confused with the imperial granaries, which stocked the grain tribute paid by the chief rice-growing provinces. The grain tribute was for consumption by the court, Peking officials, Manchus who were entitled to an allowance, and the army.

The state also had a monopoly on salt, which was in demand not only for direct consumption but for preserving food. China was divided into ten salt zones, which produced sea salt, lake salt, and mined rock salt. The government jobbed out the production and sale of salt to merchants whose function was described as "official supervision and merchant sales," or *quan du shang xiao*. (This formula was taken up again in the period 1870–1880 by the promoters of modern industry, as discussed in Chapter 7.) The salt monopoly was administered through a complicated system of licenses, quotas, and certificates which led to a great deal of smuggling, often linked with the secret societies.

As well as operating in the agricultural sector, the government was active in a number of manufacturing industries. Not only did it produce weapons and other goods for military use, but it was also involved with textiles, silk, pottery, lacquer, and metals. The state owned everything lying below the earth's surface. In some cases it operated mines and foundries directly; in others it delegated the management to groups of merchants. The government supervised the hiring of miners, decided when new mines would be opened, and fixed annual production quotas. The authorities kept a particularly close watch on the Yunnan copper mines because these supplied the mints, and on the iron mines in Shanxi and Guangdong because of their military importance.

Local officials were also responsible for roads, bridges, and inland waterways. The Grand Canal was especially important, since it was the main channel for transporting the grain tribute from the lower Yangzi to the capital without danger from pirates. It was under the supervision of three general directors who managed the Jiangsu, Henan-Shandong, and Zhili sections. Besides overseeing the maintenance of the canal, the three men superintended the annual traffic of 6,000 junks (each of which could carry about 45 tons), the recruitment of a huge body of boatmen, the distribution of transport certificates, and the loading and unloading of cargo.

As for the tribute paid to the imperial regime by China's neighbors, it was not merely symbolic. It gave the government an effective monopoly over a variety of rare goods—varnishes and essences from the tropical forests of Southeast Asia, elephants' tusks, musk, furs, minerals, and spices.

Money

Coins, known as copper cash, were manufactured by the state from an alloy of copper, lead, and zinc. They were used separately or in strings of a thousand coins. In spite of the fact that the Chinese monetary system included silver as well, in the technical sense the coppers were the only real money. Silver was really a form of merchandise functioning as money. The accepted weight of silver—the tael, or Chinese ounce—contained an average of 38 grams, though the amount varied from province to province. The value of silver ingots of a certain thickness was calculated in taels, but they were never melted down; they served simply as money on account. Theoretically, 1,000 copper cash was equivalent to 1 tael of silver, but the rate of exchange varied depending on the local economic situation, the quality of the alloy, and other factors. Furthermore, over the years copper cash consistently declined in value relative to silver.

Handicrafts and manufacturing

By 1830 or so, Chinese craftsmen had reached an extremely high technical level. Using processes which guilds or villages often kept secret, they made a wide range of silk and cotton cloth, vegetable and mineral dyes, refined alloys (needed in manufacturing gongs, for instance), lacquers, oils and varnishes, and articles of leather and bamboo. Production was distributed geographically over various proto-industrial nuclei: there were copper, salt, silver, and tin mines in Yunnan; iron mines and ironworks in Shanxi; silk-weaving centers in Guangdong, the lower Yangzi, and Zhejiang; ink and paper products in Anhui; porcelain factories in Jiangxi (particularly in the famous Jingdezhen district); cotton weavers in Jiangsu, who made the celebrated "nankeens" which were prized in England; tea products in Fujian, Hubei, Yunnan, and other areas. These manufactures were still essentially handicrafts, whether they were turned out by the guilds in the towns or by the specialized villages. (The handicrafts produced by the villages were expertly wrought, belonging to an entirely different category of skill from rural domestic handicrafts, which was associated with agricultural production.)

Thus important mining and manufacturing zones already existed in the nineteenth century. The historians of the People's Republic of China have done considerable work on the flourishing state of Chinese proto-capitalism before the Western economic penetration. There were large concerns employing several hundred, sometimes several thousand, workers among the mines of Guangxi, the potteries of Jiangxi, and the textile mills of Jiangsu. Although the coal mines of Mentoukou near Peking were under state control, the profits were shared by the landowner, the contractor who owned and worked the mine, and the sleeping partner who supplied the capital. Even when production was controlled by the powerful merchants of Canton, Hangzhou, and Nanking, they distributed the work and marketed the products. The free labor market and wage earning were already highly developed. At one end of the scale was the semipeasant miner; at the other was the professional miner earning a regular wage.

Budding capitalism was particularly obvious in the sector of trade. There were sizable capitalists among the Yangzhou salt merchants, the tea and silk merchants of Jiangsu and Fujian, and the Canton Hong merchants (a business group which had a trading monopoly with the West, as discussed in Chapter 2). One trader, Howqua, had a fortune of 26 million silver dollars in 1834. The Shanxi bankers were also among the tycoons. Exploiting China's position at the convergence of the trade routes from Central Asia, they had agents throughout the country and obtained licenses from the Ministry of Finance. The combined capital of their financial houses amounted to 200,000 taels.

But the growth of the private sector in commerce and industry was constantly restrained by the state and the ruling class. The capitalists, harassed by troublesome controls and unfavorable tax regulations, preferred to buy Confucian degrees for their sons to give them access to the class that was the main source of riches and power. The most active trading sectors were those which had developed under the domination of the administration. The holders of mining concessions, who operated the salt monopoly, and the Shanxi bankers fared best among Chinese businessmen.

Unlike Western towns from the fourteenth to the seventeenth centuries, the Chinese town was not the locus of economic and social development. Consequently it was not the nucleus of dynamic opposition to the old order. It was essentially an administrative and military center, as indicated by its geometrical layout and its surrounding walls. It was a place of residence for some members of the gentry and for everyone who gravitated to the seat of local government. It was an appendage of the "feudal-bureaucratic" society, even though its manufacturing and trading activities were sometimes considerable. Large populations, up to several hundred thousand, were found in the towns on the lower Yangzhi: Nanking, Suzhou, Yangzhou, Songjiang, Hangzhou, and Wuhu. But there never was a movement for granting charters to Chinese cities.

In the nineteenth century China was not a cluster of self-sufficient units, as some writers describe it; industrial (and even agricultural) products were marketed on a considerable scale. Long-distance trade was active in goods which were essential by nature or custom (such as salt and tea) and in those whose value was high compared with their bulk (fine handicrafts, silk, porcelain). Busy trade routes developed above all in South China, where a vast and regular system of waterways enlarged the zone over which long-distance sales were profitable. Junks on large rivers and lakes were relayed by sampans on the small canals, which were often linked by wooden slides along which the boats could be hauled. A branching network of watercourses connected the southern tributaries of the Pearl River (the river flowing through Canton). Coastal traffic was also dense on the southeastern coast.

Yet despite the vigor of the forces encouraging economic integration, the trends toward disparity and fragmentation were still more powerful. Weights and measures, the value of the tael, and the rate of exchange between silver and copper cash varied from province to province. The limited silver market and the widespread moneylending were indications of the constricted state of the economy. Interest rates of 15 to 20 percent a month were not unusual. Pawnshops were common; so were mutual credit associations, in which each member received a loan from the others in turn.

Chinese Unity

The nature of Chinese unity is somewhat elusive. It was not based on language, for there were many. Mandarin (*guanhua*) was spoken, with slight dialectical differences, throughout Northern and Central China. But the languages of the lower Yangzi (*wu* languages)—and those of Fujian, Canton, the Guangdong hinterland, and Guangxi (Hakka)—were different in quality, even though the inhabitants of these regions were also Han (ethnic Chinese). The unifying element was written Chinese (*Wenyan*), a dead language used from one end of the country to the other by the scholar-officials, who studied it when preparing for the Confucian examinations.

In fact, it was the gentry who ensured the unity of imperial China, for the educated circles were keenly aware of the unique whole that was Chinese culture. Thus in spite of the imperfect economic cohesion, it is appropriate to speak of China as a unified country. What economic integration did exist was linked with the activities of the bureaucracy and so was part of the complex equation between nation and state.

Provinces and regions

The eighteen provinces, whose outlines date on the whole from the Ming dynasty, became living units over the centuries. They were entities not only in the administrative and consequently economic fields (with their own budgets, public works, and triennial examinations), but also in their customs and social cohesiveness. Merchants living in a distant province, students going to Peking for the imperial examinations, coolies and boatmen employed in another region, all congregated in provincial brotherhoods or associations. Each province had its traditional cuisine, its own style of popular opera, and above all, an awareness of its own identity. During the great crisis of the popular rebellions from 1850 to 1870 (Chapter 4), provincial loyalty was intense, especially in South and Central China.

The differences in economic evolution, history, and geography of the various regions produced clear disparities that went far beyond mere shades of difference between provinces. Most obvious was the great contrast between North and South. The North is a wheat-

eating region (noodles and steamed bread), the South a land of
rice eaters. The North focused on continental trade, the South on
maritime trade. Because of the impossibility of navigation on the
Yellow River, the North had little experience of anything but
porterage (always excepting the Grand Canal). The South, on the
other hand, had an excellent inland waterway network. The contrast between North and South was found in many other areas as
well—for example, in the organization of secret societies, which is
described in Chapter 2. And this contrast became even stronger
during political crises, such as the Boxer rebellion, or the rivalry
between Yuan Shi-kai and Sun Yat-sen in 1912.

Key areas of the South

In the nineteenth century the liveliest part of China was the
middle and lower Yangzi basin. It was the "key area" of the economy (*chi chao-ting*), followed by the Red River basin of Sichuan
and the Xijiang basin in the far South. These three regions were
characterized by the complexity of their hydraulic engineering.
Their economic supremacy represented a fundamental shift from
the pre-Mongol period, when the center of gravity of Chinese society was the middle Huanghe basin and the old capitals of Luoyang,
Kaifeng, and Sian.

Thus in the nineteenth century Peking, the Manchu capital, was
located at a great distance from the key areas of China. But for
many reasons the government was content to stay put: political
motives connected with the historical prestige of Peking, dynastic
considerations connected with the proximity of Manchuria, and
strategic purposes connected with supervision of the northwestern
frontier.

The market economy of the key area was the most advanced in
China, largely because of the facilities provided by inland and
coastal navigation. The chief manufacturing centers were found
here, as well as the towns that were most active socially and intel-
lectually. The great majority of distinguished scholars and statesmen came from the provinces of Anhui, Jiangsu, Hunan, and
Guangdong. These southeastern provinces were the first to trade
with the countries of the West, and inevitably, it was here that the
Opium Wars broke out.

ADDITIONAL BIBLIOGRAPHY

Etienne Balazs and others, *Aspects de la Chine* (Paris, Presses Universitaires de France, 1959), vol. 1.

Derk Bodde, *China's Cultural Tradition: What and Whither?* (New York, Rinehart, 1957).

Chi Chao-ting, *Key Economic Areas in Chinese History* (New York, Institute of Pacific Relations, 1963, reprinted).

Hsieh Pao-chao, *The Government of China, 1644–1911* (New York, Octagon Books, 1966).

Michael Loewe, *Imperial China, the Historical Background to the Modern Age* (London, Allen & Unwin, 1966).

Denys Lombard, *La Chine Impériale* (Paris, Presses Universitaires de France, Que sais-je? 1967).

John Thomas Meskill, *The Pattern of Chinese History: Cycles, Development or Stagnation?* (New York, Heath, 1965).

Sybille Van Der Sprenkel, *Legal Institutions in Manchu China: A Sociological Analysis* (New York, Humanities Press, 1962).

DOCUMENTS

1. SCALES OF PUNISHMENTS AND CRIMES IN THE QING DYNASTY CODE

SOURCE: French translation: *Ta-tsing-leu-lee, ou les lois fondamentales du Code pénal de la Chine* (Paris, 1812), vol. 1, pp. 19–24.

Ordinary Punishments

The lightest punishment is applied to the transgressor with the smaller end of the bamboo, to inspire shame for his wrongdoings and to give him a desire to improve his future conduct. This first punishment has five degrees:

First		10 strokes		4 strokes
Second		20 strokes		5 strokes
Third	is supposed	30 strokes	but is	10 strokes
Fourth	to be	40 strokes	cut down to	15 strokes
Fifth		50 strokes		20 strokes

The second punishment is applied with the larger end of the bamboo. Its five degrees are as follows:

First		60 strokes		20 strokes
Second		70 strokes		25 strokes
Third	is	80 strokes	but is cut	30 strokes
Fourth	supposed to be	90 strokes	down to	35 strokes
Fifth		100 strokes		40 strokes

The third punishment is exile for a certain time, to a distance not above 500 li [about 250 kilometers], with the aim of bringing the guilty man to repent and amend his ways. This punishment also has five degrees:

Exile for	1 year	with	60 strokes	from the bamboo,
	1½ years		70 strokes	cut down as above
	2 years		80 strokes	
	2½ years		90 strokes	
	3 years		100 strokes	

The fourth punishment is perpetual exile.* It is for criminals whom the law is pleased to separate from society, in atonement for grave offences committed against it. This punishment consists of 100 strokes from the bamboo, and perpetual exile at a distance of 2,000 li, 2,500 li, or 3,000 li.

The fifth punishment is death for the criminal, by strangulation or decapitation.

Except for criminals who have committed such atrocious deeds that they must be punished by instant execution, all those who have been convicted of capital crimes will be put into prison to await the execution of their sentence, which will take place at a certain time in the autumn. The emperor will review the sentence pronounced against each guilty man, and he will ratify it if the law has been justly applied.

Crimes related to treason

Rebellion is an attempt to violate the order established by God among things here below. It disturbs the productions of the earth which follow after one another, regularly, under the influence of the spirit presiding over them, hindering their distribution among the people as ordained by the sovereign who has succeeded to the sacred throne of his ancestors. Hence to resist the emperor's power and conspire against him is to trouble the general peace and commit the most heinous crimes.

Disloyalty is an attempt to destroy the imperial temples, tombs, and palaces. The temples and tombs have been built to perpetuate the memory and house the remains of former sovereigns, and the palaces, as the residences of the reigning monarch, are no less sacred and inviolable.

Desertion is the crime of leaving the empire, or betraying its interests, to submit to a foreign power or further its designs. Those who abandon their military post, or encourage the people to emigrate, are also deserters.

Parricide is committed by a person who murders his father or mother, his uncle or aunt, or one of his grandparents. It is among the most serious of all crimes and gives proof of a thoroughly corrupt heart, because it shatters the links of nature formed by divine will.

Massacre is committed by one who murders three or more people

---

* Perpetual exile was an extremely severe punishment, because it removed man's hope of being buried on the land of his ancestors. After death his spirit was forced to wander forever.

from the same family; all other murders are included under the same name.

Sacrilege is committed by robbing temples of holy objects or stealing articles devoted to the emperor's personal use. Sacrilege also includes counterfeiting the imperial seal, administering incorrect medicine to the sovereign, or generally speaking, committing an error or an act of negligence which could endanger the safety of the emperor's sacred person.

Impiety is lack of respect and attention toward those to whom one owes one's being, from whom one has received education, and by whom one is protected. It is also impious to bring a lawsuit against close relations, to insult them, to refrain from wearing mourning for them, and to show lack of respect for their memory.

Discord in families is the severing of the natural or legal ties uniting them by blood or marriage. This term covers the crimes of ill-treatment, injury, or murder of blood relations, or of relations by marriage for whom a person would wear mourning if they died.

Insubordination is the crime committed by an inferior official when he attacks or kills his superior, and by the people when they rebel against any official.

Incest is cohabitation or overly intimate liaisons between persons who cannot marry for reasons of kinship.

As the ten crimes listed here are distinguished from all others by their atrocity, the law punishes them with the utmost severity, and when the offense is a capital one, it is never pardoned. These crimes are always direct violations of the links holding society together. Consequently they are named here in the introduction to the code, to teach the people to fear and avoid them.

2. POLITICAL LOYALTY AND SOCIAL HARMONY: THE SACRED EDICT OF THE KANGXI EMPEROR (1670)

SOURCE: English version in John K. Fairbank, Edwin O. Reischauer, and Albert M. Craig, *East Asia: The Modern Transformation* (Boston, Houghton Mifflin, 1965), p. 85.

Perform with sincerity filial and fraternal duties in order to give due importance to social relations.

Behave with generosity to your kindred to demonstrate harmony and affection.

Cultivate peace and concord in your neighborhoods in order to prevent quarrels and litigations.

Recognize the importance of husbandry and the culture of mulberry trees in order to ensure a sufficiency of food and clothing.

Hold economy in estimation in order to conserve money and goods.

Extend the schools of instruction in order to make correct the practice of scholars.

Reject false doctrines in order to honor learning.

Explain the laws in order to warn the ignorant and obstinate.

Manifest propriety and courtesy in order to make manners and customs good.

Work diligently at your proper calling in order to give settlement to the aims of the people.

Instruct your sons and younger brothers in order to guard them from evildoing.

Put a stop to false accusations in order to protect the innocent and good.

Abstain from the concealment of fugitives in order to avoid being involved in their punishment.

Pay your taxes fully in order to dispense with official urging.

Combine in the *baojia** in order to suppress thieves and robbers.

Resolve animosities in order to value your lives duly.†

---

* Mutual aid groupings of 100 (*jia*) and 1,000 (*bao*) households.
† This edict was to be read and expounded to the people of each locality twice a month.

Chapter Two

A Conjunction of Crises

In the first third of the nineteenth century, at the time when the commercial, and later political, pressure applied by the West was becoming urgent, the Chinese imperial order was facing many internal forces of opposition and a number of serious domestic crises.

Internal Opposition

Secret societies: political, social, and religious dissent

The secret societies, which in imperial China were the classic form of opposition to the established order, were extremely active during this period. Basically they were organizations of political opposition to the Manchu dynasty. They swore loyalty to the Chinese Ming dynasty dethroned in the seventeenth century, and their slogan was *Fan Qing fu Ming* (Overthrow the Qing and restore the Ming). The White Lotus Society, for instance, organized a vast insurrection in Hubei, Sichuan, and Shenxi on the northwestern frontier that lasted from 1796 to 1804. Several years later the same society attempted a *coup d'état* within the imperial palace itself.

More broadly, the societies represented several elementary forms of struggle against the established order.[1] Their equalitarian slo-

[1] See the extracts from an oath of initiation, document 1 at the end of the chapter.

gans called for "taking from the rich and giving to the poor," and some of their activities (plundering, racketeering, marauding) resembled plain banditry. But the secret societies were also the germinal spirit behind peasant movements and the source of experienced cadres for peasant risings. Their members came primarily from the poor in both town and countryside—artisans, peasants, vagrants, and the down-and-out of every sort. One unusual aspect of their social protest against the Confucian norms was feminism; in the clandestine hierarchy of the societies, men and women were treated as equals.

Finally, secret societies functioned as dissenting religious groups. They practiced cults, drawn mainly from popular traditions, which were forbidden by the Qing code and celebrated at night. They worshipped the "Old Unbegotten Mother," performed their initiation ceremonies facing the "four Easts," practiced rites of ordeal, used protective amulets, and consulted mediums.

The societies fell into two large systems that were divided into local units whose ramifications are not well known. The White Lotus group in the North was linked with units like the Nian, the Observance Society, and the Red Spears. The Triad group in the South included the Heaven and Earth Society, the Society of Brothers and Elders (Gelaohui), and the Small Knife Society. The Northern group (*jiao men*) was mainly religious and the Southern group (*hui dang*) chiefly political, but this was not a hard and fast rule.

The secret societies developed as forces of opposition within the old regime and were bound to it by many social and political links. Rich merchants and even rural gentry filled high positions in the societies, both in order to gain more control of the popular movements in their areas and to share in the plunder. Rather than attempting to crush the societies, the mandarins and their assistants tried to come to terms with the leaders, who for their part were willing to negotiate.

Dissident scholars and utopian traditions

Dissident scholars were also an active force of opposition to the imperial order during the first third of the nineteenth century. The mainstream of scholarship was toward orthodoxy and conformism. Conventional scholars had obediently turned for inspiration to the neo-Confucian system created by Zhu Xi (1130–1200) under the Song dynasty in reaction to the Buddhism of the Tang period (sixth to ninth centuries). In the climate of intellectual stagnation that this produced, the predominant literary forms were bibliographies and commentary on the Classics. An example was the work of the great bibliophile Ruan Yuan (1784–1849), who founded many academies and libraries around Canton, where he was governor-general just before the Opium Wars.

But a tradition of intellectual nonconformity also existed in China, extending back to the Han dynasty if not to the Taoist philosophers of classical antiquity. This tradition emphasized wrongdoing by the state, the need for philosophical criticism and independence of mind, and the duty to work for social justice. The nonconformist tradition was particularly lively in the seventeenth century under the last Ming emperors. Its best representatives, Huang Zong-xi, Gu Yan-wu, and Wang Fu-zhi, actively opposed Manchu power and remained faithful to the fallen dynasty. Their influence was so great that in the 1770s the Qianlong Emperor had to adopt a policy of vigorous repression, which led to the destruction of hundreds of nonconformist political and literary works. Intimidated by persecution, scholars fell back on erudition and on criticism of ancient texts: "Han learning" (*Hanxue*), whose followers tried to lay indirect emphasis on Chinese national traditions without openly defying the Manchu dynasty.

Nevertheless, unorthodox traditions remained lively, taking their inspiration from old Chinese equalitarian and utopian themes. For example, the theme of *datong* ("great unity") affirmed the harmony of the community in human relations. *Taiping* ("great peace") was a utopian vision of a third age of the world based on a notion of progress which was very different from the cyclical conception of classic Confucianism. The theme of *pingjun* emphasized equality, both in land ownership and in social conditions. The rebels of the 1850s, the reformers of 1898, Sun Yat-sen, and the Chinese Communists all drew heavily on these traditions. Scholars with neither fortune nor ambition maintained the ideal of vague, semiclandestine heterodoxy. This was the climate in which the Taiping leader, Hong Xiu-quan, and the reformer of the end of the century, Kang You-wei, received their education.

A movement for the study of politics and science

A few other intellectuals tried to lay stress on contemporary politics, foreign relations, and "statecraft" (*jingshi*). Wei Yuan

(1794–1856), who was to play an important part in the intellectual discovery of the West just after the Opium Wars, had begun as early as 1820 to study subjects outside the conservative, sterile system of neo-Confucianism. He was interested in the transportation of the "rice tribute" (he believed that it should be sent by sea instead of by the Grand Canal), in the salt monopoly, and in China's military experiences on its land and sea frontiers.

Wei Yuan was in touch with Gong Zi-zhen (1792–1849), a poet, reformer, student of population geography, and originator of a plan to exclude Westerners from Canton. Wei also knew Lin Ze-xu (1785–1851), general director of the Yellow River and governor-general of Lianghu, who was to be a prominent figure during the first Opium War. Lin was interested in hydraulic engineering, in the wider use of the fast-ripening variety of rice, and in problems of taxation. These three men belonged to the *gongyang* school of interpretation of the Confucian Classics, a tradition which stressed the unorthodox, innovating aspect of Confucius's thought. The school thus found justification in tradition for the study of contemporary affairs and the search for new ways to solve political problems.

Other original men were attracted by science. An ancient and distinguished scientific tradition existed in China, even though it was neglected by the official curriculum. Chinese mathematics, astronomy, chemistry, and medicine had developed through the centuries independently of Western discoveries, and they had reached a high level unsuspected by Western scholars until the encyclopedic research of Joseph Needham. The table of Chinese innovations that he constructed is infinitely richer than the list enumerating gunpowder, the magnetic compass, and acupuncture that Westerners usually draw up. Needham's table includes the lunar theory of the tides, equatorial astronomy of the independent position of heliacal risings, clocks, the evaluation of π, and other advanced theory. In the nineteenth century the scientific tradition, particularly in the field of algebra, was still alive in the trading towns of the lower Yangzi. Li Shan-lan (1810–1882), a mathematician and the author of an original theory of logarithms, worked in collaboration with Westerners during the *Yangwu* movement (covered in Chapter 7).

Popular literature

Intellectual nonconformity also found expression in literature. *The Flowers in the Mirror*, the famous novel by Li Ru-zhen (1763–1830), described the life of women of ability in a utopian country where the practice of foot-binding was abolished and they could take the state examinations and participate in public affairs. The social criticism is direct and explicit in this novel.

On the whole, popular literature in the vernacular was considered suspect by the authorities. It encouraged irreverence and mocked at establishment justice, praised the insubordination and independence of its heroes, gave a realistic picture of the life of the bourgeoisie and the common people, and pointed up the hypocrisy of Confucian conventions. This was true of *The Water Margin* (*Shuihu*, one of Mao Tsetung's favorite books when he was a boy), a great novel of knight-errantry about one hundred and eight bandits who righted wrongs in the marshes of Liangshanpo. It was equally true of *Rulin waishi* (*The Scholars*), of *Hongloumeng* (*The Dream of the Red Chamber*), which raised the question of freedom in love and criticized social conventions, and of *Jinpingmei*, whose libertine tone was combined with a criticism of corruption in business and administrative circles.

Entrenched resistance among peasants and minority groups

Recurring agitation in the rural areas, leading to periodic peasant revolts, was probably the most important of the social forces opposed to the imperial order. In addition, the ethnic and religious minorities of China (the Miao, the Yao, and the Moslems in the Northwest and Southwest, for example) fiercely resented the mandarins' policy of assimilation and repression. Administrators of regions inhabited by minorities exploited them even more rapaciously than their colleagues did the populations of Han zones. Officials who governed minority peoples were in league with Chinese traders who paid a low price for rare products (oils, minerals, furs, wool) and charged high for basic necessities like salt and tea. The minority populations were constantly on the verge of rebellion.

Though all these forces of political, social, and intellectual opposition were only intermittently or marginally active, they were extremely lively. They were also intrinsic to the Chinese old regime; in a sense they were built-in safety valves rather than outside movements aimed at replacing the regime. There was no equivalent to the economic, social, and ideological pressures which the bourgeoisie of Western Europe brought to bear on its monarchies in the seventeenth and eighteenth centuries. As Chapter 1 has shown, the mechanisms of Chinese society restrained business activity, and what is more, continually absorbed merchant groups into the established order.

Political, Social, and Economic Deterioration

After the long and able reigns of the two great Manchus, the Kangxi (1662–1723) and Qianlong (1736–1796) Emperors, the power of the Manchu dynasty declined during the Jiaqing era (1796–1821) and conspicuously deteriorated during the Daoguang era (1821–1851).

Political and social crises

All the signs associated by the ancient chroniclers with the fall of dynasties and the "withdrawal of the Mandate" (*geming*) now reappeared. As they had done two centuries earlier under the last Ming emperors, the mandarins became corrupt, dikes and canals fell into disrepair, and public services declined. District officials, their clerks, and their agents became greedier and more arrogant than ever, particularly when they acted as judges or tax assessors. They falsified the registers, levied swarms of additional taxes, and exacted bribes for signing receipts. Tax collectors grew rich by manipulating the "substitution rate" between rice and cash, and the exchange rate between silver and copper cash. An imperial edict of 1828 noted that in Shandong the tax collectors worked on an exchange rate of 4,000 Peking copper cash for one tael of silver, but people who wanted to pay their tax in copper cash (in other words, the poorest people) had to pay 4,260 coppers to the tael. An edict of 1829 recorded rates of 2,800, 4,000, and 4,600 when the official rate was 1,000 copper cash. This corruption not only worsened the condition of the peasants, thereby fostering agitation in the countryside, but also reduced the imperial revenue.

The system of reserve granaries declined so far that the buildings were falling into ruins and the amount of grain they still held diminished every year. A granary in the Zhili district of Hunan that was originally built to store 10,000 piculs (roughly 65 tons) contained only 6,662 in 1815. By 1861 this figure had fallen to 2,056, and the local chronicle said that most of it existed only on paper. The poor reserves still being collected were seized by the clerks and agents of the *yamen* for their own profit.

The interprovincial administration of the Yellow River was a classic example of the deterioration in public services. The mandarins in charge wavered between two policies: that of building large dikes at some distance from the river and therefore abandoning the best land permanently to the river itself, and that of building small dikes which left a dangerously narrow passage and could not stand up to floodwaters. In spite of the risks the poverty-stricken villagers preferred the small dikes and narrow passages, because excellent harvests could be reaped from the rich alluvium of the central riverbed between floods. The two types of dike were so badly coordinated that the region was unsafe in floodtime, and in 1853 flooding reached catastrophic proportions. But the cumbersome machinery of bureaucracy that administered this poor system of dikes supported 400 officials, countless engineers and coolies, and 20,000 soldiers. It provided opportunities for embezzlement, requests for fictitious credits on the basis of false reports, and other profitable forms of corruption. The budget of the interprovincial administration, one of the largest in the empire, amounted to 3 million taels in the seventeenth century and 4½ million at the beginning of the nineteenth—one-tenth of the total revenue of the central government.

The deterioration of the machinery of state was also apparent at the highest levels. Peking had not yet recovered from the He-shen affair, in which the all-powerful minister and favorite eunuch of the Qianlong Emperor was tried and convicted in 1799 as soon as the emperor was dead. The minister had accumulated a scandalously large fortune, and his possessions were confiscated. The atmosphere of demoralization and division still pervaded the court around 1830, when several Manchu circles were quarreling over the favors of the Daoguang Emperor and bickering with the most influential of the senior Chinese mandarins. The principals in this struggle were the Manchu Mu Zhang-a (1782–1856), a member of the Grand Council and the Grand Secretariat and former chairman of the Board of Censors, and the Chinese Cao Zhen-yong (1755–1835), grandson of a Yangzhou salt merchant and, like Mu, a member of the Grand Secretariat and the Grand Council. Cao was a high mandarin of the conservative type, imbedded in routine and concerned about his personal power. After his death in

1835, Mu Zhang-a gained ascendancy over the other high-ranking officials, including Lin Ze-xu, who was later very active during the first Opium War. Thus on the eve of the crisis of 1839, the leading group in Peking was neither united nor strong enough to face it, as Chapter 3 will show.

The monetary crisis

The first third of the nineteenth century was also a period of monetary crisis. Supplies of metal for minting dwindled, mostly because the Yunnan copper production was falling off and government control of mining was inadequate. These difficulties, combined with the government's poor management of financial services and of the mints, caused a deterioration in the quality of coins. Bad and false money was in wide circulation. The real exchange rate between the tael and copper cash progressively reduced the value of coppers. The accounts of a money changer's shop in Zhili show that the real rate of the tael was 920 copper cash in 1804, 1,266 in 1820, 1,365 in 1830, and 2,230 in 1850. The government's rigid monetary policy prohibited the adjustments that would have put a stop to the ever-downward fluctuations of copper. The maintenance of a completely artificial rate of exchange (1 for 1,000) worsened the crisis. Further complications were introduced by the appearance of the Spanish silver dollar on the southeast coast in the eighteenth century.

Peasant agitation and the secret societies

In the reigns of Jiaqing and Daoguang there was a resurgence of peasant revolts. A partial list can be drawn up from data given in the journal *Chinese Repository*, published in Canton by English missionaries between 1830 and 1840:

	Revolt in
1820	Guangxi
1822	Shanxi
1826	Guizhou, Taiwan
1830	Taiwan
1831	Jiangxi, Hainan
1832	Jiangsu, Hubei, Taiwan, Hunan, Guangxi, Guangdong
1834	Sichuan
1835	Shanxi
1836	Guangxi

The revolt of 1832 was a huge one which spread over the mountainous borderlands of Hunan, Guangdong, and Guangxi. Its leader was connected with the secret societies and gathered over 30,000 men to fight with him. Taking the name of Zhao the Golden Dragon, he wore the imperial yellow robes as a gesture of defiance toward the emperor. Canton authorities did not manage to overpower him until the spring of 1833, after they had corrupted some of his lieutenants.

The secret societies were extremely active during this period, particularly the Triad and its branches in South China. They set themselves up as leaders of discontented peasants, organized attacks on *yamen* and official transport, defied the authorities, and terrorized all who refused to pay them tribute. From a sociological point of view there was no clear distinction between them and pirates. River pirates were numerous in the South, while sea pirates had countless bases along the coasts of Guangdong and Fujian and mingled easily with fleets of fishing boats. In 1806 a fleet of a hundred pirate ships with ten thousand men attacked Taiwan. The mandarins of the southeastern provinces were too occupied with rivalries among themselves to act in concert against the pirates, who attacked merchant convoys as they pleased throughout the South China Sea.

The government also had to deal with rebellions among the ethnic minority populations: a Tibetan revolt in Kokonor in 1807, a revolt of the Yao in Guizhou in 1833, and a great Moslem rising in Turkestan in 1825–1828. The Mongol general Chang-ling, who fought under a "banner" allied with the Manchu aristocracy, took three years to overcome the Moslem leader Jehangir (a Khwadja Turk) and win back the oases of Kashgar, Khokend, and Yarkend.

The population increase and internal migrations

Demographic pressure aggravated China's political and social crises. As shown by statistics from the Ministry of Revenue in Peking, the population had been growing steadily since the eighteenth century. Probably these figures are not wholly accurate; sometimes the data for migrants and ethnic minorities were not recorded by the authorities. The most competent specialists say that the government statistics are lower than the real ones, and that they point to a general tendency:

	Population		**Population**
1770	213,613,163	1815	326,574,895
1780	277,554,413	1820	353,377,694
1790	301,487,114	1825	379,885,340
1800	295,273,311	1830	394,784,681
1805	332,181,143	1835	403,052,086
1810	345,717,214	1840	412,814,828

The fact was that the prosperity of the country under the first Manchu emperors had caused a great population increase, while the amount of land under cultivation did not expand by very much. According to official figures, there was total stagnation in this area of the economy: 741 million mu under cultivation in 1766 and 737 million in 1833. In general 1 mu is 0.165 acre, but the mu in the government figures was a fiscal mu, calculated according to a complicated system of equivalent values on the basis of the different categories of land which were taxed. The government statistics omitted the land which was officially exempt from the land tax because it had just been brought into cultivation. This was precisely the property which most affected the demographic relation between population and farmland. And of course, the figures of the Ministry of Revenue did not include the land which escaped taxation either through fraud or through favoritism, that belonging to the richest families, or in other words, the largest estates and the most fertile farms. But when corrections are made for these factors, it still seems likely that the total land under cultivation, and above all the crop yield, did not increase in proportion to the population.

The effects of demographic pressure were no doubt partially allayed by the introduction of crops from America. The arrival of the sweet potato and corn enabled peasants to bring large new areas into cultivation in the hills of Central China, in the mountainous borderlands of the West and Southwest, and especially in Yunnan. Peanuts could be grown in the sandy wasteland of Guangxi and Hainan; nonirrigated crops had been progressing since the seventeenth century in the South, where they were alternated with rice. This extension of farming activity caused large peasant migrations within China, particularly toward the Han basin and toward the hills surrounding the middle Yangzi basin (Hunan, Hubei, Jiangxi). A third center of immigration developed for political reasons: population began to flow back into Sichuan, which had become depopulated in the seventeenth century at the time of the great rebellion led by Zhang Xian-zhong and the repression that followed. All these migrations resulted in very uneven population shifts in the various provinces. The population of Sichuan grew by 415 percent between 1787 and 1850 (from 8 million to 44 million inhabitants), that of Yunnan by 113 percent owing to the introduction of corn), that of Hubei by 77 percent (because of the colonization of the Han basin), and that of Guangdong by 75 percent. In Hunan, on the other hand, population rose by only 28 percent, because people left there to go to Sichuan, and in Zhili the increase was a mere 2 percent.

Progress in agriculture not only failed to keep pace with the increase in population but sometimes also had destructive ecological repercussions. Growing corn on the hitherto uncultivated hillsides of the Southwest eroded the land and affected the hydrographical balance so that there were more floods. Indeed, for some unknown reason agricultural catastrophes seem to have proliferated at the beginning of the nineteenth century. Sixteen floods of the Han were recorded between 1821 and 1850, compared with six between 1796 and 1820. Using records from local chronicles, the historian Ho Ping-ti has demonstrated that the total number of districts affected by famine, drought, floods, typhoons, epidemics, and locusts was on the increase.

	Disasters in
1790–1799	25 districts
1800–1809	52 districts
1810–1819	55 districts
1820–1829	49 districts
1830–1839	136 districts

It is generally reckoned that between 1780 and 1800 the overall relationship between demography and economic activity was upset. Until the middle of the eighteenth century demographic growth had been satisfactorily combined with economic growth, but at that point resources began to dwindle relative to the needs of a rapidly increasing population. Contemporary observers were keenly aware of the deteriorating situation. They saw the growing numbers of unemployed and noted that the "rice bowls" like the provinces of Jiangxi and Hunan could hardly meet their own needs. "Since the end of the reign of Qianlong" declared the scholar and reformer Gong Zi-zhen in 1820, "officials and common people have been sliding rapidly toward a state of distress. Those who are neither scholars nor farmers nor artisans nor merchants represent nearly half the population. . . . In general, the rich have become poor and the poor are starving. . . . The provinces are on the threshold of a convulsion which will come not in a few years, but in a few months, if not in a few days."[2]

The same anxiety was expressed by Hong Liang-ji (1746–1809), who pointed out in 1793, five years before Malthus, that the balance between population and resources had been disturbed and that population growth was accelerating in spite of epidemics and natural disasters. He recommended that more land be brought under cultivation, that the population disperse from the towns to the countryside, that convents and other centers of idleness be closed, and that production of luxury goods be forbidden.

Two generations later, the scholar Wang Shi-duo (1802–1889) wrote with melancholy: "The evils of over-population force people to plant cereals in the mountains and cultivate sandbanks. All the centuries-old forests of Sichuan have been cut down and transformed into crops. Yet there is not enough for everybody. This proves that the resources of Heaven and Earth are exhausted."[3] The general tendency toward impoverishment can be traced in Wang's own family: his great-grandfather had been a rich merchant, but his father was a simple apprentice.

Thus in the first third of the nineteenth century, the deterioration in political, social, and economic conditions already heralded the great wave of popular rebellions of the years between 1850 and 1870.

The Closed-Door Policy

In the years before 1830 the Chinese imperial authorities practiced a strict closed-door policy toward the West, particularly in the fields of trade and religion.

The Cohong: A system for controlling foreign merchants

Since the middle of the eighteenth century trade relations had been organized according to the "Canton system," for Canton was the only port open to Westerners. In that city a group of Chinese firms known as the Cohong (the Cantonese form of *gong hang,*

[2] Quoted by Ho Ping-ti, *Studies on the Population of China, 1368–1953* (Cambridge, Mass., Harvard University Press, 1959), p. 273.
[3] Ibid., p. 274.

"officially authorized firms") had the monopoly on trade with the West. The Cohong fixed the prices and the volume of trade. It was responsible to the governor-general of Liangguang and above all to the *hoppo*, the Canton customs superintendent. The *hoppo* was notoriously corrupt; the Hong merchants, members of the Cohong, paid huge bribes to him.

The Cohong was personally responsible for the activities of foreigners (both commercial and general), a position which brought this group large profits and made it a highly influential trading aristocracy in Canton. A special district of the city, the "Thirteen Factories," was reserved for the English and American traders who came to buy products like silks, nankeens, and tea, which in the eighteenth century had become the national drink of their countries. In 1793 the British sent Lord Macartney to Peking in a vain attempt to relax this rigid system.

In reality, "control," in the way that this word was used by the Chinese bureaucracy, is a more accurate term than "closed door." A similar system was imposed in the Chinese Middle Ages, when the Arab merchants in Canton had to live in a particular district of town and obey special regulations.

At the beginning of the nineteenth century the West began to penetrate the Chinese market in spite of the restrictions imposed by the Canton system. Foreign purchases stimulated the production of porcelain, cotton, silks and brocades, and above all, tea.[4] Many trade routes, all converging on Canton, were organized to bring the goods from Jiangxi, Fujian, and the middle Yangzi basin. Transport was by river boat and porterage, and these trade routes employed countless coolies and boatmen. Until about 1820, when opium smuggling became important, Western purchases were made in the Spanish silver dollar—the carolus. The coins were minted in Mexico and brought to the Far East by Spaniards from the Philippines, by the Dutch, who had permission to put into Japanese ports, and by Western merchants in Southeast Asia. It has been calculated that by 1810 a total of 350 million dollars had been introduced into China through these routes since the seventeenth century.

[4] The very form of the word *tea* reflects the fact that Westerners were in direct contact with South China long before the "opening" of 1840. It represents the pronunciation of the Chinese word *cha* in the province of Fujian, where a dental, not an affricative, consonant is used. On the other hand, the peoples of Eastern Europe and the Middle East (Persia, Russia, etc.) knew tea in the form that was imported by caravan from Northwest China, and they adopted the pronunciation of the Northern Chinese: *tchai*.

Restrictions on the Christian missions

Christian missionaries were also under close supervision. In the seventeenth and eighteenth centuries, Jesuits were admitted to the court under the last Ming emperors and the great Manchu emperors. Their learning in mathematics, astronomy, cartography, and artillery, and the zeal that they showed in translating Western scientific and technical works into Chinese, won them an influential position. They were given official appointments as astronomers, cartographers, and doctors. They converted senior mandarins and managed to form large groups of Roman Catholics in the North, in Sichuan, and in Fujian. But during the eighteenth century—particularly after Rome had settled the famous Rites Controversy by deciding that Chinese customs were not to be tolerated—the situation of Catholicism in China became much more difficult.

No more priests were admitted to the empire; the last Jesuit astronomer died in Peking in 1805 without being replaced. By 1830 only a few small, scattered Catholic communities containing one or two hundred thousand people were left in China. The Lazarists (successors to the Jesuits, whose order was dissolved) and the Franciscans did their best to remain in contact with these groups by entering the country secretly.

In the eyes of the Confucian mandarins, public order was indivisible and ideological loyalty went hand in hand with political obedience. To them Christianity was comparable to other unorthodox and subversive cults, particularly to the legitimist and anti-Manchu secret societies. The imperial order oppressed Christians for the same reasons that it did members of other cults. Under the Jiaqing and Daoguang Emperors, in whose reigns the Triad and the White Lotus Societies revived and expanded, persecution of all unorthodox politico-religious forces became more severe. Roman Catholic communities were dissolved and priests were driven away or put to death. Eight hundred Christians were arrested in Guizhou in 1815. The last Roman Catholic church in Peking, the Beitang, was closed in 1827. Land given to Christian churches in the seventeenth century by rich converts had been confiscated long ago. When the treaty of 1860 stipulated that China should give it back, the difficulties were virtually insoluble.

The Protestants were unable to take over from the Roman Catholics, in spite of attempts by Protestant missionaries to penetrate China through the British and American factories in Canton. Foreign merchants in Canton employed several British, American, and German missionaries as interpreters—men like Robert Morrison (1792–1834), the author of a complete translation of the Bible, and Karl Gützlaff, a Pomeranian Lutheran who actively supported the British in the first Opium War. The missionaries published an interesting journal in Canton, the *Chinese Repository* (1832–1851), and in 1835 they opened a hospital. They made a few Chinese converts, one of whom was the famous Liang A-fa (1789–1855), a lay preacher who had an influence on the Taiping leader Hong Xiu-quan later in Canton. But the importance of Protestantism in this region was still minor around 1835.

Foundations of the closed-door policy

The policy of partially closing the country arose mainly from the anxiety to protect the political and social regime. The dominant scholar-official class distrusted foreign merchants because it distrusted all merchants, since the Confucian scale of social values put merchants at the bottom. In the same way, the officials distrusted Christianity because they distrusted all unorthodox cults.

The closing of the country can also be traced to a feeling which was more deeply rooted—a conviction that China had nothing to gain and much to lose by opening the door to Western traders and missionaries. The famous letter of the Jiaqing Emperor to George III[5] expressed this feeling. Chinese domestic trade was self-sufficient, as the Lazarist Evariste Huc noted in 1844 after a long inland journey through China: "One excellent reason why China is only moderately fond of trading with foreigners is that her home trade is immense. . . . China is such a vast, rich and varied country that internal trade is more than enough to occupy the part of the nation which can perform commercial operations . . . there is everywhere to be seen movement and a feverish activity which is not to be found in the largest towns of Europe."[6]

Moreover, China was not so isolated that its rulers had not meditated on the experiences of Japan and India. In Japan, the "Christian century" (1550–1650), during which the missionaries had been largely tolerated, ended in serious political trouble when groups of Christian converts rebelled against the imperial power. In India, trade first with the Portuguese, then with the British opened

---

[5] Document 2.
[6] Père Huc, *L'Empire chinois* (Paris, 1879), pp. 153–154.

the way in the middle of the eighteenth century for political penetration by the British East India Company, and ultimately for the conquest of India. Both precedents were well known to those in charge of imperial policy.

The hypothesis that the closed-door policy was the expression of a defensive reaction rather than a systematic and xenophobic hostility toward everything foreign is confirmed by the fact that the policy did not apply to Russia. From the seventeenth century on, relations between China and Russia were based on equal participation by each side. In 1689, after the Cossacks had arrived in East Siberia, the two countries signed a treaty at Nertchinsk to regulate their frontier traffic. They conducted a brisk and well-balanced trade, mainly an exchange of tea for furs. A permanent Russian mission which was religious, commercial, and political opened in Peking. The fact that the two nations were contiguous gave China a strong motive for establishing formal relations. Moreover, the slow, gradual way in which the Russians moved into Siberia enabled the Chinese to adjust to this foreign neighbor even while they tirelessly resisted the foreigners from Western Europe on their southern coast.

Increasing Pressure from the West: 1820–1835

When the Napoleonic Wars were over, the dynamic expansion of the Western economies once again drove Western traders abroad, especially in the direction of the Far East. But policies such as the British doctrine of "free trade" were clearly incompatible with the Chinese conception of "controlling barbarians." In 1816 Britain made another attempt to improve relations with China through the mission of Lord Amherst to Peking. He encountered the same quarrels over ceremony (particularly regarding prostration—the *koutou* or "kowtow" before the emperor), and the same ultimate refusal, that Lord Macartney had experienced in 1793. But the British founded Singapore in 1819, bringing their base for trading and military activities in the Far East considerably nearer to the Chinese coast. The West was knocking at the door.

Development of opium smuggling

Under the growing pressure for trade, the purchases made by British and American firms in Canton were multiplying. The Westerners were increasingly anxious to balance their trade with China. They did not want to go on paying for goods with silver, but the Chinese showed almost no interest in Western products because their own output was so varied. The economic bind led the British and American merchants into the large-scale smuggling of opium, a product that was forbidden in China except for medicinal use. The British Hong, or companies that were authorized to operate in Canton (such as Dent and Company and Jardine and Matheson), bought opium in Bengal, where it was produced cheaply by the subjects of the British East India Company; the American Hong bought it in Turkey. In this sense, the opium trade was an unhealthy extension of what in the eighteenth century had been known as "country" trade.

Between 1820 and 1835 opium smuggling developed all along the South China coast:

	No. of crates smuggled[7]
1820–1825	9,708 crates per year
1825–1830	18,712 crates per year
1830–1935	35,445 crates per year

Opium was unloaded in about a dozen seaports on the southeast coast, particularly ports in Guangdong and Fujian, and was dispatched in every direction. It was sold in Guangxi as far as Guilin and toward Guizhou; in Hunan as far as Changsha; and in all the Guangdong, Jiangxi, and Fujian hinterlands. It reached the lower and middle Yangzi basin once smugglers began operating in the neighborhood of Shanghai and Zhenjiang.

Troubles caused by the opium trade

Opium had been known in China since the Chinese Middle Ages, but for a long time only as medicine. Now the drug became a vice. The first to take it were young men from rich families, but in the towns it spread rapidly among all men under forty: small shopkeepers, peddlers, Taoists and geomancers, low-ranking officials in the public service, the lowest grades of *yamen* employees, the servants of the mandarins, and the entire army. Essentially it affected the services sector, where too many men were employed to do too

---

[7] The figures are approximations. Depending on the region where the crates came from, they varied in weight from 100 to 120 "catties" (Chinese pounds) each, or about 60 to 72 kilos.

little work and had plenty of free time. Around 1835, senior officials and generals assumed that 90 percent of their staffs were opium smokers. Estimates of the total number in the population were various and imprecise: Lin Ze-xu reckoned that there were 4 million opium smokers in China, while a British doctor in Canton set the figure at 12 million. Because of opium, business slowed down, the standard of living fell, and public services no longer worked smoothly.

Lin Ze-xu, a high-ranking official who later played a leading role in the opium crisis, calculated in 1839 that 100 million taels were being spent each year by Chinese opium smokers, while the government's entire annual revenue was approximately 40 million taels. "If we continue to allow this trade to flourish," he wrote, "in a few dozen years we will find ourselves not only with no soldiers to resist the enemy, but also with no money to equip the army."

The development of smuggling and the consumption of opium led to a shortage of silver that had an erosive effect on the monetary system. The sale of Chinese goods to Westerners no longer balanced Chinese purchases of opium. The difference was made up by the export of Chinese silver, prized by Westerners for its fine quality, particularly as the world silver market was in a period of contraction. In 1837 opium represented 57 percent of Chinese imports. Between 1828 and 1836 China exported 38 million Spanish dollars in silver—4½ million during the fiscal year 1835–1836 alone.

The outflow of silver contributed to the disturbances in the exchange rate between silver and copper that were crippling the Chinese economy. The loss of silver to the West aggravated all the problems connected with the drop in copper production in Yunnan and the deteriorating quality of copper coins. The rate of exchange between copper cash and the tael, theoretically 1,000 to 1, rose to 1,600 and 1,700 to 1 in 1838. The depreciation of copper was particularly severe in South China.

Opium smuggling by the British and Americans, together with other activities of the foreign firms in Canton, created a problem of authority that challenged the ability of the state to rule. Canton and the ports of the Southeast which were frequented illegally by foreign vessels were becoming centers of insubordination and corruption. Smuggling was carried out by means of a vast network of Chinese clients and Chinese systems of complicity. Many Chinese mandarins and merchants were eager to grow rich through trade with foreigners even if it meant defying imperial interdictions. The greediness of the officials of the *hoppo*, the customs office in Canton, was notorious. And in the entourage of the governor-general of Canton, Deng Ting-zhen (apparently an honest man himself), it was the practice to accept a bribe of 80 taels per crate of opium for turning a blind eye to smuggling in the port of Canton. Westerners also had the help of certain Chinese who dealt with the factories and had learned a little English. Some of these "traitors to the country of the Han," as the government called them, were connected with the missionaries. The Reverend Karl Gützlaff, the boisterous Pomeranian Lutheran who championed the British intervention in 1840–1842, had a large group of agents and interpreters whom he placed at the disposal of British troops during the war.

In short, Canton was a center of dissidence that presented a serious threat to the established order, even to the point of undermining the political loyalty that was founded on the relation between emperor and subject. Since the beginning of the nineteenth century the imperial authorities had tried to subdue this hotbed of disorder and subversion, but they were helpless. The legal penalties in the edict of 1800 for participating in the opium trade were enforced many times over against both traders and consumers. To no effect; the evil grew steadily.

Rising tension in Canton

Around 1830 there was constant friction between the personnel of the British factories and the Chinese authorities, especially over questions of unpaid debts and conflicts of jurisdiction. The Westerners in general were baffled by Chinese law and refused to submit to Chinese legal proceedings, particularly because these permitted the use of torture. The Chinese authorities were irritated by the extension of smuggling and all its consequences.

In 1834 the House of Commons decided not to renew the British East India Company's monopoly on trade in the Far East. The way was now clear for free trade. Lord Napier was sent to Canton to negotiate more favorable conditions for British companies, but his mission was a failure. Although his successors, Davis and Charles Elliot, practiced a wait-and-see policy, they supported the British Hong of the Canton factories no matter how open their smuggling or their general defiance of the Chinese authorities. Tension mounted, and in 1839 war broke out.

Causes of the Opium Wars

It would be an oversimplification to analyze the crisis of the Opium Wars and the great change in the Chinese historical process which began in 1840 merely in terms of Chinese stagnation and Western dynamism. In the middle of the nineteenth century China was neither passive nor inert, although the rhythm and the forces at work behind its evolution over two thousand years were very different from those operating in Western history. China had developed slowly over the ages, particularly after the arrival of the Ming dynasty in the fourteenth century. Agriculture made great progress with the introduction of American crops in the sixteenth century, and demographic patterns were profoundly transformed (population may have increased as much as four times under the Ming and the Qing). The machinery of state evolved steadily, as when the "single whip" tax was created at the end of the Ming dynasty, and when the Grand Council was formed in the eighteenth century.

Around 1830 rich and complex ideological currents were at work in China. The chief characteristic of the economy was the contradiction between state planning and the growth of private commercial capitalism. At the same time, government authority was weakening, government services were deteriorating, and social tension was mounting in the rural areas.

The internal crisis which had been coming to a head since the reign of the Jiaqing Emperor was not simply a classical instance of the withdrawal of the Mandate of Heaven. It was combined with an external crisis of a new sort, without precedent in the history of China. The foreigners who were determined to open China were not simply "barbarians" on its frontiers. They were Westerners at the time of the Industrial Revolution, members of a society whose historical development had reached a totally different level in a totally different direction. The characteristics of China's circumstances in 1840, and of the history of modern China in general, stem from the conjunction of these two crises.

ADDITIONAL BIBLIOGRAPHY

Etienne Balazs, *La Bureaucratie céleste* (Paris, Gallimard, 1968).
Jean Chesneaux, *Les Sociétés secrètes en Chine, XIXe–XXe siècles* (Paris, Julliard, 1965).

Ho Ping-ti, *Studies on the Population of China, 1368–1953* (Cambridge, Mass., Harvard University Press, 1959).

DOCUMENTS

1. CLANDESTINE SOLIDARITY AND REFUSAL OF THE ESTABLISHED ORDER: EXTRACTS FROM THE OATH OF INITIATION TAKEN BY MEMBERS OF THE TRIAD

SOURCE: *The Chinese Repository* (Canton, January–December 1848), vol. 17, pp. 282–287.

After entering the Great Brotherhood, you swear not to oppose the heavenly relations, nor alter your mind by violating this oath, nor plan any injury against a brother: if you do, may the god of Thunder utterly destroy and exterminate you. . . .

After entering, you swear not to vilify the laws or acts of the Association, nor introduce into company of the Brotherhood those who are not members, nor secretly disclose its principles: if you do, may your body be cut in pieces.

After entering, you swear, if you are a father, not to reveal the laws of the Brotherhood to your son, if an elder brother, not to tell them to your younger brother, nor to disclose them to your relations or friends: if you do, may you die under the sword.

After entering, you swear you will not oppress the weak by employing the strong, nor the poor by means of the rich, nor the few by the many: if you do, may you die by myriads of knives. . . .

After entering, you swear that whoever of your brethren meets with pressing difficulties, you will faithfully and disinterestedly rescue him: if you do not, may you be cut into myriads of pieces by thousands of swords. . . .

After entering, you swear that if you fill the situation of writer or policeman in the government offices, you will faithfully and diligently assist a brother in trouble: if you concoct any artful plans in this position, may the god of Thunder utterly destroy and exterminate you. . . .

After entering, you swear that should a brother become prosperous, you will not stop him in his path to extort from him: if you do, may you die by the sword. . . .

After entering, you swear you will not, on returning home, secretly discard your oath: if you thus privately release yourself from it, may you be struck down to Tartarus* and never undergo any transmigration.†

---

* That is, become a Manchu, a member of the dominating and disdained nationality.
† A sign of the Buddhist influences in the secret societies.

2. The Ch'ien Long Emperor: A decree

Source: Harley F. MacNair, *Modern Chinese History* (Shanghai, Commercial Press Ltd., 1923), pp. 2–9.

You, O King, from afar have yearned after the blessings of our civilization, and in your eagerness to come into touch with our converting influence have sent an Embassy across the sea bearing a memorial. I have already taken note of your respectful spirit of submission, have treated your mission with extreme favor and loaded it with gifts, besides issuing a mandate to you, O King, and honoring you with the bestowal of valuable presents. Thus has my indulgence been manifested.

Yesterday your Ambassador petitioned my Ministers to memorialize me regarding your trade with China, but his proposal is not consistent with our dynastic usage and cannot be entertained. Hitherto, all European nations, including your own country's barbarian merchants, have carried on their trade with Our Celestial Empire at Canton. Such has been the procedure for many years, although Our Celestial Empire possesses all things in prolific abundance and lacks no product within its own borders. There was therefore no need to import the manufactures of outside barbarians in exchange for our own produce. But as the tea, silk, and porcelain which the Celestial Empire produces are absolute necessities to European nations and to yourselves, we have permitted, as a signal mark of favor, that foreign *hongs* should be established at Canton, so that your wants might be supplied and your country thus participate in our beneficence. But your Ambassador has now put forward new requests which completely fail to recognize the Throne's principle to 'treat strangers from afar with indulgence,' and to exercise a pacifying control over barbarian tribes, the world over. Moreover, our dynasty, swaying the myriad races of the globe, extends the same benevolence toward all. Your England is not the only nation trading at Canton. If other nations, following your bad example, wrongfully importune my ear with further impossible requests, how will it be possible for me to treat them with easy indulgence? Nevertheless, I do not forget the lonely remoteness of your island, cut off from the world by intervening wastes of sea, nor do I overlook your excusable ignorance of the usages of Our Celestial Empire. I have consequently commanded my Ministers to enlighten your Ambassador on the subject, and have ordered the departure of the mission. I have ever shown the greatest condescension to the tribute missions of all states which sincerely yearn after the blessings of civilization, so as to manifest my kindly indulgence. I have even gone out of my way to grant any requests which were in any way consistent with Chinese usage. Above all, upon you, who live in a remote and inaccessible region, far across the spaces of ocean, but who have shown your submissive loyalty by sending this tribute mission, I have heaped benefits far in excess of those accorded to other nations. But the demands presented by your Embassy are not only a contravention of dynastic tradition, but would be utterly unproductive of good result to yourself, besides being quite impracticable. I have accordingly stated the facts to you in detail, and it is your bounden duty reverently to appreciate my feelings and to obey these instructions henceforward for all time, so that you may enjoy the blessings of perpetual peace. If, after the receipt of this explicit decree, you lightly give ear to the representations of your subordinates and allow your barbarian merchants to proceed to Chêkiang and Tientsin, with the object of landing and trading there, the ordinances of my Celestial Empire are strict in the extreme, and the local officials, both civil and military, are bound reverently to obey the law of the land. Should your vessels touch the shore, your merchants will assuredly never be permitted to land or to reside there, but will be subject to instant expulsion. In that event your barbarian merchants will have had a long journey for nothing. Do not say that you were not warned in due time! Tremblingly obey and show no negligence! A special mandate!

Chapter Three

The Opening
of China

The Opium Wars, which occurred in 1839–1842 and 1856–1860, were fought primarily to determine the relations between China and the West. Yet they not only profoundly changed the international circumstances of the Middle Kingdom, but also transformed the conceptions held by the Chinese themselves about their place in the world. The new demands on China made by the victorious West created internal problems that had far-reaching consequences, particularly for the Chinese economy.

Chinese Reactions to the First Opium War

Government debate on the opium problem

The pressure exerted by the British to open China, and the increase in opium smuggling between 1835 and 1838, raised issues that the Chinese tried to approach in the traditional way. Since the classic Western distinction between domestic and foreign affairs did not exist in China, the imperial authorities still refused to treat the Westerners as foreign nationals. In his diary Lin Ze-xu, one of the chief figures behind the Chinese resistance to foreign demands, constantly referred to the British as "rebels." In his view their activities in Canton disturbed the established order and upset the harmony of political and social relations. He and other Chinese authorities believed that harmony should be restored by eliminating the causes of disorder, not by negotiating with the "red-haired barbarians" on a diplomatic basis.[1]

Meanwhile opium smuggling had become an ever-expanding threat to the equilibrium of Chinese society. The volume of this trade suddenly increased in the period 1830–1835, and increased again when the monopoly of the British East India Company in the Far East was brought to an end.

In accordance with Chinese political tradition, the authorities opened a "debate" among local mandarins and senior officials of the central government on the political problems raised by Canton, opium, and the outflow of silver. The debate lasted nearly two years, from 1836 to 1838. Memorials addressed to the throne in the Confucian tradition proposed various solutions: a minority party favored an uncompromising stand against the opium traffic, while a more conciliatory group suggested that the opium trade should be made legal in the hope that it would be easier to control. The hard-line party won, and in 1839 an imperial statute in thirty-nine articles levied extremely heavy punishments (including the death penalty) both for trading in and for consuming opium.

Lin Ze-xu in Canton

Lin Ze-xu, a strict Confucian who had played an active part in the controversy, was sent to Canton as special commissioner to see that the new rules were applied. Lin belonged to the group of scholars (described in Chapter 2) who were interested in contemporary affairs and in Western science and techniques, particularly geography and military strategy. Although not a narrow-minded traditionalist, he was a man of principle who favored taking severe measures against Western traders.

In Canton Lin came into violent conflict with the British which resulted in the military expeditions known as the first Opium War (1839–1842). In actual fact, the measures he took when he arrived in the spring of 1839 were aimed just as much at the Chinese accomplices and clients of the foreign firms as at the firms themselves. In two months he made 1,600 arrests and confiscated 11,000 pounds of opium—actions which emphasize once more that

---

[1] See his letter to Queen Victoria in document 1 at the chapter end.

from the Chinese point of view the crisis leading up to the Opium War was a question of domestic policy, if not a simple police matter. He conducted a great ceremony of ritual expiation in June when, after forcing the foreign factories to hand over about 20,000 crates of opium, he had them destroyed and their ashes scattered over the sea. It was when Lin gave the order that Canton should be closed completely to foreign trade that Britain opened hostilities. The fighting began in the South and then moved to the region near the mouth of the Yangzi, where the British overcame the imperial troops with ease.

The conciliators prevail

The British victories coincided with a counteroffensive by the party within the government that favored a conciliatory attitude. Lin Ze-xu had tried to settle the opium question by treating it as an essentially internal problem; he came into conflict with the British solely insofar as they were responsible for internal disturbances in South China. But he had provoked a retaliation which he had been unable to meet. In September 1840 he was recalled in disgrace and sent into exile in the Northwest. His friend Wang Ting, a member of the Grand Council, committed suicide in protest. To replace Lin Peking appointed Qi-shan, a Manchu aristocrat related to the emperor. To a large extent the antagonism between the conciliatory party and the party opposed to compromise reflected the antagonism between Manchu aristocrats and Chinese senior officials.

The Manchu plenipotentiaries Qi-shan and his successor Qi-ying negotiated the Treaty of Nanking in 1842. Meanwhile the British troops occupied strategic positions on the coast: Amoy, the Zhoushan (Chushan) Islands, the bay of Hangzhou, Shanghai, and Zhenjiang. The treaty, which was highly advantageous to Britain, repudiated the policy of resistance advocated by Lin Ze-xu.

The new policy of conciliation was favored not only by the Manchus, who were uncertain of their political backing and unwilling to provoke a military reaction, but also locally in Canton by the bourgeoisie, the Hong merchants, the brokers and traders, and all people connected with the Western factories, since they all hoped to profit from an enlargement of foreign commerce. These Canton circles supported the Manchu decision in the spring of 1841 to pay the British a "ransom" of 6 million Mexican dollars for the town instead of trying to defend it.

Gentry and peasants oppose the British

The local scholars and rural gentry, on the other hand, were bitterly hostile to the foreigners and supported the policy of resistance. They organized and financed irregular military units known as "corps to reduce the British to a harmonious attitude." Some of these had been recruited among professional soldiers and were commanded by officers. Others were directly under the leadership of the gentry, and still others were companies of village militia which had grown up more or less spontaneously. In May 1841, when the siege of Canton had not yet ended in the "ransom," these irregular groups multiplied and showed considerable fighting spirit.

The most serious incident occurred on May 29 and 30 near the village of Sanyuanli. Several thousand peasants armed with pikes, scythes, and bamboo rods surrounded an Anglo-Indian battalion which had been looting the countryside, desecrating tombs, and molesting women. The battalion escaped only after the intervention of the prefect of Canton, a supporter of the conciliation policy. The British losses were slight, but the effect on Chinese morale was considerable. The memory of Sanyuanli has remained one of the favorite themes of modern Chinese nationalism.[2] It greatly strengthened the militia movement, and in July over 20,000 men from 103 villages were mobilized in that district with the help of the gentry.

In other regions of China the same popular resistance appeared sporadically, always through the joint action of the local gentry and the village militia. British units were harassed, and warships were attacked and sometimes burned, in Fujian, in the neighborhood of the town of Dinghai in the Zhoushan Islands, and in the vicinity of Ningbo. The first Opium War made the gulf between the imperial power and the popular forces still more obvious than before.

The Treaty Ports and Their Influence

The treaties of 1842 to 1844

The Treaty of Nanking of 1842, the "supplementary treaty" between China and Great Britain in 1843, the treaty between France

---

[2] See document 2 for a poem about the battle.

and China signed at Huangpu (Whampoa) in 1844, and the treaty between China and the United States, also signed in 1844, radically modified the West's conditions of access to China and the scope of Western activities there. Some terms of the treaties concerned Britain only, in that country's capacity as a belligerent power. For example, the island of Hong Kong was ceded to Britain, China agreed to pay an indemnity of 21 million Mexican dollars, and British troops were to occupy the Zhoushan Islands until the sum was handed over. Owing to the so-called most-favored-nation clause, the various advantages obtained by each power accumulated and formed the basis of the "unequal-treaties system" which gradually developed during the nineteenth and early twentieth centuries.

Five Chinese ports—Canton, Shanghai, Ningbo, Amoy, and Fuzhou—were declared "treaty ports." Foreign merchants and consuls had permission to reside and operate freely there. The Cohong system was abolished. Chinese customs duties were limited to 5 percent—which was 60 or 70 percent lower than the previous tariffs. In each treaty port the Westerners were granted extraterritoriality, which meant that they were subject only to the legal jurisdiction of their consul. They could buy land and open schools—a privilege particularly advantageous to the missionaries, though they were not specifically mentioned in the treaties. Finally, the warships of the foreign powers could anchor in the treaty ports, and could enter any Chinese port "when the interests of trade demanded."

China was therefore "open," that is, the treaties obliged the Chinese government to allow foreign activities to develop in the five ports. In the years following the first Opium War, the Westerners strengthened their positions inland by securing the concessions, or privileged zones, in the treaty ports and the control of the customs, neither of which had been provided in the treaties of 1842 to 1844.

The formation of the concessions

The concessions were privileged zones which, in some treaty ports, became real foreign enclaves exempt from Chinese authority. They originated in the treaty rights granted to foreigners to reside in the open ports. In 1845 the Chinese prefect of Shanghai concluded the land regulations—an agreement with the British consul determining the zone where the British could lease or buy land. In 1849 France negotiated a similar agreement for a second district of

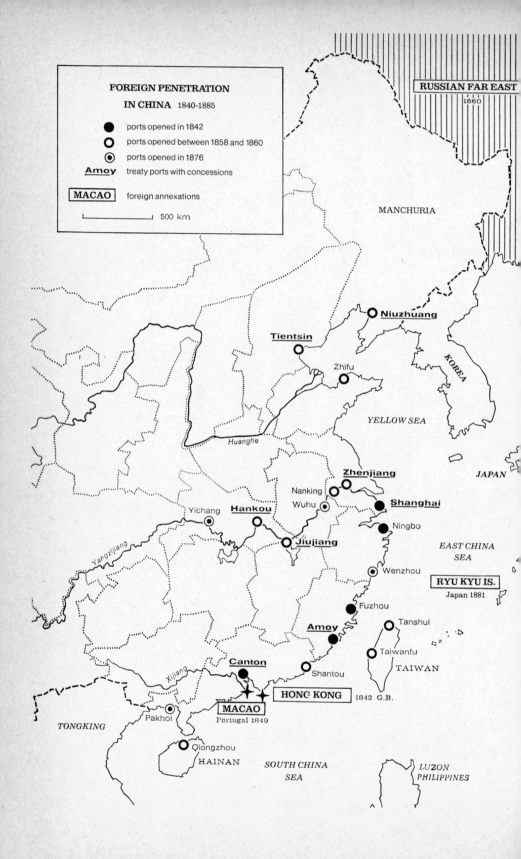

FOREIGN PENETRATION
IN CHINA 1840-1885

● ports opened in 1842

○ ports opened between 1858 and 1860

◉ ports opened in 1876

Amoy treaty ports with concessions

MACAO foreign annexations

500 km

RUSSIAN FAR EAST
1860

MANCHURIA

Niuzhuang

Tientsin

Zhifu

KOREA

YELLOW SEA

JAPAN

Huanghe

Zhenjiang

Nanking

Wuhu

Shanghai

Yichang

Hankou

Ningbo

Yangzijiang

Jiujiang

EAST CHINA
SEA

Wenzhou

RYU KYU IS.
Japan 1881

Fuzhou

Tanshui

Amoy

Taiwanfu

TAIWAN

Canton

Shantou

HONG KONG 1842 G.B.

MACAO
Portugal 1849

Xijiang

TONGKING

Pakhoi

Qiongzhou

HAINAN

SOUTH CHINA
SEA

LUZON
PHILIPPINES

the town, and later the United States followed suit. Each of these zones was on the banks of the Huangpu.

After gaining the right to live in their own district, the British moved on to obtain a second series of related privileges in 1854. This was at the time of the legitimist revolt of the Small Sword (described in Chapter 4) and the eclipse of imperial authority in Shanghai. The British created an autonomous political body, the municipal council, on the territory of their concession. The council was elected by holders of land leases. It administered a budget, carried out municipal and town planning activities, provided a police force, and levied taxes.[3] It had the power of mobilizing foreign residents, and in 1853 during the Ming legitimists' revolt in Shanghai it formed the Shanghai volunteer corps, a sort of bourgeois militia. Thus the concession, an entirely original social institution, was built up empirically and unilaterally, grafted like an excrescence onto the Chinese political and social body. The Chinese authorities were consulted only as to its boundaries, not as to its political status. The fact that Chinese sovereignty was being encroached upon became particularly obvious when the concessions, which were originally almost empty and were intended as a sort of "reserve" for foreigners, were suddenly peopled by tens of thousands of Chinese refugees owing to the Taiping war. And once they lived in a concession, the Chinese were exempt from the authority of their own government.

The act of 1854 defining the new municipal authority was drawn up by the consuls of Great Britain, the United States, and France. The fusion between the British and American concessions lasted (the joint concession became known as the "international concession"), but the French concession quickly regained its independence. The first sign of administrative autonomy appeared in 1856, when the residents of the concession voted on a budget for roads and bridges. A proper municipality was created in that concession a little later on. Further south, the foreign residents in Amoy settled on the island of Gulangyu opposite the harbor around 1850, forming the embryo of a new and completely international concession. In the three other ports opened in 1842, on the other hand, the right of residence granted to foreign consuls and merchants was not given such a broad interpretation. Fuzhou and Ningbo were smaller, and the colony of Hong Kong ensured conditions of resi-

[3] Document 3 gives the regulation establishing the council and describing its duties.

dence for the foreign merchants in the Canton region which were even better than in the concessions.

Foreign control of the Shanghai customs

The political unrest of the 1850s also made it easier to bring the Shanghai customs under foreign control. In the period 1852 to 1853 the British consul in Shanghai, Rutherford Alcock, demanded that foreign merchants be exempted from paying customs dues, because they were in financial difficulties owing to the Taiping war and the decrease in trade. When the Small Sword revolt broke out in Shanghai in 1853, the rebels drove the prefect out of town. The Western consuls decided to collect customs dues themselves, at least in the form of promissory notes. When the prefect, Wu Sam-qua (a former Hong merchant in Canton), returned in 1854, the consuls persuaded him to entrust the collection of customs dues in Shanghai to a permanent body of foreign inspectors. In exchange they guaranteed that the arrears of the past two years would be paid. The inspectors would be proposed by the consuls and appointed formally by the prefect, to whom they would hand over the taxes they collected.

An important part of the Chinese machinery of state thereby came under foreign control. It began as a local expedient but quickly became a permanent system. In the years that followed, it was extended to the whole of China.

Shanghai: A cosmopolitan society

Even at this early stage, the society in the treaty ports was as original as the political status of the ports themselves. This was especially true of Shanghai, which had been the smallest of the five ports before the Opium War, but which now mushroomed owing to the immense economic potential of the Yangzi basin.

Between 1850 and 1860 Shanghai had a foreign population of over a thousand, most of them connected with the consulates or with the large British and American firms—the Hong, like Jardine and Matheson, Dent and Company, and Russell and Company. Their heads, the *taipan*, were the real masters of the town. They were industrialists who had come to China to make rapid fortunes and did not encumber themselves with moral scruples or with any concern for long-range city planning. The Shanghai of the twentieth century, with its narrow streets and overcrowded buildings, still bears traces of their improvisations and their basic indifference. The Hong which had grown rich on the opium trade in the preceding years had generally had six departments: tea, silk, "Manchester articles" (British-made textiles), freight and insurance, landed property, and "miscellaneous" (chief of which was opium). Land speculation was extremely active. In 1852 an acre of land in the international concession was worth 50 pounds sterling; in 1862 it was worth 10,000 pounds.

The atmosphere of feverish business activity was reflected in the town landscape, with its rows of warehouses, or godowns, its red-brick bungalows in British colonial style, and its office blocks on the banks of the Huangpu (the Bund). The life of the semicolonial foreign community was chronicled by the English-language press of the time: the *North China Herald* was founded in 1850, at roughly the same time as the *Friend of China* and the *China Mail* of Hong Kong, founded in 1841 and 1845 respectively.

A world of Chinese clients and assistants grew up around the foreign community, ranging from compradors and interpreters to coolies and servants ("boys," "amahs," etc.). The compradors, managers to whom the Hong entrusted business transactions with the Chinese, were largely autonomous and formed the nuclei of a Chinese business bourgeoisie linked with modern capitalism. Many of them—and generally speaking, many of the traders and intermediaries who flourished in the shadow of the Western Hong—came from other regions of China, such as Ningbo. Most of all, they came from Canton, where Chinese had dealt with foreigners for a third of a century. These men whom the imperial authorities had called "Chinese traitors" provided the first Chinese executive staffs in the consulates and in the Shanghai Hong. John K. Fairbank has spoken of the "Cantonization" of Shanghai between 1850 and 1860. A case in point was the transformation of Wu Sam-qua, the former Cohong merchant, who managed to become prefect of Shanghai so that he could continue his fruitful business with the Westerners.

The society of Shanghai, and that of the open ports in general, had an artificial quality because it was outside the Chinese social organization. In Shanghai's busy streets Chinese from all provinces mingled with foreigners of all nationalities. Besides the Westerners there were many Indians, whom the British had brought over as servants or policemen. In its melting-pot diversity Shanghai society had some points in common with the United States or Australia during the same period. Its composite multitude used a sort of hybrid language known as pidgin English, made up of corrupt forms of English words, Malay expressions brought in by sailors (like *godown*), and Chinese terms borrowed from the local dialect.

Piracy

By a series of barely perceptible shadings the world of the compradors, the interpreters attached to the consulates, and their hangers-on graded into a murky assortment of vagabonds who had come to look for easy profits in a new, inadequately controlled environment. Shanghai had a floating population of deserters from various navies and merchant marines (from the West, the Philippines, and Macao), as well as smugglers and adventurers from Ningbo and Fujian who formed regional gangs. This underworld supplied the clientele for countless opium dens, brothels, and gambling dens. The treaty ports, and especially Shanghai, contributed to the disintegration of Chinese society; they formed a sort of historical no-man's-land free from control by the regular Chinese authorities and detached from China. The foreigners for their part had neither the power nor the wish to create social structures as stable as those in their own countries.

One result of this social license was the increase in piracy on the southeast coast after the Opium Wars. China had turned its back on the sea for several centuries, and at the time of the Cohong the only traffic in the coastal regions was local trade. The opening of the five ports and the resulting development of large-scale trade was paralleled by the development of piracy, particularly around Ningbo and the archipelagos off the coast of Zhejiang. Pirates in gangs several hundred strong often sailed in fleets of lorchas—boats that were typical of the society of transition, with Western hulls and Chinese rig. Some of the gangs were in league with the Portuguese of Macao. The British navy fought some hard battles with the pirate fleet between 1850 and 1860 but was unable to wipe them out.

The Christian missions

In 1842 the Treaty of Nanking gave legal sanction to Christian missions in the ports. The Protestants took advantage of it by preaching the Bible, opening dispensaries and schools, and training catechists (who were often Cantonese). In 1844 the Daoguang Emperor issued an edict of tolerance toward Roman Catholics, after which the Jesuits settled at Xujiahui (Zikawei) in the suburbs of Shanghai. Lazarists and members of the foreign missions were also numerous in the five ports. They often traveled inland even though this violated the terms of the treaty, which required foreigners to *reside* in the five ports and thereby set a limit of one day on any trips to the interior. Between 1842 and 1856 about fifteen Catholic missionaries were arrested far inland and expelled from the country. Even so, nearly a hundred Catholics actually lived inland, benefiting from the tolerance of the mandarins and their anxiety to avoid conflict with the European powers. Strictly speaking, the 1844 edict of tolerance applied only to Chinese Catholics throughout the country.

Foreign trade in China

The business activities of foreigners, who were now freed from the "Canton system," were organized around the treaty ports, where tea and silk could be bought and cotton fabrics sold. Since the five ports lay between Shanghai and Canton along the southeast coast, the trading inclinations of the Westerners fitted in with the economic map of China. (Later, as Chapter 9 will describe, the Europeans managed to remodel that economic map, beginning around 1895 with the "breakup," the railway concessions, and the zones of influence.) Through the treaties of 1842 to 1844, the West sought access to the most developed regions of China, where the economy was naturally liveliest.

Between the two Opium Wars, however, trade did not expand as rapidly as the promoters of the open-door policy had hoped. The market was still limited to the treaty ports and the neighborhood surrounding them, and the Chinese economy was still largely self-sufficient in the basic necessities. Inland, the famous "Manchester articles" such as cotton fabrics could not compete with the local thread and cloth, which were cheaper and better adapted to Chinese habits. In 1850 Chinese imports of British manufactured goods were much lower than in 1844. Over the period 1843–1857 the value of Chinese purchases increased only from 1,750,000 to 2,450,000 pounds sterling.

On the other hand, the freight business of the British merchant navy along the Chinese coasts flourished. Chinese vessels, both junks and lorchas, joined in, buying a "colonial license" in Hong Kong partly because they hoped it would give them better protection from pirates, but mostly because it enabled them to avoid close supervision by the mandarins. The inshore traffic was a real "foreign invasion of coastal traffic," as John K. Fairbank has termed it.

This was also the time when coolies were shipped like cattle beyond the Pacific by unscrupulous shipping companies and recruiters of manpower. Poor peasants and the down-and-out elements of the towns were lured by seductive advertisements, particularly in Macao and Amoy. The men were sent to the great plantations of Cuba or Peru, and to Australia, where they were worked like slaves for a short time. Or rather, those who survived the trip were worked, but the conditions on board were so appalling that the death rate was high.

The opium trade continued to prosper; Western negotiators had deliberately avoided any mention of it in the early treaties. China's exports increasingly exceeded imports; in 1853, for example, British purchases in China were three times larger than sales. Opium made it unnecessary for Western firms to bring silver to China to balance their deals. In 1842 Westerners sold 33,000 chests of opium in China, while in 1850 the figure was 52,000. After the harsh ordeal they had had to undergo between 1841 and 1843, the mandarins were even more reluctant to oppose the trade than they had been before the war.

Economic effects of the treaty ports

How much was the Chinese economy affected, in whole or in any part, by the boom in the treaty ports? Historians have described the economic progress of the ports in detail, but they have had much less to say on the broader subject.

The tea- and silk-producing regions, particularly Zhejiang and Fujian, certainly benefited from the increase in foreign purchases. Between 1845 and 1858 exports of silk from Shanghai rose from 6,000 to 85,000 bales and tea exports from 3,800,000 to 51,-300,000 pounds. On the other hand, exports of tea from Canton fell from 76,000,000 to 24,000,000 pounds over the same period. In other words, Canton no longer handled all the South China tea exports. The consequent decline in inland traffic between the lower

Yangzi and Canton ruined the population of boatmen, porters, and
coolies who lived on it. These unemployed groups subsequently
played an important part in the Taiping rebellion which broke out
in the Cantonese hinterland.

The opening of the ports seems to have had no effect on handicraft production. Chinese handicrafts stood up well to competition
from imported goods, except in a few regions like the districts
around Canton that specialized in silk spinning and weaving. Contemporary chronicles report that people were already without work
there around 1850, and their numbers went to swell the Red Tur-
ban insurrection in those districts in 1854.

Monetary disturbances

The monetary crisis provoked by foreign economic activity
around the treaty ports was severe. The sudden rise in the volume
of trade resulted in a shortage of the carolus, the old Spanish silver
dollar that had been used in Chinese coastal regions since the eighteenth century. When it began to appreciate out of proportion to its
weight in silver, it became even scarcer because of hoarding. In
Canton, the shortage of currency was so acute in 1853 that the
Spanish dollar was abolished as a unit of account. With the agreement of the Chinese authorities in Canton, the carolus was replaced
by the Mexican silver dollar ("the republican"). In Shanghai,
where speculation in the carolus had put it on a par with the tael,
the carolus was abolished and the Mexican dollar was officially
introduced in 1857. The unit of account in Shanghai, however,
became the tael, that is, a certain weight in silver and not a currency in the strict sense. To complicate matters further, customs
duties in the treaty ports were paid in yet another unit of account,
the "customs tael," a fictitious unit used mainly in the business
world.

Aggravating these currency disturbances tied up with the opening of China were the effects of the internal crisis in the Chinese
monetary system. As it had been doing since the beginning of the
nineteenth century, Chinese copper cash continued to lose value
relative to silver currency, owing to bad administration in general,
an inadequate supply of copper, and the hoarding of silver because
of troubles and rebellions. Between 1850 and 1855 the rate of
exchange in some districts was as high as 2,000 copper cash for 1
tael. The government was reduced to striking iron coins (which

were heavy to handle and rapidly became disfigured by rust), introducing "large copper coins" worth ten ordinary ones, and in 1853, even issuing paper money.

The Intellectual Discovery of the West

The West had existed on the Chinese intellectual horizon since the arrival of the Jesuit missionaries in the sixteenth century. With the Opium Wars, however, the intellectual discovery of the West acquired a new meaning, and in many respects a disturbing one. The West presented a challenge to Chinese tradition and the imperial power; it created issues that concerned the whole nation. It was no longer merely a subject for abstract study by a few scholars, but a problem for general anxiety.

Lin Ze-xu and Wei Yuan

The study of the West was given special encouragement by Lin Ze-xu, the imperial commissioner of Canton who destroyed 20,000 crates of British opium in 1839. Lin's opposition to British trade and British smuggling did not arise from a conservative and backward-looking cast of mind, but from a desire to promote Chinese national defense. He acknowledged the military superiority of the West. "After all," he wrote to a friend in 1842, "ships, guns and a water force are absolutely indispensable. Even if the rebellious barbarians had fled and returned beyond the seas, these things would still have to be urgently planned for, in order to work out the permanent defense of our sea frontiers. Moreover, unless we have weapons, what other help can we get now to drive away the crocodile and to get rid of the whales?"[4]

During his term of office in Canton Lin Ze-xu collected all sorts of information about the West—missionary tracts, commercial treatises, geographical descriptions; whatever was available. He had the material translated, studied it, and passed it on to his friend Wei Yuan who, like Lin, was a member of the circle of reformers known as the "contemporary affairs" group. Wei Yuan used Lin's material to compile his *Atlas of the Countries Beyond the Seas*, first

---

[4] Ssu-yu Teng and John K. Fairbank, *China's Response to the West* (Cambridge, Mass., Harvard University Press, 1954), p. 28.

published in 1842. Revised several times, it eventually had 100 chapters, which were studied zealously by scholars and officials of the following generation.

Wei Yuan's aim was not a disinterested search for knowledge; he wanted to develop concrete policies to defend China against the barbarians. He suggested, for instance, that France or the United States be used against Britain and that Russia be used against British India, thus raising the old Chinese method of "using barbarians to control barbarians" to the level of world diplomacy. He also believed that the main effort should be to create a defensive strategy inland, a strategy which should include the waterways. In his view it had been a mistake to concentrate the fighting in the coastal areas during the war of 1840–1842. Wei was also in favor of building a modern arsenal near Canton.

The conciliators: *Xu Ji-yu*

Other scholars who studied the West were supporters of the policy of conciliation followed by the imperial government after the treaties of 1842 to 1844. One such scholar was Xu Ji-yu (1795–1873), the governor of Fujian. Xu was responsible for relations with foreigners at Amoy and Fuzhou, the two open ports in the province. With the help of materials supplied by foreign missionaries, he published *A Description of the Ocean Circuits* in 1850. His book was shorter but more accurate (particularly in its maps) than the geography of the world by Wei Yuan.[5] His approach was the opposite of Wei Yuan's: Xu's aim was to learn more about the Western countries in order to cooperate with them more effectively in the context of the treaties of 1842 to 1844.

Scientific relations

Relations between China and the West also developed in the scientific field during the opening-up period. Some of the Protestant missionaries who had settled in the open ports and in Hong Kong had a sound training in medicine; others were proficient in mathematics.

Books on modern medicine and surgery were translated by people connected with the hospitals established in the open ports by the

[5] See Xu's account of Great Britain in document 4.

China Medical Missionary Society (founded in Canton in 1838). Chinese doctors and surgeons were trained to practice Western medicine. Vaccination was introduced into Canton at the beginning of the nineteenth century by Pearson, an East India Company doctor, and spread from there throughout South China. You He-chuan, a doctor trained by Pearson, was said to have vaccinated a million people.

In Shanghai the missionary and mathematician Alexander Wylie became associated with a group of scholars from the lower Yangzi, the best known of whom was Li Shan-lan. They continued the translation into Chinese of the works of Euclid, taking it up again at the exact point (Book VII) where Matteo Ricci had left off at the beginning of the seventeenth century. Between 1855 and 1859 Li Shan-lan, with the help of missionaries, translated the astronomical treatise by Herschel, as well as works on mechanics, differential and integral calculus, and botany. Li was not only a translator but himself a mathematician who specialized in algebra and logarithms. After 1860 he worked at the Tong Wen Guan, founded in Peking by the imperial government in connection with the reform movement known as *yangwu* (see Chapter 7).

The Second Opium War

The Western countries were dissatisfied with what they had acquired through the treaties signed between 1842 and 1844. They had not achieved their aims in China, either locally in Canton or in the country as a whole.

The Canton crisis

In Canton, which had been the traditional base for foreign activities in China since the eighteenth century, Westerners were annoyed by the refusal of the authorities to grant them access to the walled city—the political and commercial center of the town. A raid carried out by the British in 1847 ended in a Chinese promise to open the city in 1849. But popular resistance to the West, supported by the local gentry, continued. Clashes frequently broke out between the British or Indians and the militia of the "school for attaining harmony," as the federation of anti-British groups in Guangdong was called. The federation, backed by the gentry, was

strongly rooted in the villages. In 1849 this militia organized a mass
mobilization in opposition to opening the city to the British. The
call to arms was approved by the new governor-general of the South,
Xu Guang-jin, a friend of Lin Ze-xu, and by the new governor of
Canton, Ye Ming-zhen, who also belonged to the hard-line faction.
The village troups were reinforced by the urban militia, which was
financed by the Canton merchants (the former Cohong, deprived of
commercial privileges after the treaties of 1842). Britain gave way
and temporarily abandoned the attempt to enter the walled city of
Canton.

But the British failure merely intensified British dissatisfaction.
War was approaching, fostered not only by the desire to open Canton but also by broader Western aims. Foreign trade with China
had not developed as much as the West had expected. The lucrative
opium trade was still illegal. Westerners turned their attention to
the Northern and inland ports, thinking that these would offer
much more scope for foreign business than the five ports of the
Treaty of Nanking. They also wanted to negotiate directly with
Peking. The central government had handed over responsibility for
"barbarian affairs" to senior officials, whose powers and hierarchical positions were inadequately understood by the foreigners. All
these points were included in a joint paper presented to the authorities in 1854 by the ministers of France, Britain, and the United
States, demanding that the treaties be revised.

The hard-line faction regains power

Peking refused to alter the treaties in any way. At court, changes
were taking place that undermined the supporters of conciliation,
who had been in power since the eviction of Lin Ze-xu in 1841.
Their principal leaders, the Manchus Qi-ying, who had signed the
treaty of 1852, and Mu Zhang-a, Grand Secretary and head of the
Grand Council, were steadily losing ground. The appointments of
Xu Guang-jin as governor-general of the South, and of Ye Ming-
zhen to Canton in 1848 in place of Qi-ying, were victories for the
supporters of the hard line. When the Daoguang Emperor died in
1850 the whole party of Mu Zhang-a was dishonored, and heavy
fiscal punishments were levied against the members. Apart from
their failures in foreign policy, they were blamed for domestic upheavals such as the Taiping rebellion, which had just broken out.
The new Xianfeng Emperor, who was violently hostile to foreign-

ers, gave leading posts to men like Qi Jun-cao, a Chinese mandarin of the old school.

But the Manchu aristocracy tended to concentrate power in its own hands as successive dangers arose from within or without. Under the Xianfeng Emperor the real center for policy making was not the Grand Council and the Grand Secretariat but an unofficial body, the "council of princes." Its real head was the Manchu aristocrat Su-shun, who was responsible for government finance and served as chairman of the Ministry of Ceremonies. Although Su-shun was hostile to Qi Jun-cao because the Manchu wanted to keep the power within the council of princes, he also favored the hard line against foreigners. This shows that the opposition between the resistance and the conciliation parties did not correspond exactly to the cleavage between the Chinese and the Manchus. However, most of the supporters of the hard line were Chinese mandarins (examples were the mandarins Lin Ze-xu, Qi Jun-cao, Xu Guang-jin, and Ye Ming-zhen, who was appointed Grand Secretary in 1856, although he continued to live in Canton).

Thus the political divisions high in the administration and in the entourage of the emperor reflected the acuteness of the international problems and the rivalry between the Chinese and the Manchus. In addition, however, they were the result of personal power struggles between factions. An example was Su-shun's plot in 1859 against a highly influential Manchu, the Grand Secretary Po-jun. Su-shun managed to implicate him in a scandal concerning fraud in the imperial examinations, and succeeded in having him condemned and beheaded.

The political situation at court was further complicated by problems arising from the repression of the Taiping rebellion. Some Manchus, especially the group centered around Su-shun, were in favor of giving political promotion to the most dynamic elements of the Chinese gentry—men like Zeng Guo-fan, whose local militia led by landowners had halted the rebel advance. But the traditionalists among the Chinese senior officials, such as Qi Jun-cao, were unwilling to make room for young and turbulent rivals.

The second Opium War and the treaties of 1858 to 1860

Weakened by factionalism, the imperial government was incapable of determined resistance to the French and the British during the second Opium War (1856–1860). Both powers were determined to impose their views on Peking by any available method. They made the most of minor incidents, such as the arrest on piracy charges of the crew of the lorcha *Arrow*, who claimed that they were covered by a license bought in Hong Kong which had expired a week earlier. Another incident was the arrest and execution of a French missionary, Father Chapedelaine, in an inland province where he had no right to be, according to the treaties of 1842 to 1844.

The war began in the South with the bombarding of Canton and the burning of its British factories. In spite of Ye Ming-zhen's stubborn efforts to defend the town, it was captured in 1858. The war continued in the North from 1859 to 1860, when French and British troops attacked Peking with the aim of forcing the emperor to ratify the treaty drawn up in 1858. The foreigners captured and looted the capital, including the famous summer palace. ("Two bandits, France and England, entered a cathedral in Asia," as Victor Hugo described it.)

One result of the Chinese defeats was that the conciliation party returned to power, and a part of the council of princes joined forces with it. Qi-ying, whose name was a symbol of the search for an agreement with the West, was recalled and sent to take part in the negotiations. While the French and British advanced on Peking, the court fled to Jehol in a timid attempt at resistance which had no sequels. The princes' return to the conciliation policy was motivated above all by the desire to save the dynasty and the regime. But some people, among them some senior Chinese officials, were already thinking about the possibility of getting Western help against the Taiping and other popular rebellions, and in general about implementing a policy of carefully controlled modernization. The failure of the hard-line conservative faction of the Opium War period prepared the way for the "foreign matters," or Westernization, movement (*yangwu*) of the years 1860 to 1890.

The treaties signed in Tientsin and Peking from 1858 to 1860 represented an even worse defeat for China than those of 1842 to 1844. Eleven more ports were opened, including Tientsin and Hankou. Western vessels were allowed access to certain inland waterways, and Western missionaries and merchants were granted the right to travel about the country and to buy land. The importing of opium was made legal. Foreign goods were allowed to circulate in the country and were exempt from the transit tax (*lijin*), which was replaced by a lump-sum payment in the form of a surtax of 2.5

percent. France and Britain each received a war indemnity of 8 million taels. They acquired the right to send permanent diplomatic missions to Peking. Russia meanwhile had taken advantage of the crisis to occupy vast territories in the Northeast; the Treaty of Peking (November 1860) confirmed the Russian acquisition of the northern bank of the Amur and the eastern bank of the Ussuri, where Muraviev had already founded Vladivostok.

The period of the Opium Wars and the opening of China fundamentally transformed the relations between China and the Western powers. As for domestic affairs, the defeats suffered by the Manchu power were the outward expression of its political inability to win support among the most vital elements of the populace. The resistance at Sanyuanli in 1842 (which recurred in 1857) did not spread. The hasty capitulation of the imperial power made its weakness still more obvious and contributed to the outbreak of anti-Manchu peasant movements in the years between 1850 and 1870.

ADDITIONAL BIBLIOGRAPHY

Chang Hsin-pao, *Commissioner Lin and the Opium War* (Cambridge, Mass., Harvard University Press, 1964).

John K. Fairbank, *Trade and Diplomacy on the China Coast: The Opening of the Treaty Ports, 1842–1854* (Cambridge, Mass., Harvard University Press, 1953).

Ch. Maybon and J. Fredet, *Histoire de la concession française de Changhai* (Paris, Plon, 1929).

Frank Wakeman, *Strangers at the Gate: Social Disorder in South China, 1839–1861* (Berkeley, University of California Press, 1966).

Arthur Waley, *The Opium War Through Chinese Eyes* (London, Allen & Unwin, 1958).

Wei Tsing-sing, *La politique missionnaire de la France en Chine, 1842–1856* (Paris, Nouvelles Editions Latines, 1960).

DOCUMENTS

1. MORAL AND SOCIAL CRITICISM OF BRITISH OPIUM SMUGGLING: LIN ZE-XU'S LETTER TO QUEEN VICTORIA (1839)

SOURCE: English translation by Arthur Waley (from Lin Ze-xu's diary). *The Opium War Through Chinese Eyes* (London, Allen & Unwin, 1958), pp. 28–31.

The Way of Heaven is fairness to all; it does not suffer us to harm others in order to benefit ourselves. Men are alike in this all the world over; that they cherish life and hate what endangers life. Your country lies twenty thousand leagues away; but for all that the Way of Heaven holds good for you as for us, and your instincts are not different from ours; for nowhere are there men so blind as not to distinguish between what brings life and what brings death, between what brings profit and what does harm. Our Heavenly Court treats all within the Four Seas as one great family; the goodness of our great Emperor is like Heaven, that covers all things. There is no region so wild or so remote that he does not cherish and tend it. Ever since the port of Canton was first opened, trade has flourished.* For some hundred and twenty or thirty years the natives of the place have enjoyed peaceful and profitable relations with the ships that come from abroad. Rhubarb,† tea, silk are all valuable products of ours, without which foreigners could not live. The Heavenly Court, extending its benevolence to all alike, allows these things to be sold and carried away across the sea, not grudging them even to remote domains, its bounty matching the bounty of Heaven and Earth.

But there is a class of evil foreigner that makes opium and brings it for sale, tempting fools to destroy themselves, merely in order to reap profit. Formerly the number of opium smokers was small; but now the vice has spread far and wide and the poison penetrated deeper and deeper. If there are some foolish people who yield to this craving to their own detriment, it is they who have brought upon themselves their own ruin, and in a country so populous and flourishing, we can well do without them. But our great, unified Manchu Empire regards itself as responsible for the habits and morals of its subjects and cannot rest content to see any of them become victims to a deadly poison. For this reason we have decided to inflict very severe penalties on opium dealers and opium smokers, in order to put a stop forever to the propagation of this vice. It appears that this poisonous article is manufactured by certain devilish persons in places subject to your rule. It is not, of course, either made or sold at your bidding, nor do all the countries you rule produce it, but only certain of them. I am told that in your own country opium smoking is forbidden under severe penalties. This means that you are aware of how harmful it is. But better than to forbid the smoking of it would be to forbid the sale of it and, better still, to forbid the production of it, which is the only way of cleansing the contamination at its source. So long as you do not take it yourselves, but continue to make it and tempt the people of China to buy it, you will be showing yourselves careful of your own lives, but careless of the lives of other people, indifferent in your greed for gain to the harm you do to others; such conduct is repugnant to human feeling and at variance with the Way of Heaven. . . .

The laws against the consumption of opium are now so strict in China that if you continue to make it, you will find that no-one buys it

---

* That is, since the port was opened in the middle of the eighteenth century to British trade under the Canton system of the Cohong.

† At that time the Chinese were convinced that "red-haired barbarians" could not do without Chinese rhubarb, for use as a laxative.

and no more fortunes will be made. Rather than waste your efforts on a hopeless endeavour, would it not be better to devise some other form of trade? All opium discovered in China is being cast into burning oil and destroyed. Any foreign ships that in the future arrive with opium on board, will be set fire to, and any other goods that they are carrying will inevitably be burned along with the opium. You will then not only fail to make any profit out of us, but ruin yourselves into the bargain. Intending to harm others, you will be the first to be harmed. Our Heavenly Court would not have won the allegiance of innumerable lands did it not wield superhuman power. Do not say you have not been warned in time. On receiving this, Your Majesty will be so good as to report to me immediately on the steps that have been taken at each of your ports.

2. POPULAR POETRY IN PRAISE OF THE PEASANT RESISTANCE AT SANYUANLI AGAINST THE BRITISH ARMY

SOURCE: Frank Wakeman, *Strangers at the Gate: Social Disorder in South China, 1839–1861* (Berkeley, University of California Press, 1966), p. 20. (From the anthology in Chinese compiled by A. Ying, *Literature of the Opium War.*)

> They roared like thunder before Sanyuanli:
> A thousand, ten thousand, assembled at once,
> Righteousness behind rage, and rage behind the braves,
> While the villagers' force broke the enemies' ranks.
> Fields and villages—all must be manned.
> None waited for the drum's snare to awaken his zeal.
> Wives were of one mind with their heroic men,
> Mattocks and hoes turned to weapons at hand.
> Around the hamlets, far and near, flashed the
> Banners of every colour and hue.
> One brigade, then a hundred, over the hills beyond,
> While barbarians looked on and suddenly paled.

3. THE CONCESSIONS AS *de facto* AUTONOMOUS TERRITORIES: REGULATION VIII OF THE INTERNATIONAL CONCESSION OF SHANGHAI (1845)

SOURCE: *Report of the Hon. Richard Feetham, CMG, to the Shanghai Municipal Council* (Shanghai, 1931), vol. 1, p. 74.

It being expedient and necessary for the better order and good government of the Settlement that some provision should be made for the appointment of an executive Committee or Council, and for the construction of public works, and keeping the same in repair; and for cleaning, lighting, watering and draining the Settlement generally; establishing a watch or Police force therein; purchasing and renting lands, houses and buildings for Municipal purposes; paying the persons necessarily employed in any Municipal office or capacity, and for raising money when necessary by way of loan or otherwise for any of the purposes aforesaid, the Foreign Treaty Consuls, or a majority of them, shall during the month of February or March each year, and so early in the same as possible, fix the day for the election of the Executive Committee or Council, in manner hereinafter provided, giving fourteen days' notice of the same, and shall also during the said months give notice of a public meeting to be held within twenty-one days of such notice, to devise ways and means of raising the requisite funds for these purposes; and it shall be competent to such meeting duly assembled, or a majority thereof, including proxies for absent owners of land, to impose and levy rates and issue licences for the purposes mentioned in the Bye-laws, and to declare an assessment in the form of a rate to be made on the said land or buildings; provided always that the proportion between the tax on land, and on houses or buildings, shall not exceed one-twentieth of one per cent. on the gross value of land to one per cent. on the annual rental of houses; and it shall also be competent to the said meeting, or a majority thereof as aforesaid, to impose other rates and taxes in the form of dues on all goods passed through the Chinese Custom House by any person or persons resident within the said limits, or land, shipped or transhipped at any place within the said limits; provided the said rates or taxes levied in the form of dues shall in no case exceed the amount of one-tenth of one per cent. on the value of the goods so passed, landed, shipped or transhipped, and in such other forms as may appear requisite and necessary for the purposes aforesaid.

4. DESCRIPTION OF GREAT BRITAIN IN THE MANUAL OF WORLD GEOGRAPHY BY XU JI-YU (1848)

SOURCE: English translation by Ssu-yu Teng and John K. Fairbank in *China's Response to the West* (Cambridge, Mass., Harvard University Press, 1954), pp. 42–43.

The population of England is dense and the food insufficient. It is necessary for them to import from other countries. More than 490,000 people are engaged in weaving. The weaving machine is made of iron, and is operated by a steam engine, so it can move automatically. Thus labor is saved and the cost of production is low. Each year more than 400,000 piculs [1 picul equals 133 lbs.] of cotton are used, all of which are shipped in from the five parts of India and America. . . . Silk is purchased and shipped from China and Italy. The work of manufacturing guns, cannon, knives, swords, clocks, watches and various kinds of utensils and tools for daily use is done by about 300,000 people. Each year the income from the various products is worth approximately ten million taels or more. Their commercial ships are in the four seas; there is no spot which they do not reach. The great profits go to the merchants and dealers, while the workers are poor.

The English procedure of legal enquiry is that, when there is evidence of crime, the offender is arrested or sent to court. When he is about to be examined, six persons of good reputation are first selected from among the common people and the offender is also ordered to select six persons for himself. Together the twelve persons make the enquiry, and decide the merits of the case before they report it to the judge. The judge then examines it and the law is executed. . . .

England consists merely of three islands, simply a handful of stones in the western ocean. Her area is estimated to be about the same as Taiwan and Ch'iung-chou (Hainan). . . . Even if the soil is all fertile, how much can be produced locally? The reason for her becoming suddenly rich and strong, exerting political influence here and there beyond tens of thousands of li is that in the west she obtained America and in the east she obtained the various parts of India. The land of America hangs isolated on the globe, and since ancient times it has been little known. In the Wan-li period [1573–1620] of the Ming, it was discovered, and then a rich soil of ten thousand li was added to Great Britain, soon making her immensely rich. Even though the land of America is separated from England by ten thousand li, the British are skilled in ocean navigation, and make the voyage as easily as crossing a marshy ground with weeds. When the southern part was ceded to the United States of America, the northern part [Canada] which, though vast, is as barren and cold as Chinese Mongolia, [was retained by the British]. After England lost this part [the United States], she almost lost her prosperity [literally: her color].

Chapter Four

Popular Movements in the Mid-Nineteenth Century

Around the middle of the nineteenth century the Chinese empire was severely shaken by a series of popular movements that were both political and social in nature. They began between the two Opium Wars, and some continued until 1875. They included the Taiping revolution (the most important), the Nian rebellion in North China, the Moslem risings in the West, and many other minor movements, usually led by secret societies.[1] By 1860 every one of the empire's eighteen provinces had been affected by at least one of the rebellions.

Roots of the Popular Movements

The various movements expressed a diversity of local conditions and local discontents. They fitted into the cyclic phase of dynastic decline which China had entered at the beginning of the nineteenth century. They also belonged to a historical context heavily influenced by the two Opium Wars and the "opening." And they reflected the fundamental fact that China had stopped developing as though in a vacuum; from now on, these and all other internal developments were tied up with the evolution of international affairs.

[1] The brief chronology on pages 383–384 shows the sequence of these rebellions and their relation to the Opium Wars.

The worsening of the political and social crisis

Some of the causes behind the popular movements were connected with "signs preceding the fall of dynasties"—the same signs recorded by the Chinese annalists before the fall of the Tang in the ninth century and that of the Ming in the seventeenth. The weakening and decline of the imperial regime were obvious between 1830 and 1840, for the bureaucratic machine became so inefficient that public works deteriorated. In 1852–1853, for instance, neglected dikes caused the Huanghe to burst its banks in the region of Kaifeng. The river changed course to flow into the sea north of the Shandong peninsula, 800 kilometers from its former mouth, and vast areas were devastated.

In addition to the hardships created by the incompetence of the social machine, droughts and other agricultural disasters caused great suffering. There were famines in Henan in 1847, in the middle Yangzi basin in 1849, and in Hunan around 1850, when people fought over scraps of food that were usually fed to the pigs.

The peasants became more and more resentful of the land tax and cynical about their obligations to the landowners. The officials continued to manipulate the "substitution rate" between rice paid in kind and taxes paid in silver or in copper cash. Poverty increased. In the period 1840–1850 the provinces of the middle Yangzi basin were able to pay the central government only 50 to 70 percent of their tax quota, while the province of Jiangsu could raise only 50 to 60 percent.

Zeng Guo-fan describes the crisis

The worsening conditions were analyzed in a "memorial to the throne" handed in on February 7, 1852, just before the Taiping took Nanking. The paper was written by a senior mandarin, Zeng Guo-fan, one of the leaders who emerged during the Taiping crisis. He said:

> The distress among the people cannot appeal to the emperor . . . the silver price is too high so it is difficult to pay taxes. . . . In former days a tael was worth two thousand cash; then a picul of rice could get three tael of silver. Nowadays one tael of silver is worth two thousand cash and one picul of rice only gets one tael and a half of silver. In former days to sell three pecks of rice could pay the land tax for one *mou* and still have something left. Nowadays

to sell six pecks of rice to pay the land tax for one *mou* is still not enough. . . . Secondly, the thieves and bandits are too numerous and it is difficult for good people to live peacefully. . . . People cannot help but appeal to the officials. When the officials go in to arrest, an announcement is proclaimed in advance and till the government [force] reaches the spot the local gentry usually tell a lie that the bandits have fled. The officials then burn the people's houses in the neighborhood for demonstration before they leave, while the soldiers and the government servants will illegally extract money and property from the suffering host, and load up fully before they return, and yet actually the bandits have not fled. . . . the soldiers in ordinary times all have connections with the bandits. . . . The third one is that the unjustified imprisonments are too many, so it is difficult for people to redress their grievances. . . . When one family has a long-pending case ten families become bankrupt. When one person is falsely charged a hundred persons will be involved in his suffering.[2]

Influence of the Opium Wars

Zeng's description of the poverty caused by the rise in the value of silver compared with copper cash accentuates one of the direct connections between the Opium Wars and the great political and social movements between 1850 and 1870. Besides aggravating the monetary crisis, these wars exacerbated many of the other problems that China already had: corruption, overtaxation, neglect of the dikes, and so on.

Opening the ports, particularly the port of Shanghai, also shifted the axis of trading relations within the country itself. Foreign trade with the Yangzi regions was now carried out through Shanghai. Products of these regions had previously been sent south by boat or by porterage along the roads linking the southern tributaries of the Yangzi with the rivers flowing into the bay of Canton. When Canton's monopoly was broken, hundreds of thousands of coolies and boatmen were suddenly ruined. They supplied the Taiping with some of their best recruits.

In addition, some historians have given emphasis to the operations launched in 1842 by the British navy against piracy on the coasts of China. It may be that pirates and their underworld con-

[2] Quoted by Teng Ssu-yu in *New Light on the History of the Taiping Rebellion* (Cambridge, Mass., Harvard University Press, 1950), p. 44–46.

federates who were driven inland also swelled the troops of the secret societies and other movements opposing the established order.

Politically speaking, the Opium Wars prepared for the success of the great popular movements. They helped to discredit the establishment—the Manchu dynasty, the mandarinate, and the army. A popular proverb in South China at the time said: "The people are afraid of the mandarins, the mandarins are afraid of the foreign devils, but the foreign devils are afraid of the people." When the imperial authorities signed the Treaty of Nanking in 1842 without having exhausted all possibilities of resistance, they proved their weakness. According to the Manchu Wu Lan-tai, a leader of the Army of the Green Standard, the troops never recovered from their defeat in the "barbarian affair" (the first Opium War). They no longer obeyed orders, they considered retreat on the eve of battle as an "old habit," and they called the abandonment of fortified towns a "routine affair."

The combination of a classical type of political and social crisis and the effects of Western penetration was particularly obvious in China south of the Yangzi. That was the region where the Westerners had settled and where the "challenge" with which they confronted China was most apparent. A popular movement of resistance to the West developed there—a movement which gave the village militia an awareness of their own strength, and consequently enabled them to measure how rapidly the dynasty was losing the Mandate of Heaven. That was also the region where Manchu power was least firmly established and where resistance by supporters of the Ming had lasted longest in the seventeenth century. The areas south of the Yangzi were in any case less thoroughly Sinicized than North or Central China. South China was the cradle of the Taiping rebellion, which was the most lasting and most highly organized of the antidynastic movements of the time, as well as the most original in political and ideological content.

Origins of the Taiping Movement

Guangxi and Hong Xiu-quan

The Taiping revolution originated in Guangxi in South China. This poverty-stricken province, colonized relatively late by the Chinese, was afflicted by rivalry between different racial groups: the non-Chinese population (such as the Yao), which had settled there before the Han arrived, the first Chinese settlers (the Bendi), who had taken over the best land, and the Chinese families (the Hakka) who had come from Central China at a much later date and had been relegated to the poorer land. Relations were particularly bad between the Hakka and the Bendi. Outbreaks of peasant unrest had been frequent throughout the first half of the nineteenth century. At the same time, Guangxi was the hinterland of Canton, a part of China already extensively influenced by Western activities, particularly those of the Protestant missions. The conjunction of archaism and modernism which was characteristic of the Taiping movement as a whole was apparent in the geographical situation of its birthplace.

The same was true of the man who founded the movement, the village schoolmaster Hong Xiu-quan (1814–1864). Born to poor peasants of Hakka origin, he grew up in a traditionalist rural society where primitive popular systems of belief were to be found alongside the official Confucian ideology. He had twice failed the Confucian examinations and had had some contact with the Anglo-Saxon missionaries in Canton. An embittered and neurotic man, Hong thought he had found confirmation in the Bible for the visionary hallucinations that he believed conferred on him a divine and liberating mission. He began to preach around 1843 and gradually attracted a small group of determined men. They included the schoolmaster Feng Yun-shan, also a Hakka, the charcoal dealer Yang Xiu-qing, and the woodcutter Xiao Chao-gui, both former coolies and porters who were out of work as a result of the slump in trade between the Yangzi and Canton. A fourth follower was Shi Da-kai, another Hakka who had also failed the official examinations and who was especially interested in military questions. Wei Chang-hui, who joined the group later, was a rich landowner and moneylender who was popular among his Hakka compatriots because of his philanthropic activities in times of famine. These six men led the movement. With one exception they came from poor peasant families, but they had all held jobs which opened wider horizons for them. In effect they formed a "pre-proletariat," as the historians of the People's Republic of China put it.

The God Worshippers

Around 1845 the movement founded by Hong Xiu-quan grew larger and became the highly pugnacious Society of God Worshippers, which began fighting the private militia of the landowners. The God Worshippers gathered all the rebellious and discontented social elements in Guangxi: miners, charcoal burners, landless peasants, underprivileged Hakka, and the usual members of secret societies—geomancers, smugglers, bonesetters, disbanded soldiers, deserters, and impressed soldiers.

The political and religious ideology of the future Taiping could already be seen in Hong's movement. The influence of the Bible was apparent in the God Worshippers' adoption of the Ten Commandments, in their monotheism, in the liberating mission entrusted to Hong by God the Father, and in their doctrine of the equality of all men as the sons of God. (The idea of equality was sacrilege according to the Confucian tradition, which regarded the emperor alone as the Son of Heaven.) The God Worshippers were probably closer to the militant aspects of the Old Testament than to the loving spirit of the Gospels. Hong stayed in Canton again in 1847 and got to know more about Christianity. He composed "Songs for Saving the World" for his disciples and wrote "A Teaching for Awakening the World," whose equalitarian Messianic note echoed old Chinese peasant traditions of primitive collectivism: "May all humanity become a great family once more, enjoying Peace and Harmony together."

Hong and the secret societies

Much has been said about the connection between the Society of God Worshippers and the secret societies of the Triad type, which were numerous and influential in South China at that time. The God Worshippers were close to the secret societies in many ways. They developed from the same social and ideological foundations that inspired opposition to the established order through peasant uprisings and insubordination. As in the case of the secret societies, the leaders of the God Worshippers came from the peasants—particularly from the marginal members of rural society who were relatively mobile and advanced, such as traveling artisans, failed scholars, and smugglers. In spite of their borrowings from Christianity, the God Worshippers were influenced by the same peasant traditions of equality as the secret societies. In both cases they were involved in a political and military struggle against the central power—the Manchu dynasty in Peking.

Moreover, many members and leaders of the Triad and other secret societies in the South joined the God Worshippers between 1848 and 1850. Some, like the Triad leader Luo Dao-gang, became permanent members. Others later withdrew, like Luo's seven colleagues, the most prominent members of the Triad in Guangxi, who served Hong for a while but eventually decided that they wanted more freedom of action.

Hong breaks with the secret societies

As the rebellion developed, however, the God Worshippers and the secret societies increasingly differed on the question of its goals. By tradition the secret societies claimed to uphold Ming rights to the throne ("Overthrow the Manchus and restore the Ming"). Hong and the other leaders of the God Worshippers, on the other hand, quickly came to envisage founding a new dynasty.

For a time this fundamental dispute remained in abeyance. Hong apparently eased the situation by making one of the supporters of the Ming a leader of the movement, second to himself. Hong Da-quan, as he was called, also had the title of Tiandewang, King of Heavenly Virtue, which came from the mythology of the secret societies. Some historians deny that he existed, but in fact he appears to have played an important part in the leadership of the rebellion between 1849 and 1851. Callery and Yvan, interpreters at the French consulate in Canton, published an account of the origins of the Taiping movements in 1852. Their book, based on eyewitness reports, gave him the chief role; he was even pictured in the frontispiece, wearing traditional Ming dynasty dress.

The compromise reflected in this joint leadership could only be provisional. The partisans of Ming restoration were expelled by Hong or abandoned that goal, and the God Worshippers followed another direction by proclaiming a new dynasty which they called the Taiping Tianguo (Heavenly Kingdom of Great Peace). The break became complete when Hong Da-quan, the King of Heavenly Virtue, disappeared in 1851, probably captured by imperial troops.

Actually, the name *Taiping* (Great Peace, or more accurately, Great Social Harmony) had belonged to the traditions of Chinese secret societies for thousands of years. The unorthodox canon of the Yellow Turbans, who overthrew the Tang dynasty in the second century A.D., was called *The Book of the Great Peace*. Thus the God Worshippers had opted for a political goal which, though it conflicted with the goal of the secret societies, was inspired by the same traditions of peasant utopianism.

The Heavenly Kingdom of Great Peace

In 1850 the God Worshippers concentrated their troops and entrenched themselves in their camp at Jintian. Preaching had given way to rebellion. Tens of thousands of people joined them— peasant militia, especially of Hakka origin, whole clans, Miao and Yao tribes, groups of pirates, units from secret societies.

The troops won several victories against the imperial troops, and at the beginning of 1851 Hong Xiu-quan proclaimed the Taiping state, the Heavenly Kingdom of Great Peace, and called himself the Heavenly King. In September 1851 the Taiping took their first forti- fied city: Yong'an in Guangxi, where they stayed until the spring of 1852 to consolidate their organization.

To emphasize their messianic and universal nature, Hong as- signed the "four cardinal points" of the Chinese esoteric tradition to his lieutenants. Xiao the woodcutter was the Western King, Yang the charcoal dealer the Eastern King, Feng the schoolmaster the Southern King, and Wei the rich merchant-landowner the Northern King. Shi Da-kai, the Hakka who, like Hong, had failed the Con- fucian examinations, was Assistant King.

In April the troops left Guangxi. What had begun as a local rebellion was now an army marching against the imperial power. On Lake Dongting in Huan the Taiping captured a large flotilla and used it to take the great towns on the Yangzi. Wuchang fell in January 1853, Jiugiang in February, Nanking in March. Nanking was given the name Tianjing (Celestial Capital) and served as the Taiping capital until their collapse in 1864.

Characteristics of the Taiping Movement

In all, the Taiping movement was a social crusade expressing the poor peasants' desire for equality, a national campaign against the foreign dynasty occupying the throne in Peking, and a modernist trend that developed in response to the challenge presented by the West through the Opium Wars.

The peasants and the Taiping

For centuries the landowners and officials had been the "natural" social adversaries of the Chinese peasants, and now the peasants joined the Taiping to fight them. In the original group of God Worshippers there were many poor peasants from Guangxi. The Western King, Xiao, the Southern King, Feng, and Hong, the Heavenly King himself, were members of the peasantry. So were the future Faithful King, Li Xiu-cheng, who was commander-in-chief of the Taiping armies from 1859 to 1864, and his cousin, Li Shi-xian, who tried to continue to resist in 1865, after the fall of the Celestial Capital of Nanking.

As they gradually advanced through Central China and toward the lower Yangzi, the troops of the Great Peace were supported by spontaneous uprisings among the peasants. The most unpopular officials and landowners were put to death. The *yamen*, the grain registers, the land registers, loan contracts, and other moneylenders' documents were burned. A contemporary chronicle says that when the troops entered a rich house or one belonging to an important family, they were required to dig down three feet into the ground (to uncover their valuables). But they took nothing from the peasants; indeed, they gave the poor what clothes and other spoils they had acquired, and they announced that taxes would be postponed for three years. Because the poor could not better their lot except under the Taiping, they vied with each other to welcome the army of the Great Peace, whereas they went on strike when the imperial troops arrived.

The struggle against the Manchus

The Taiping movement aimed to liberate China from Manchu domination. New members proved their allegiance by cutting off their queues, which the Manchu dynasty had required the Chinese to wear ever since it came to power in the seventeenth century. The Taiping let their hair grow and were often called the "long-haired rebels."

The first proclamations of Hong, Feng, and Yang in 1851–1853 were strongly nationalistic.[3] They accused the Tartar dynasty of incompetence in governing China, of exploiting the country, and of having provoked its misfortunes at home and abroad. The choice of Nanking for the Taiping capital, which was probably a grave strategic error, had political significance. Nanking was the capital of the first Ming Emperors, who restored Chinese national independence in the fourteenth century after the domination of another barbarian dynasty, the Mongol.

Because of the movement's profoundly national character, many educated and well-to-do people who had no real reason to give their support to a group of poor peasants joined the Taiping. These people were represented in the Taiping leadership by the rich merchant-landowner Wei and by Shi Da-kai, the dissident scholar. The patriotic scholars who, like Shi, were enemies of the Manchus helped to run the Taiping administration smoothly in the huge regions that were under their control until 1864. They drafted proclamations, manufactured weapons, and saw to all the complex operations that keep a real state going. These tasks were far beyond the capacity of the peasants from Guangxi who had originated the movement.

Modernist trends in the Taiping

The originality of the Taiping revolution lay in the modernist impulses that were blended with its traditional themes of popular revolution and anti-Manchu nationalism. This is the meaning of the political act of founding a new dynasty; the Taiping did not merely attempt to restore Ming legitimism (as the Triad did in Shanghai between 1853 and 1855).

The Taiping movement belonged to the context of the Opium Wars and reflected the new problems arising from the sudden impact of the West and its technological, scientific, and social advances. Hong, the Heavenly King, was not merely a simple schoolteacher from a backward Chinese province. He had lived in Canton among the missionaries and in the general atmosphere of a

[3] See the proclamation of 1853 in document 1 at the chapter end.

large port frequented by foreign steamships and well supplied with foreign goods. The borrowings from Christianity which were of such importance in the Taiping religion were the concrete expression of an underlying historical process: the search for the "secret" behind the superiority of the Westerners. In this sense, the Taiping are related to many other acculturation movements in the modern Afro-Asian world. They have common ties, for example, with the syncretic sects of the South Sea Islands (the cargo movement) and Central Africa (the Black Christs), which also combined elements from native religions and Christianity, and which also aimed at social liberation and the acquisition of modern techniques.

The link between Christianity and social and technical progress was apparent in the versatile figure of Hong Ren-gan, a cousin of the Heavenly King. He spent a long time in Canton and Hong Kong, became a Protestant convert, and worked as a catechist in an English mission from 1855 to 1858. A student of medicine and astronomy, he sympathized with the Taiping movement from the beginning. He was appointed prime minister by his cousin when he joined the movement in Nanking in 1859. Hong Ren-gan drew up a general program of reforms inspired by the West: modernization of the educational curriculum, the conversion of monasteries into hospitals, and the development of steam navigation, commercial banks, a railway system, and a modern postal service. These plans, however, were put forward at a time when the Heavenly dynasty was on the wane, so that they could not be carried out.

Hong Ren-gan was not an isolated figure; all the Chinese intellectual circles that were most sensitive to the question of modernization were in touch with the Taiping. Rong Hong ("Yung Wing"), the first Chinese student to get a degree from a foreign university (he was at Yale from 1850 to 1854), visited the Taiping in 1859 and suggested that they follow a policy of systematic modernization. He refused to work for them, however; he preferred his private business.

The Taiping and the foreigners

Westerners were well received in the zone controlled by the Taiping rebels. In a spirit of friendship which contrasted with the haughty mistrust of the imperial mandarins, the Taiping gave Westerners the title of "foreign brothers." Missionaries, especially Protestants, made frequent visits to the Taiping zone, and all seem to have gained favorable impressions.

The Taiping would willingly have established friendly relations with the foreign powers; in his messages Hong stressed that equality exists between nations as it does between men. But the Westerners, doubtless after briefly considering the possibility of a *modus vivendi* with the Taiping, preferred to draw nearer to the imperial court after the second Opium War, and ultimately they joined in the repression of the revolution. Isolated individuals among the foreigners did respond to the political overtures of the Taiping. One Englishman, Lindley, organized a small military unit of foreign volunteers, most of them deserters or adventurers, to fight with the army of the Faithful King.

The Taiping political and social system

The primitive rural collectivism of the Taiping social organization was linked with the utopian tradition of Chinese peasant movements. According to the rule laid down by the Taiping in 1853, the land belonged to everyone and was cultivated for everyone, while each family was allotted a plot whose size depended on the age of the members.[4] Once everybody in a producer's collective (consisting of twenty-five people) had been provided for, surplus rice and meat were put into Heavenly storehouses. The leaders of the army and the administration were given food, as well as money drawn from the Heavenly treasuries. Amassing private wealth was forbidden, however.

Artisans were organized into Heavenly battalions (such as carpentry, weaving, or engraving) whose products went to the state. Heavenly controllers supervised the manufacture of gunpowder, iron, copper, and their by-products. The tendency of the Taiping was to organize industrial production into a broader manufacturing system than that of traditional individual handicrafts. Industrial products were collected in state depots and distributed by Heavenly compradors (*tian maiban*). "The peasants' grain, the artisans' handiwork, the merchants' capital all belong to the Heavenly Father and ought to be handed over to the treasury," a proclamation said. Work was a social obligation, idleness a sin.

The Taiping political system, at least in principle (for no one knows how far the principles were applied), was very simple. It was

---

[4] The law, entitled "Agrarian system of the Heavenly dynasty," is given in document 2.

inspired by the ancient *Zhouli* (*Rites of the State of Zhou*), a canonical text said to date from the eleventh century B.C. Military and civilian structures were intermingled in the Taiping administration. Each family provided a soldier. Twenty-five families were led by two *sima* (an ancient Chinese title) who were responsible for vital statistics, justice, religion, and military affairs. An intermediary hierarchy led up to a unit of 13,156 families, headed by an army general. The officials in the hierarchy were elected, according to the first rules laid down by the Taiping. Apparently they were also recruited by a competitive examination of the traditional Chinese type, in which the Confucian canons were replaced by the Taiping sacred texts. At the top of the hierarchy was the Heavenly court, originally composed of the six leaders of the directorate set up in 1851 after the capture of Yong'an. The number of "kings" (*wang*) increased rapidly, however, while the members of the founding group disappeared. The Heavenly King, Hong, was accorded more and more omnipotence.

There were many other links between the Taiping political system and Chinese popular traditions. Both emphasized "moral rectitude" and "reverence." Both were pervaded by rebellious romanticism, nourished by memories of novels like the *Shuihu*— tales of knight-errantry from the Chinese Middle Ages.

Although the political and social organization of the Taiping was archaic in many ways, in others it was very modern. The Taiping replaced the traditional lunar calendar with a calendar based on the solar system, which resembled the Western version except that a year consisted of 366 days and the months of 30 and 31 days alternately. The Taiping approach to the emancipation of women was also advanced. Women could take the public examinations; they fought in the army, in separate units; they had the same education as men; they married freely. Customs like foot-binding and buying slaves for servants were severely punished. An English traveler who visited Nanking found that the women went freely about the streets on foot or horseback. Unlike other Chinese women, he wrote, they seemed unafraid of foreigners and did not try to avoid them. But as the Taiping leaders grew more accustomed to power, they fell away from the feminist ideal. Some of them acquired vast harems, whose luxury contrasted sharply with the austere way of life which they demanded of their subjects.

Religion: A fusion of eclectic elements

The characteristic of the Taiping religion which most struck contemporaries was the Christian elements it included: monotheism, the Ten Commandments, the divinity of Christ, the duality of heaven and earth, the existence of Satan. The Taiping adopted both the Old and the New Testaments. They read passages from the Bible during their religious ceremonies, wrote commentary on it, and asked questions about it in their examinations.

These borrowings from Christianity, however, seemed seriously incomplete to Westerners. For example, the Taiping omitted a rite of such vital importance as the Eucharist, and they had no clergy distinct from the mass of the laity. They combined components of Christianity with other elements from ancient Chinese traditions and from popular religion. The name they chose for God, *Shangdi*, is found in the oldest Chinese canons. They believed in the eighteen hells and thirty-three heavens of Buddhist mythology. And they made offerings of food on ritual feast days in the tradition of village and family cults.

In fact, these disparate elements were fused into a closed and complete religious system. Its diversity reflected the contradictions inherent in the Taiping movement, yet it had a unity of purpose which was a powerful political and ideological weapon against the imperial power and Confucian orthodoxy. For Hong and his supporters, the divine mission of the Taiping was inseparable from their political mission: the Manchus had to be driven out so that the kingdom of God could be established on earth. From the beginning, and throughout the victorious Taiping march between 1850 and 1853, the zealously monotheistic troops destroyed the Confucian tablets hanging in public places and threw down the idols on family and village altars. This militant iconoclasm was a challenge to the established order and to the popular traditions of the past. The messianic outlook of the Taiping was deeply equalitarian. It came into direct collusion with the Confucian view of the unchangeable hierarchical divisions of the human condition. Indeed, the imperial mandarins who later supervised the repression of the movement reproached the Taiping with having called each other "brother" and "sister," for to the Confucians this seemed a real crime against society.

The social aim of the Taiping was to found a complete and integrated society where the religious and temporal orders, and the military and civilian worlds, were merged into one—making a true theocracy. All their political and economic institutions were called "heavenly" or "holy": the treasury, the rice granaries, the capital, and the dynasty. Hong, the Heavenly King, was the instrument of the divine mandate which the Taiping had to fulfill. According to his own revelations he was the son of God—the younger brother of Jesus Christ—and Taiping theology slightly rearranged the Trinity to accommodate him.[5] In the context of the Opium Wars, Hong's claim to the same status as Christ's implied the claim of basic equality between the Chinese and white peoples. This insistence on religious equality resembles the approach of the Congolese Black Christ movement, which attacked the privilege of whites in the field of revelation.

Taiping morality, which was both civil and religious, was demanding. Opium, gambling, prostitution, and adultery were all forbidden as serious sins. Everyone was under a sacred obligation to work, to perform the ceremonies of the cult, to fight the enemies of the Heavenly Kingdom, and to obey the will of God and the mission of Hong. This militant, puritanical religious morality recalls the early stages of Islam, or the attitude of the peasant armies of the Reformation in Germany, as much as it does early Christianity. Certainly the Taiping left little room in their beliefs for Christian charity.

The application of the Taiping system

How far was the political, economic, and religious system of the Taiping effectively put into practice in the regions they controlled? With its theological complexity and attention to detail, the system was more like a utopian description aimed at mobilizing the masses than a plan which could be applied to concrete situations. As would be expected, the Taiping system proved impossible to translate completely into action. In the first place, it required conditions of peace and political stability, whereas the boundaries of the zone controlled by the Taiping were constantly shifting with the tide of battle between 1852 and 1864. Second, there was a considerable difference between the original nucleus of the faithful adherents to the Great Peace, who had come from Guangdong or Guangxi, and the population of the lower Yangzi over whom they assumed au-

[5] Document 3 is a passage from Hong's commentary on Saint John.

thority. The latter were rather like subjects, lukewarm in their political and religious support compared with the rebels from the Southwest. The fusion between the two elements was never complete, and in fact the division between the leaders and the led widened rapidly in Nanking until in 1856 it became really serious. The political customs of the Taiping court drew further and further away from the original principles of the movement.

Life in the Taiping zones, however, does seem to have been influenced by the Taiping system, particularly in economic and social matters. All Western travelers were struck by the cordiality, simplicity, and prosperity of the people there, in contrast to the inhabitants of areas under imperial rule.[6] Although complete collectivism did not exist on the land, the peasants were freed from their heavy obligations to the landowners (with the possible exception of the regions conquered last, between 1861 and 1863). The fact that the state still levied taxes proves that the land law of 1853 had not been completely put into practice, but the taxes were light. Visitors like Lord Elgin in 1854 noticed the Heavenly granaries and Heavenly warehouses. However, they seem to have been used for storing supplies and valuables seized in conquered towns rather than for stockpiling the products of Taiping agriculture and handicrafts.

Taxes on commerce were simplified and lightened, particularly the inland customs tax, and trade appears to have been brisk. The attractive market represented by the Taiping zones, and the facilities they offered, contributed to Western sympathy for the rebels, which was expressed in a neutralism that the Westerners were slow to abandon.

Foreign accounts were also unanimous in praising the discipline of the Taiping, the simplicity of their manners, and the vigor of their religious faith in the liberating mission. Visitors noted, too, that measures like the emancipation of women and the prohibition of opium were effectively carried out. When the Taiping state collapsed in 1864, hundreds of thousands of Heavenly followers preferred death to surrender.

[6] One missionary's account is in document 4.

The Taiping from 1853 to 1859: Stabilization and Crisis

The Taiping movement was, simultaneously, a movement opposing the imperial order and an attempt to build a new order in China. Insofar as it was a centrifugal, destructive force, attacking both the traditional social order and the Manchu dynasty, the activities of the Taiping were essentially mobile and warlike. Heavenly troops crossed districts and provinces, striking at the enemy rather than attempting to occupy the land. This military vigor, which emerged early during the march of 1850 to 1852, was maintained until the end. The high quality of their armies, their fanatical determination, the discipline which impressed all foreign observers, the outstanding military ability of leaders like Shi Da-kai, Li Xiu-cheng, and Chen Yu-cheng—all enabled the Taiping to hold their own against the imperial troops for many years. From beginning to end, their history is largely a military history.

But the Taiping were also builders, or at least wanted to be. They wanted to create a new power symbolized by a new dynasty. Here lay the radical difference between them and the other peasant movements, such as that of the Nian, to whom the Taiping were very close in both time and geography. The Taiping had a capital to defend—the Heavenly city of Nanking, to which the imperial troops laid siege in 1853 from two large camps which they set up downstream on either bank of the Yangzi. The Taiping had a government to manage, with all the troubles attendant on quarrels between rival factions. Indeed, it was the struggles for power between factions as much as the Taiping military expeditions that fixed the rhythm of the movement's history.

Failure to capture Peking

The contradiction between the military need for mobility and the political need to settle in one place became obvious when the Taiping arrived on the Yangzi at the end of 1852. After the capture of Wuchang, Hong and his companions decided to go downriver as far as Nanking. Being natives of the poor, mountainous regions of Guangxi, they were no doubt attracted by the prosperity and easy life of the manufacturing and rice-growing regions in the lower Yangzi. Many Chinese historians consider this a great mistake, a real political and strategic "deviation." They argue that if the Taiping had marched on Peking straightaway, the Manchu government would have been unable to resist.

The Taiping organized the "Northern expedition" much later, in May 1853. It was entrusted to Lin Feng-xiang, a veteran from Guangxi whom Hong had appointed head of his Heavenly guard. Soon after the march began, Lin came up against resistance from the imperial troops. He detoured westward and crossed the Huanghe, but did not manage to take the town of Kaifeng in spite of help from reinforcements commanded by Li Kai-fang. By October the expedition had only reached Tientsin. Accustomed as they were to the climate of Guangxi, the Taiping soldiers found the harsh Northern winter very difficult. The imperial troops, commanded by General Senggelinqin, a Mongol prince, gradually pushed the Taiping southward. The Northern expedition was routed in 1854, and its last remnants were annihilated in the spring of 1855. They did not find the support among the peasants of North China that the army of the God Worshippers had received in the South when it was advancing toward the Yangzi.

Although the imperial troops did halt the Taiping's northward drive, the Army of the Green Standard in Central China never recovered from the beating it received during the first Taiping offensive in 1850–1852. The scholar-officials and rural gentry in the provinces closest to the uprising, particularly in the province of Hunan, took charge of defenses at the local level. The most active leader was Zeng Guo-fan, who launched a vigorous military, political, and ideological counterattack on the Taiping (covered in Chapter 5).

In 1854 and 1855 the counteroffensive of the local ruling classes began to bear fruit. At that time the Taiping had lost none of their dynamism and military vitality. Twice they managed to take the large town of Wuchang, the key to Central China (they occupied it first in January 1853 when they arrived on the Yangzi, though they could not hold it). But Zeng Guo-fan resisted them much more effectively than the first imperial armies that had been sent against them. He prevented them from entering Hunan, eventually took Wuchang back from them, and won the battle for Jiangxi from one of their best generals, Shi Da-kai. The outcome was still uncertain, however. In 1855 Shi Da-kai managed to immobilize Zeng's flotilla on Lake Poyang, sink the admiral's flagship, and attack his camp; Zeng himself narrowly escaped.

Stabilization of the rebel state

During the first years after the establishment of the Heavenly capital at Nanking, the Taiping state was strong enough for the Westerners to adopt an attitude of neutrality toward the conflict. In 1853 and 1854 diplomatic missions visited Nanking. Bonham was sent by Great Britain, de Bourboulon by France, and McLane by the United States. Nanking was a prosperous city; at the end of 1853 the Taiping had a stock of 2 million piculs of rice there. The Reverend E. C. Bridgman who accompanied Commissioner Mc-Lane in 1854, wrote: "All the people we saw were well-clad, well-fed, and well provided for in every way. They all seemed content, and in high spirits, as if sure of success." [7]

The crisis of 1856 and the rise of the military leaders

In 1856, however, the Taiping movement was shaken by a serious crisis of leadership which was almost its undoing—and which in fact may have been the long-term cause of its final failure.

The unity of the Taiping "directorate" seems to have been short-lived. Of the six *wang* created originally at the capture of Yong'an, two—the Western King, Xiao, and the Southern King, Feng—died in the field in 1852. The Heavenly King, Hong, whose mind was probably not entirely normal, left more and more real power to the Eastern King: Yang, the former charcoal dealer. An energetic organizer, Yang created a powerful faction and managed to fill posts in the central administration with more than seven thousand of his supporters. To counterbalance his influence the Northern King, the merchant-landowner Wei, built up a following from members of his own wealthy clan and the natives of his region. Hong himself looked mainly to his brothers and cousins for support. Family, regional, and personal allegiances were taking over from the original solidarity among the God Worshippers.

In 1856 it seems that Hong, his jealousy and anxiety aroused by the growing authority of Yang, spoke of it to Wei. Wei organized the massacre of tens of thousands of Yang's supporters and their families.

In order to restore the balance, Hong then had Wei's supporters

[7] F. Michael and Chang Chung-li, *The Taiping Rebellion* (Seattle, University of Washington Press, 1966), vol. 1, p. 75.

killed. He also tried to attack the last survivor of the six original *wang*, Shi Da-kai. The members of Shi's family were massacred, and he himself barely escaped. Shi withdrew his allegiance to the Heavenly King, and at the head of several hundred thousand men he fought the Manchu armies in West China on his own account until his death in 1863.

These quarrels and bloodshed probably reflected policy schisms as well as rivalries between factions. The charcoal dealer Yang, the Eastern King, was the chief representative of a radical policy, which no doubt earned him the animosity of the wealthy circles supporting the Taiping. The Northern King, the rich merchant and moneylender Wei, was a member of these circles. When the two groups had wiped each other out, Hong remained alone at the head of the Taiping state. He governed through his two elder brothers, whom he made *wang* though they were vain and incompetent.

The military leaders who had remained more or less loyal to Nanking moved up to the first rank, particularly after the departure of Shi Da-kai. Li Xiu-cheng, a poor peasant from Guangxi, had until then been given only secondary responsibilities in the army. But he and his men managed to break through the encirclement of the imperial troops in Anhui, and he was made commander-in-chief of the Northern sector. He was the main craftsman of a military alliance between the Taiping and the Nian rebels, whose influence in his sector was considerable. (The ideological differences which had at first formed an obstacle to a *rapprochement* between the Taiping and the secret societies gradually became less important as the Taiping movement developed into a purely military conflict.) Farther south Chen Yu-cheng, the commander of the Southern front, mounted a counterattack in the Yangzi region. But he could not prevent Zeng, the leader of the local provincial army fighting the rebels, from taking back Jiujiang in 1858. This was the last important Taiping base in the region.

The years 1856 to 1859, which were a period of defensive strategy and priority for military affairs among the Taiping, were also the years of the second Opium War. Although the Westerners had earlier considered the possibility of cooperating with the Taiping, they now decided against it. Meanwhile the peasants too had turned away from the Taiping. The original upsurge of sympathy with the Great Peace as a liberating force had disappeared. The Nanking regime had become mainly an additional burden for the peasants because of the upkeep necessary for armies whose sphere of activities and, consequently, supply bases were steadily shrinking.

The Taiping from 1859 to 1864:
New Upsurge, New Defeat

The Taipings rally under Hong Ren-gan and Li Xiu-cheng

The arrival of Hong Ren-gan, the Heavenly King's colorful cousin, in Nanking in 1859 provided the Taiping with the political head who had been missing since the massacre of 1856, the departure of Shi Da-kai, and the worsening mental health of the Heavenly King. The cousin was immediately appointed prime minister. His ambitious program of modernization (page 95) included a policy of opening the Taiping zones to the West. He got his former master in Canton, the American missionary Issachar Roberts, to come to Nanking and help him.

Hong Ren-gan also tried to reform the Heavenly State. He wanted to get rid of the provincial and family cliques, fight corruption and indolence, and put competent men of firm religious faith into the important posts.

In the military field, he proposed that the two best Taiping generals, Li Xiu-cheng (the Faithful King) and Chen Yu-cheng (the Heroic King) should attack the middle Yangzi, using a pincer movement to the north and to the south. The first phase of the operation succeeded, and the blockade of Nanking was broken. But the two generals did not manage to coordinate their movements as far as Wuchang, the ultimate object of the campaign. Zeng and his Hunan army still had the upper hand; in 1860 and 1861 they inflicted a sound defeat on the Heroic King and took back Anqing, the capital of Anhui.

Nevertheless, the Taiping benefitted from the bad relations between the provincial armies of the rural gentry and the Manchu dynastic armies. Zeng, commander of the former, was in favor of a mobile strategy, whereas the Manchu generals put their trust in the camps which they had established opposite Nanking on the Yangzi. In 1860 Li, the Faithful King, managed to destroy these imperial bases. In several brilliant campaigns he occupied almost all of south Jiangsu and Zhejiang, including rich towns like Suzhou (where he set up his headquarters), Changzhou, and Hangzhou. He thus obtained new resources in men, money, and supplies, for some regions in this area produced large quantities of tea and silk and had profitable dealings with foreign trading firms.

The policy of diplomatic opening to the West that was being attempted by Hong Ren-gan in Nanking went hand in hand with a military and economic opening in the same direction. From 1860 to 1862 Western trade in the Taiping zones was extremely active, fostered in particular by the flexibility of the Taiping fiscal system compared with that of the mandarin bureaucracy.

But the new upsurge of the Taiping movement did not last long. In Nanking the Buckler King (as Hong Ren-gan was called) was not able to check the tendency toward factions, pleasure seeking, nepotism, and corruption. And in the field he could neither convince the generals that they were subject to civil authority nor put a stop to their rivalries (for instance, to the simmering feud between the Faithful King and the Heroic King). In 1861 he lost his prime minister's seal. Hong, who was becoming more and more irresponsible, multiplied the numbers of *wang* by several hundred. They became a true neofeudal body, greedy for riches and power.

Taiping decadence

The Heavenly Kingdom of Great Peace had lost most of the militant energy which had been its chief characteristic at the time of the march on Nanking from 1853 to 1855. It was no longer a movement founded on the determination of the mass of the people to undertake collective action; it had become a political-military apparatus interested in ensuring its own subsistence and maintaining the positions it had won.

After attacks by imperial troops, the Taiping evacuated the regions of Central China which they had conquered at the start with the help of a strong popular movement. In the zones lying further to the east (see map, page 109) that they conquered around 1860, their power resulted purely from military supremacy. In spite of the large trading and manufacturing centers in these rich regions, the Taiping generals, including Li Xiu-cheng, put pressure mainly on the villages to furnish the supplies needed by the army and the heavenly administration. They left the landowners and tax collectors undisturbed, for the utopian equalitarianism of the 1853 land law was forgotten.

The political and military apparatus of the Taiping was in the hands of "elder brothers," who had come by the hundreds of thousands from Guangdong and Guangxi in 1851. They had a keen sense of their privileged position and of provincial solidarity (through their dialect, for example), and they were cut off from the peasant masses at whose expense they lived (the "new brothers"). The Taiping regime had deteriorated socially, politically, and ideologically. Its religious beliefs were fading away, and its anti-Manchu propaganda had lost conviction. To win supporters for loyalism and neo-Confucianism, Zeng Guo-fan made skillful use of the disenchantment with the Taiping that was felt by the masses.

Western intervention and the fall of Nanking

In spite of the trading benefits offered the West by the Taiping, in 1860 the Western powers gave up the policy of neutrality that they had tentatively followed at first. Their long-term political commitment was in support of the Manchu regime, which had just promised them new advantages by the terms of the Tientsin treaties. This was the first of a long series of foreign interventions on the side of the conservative forces in Chinese political struggles. In the future, for example, foreign powers would back Yuan Shi-kai against Sun Yat-sen in 1912 and the Guomindang against the Communists in 1930. Now, although the support of the West was not the sole reason for the Taiping defeat, it did strengthen the offensive capacity of the imperial troops (see Chapter 5).

When Zeng Guo-fan took back Anqing, upstream from Nanking, in 1861 and made it his headquarters, the balance of military power tipped decisively in favor of the imperial troops. Li Xiucheng tried to delay defeat by several daring campaigns. But he was quickly driven out of his capital, Suzhou, and those who had supported him were slaughtered by the army of occupation. In 1862 and 1863 Zuo Zong-tang recaptured Zhejiang from the Taiping. Nanking fell in the summer of 1864, and the occupation involved terrible bloodshed. Tens of thousands of leaders, soldiers, and civilians were massacred by the imperial forces.

For a time some of the leaders who had escaped the disaster tried to return to the more mobile military strategy used at the start by the God Worshippers. The remains of the Taiping armies continued to fight on the borders of Fujian in 1864 and 1865, occasionally capturing towns but never managing to hold them. Other units headed southwest to the borders of Vietnam and later became the Black Flags. But each case involved guerrilla warfare resembling banditry, in contrast to the grandiose visions of the Heavenly Kingdom of Great Peace.

The imperial troops' reign of terror after their victories (it has been said that several million people died) explains why the Taiping movement ended abruptly, and why the enormous popular appeal of its political and ideological synthesis did not inspire similar movements. Yet in spite of its failures, its unresolved ideological contradictions, and its degeneration from 1856 onward, the Taiping movement remained highly popular in Chinese tradition. Survivors of the "Great Peace" enjoyed considerable prestige among the peasants and kept its memory alive. Sun Yat-sen, for example, was greatly stirred as a child by the stories told him by an uncle who had belonged to the Taiping.

The Nian

Social foundations

As an overt rebellion, the Nian movement extended from 1853 to 1868. It was led by a secret society (*nian* means "bands") that was probably a ramification of the White Lotus Society, which itself had existed in North China since the end of the eighteenth century. The Nian were related to other secret societies by their mythology (all had such mystic concepts as the eight diagrams and the five lodges), by the titles they adopted (for example, the head of a band was a "master of the mountain"), and by their predilection for the color red. Their uprising took place in one of the border regions which have always counted for a great deal in the history of popular movements in China (as well as in the war against Japan in 1937–1945). Theirs was the poor, sandy, underadministered area stretching along the borders of the provinces of Anhui, Jiangsu, Henan, and Shandong. Village solidarity was strong, the population was scattered, and the horse, an unusual animal in China, played a large part in peasant life on these bleak plains.

Around 1855 Nian units began to clash with the police, plunder the *yamen*, attack prisons, ambush official convoys, and hold rich merchants, moneylenders, and landowners for ransom. It was essentially a peasant movement, one which was joined by villages, families, and whole clans. It also gained supporters from marginal groups in rural society like salt smugglers (the supreme head of the Nian, Zhang Luo-xing, was one), disbanded soldiers and deserters

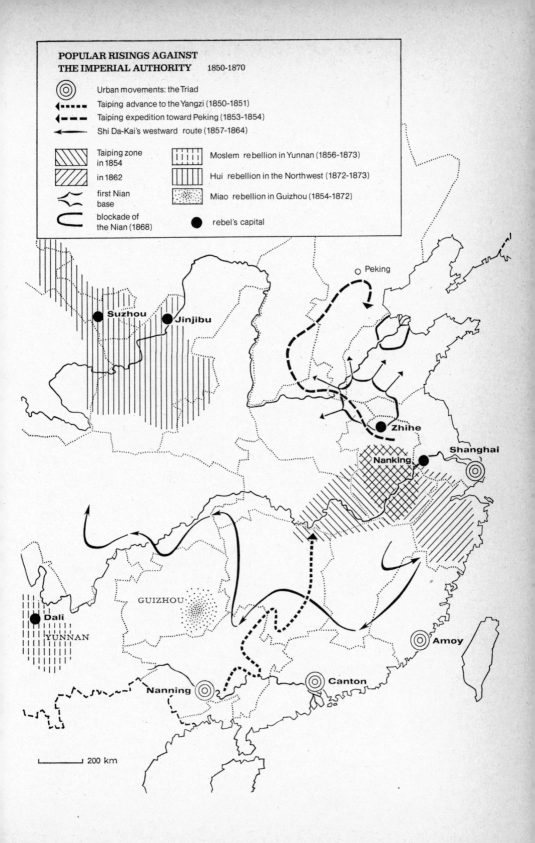

POPULAR RISINGS AGAINST
THE IMPERIAL AUTHORITY   1850-1870

◎ Urban movements: the Triad

◀┅┅ Taiping advance to the Yangzi (1850-1851)

◀╍╍ Taiping expedition toward Peking (1853-1854)

◀— Shi Da-Kai's westward route (1857-1864)

▨ Taiping zone in 1854

▨ in 1862

first Nian base

blockade of the Nian (1868)

▥ Moslem rebellion in Yunnan (1856-1873)

▥ Hui rebellion in the Northwest (1872-1873)

Miao rebellion in Guizhou (1854-1872)

● rebel's capital

○ Peking

● **Suzhou**   ● **Jinjibu**

● **Zhihe**

Nanking ●   ◎ **Shanghai**

GUIZHOU

● **Dali**

YUNNAN

◎ **Amoy**

Nanning ◎   ◎ **Canton**

⊢——⊣ 200 km

(who were particularly numerous in the context of the war against the Taiping), frustrated or warped members of the rural gentry, jobless scholars, and students who had failed the examinations. The educated men who joined the Nian movement were extremely useful, because they performed intelligence work among minor employees at the *yamen* and noncommissioned officers in the imperial troops. The remarkable efficiency of the operations organized by the Nian was often due to the high quality of the information these men obtained.

Banditry and guerrilla activities

The Nian organization was both flexible and strong. It was decentralized and included three different types of units, though not much is known about the connection between them. One consisted of fortified earth-walled villages where the peasants, who had all joined the rebellion, continued to farm in the periods when they were not needed as guerrillas. Another was the "banners," highly mobile groups of cavalry who formed the spearhead of offensive action against the imperial armies. A third unit was made up of "lodges" bound by an initiation oath and ritual ceremonies. Like the Taiping, this much more rudimentary movement had a certain nationalist and anti-Manchu tinge. The Nian leader, Zhang Luoxing, bore the title "Lord of the great Han alliance" (*Han* meaning members of the Chinese race, as opposed to the Manchus).

Economically, the Nian movement can be defined as a primitive form of "class expropriation." The Nian seized goods carried by private or government convoys, raided the stock of imperial granaries, and stole from wealthy families. They kidnapped rich people and exacted huge ransoms, and they worked the protection racket on moneylenders and merchants. The operations of these "robbers and dispensers of justice" were profitable to Nian supporters, who received shares of the plunder. The Nian leaders themselves grew rich, amassing huge clandestine fortunes while disposing of Nian loot through smugglers and a network of receivers. (This "primitive accumulation of capital" by pillaging was not peculiar to China; the robber bands of Elizabethan England were in the same business.)

The Nian were also engaged in waging war against the established order. For fifteen years they held their own against the imperial armies in North China, severely defeating them many times. In weaponry they combined cannons and muskets with pikes and bamboo spears, the traditional arms of village militia. Their great superiority lay in their cavalry (numbering as many as 20,000 horses), which gave them the mobility to surprise or out-distance the heavy regular troops of the imperial army. Thus the Nian could fall on the enemy without warning or vanish in front of them. One historian has compared their strategy of mobile warfare with that of Mao Tsetung ("The enemy advances, we retreat. The enemy camps, we harass. The enemy tires, we attack. The enemy retreats, we pursue").

The Nian and the Taiping

The history of the Nian rebellion can be divided into two com-pletely different stages: its development parallel with the Taiping revolution, and its survival after 1864 when the Taiping had been defeated. During the first period, the imperial authorities could spare only the traditional Army of the Green Standard and the Manchu Banners to fight against the Nian. Since both were slow and poorly trained, the Nian stood up to them and began to ad-vance. They benefited greatly from the Taiping struggle against the same enemy in Central China. The zones of action of the two groups were only a few hundred kilometers apart. Great differences existed between the Nian and the rebels at Nanking; the Nian had no original political and religious ideology, and they lacked the militant reforming spirit of the Taiping (the Nian were great opium smokers, for example). Yet the political and military interests of the two groups were the same. The Nian profited from the fact that most of the government troops were being used against the Taiping, while the latter were looking for allies who could relieve them on their northern flank.

In 1854–1855 the Nian tried to assist the Taiping expedition sent against Peking; they saved the survivors from disaster and absorbed them. In 1856 the Faithful King, Li Xiu-cheng, attempted to coordinate his action more systematically with that of the Nian. Their leader, Zhang Luo-xing, was given the title of *wang*, and the political *rapprochement* was symbolized by the decision of the Nian to let their hair grow. Several campaigns north of the Yangzi led by the Heroic King and the Faithful King were combined effec-tively with the action of the Nian, which undoubtedly helped the Heavenly state to survive longer. In 1862 and 1863, when the final Taiping crisis arose, Li Xiu-cheng tried to organize a combined diversionary operation with the Nian in the direction of Shenxi. He hoped to gain support from the Moslem rebellion there, but the maneuver came too late to save the Taiping, and Nanking fell almost immediately.

The association between the two movements had been more fruitful for the Nian than for the Taiping. Their network of fortified villages developed steadily during the first period, giving them a strong infrastructure complementing the mobile action of the rebels' cavalry units. The imperial forces struck at the Nian several times without reducing their war potential. The "nest" of Zhihe on the northern border of Anhui was occupied by the imperial troops in 1852, in 1856, and again in 1863, without inflicting irreparable losses on the Nian. The Manchu troops were incapable of maintaining a permanent foothold among the village structures.

Zhang Luo-xing, the ally of the Faithful King, died in the attack of 1863. His successors continued the struggle, however, and in 1865 had the good fortune to inflict a thorough defeat on the Mongolian cavalry. Senggelinqin, considered the best general in the empire, was killed in that action. He had been overconfident about the effectiveness of classical strategy against the Nian and made no attempt to adapt his tactics to the flexible, mobile guerrilla warfare of his peasant adversaries.

Nian victories and final defeat

On a short-term basis, the fall of the Taiping in 1864–1865 helped the Nian. The remains of the army and the leaders who escaped the Nanking disaster joined the rebels from the North. Lai Wen-guang, one of the *wang* of Nanking who had not surrendered, became the best Nian leader during this period.

Around 1865 and 1866 the Nian were at the zenith of their power. They held off the imperial troops and overran all North China, from Hubei to Shandong. In their boldness they tried to cut off the big town of Kaifeng on the Huanghe and surround it with water by breaching the dikes. In 1866 they divided into two groups: the eastern Nian attacked the Grand Canal and its stocks of rice and military equipment, and the western Nian marched toward Shenxi, where they hoped to join forces with the Moslems in revolt (the Hui).

But the imperial forces were now freed from the war with the Taiping, and they were strengthened by the experience accumulated in ten years of fighting under Zeng Guo-fan and other leaders. Zeng's political and military strategy, continued by Li Hong-zhang, eventually bore fruit against the Nian. The eastern Nian were encircled and destroyed in 1867 and 1868. The western Nian, whose ride to Shenxi had not produced the expected results, tried to get back to their former strongholds on the Huai; they were destroyed in their turn by the armies of Li in 1868.

The Moslem Rebellions

A succession of religious rebellions lasting more than a quarter century in various regions of China inhabited by Moslems (the Southwest, the Northwest, and Turkestan) all but fulfilled the old popular prediction that the next Chinese dynasty would be a Moslem one.

Chinese and Moslems clash in Yunnan

In Yunnan the rebellion began around 1853 with conflicts between Moslem and non-Moslem tin miners. The local officials, who for a long time had discriminated against the Moslems, suddenly took action in May 1856 and organized a brutal massacre. The Moslems in turn rose in open rebellion and founded a sultanate based in the town of Dali.

The movement was led by three men: Ma De-xin,[8] a Koranic priest who had made the pilgrimage to Mecca and visited Constantinople and Alexandria; Ma Ru-long, the brother of a miner who died in the clashes of 1853; and Du Wen-xiu, a young scholar of Moslem origin. The first of the three was the religious leader, the second was the military leader, who managed to persuade most of the province to revolt, and the third took the name of Sultan Suleiman and assumed political leadership of the dissident state of Dali.

The rise and fall of the sultanate of Dali

Although the rebellion was born of friction between Moslems and non-Moslems, it quickly took on an anti-Manchu and anti-dynastic coloration. Du Wen-xiu tried to rally all discontented

---

[8] Chinese Moslems often have the surname *Ma*, the first syllable of the Chinese name for Mohammed, with the character for horse (*ma*).

groups, making no racial or religious distinctions. The oath taken by the rebels declared: "To wash away dishonor it is absolutely necessary to bring about the union between Moslems and Han Chinese. . . . our army has three tasks: to drive out the Manchus, unite with the Chinese, and drive out traitors." [9] Many Han Chinese and Yi aborigines joined the rebels.

In spite of initial success (they laid siege to the provincial capital, Kunming, for two years), the two Ma succumbed to invitations from Peking to abandon the rebellion in exchange for high posts in the imperial army. Du Wen-xiu went on with the struggle and held his own against the Manchu armies for more than twelve years. His troops were reinforced by Miao and Yi aborigines, by numerous peasants, and by units of women led by his own daughter.

In 1862 the sultan promulgated a simple, strict code of military administration which stressed the popular nature of the rebellion and contrasted with the conventional hierarchy and slovenly discipline of the Manchu Banners: plundering was forbidden, supplying food for the army was controlled by the people, the abuse of power was punished. He encouraged handicrafts and founded Moslem schools.

From 1868 to 1869 Du Wen-xiu laid siege to Kunming for the second time. The imperial troops had already begun to reconquer the province, destroying everything in their path. Dali fell in 1873 and Du was executed. The suppression was savage. The official chroniclers themselves estimated that over half the population of the province perished. The dead included the versatile high priest Ma De-xin, who was executed by the Manchus in 1874 for his role in initiating the rebellion even though he had later supported Peking.

The Hui revolt and its suppression

The revolt of 1863 to 1873 in the Northwest was ethnic as well as religious. The Chinese Moslems, who were numerous in the provinces of Shenxi and Gansu, were not Han but Dungans (Hui). One of the last expeditions launched by the Taiping to free Nanking got as far as Shenxi in 1861. Its example encouraged the Moslems to rebel, for they had long been in conflict with the Han Chinese, particularly the mandarins and merchants. The revolt was

[9] *Huimin qiyi(The Moslem Revolt)* (Shanghai, 1952), vol. 2, p. 127.

led by Ma Hua-long, one of the heads of a Moslem reform movement called the "new doctrine." From 1862 to 1865 the uprising
spread rapidly to the whole of Gansu and Shenxi, until in 1866
Peking called on Zuo Zong-tang for help.

Thus the Manchu authorities were again forced to entrust the
defense of the empire to the Chinese provincial gentry. To fulfill
this new task, the gentry greatly expanded their political and military staff. They had grown hardened to war during the suppression
of the Taiping, and Zuo's methods in the Northwest were as brutal
as those of the imperial troops in Yunnan. "If I do not destroy
them," Zuo said, "if I leave a branch or a root, I run the risk of
their destroying me in turn." In 1866 and 1867 he managed to
prevent the western Nian from joining forces with the Hui. Year
after year he advanced steadily westward, wiping out the entire
Moslem population. In 1870 he reached Suzhou, the last strong-
hold of the rebels, and took it after a siege of three years. The
Chinese historian Fan Wen-lan estimates that several million soldiers and civilians died in his campaigns.

The revolt of Yakub-beg

After the capture of Suzhou, Zuo Zong-tang continued his advance toward the West, which was in full rebellion. In Chinese
Turkestan, Moslem movements still formed around the noble family of the Khwadja, the princes of Kashgar, although China had
established dominion over the whole region in the eighteenth century. A Khwadja prince, Jehangir, had led a revolt against the
Chinese in 1826 and 1827. It was the expression of the nationalistic
antagonism between the Uighur Turks and the Chinese garrisons,
and was also in a sense a holy war directed by the Moslem "White
Mountain" sect, which was loyal to the Khwadja family.

In 1862 the Western oases had again seceded under the leadership of Yakub-beg, prince of the ruling family at Khokend. Around
1873 he became master of a huge area south of the Tianshan mountains. He took advantage of the Sino-Russian conflict in Central
Asia and also received encouragement from Great Britain, which
favored the creation of a buffer state in the area. The sultan of Constantinople, to whom Yakub-beg had paid homage, acknowledged
his title of prince of Kashgaria. But the armies of Zuo Zong-tang
occupied the oasis of Hami, the key to the West, and then moved
steadily toward Turkestan. In 1877 the kingdom of Yakub-beg

collapsed and by 1878 all the towns in the region were once more occupied by Zuo. Turkestan lost its autonomy and came under direct Chinese administration. In 1885 its territory became a new province, Xinjiang ("new territory").

Minor Rebellions

Besides the Taiping, the Nian, and the Moslems, the imperial authority came up against innumerable shorter and more localized popular movements in the period between the first Opium War and the Sino-French War.

Revolt of the Miao in Guizhou

Some of the movements were launched by ethnic minorities like the Miao, who revolted in southeast Guizhou in 1854. The rebels entrenched themselves in the mountains and from there attacked the Manchu garrisons and Chinese officials, merchants, and land-owners. They worked in cooperation with the local secret societies, and their movement was given a new impetus in 1859 when wandering troops under Shi Da-kai arrived in Guizhou. But Shi Da-kai was heading for the rich province of Sichuan rather than trying to create a solid organization of all the enemies of the Manchus.

In 1865 the imperial armies of Hunan and Sichuan, freed from the necessity to fight the Taiping, began penetrating Guizhou. They forced their way through the mountain passes leading to the Miao districts, where hard fighting went on until 1873. After twenty years of war and massacres, the governor of the province estimated that Guizhou had lost nine-tenths of its population.

Rebellions of the Triad

In the towns, the societies affiliated with the Triad organized several rebellions in the period preceding the second Opium War. The Small Knife Society controlled the city of Shanghai for two years, from 1853 to 1855. These rebels, led by boatmen, porters, and shopkeepers, proclaimed the restoration of the Ming dynasty. It was only a symbolic restoration, however, since they had no pretender to the throne. The imperial troops scattered them with the help of the Westerners. In Amoy another branch of the Small Knife

Society took over for a few months in 1853. And in Canton in 1854 the Red Turbans, who were also affiliated with the Triad, began a rebellion which was not restricted to that city but included the chief neighboring towns of Foshan, Henan, Sanshui, and Shunde. These rebels, who likewise proclaimed their allegiance to the Ming dynasty, were chiefly supported by coolies, boatmen, and craftsmen. The gentry and the rich merchants championed the Manchus, subsidized them, and helped them organize the resistance. The rebels converged on the walled city of Canton but could not take it; they were routed by the authorities after fighting which lasted for several months.

Sporadic action by the secret societies

The risings at Shanghai, Amoy, and Canton and the role of the secret societies in them were not a matter of chance. At the time of the Opium Wars and during the period that followed, the turmoil caused by these clandestine political-religious groups continued without interruption. Since the opening of China to the West their social base and their possibilities of recruitment had become much larger. They attracted transport workers (porters and boatmen) who were thrown out of work by the shifting of the trade routes (especially in the South) and later by the development of steam navigation (particularly in the Yangzi basin). They were also rallying points for peasants affected by the land crisis and by the destruction resulting from the civil wars and the suppression of the large rebellions. Disbanded soldiers, marauding soldiers, and deserters likewise flocked to the secret societies, for after the wars against the Taiping, the Nian, and the Moslems were over, the army disbanded many troops. The conjunction of these groups was especially obvious in the middle Yangzi basin between 1860 and 1880, where the powerful Society of Brothers and Elders had the lead over the other societies in the South (such as the Triad and the Heaven and Earth Societies). The Brothers and Elders Society was particularly influential among boatmen (it was also called the Society of Lakes and Rivers) and among vagrant soldiers.

The North was the domain of the White Lotus and its various affiliates—the Eight Diagrams, the Observance, and the Big Sword Societies, as well as the Society of the Righteous Fists (the Boxers), which was in existence long before the Boxer rebellion at the end of the century (described in Chapter 9). The Northern secret societies were confined almost exclusively to the rural population, whereas the social base of the Southern ones was more complex and more closely linked with recent military and economic developments.

The secret societies untiringly organized rebellions and attacks on the *yamen*, the public granaries, and the prisons. They sacked the houses of the rich and destroyed rent registers. Their watchwords were "Overthrow the Qing and restore the Ming," and "Let us practice justice ourselves in the name of heaven." Their confused social protest and their struggle against the imperial power and the Manchus were not clearly differentiated.[10]

The Chinese historian Wang Tian-jiang has drawn up a provisional list of the movements of agitation led by the secret societies:

	1860–1870	1870–1885
Hunan	27	25
Hubei	7	7
Sichuan	2	—
Guizhou	—	6
Guangdong	—	4
Guangxi	—	1
Yunnan	—	1
Jiangxi	6	4
Fujian	1	—
Zhejiang	—	2
Jiangsu	1	—
Henan	2	3
Zhili	2	—
Gansu	1	1
Shandong	—	1

The turbulence generated by the societies was tenacious, diligent, and countrywide, but it was also episodic. Most of the movements listed by Wang Tian-jiang involved a few hundred men, or sometimes only a few dozen.

The insurrections launched by the secret societies were never clearly distinguishable from ordinary pillaging and banditry. A chain of complicity—a succession of barely perceptible gradations —existed between the clandestine hierarchies of the White Lotus, the Triad, and their affiliates, and the robber bands who lived by plundering and murdering. In Manchuria, for instance, the *mafei* ("bandits on horseback") made long-distance raids like those of the Nian. The imperial authorities were forced to organize military campaigns against them around 1870, but in spite of government

---

[10] See document 5 for an account of the birth of a secret society.

action the bandits on horseback continued to exist. At the other end of China the Black Flags of Guangxi, who intervened in Tongking when the French attacked in 1884 and 1885 (Chapter 6), were also characteristic of the permanent collusion between secret societies and robber bands. The result was that although the secret societies were popular among the peasants because they were enemies of the established order, they were also feared by the peasants because of their exactions and domination.

At the other end of the social scale, no clearly defined boundary existed between the secret societies and the leaders of the established order—mandarins, army leaders, and gentry. Some of the heads of secret societies came from upper-class circles and remained in close contact with them. Some important people gained admittance to the secret societies in order to extend to the social groups represented by the societies. Zuo Zong-tang, who conquered the Nian and the Moslems, was said to have held a high rank in the Society of Brothers and Elders. This frequent collusion between the secret societies and the leaders of the country was confirmed by the fact that rebel leaders often changed sides and supported the authorities, then returned to the rebels, then joined the authorities once more, depending on what they stood to gain. Thus there was constant interpenetration between the ordered world and the world of rebellion. Between 1860 and 1865 Song Jing-shi, the head of the Black Banners (a branch of the White Lotus), led a large peasant revolt in Shandong. Eventually he submitted to the authorities, later took up arms against them once more, and later still gave up the revolution and lived a peaceful village life for several decades more.

Of course, popular discontent with the established power often found expression in forms more diluted than the flare-ups of the secret societies or the wars waged by the Taiping and the Nian. Chinese chronicles, particularly the local ones, mention innumerable conflicts arising between peasants and their landlords, especially when harvests were bad or taxes were heavier than usual. These spontaneous outbursts were directed variously against the authorities, the tax collectors, and the requisitioning of forced labor. In time of famine, peasants would frequently attack the public granaries or the private storehouses of rich landowners and money-lenders.

Failure of the Popular Movements

The large and small movements of insurrection, the countless forms of opposition, and the centrifugal forces, which were at work from one end of the country to the other were the outward signs of an immense political and social crisis. It was an upheaval on a scale rarely equaled in the history of China or even the history of the world; it recalls the ravages of the Thirty Years' War. Tens of millions of men took part in the rebellions. The suppression of the revolts caused more bloodshed than was produced by their direct effects, even allowing for the exaggerations of the mandarins, who were always anxious to reassure the central power and magnify their own role.

Scattered rebellions linked with ancient China

All these insurrections were unable to overthrow the Manchu power, in spite of simultaneous threats from Western pressure and the unspoken hostility of the gentry. Around 1870 the imperial power re-established itself once more for the last time; Chinese historians refer to this as the Tongzhi Restoration (Chapter 5).

The failure of the great mid-nineteenth-century popular risings has sometimes been explained by their lack of strategic coordination. Those responsible for them were aware of the importance of integrating their activities and made serious efforts in this direction. The military cooperation between the Taiping and the Nian certainly gave longer life to both movements. The Moslem rebellion in the Northwest and the Miao rising in Guizhou were repercussions of the far-distant Taiping expedition. Du Wen-xiu, the sultan of Dali, declared when he took power: "The Taiping will become our allies, we will help each other, we will destroy our enemies by our combined efforts." [11] Even when the cooperation did not work well, there was a noticeable lack of conflicts and rivalries between the various rebellions.

More important still was the lack of homogeneity among the movements, especially from the ideological point of view. They had diverse intentions: the renewal of Islam, the assertion of Ming legitimism, the pursuit of banditry with a vague coloring of equalitari-

[11] *Huimin qiyi*, vol. 1, p. 298.

anism, or the creation of a modernist peasant utopia on which a new dynasty could be founded. In the long run, it was not possible to combine any one of the movements with any other, and a coalition of their military projects, even if they had been better coordinated, could not have produced anything durable.

In short, the centrifugal forces were at work only within the old regime, in accordance with the traditional dynamics of Chinese politics. Mainly they reflected the difficulties in the workings of the old regime, not the development of new economic and social structures capable of challenging the regime from without. Even the modernism of the Taiping was still only a confused aspiration resulting from the impact of the West on China. Its specific base within Chinese society was extremely limited. Modern aspects were entirely lacking in the other movements, except for the Islamic reformism of the Moslems, which was a vague and distant echo of the political and religious changes in the Moslem states in the Middle East around 1860.

The intermediary position of the villages

A further confirmation of the fact that the movements in China remained within the old regime is that they were incapable of dissociating themselves from it in political practice. Their leaders shifted back and forth between the imperial cause and their revolutionary crusades too often for it to be an anomaly peculiar to individuals. It happened in the case of the Nian, the Moslems, and the Taiping (after his capture, the Faithful King eventually offered his services to Zeng Guo-fan). In Chinese tradition the holding of rebel power was as much a way to legal power as an alternative to it.

Moreover, in the areas under their control the rebels attempted to draw on the villages for men, materials, and provisions, but they did not really try to create new power of a truly popular nature. The great Chinese rebellions of the mid-nineteenth century were popular risings in that their leaders came from the people and had wide popular support at the outset. But they do not appear to have been associated in any lasting way with the mass of the people—in other words, with the villages and their political machinery. The movements of insurrection were the domain of minority groups, and their most active members often came from the nonagricultural population.

The struggles between the rebels and the authorities, particularly when they lasted for a long time, took place above the level of the villages, which were in a sense a "third force." The villages had their own rural militia, which often supported the rebels at first because the exactions of the government and the privileged classes were such a burden. But the villages quickly became disappointed, and the mandarins were able to re-establish their power in the countryside through the rural gentry. This happened in the cases of the Taiping, the Nian, and the Red Turbans. In spite of their vigor, none of these revolts were able to shatter the traditional mold of Chinese rural society, or to sever the innumerable threads by which the rural gentry had controlled the villages for centuries. The instruments of control were not only the land tax and forced labor, but the gentry's intellectual prestige and their moral authority based on their good works, administrative supervision, arbitration of private disputes, and overseeing of public works. In spite of the vast numbers of people they mobilized, the peasant revolts did not take on the nature of a peasant revolution; this did not happen until the twentieth century.

The respite enjoyed by the Manchu authorities between 1860 and 1870 was also due to the reversal of the policy adopted by the foreigners toward them. The privileges obtained by the Westerners in China as a result of the two Opium Wars implied the existence of a central power which was both relatively strong and relatively docile. The help which the British and the French gave the imperial cause in the struggle against the major rebellions may not have been decisive, but it made an appreciable contribution to the temporary success of the Restoration.

ADDITIONAL BIBLIOGRAPHY

Callery and Yvan, L'Insurrection en Chine, depuis son origine jusqu'à la prise de Nankin (Paris, 1853).

Chiang Siang-tseh, The Nien Rebellion (Seattle, University of Washington Press, 1954).

A. Lindley, Tai-ping Tien Kwoh: The History of the Tai-ping Revolution (London, 1866, 2 vols.).

Thomas Meadows, The Chinese and Their Rebellions (London, 1856).

Franz Henry Michael and Chang Chung-li, The Taiping Rebellion. Vol. I: History (Seattle, University of Washington Press, 1966).

Vincent Yu-chung, Shih, The Taiping Ideology: Its Sources, Interpretations and Influences (Seattle, University of Washington Press, 1967).

Wen Djang-chu, The Moslem Rebellion in North-Western China, 1862–1878 (Paris, 1966).

DOCUMENTS

1. THE TAIPING APPEAL TO CHINESE NATIONALISM AGAINST MANCHU DOMINATION: EDICT OF 1853

SOURCE: English version of J. C. Cheng, *Chinese Sources for the Taiping Rebellion* (Hong Kong, Hong Kong University Press, London, Oxford University Press, 1963), p. 72.

We consider the world as China's, not the Tartar's; clothes and food as China's, not the Tartar's; sons, daughters and people as China's, not the Tartar's. It is regrettable that the Ming dynasty failed in their duties as rulers and the Manchus availed themselves of the chaos, defiled China, stole China's territory, raped and maltreated China's sons and daughters. Yet if China, which extends in the six directions and covers the nine provinces, calmly allows them to molest her without any reaction, can she be said to possess men worthy of the name? . . . China is the head, and Tartary the foot; China is the Holy Continent, and Tartary that of evil spirits. Why do we call China the Holy Continent? The Heavenly Father and August God is the True God, and Heaven, earth, mountains and seas were made by Him. Thus, formerly, the name Holy Continent was given to China. Why do we consider the Tartars evil spirits? The snaky devil Yen-lo is an evil spirit and the Tartar demons worship him and his like. Thus, now, we consider the Tartars evil spirits. . . . Fortunately the Heavenly doctrines have triumphed and China has hopes of recovering. As the minds of the people seek a remedy, there are sure signs of the annihilation of Tartary. The Tartars' sins are full; August Heaven has lost patience and has commanded our Heavenly King to display respectfully the grandeur of Heaven to raise the banner of righteousness, sweep away the evil demons, clear China thoroughly and execute reverently Heaven's punishment. . . . We raise the army of righteousness in order to wreak the vengeance of God on high on those who have deceived Heaven, and to liberate the masses below for the sake of China. We ought to clear away all traces of the Tartars and enjoy together the joy of Universal Peace. Those who obey Heaven shall be amply rewarded, and those who oppose Heaven shall die conspicuously. This is hereby proclaimed to all under Heaven so that everyone may hear and know of it.

2. THE AGRARIAN UTOPIANISM OF THE TAIPING: THE LAND LAW OF THE HEAVENLY DYNASTY (1853)

SOURCE: J. C. Cheng, *op. cit.*, pp. 39–41.

The distribution of land is made according to the size of the family, irrespective of sex, with only the number of persons taken into account. The larger the number, the more land they shall receive; the smaller the number, the less land they shall receive. The lands assigned are of various grades of the nine categories. If there are six persons in the family, three shall receive good land, and three shall receive bad land:

half good and half bad. All lands under Heaven shall be farmed jointly by the people under Heaven. If the production of food is too small in one place, then move to another where it is more abundant. All lands under Heaven shall be accessible in time of abundance or famine. If there is a famine in one area, move the surplus from an area where there is abundance to that area, in order to feed the starving. In this way the people under Heaven shall all enjoy the great happiness given by the Heavenly Father, Supreme Lord and August God. Land shall be farmed by all; rice, eaten by all; clothes, worn by all; money, spent by all. There shall be no inequality, and no person shall be without food or fuel.

No matter whether man or woman, everyone over sixteen years of age shall receive land. If there is any land left, those who are fifteen and under shall receive a half share. For instance, a person over sixteen receives one *mow* [2 mou—0.1518 acre] of the superior-superior category. If a person over sixteen receives three *mow* of the inferior-inferior category, one who is fifteen or under shall receive a half share and thus get one and a half *mow* of the inferior-inferior category.

Everywhere in the empire mulberry trees shall be planted beneath the walls. All women shall raise silkworms, spin cloth and sew dresses. Every family in the empire shall have five hens and two sows, without exception. At the harvest the platoon-chief shall supervise the section-chief in storing away the amount of new grain needed for the twenty-five families and surrendering the rest to the public storehouse. The same applies to wheat, beans, nettle-hemp, cloth, silk, chickens, dogs and so on; it applies to money also. For under Heaven all belongs to the great family of the Heavenly Father, Supreme Lord and August God. In the Empire none shall have any private property, and everything belongs to God, so that God may dispose of it. In the great family of Heaven every place is equal, and everyone has plenty. This is the edict of the Heavenly Father, Supreme Lord and August God, who especially commanded the T'ai-P'ing True Lord to save the world.

But the platoon-chief shall keep an account of the amount of money and grain, reporting it to the treasurer, disburser and receiver. In every twenty-five families there shall be established a public storehouse and a chapel, where the platoon-chief shall reside. In every twenty-five families all matters, such as marriage and birth celebrations, shall be at the expense of the public storehouse. But they shall be controlled, and prohibited from spending one cash more than the limit.

In case of marriage a family is given 1,000 cash and 100 catties of grain. In the empire everything shall be uniform. In everything expenses shall be economized lest there should be wars and calamities. In the empire marriages shall not be made in accordance with wealth. In every twenty-five families the services of blacksmiths, carpenters and stone-masons shall be provided by the section-chiefs and privates, during their leisure after farming. All platoon-chiefs shall take charge of affairs, among their respective twenty-five families, such as marriage, birth and other celebrations.

3. THE SYNCRETIC THEOLOGY OF THE TAIPING: COMMENTARY BY HONG XIU-QUAN ON THE FIRST EPISTLE OF ST. JOHN (1863)

SOURCE: J. C. Cheng, *op. cit.*, pp. 88–89.

There is only one Supreme God. Christ is the First Son of God. The Son was born of the Father, originally one and only one body. But the Father is the Father; the Son, the Son; one in two, and two in one. As to the Holy Spirit of the Eastern King,* Almighty God issued an edict appointing him to be the spirit. The Eastern King is a beloved Son of God, and, together with the Great Elder Brother and Myself, was born of the same Mother. Before the beginning of Heaven and Earth, all three of us were of the same Father, as the Heavenly Father God is the one and only True God. The one and only True God says: "Beside Myself, thou shalt have no other gods." The Holy Ghost is really God. If there were to be another Holy Ghost, there would be another Divine Being. Even the Holy Ghost and Wind is also the Wind of the Holy Ghost and God, nor is the Wind the Holy Ghost. The Wind is the Eastern King, the Wind Maker in Heaven. The Holy Ghost is the Holy Ghost; the Wind, the Wind; one in two, and two in one. The Son was born of the Father, originally one and only one body. But the Father is the Father; the Son, the Son; either united into one, or separated into two. Now God has sent down the Eastern King into the world, and descended upon the Eastern King as the Holy Ghost. The King's original title was the Wind and Comforter. The Father knows that there are some mistakes in the records of the New [sic] Testament, and thus has sent down the Eastern King as a witness that the Holy Ghost is the Wind of God, the Eastern King. He also knows that the people on earth mistakenly think that Christ is God. Thus God sent down the Eastern King to prove the existence of the Divine Father. Thus Christ has sent down the Western King to prove the existence of the First Son. Hence, the Father is the Father; the Son, the Son; the Elder Brother, the Elder Brother; the Younger Brother, the Younger Brother; one in two, and two in one. Immediately upon their descent the titles and ranks have been fixed. If you should suppose that Christ is God, there would be another God. How could the mind of the Great Elder Brother be at ease? Now the Great Elder Brother descended upon earth, and issued an edict introducing Me Myself: "My brother Xiu-quan, you shall not call yourself Emperor (God); only the Father is indeed the Emperor (God)." The Great Elder Brother then spoke as the Son of the Father. Moreover, I Myself† ascended to the High Heaven, saw the Heavenly Father, the Heavenly Mother, the Great Elder Brother and the Heavenly Sister-in-law many times. The proofs and evidence are just too many. In Heaven and on Earth it is the same. The things heard are not quite equal to those seen.

* Yang Xiu-qing, who in this way was incorporated into the Trinity.
† That is, Xiu-quan, the Heavenly King, who proclaimed himself to be the younger brother of Christ.

4. THE FRATERNAL LIFE OF THE TAIPING IN NANKING DURING THE FIRST PHASE OF THE REBELLION: AN EYEWITNESS ACCOUNT BY A ROMAN CATHOLIC MISSIONARY

SOURCE: Roger Pélissier, *La Chine entre en scène* (Paris, Julliard, 1963), pp. 76–77. The extract is a letter written by Father Clavelin, quoted in *Mémoires sur l'état actuel de la mission du Kiangnan, 1842–1855*, followed by *Lettres relatives à l'insurrection, 1851–1855* (Paris, Julien et Lanier, 1855).

Straight after the Heavenly King come five people, prime ministers, who have also assumed the title of king, as in the past. In the case of one of them it is said to be a purely honorary title. As a means of distinguishing one from another, each of the others has added one of the four points of the compass to his title of king. The ministers whom we saw formed the second rank. All the inhabitants are divided into groups of ten thousand. Only one group of three thousand women, for example, has a man as its head to communicate with the ministers. While we were with one of them, this leader came to hand over a request to him, worded as follows: "The sisters of such-and-such division ask for more clothes, because it has become colder." The minister immediately replied: "Look into it, and do what is necessary."

Community life in Nanking is shown in its most revealing aspects and in the broadest possible meaning of the term, but morals do not suffer in the least, far from it; any attack on morals, like pillage, is irremissibly punished by death. A light burns during the night in each post occupied by women, and one of them stays on guard and beats a little tambourine every now and then.

The chief leaders are probably extremely anxious to maintain a hierarchy, and to make it respected. A cannon shot indicates their departures and arrivals. Music is played during their meals, yet we saw not only the secondary leaders, but also members of the people approach them absolutely freely.

No one could deny that something in the way they treat one another justifies the name of brothers which the people from Guangxi use when addressing one another. There is still the feeling of a family about them even now. Thus all the houses are owned in common; food and clothes are deposited in public storehouses; gold, silver and precious things are taken to the public treasury. Nothing can be bought or sold; consequently money would be useless in the hands of a private individual. It was impossible for us to obtain costumes like the ones that the Guangxi-ren wear at the moment. The leaders are responsible for meeting the various needs of their subordinates. It really is an admirable thing that a population swelled by the invasion to over a million can be fed and clothed regularly like this, as we saw with our own eyes, and what is more, in the middle of a civil war, with an enemy camp opposite laying siege to the town. . . .

As for us, we were given plain food, true enough, but plenty of it, and treated like honored guests. Several times the secretaries, our friends, shared our meals. They said a prayer to the Heavenly Father before and afterwards; we said the Benedicite and grace.

Twice a day, gathered in a large room or hall, the people from Guangxi pray to the Shangdi (the Chinese term for God). Ten cannon shots are fixed when the Heavenly King prays. For our part, we performed our spiritual exercises among them in complete liberty. My catechist in particular said as many prayers as fifty people from Guangxi.

We asked them how they treated people who do not want to pray with them. This was the reply: "Those who want neither to pray nor to renounce idols are put to death; those who believe in nothing and pray to nothing are left alone, though often at the price of a few strokes of the rod; but if they massed together, we would put them to death too."

5. A SECRET SOCIETY IS BORN (1858)

SOURCE: French translation by Jean Chesneaux, in *Les Sociétés secrètes en Chine* (Paris, Julliard, 1965), pp. 83–85. Chinese text in the periodical *Jindaishi ziliao*, 1955, no. 3.

The bandits of the Gold Coin Society began their activities in the early years of the reign of the Xianfeng Emperor. A man called Zhao Qi, who was about thirty years old, had a restaurant in his native village of Quincang in the district of Pingyi. He was well versed in the techniques of wrestling and boxing, and his friends were all boxers or athletes.

When his friends were in need, Zhao Qi gave them money or helped them with presents. Consequently his name was known to the North and to the South, as far as the borders of the province of Fujian. Many convicts accused of common-law offenses came to him for protection. He was known as Zhao-da-ge (Zhao the big brother).

In the eighth year of the reign of the Xianfeng Emperor (1858) a man called Mu Yuan, who could write characters well, loved reading the biographies of the heroes of old, and who was brave and vigorous, dreamed on the night of August 15 that there were two moons in the sky. Next day he went to see Zhao Qi and asked him about his dream. Zhao Qi replied: "The two moons from the word *peng* (friend); friend means belonging to the same category." Zhao then quoted a passage from the *Classic of Changes** and said: "You have great ambitions, and your dream will materialize." The two men became closer and closer friends.

Later Xie Gong-da, Zhu Xiu-xian, Chen Shi-yi, Zhou Xiong (who was a brush seller from Huzhou), a man from Shandong province who was condemned to serve in the army at Mengzhou, and a coppersmith called Huang Xiu-jin all joined Zhao Qi and Mu Yuan. The eight men were united by the ties of sacred brotherhood. They shared out the eight sacred diagrams among themselves.

---

* One of the Five Classics, highly esoteric in character.

Later Zhao Qi declared: "We are united in life and in death; we hope that our ties will last a long time. Today the long-haired rebels* are spreading through Jiangsu and Zhejiang. We will probably be separated again. When this happens, what can we adopt as a rallying sign?"

During the meeting one of those present declared: "I have thought of something. We will ask the deity if it is suitable for us."

At that moment an opera was being performed in the temple at Qiancang, and this was how the term *Jin-qian* (gold coin) came to be suggested. The people replied: "Very good!" and the deity's reply was also satisfactory.

They took sixteen coins of the Kangxi Emperor; they tied them together, with the side bearing the word "hand" on the inside, then they fastened them inside their clothes with ribbons.†

Each year at the same date they organized a big feast and had plays performed. The people appreciated this greatly.

More and more vagabonds joined them, as well as people who had great riches but who were excluded from power. They made raids on the villages and no one dared stand up to them. Thus the power of the Gold Coin Society grew greater and greater.

---

* The Taiping.
† The coins had a hole in the middle.

Chapter Five

Restoration of Imperial Order: *1860-1885*

In October 1860 when the British and French signed the agreements with the imperial regime that were known as the Peking conventions, the Manchu dynasty seemed on the verge of collapse. French and British troops had burned the summer palace, and most of the provinces were in a state of insurrection. The Taiping had won control of the richest regions in China and were extending their conquests. The expedition of Shi Da-Kai had aroused the Miao to revolt in Guizhou once more. Yunnan was a prey to the Moslem rebellion. The army was disorganized and the treasury was empty. The high-ranking mandarins who had fled to Jehol with the emperor were panicked and quarreling among themselves.

Yet during the fifteen years which followed, unity and order were apparently re-established by the imperial regime. Scholars of the time considered the reign of Tongzhi (1862–1874) as an era of "restoration" (*zhongxing*). This term was applied to a period in the traditional cycle of a dynasty when its decline is temporarily halted. Decay is replaced by a fleeting renewal of strength—a last show of brilliance before the ultimate catastrophe.

The Tongzhi Restoration was not merely a return to the old order; it involved the creation of a new program to meet the problems raised by the rebellions and the challenge from abroad. It defined a form of conservatism based on certain political forces whose effects left their mark on the entire history of modern China.

Restoration of the Central Power

The reprieve granted to the Manchu dynasty was due mainly to the sudden change in the policy of the foreign powers toward it after the second Opium War. The Peking conventions further extended the privileges granted to the foreigners by the treaties of Tientsin in 1858. Since these privileges were considerable, it was in the interest of the foreign powers to uphold the imperial regime against the Taiping. At the time they were not in a position to play a direct part in the political intrigues of the Manchu court. But they were glad of the *coup d'état* which, on the death of the Xianfeng Emperor, eliminated the leaders who took a hard line against the West.

The Westerners refrained from any action likely to embarrass the new government, and as soon as it appeared to be stable, they offered their help. The best guarantee of the government's good will seemed to them to be the role played in it by Prince Gong. He had signed the Peking conventions and on January 20, 1861, he created the foreign ministry which the Westerners had wanted for a long time. Its title was Zongli Geguo Shiwu Yamen (Office for the General Administration of Affairs with All Countries, usually found in the abbreviated form of Zongli Yamen). The foreign powers considered Gong an open-minded and enlightened man.

The imperial succession

When the Xianfeng Emperor died on August 22, 1861, his son was only five years old. Both the empress consort Ci-an, and Ci-xi, the mother of the new emperor, became Empress Dowagers. The stake in the political struggle was the council of regents. The supporters of the policy of conciliation with the foreigners, Prince Gong and Wen-xiang, had stayed in Peking after the negotiations with the French and the British. The members of the hard-line "war party," who had followed the court into exile in Jehol during the foreign invasion, were intriguing around the body of the dead emperor. Their leaders, the Manchu princes Cai-yuan, Duan-hua, and Su-shun, published an edict naming them as regents.

Ci-xi, the new emperor's mother, knew that if these three princes gained the upper hand she risked losing not only her power but also her life. She managed to gain possession of the imperial seal, without which no edict of the new government was valid. Ci-xi, with Ci-an, got back to Peking long before the regents, who were ceremonially obligated to follow the slow progress of the emperor's coffin.

A *coup d'état* was plotted with the connivance of Prince Gong and his supporters. In reply to a flood of carefully inspired petitions, edicts were issued that stripped the most powerful opponents of their offices. On November 8, 1861, Prince Cai-yuan and Prince Duan-hua were accused of high treason and ordered to commit suicide, while the third prince, Su-shun, was beheaded. The next day an edict put a stop to reprisals against the other conspirators. Thus the leaders alone had been punished; this moderation contributed to the success of the Restoration, for it helped to eliminate quarrels among different factions and emphasized the joint interests of the Chinese and the Manchu bureaucracy.

The new government was set up early in November. Ci-xi and Ci-an became sole regents, in violation of the dynastic custom forbidding women to reign. Prince Gong was appointed "prince councillor to the government" and became a member of the Grand Council, which was reshuffled. The new reign was called Tongzhi (Union for Order), to convey both its aim, and the determination to cooperate which united the leading groups. In fact, a relatively homogeneous group was brought to power by the *coup d'état*.

The new sovereigns

Unlike earlier "restorations," that of Tongzhi owed nothing to the virtue or the energy of the emperor. His sole merit lay in being the legitimate heir to the throne; he was too young and too weak to play his own part. Although she had great personal ambition, his mother Ci-xi was not then in a position to wield power. While the Xianfeng Emperor was alive she had grown accustomed to political intrigue and had learned how to find allies among the factions dividing the court. She had no knowledge of government routine, however, and no experience in handling men or affairs. Not until 1865 did she gradually rise to a position of supreme power, usurping the influence of the other Empress Dowager, Ci-an, and even daring to dismiss Prince Gong. Though Gong came back into favor a few weeks later, he never regained the title of prince councillor to the government.

Ci-xi did not exercise a despotic authority until after the death of the Tongzhi Emperor in 1874. Even then she still had rivals, until the death of Ci-an and the final disgrace of Prince Gong in 1884 enabled her to set herself up as an autocrat. During the reign of her son, Ci-xi's thirst for power and taste for political machinations had some influence on government actions. But the substance of her role consisted above all in vigorously upholding the continuity and the rites of the imperial institution. The insistence of both Ci-xi and Ci-an on the importance of this institution gave meaning and legal sanction to the work of restoration undertaken by others.

Senior officials of the central government

The real artisans of the Restoration were a few senior officials in the capital and in the provinces.

In Peking the chief figure was Prince Gong (1833–1898). The brother of the Xianfeng Emperor, he had won his political position through his talents as a diplomat. Early in his career he had been extremely hostile toward the West. After frequent negotiations with the British, however, he became an Anglophile and advocated a relative degree of modernization for China. Until 1884, apart from his brief overthrow by Ci-xi in 1865, he was chairman of the Zongli Yamen and Grand Councillor.

Within the Grand Council Prince Gong had the support of Wen-xiang (1818–1876), who was a still more able statesman than Gong himself. Chinese and foreign contemporaries had the greatest esteem for Wen-xiang, a Manchu whose honesty, sense of duty, perspicacity, and broad-mindedness earned him widespread respect. As well as belonging to the Grand Council, he was chairman of the Ministry of Public Works and of the Ministry of Civil Office, both of which were key posts in the work of rebuilding launched by the Restoration.

Shen Gui-fen, who was admitted to the Grand Council in 1867, and Li Tang-jie, a neo-Confucian theorist who became vice-chairman of the Ministry of Ceremonies, chairman of the Board of Censors, and then Grand Councillor, were two of the high-ranking officials who ensured the success of the Restoration in Peking. Until 1874, in spite of rivalry among factions at court, Prince Gong and his colleagues managed to control the central government and impose its authority on the great provincial mandarins.

Senior officials in the provinces

The most outstanding and controversial figure in the government was one of the provincial leaders of the Restoration. Zeng Guo-fan (1811–1872), whose military successes against the Taiping were described in Chapter 4, dominated his time and became a symbol of it. He has been praised extravagantly by generations of conservatives and denounced as a traitor by generations of revolutionaries. A native of the province of Hunan, Zeng came from a humble family of scholars. He passed the metropolitan examinations in 1838 and held several official posts, attracting attention by his determination and the high quality of his literary style. In 1852 he retired to Hunan for the mourning period required by the death of his mother. While he was there, an imperial order put him in charge of recruiting a militia to fight the Taiping. He organized it, disciplined it, and gave it military training of a kind totally unheard-of until then.

The success of the Hunan army gave a decisive impetus to Zeng's career. In 1860 he was imperial commissioner responsible for the suppression of the Taiping and governor-general of Liangjiang, a post which he occupied except for two brief intervals until he died. He was also a member of the Grand Secretariat. Zeng was a man of integrity who set himself extremely high standards. He was frugal, brave, and tenacious. He was gifted with considerable insight and knew how to choose his assistants, many of whom later rose to high position. His clear, unerring intellect enabled him to grasp the essential points of a situation and arrive at sound judgments. In the eyes of his contemporaries, Zeng Guo-fan—general, administrator, economist, moralist, and writer—was the perfect example of the Confucian sage.

Zuo Zong-tang (1812–1885) also embodied the ideal of the statesman in a Confucian society. More ardent in temperament than Zeng, he was less of a scholar and thinker, and possibly more imaginative. He had failed the metropolitan examinations and was tending his land in his native province of Hunan when he was summoned in 1852 to help fight the Taiping. He was put in charge of organizing and leading the military operations in the Yangzi provinces, where he revealed great qualities as a leader, strategist, and administrator. In 1861 Zuo was made governor of Zhejiang; two years later he became governor-general of Zhejiang and Fujian. He was posted to Shenxi-Gansu from 1866 to 1880 and to

Liangjiang from 1881 to 1884. He became a member of the Grand Secretariat in 1873 and was called to the Grand Council twice, in 1881 and 1884. It was Zuo who crushed the Nian insurrection and the Moslem rebellions in the Northwest. He also tried to restore the agrarian economy and set up modern enterprises (see Chapter 7).

Li Hong-zhang (1823–1901) was not outstanding for his moral virtues since he was both conceited and corrupt. However, he had great military ability, formidable skill in politics, and exceptional flexibility and brilliance of intellect. He was one of the principal figures of the Restoration period, though he was less prominent than Zeng Guo-fan or Zuo Zong-tang. In 1853 he raised a militia in his native province of Anhui which won a few victories against the Taiping. Following the advice of his friend and protector Zeng Guo-fan, he quickly turned his militia into the Huai army, on which he founded his personal power. He was appointed governor of Jiangsu in 1862 and governor-general in 1865. He was transferred to Huguang in 1867 and in 1870 was given the strategic post of governor-general of Zhili, where he remained until his disgrace in 1895.

Other less illustrious people contributed to the work of the Restoration in the provinces: Luo Bing-zhang in Sichuan, Ma Xing-yi in the lower Yangzi provinces, Guo Song-dao and Jiang Yi-li in Guangdong, and Ding Bao-zhen in Shandong. All had the reputation of being efficient administrators.

More opportunity for the Chinese bureaucracy

The reign of Tongzhi certainly profited from the fact that an exceptionally large number of energetic and intelligent men were in important posts. It seems that throughout the crisis in the Qing state around 1860, the traditional rules of balance in numbers between Manchu and Chinese officials were less strictly observed than they had been in the past. Now the balance was tipped in favor of the Chinese, not simply because individual competence was given more weight in appointments, but because it was politically necessary to acknowledge the importance of Chinese help against the rebellions. The Manchus, including the members of the imperial clan, were slightly in the majority on the Grand Council, but the Chinese outnumbered them in provincial administrative posts.

The increased opportunities for Chinese with ability no doubt helped to win over the elite to the dynasty. The constant efforts of the leading mandarins to find and recruit "men of talent" promised a rapid and brilliant career to young men with ambition. Each of the important figures in the Restoration had a team of private secretaries: Zeng Guo-fan employed eighty, and Li Hong-zhang almost as many. They acted as a brain trust and, through their family relationships, gave the officials a kind of following, a local base for their credit and their influence. Particularism was not always as obvious as it was in the entourage of Zeng Guo-fan, who was justly accused of partiality toward the Hunanese. But regionalism was certainly the main feature of the political-military circles which gathered around the chief provincial mandarins. As long as the regional leaders carried out the orders of the central government, personal and regional loyalties were not a source of disunity; quite the opposite. They ensured that decisions from the top were executed effectively, with less wear and tear on the bureaucratic machine.

Loyalty of the provincial leaders

The government born of the *coup d'état* of November 1861 would have been incapable of re-establishing the central power without the allegiance and cooperation of the provincial leaders. Zeng Guo-fan, Zuo Zong-tang, and Li Hong-zhang have often been denounced as prototypes of the warlords of the Republican era. The comparison is justifiable in some respects, but these people remained loyal to the empire during the crisis of 1860–1861; they accepted the new authorities.

The work of political and military recovery which was the chief characteristic of the reign of Tongzhi had in fact begun several years earlier, initiated by gentry and certain officials in the Yangzi provinces. The movement took shape between 1853 and 1856, at the time when the Taiping empire based in Nanking developed organizational difficulties and gradually lost its revolutionary drive. For men like Zeng Guo-fan or Hu Lin-yi (governor of Hubei from 1856 to 1861), the problem was not one of overcoming the Taiping in the military field, but of conquering the Taiping politically and morally.

Although their material strength lay in their armies, the provincial leaders who came to prominence in the struggle against the Taiping were not army officers in the Western sense of the term. They were mainly civil officials, products of the examination system, who had managed to rise owing to their capability in both civil and military affairs. Their reputations were built on their literary talent and their fidelity to the moral code. As they were thoroughly imbued with Confucianism, they hoped to preserve the social order and the conception of the state, which in their eyes was a more certain guarantee of the continuance of their power than was purely military success. Similarly, they won the trust of the gentry, the scholars, and the officials by their concern to protect a stable society based on the *li* (the rites of principles of social customs, in conformity with the doctrines of the Confucian Classics).

From a purely ideological point of view, it was inconceivable for the Confucian state to be without an emperor at the summit of the social hierarchy. There had to be a central, superior authority who transmitted the rites and supervised their observance. And from a practical point of view the provincial leaders realized that if they were to carry out effective action, it must be coordinated. Above all, they knew they must have the approval and good will of the foreigners, if not their material help, for it was impossible to fight on two fronts. Thus in spite of overtures made to them by the "war party," the great provincial mandarins upheld Prince Gong and his friends. The Confucian qualities of the men led by Gong may not have been greater than those of their rivals, but Gong wanted to negotiate an agreement with the foreign powers, and he managed to do it.

Balance between central and regional authority

The Restoration statesmen never formed a unified group; they were not a species of political party capable of taking over the key posts. They were split by personal antipathy, like that between Zeng Guo-fan and Zuo Zong-tang, and by power struggles, like those between metropolitan and provincial officials. They had to share authority with people who rejected many of their convictions. But their aims and interests were fundamentally identical: they wanted to suppress rebellions and ensure the survival of the old political, economic, and social regime. This was the basis on which the government was able to achieve stability.

During the reign of Tongzhi there was a halt in the growth of the centrifugal tendencies which had predominated in the preceding period and which began again afterward. The traditional balance between central and provincial authority was temporarily re-established. Skillfully, and because they had to, Prince Gong and the regents allowed the great provincial mandarins a voice in the central government. Zeng Guo-fan, for example, was a member of the Grand Secretariat and was called to Peking several times for special consultations. Most of the senior officials in the capital also had posts in the provinces. These practices helped to reinforce the foundations of the government, while the Confucianism of the senior officials led them to subordinate their private interests to collective ones. The collective interests protected by official Confucianism were those of the gentry and the landowners, who heartily welcomed the assumption of power by such men.

The task of the new government

The recapture of Anqing in Anhui on September 5, 1861, was a turning point in the campaign against the Taiping. A series of imperial victories followed. Foreign opinion and the opinion of Chinese scholars were unanimous in laying them to the credit of the new government. Zeng Guo-fan wrote in a letter to his brother: "There is hope of a national renewal."

In 1862 the consolidation of the central power, due to the *entente* with the foreigners, the arrival of new leaders, and the rallying of gentry and officials, enabled the government to begin the serious work of restoration. Its task was twofold: to re-establish order at home and to strengthen Chinese power abroad. The first aspect involved the suppression of popular movements, the rehabilitation of the recaptured territories, and the reorganization of the territory as a whole.

Suppression of Popular Movements

The suppression of the popular movements, which historians have traditionally presented as the glory of the reign of Tongzhi, was a long and difficult undertaking still unfinished on the emperor's death. The country was never at peace in his reign. When he died, a new rebellion was in full swing in Turkestan and sporadic popular risings were still endemic. The Restoration had nevertheless defeated the four chief movements threatening the Qing state, thanks to the new military and political techniques devised by the government.

Victory over the Taiping

Although the imperial troops had been engaged against the Taiping for several years, the fall of the Taiping empire was relatively quick once it began. After the conquest of Anqing in September 1861, the military campaign was punctuated by the reconquest of Jiangxi, Zhejiang, Anhui, and the lower Yangzi valley by Li Hongzhang and Zuo Zong-tang.[1] The rebels were caught in a vise, and Zeng Guo-quan laid siege to Nanking. Suzhou was recaptured at the end of 1863, Changzhou at the beginning of the following year. Nanking fell on July 19, 1864, to Zeng Guo-fan, who had come to his brother's help. The Taiping empire collapsed, and with it the most serious threat to Qing power.

The campaign against the Nian

The military effort was then directed against the Nian, whose power was steadily growing. In 1864 the imperial troops, commanded by one of their best generals, the Mongol Senggelinqin, lost control of the situation in Shandong. During the following year they were crushed in a brutal defeat in which Senggelinqin was killed.

Panic-stricken, the government put Zeng Guo-fan in command of all the troops in Shandong, Henan, and Zhili, while Li Hongzhang replaced him temporarily as governor-general of Liangjiang. All military resources were mobilized. Nine more garrisons were established in the provinces at the center of operations—Shandong, Anhui, Jiangsu, and Henan. Fortifications, dikes, walls, canals, and trenches were rapidly constructed at strategic points along the Yellow River and the Grand Canal. But the Nian still advanced. In the autumn of 1866 their troops—which up till then had worked mostly in small bands—managed to organize themselves into two main forces, one to the west, based in Shenxi, and the other to the east, operating in Shandong, Henan, Hubei, and Jiangsu.

At the beginning of 1867 converging offensives by the Nian armies were directly threatening the capital itself. Zeng Guo-fan, well aware of the failure of his efforts and of the criticism leveled against him, handed over his command to Li Hong-zhang. In face of the imminent danger the government called in all the great mili-

---

[1] Document 1 at the end of the chapter gives an account from Li's memoirs.

tary leaders. After many reverses and surprises, the eastern Nian seem to have been neutralized, more or less, in December 1867. But in January 1868 they reappeared in full force in Zhili, working in conjunction with the western Nian, who had crossed Shanxi and were advancing on Peking. Zuo Zong-tang was placed at the head of the troops in Zhili, and Prince Gong was put in charge of defending the capital. Each time they failed, punishments and threats were dealt out to the leaders of the imperial troops. In May Li Hong-zhang was told that he had one month in which to "finish off" the Nian. The death of the leader of the western Nian, Zhang Zhong-yu, who was drowned during a retreat, marked the end of the revolt. The defeat of the Nian was officially proclaimed on August 27, 1868.

Operations against the Moslems

The victory over the Nian enabled the government to concentrate on the Moslem rebellions in the Northwest and in Yunnan. In November 1868, Zuo Zong-tang arrived in Sian as governor-general of Shenxi and Gansu. At the end of 1869, the rebels had been chased out of Shenxi and the province appeared to have been pacified. It took much longer to obtain the submission of Gansu and Ningxia, and more cruelty was involved. At the beginning of 1871, after a year of sieges and repeated attacks, Jinjibu, the "Medina of Chinese Islam," surrendered under its leader, Ma Hua-long. The town was razed to the ground and the inhabitants were slaughtered in a hideous massacre. The victory gave the upper hand to the imperial troops. Over the next three years, the citadels of the rebellion were won back by force and persuasion. The last, Suzhou in the far west of Gansu, fell in November 1873. The punishment meted out to the besieged was even more atrocious than the horrors committed at Jinjibu.

The pacification of Yunnan was brought to a successful conclusion during the same period. Dali fell and Du Wen-xiu committed suicide in January 1873, after many years of fighting and negotiations led by the Moslem Ma Ru-long, who had gone over to the other side, and Cen Yu-ying, the commander of the Qing troops.

As for the local movements in Guangdong and the Northeast, they were more or less put down by 1868. In Guizhou the revolt of the Miao and the Moslems was not subdued until 1872–1873.

Forming the regional armies

The battles against the Taiping dealt the final blow to the regular troops of the eight Manchu Banners and the Chinese Army of the Green Standard. They had been deteriorating since the end of the preceding century, and all efforts to reorganize them into a "disciplined army" (*lianjun*) had been in vain. Their upkeep was still a strain on the budget, however; the 40 million taels that they cost each year was half the imperial government's annual income.

The troops who overcame the rebellions were regional armies recruited, trained, commanded, and maintained by the Chinese officials and gentry. The practice of using local militia, "private armies," to make up for the deficiencies of the regular troops was not new; both the Ming and the Qing had often resorted to it in times of crisis. The militia which fought the Taiping were in fact raised by order of the emperor. They showed considerable differences from the militia that had been used before, however. They were larger, stronger, more coherent, and more independent. Moreover, once the rebellions had been suppressed, the regular army was not strong enough to prevent trouble when the militia were disbanded. There was nothing to counterbalance the power of the regional troops.

The most famous of these was the Hunan army (*Xiang jun*), which Zeng Guo-fan began to assemble in January 1853. He combined two small units that had been mustered by local gentry, and set up training camps for recruits in each district of the province. The basic unit of the Hunan army was a battalion of five hundred men with five officers and, for additional mobility, its own commissariat and administrative staff. The weapons used by the troops were not uniform, but by 1864 each battalion had several squads armed with foreign rifles.

Not only did Zeng Guo-fan want to create a seasoned army with advanced technical ability, but he also paid great attention to its moral indoctrination and its cohesion. He transposed to it the principles ruling the Confucian family. The method he used for choosing officers laid greater stress on personal loyalty than on devotion to the national cause, although it did in fact select the most capable men. The organization of the battalion was paternalistic. The officers were called "fathers," the noncommissioned officers "younger brothers," and the soldiers "sons." Recruits had to be peasant volunteers from the neighborhood, with a good name in their villages. In many cases officers and men came from the same village, or even the same clan. Opium smoking and gambling were forbidden. Both rations and wages were three times what was customary in the regular army, and the battalion commander was responsible for holding back part of the soldiers' pay to send to their families. In 1856 Zeng's army had 60,000 men, all from Hunan. Later the number doubled. Men from other provinces were allowed to join, but 83 percent of the officers still came from Hunan.

Since 1853 Li Hong-zhang had been in command of a fairly large militia raised in Anhui. At the end of 1861 Zeng Guo-fan, anxious to avoid suspicion and possible disgrace by gathering too many men under his command, made Li responsible for organizing another army. Composed of Li's own militia swelled by more recruits from Anhui, it was intended to relieve Shanghai. The rules of the Huai army (*Huai jun*) imitated those of the Hunan army, although the Confucian indoctrination was not so thorough. Several battalions belonging to Zeng Guo-fan were responsible for its military training. Since the Huai army was recruited on the borders of North China and South China, its soldiers were used to eating noodles or bread as well as rice. They could therefore march longer and farther than the Hunan army of Zeng Guo-fan, whose men did not take easily to any food but rice.

The Chu army (from Hunan and Hubei) was formed by Zuo Zong-tang, who started in 1860 with 5,000 men from Hunan. Its numbers grew rapidly, swelled by soldiers from other regions. It formed the nucleus of Zuo Zong-tang's troops throughout his campaigns. Order and discipline were strictly enforced. Zuo's austere way of living was held up as an example; he was said to share the same food and lodgings as his men. Other smaller armies also played their part in subduing the rebellions. For example, the Tenacious army (*yi jun*), made up of men from Shandong and Anhui, fought in Henan and was maintained as a separate unit until 1928.

Financing the new armies

The strength of the armies was due to their organization, their morale, and above all, the logistic base which their leaders assured them. This base was all the more remarkable considering that the regions over which the troops marched had been sorely tried by war, and that the central government, which could not even maintain the regular army, was of little help.

At first, money came from contributions by the local gentry and merchants. In fact throughout the suppression of the Taiping rebellion, the province of Hunan maintained the Hunan army. As his account in document 1 explains, Li Hong-zhang organized the Huai army by means of funds supplied by Shanghai and Jiangsu businessmen. Such voluntary contributions were not enough to keep the armies going, however; nor were the subsidies levied on ordinary fiscal revenues which the throne occasionally ordered the magistrates to supply. The treasury of the regional armies was stabilized in two ways: by the creation of new taxes and by the levying of local taxes under military supervision.

New surtaxes were added to the land tax and the grain tribute, and the additional revenue was made available to the provinces. Special dues were levied on markets and from shopkeepers. Loans were obtained from the provinces which had suffered least from the wars. Compulsory contributions were exacted from wealthy men, who were rewarded by grants of titles, rank, or extra places in the examination quota.

But these methods were not enough, and a new tax called the *lijin* was created. Sometimes it was collected at *lijin* barriers on goods in transit, and sometimes it was imposed on merchants at the place of sale. It was originally meant to be an *ad valorem* tax (of 1 to 1,000, as its name indicated). On articles of consumption, however, it was soon calculated at a fixed rate by weight on each piece.

The *lijin* was first introduced in 1853 in Yangzhou by the commander of the local militia. It was quickly extended to the other districts of Jiangsu and then to the rest of the country. By 1860 the *lijin* existed in every province except for Yunnan, where it was introduced in 1874, and Heilongjiang, where it arrived in 1885.

The administration of the *lijin* suffered from rule-of-thumb application. The rates varied greatly depending on the district, but they were generally high (10 percent, on an average, in Jiangsu). Because of the corruption and inefficiency of the bureaucracy, the same goods were sometimes taxed many times on their way from the producer to the consumer. On the Grand Canal between Jinjiang and Hangzhou, there was a *lijin* barrier every 20 kilometers.

The tax aroused violent criticism and opposition from the moment it was introduced, yet it was constantly extended because it provided considerable revenue. It was estimated that the *lijin* covered over a third of the expenses of the troops which suppressed the Taiping. It was collected with the cooperation of the gentry and the merchants. As long as the campaigns against the rebels continued, the income from the *lijin* was left almost entirely in the hands of the provincial authorities to meet the needs of local defense. Later on, although the central treasury claimed a share, much of the revenue from the *lijin* still went straight to the provinces, thereby helping them to maintain their independence from Peking.

As for other sources of revenue, the customs, under sound foreign administration, regularly brought in large payments. Most of these funds were also spent on military operations.

For the military leaders, the difficulty was to get hold of the various revenues for the use of their own personal armies. The best way was to obtain an appointment to the civilian post of governor or governor-general. Although the throne was reluctant to concentrate military and civil power in the hands of one man, there was often no alternative, because the existence of the dynasty depended on the regional armies. Under the Restoration the chief military leaders were also among the most influential senior officials of the empire. Possibly the most skillful of them all was Li Hong-zhang, who obtained the governorship of Jiangsu and then that of Zhili, thus securing control of the largest customs revenues. This bountiful source of funds greatly benefitted the Huai army.

Supplies

The supplies for each army were quite well organized. During his campaigns in the Northwest, Zuo Zong-tang received funds regularly through a powerful Shanghai merchant, Hu Guang-yong, who had set up a banking system. In the more distant regions, however, the transport of supplies was difficult and it was not always possible to buy or pillage in the countryside. Zuo restored to a process traditionally used by Chinese armies in frontier regions, with results that had psychological value as well as practical benefits. When the soldiers took up their winter quarters, they were allotted fields which they cultivated. The harvest ensured them their ration for the following year, and the official propaganda could boast of these soldier-laborers who spared the population. In point of fact, in many cases the owners of the land had been driven away or massacred.

Transport

Troop transport was also a problem. Zeng Guo-fan created a fleet of war and transport vessels on Lake Dongting in 1854, but it was wiped out by the Taiping. He immediately launched another, which included junks and sampans armed with foreign guns. From 1862 onward, transport of the Hunan army on the Yangzi was usually carried out by steamships that were either bought or rented from foreigners. In 1865 Zeng Guo-fan and Feng Yu-lin organized the Yangzi fleet, with 800 officers and 12,000 men, as an auxiliary force supporting the army.

Morale of the troops

Although largely superior to that of the regular troops, the logistic support of the regional armies of the Restoration was limited because the resources of the country itself were limited. In addition, a large proportion of these resources were devoted to the upkeep of traditional troops. This explains why the new armies never grew really large, and why pillage and banditry remained part of the soldiers' habits.

The relative material security enjoyed by the soldiers facilitated their indoctrination and the military success of their armies. They were more disciplined than the regular army and obtained a slightly less hostile reception from the populace. In any case—and this was an innovation—their leaders paid great attention to the ideological role which the armies had to play. The troops of Zeng Guo-fan sang songs with titles like "Love the People" and "The Oppressed Joyfully Welcome the Emperor's Troops." Soldiers and officers were liable to heavy punishments if they treated civilians unjustly.

Strategy

The emphasis given to the morale of the troops was part of the military and political strategy which was a decisive factor in the victories over popular rebellions. The great regional leaders of the Restoration detected the motives, the strengths, and the weaknesses of each insurgent movement and adapted their strategy to suit. Nevertheless, all the campaigns were based on the same principle, which Zuo Zong-tang put as follows: "A strategy of pacification which is not founded on extermination and succor simultaneously is impossible." In each case the strategy of the new armies led to a succession of victories culminating in a turning point like the recapture of Anjing or Jinjibu, where the preliminary work of rebuilding could begin. From then on, although setbacks did occur, the sources of rebel troops gradually dried up.

After the capture of Nanking in 1853, the provincial leaders began to analyze the Taiping insurrection. They made its weaknesses in military leadership, civil administration, and ideology their strong points. For one able general like the Taiping's Li Xiucheng, the Restoration camp had fifty capable officers. Whereas the Taiping restricted themselves more and more to seizing towns, which they sometimes abandoned after plundering them, the Restoration leaders were careful to administer conquered territory, especially in the rural districts, and give immediate help to the farming economy.[2] As for the Taiping religion, many people were indifferent to it and most scholars rejected its theology, whereas they welcomed the regenerated Confucianism of Zeng Guo-fan. The leaders of the Restoration armies had real faith in their cause and carried their troops along with them, whereas the cohesion and the morale of the rebels wore thin as the years went by.

The strategy of the Nian was much more mobile than that of the Taiping. In the regions under Nian control, "people" and "rebels" were thoroughly intermingled, making political work more difficult than in the Taiping regions. Yet it was essential to undermine the Nian's popular support, for that was their chief strength. In the summer of 1865 Zeng Guo-fan formulated a new strategy. From a military point of view, his plan was one of defense. Instead of wearing out his troops by following the enemy, he decided that "rivers must become frontiers, and small areas must be surrounded." His plan was eventually successful in blocking the retreat of the Nian toward the West. From a political point of view, Zeng's strategy aimed to turn the villagers away from their leaders by "strengthening the walls and clearing the countryside." As the villages in the Nian regions all had walls around them, the Restoration forces had to occupy them and supervise them strictly in order to cut the rebel troops off from their supply base. To win the confidence of the population, a system of rewards and identity cards was introduced, inhabitants were enrolled in the Huai army at good pay, food and supplies were distributed, and land was brought under cultivation.

The strength of the Moslem rebellions lay in holding the towns in poor, sparsely populated areas pervaded by religious fanaticism. These rebels made considerable use of racial and cultural antagonisms as well as discontent arising from popular abuses. The Restoration army's military drive was aimed at the Hui fortresses.

[2] See document 2 for a contemporary account of the Restoration's agrarian policy.

Its political strategy was based on the traditional maxim, "Make no distinction between Chinese or Moslem, but only between good and bad." In Shenxi and Gansu, Zuo Zong-tang tried to put an end to the worst abuses in taxation, and to right the wrongs caused by the administration. Whereas the Taiping and Nian leaders had been mercilessly executed, different methods were used with the Moslem leaders. In the central provinces, the gentry's support of the Qing frequently undermined the power of the rebel leaders. But in the Moslem regions, the gentry and the rebel leaders were generally the same people. The central power was unable to re-establish its authority without the collaboration of the elite. As the rebel leaders fought local abuses rather than the Qing state and society, it was possible to come to an understanding with them. Chinese officials who had collaborated with the rebels were executed, but the Moslem gentry and leaders were mainly pardoned.

Foreign help

The role of foreign help in the success of the imperial cause was, and still is, a highly controversial subject.[3] Certain historians argue that since foreign subsidies amounted to little in material terms, foreign support was a negligible factor and the mobilization of forces at home was decisive. Other writers who focus on the long-term consequences of resorting to foreign aid maintain that the Restoration statesmen were able to triumph over the popular movements only by "selling China to the foreigners."

From a statistical point of view, foreign help was not substantial. Twenty-one loans (fifteen of them during the reign of Tongzhi) from foreign merchants or foreign banks in the open ports have been listed between 1853 and 1874. They were contracted by provincial officials and were almost all secured by the revenues of the maritime customs. They were short-term loans ranging from four months to one year. The rate of interest usually varied between 8 and 15 percent annually, a lower rate than that generally asked by Chinese bankers at the time. Li Hong-zhang was directly responsible for three of the loans, Zuo Zong-tang for two. The total amounted to about 7 million taels, whereas the estimated cost of the suppression of the Taiping rebellion alone was 250 to 300 million taels.

[3] In document 1 Li Hong-zhang describes one kind of foreign aid.

The troops supplied by the foreigners never exceeded three thousand men. In June 1860 a contingent of about a hundred adventurers, commanded by the Americans Frederick Townsend Ward and Burgevine, joined the imperial troops in spite of the disapproval of the consuls, who still advocated neutrality. In the following year Chinese soldiers swelled the numbers of this unit, and it became known as the Ever-Victorious army. Foreign businessmen, changing their policy completely, asked for its help in defending Shanghai against the Taiping. When Ward died, the British Major Charles George Gordon took command in March 1863, carrying official orders from his government to help the imperial troops. The French and British navies also took part in the fighting. Other mixed units were formed, such as those under the orders of the French officers Giquel, Tardiff, and d'Aiguebelle. The foreign community paid subsidies, and missionaries frequently offered their help in the cooperation between Westerners and the imperial cause. But the action of foreign troops was limited to the lower Yangzi region, and after 1864 the imperial authorities did not call on them.

It is hard to maintain, as some foreigners disdainful of Chinese talents did at the time, that these contingents saved the Qing. Their Western officers were always under the authority of the imperial government, and none of them ever held the rank of commander-in-chief. The few foreign ships which were hired or bought could hardly be used in the operations against the Nian or Moslem guerrillas. No estimate exists of the amount of arms supplied; these were no doubt considerable, even in a distant region like Yunnan, where one of those responsible for the conquest of Tongking, the French merchant Jean Dupuis, crossed the border in 1868. (The Taiping also used arms and men from the West, though in smaller numbers.) In all events, the superiority conferred on the imperial cause by foreign help lay not so much in the number of men involved as in the fact that reinforcements were available if needed. This was particularly true from 1860 onward, when the Western governments were always ready to facilitate matters. Equally, the role of foreign aid ought to be measured by the destructive power of European weapons and by their psychological effect on a population accustomed to fighting with knives and sticks.

The Restoration statesmen were reluctant to call on foreign governments for help, knowing that it would open the way to intervention and interference. As Zeng Guo-fan wrote in 1860, "From time immemorial barbarian assistance to China, when crowned with success, has always resulted in unexpected demands." The foreign governments and residents never considered Li Hong-zhang, Zuo Zong-tang, Zeng Guo-fan, and Prince Gong as instruments in their hands. On the contrary, they saw them as "Chinese patriots" defending the interests of their country, patriots who were mistrustful of and sometimes hostile to the West. Generally speaking, the Restoration refused direct help from foreign governments. But by dealing with Western merchants and by recruiting technicians, it strengthened and enlarged the foreign economic base in China. The immediate effect was to encourage the foreign powers to allow the Manchu regime to regain some measure of its authority. They did not, therefore, create difficulties for the government in its wars against the popular movements, and this was an important factor in the government's ultimate success. But the foreigners' aim was to ensure a minimum degree of stability for the established power. In the outlying regions of the Chinese empire the foreign powers were not so cooperative (see Chapter 6). The British and Russians did not hesitate to give their support to the revolt of Yakub-beg in 1872–1873.

In the absence of an energetic central government capable of keeping foreign ambitions in hand, the Restoration policy of economic concessions offered countless pretexts for foreign interference and demands for further privileges. In 1870, for example, pressure from foreign merchants in Shanghai helped prevent the ratification of the Alcock Convention revising the customs tariffs in China's favor. At a practical level, the attitude of the Restoration toward the foreigners provided its statesmen with the respite they needed to strengthen their own power and that of the Qing. But it eventually led to the result which they themselves predicted in their warnings against foreign aid; increased penetration by the "barbarians."

Thus to suppress the popular movements, the Restoration used methods which were likely to boomerang in the future: new armies which were answerable to their leaders rather than to the government, heavy taxes on trade, which was still underdeveloped, and conciliation of the West. It doubtless had no choice, but the risks were considerable, particularly if the government did not succeed in consolidating its power in a country exhausted by war.

The Work of Reconstruction

Vast regions had been laid waste by the long military campaigns. From an economic point of view, the worst damage resulted from the depopulation of the rich areas, particularly the irrigated lands of south Jiangsu and the Bay of Hangzhou. As foreign observers described the Yangzi valley:

> Smiling fields were turned into desolate wildernesses; "fenced cities into ruinous heaps." The plains of Kiang-nan, Kiang-si and Cheh-kang were strewn with human skeletons; their rivers polluted with floating carcasses; wild beasts descending from their fastnesses in the mountains roamed at large over the land, and made their dens in the ruins of deserted towns. . . . no hands were left to till the soil, and noxious weeds covered the ground once tilled with patient industry.[4]

According to another account, "The wretched inhabitants of the districts which Gordon has lately recovered have been driven to cannibalism to satisfy the cravings of hunger." [5] Zuo Zong-tang said of Zhejiang: "Men and beasts have disappeared, the land is deserted." Most of Guizhou, Yunnan, and the Northwest were in a similar state, as well as several regions in the North China plain. Shenxi had lost nine-tenths of its Moslem population and Gansu two-thirds, amounting to three million inhabitants; the rest had been deported. Half the population of Yunnan had been wiped out; except in three districts, everything had been destroyed. Five million had died in Guizhou; the Miao, stripped of their lands, became tenant farmers or took refuge in the mountains. In a local rebellion like that of the Hakka, five or six hundred thousand were killed.

The program conceived by the Restoration to repair the terrible damage is summarized in a maxim which the statesmen liked to repeat: "Assure the people's livelihood; fortify popular sentiment" (*An min sheng gu min xin*). On one hand, material reconstruction was begun, with a view to achieving economic recovery, and on the other, political and ideological reconstruction was undertaken to prevent rebellion from breaking out again.

[4] *Journal of the North China Branch of the Royal Asiatic Society* (1865), vol. 2, p. 143.
[5] *North China Herald*, April 30, 1864.

Principles of material reconstruction

The aim of the Restoration was to create a stable, austere agrarian society, in which frugality was a virtue and strict limitations were imposed on government spending, on luxury in the ruling classes, and on the material aspirations of the peasants. Frugality by no means implied social equalization; the ideal was for each person, staying within his class, to amass nothing and be self-sufficient. Zeng Guo-fan wrote his son that his new daughter-in-law should look after her own house and spin, weave, and sew for her own family—that she should not regard herself as exempt by birth from labor and austerity.

Until 1872 there was no attempt on the part of the government to develop a modern economy, and nothing to compare with the program launched by the Meiji reform in Japan. An increase in production and national wealth would have disorganized the Confucian social hierarchy on which the power of the traditional ruling classes was founded. In accordance with an ancient formula, the senior officials stressed the need to reconcile the interests of "state finances" and the "people's livelihood" (*guo ji min sheng*); both were to be maintained, not increased. To achieve this end the best method seemed to be to apply the Confucian principle of political economy: "Respect agriculture and scorn trade" (*Zhong nong bing shang*).

The Restoration leaders were above all determined to bring about the rebirth of the agricultural economy. Their program took three main directions: enlargement of the cultivated areas, expansion of public works, and reduction of the land tax. The provinces which benefited most of all were those affected by the Taiping insurrection.

Reclaiming and expanding farmland

The wars had caused extensive migrations of the rural population, and much land lay abandoned. As soon as a region was reconquered, the imperial administration set about bringing it back under cultivation.

Hungry peasants often flocked spontaneously to the rich areas and began farming straightaway. Until the middle of the century they had been moving away from the overpopulated region of the lower Yangzi to work the mountainous territory farther inland, but now the migration flowed in the opposite direction as the irrigated land attracted peasants from the poor regions. Farmers from Henan and north Jiangsu repopulated south Jiangsu and north Zhejiang. South Anhui was recolonized by people from the north of the province, from Hubei, Hunan, Henan, and south and central Zhejiang. In Jiujiang, Jiangxi, the population increased from 8,000 to 40,000 in the space of six months. At the end of 1866 the governor of Zhejiang reported that in most of his districts, agriculture and silkworm culture were flourishing.

Some official measures also encouraged repopulation. Zeng Guofan settled some of his demobilized soldiers in Hunan, giving a plot of land to each. Soldiers from the Huai army were settled in Anhui in the same way. In Jiangnan, officials seized the abandoned land and sold it cheaply, giving preference to those who paid cash. They also set up a system of loans for tools and seeds, repayable in three years. In some districts the rent for a farm was reduced to three-tenths of the harvest. To repopulate the Nanking neighborhood, labor was attracted there from the north bank of the Yangzi. The farmers then crossed back over the river secretly, taking seed, animals, and tools, to cultivate the land lying fallow in their own home territory. After pursuing them in vain, the authorities sanctioned the accomplished fact and granted the peasants north of the river the right to cultivate "ownerless wasteland" as their own. In Guizhou, "recolonization offices" were made responsible for resettling the peasants and supplying them with free tools and food until the first harvest.

The Restoration also encouraged the cultivation of unclaimed land in the border regions. Theoretically, Chinese immigration to Manchuria was forbidden, but clandestine colonization was now legalized and subjected to taxation. Zuo Zong-tang settled soldiers in Xinjiang and offered inhabitants who had moved off their land the equipment they needed to start farming again and to enlarge the area cultivated. In Inner Mongolia colonization developed rapidly under the authority of the princes and with the blessing of Peking.

Not enough data are available to determine how much land was brought under cultivation during the reign of Tongzhi. It can only be said that abandoned land was reclaimed and new farmland was opened up. Since millions had been killed in the war, a delicate balance was established once more between population and agricultural resources, a balance which facilitated the return to order.

Modifications in land ownership

The Confucian ideal of the Restoration implied the re-establishment of a majority of peasant landowners. The results of the agrarian policy appear uneven on this point; the situation varied from district to district and from village to village. In some regions of Jiangsu, Anhui, Fujian, and above all Zhenjiang, more peasants than before owned land in the form of very small farms of less than a hectare. At Zhenjiang in Jiangsu, the big landowners disappeared along with the Taiping, and only peasant landowners were left. In many places, however, the peasants who had bought or had been given land were dispossessed when the former owner returned, sometimes many years after his eviction by the Taiping. As the old title deeds had often been burned, some people took the opportunity of seizing the possessions of relations or friends who had died.

Above all, however, the drop in the price of land enabled the rich to acquire more. Bureaucrats and army officers built up vast domains. "Contractors" also appeared who bought large stretches of land and rented them to tenant farmers without the traditional guarantee of life tenure. A clear trend emerged toward the concentration of land ownership, though at the present stage of research it is impossible to determine the scale of this phenomenon.

Progress of agricultural techniques

The question of agricultural techniques was examined, with a view to enlarging the total yield rather than improving individual productivity. Zuo Zong-tang was able to increase cotton production and silkworm culture in Zhejiang and Fujian, as well as livestock raising, wool production, and reforestation in Shenxi and Gansu. Local officials also introduced new methods of farming.

Public works

In the provinces reclaimed from the Taiping, "reconstruction offices" were set up to mend city walls and temples. With the help of the gentry, the reserve granaries were repaired and many extra granaries were created in order to fight famine. The most urgent task of all, however, was to get the waters under control. Dikes and canals had been neglected during the years leading to the rebellions, and they had been badly damaged since. In Zhili, Shandong, Shenxi, and Sichuan, the officials launched vast enterprises to repair hydraulic works and recover dried-out and flooded land. Vast stone reservoirs were constructed, and dikes were rebuilt along the seacoast.

The Restoration also attacked the problem of the Huai and the Yellow River floods, but to no effect. An interprovincial office that was set up in 1866 to bring the Huai under control did no more than study plans. Between 1851 and 1855 the Yellow River had changed its course and flowed northward, creating a series of catastrophic floods. At the beginning of the reign of Tongzhi, provincial officials tried to drag the riverbed and repair the dikes. The river flooded again in 1866, however, and the governor of Shandong set the flood victims to work on a vast reclamation project. Countless plans were put forward for getting the river under control, including Zeng Guo-fan's detailed scheme for returning it to its former southern course by coordinating the efforts of the provinces bordering on it. None of the plans were carried out. The money was spent on the upkeep of the armies. Serious flooding occurred again in 1867–1868, and makeshift remedies were again applied.

Reduction of the land taxes

Since tax abuses were one of the targets of the popular movements, and since overtaxation could hamper the resumption of agriculture, the Restoration reduced some of the taxes that directly affected farmers. During the Taiping rebellion the governors of the Yangzi provinces made a temporary reduction in the surtaxes supplementing the grain tribute. Between 1863 and 1866 the quota and the surtaxes in force in several districts of Jiangsu and Zhejiang were cut by 10 to 30 percent. Yet the grain tribute remained a source of abuse and corruption. Although the court preferred to have it paid in stocks of rice to feed Peking, local authorities more and more frequently exacted payment in silver, thus increasing the opportunities for making illicit profits. This practice was harmful to the taxpayer; in fact the substitution rate, fixed once and for all, was normally higher than the real price of rice.

It is reckoned that during the reign of Tongzhi, land taxes were cut by 30 percent compared with the years between 1840 and 1850. Total or partial rebates were often granted in disaster areas. In some cases the central government took action, without waiting for the pleas of the victims. A more important step, however, was the permanent reduction of the land tax in certain areas. Hu Lin-yi set the example in Hubei before 1860. In 1864 surtaxes were abolished in Shandong. Tax cuts were granted to several districts in Zhejiang and to Canton. Jiangsu was the province which received preferential treatment, because it had suffered more than any other from excessive taxation and from the ravages of war. Li Hong-zhang, Zeng Guo-fan, and especially Feng Gui-fen all played a part in the Jiangsu tax reform, which the official chronicles treat as one of the glories of the reign of Tongzhi. An edict of July 1863 allowed a reduction of two-thirds in the basic rate.

Yet many of the benefits of tax reform in Jiangsu were not felt by the peasants. Defective regulations by the authorities sometimes did not take surtaxes into account.[6] The rise in the price of silver canceled out part of the taxpayers' profits. No land register had been drawn up, and since the new tariffs had not been published, the magistrates and the local gentry often took advantage of the rural population by collecting payments at the old rate and pocketing the difference. Lastly, in spite of the orders given by Feng Gui-fen, the reduction of the land tax was not accompanied by a reduction in rents. Thus the tenant farmers who formed the majority of the peasant population in Jiangsu did not benefit from this form of tax relief.

The neglect of the social and political problem posed by the exploitation of peasants by the big landowners limited the achievements of the agrarian reconstruction. In fact, the rehabilitation of agriculture hardly bettered the "people's livelihood" at all, because it was not accompanied by developments in other sectors. Its modest benefits were consequently whittled down or completely swallowed up.

Obstacles to the development of trade

The Restoration did nothing to develop traditional trade; in fact, it increased the taxes which burdened it. The *lijin* was maintained, in spite of opposition, because the provincial administrators and some of the gentry found it profitable. A generous proportion of its fairly large revenues were made available to the provinces. It was collected with the help of the gentry, who were responsible for

---

[6] Document 2 describes this and other tax inequities.

getting together and handing over the *lijin* payments of the guilds and associations.

Under the Restoration the administration of the *lijin* was improved. Annual reports were required, the number of *lijin* barriers was cut down, abuses were punished, and control over the collection was transferred from the district to the provincial authorities. Nevertheless, the tax hindered the expansion of trade and was a burden on agriculture as well. Nothing could be gained from sending goods elsewhere, because they were taxed in proportion to the distance covered. Therefore trade could not expand much, and manufacturers had no incentive to produce more by introducing division of labor or technological improvements.

For the merchant, the *lijin* represented a lost opportunity; for the peasant, it was both a real loss and a lost opportunity. Since the peasant was the chief consumer either when he bought goods himself or when he paid rent and taxes and thus enabled the gentry to buy goods, he paid tax on every purchase. On the other hand, since he was the chief producer, his profits could not increase because the *lijin* set a limit on the market. The *lijin* accentuated the stagnation of trade and the tendency toward subsistence farming, thereby affecting output and the standard of living. It slowed down the development of a merchant class capable of launching industrial enterprises.

Transportation and communications

Efforts were made in the field of transportation, particularly in connection with measures to fortify Peking by sea and ensure its food supply. The Grand Canal was opened once more, though it remained in poor condition, and took up the functions it had fulfilled before 1853. There was growing interest in the use of steamships for coastal traffic. For one reason, the droughts and floods of 1867 and 1868 made it necessary to convey the grain tribute by sea. For another, private merchants preferred to use the ocean route in order to avoid paying the *lijin*. In 1867 scholars from the Southeast took a steamship to Peking to sit for the examinations. Steamships, which belonged to foreigners, gradually replaced the big seagoing junks. The first Chinese company was the China Merchants' Steam Navigation Company, founded in 1872.

There was active opposition, however, to the introduction of steamships for inland water transport, to the building of railways,

ʿe introduction of a telegraph system. Most Restoration
ʾelieved that the domestic economy and the social order
ᴜe ruined by such innovations, and that they were a serious
ᴀreat to Chinese security.

Foreign trade

The government did not try to turn the development of foreign
trade to account or to encourage Chinese exports, for example, to
pay for supplies of arms. The customs revenue covered military
expenses, but the official attitude was summed up in a remark by
Wen-xiang to Robert Hart: "We would gladly pay you all the increased revenue you have brought us, if you foreigners would go
back to your own country and leave us in peace as we were before
you came."[7]

Mines

The mines aroused some interest. Officials in Zhili encouraged
the private operation of coal mines near Tientsin. Efforts were
made to start copper mining again in Yunnan. Capital, technicians,
and initiative were lacking, however. In general the Restoration
leadership utterly ignored industry, except in the military field (see
Chapter 7).

Public finances

The government's contempt for economic development adversely
affected the "people's livelihood" that the Restoration officials were
concerned to stabilize, and it did nothing to improve the "state
finances" that they wanted to bring into balance. The officials believed that the increase in public expenditure was temporary, so
they applied makeshift remedies to counteract it. The tax systems
which had been swept away by the popular rebellions were set up
once more with no thought of simplifying them or making them
uniform. Tax reform consisted merely of publishing quotas, asking
for reports, and appointing officials who were assumed to be men of
integrity. Tax receipts grew, but they were still inadequate.

During the reign of Xianfeng the monetary system had been

---

[7] J. Bredon, *Sir Robert Hart* (New York, 1919), p. 221.

totally disorganized by the fall in the value of copper, the manufacture of iron coins, and the introduction of nonconvertible paper
money. To provide the economy with the financial tools needed to
achieve recovery and expansion, it would have been necessary to
control and systematize the issue of banknotes, reform the tael system by introducing a Chinese silver coin, and reform copper cash.
Zeng Guo-fan suggested that the exchange rate between copper and
silver be fixed officially, but considering the dislocation of the economy, this was impractical. The government's only gesture toward
revising the monetary system was to try in 1867 to rehabilitate
copper cash by ensuring that the new coins struck were identical
with the old ones, so that their value in relation to silver could be
stabilized. The supplies of metal were inadequate, however; virtually no copper was produced in Yunnan and Japanese copper
was expensive. The reform did not achieve the expected results—
although the value of copper cash did rise slightly, and inflation
does not seem to have continued at the same rate as during the
previous reign.

Economic policy during the reign of Tongzhi was essentially
conservative. The aim of the economic reconstruction measures
was above all to re-establish the agrarian foundations of the traditional state. Meanwhile political and ideological reconstruction was
directed at re-establishing the state's authority.

Political and ideological reconstruction

As soon as fighting stopped in a region, the responsibility for
reconstruction fell upon the officials. The Restoration made substantial efforts to improve its bureaucracy. No administrative reforms were carried out, except for the creation of the Zongli
Yamen and the customs administration. But consistent with the
Confucian principles guiding politics as a whole, the aim became to
recruit "men of talent" and to keep them under control. The Restoration leaders believed that laws and regulations were useless,
that everything depended on the quality of the men involved.

The examination system was re-instated, so that it became once
more the only road to power and prestige. Certainly it had the
advantage of providing well-educated officials who were imbued
with Confucian morality. It discouraged the gentry from turning to
unorthodox intellectual or political pursuits, while at the same time
it offered a future to men of ambition. The examinations were

made more useful by the inclusion of subjects with a direct bearing on problems of government and administration. In 1862 an edict declared that candidates could be questioned on modern political subjects. At the next session a young man, Zhang Zhi-dong, received high praise for his essay on the Taiping rebellion.[8]

When a province was recaptured, the first concern of the authorities was to work through the backlog in examinations. The quota of degrees allotted to each province was increased as a reward for contributions paid to help suppress the rebellions. The increases could be temporary or permanent. The permanent increase in quotas for the district examinations has been calculated as 4,648 places, bringing the total up to 30,113. This expansion did not jeopardize the quality of the examinations, for there were over 2 million candidates. In fact the results were beneficial, because good Confucian officials were needed, particularly to replace corrupt army officers and merchants. The merchants had generally bought official titles and ranks. These sales were not stopped, as they were profitable to the Treasury; prices fell, and sales became still more numerous. But on the advice of Zuo Zong-tang, those who acquired titles had to take an examination before being allowed to assume office.

Local officials

Once appointed, officials were closely supervised. Regular inspections were resumed, and superiors were encouraged to check the work of their subordinates and send in reports. The Board of Censors, which controlled the network of supervision, was vigilant in the struggle against corruption. In the case of officials in the middle and lower ranks, strictly applied rules prevented them from staying more than two or three years in the same post or from holding a post in their native province. The choice of good district magistrates was a constant worry, because it was through them that the government reached the people. Numerous memoirs and edicts set out the line of conduct they were supposed to follow. The *Local Magistrates' Manual* was formally reprinted with a preface written by Li Hong-zhang. The ideal official was an administrator of all-round competence, embodying the Confucian doctrine. In the district administrative system the official's judiciary power was his chief means of control over the population. An effort was made to

[8] Zhang became one of the leading statesmen in the period following 1885 (Chapter 8).

eliminate the frequent abuses, to remedy the slowness of justice, to prevent interference by the *yamen* clerks who often blocked the normal progress of legal proceedings, to apply the law without allowing the police to use it as a way of repressing the population, and to prevent overly harsh punishments. During the reign of Tongzhi the general quality of the bureaucracy seems to have improved. The publicity given to the improvements helped to rally the support of the local elite, whose cooperation was just as necessary for any achievements in political reconstruction as that of the officials.

Control in the countryside

The Taiping had estranged the gentry from their cause by attacking economic, legal, and social privileges of the elite. The Restoration quickly re-established these and used the gentry in the system for controlling rural society. Land was given back to the original owners, and reductions in the land tax were designed to lighten the burden on landowners. The right of appeal to the throne against local and provincial officials was confirmed. The examinations were re-instated, and rewards and honors were distributed to families who had remained loyal during the rebellions.

The gentry became an essential element in the community organizations that were designed to keep the population in hand. These were of two kinds: the *baojia* system of security units, and the *lijia* system of units for the collection of taxes and fulfillment of labor services. Their purpose was to maintain social conformity and to provide the channel through which the state, with its limited number of officials (40,000 for 400 million inhabitants), could collect a share of food, money, and labor from the villages.

Each district kept a register of the population. Ten households formed a *pai*, one hundred households a *jia*, and one thousand a *bao*. Members of these units were collectively responsible for the conduct of each person. At each level the families elected a head who was theoretically their spokesman with the authorities. Since their choice was submitted to the local magistrate for approval, however, the leaders were more like instruments of the central power. In the *lijia* system, ten households formed a *jia* and one hundred and ten a *li*. The heads of the *jia* and the *li* were agents appointed by the magistrates to levy taxes, take the census, distribute labor services.

Both systems, and particularly the *baojia* organization, had been on the decline since the beginning of the nineteenth century. The Restoration made a point of re-instating them, apparently with success. They cost less and were more efficacious than a militia. They were more easily accepted by the population because they were an integral part of the family and clan system which ruled the life of society and the individual. Theoretically the *baojia* and *lijia* were different from each other and did not correspond to towns or villages. But in practice, the same people were often at the head of the various units. These leaders were chosen from the most influential figures in the village community, and the most prominent among them were the gentry. They were the instruments through which the state exercised its authority in the country districts.

The restoration of Confucianism

Political reconstruction through the re-establishment of administrative and legal control was consolidated by ideological reconstruction which emphasized the rebirth of Confucian knowledge. Confucianism protected the institutions and values underlying the position of the gentry. In addition, the statesmen believed that it would facilitate a renewal of obedience in the people, the Sinicization of minority races, and the training of the "men of talent" needed to govern the country.

Besides the revival of the examination system, schools were repaired and reopened. Private donations flowed in for village schools and for academies where scholars who were district graduates could go free of charge to prepare for further examinations. High-ranking provincial officials all brought honor upon themselves by founding famous academies. Those which Zuo Zong-tang reorganized or created in Shenxi and Gansu offered special scholarships to the Hui and the Mongols. The academies once more became centers of intellectual life. In the most important of them the great scholars of the time taught the "true" Confucian doctrine, basing their work on the critical and comparative study of the texts. They also directed the publication of large collections of scholarly works.

The authorities and the scholars concentrated on rebuilding the libraries as well. Sometimes they had to send as far as Japan to repurchase copies of works which had been lost. They had the Classics and the Histories reprinted, and they organized lectures for the people to explain the principles of morality embodied in these writings. Contemporary accounts bear witness to the fact that

Confucian teaching was extended to the most underprivileged sectors of society.

Sentiments or doctrines that fell outside the Confucian frame of reference were firmly discouraged. Official proclamations inveighed against novels, the theater, gambling, and popular religious beliefs. The secret society of the Brothers and Elders was forbidden everywhere. Within Confucianism, the interpretation of Zhu Xi was regarded as the only orthodox approach. The principles of Song neo-Confucianism had been elaborated in the eighteenth century by a philosophic and literary circle, the Tongcheng School (called after the town in Anhui from which its founders came). This school blossomed anew under the Restoration. It stressed moral values, contempt for material conditions, and the use of a clear, concise literary style exemplified by Tang and Song authors. The Tongcheng School dominated almost all political thought and literature during the years 1860 to 1885.

Strengthening China's Position Abroad

The suppression of rebellions and the work of reconstruction more or less restored order within the country. But this was not the sole task which the Restoration statesmen had set themselves. China's power also had to be re-established abroad.

Revival of the tribute system

The restoration of the prestige of the Qing and the reopening of routes which had been closed by war made it possible to re-establish the tribute system with the "dependencies." These neighboring countries were pleased to send their tribute to Peking once more in exchange for protection against foreign attacks. Korea, the Ryukyu Islands, and in 1869, Vietnam all dispatched regular embassies to the emperor.[9]

New diplomacy toward the West

Most Chinese officials, strongly supported by the gentry, still believed that the barbarians should be pushed back into the sea. But a

[9] Document 3 is a letter from the king of Vietnam to the emperor which accompanied one consignment of tribute.

small though powerful minority, which included Prince Gong, Wen-xiang, Li Hong-zhang, Zeng Guo-fan, and Zuo Zong-tan, felt that it was impossible to go backwards, that the best solution was to put relations with foreigners on a normal footing in order to set limits on their encroachments.

The creation on January 20, 1861, of the Zongli Yamen, a ministry with a membership varying between three and eleven, was a manifestation of this policy. The new institution, partially financed by the customs, had control over the overseers in the ports and received a copy of all documents concerning foreign affairs, including those addressed directly to the throne. The formation of this ministry, which was clearly anxious to enlarge its own importance by developing foreign relations, coincided with the adoption by the West of a "policy of cooperation" intended to obtain lasting benefits by avoiding a head-on clash with the imperial power.

The Zongli Yamen sided with the foreign diplomats against overly greedy merchants and missionaries, and equally against archconservatives in the central government and the provinces. Its method of action was to apply treaties to the letter. Its officials studied individual rights so that they could back up their arguments. In 1864 an American missionary, W. A. P. Martin, translated Wheaton's work on international law at the request of the Zongli Yamen. Foreign demands based on the law of the treaties were granted regardless of the immediate consequences for China, because the Zongli Yamen felt that in the long run the national interest depended on the inviolability of the treaties. On the other hand, the ministry consistently opposed foreign activities which were not specified in the treaties.

The frailty of "self-strengthening"

The Zongli Yamen policy of strict treaty interpretation, outlined by Qi-ying in 1845, tended to make the treaties into a protective wall for the Chinese government. They became the point beyond which no further concessions would be made to foreigners. Such a policy could succeed only if Chinese power was strong enough to command foreign respect. Consequently the Restoration statesmen launched a policy of "self-strengthening" (*ziqiang*), which was intended to modernize the state's means of defense (see Chapter 7). They distrusted the West's "policy of cooperation," for it did not prevent constant foreign intervention in the outlying areas of China or innumerable incidents provoked by Westerners inside the empire.

The strengthening, however, had no effect at all. Though small points were won from time to time owing to the skill of imperial negotiators, China was still in a position of weakness relative to foreign countries. In 1870 the British Parliament, yielding to pressure from merchants, refused to ratify the Alcock Convention, a carefully negotiated treaty revision which was not wholly disadvantageous to China. This failure nullified the efforts of ten years on behalf of a diplomatic policy which lacked the material means to match its ambitions. Moreover, it was a policy which the Chinese public neither understood nor supported, as was proved by the Tientsin massacre in the same year (Chapter 6).

Consequences of the Restoration

Strengthening of the gentry

In view of the weakness of the Manchu army and bureaucracy, the Qing could not re-establish their power without rallying the Chinese elite to their cause. They did so by setting themselves up as the defenders of a Confucian state with institutions and values which supported the scholar-officials. The work of the Restoration was carried out for the gentry's advantage, with the gentry's help, and under the leadership of men belonging to the gentry. The Restoration strengthened the gentry numerically, economically, socially, and politically.

The increase in the number of successful candidates for degrees and in the sale of ranks quickly compensated for the losses due to war, so that the gentry grew as a class. It has been reckoned that before the Taiping rebellion, the number of men holding official titles was about 1,100,000, whereas afterwards it was about 1,450,000. Since the legal privileges of the gentry were also extended to wives and to children who were under age, the actual size of this class was closer to 5,500,000 before the Taiping rising and 7,200,000 after it. In reality, the prestige of the scholar was reflected on his extended family: his brothers, grown-up sons, and parents all enjoyed an importance that set them above the common run because of his achievement. The number of privileged people therefore grew considerably.

The gentry's geographical distribution had always been irregular, and it became more uneven after the Taiping uprising. Before it, the proportion of scholar-officials and their closest dependents varied between 0.7 percent of the population in Anhui to 3.5 percent in Yunnan. After the Taiping, it varied between 0.6 percent in Sichuan to 5 percent in Zhejiang. The proportion of gentry fell in Guizhou, Yunnan, and Sichuan, remained the same in Guangdong, and increased more than threefold in Shenxi and Gansu. These changes were signs of the weakening of government control over the gentry's numbers and distribution. In its effort to win their support, the central power risked losing control of their actions. Their economic and social position had become stronger. The concentration of land ownership and the lightening of taxation which had followed the suppression of the rebellions had been largely to their advantage. The maintenance of the *lijin* guarded against the development of a merchant class able to assert itself by the power of wealth alone. With their official ranks, the gentry still represented the summit of the social hierarchy, and they continued to impress on all of society their conviction that they alone deserved authority because of their education. The merchants were a much smaller group, and in any case they did not try to form a separate class. Their ambition was to pass the examinations, or if they could not, to buy the titles and ranks which would qualify them for membership in the gentry. Once they had, they hastened to make use of their new position to humble their rivals.

The Restoration's reinforcement of the political role of the gentry enabled them to make the fullest possible use of their economic and social privileges. The members of the bureaucracy were once more drawn entirely from the gentry, who took on once more their former position as local intermediaries between the central authorities and the population. Whether they held official posts or simply helped the magistrate to manage his district, they were on the spot to get the best buys, to secure exemption from taxation in times of disaster, to lay hands on public funds, and to increase the peasants' economic burdens without running the risk of being prosecuted.

The birth of regional militarism

The political strength acquired by the gentry under the Restoration was backed up by the military forces which they had created. The monarchy had to make concessions to the gentry in order to obtain the services of their armies. Although these new armies were superior to the traditional imperial troops, some of their characteristics were a potential threat to the state. Since they were not under the control of the Ministry of War the central government's only means of exerting authority over them was through the provincial commanders. "The army belongs to its general" was a proverb often heard at the time. The troops were recruited over a restricted geographical area, and they concerned with protecting regional interests above all else.

Although the regional armies had very close links with the civilian bureaucracy, the phenomenon of political-military collaboration gradually changed in meaning. At first the armies were in the hands of the civilian power—of the local officials and the gentry, who kept them supplied, commanded them, and disbanded them if necessary (in 1864, for example, Zeng Guo-fan demobilized a large part of the Hunan army). As time went on, the situation was reversed. Standing armies had to be available to suppress popular movements, and they became organized forces which were much less docile. The civil power and the gentry were no match for this military power, which was concentrated in the hands of a few regional leaders.

Lastly, the provincial armies were partially dependent on the foreigners for their equipment and their training. The result was that they were strong, but only on condition that they did not have to fight the Westerners.

Limitations of the Restoration achievements

The Restoration of Tongzhi cannot be called a failure because, as Chinese tradition itself indicates, a "restoration" is only a respite before the irremediable fall of a dynasty; what can be said is that the respite was a brief one. The very forces to which the Restoration looked for support set a limit on its accomplishments.

Four large popular rebellions were suppressed between 1862 and 1873, but in 1873 Yakub-beg was master of the whole Tarim basin, from Pamir to Lob Nor. After some difficult expeditions, Zuo Zong-tang managed to win back the whole of Turkestan in 1878 and to restore peace, although to do so he had to borrow 13,750,000 taels from the foreigners, which was twice the total amount borrowed during the preceding reign. As before, sporadic agitation continued in rural districts. Four consecutive years of natural disasters in 1876 to 1879 caused hideous misery. Ten million people died in floods and famines (5 million in the province of Shanxi alone in 1877).[10] The extent of the disaster proved the inadequacy of the flood-control measures which were carried out at great expense during the reign of Tongzhi.

The peasants went further into debt, and the entire agrarian situation worsened. The Restoration left this fundamental problem untouched, and in fact could not do otherwise, since its aim was to re-establish order—or in other words, to restore the power of the gentry and the landowners. If the gentry had found resources elsewhere in compensation, they might eventually have abandoned the ownership of the land to the peasants, but the country's economic development was inadequate.

The fact was that the Confucian ideal which guaranteed the privileges of the gentry was linked to an agrarian economy of austerity, tending toward subsistence farming. As a system it allowed little or no savings and did not encourage industrial or commercial enterprise. Demographic pressure and the permanent threat of famine reinforced the trend to self-sufficiency. With his tiny plot, a peasant had barely enough to feed himself once he had paid his rent and taxes. At best he earned enough to buy salt and replace an agricultural tool; he usually made his own clothes.

Owing to the Restoration, the gentry acquired more land. In this respect their economic situation was strengthened compared with that of the peasants. But they were also more numerous than they had been in the past, and so were the inequalities in their fortunes. The majority of the gentry had probably grown no richer, and their available funds were still scanty. Possibilities for investment and economic development depended on a small number of rich merchants. The few members of the gentry who were wealthy enough to become entrepreneurs did not want to endanger the social order by launching modern enterprises.

New political problems

The Restoration had re-established the central government and local control, but new problems quickly arose concerning the balance between central and regional power and between civil and military power. After the death of Zeng Guo-fan in 1872 and the

[10] A missionary's account of famine in Shanxi is given in document 4.

end of the large risings in China, the regional leaders no longer needed to work together so closely, or to obey orders from the court as strictly as they did when they faced a common danger. With the help of his army, which he built up and watched over with jealous care, Li Hong-zhang became strong enough to escape altogether from bureaucratic control.

The throne tried to divide in order to rule, making the most of differences that arose between military leaders and encouraging a form of opposition termed *qingyi* (see Chapter 1). Scholars and officials of the middle and lower ranks composed petitions, satires, and poems criticizing government decisions or proposals, and attacking their colleagues in the name of Confucian orthodoxy and the public good. The action of the *qingyi* became more and more violent between 1870 and 1885, when it was led by a small, influential circle, the *qingliu* ("purification") group. Its members were young officials from the six ministries, the Board of Censors, and the Hanlin Academy who had obtained senior posts in the central administrative bodies strictly through the regular channel of examinations. They protested against the usurping of diplomatic, military, and financial power by the regional leaders, whose "self-strengthening" policy, they said, was ruining the country. They advocated an uncompromising stand that did not stop short of war with the foreigners.

The prestige of the *qingliu* was considerable among the many members of the bureaucracy and the gentry who were jealous of the growing power of men like Li Hong-zhang. The purification group also played involuntarily into the hands of the Empress Dowager Ci-xi. When her son, the Tongzhi Emperor, died on January 12, 1875, she maneuvered to put her three-year-old nephew on the throne under the reign name of Guangxu. In this way she could be appointed regent, although the law stipulated that the successor should be a generation younger than the dead emperor, and that the widow, not the mother, should become regent. Li Hong-zhang and Prince Gong opposed Ci-xi's scheme, and she looked for support to the *qingliu* group. In these conditions imperial policy constantly wavered between the enlightened modernism of the supporters of "foreign matters" (*yangwu*) and the reactionary conservatism of the *qingliu*. The authority of the government was consequently weakened at a time when China had to face the growing threat of the challenge from abroad as well as difficulties at home.

The economic system underlying the supremacy of the gentry was no longer able to supply a growing population with the means of subsistence, produce the resources that were necessary to crush popular rebellions, or stand up to the shock of foreign penetration. But the gentry, aware that abandonment of the system was political suicide, did all they could to perpetuate it, even calling on foreign help against the peasants. The result was that they kept China in a state of weakness and economic stagnation, and in the long run their conservatism worked against them. Some of the gentry were conscious of the dead end facing them and tried to avoid it, but Western penetration of China was beginning to foreclose all possible solutions.

ADDITIONAL BIBLIOGRAPHY

Ch'u T'ung-tsu, *Local Government in China Under the Ching* (Cambridge, Mass., Harvard University Press, 1962).

Lloyd Eric Eastman, *Throne and Mandarins: China's Search for a Policy During the Sino-French Controversy, 1880–1885* (Cambridge, Mass., Harvard University Press, 1967).

Frank Henry Haviland King, *Money and Monetary Policy in China, 1845–1895* (Cambridge, Mass., Harvard University Press, 1965).

Stanley Spector, *Li Hung-chang and the Huai Army: A Study in Nineteenth-Century Chinese Regionalism* (Seattle, University of Washington Press, 1964).

Mary Clabaugh Wright, *The Last Stand of Chinese Conservatism: The T'ung-chih Restoration, 1862–1874* (Stanford, Calif., Stanford University Press, 1957).

DOCUMENTS

1. THE SUPPRESSION OF POPULAR MOVEMENTS: ORGANIZATION OF THE DEFENSE OF THE LOWER YANGZI (1891)

SOURCE: Extract from a memorial by Li Hong-zhang, translated into English by Stanley Spector in *Li Hung-chang and the Huai Army* (Seattle, University of Washington Press, 1964), pp. 64–65, taken from "Memorials" in Li Wen-chung, *Collected Works*, 71/50. In this text, dated May 22, 1891, Li recalls the merits of Ying Bao-shi, an official and a native of Zhejiang, who became one of his trusted assistants in the Jiangsu administration.

In the eleventh year of Xianfeng [1861], the capital of Zhejiang fell to the rebels, and with the exception of Shanghai, which was the key to the entire situation, all of the southeast also fell. Ying Bao-shi consulted with the officials and gentry and built up a united defence bureau. He raised revenues, summoned volunteers, and maintained contact with the outside world. Shanghai had become an isolated city, and in view of the more than one million refugees in the city and the importance of its foreign trade and revenues, Ying did his best to hold the city. He consulted the officials, gentry and people, and persuaded them to receive the *Huai jun*, contribute funds and hire steamers. So great were Ying Bao-shi's efforts that the eastward journey of my armies was actually the culmination of his efforts. And the eastern journey of my armies was the turning-point of the situation. . . . When he took steamers up the river to welcome me, jealous people hampered him, and the English consul, Meadows, tried to dissuade him. But Ying was fairly well acquainted with the foreign leaders and explained to them why he should go. He succeeded in persuading Admiral Hope,* and went further, paying money to the foreign merchants. As a result, the foreigners became willing to furnish him with steamers and to transport munitions and horses in the same boats. At Anhui, he did everything to my satisfaction. This use of steamers may be credited solely to Ying Bao-shi.

2. The agrarian policy of the Restoration: Reduction of the grain tribute (1881)

Source: Extract from the *Chronicle of the Districts of Wuxi and Jingui* (1881), translated into English by Chang Chung-li in *The Income of the Chinese Gentry* (Seattle, University of Washington Press, 1962), p. 135.

Local chronicles are an important source of information on the economic and social history of imperial China. They were compiled at irregular intervals by scholars recruited and paid by the local gentry. They include information and documents on the topography, climate, agriculture, handicraft industry, administration, customs, education, successful candidates in the examinations, and well-known figures in the area.

It used to be the practice of the grain tribute collectors to receive the tax partly in cash and partly in kind. However, it is more convenient for the small owners to pay in kind rather than in cash, since what is produced by the land is grain and not cash. After the [Taiping] war, the majority of the granaries stand in ruin and have not been reconstructed. Therefore only cash is now being collected, a situation arising out of necessity. In the years of Daoguang and Xianfeng [from 1821 to 1861], for one picul of grain tribute, Suzhou and Songjiang people had to pay six to seven thousand copper cash, while Changzhou and Zhenjiang people had to pay four to five thousand cash. This rate refers to commoner households. *For the gentry households (shen-hu), the rate differed with the degree of strength* [of gentry members] *and the size of their landholdings.* . . . After the war, rehabilitation measures have been undertaken. Not only has the tax quota been lowered; officials are also forbidden to overtax. The regulation is that for 100 per cent of tax quota, 30 per cent is added [to defray the cost of collection], and for both gentry and commoners, *the rate in cash for each picul is*

* A British admiral who commanded part of the foreign troops in Shanghai.

set at 4,500 [without regard to market price]. . . . For second-grade land, the rent amounts only to five pecks [per *mu*] and according to the market price amounts to a little over 1,000 cash. The grain tribute, although it amounts to only six-tenths of a peck [per *mu*], is computed at more than 250 cash, thus taking away a quarter of the owner's income. Some large owners are probably good at mercantile activities and do not rely solely on rent income, but I have heard of those who by their own will computed the grain tribute *at the rate of 2,500 cash* (approximately in line with the market price per picul of rice) *and forced the officials to accept it*. . . . The small owners have only a few to several ten *mu* of land. After a year's hard labor, the proceeds are not enough to support a family of eight mouths. They do not have cash to pay for the grain tribute. They have therefore been forced to sell rice for daily meals at a low price. [*Italics added*]

3. LETTER FROM THE SOVEREIGN OF VIETNAM TO THE EMPEROR OF CHINA, ACCOMPANYING THE ORDINARY TRIBUTE IN 1881.
SOURCE: A. Couvreur, *Choix de Documents*, pp. 211–215.

Your servant Nguyen Tu-duc [1830–1883], King of Vietnam, bowing his head to the ground and hitting the dust with his forehead, salutes you and begs you to hear him.

Respectfully contemplating the ever-increasing brilliance of the Pole Star [the emperor], I offer him a present of gold from the south. Crossing, in thought, the mountains rising tier upon tier 10,000 li away, I turn in happiness toward the Sun.

I who write this letter consider that thanks to the unity of government and the influence of the one and only culture in use everywhere under the sun, between the four seas, the southern countries, although they are far away, depend on China and must offer her their products as legitimate tribute.

In the midst of the smoke of the perfumes arranged in my room, my spirit flies toward the palace of Son of Heaven. I respectfully contemplate this great Emperor, this august Majesty, this dazzling light ceaselessly illuminating the nations and extending its beneficent action; this prince, always faithful to duty, who imitates the principle of everything; this unique and sovereign head of all peoples, who answers perfectly to the ideal outlined in the *Spring and Autumn Annals*;* who, a conscientious follower of the nine rules of the *Doctrine of the Mean*,* loves princes and treats foreigners with generosity; who has received the imperial mandate to be the model of all provinces; who captures the hearts of all his subjects by his lovable virtues; the great man whom it is useful to see; the Son of Heaven who in return for his blessings, receives from each a tribute.

I consider that our country, burnt by the sun, has for a long time been among the number of frontier kingdoms which are tributaries of

* Titles of Confucian classics.

China. Those who occupy lands under the control of the Emperor should be careful to give him their cooperation from age to age. Now that the plague [the rebellions] which was laying waste our frontiers has just been dispersed, that all the princes are gathering at the imperial court, that no wave appears on the sea of Zhou* and that the offerings of all tributary peoples are collected together in the hall of Yu [the imperial palace], I, your servant, trusting in the imperial goodness, submit respectfully to the custom of the princes who all offer presents, and on the point of sending off my envoys, I imagine myself to be in the presence of the Emperor. I rejoice that the rays of the Sun and the Moon [the Guangxu Emperor and the regent, Ci-xi] have scattered the clouds of war forever. I hope that we will maintain peace by always remaining obedient to the leadership of our chief, and by never resisting him. Your servant, contemplating the Heavens and the Emperor, experiences a deep feeling of respectful fear.

I have told Nguyen Thuat and my other envoys to give you the list of presents making up my ordinary tribute. I am writing you this letter as well, which will be presented to you at the same time.

4. The famine of the winter of 1878 in Shanxi

Source: Timothy Richard, *Forty-five Years in China* (London, T. Fisher Unwin, 1916), pp. 129–132. Timothy Richard (1845–1919) was an English missionary who had a certain influence on the reformist movement at the end of the nineteenth century.

January 28, 1878

Started on a journey south through the centre of the province to discover the severity of the famine. I rode on a mule, and had a servant with me, also on a mule.

Before leaving the city [of Taiyuan, capital of Shanxi] we could not go straight to the south gate, as there was a man lying in the street about to die of starvation, and a crowd had gathered round.

January 29. 140 li south

Passed four dead men on the road and another moving on his hands and knees, having no strength to stand up. Met a funeral, consisting of a mother carrying on her shoulder a dead boy of ten years old. She was the only bearer, priest, and mourner, and she laid him in the snow outside the city wall.

January 30. 270 li south

Passed two men apparently just dead. One had good clothes on, but had died of hunger. A few li further there was a man of about forty walking in front of us, with unsteady steps like a drunken man. A puff of wind blew him over to rise no more.

---

* A quotation from the classics meaning that the empire enjoyed good government under a wise emperor.

January 30. 290 li south

Saw fourteen dead on the roadside. One had only a stocking on. His corpse was being dragged by a dog, so light it was. . . .

In the midst of such universal suffering, the wonder was that there was no robbery of the rich. But today this was explained, for there were notices put up in the villages saying that by order of the Governor, if any person attempted robbery or violence, the head-men of the town or village were empowered to put the robbers to death at once. The result was a wonderful absence of crime. The only tears I saw shed by the patient sufferers were those of the mother burying her boy.

February 1. 450 li south

Saw six dead bodies in half a day, and four of them were women: one in an open shed, naked but for a string round her waist; another in a stream; one in the water, half exposed above the ice at the mercy of wild dogs; another half clad in rags in one of the open caves at the roadside; another half eaten, torn by birds and beasts of prey. Met two youths of about eighteen years of age, tottering on their feet, and leaning on sticks as if ninety years of age. Met another young man carrying his mother on his shoulders as her strength had failed. Seeing me looking at them closely, the young man begged for help. This is the only one who has begged since I left Taiyuanfu.

Saw men grinding soft stones . . . into powder, which was sold for from two to three cash per catty [1⅛ lb.] to be mixed with any grain, or grass seed, or roots and made into cakes. I tried some of these cakes, and they tasted like what most of them were—clay. Many died of constipation in consequence of eating them.

February 2. 530 li south

At the next city was the most awful sight I ever saw. It was early in the morning when I approached the city gate. On one side of it was a pile of naked dead men, heaped on top of each other as though they were pigs in a slaughter-house. On the other side of the gate was a similar pile of dead women, their clothes having been taken away to pawn for food. Carts were there to take the corpses away to two great pits, into one of which they threw the men, and into the other the women. . . .

For many miles in this district the trees were all white, stripped clean for ten or twenty feet high of their bark, which was being used for food. We passed many houses without doors and window-frames, which had been sold as firewood. Inside were kitchen utensils left untouched only because they could not be turned into money.

February 3. 600 li south

Saw only seven persons today, but no women among them. This was explained by meeting carts daily full of women being taken away for sale.

Chapter Six

The Foreign Presence in China: *1860–1885*

During the quarter century between the Opium Wars and the Sino-French War, the Western powers consolidated their political, economic, and religious foothold in China. But the increasing strength of their position aroused lively resentment among the Chinese, particularly toward the missionaries. The Sino-French War of 1884–1885 and the accompanying wave of hostility toward France were the immediate consequence of French intervention in Tongking and the long-term result of friction between the Chinese and all Westerners.

The Westerners' Foothold in Politics

Treaty ports and concessions

Around 1870 there were about fifteen "treaty ports." Five more were opened in 1876, when the Zhifu Convention was signed between China and Great Britain after the death of an English interpreter on the Sino-Burmese frontier. British concessions had grown up in seven of them—in Canton, Hankou, and Tientsin, among others—and French concessions in three (see map, page 66). In addition there was the international concession in Shanghai. The

Chinese government had virtually no control over these enclaves, since the provisional institutions that the foreigners created to run them at the time of the Opium Wars had developed and gained strength over the years.

The international concession in Shanghai, formed in 1863 by the fusion of the British and American concessions, was administered by a municipal council elected each year by foreign landowners or leaseholders whose estate or lease exceeded the value of 500 taels. The decisions of this miniature government had to be approved by the consular corps, as well as by an annual general meeting of electors which was something like a Parliament. The municipal council had a police force, which in time of trouble was reinforced by the Shanghai volunteer corps (made up of foreign residents only). The council levied taxes, and its activities were managed by three departments: public works, finance, and police. Chinese residents in the concession (20,000 in 1844 and 125,000 in 1885) were not represented at the assembly, although they were heavily taxed. They were subject to jurisdiction in a mixed court, created in 1864, that had both Chinese and Western judges. The system set up provisionally at the time of the Opium Wars had become a real merchant republic dominated by the *taipan* oligarchy (*taipan* was the Chinese name for the heads of foreign firms). The affairs of the town were conducted for the benefit of the foreign residents and with an almost total disregard for Chinese interests, as was shown by the famous *Ocean* incident in 1875.[1]

The French concession was organized on similar lines. It was run by a municipal council elected by foreign residents. The council's actions were controlled by an annual meeting of foreign residents and by the French consul. It had the right to form a police force, to use revenues from taxation, and to construct and maintain public works. As in the international concession, the Chinese (who numbered about 40,000 in 1885) could neither vote nor stand for election, although they had to pay taxes. Plans to combine the French and the international concessions failed several times because of French opposition.

The political structure of foreign life in China was not limited to the concessions but included the foreign law courts, the foreign postal service, and above all, the organization of the customs. In a number of important geographical and administrative sectors, for-

[1] Described in document 1 at the chapter end.

eign authority had replaced or was added to the authority of the Chinese state.

The consular courts

In line with the principle of extraterritoriality, consular courts were set up in the main open ports. These courts served not only the first foreign powers to benefit from the treaties—France, Great Britain, and the United States—but other countries to whom the same advantages were extended owing to the most-favored-nation clause (Prussia, Denmark, Holland, Spain, Italy, Austria and Hungary, and Belgium). Nationals of countries who had not signed a treaty could declare themselves under the protection of a treaty power and take advantage of its consular court. Britain was the only country to set up a court of appeal in China, established in 1865. Appeals against decisions taken by the French, Dutch, or Spanish consular courts had to go to Saigon, Batavia, or Manila. For other powers the legal situation was vaguer still, so that the Chinese who were liable to trial by a consular court (a trial involving a foreigner) were placed in a position of obvious inferiority. Foreign post offices were also set up in the main ports to dispatch mail sent from Europe to foreign residents throughout China. This again was a de facto measure which had not been provided for by the treaties.

Control of the customs

At the beginning, foreign control over the Chinese customs was local and temporary: the foreigners took charge of the Shanghai customs service during the Small Knife rebellion. But as often happened in the history of the unequal-treaties system, the temporary expedient turned into a permanent institution.

In 1861 the inspector of customs in Shanghai (a foreigner) became the inspector general of imperial customs. He was H. N. Lay, an Englishman, who was replaced in 1863 by another Englishman, Robert Hart, a former interpreter at the British consulate in Canton. Hart was directly responsible to the Chinese Foreign Ministry created in Peking just after the Treaty of Tientsin, the Zongli Yamen. For this reason customs headquarters were transferred from Shanghai to Peking in 1865. In every important port Hart had well-paid customs commissioners, all foreigners, under his command. Each commissioner directed a large staff. The total number of customs employees in 1864 was 400 Westerners and 1,000 Chinese, and it rose to 500 Westerners and 2,000 Chinese in 1885. The commissioners in the ports were supposed to be under the supervision of the customs superintendent, a Chinese local official, but in fact only Hart's authority counted. Consequently he had the direction of a powerful, completely autonomous administrative body.

The work of the customs service did not consist solely of collecting import and export taxes, harbor dues, and coastal taxes. It also included quarantine, the study of epidemics in the ports, coastal geographic surveys, the upkeep and improvement of harbors and rivers, and aids to navigation (lighthouses, buoys, and beacons). An embryonic public postal service was created by the customs service in 1878 and later became an independent organization. Thus an entire sector of Chinese administrative and economic life was taken over by the Westerners.

Western intervention in the customs arose from complex considerations. Foreign merchants wanted to make sure that the low tariffs imposed on China in 1842 were respected. They also wanted the coastal navigation set in order, for at the time of the Opium Wars it had been invaded by smugglers, military adventurers, and irregular traffic of all kinds. Well-established Western firms with influence in London aimed to eliminate their less respectable rivals through tighter control of Chinese foreign trade.

The creation of the customs service was also a result of the policy of support for the Manchus adopted by the Westerners after the second Opium War (and illustrated, for instance, during the suppression of the Taiping). Once the Westerners had acquired the essential advantages that were granted in the treaties, it seemed preferable to maintain and strengthen the imperial government which had negotiated the treaties. The adoption of this policy of support coincided exactly with the turnaround in policy carried out by the British in India with regard to the India princes. After the Sepoy Mutiny (1857–1859), the British abandoned their program of cutting down the powers of the princes and gradually eliminating their authority. Instead they began strengthening the princes' power and appointed a Resident as assistant to each prince to ensure his cooperation.

The Chinese customs service, administered with great efficiency under the leadership of an outstanding man, brought the empire a large and regular income which had not been whittled away by the usual misappropriations of the mandarins. Customs revenues totaled 8 million taels in 1864 and 15 million in 1886, when they amounted to nearly a quarter of the government's income.

In addition Hart, who served as inspector general until 1908, asserted his authority more and more until he came to act as a highly influential unofficial counselor, almost like a Resident, to the imperial state. His famous memorandum of 1866 to the Chinese government was a regular "manual of good conduct" (in the words of the Chinese historian Hu Sheng) for both home and foreign policy. Hart played an important role in the negotiations leading up to the Zhifu Convention in 1876 and the settlement of the Sino-French War in 1885. He also had a say in high government appointments. In 1867, for instance, both of the candidates whom he proposed for the posts of governor-general of Sichuan and Yunnan-Guizhou were appointed.

Hart was not the only influential foreigner in the Chinese machinery of state. In 1868 the first Chinese diplomatic mission to be sent abroad was led by an American diplomat, Anson Burlingame, who was supposed to represent the Peking government in the West. Similarly, Western military counselors to the army were made available to the imperial faction, particularly by France and Great Britain. These advisers equipped and trained troops fighting the Taiping and the Nian after 1860, but their activity outlasted the two rebellions by far. The British diplomat and Sinologist T. F. Wade translated the British infantry manual into Chinese, and it was widely distributed in the Chinese army between 1870 and 1880.

Western Economic Activity

Large-scale foreign trade in China

Trade was still the chief economic activity of Westerners in China. From 1860 on, the zone of operations for foreign merchants was considerably enlarged by the opening of numerous ports in North China and in the interior. In addition the Zhifu Convention made provisions for some ports in the middle Yangzi basin to be used as ports of call by foreign ships, although they had not been formally opened. Foreign goods circulating in the interior were also exempt from the inland customs duties (*lijin*) instituted by the imperial authorities to finance the suppression of the Taiping movement. The only payment required of foreigners was a moderate surtax on inland traffic. Between 1870 and 1880 steam navigation appeared not only on the coastal routes but also on Chinese inland waterways. British and American steamships completely replaced the clippers (sailing ships with iron hulls) which had won renown in the opium smuggling at the beginning of the century. In 1885 there were eleven large British and American steam navigation firms in Shanghai and Hong Kong. The two biggest, Jardine & Matheson and Butterfield & Swire, had offices in both ports. In the Yangzi basin the early steamboats traveled upstream as far as Hankou and Yichang, stopping at the rapids leading to the rich province of Sichuan. In 1868 the Shanghai chamber of commerce (a British organization) financed a reconnaissance expedition to explore the economic possibilities of the upper Yangzi.

The scope of operations carried out by Western firms also grew larger, as the table shows.

Western trade	1871–1873	1881–1883
Sales		
Opium (hundredweight)	37,408	42,777
Raw cotton (″)	151,491	106,373
Cotton yarn (″)	37,791	118,020
Cotton fabric (yuans)	32,013,727	28,493,915
Paraffin (gallons)	—	176,513,915
Iron and copper (hundredweight)	142,806	273,717
Purchases		
Tea (hundredweight)	1,022,159	1,238,145
Silk (″)	37,529	39,345
Soya beans (″)	57,506	84,760

Opium (whose volume corresponded exactly to that of cotton yarn and silk) was still extremely important, as were cotton fabrics. Chinese purchases of yarn, used by artisans for weaving, rose steeply. So did purchases of metal and metallurgical products for use both in fitting out the open ports and in building modern industrial concerns under the patronage of the Chinese authorities. Purchases of paraffin doubled, and supplied the foreign concessions as well as the interior, where it rivaled the use of oil for lighting. Tea and silk were still China's principal exports, with the addition of soya beans (and small quantities of hides, hog bristles for brushes, and dried eggs from Hubei and Sichuan). Foreign trade was beginning to absorb products from the interior instead of being confined to tea and silk from the Southeast, which had been the only zone of activity at the time of the Opium Wars.

Relative stagnation

Although foreign trade was active, it had not come up to the expectations of the "old China hands" and the big British firms in Shanghai which from 1839 on frequently exerted pressure on the diplomacy of the Foreign Office. Exports increased from 106 million yuan in 1871–1873 to a mere 126 million yuan in 1881–1883; imports fell from 110 million to 108 million over the same period. Relative stagnation was also apparent in the foreign traffic in the main ports:

Traffic (in customs taels)	**1870**	**1880**
Shanghai	90 million	88 million
Canton	28 million	30 million
Hankou	18 million	21 million
Tientsin	15 million	16 million

The preceding table on Western sales and purchases also revealed a drop in sales of foreign raw cotton and cotton fabrics, both products in which home manufactures stood up fairly well to competition. (The same was not true of cotton yarn, where the difference in cost between handicraft goods and industrial products was much greater.) Foreign purchases of tea and silk showed only a modest increase, because these Chinese products no longer dominated the world market as they had at the beginning of the nineteenth century. Now they had to compete with Indian tea and Japanese silk, which were often better processed and more accessible.

Foreign trade in China was vulnerable and fluctuating. For example, it was severely affected by the economic crisis of 1865–1866 (which caused Dent & Company, one of the oldest British *hong* in the Far East, to go bankrupt), and by the slump of 1872–1873.

Other foreign business activities included coastal transport, the shipment of goods from one port to another (particularly in the Yangzi basin), insurance underwriting, and the beginnings of industrial development. The largest firms combined several kinds of business by means of subsidiary companies. Jardine & Matheson, for example, had a steamship line, four import-export firms, three insurance companies, a sugar refinery, and a silk mill. The Chinese name for these concerns, as a sign of their link with the head office, was that of a comprador (Yi-he, or in Cantonese, Ewo) who had worked for William Jardine in Canton during the heyday of the opium trade. The development and the growing complexity of the business world, which at that time was dominated by British financiers, led to the foundation in 1864 of the Hong Kong and Shanghai Bank, which combined the functions of bank of issue, depositing bank, and merchant bank.

The Western business world in China provided readers for many foreign newspapers in Hong Kong, Shanghai, Fuzhou, and Amoy. The *Celestial Empire* appeared in 1874 to compete with the older *North China Herald*; the *Shanghai Mercury* began in 1879, and about thirty other shorter-lived papers were started up at one time or another. The foreign press in China was almost exclusively British in financing, management, and composition (three attempts to launch French papers were unsuccessful). This was a further confirmation of British predominance in every domain of foreign penetration in nineteenth-century China.

The first foreign industry

According to the Chinese economist Yang Zhong-ping, 61 industrial concerns were founded in China by foreigners between 1860 and 1885. Before that 10 British and 3 American concerns had already been established between the two Opium Wars. Most of these 13 pioneers were located in Shanghai, and almost all of them were printshops or shipyards.

The 61 newer industrial firms fell into four categories: there were 14 shipyards and ship repair shops, 10 workshops processing goods for export (including brick-tea factories, shops for pressing hides, and plants for drying eggs), 23 concerns that filled the everyday needs of the foreign communities and concessions (waterworks, gasworks, icehouses, soap factories, printing and publishing works), and 14 factories in which attempts were already being made to use cheap labor and Chinese raw materials in producing goods for the local market (for example, there were 6 silk mills, all in Shanghai).

The majority (47) of the first foreign factories were British, 6 were Russian (most of them brick-tea factories), 4 were German, 2 were French, and 2 were American. As for location, 34, or over half, were in Shanghai, 5 were in Hankou, 4 in Canton, 4 in Amoy, 3 in Fuzhou, 2 in Hong Kong, and 2 in Shantou. Thus the great majority were on the southeast coast, where the foreigners had been for the longest time.

Plans for Western economic penetration

Apart from a few exceptions, like the shipyards owned by Jardine & Matheson and by Farham & Company, the foreign factories were all small enterprises which counted for little in Chinese economic life. But they prefigured the form which foreign economic penetration would take during the period that followed. The same was true of foreign mines. In the period 1870–1875, the famous German geologist Ferdinand von Richthofen conducted exploratory expeditions on the coal-producing plateaus of Shanxi at the request of the British organization, the Shanghai chamber of commerce. The first foreign attempts to invest in railways also foreshadowed the period to come. In 1863 the British officer Charles George Gordon had just taken back Suzhou from the Taiping, and a group of British and American businessmen from Shanghai presented the governor of Jiangsu, Li Hong-zhang, with a plan for a railway from Shanghai to Suzhou. Li refused, however. In 1865 another group of foreign merchants in Shanghai proposed to build a line from Shanghai to Wusong, the town located at the junction of the Huangpu (the river flowing through Shanghai) and the Yangzi. The line lay in an army-occupied zone which Western troops had just evacuated, on payment by the Chinese of the indemnity imposed on them after the second Opium War. The line was eventually built in 1875, only to be destroyed almost immediately by the Chinese. Both of these early projects for railways were closely linked with the foreign military presence in China.

The Chinese coolie traffic was still flourishing. It was highly profitable for the recruiting agencies and the shipping companies, just as it had been in the period 1840–1850. And it continued in conditions which were just as primitive as they had been in that decade. Sometimes the coolies were taken on as workers "under contract" (in fact they were short-term slaves), particularly when they were destined for Latin America or the Caribbean Islands. When they were sent to California or the western colonies in Southeast Asia, they were treated as free emigrants. The coolie traffic was especially lively in Macao, Canton, and Amoy. The recruiting agents took advantage of the coolies' naïveté, made them sign a contract, shut them up in barracks where their wretched food was deducted from their future salaries, and then packed them into cargo boats. It was not unusual for the victims to revolt and turn to piracy.

Cultural and Religious Activities

Protestant missionaries

Like British and American merchants, Protestant missions appeared in China at the beginning of the nineteenth century. At first they had to remain on the edge of things, in Singapore or in the foreign-factories area of Canton. Later they settled in all the large ports as they were opened. The China Inland Mission (British) was established in Shanghai in 1865, the London Missionary Society was based in Canton and the Yangzi basin, the British Baptists were in the North, the Presbyterians settled in Shanghai, and the Methodists installed themselves in Fujian and Jiangsu. Their dispersal reflected the decentralized nature of British and American Protestantism. In 1880, 132 different missions were established in 79 towns.

The Protestant missions did not have large staffs. Around 1860 there were a few hundred Protestant missionaries in China, and by 1885 there were slightly over a thousand. The number of conversions was not particularly encouraging; according to the missionary census of 1896, China had 6,753 practicing Protestant converts in 1869 and about 30,000 in 1885. The vast majority of these new Christians belonged to the sections of the urban population which were linked economically and socially with the West. They were office workers, interpreters, shopkeepers, and coolies (some of whom, the "rice Christians," were drawn to the missions for material reasons).

Medical and scientific activities

The Protestant missions, which associated religious conversion with the diffusion of Anglo-Saxon forms of civilization, concentrated their work in the towns. They supported numerous hospitals and translated Western medical works. They opened schools, like the Anglo-Chinese Methodist College in Fuzhou and St. John's College (later a university), founded in Shanghai in 1879 by American Episcopalians. Around 1885 the missionary schools had 17,000 pupils. The missionaries had their own printing plants, such as those of the Episcopalian Methodists in Fuzhou and the Presbyterians in Shanghai, and they published Chinese-language tracts, pamphlets, and regular newspapers like the *World Magazine* in Shanghai.

Several of the Protestant missionaries were distinguished scholars of Chinese. James Legge, for example, translated the Confucian canons into English. Alexander Wylie, the specialist in Chinese literature, translated the Gospels into Chinese. Both men belonged to the London Missionary Society. Other missionaries developed an absorbing interest in Chinese politics. Timothy Richard was associated with influential members of the reformist party in Peking, and in 1877 he was instrumental in getting help to the famine victims in Northwest China.

From 1860 on, the Protestant missionaries played an active part in the translation offices set up in Shanghai and Peking in the context of the *yangwu* movement (Chapter 7). W. A. P. Martin (1827–1916), appointed head of the Tong Wen Guan in 1870, was an American Presbyterian who had worked at the American legation in Peking in 1859–1860. He founded a Christian mission and a mission school in the capital and translated a classic work on international law into Chinese. He was a friend of Robert Hart, who encouraged him to accept the high appointment offered to him by the imperial government.

Thus the intellectual and social influence of British and American Protestantism in China was out of all proportion to its modest numbers. Moreover, it was closely associated with the economic and political activities of the foreign powers.

Roman Catholic missionaries

Roman Catholicism, on the other hand, was established in the country districts, not in the towns. It covered the whole of China, not merely the open ports; in fact the largest Catholic population was in the province of Sichuan. Catholic missionaries were fewer in number than the Protestants. The foreign missions in Yunnan, Guizhou, Sichuan, and Guangdong; the Franciscans in Hubei,

Hunan, Henan, Shenxi, Shandong, and Shanxi; the Lazarists in Zhili, Zhejiang, and Jiangxi; the Jesuits in Zhili and Jiangnan; the Dominicans in Fujian—all these represented a total of about 600 missionaries in 1885. The Chinese Roman Catholic clergy, however, numbered 167 priests in 1865 and 335 in 1886. Furthermore, there were half a million Chinese Catholics.

Unlike the work of the Protestants, the activity of the Catholic missionaries was rarely connected with the economic and technical penetration of China by the West, based on the open ports. The only Catholic organization which fell into this category was the Observatory of Xujiahui (Zikawei) in the suburbs of Shanghai. Its Jesuit directors specialized in meteorology and typhoon forecasting, and their work was highly important in the activity of the port.

The great majority of Catholic missionaries lived in the villages and small towns of the interior. There they were in contact with the Confucian gentry and local officials, not with the modernized urban population of Chinese society. The contact was not easy.

Conflict between Catholics and mandarins

After the treaty of 1860 the presence of Catholics was legal throughout the country. In each province they had the right to appeal to the senior mandarins when they considered themselves wronged, and if they did not receive satisfaction, they could turn to their own government in France or Italy. Consequently on the slightest provocation they sent in requests for heavy indemnities (nearly 900,000 taels for thirty-four incidents between 1861 and 1870), and if the mandarins ruled in the Catholics' favor, the local gentry had to collect money to pay these sums. The treaties of 1858–1860 also declared that the Catholic missions had the right to reoccupy land which they had acquired by purchase or gift in the seventeenth and eighteenth centuries, before the edicts proscribing Roman Catholicism. The Catholics enforced this clause without much tact, at the price of countless quarrels with the new Chinese owners of the land. The Jesuits, for example, built the Xujiahui Observatory on the former estate of the Xu (Zi) family, to which Paul Xu Guang-qi, the scholar and assistant of Matteo Ricci, had belonged. The Lazarists reoccupied their old church, the Beitang, in the north of Peking near the imperial palace.

The Catholic missionaries aspired to local political influence everywhere, particularly in the distant provinces of the Southwest.

The apostolic vicar of Guizhou, Monsignor Faurie, tried to arbitrate political rivalries, act as peacemaker in cases of social disorder, and recommend candidates for high posts in the provincial administration. The "right of protectorate over Roman Catholics" exercised by France was also a source of friction. Missionaries sometimes extended it without due consideration to undesirable people or to people whom the courts had judged guilty and who appealed to the missionaries in order to escape the jurisdiction of the mandarins. Catholic orphanages were regarded by the Chinese, with their tradition of ancestor worship, as antisocial institutions in which the orphans could no longer take part in their traditional family rites. Many small children arrived at the orphanages in very poor health and were no sooner baptized than they died, thus giving rise to still darker suspicions.

Chinese Reactions

The dynamic expansion shown by the Westerners in every field since the opening provoked different reactions in China. Some of the chief statesmen, senior officials, and intellectuals believed that the challenge of the West should be taken up, that a plan for modernization should be defined which would not compromise Chinese integrity. They belonged to the *yangwu* movement (described in Chapter 7), which contended that in the immediate future at least, the treaties should be accepted and cooperation with the Westerners should take place within the context created by the treaties. But among Chinese local leaders, among the vast majority of Confucian scholars with traditional training, and among the mass of the people, the political, economic, and religious influx of the West aroused irritation and hostility. Thus most Chinese opposed the official line of conciliation adopted by the central government.

Conflicts arising from the concessions

In 1874 the enlargement of the territory of the French concession in Shanghai provoked violent rioting. For several years the French municipal authorities had planned to build a road through a piece of land occupied by a pagoda and a cemetery belonging to the Ningbo Guild—the corporation of Shanghai merchants who were natives of Ningbo. The guild, with the support of Chinese public opinion, had tried repeatedly to persuade the French to modify their project, but in vain. In a sudden outburst a Chinese crowd rioted, gave some foreigners a rough handling, and sacked and burned some French buildings. The affair ended in a compromise: the French abandoned the construction project, but China had to pay a heavy indemnity for the acts of violence committed. (Six Chinese were killed by the French police during the suppression of the rioting; the French had no fatalities.)

This violent incident was exceptional in the history of Shanghai during the nineteenth century. The Chinese population of the town had settled there only a short time earlier and had not the same collective defenses against foreign ways as the towns in the interior with their gentry-led ruling class. Even in Shanghai, however, the existence of concessions, consular courts, and extraterritoriality resulted in constant friction and humiliation for the Chinese. The *Ocean* incident (document 1) is only one of many occasions when foreign attitudes produced lasting bitterness and resentment. The municipal rules of the concessions were often contrary to Chinese customs or based quite simply on racial discrimination, such as the rule forbidding Chinese to enter the parks or gardens in the concessions.

Gunboat policy

One of the most important rights obtained by Westerners, that of sailing warships on inland waters, was also one of the most widely resented by the Chinese in the inland regions. (Only the fraction of the population that lived in the treaty ports was in direct contact with the actual machinery of unequal treaties, concessions, customs, and extraterritoriality.) The gunboat policy (the official term used at the time) was designed to intimidate the authorities and the public and to make them aware of the dominant position which the West intended to occupy in all China.

Hardly a year passed without a demonstration of strength by France or Britain on the Chinese coast or in the Yangzi basin. In November 1868, after rioting broke out against the Protestant mission in Yangzhou, the British minister in Peking, Rutherford Alcock, sent four gunboats to Nanking and stationed two more opposite Yangzhou. At the same time a conflict arose between the Taiwan authorities and a British trading firm on the subject of camphor, over which the island traditionally had a monopoly. British gunboats attacked the port of Anping on the north coast and killed seventeen Chinese soldiers. In 1869 the French minister in Peking, Julian de Rochechouart, made what amounted to a military tour on the upper Yangzi in the hope of impressing local mandarins and putting an end to the antimissionary agitation which was developing. He obtained the opposite effect, however, as the Tientsin massacre showed in 1870.

Failure of the Wusong railway

Western plans for setting up modern transportation and communication facilities also created friction. A railway from Shanghai to Wusong was built by trickery in 1875, for the land was bought under other pretexts. As soon as an accident occurred, public opinion exploded. The steel rails crossed the fields with no concern for the tombs of the peasants, and they also violated the rules of *feng-shui* (harmony between the natural and the social worlds, implying that human construction should be adapted to the features of the landscape). According to the peasants, the engines threatened and irritated the subterranean dragon whose body carries the world of men. The local gentry gave their support to the popular agitation against the railroad, and the Chinese government bought back the line in 1877 in order to destroy it.

The first plans for telegraph lines provoked similar resistance. It was not until 1881 that the government permitted a Danish company to open a line through Peking, Tientsin, and Shanghai.

Popular hostility toward the missionaries

Local conflicts between the missionaries and the authorities were the most frequent grounds for the use of gunboat policy. Both Roman Catholic and Protestant missions, which had been granted freedom of action in 1860, operated in a context of contentiousness which often erupted into riots.

Hostility to Christianity had been traditional among the mass of the Chinese people and the Confucian scholars since the seventeenth century. In the years just after the treaties of 1858–1860, which officially reopened China to the Christian missions, this tradition took on new vigor. National humiliation was added to the old ideological antagonism between the scholars and the missionaries, whose activities threatened the intellectual influence and the social position of the gentry. Many Catholic missionaries had a self-praising, self-satisfied attitude based on the allegedly privileged status of their church. After 1860 three main Catholic cathedrals were built in Canton, Tientsin, and Peking. The first was erected, symbolically, on the site of the *yamen* of the viceroy Ye Ming-zhen, the tenacious and unfortunate enemy of the British during the siege of 1856. The second, located in the town where the humiliating treaty of 1858 had been signed, replaced a Confucian temple (which was demolished to make way for it) and was placed under the patronage of Our Lady of Victories. The third was built on a piece of land given to the Jesuits in former times by the Kangxi Emperor. Its towers dominated the imperial palaces of the Forbidden City and for the Chinese became a symbol of Western religious arrogance.

The hostility of the scholars

Between 1860 and 1870 Confucian scholars issued tracts, placards, and pamphlets containing anti-Christian propaganda. Engravings mocked church services by showing the participants as pigs and goats, the most contemptible of all animals in the Chinese view. Christianity was denounced not only for its collusion with "foreign devils" but also for its intrinsically heterodox and perverse nature, which was likely to corrupt the Chinese social order.

A short book written around 1860 by a scholar from Hunan, a traditionalist province, was distributed throughout the country. Its author, who signed himself "the most despairing man in the world," entitled it *Authentic Statement Designed to Eliminate Heterodoxy (Bixie Jishi)*. It was a mixture of theological criticism, obscene anecdotes, a denunciation of the difference in customs between the West and the East (for instance, the weekly day of rest), and accusations of kidnapping and sorcery. It appealed to the public to form a popular militia capable of fighting Christian propaganda and driving out the missionaries.

Incidents between 1860 and 1870

This climate of hostility bred incidents of violence. Sometimes they involved only pillage, burning, and other property damage. But sometimes people died in them: a partial record covering thirty-three incidents between 1861 and 1869 lists the deaths of three Catholic priests and one hundred and thirty Chinese Christians. Only five of the reported incidents affected Protestant missions; the rest were Catholic. Most of the incidents occurred in distant prov-

inces of the interior, because the Catholics were active over a much
larger area than the Protestants. Ten incidents were reported in
Guizhou (a record figure linked with the behavior of Monsignor
Faurie, who was particularly unpopular), four in Hunan, and four
in Sichuan, both of which were traditionalist provinces with almost
no commercial links to the West. Three were reported in Fujian,
and two each in Henan, Anhui, and Guangxi.

In these incidents the demonstrators attacked missionaries,
churches and other buildings belonging to the missions (Hengzhou
in Hunan, 1862, Taiwanfu, 1868), and Chinese converts and their
homes. Orphanages were often assailed, as in Nanchang, Jiangxi, in
1862. The incidents all began as sudden reactions on the part of a
crowd which had gathered without warning. At Yangzhou in 1868,
ten thousand people attacked the China Inland Mission. Several
hundred gathered at Taiwanfu in the same year, when the rumor
went around that missionaries used magic potions to bring about
conversions.

Confucian scholars seem to have inspired many of these incidents. In Nanchang and in Xiangtan in 1862 the anti-Christian
rioting coincided with the triennial examinations of Jiangxi and
Hunan, which attracted many scholars, their families, and friends
to the provincial capitals. The role of the gentry in the Yangzhou
rioting in 1868 has also been proved. In every case the local authorities seem to have sat back and let things happen. When the
missionaries insisted on having protection, the authorities supplied
it reluctantly. Foreign consuls and ministers protesting acts of violence toward missions or missionaries had to appeal directly to top
officials (governor-generals, members of the central government)
to obtain apologies and the payment of indemnities (which were
usually heavy: 400,000 taels for thirteen incidents between 1862
and 1869).

Incidents occurred constantly during the ten years following the
Treaty of Tientsin, and they were particularly numerous in 1868
and 1869 (ten in one year alone). Thus the massacre of June 1870
at Tientsin was not an isolated catastrophe but the culmination of a
far-reaching crisis.

The Tientsin massacre

In Tientsin, a town where memories of the negotiations of
1858–1860 were still particularly vivid, public opinion was inflamed against the missionaries, especially against the orphanage

of Saint Vincent de Paul. Tension was increasing, and the local authorities suggested to the French consul that a joint inquiry be carried out with a view to halting the rumors of kidnapping and other abuses circulating against the missions. The discussion grew acrimonious, however. In irritation the consul opened fire, and violent rioting ensued. Among the dead were twenty-one Westerners, including the consul and ten nuns, and about thirty Chinese Christians. The consulate, the church, and the other buildings belonging to the missionaries were burned by the mob.

The Chinese government, anxious to preserve its policy of cooperation with the West, paid an indemnity of 490,000 taels, executed eighteen suspects, and took their rank away from the two local mandarins. These measures still fell short of French demands. But war had just broken out between France and Prussia, and the French claims to damages could not be backed up by the armed demonstration which was usually inevitable in such circumstances.

The Chinese authorities wanted to take this opportunity to tighten government control over the missionaries. In 1871 a draft regulation was submitted to the foreign powers by the Zongli Yamen (Foreign Ministry). Its eight articles proposed to abolish orphanages, to require Chinese Christians to register with the local authorities, to forbid direct appeals by missionaries to the provincial authorities, to outlaw all further building contrary to the rules of *fengshui*, and similar measures. The foreigners refused outright.

The Tientsin crisis, and the entire antiforeign movement between 1860 and 1870, burdened the Chinese government with a problem of internal politics which was virtually insoluble. If it did not firmly put down demonstrations and riots against the missionaries, the government ran the risk of displeasing the foreign powers, whereas it was the policy of the *yangwu* movement to stay on good terms with them. But if it was too firm with the rioters, the government risked losing the support of the masses and the gentry. The imperial power could not afford to take the risk, because it was just emerging from the serious social crisis in which it had barely managed to overcome the great mid-century popular risings. Chinese intervention against France on Vietnam's behalf in 1884 was an attempt to escape from this political impasse.

The Sino-French War

The *yuangwu* policy adopted by the Chinese government in 1860 was closely linked to the search for a way of getting along with the West on the basis of the treaties of 1860. Conciliation of the foreigners had not, however, lived up to the hopes of Chinese statesmen. In spite of all the government's efforts and gestures of good will, in 1869 the foreign powers refused a Chinese proposal, presented in accordance with the 1858 agreements, to revise the treaties. Above all, the foreigners were bringing increasing pressure to bear in the peripheral areas of the Chinese world, while the Zhifu Convention continued the process of undermining Chinese sovereignty that was initiated by the unequal treaties of 1842 and 1860. This evolution taken as a whole led China to begin resisting the encroachments of the foreigners for the first time since 1839, and of going to war when the French attacked Tongking.

Russian pressure in Central Asia

In Central Asia the interventions of the foreign powers were linked with the Moslem rebellion (covered in Chapter 4). While Britain openly supported Yakub-beg in southwest Turkestan, Russia took the opportunity to annex the northern part of the same region in 1871: the Ili territory and the Kouldja Oasis, the "Gates of Dzungaria," a strategic zone of the utmost importance for communications in Central Asia. It was the beginning of a program for dividing a Chinese territory into "zones of influence" controlled by rival powers, a policy which became generalized at the end of the nineteenth century. Russia promised, nevertheless, to evacuate the Ili zone as soon as Chinese authority in the region was restored. At first, in the Treaty of Livadia of 1879, which was signed after the liquidation of the principality of Yakub-beg by Zuo Zong-tang, the Russians agreed to give back only a small part of the area. But in 1881 China managed to recover almost all of it.

Japan, which had been modernized by the Meiji revolution (1868), quickly followed the example of the other foreign powers and became active on the Chinese eastern seaboard. In 1874 a samurai unit attacked Taiwan but did not occupy the island permanently. In 1875 Japan permanently annexed the Ryukyu Islands, a tributary kingdom of China that had also been linked to the Japanese fief of Satsuma since the sixteenth century. China had to acknowledge the *fait accompli* in 1881.

Foreigners in Korea

Foreign ambitions on the Chinese borders were also directed toward Korea between 1870 and 1880. A tributary kingdom of China in the classic sense, Korea became within the space of a few years the object of attacks or shows of naval strength from France (1866), Russia (1869), the United States (1867 and 1871), and Japan (1875 to 1876). This rivalry between the powers was like a prelude to the "battle of the concessions" which occurred later, around 1895–1900, for control of China's resources. In 1876 Japan seemed to have won the upper hand in Korea for the time being by imposing a treaty which opened three Korean ports.

China was unwilling to give up its special relations with that country, however. In 1883 Li Hong-zhang, who was directing Chinese diplomacy at the time, sent a Resident to Seoul, Yuan Shi-kai (later president of the Chinese Republic in 1912). At the same time Li encouraged Korea to sign treaties with other foreign powers in order to counterbalance Japanese influence. He wanted Korea to have a Western political counselor who could play a role in Seoul similar to that of Robert Hart in Peking. Hart and Li chose von Möllendorf, an official in the customs service. Korea was thus "open."

Rise of the *quingliu* group

The failure of China's policy of conciliation with the West once more increased the influence of diplomats who advocated a hard line against foreigners. This viewpoint had predominated in 1839 and in 1856–1858, and now it was represented by the *qingliu dang* ("purification clique"). Around 1880 the group had great power at court, in the Grand Council, and in the Grand Secretariat (see Chapter 5). It put up vigorous opposition to the Treaty of Livadia, which had agreed to the annexation of the Ili territory by the Russians. The *qingliu* clique even obtained the death sentence for Chong-hou, the Manchu official who had led the negotiations (in the end he was pardoned, however). At the clique's insistence, negotiations were reopened with Russia and resulted in the return of the Ili region to China in 1881. When France attacked China in

1883, the *qingliu* group was strong enough to impose a firm line on government policy.

French intervention in Tongking

Vietnam, whose southern provinces had been amputated by French annexations from 1862 to 1867, was one of China's oldest tributary countries, and one of those most closely linked to the Chinese world by political and economic ties. China still considered itself jointly responsible for affairs in that country, although France imposed a treaty in 1874 on the court of Hue which announced the rupture of ties between Vietnam and China. Tu-duc, the emperor of Annam, asked for Chinese help in 1879 against the hordes of bandits, and in 1881 he sent the traditional tribute to Peking (his covering letter is in document 3 at the end of Chapter 5). Trade by land and sea was brisk between the two countries. Chinese irregular troops, the Black Flags (whose leader Liu Yong-fu had been affiliated with the Triad and influenced by the Taiping), occupied a large part of the Tongking delta, with the agreement of the Vietnamese government.[2] These troops obstructed French plans for commercial expansion in the region.

The long-standing French designs on Tongking crystallized in 1882, when Henri Rivière occupied Hanoi and clashed with the Black Flags, who killed him in 1883. China considered itself directly concerned in the defense of Tongking. With the agreement of Peking, the governors of Guangxi, Yunnan, and Guangdong, the provinces adjoining Tongking, sent several small contingents of troops there in 1881 and 1882. Considerable differences of opinion existed within the government, however, as to the line of conduct to be followed.

Li Hong-zhang's policy of compromise

Some people, and especially Li Hong-zhang, one of the most prominent leaders of the *yangwu* movement, believed that China should maneuver, play for time, and avoid a head-on clash with France which would endanger the policy of "self-strengthening" and modernization followed after 1860. Li tried three times to im-

---

[2] Liu's threats against the French are presented in document 2 at the end of this chapter.

pose this policy of appeasement by taking negotiations with France into his own hands. At the end of 1882 he signed an agreement with the French diplomat Bourée which provided for the neutralization of Tongking and its division into two zones of influence, one French and one Chinese. When Bourée was disowned by Paris, Li continued the same policy and maneuvered in 1883 to avoid taking the leadership of the Chinese armies sent to Tongking. Instead of going directly to Canton, he stopped in Shanghai to negotiate with another French diplomat, Tricou, but to no effect. In 1884 he opened negotiations for the third time, and these ended in the Li-Fournier agreement providing for the withdrawal of Chinese troops. But the Bac-lé incident precipitated the war between France and China which Li had tried so hard to avoid.

The Chinese position hardens

Li's patient search for a compromise provoked violent attacks from his political enemies in 1883 and 1884. They voiced their criticisms by the traditional means of "pure criticism" (qingyi). The qingliu clique addressed countless memorials to the throne and endlessly denounced the Li-Fournier agreement. In 1884 it obtained the transfer of the governor of Yunnan's headquarters to Vietnamese soil and persuaded the government to encourage large numbers of Black Flags to move into Vietnam. Early in 1884 there were 50,000 Chinese in that country.

This hard-line policy was supported by the Empress Dowager Ci-xi. In 1884 she ended a rivalry of long standing and brought about the disgrace of Prince Gong, head of the Zongli Yamen and an upholder of the moderate line. He was deprived of his office by what amounted to a coup d'état that strengthened the antiforeign party. Between 1883 and 1885 the Sino-French War was at the heart of the complicated ramifications of Chinese home politics. For between the two factions of Li Hong-zhang and the quingliu clique lay countless intermediate approaches. Zuo Zong-tang, for example, was a member of the modernization movement from 1860 to 1870, but in 1885 he advocated resistance—without, however, becoming one of the quingliu clique.

Settlement of the war

War broke out in the summer of 1884 when Admiral Courbet bombarded the port of Fuzhou without warning and destroyed the modern fleet which China had just created there with the help of French technicians. Li refused to put his Huai army at the disposal of the Fujian authorities, an episode illustrating the rise of provincialist and centrifugal tendencies in Chinese politics. Neither side made a formal declaration of war, but in 1885 hostilities spread to the whole of South China. Taiwan was blockaded and partially occupied by the French navy under the command of Courbet, who also occupied the Pescadores islands and declared that rice was war contraband. The French obtained only limited successes, however, and suffered some defeats, such as that at Langson.

The Treaty of Tientsin in the spring of 1885 ratified China's renunciation of all rights to Vietnam, which became a French protectorate. Southwest China was opened to French trade. The fact that the French did not ask for an indemnity was considered a success for the Chinese negotiators. But the Chinese acknowledged France's right to be consulted and to offer its services if and when China decided to undertake a policy of railway development. The treaty was a formula of compromise which postponed the achievement of French ambitions, although it allowed for them in principle. It prepared the way for the breakup of 1898 and the West's sudden expansion in the fields of mining and railroad construction in China.

Renewal of popular movements against the West

The Sino-French War occasioned a further outbreak of anti-foreign political agitation, particularly in South China and around Canton. As in 1841, 1865, and 1868–1870, the peasants held excited meetings, xenophobic pamphlets were circulated, and the local gentry actively encouraged the turbulence. Roman Catholic and Protestant chapels were attacked from 1883 onward. After the French bombardment of Fuzhou, the agitation was intense. Several dozen missionary chapels and buildings were pillaged and Chinese Christians were molested. In Hong Kong a general strike of harbor workers broke out at the beginning of 1885 when the vessel *La Galissonière* wanted to put in for repairs. The strike, led by the triad, forced the British authorities to refuse to repair the French warship, which had to go on to Japan. This was the first collective action of a political nature on the part of the Chinese proletariat. Other anti-French riots broke out in the port of Wenzhou opposite Taiwan.

Although these movements were popular in nature, they were encouraged by the local officials and the Confucian scholars. In September 1884 Zhang Zhi-dong, one of the militant members of the *qingliu* clique, whose nomination to the post of governor-general of Canton was a success for the hard-line party, published a vigorously anti-French proclamation which was an appeal for a mass rising: "The French have come unjustly to make war in our country . . . those among you who have patriotic feelings should stop French ships to attack them, or enlist in the French army to destroy their ships . . . or get taken on as pilots, to lead their ships onto reefs."[3]

On a short-term basis, the 1885 treaty with France did not impose as severe concessions on China as the agreements that grew out of the two Opium Wars. The system of unequal treaties became no worse, or at least not straightaway (although the treaty of 1885 did open the way for foreign railway expansion). But the new defeat of the imperial power came after twenty years of efforts to "strengthen the country" and modernize it. The defeat made it obvious what little impact the efforts had had. This is why the public was particularly sensitive to the new proof of incompetence which the imperial government had just given. The prestige of the state was severely damaged. In his autobiography Sun Yat-sen says that it was after China's defeat by France that he made it his goal to overthrow the Qing dynasty and establish a republic.

ADDITIONAL BIBLIOGRAPHY

George Cyril Allen and Audrey Gladys Donnithorne, *Western Enterprise in Far Eastern Economic Development* (London, Allen & Unwin, 1954).

Paul A. Cohen, *The Missionary Movement and the Growth of Chinese Antiforeignism, 1860–1870* (Cambridge, Mass., Harvard University Press, 1963).

Kenneth Scott Latourette, *History of Christian Missions in China* (London, S.P.C.K., 1929).

Kwang-ching Liu, *Anglo-American Steamship Rivalry in China, 1862–1874* (Cambridge, Mass., Harvard University Press, 1962).

Stanley Fowler Wright, *Hart and the Chinese Customs* (Belfast, Mullan, 1950).

[3] Quoted by J. Silvestre, *L'Empire d'Annam*, p. 354.

DOCUMENTS

1. The exercise of British consular jurisdiction in Shanghai: the *Ocean* affair (1875)

Source: E. Hauser, *Blancs et jaunes à Shanghai* (Paris, La Nouvelle Edition, 1945), pp. 73–75. (Based on British documents belonging to the international concession.)

The British steamer *Ocean* collided with the *Fusing*, a Chinese steamer, on April 4, 1875, somewhere in the Yellow Sea between Shanghai and Tientsin. The weather was fine, the sea calm. No-one denied the fact that the collision was due to an error in seamanship on the part of the *Ocean*. The English steamer hit the *Fusing* on the starboard side, and she sank a few minutes later. There was panic on board the Chinese vessel, and a rush for the lifeboats which the crew could not control. Before the *Fusing* sank, only one of the lifeboats could be put to sea, saving twenty-six people. Other passengers and members of the crew jumped overboard and were picked up by the *Ocean*; sixty-three passengers and crew were lost with the *Fusing*.

The Chinese steamer belonged to China Merchants Steam. The six officers were Europeans; the rest, members of the crew and passengers bound for Tientsin, were Chinese. All the Europeans were saved, except for the third engineer. Among those lost were several junior Chinese officials from the province of Jiangsu, three members of the Rice Commission, a few civilians and servants, five employees of the Purser's office, and twelve crew members.

The poverty-stricken families of some of the victims inquired as to the treatment they would receive. They began by asking the Chinese company to take their interests in hand; Mr Tong, director of China Merchants Steam, wrote to Captain Brown, in command of the *Ocean*, to ask him how he intended to settle the damages. The only reply he received were the two initials, W.B., written in Mr Tong's notebook. They stood for William Brown, and meant that he had received the letter.

The affair was taken to the British consul, Mr W. H. Medhurst, who was an interpreter when Captain Balfour was consul. The consul advised the plaintiffs to get a British lawyer to defend them.

The hearing of the case *The Chinese lost in the collision between the steamers Fusing and Ocean* was opened with due solemnity on June 11 at the British consulate in Shanghai, with Captain William Brown of the *Ocean* as the defendant. Her Majesty's consul and the *daotai**
Fung presided, that is, saw to it that the interests of the plaintiffs were respected. William Brown was defended by two lawyers, Mr Wainewright and Mr Hannen, both Englishmen; two others, Mr Drummond and Mr Eames, represented the families of the victims.

The room was crowded with Chinese men, women, and children

---

* The intendant of circuit (*dao*).

from the victims' families. They waited, calm and restrained, having put their trust in Mr Medhurst and in the austere dignity of British justice. It was the most serious, perhaps the only really serious, affair to come before the consul for many years; the atmosphere was oppressive, tense, and impatient.

Action was brought for damages amounting to 63,000 taels—1,000 taels for each victim. The court was sitting in compliance with stipulations laid down by the Treaty of Tientsin, so the third engineer was struck off the list because he was European; the stipulations of the treaty applied solely to plaintiffs of Chinese nationality. Then the facts of the case were set out, down to the most minute detail, the witnesses were questioned and heard at length . . . and the case was adjourned.

One month after the first hearing, the second began with an extremely unfortunate incident. The *Ocean*, which had been at anchor in the harbor, representing a security for the plaintiffs, calmly applied to the customs for permission to leave. Permission was granted the day before the hearing by the clerk of the merchant navy, who was on the staff of the consulate and whose office was in the same building. The director of the Chinese line got wind of this and made a desperate appeal to the consul, Mr Medhurst, beseeching him to prevent her departure. His letter, which was read at the hearing, ran as follows:

"We have heard that permission to leave has been granted by the customs and that the *Ocean* is preparing to leave. . . . The vessel ought not to be allowed to lift anchor. The representatives of the families of the Chinese victims are besieging our offices with their complaints. . . . If the British steamer is allowed to put to sea, what will be the guarantee that the damages granted by the court will be paid?" With weighty candor, the Chinese added: "The case is one which concerns foreigners as much as Chinese."

Her Majesty's consul cleared his throat. He declared that action had been brought against the captain of the *Ocean*, and therefore had nothing to do with the vessel herself. He had not the power to alter his opinion.

The *Ocean* left the harbor; there was no possible doubt here, as the consulate had granted permission to leave. The plaintiffs' lawyer, whose conception of justice was outraged by this, stood up and declared that given the facts, his clients could hold the representative of Her Majesty's government responsible for the damages. To this the consul replied: "In fact you are holding *me* responsible!"

After this incident, which made a considerable impression on all the Chinese present, the court withdrew to discuss the case . . . and to have lunch.

When the hearing was opened once more in the afternoon, Mr Medhurst, the consul, read the sentence:

"We have had great difficulty in coming to a decision. This is what has been decided and agreed upon by all present. We consider that the loss of life was due to a fault in seamanship on the part of the *Ocean*, for which her captain must be held responsible. Consequently we have decided that owing to his negligence, he is liable to make up the losses caused to the families concerned," etc.

The end of it was that Captain William Brown was condemned, in all seriousness, to pay the plaintiffs 300 (not 1,000) taels for each passenger who was drowned, and 100 taels for each servant or crew member. This amounted to a total of 11,000 taels (not 63,000).

When, after hearing this solemn parody of justice, the afflicted families tried to obtain the ludicrous compensations allocated to them, Her Majesty's consul informed them that his government had not granted him the necessary powers, and that unfortunately he had not the means of enforcing the sentence. He regretted to say that he had done all he could. To do more was to exceed his orders.

2. POPULAR REACTIONS TO FRENCH INTERVENTION IN TONGKING: AN APPEAL BY LIU YONG-FU, LEADER OF THE BLACK FLAGS (1883)

SOURCE: Hosea Ballou Morse, *The International Relations of the Chinese Empire* (London, Longmans & Co., Ltd., 1910), vol. 2, pp. 474–475.

You French brigands live by violence in Europe and glare out on all the world like tigers, seeking for a place to exercise your craft and cruelty. Where there is land you lick your chops for lust of it; where there are riches you would fain lay hands on them. You send out teachers of religion to undermine and ruin the people. You say you wish for international commerce, but you merely wish to swallow up the country. There are no bounds to your cruelty, and there is no name for your wickedness. You trust in your strength, and you debauch our women and our youth. Surely this excites the indignation of gods and men, and is past the endurance of heaven and earth. Now you seek to conquer Annam, and behind the dummy of international commerce cast the treaty aside and befool the world, that you may satisfy your lust for blood, capture cities, storm towns, slaughter Mandarins, and rob everybody. Your crimes are unspeakable. Not all the water in the West River would wash out your shame. He who issued this proclamation has received behest to avenge these wrongs. He has taken oath to exterminate you with an army which bears Ni ("justice") on its banners. His first desire was at once, with the speed of the thunderbolt, to descend on your rabbit holes and exterminate you without pity like the vermin you are. Such would raise rejoicing in the heart of man, and would be a symbol of Heaven's vengeance. But Hanoi is an ancient and honourable town. It is filled with honest and loyal citizens. Therefore could he not endure that the city should be reduced to ruins, and young and old be put to the sword.

Therefore now do I, Liu Yong-fu, issue this proclamation. Know, ye French robbers, that I come to meet you. Rely on your strength and rapine and lead forth your herd of sheep and curs to meet my army of heroes and see who will be master. WAI-TAK-FE, an open space, I have fixed on as the field where I shall establish my fame. If you own that you are no match for us; if you acknowledge you carrion Jews are only fit to grease the edge of our blades; if you would still remain alive, then behead your leaders, bring their heads to my official abode, leave our city, and return to your own foul lairs. Then I out of regard for the lord of Heaven, for humanity, and for my commission from Government to maintain peace, will not slaughter you for mere personal gratification. But if you hesitate and linger on, hankering for what you cannot take, one morning my soldiers will arrive, and with them dire misfortune for you. Take heed and yield while yet you may. Be not as mules and involve yourselves in ruin. Let each man ponder this well, while yet he may save himself from death.

Chapter Seven

The Modernization Policy

Chinese historians call the official program of modernization that was shaped by the Restoration statesmen after the second Opium War the "foreign matters movement," or *yangwu yundong*. This expression was used at the time to refer to anything concerning foreigners, from diplomacy to industrial machinery. The first manifestation of *yangwu* as a movement was the creation of an armaments industry in connection with the "self-strengthening" (*ziqiang*) policy. Then, in accordance with the watchword "wealth and power" (*fuqiang*), came the development of communications, mines, and the textile industry.[1]

The evolution of *yangwu* took place in a context of general economic development. Alongside the Restoration achievements, which were the work of a few high officials rather than of the government, modern enterprises launched by private initiative appeared. Owing to obstacles at home and abroad, the modernization of China progressed slowly, but it created social changes and new problems which raised questions about the very basis of the traditional order.

---

[1] Refer to the chronology at the back of the book to see the two phases of the *yangwu* movement in relation to other events.

Beginnings of Modernization: *Ziqiang* (1860–1872)

Achievements during the first Opium War

At the time of the first Opium War scholars and senior officials began to realize that China would benefit by borrowing certain techniques from the West in order to defend itself against Westerners (see Chapter 3). Lin Ze-xu and his entourage were the pioneers in this respect. They set up translation offices, Lin himself compiled a description of the West, the *Chronicle of Four Continents*, and his friend Wei Yuan published the *Atlas of the Countries Beyond the Seas*. This group also attempted to imitate English guns and cannons and improve shipbuilding, on the assumption that it was essential to "learn their superior technology in order to control the barbarians," as Wei Yuan put it. At that time it was the military aspect of Western superiority which seemed the most overwhelming, so Lin Ze-xu and Wei Yuan gave priority to the acquisition of modern weapons to resist foreign invasion. However, they were also aware of the importance of trade and industry in the growth of national power.

Although Wei Yuan stressed the difference between the political regimes in China and the West, it never occurred to him, any more than it did to Lin Ze-xu, that the traditional system of government should be modified. On the contrary, all the reforms advocated by both men were aimed at strengthening it by correcting its faults and eliminating abuses. Actually, the ideas of the enlightened thinkers at the time of the Opium Wars could provide material for contradictory political currents. On the one hand they emphasized the need to modernize the economy and resist the enemy. On the other they defended the traditional social and political order, buttressed by adequate military power. The events of the Xianfeng Emperor's reign brought the second aspect of these ideas into prominence.

Provincial achievements under the Xianfeng Emperor

To re-establish the imperial power that was endangered by popular rebellions, some of the high-ranking mandarins launched a program of "self-strengthening" (*ziqiang*) aimed principally at building modern military potential. Their conceptions were inspired by Lin Ze-xu and Wei Yuan. Some of them (for example, Zuo Zong-tang, Hu Lin-yi, and Feng Gui-fen) worked with these two leaders, and some were linked with them through family ties (Shen Bao-zhen, for example, was Lin's son-in-law).

During the reign of the Xianfeng Emperor the "self-strengthening" policy took the form of a series of actions by officials in the provinces occupied by the Taiping. They spread the use of Western arms, and for several military operations they hired foreign steamers (see Chapter 5). Between 1853 and 1860 small arsenals and shipyards, managed by Zeng Guo-fan and Zuo Zong-tang, among others, were opened in Hunan and Jiangsu. But in spite of a few technical improvements in manufacturing, these enterprises were still too traditional in style to be able to meet the needs of the militia. As the campaigns advanced, the regional leaders became aware of the decisive importance of modern weapons. The high price of foreign arms was an incentive to try to make them at home. With this aim Zen Guo-fan created an arsenal at Anqing when he set up his headquarters there in 1861. Without a single foreign machine, his entirely Chinese personnel managed to copy Western models of firearms and ammunition; they even made a steamship. For technical and financial reasons, however, the production of the most modern arms got no further than the experimental stage.

The policy of *ziqiang*

The end of the second Opium War opened new prospects for the military industry, while the intensification of the struggle against the Taiping made the leaders draw up plans on a still larger scale. As Chapter 5 discussed, the policy of cooperation inaugurated by the foreign powers after the Peking agreements enabled the Manchu government to call on the West for considerable help. There was a growing conviction in official circles directly involved in the war, and also among those in contact with foreigners, that to maintain power, a minimum of techniques had to be borrowed from the West.

Feng Gui-fen (1808–1874) developed these ideas in 1861 in his *Personal Protests from the Study of Jiao-bin*. This was a collection of forty essays on the modernization of China covering such topics as government, finance, education, and foreign relations. The author, a scholar from Suzhou and a former assistant of Lin Ze-xu, was one of the gentry who organized the defense of Jiangsu against the Taiping. In 1861 he presented the manuscript to Zeng Guo-fan, who praised it highly. Owing to either modesty or prudence, however, Feng refused to have it published during his lifetime, so that the first edition was not issued until 1883. Copies of the manuscript were circulated during the Restoration, however, and inspired the statesmen of the time. Feng Gui-fen himself was able to apply some of his plans when he worked as an adviser in the private secretariat of Li Hong-zhang.

The ideas of Feng Gui-fen

Feng Gui-fen accepted the foreign presence in China and the treaties of Tientsin. He acknowledged that his country was from that time onward a part of the system of world politics and that it was impossible to return to isolation. His main concern was to prevent the situation from growing worse. He believed that it was essential to study the West in order to negotiate effectively with the foreigners instead of relying on interpreters, who were only "stupid and silly 'linguists.' " In addition, a modern military force had to be created by building more arsenals and shipyards with the help of foreign technicians.[2] "Only thus will we be able to pacify the empire; only thus can we play a leading role on the globe; and only thus shall we restore our original strength and redeem ourselves from former humiliations,"[3] Feng wrote.

Feng's ideas were contradictory on many points. Although he affirmed that "what we then have to learn from the barbarians is only the one thing, solid ships and effective guns," he emphasized the importance of studying science, particularly mathematics. He proposed that the traditional system of education should be remodeled, leaving plenty of room for scientific subjects. He demonstrated the economic advantages of mechanized industrial production, yet maintained that the cultivation of tea and silk "was the great source of prosperity" for China and that there was "no other way to enrich the country." He denounced the abuses of the monarchy, the growing distance between the people and the sovereign, and showed that in the West these failings were less pro-

[2] Extracts from Feng's book are given in document 1 at the chapter end.
[3] Ssu-yu Teng and John K. Fairbank, *China's Response to the West: A Documentary Survey, 1839–1923* (Cambridge, Mass., Harvard University Press, 1954; New York, Atheneum, 1963), p. 54.

nounced; he did not, however, suggest any political reforms. He had no desire to abandon "Chinese ethics and the principles of Confucius"; on the contrary, for him the study of the West was a way of restoring its former brilliance to the traditional civilization of China.

Feng Gui-fen's attitude toward the West was somewhat ambiguous. He wanted China to be able to make the machines it needed as quickly as possible, without help from abroad. He was outraged by the foreign invasion, but since he was looking merely for a way to "control the barbarians," not to repel them, he believed that trust and good faith were the best policy. The military strength he advocated was to be used to crush rebellions. As regards foreign policy, military power was merely an instrument of dissuasion, for "The bandits [Taiping] can be exterminated, but it is impossible to do so with the barbarians."

Characteristics of *ziqiang*

The aspect of Feng Gui-fen's thought which was put to fullest use by his contemporaries was his proposed policy of improving relations with Western countries and utilizing Western technology to defend the traditional state. They called this policy by a name borrowed from the *Classic of Changes*, which Feng had been the first to apply to problems of modernization: *ziqiang* (to strengthen oneself, or self-strengthening).

Ziqiang was advocated by Restoration officials first of all for reasons of domestic policy, to ensure the imperial camp's military superiority over the popular movements. The armaments industry they launched began to develop as soon as it became possible to secure foreign help. At first it consisted chiefly of fairly small factories in Jiangsu and Zhejiang, where action against the Taiping was concentrated. Between 1865 and 1867 the four major achievements under the reign of the Tongzhi Emperor were initiated: the Jiangnan, Nankang, Fuzhou, and Tientsin arsenals. Others were established later in most of the provincial capitals.

The first modern arsenals

While their experience on the battlefield convinced the provincial leaders of the virtues of modern weapons, it took the *coup d'état* of 1861 to bring men into the central government who were ready to produce these weapons, if necessary with the help of the Westerners themselves. In 1862 Prince Gong and Zeng Guo-fan explained to the throne the need for manufacturing the new weapons in China and for calling on foreign technicians to direct the work, at least temporarily. Zuo Zong-tang was the last of the regional officials to attempt production using Chinese engineers exclusively. In 1864 he commissioned them to build steamships in Hangzhou, and their failure obliged him to change his approach.

The provincial leaders began to organize small enterprises under the supervision of Western engineers. In 1862 Li Hong-zhang appointed Halliday Macartney, a former British army doctor, to recruit workmen and start manufacturing rifles and ammunition in the neighborhood of Songjiang. In the following year, when Li settled in Suzhou after the recapture of that town, he had the factory transferred there, enlarged it, and set up two more small arsenals.

The Jiangnan arsenal

The success of the Suzhou experiment was an encouragement to try building still larger enterprises. Zeng Guo-fan, who was disappointed by the results obtained at his arsenal at Anqing, sent a Chinese educated in America, Rong Hong (Yung Wing), to buy machinery abroad for a factory to be set up in Shanghai. In 1865 Li Hong-zhang was appointed governor-general of Liangzhang and consequently assumed direct control over the military installations in Jiangsu, including Shanghai. He gave Zeng considerable scope for the arsenal. Before the year was out, Li acquired shipyards and arsenals founded by foreigners in Shanghai and had the equipment from the two arsenals in Suzhou transferred there. The arrival of foreign machinery resulted in further expansion, and the enterprise became known as the Jiangnan arsenal. Zeng Guo-fan's primary purpose had been to establish a shipyard, but the campaigns against the Nian made it necessary to give priority to manufacturing rifles and ammunition. In 1867 the shipyard project was taken up again, and in the following year the first gunboat left the yard. Several ships were built, but production fell in 1875, and only one was launched between then and 1885. Only three out of the total number were large vessels.

The other work of the arsenal was booming, however. In 1875 the Jiangnan arsenal was one of the largest in the world and growing steadily larger. It had repair ships, mechanical engineering works, depots, a shipyard, arms and ammunition factories, a translating department, cartographers' offices, and a language school. It was also responsible for importing arms from abroad. A trusted assistant of Li Hong-zhang, the Shanghai customs superintendent Ding Ri-chang, directed the enterprise, with eight foreign engineers under his command. In 1890 over two thousand workmen were employed there. The building costs had amounted to 540,000 taels; the upkeep, paid out of the revenues of the Shanghai customs, was 300,000 to 600,000 taels per year.

The Nanking arsenal

When he assumed the post of governor-general in 1865, Li Hong-zhang had the Suzhou arsenal run by Macartney transferred to Nanking. Although the Nanking arsenal, which made only arms, was a smaller operation than the Jiangnan works, its production was more varied and its weapons were technically superior. It supplied the equipment of the Huai army. When Li Hong-zhang became governor-general of Zhili in 1870, he called on Macartney to equip the Dagu forts with guns. But the cannons made by the arsenal exploded, killing two soldiers, and Li had to accept the resignation of his British adviser. This unpromising start, combined with the fact that Li was too far away for effective supervision, prevented the arsenal from progressing as well as that of Jiangnan.

The Fuzhou arsenal

The Fuzhou arsenal was founded in 1866 by Zuo Zong-tang.[4] After the failure of his shipyard at Hangzhou in 1864, two French officers, d'Aiguebelle and Giquel, suggested that they be put in charge of building steamships like the French ones. Zuo asked them to draw up a plan, which he submitted to the throne. Imperial approval was granted on July 14, 1866. In October Zuo was ordered to leave for Shenxi to suppress the Moslem rebellion. He arranged for Shen Bao-zhen, the son-in-law of Lin Ze-xu, to direct the work and left several trusted subordinates as assistants. Zuo, d'Aiguebelle, and Giquel also drew up a plan for future production projects. As soon as the arsenal had been completed, it was to build

4 Zuo's reasons for creating it are given in document 2.

two 150-horsepower steamships and five 80-horsepower steamships on a budget of 3 million taels provided by the Fujian customs, all in the space of five years.

The original installations covered about 20 hectares at the mouth of the Min River; they were enlarged several times and by 1874 covered 47 hectares. Besides the docks, yards, and workshops used for shipbuilding, they contained an arms and ammunition factory, metalworks producing laminated iron, a translation department, and a school where French, English, mathematics, drawing, and navigation were taught. In 1874 two thousand Chinese and fifty-two Europeans were employed there. But most of the equipment was imported from France; even the ships' engines were second-hand French ones, whereas Giquel had promised to make them in China. Work began in January 1868. By July 1874, 5,356,948 taels had been spent; fifteen ships, including one with 250 horsepower, had left the yard. The establishment had become larger than planned, but it had proved impossible to abide by the five-year plan. The cost of each ship was several times more than the price of foreign vessels which could be bought in China. However, the quality was slightly better, although it did not come up to that of the good Western warships.

The Tientsin arsenal

The creation of the arsenals at Jiangnan, Nanking, and Fuzhou provoked fears at court that the Chinese mandarins would arrogate too much power to themselves in the South. A Manchu dignitary, Chong-hou, was given orders to establish an arsenal at Tientsin. It was opened in 1867, with an Englishman, Meadows, as technical director. But it remained a mediocre powder factory until Li Hong-zhang, who became governor of Zhili in 1870, took charge. Li dismissed Meadows, increased the number of foreign machines and technicians, enlarged the plant, and expanded production. The arsenal made rifles as well as ammunition, and it had a technical training department. Like the Jiangnan arsenal, it also imported foreign arms.

Small provincial arsenals

The difficulties involved in transporting arms and the desire of local authorities to "strengthen" their own power led to the creation

of many small arsenals in the various provinces where rel
broken out. In 1869 Zuo Zong-tang opened an arms
Sian, later transferring it to Lanzhou. An arsenal was als
Yunnan. Both of these closed down after the end of mili
tions. Others were set up in Shandong, Canton, Fujian, ..., ...
Sichuan for varying lengths of time. The arsenal in Hubei, which
expanded considerably after 1889 with the help of Zhang Zhi-dong,
was the only one of any importance.

Aims behind the military industries

The effort to develop military industries has given rise to many
controversies among historians concerning both the aims and the
economic and social consequences involved. As regards the aims,
a distinction should be made between the intentions and the reality.
In the minds of their founders, the four great arsenals of the reign
of the Tongzhi Emperor were not intended solely to serve the
armies that were busy repressing the popular rebellions. They were
also intended to enable China to resist the foreigners. They were
created after the crushing of the Taiping rebellion, the most dangerous of all for the Manchu power, and reflected a determination
to achieve national recovery not only at home, but also in foreign
relations.

This accounted for the emphasis on building a navy, though its
usefulness was slight in terms of fighting the Nian and the Moslems
in regions far inland. Zeng Guo-fan wrote in 1865: "Obviously
rifles are important and there is an urgent need for them, but
steamships are just as important and must be built as quickly as
possible. This achievement will show the foreigners that we are
strengthening ourselves and will bolster the morale of our compatriots."[5]

As document 2 demonstrates, Zuo Zong-tang considered resistance to the foreigners from an economic as well as a military point
of view. Li Hong-zhang went further still, praising the economic
and social progress introduced by mechanized production. Speaking of the machinery he had ordered for the Jiangnan arsenal, he
wrote in 1865: "These foreign machines can also build machines
for ploughing, weaving, printing, and making pottery. All these

[5] The citations from Restoration leaders given in this section come from *Zeng
Wen-zheng gong shuzha*, 25/15 b and 10/5 b-6; *Li Wen-chong gong quanji, zougao*,
9/34 b.

things improve the standard of living of the people and are for everyday use. These machines are not only for producing arms and ammunition. The admirable thing about these machines is that they lessen human work and the consumption of raw materials, using the energy of fire and water."

However, the argument that mechanization contributed to general progress was rarely used by the supporters of *ziqiang*. Their main theme was the defense of national interests against Western penetration by the development of military industries. Moreover, the court doubtless hoped that fear of new Chinese power would limit the Western demands when the treaties were next revised. But the possibility of using the military potential to drive out the Westerners was not envisioned either by the court or by Li Hong-zhang, Zeng Guo-fan or Zuo Zong-tang. Zeng summarized their strategy in these terms: "To begin with we must keep our distance from the foreigners, but then we must approach them." Thus the growth of military power was conceived of as a temporary measure to prevent the foreigners from further encroachment until the restoration of national prestige enabled friendly relations to be established on an equal footing.

Political effects

However, the arms industry created by the supporters of *ziqiang* did not have the slightest deterrent effect on foreign activity in China. The industry was born of the wars of repression against the popular movements, and until 1884 its essential task was to supply the armies fighting the rebels. Actually, nothing favored foreign penetration more than the maintenance of order.

Furthermore, modern arms strengthened the authority of the provincial leaders far more than they did that of the central government, with whom the foreign powers were dealing. Three of the principal arsenals were directly controlled by Li Hong-zhang and administered by his trusted assistants; after the death of Zeng Guo-fan their output served almost exclusively to equip Li's troops. Each time he took a new government post, he was careful to set up a large arsenal nearby, and he retained close control over those which he could not move. Meanwhile Zuo Zong-tang managed to remain master of the Fuzhou arsenal. Each man acted only on his own account; the refusal of the regional leaders to cooperate among themselves was one of the causes of the Chinese defeat in the Sino-French War.

The dependence of the armaments industry on provincial leaders who were in constant rivalry with one another enabled the foreigners to establish tutelage over the new arsenals and to profit from their development. Li Hong-zhang's works used British technicians and machinery; France supplied Zuo Zong-tang with the equipment and staff he needed at Fuzhou. In 1862 Zeng Guo-fan boasted that within two years China would be able to dispense with foreign engineers. But except in small arsenals like the one at Lanzhou, Western cooperation was still necessary. One reason was that men capable of replacing the Western technical directors had not been trained. In addition, once it had been decided to copy foreign models, the founders of the arsenals felt that only Westerners were capable of keeping pace with the constant improvements in European military technology. Thus constraints were imposed both by the foreign model and by the presence of foreign experts, who were usually scornful of local techniques and resources. As a result the factories came to import not only machinery but also the raw materials needed for production. Meanwhile imports of foreign-made arms did not lessen, so that the *ziqiang* worsened the trade deficit. To pay the bills, the provincial leaders had to turn more and more to loans from abroad: between 1867 and 1881 Zuo Zong-tang borrowed a total of 15,750,000 taels in five loans. The growth of Chinese military potential was thus entirely dependent on foreigners. It was profitable business for the big arms manufacturers, such as Armstrong, Krupp, and Schneider, but when the time came, their governments could limit or cut off supplies and so had the Chinese army at their mercy. Many factors contributed to the technical backwardness of the Chinese arsenals, among which were the outdated equipment sold them by Westerners and the hollow promises made by foreign directors. For in spite of the foreigners' assurances, no complicated machinery was manufactured in China.

Only one aim of *ziqiang* was achieved: the equipping of troops sent against the rebels. The other—to create a force which could discourage threats from abroad—was not pursued seriously. Instead of ensuring China's independence of foreigners, the arms industry relied on them. This fact adversely affected the social and economic results of *ziqiang*.

Social and economic effects

The chief merit of the modern arsenals was that they introduced mechanized production in China. But the technical revolution which they brought about was extremely limited, because there were so few machines that many operations were still carried out by hand. Working conditions in the arsenals were not radically different from those of the specialized workers and apprentices in the big potteries and silk factories, except that the arsenal employees were not under the control of the corporations.

At the Jiangnan arsenal in 1867, workers were paid between 0.1 and 0.2 Chinese dollars a day—four to eight times as much as the agricultural workers and coolies in the region. The arsenal workers' wages were paid to them directly, and they were supposed to work only eight hours a day. Conditions were not so liberal elsewhere; in Nanking they worked eleven hours a day, in Tientsin eleven and a half. But those workers had a day off every fortnight, a practice which was completely unknown in traditional industries. Although they were a small group, numbering between 5,000 and 6,000 in 1872, the arsenal workers can be considered as the beginning of a Chinese working class supervised by Chinese employers. Most of them were from the provinces of Guangdong, Jiangsu, and Zhejiang, where they had been employed in building and repair workshops set up by foreigners in the ports, particularly in Hong Kong. When Zuo Zong-tang established the arsenal of Lanzhou in 1872, he had workers brought from Canton, for they were famous for their skill. Not all the workers had had previous experience in foreign workshops, however. The development of the armament industries contributed to a gradual rise in the technical level of Chinese manpower.

Ziqiang did not result in the emergence of a bourgeoisie alongside the proletariat. The arsenals, which required an investment of more than 32,000,000 taels between 1865 and 1885, were financed entirely by the state, mainly out of revenue from the customs and the *lijin*. About 27,500,000 of the government's investment went to the four big arsenals, so that those plants absorbed an average of 2.2 percent of the annual state budget. (In Japan at the same time, 13 percent of the budget was devoted to industrialization.) And an injection of capital into a field as sterile as armaments brought no economic benefit. Since the raw materials were imported, the creation of arsenals did not stimulate the development of subsidiary industries, or at least, not until 1875. Since output was low, and the state maintained an absolute monopoly over production and sales, a fruitful arms trade could not develop. Lastly, the management of the arsenals had nothing in common with the administration of a modern enterprise; it was a traditional bureaucratic system in which the notion of profitability was barely taken into account. It suffered from the same ills as the rest of the imperial administration. Corruption and embezzlement enabled some officials to amass large fortunes. And these abuses prevented the introduction of new methods of administration and accounting and contributed to the growing deficits and inefficiency of the arsenals.

Intellectual aspects of *ziqiang*

In view of the backwardness of the entire Chinese economy and the bureaucratic nature of the arsenals, the industrialization linked with *ziqiang* was unlikely to generate new ideas or new ways of thinking. For the Restoration statesmen, the self-strengthening policy involved nothing more than borrowing techniques from the West, mainly techniques for making rifles, cannons, and ships.

The approach characteristic of their attitudes is illustrated in their creation of the first modern Chinese school, the Tong Wen Guan (literally Translation Office, though it was in fact a language school). It was founded in Peking in 1862, at the request of Prince Gong and Wen-xiang, to train the interpreters needed by the Zongli Yamen. At first the school taught languages alone—English, Russian, and French—as the techniques needed to ensure the smooth working of diplomacy. A similar institution was opened in Shanghai in 1863 (it later became the school connected with the Jiangnan arsenal), and another in Canton the following year. In 1867 Prince Gong had a scientific department added to the Peking school in order to educate the engineers needed by the arsenals.[6] Li Shan-lan was invited there to teach mathematics, Xu Ji-yu (see Chapter 3) became director, and W. A. P. Martin, an American missionary recommended by Hart, headed the institution. The students, who went on to join the civil service, still spent more than half their time on traditional Chinese studies. The schools connected with the Jiangnan and Fuzhou arsenals were of the same type; the "Western knowledge" (*xixue*) taught there was confined to technical and language studies. One of the most outstanding thinkers of modern China, Yan Fu (1853–1921), was educated at the Fuzhou arsenal school from 1867 to 1876. By and large, however, these schools offered a mediocre education to a few dozen technicians each year, so they had a very limited influence.

The translation offices attached to the Jiangnan and Fuzhou ar-

---

[6] Wo-ren's arguments against teaching science in the school appear in document 3.

senals were more important. They produced Chinese editions of a considerable number of scientific works, which aroused interest and curiosity in scholarly circles. Among the forerunners of this awakening to scientific subjects were Hua Heng-fang and Xu Shou, two scholars from Wuxu who had begun to hold gatherings with their friends around 1850 to carry out experiments and study mathematics, physics, and chemistry. Zeng Guo-fan heard about the scholars and invited them to Nanking in 1864. Later they founded and ran the translation office of the Jiangnan arsenal with the help of an American missionary, John Fryer, who also designed and built boats.

From *Ziqiang* to *Fuqiang*

The industrialization linked with *ziqiang*, or self-strengthening, was not the only economic change to occur in the years following the Peking conventions and the crushing of the Taiping. For in spite of the efforts of the Restoration leaders to achieve *fuqiang*, or wealth and power, the traditional economy represented by agriculture and handicrafts began to disintegrate. In some agricultural sectors commercialization developed, making room for a new type of production and enabling the merchants to amass some capital. These modifications were the result of both the advance of Western penetration and the upheavals in the countryside arising from the popular movements.

Decline of the handicraft industry

In the rural districts, the chief phenomenon was the tendency toward the dissociation of agriculture and family handicraft production. The Chinese rural economy had been founded on the close association between the two. Now the peasants still made what they needed for themselves, but in many places they gradually gave up producing goods to sell.

Textile manufacturing, by far the most important of the handicraft industries, was the earliest victim. First, foreign yarns replaced local yarns and thus broke the link between the crafts of spinning and weaving. Then foreign cotton fabrics supplanted locally made fabrics, breaking the connection between weaving and agriculture. This was the beginning of a trend resulting from a decline in the manufacturing costs of foreign products. With mechanization came great leaps in productivity, so that the cost of making British cotton fabrics fell by 80 percent between 1850 and 1870. In addition, the opening of the Suez Canal in 1869 cut the cost of transportation between Europe and China. In 1871 the introduction of telegraph service between Shanghai, Hong Kong, and London accelerated the circulation of trade news.

During the same period the price of Chinese raw cotton rose, owing to an increase in demand. Exports of American cotton had been cut off by the Civil War, and British factories bought their supplies in India, where a textile industry was also developing. India consequently had less surplus cotton to dispose of in the Far East. Suddenly Chinese cotton had no competition on the home market, and it could command good prices from the new Japanese textile industry. China, which until then had imported cotton, now began to export it at the expense of the handicraft industry at home. The domestic price of raw cotton did not fall, whereas increasing foreign competition pushed down the price of finished goods. As a result the profits of Chinese craftsmen tended to disappear completely.

Between 1867 and 1885 China's annual imports of yarn rose from 33,000 to 387,000 piculs. Before 1860, imports of foreign yarn had brought local production to a halt only in the neighborhoods of Canton and Shanghai. Between 1860 and 1885 the phenomenon spread through the coastal provinces as far as Shandong and the middle Yangzi basin. In most cases, however, the peasants went on spinning to meet their own personal needs.

The ruin of the handicraft industry in weaving, which began in the 1870s, was a slower and a more varied process. It first became apparent in the areas around some of the open ports—Ningbo and Niuzhuang, for example. But in regions with a long handicraft tradition, the use of foreign yarns brought rapid expansion as the peasants who could no longer spin turned to weaving. With rising production the price of local woven cloth fell, until it was often cheaper and higher in quality than imported cloth. Exports increased four times over between 1872 and 1885. Weaving became an entirely commercial process in many areas: around Nantong in Jiangsu, in the Shashi region of Hubei, at Foshan and Xinning in Guangdong, in the neighborhood of Chongqing and Leshuan in Sichuan, at Xingyi in Guizhou, and at Gaoyang and Baochi in Zhili. The peasants who did the weaving were dependent on the town not only as a place for selling their goods, but also as a supply center where they bought raw materials. These changes were not the result of natural evolution in the home weaving industry; they were imposed by the pressure of Western capitalism, and they made the industry dependent on the West.

The growing diversity of imports from 1860 on affected other branches of the handicraft industry. Along the coast, Chinese iron was replaced by lower-cost, higher-quality foreign iron. The great traditional center of the metal handicraft industry also suffered. Wuhu in Hunan had fourteen forges in the period 1850–1860, but after 1880 only one was left. By 1870 the market for the Shanxi forges was confined to the Northern provinces, and many had had to close down. Paraffin, which was two or three times cheaper than vegetable oils, began to replace them for lighting; in 1884 Zhang Zhi-dong lamented the decline of the Sichuan oil mills. In many sectors imported products were in competition with local products, and the handicraft industry was surviving only by cutting wages to the basic minimum and increasing working hours to the limits of human endurance.

In contrast, the production of goods which were Chinese specialties, or which were linked with national customs, continued and prospered. These included porcelain, fans, firecrackers, paper money for the dead, bamboo tools, drugs and medicines, lacquer ware, agricultural tools, tinware, and copper ware. Some sectors which were already fairly well commercialized also prospered and developed further. Between 1860 and 1885 this was the case for the silk and tea industries in particular. Their progress was stimulated by the expansion of foreign trade, although such progress meant that they had to share in the fluctuations of the world market.

Specialized and commercialized agriculture

As a result of the dislocation of the traditional rural economy and of China's participation in international trade, specialized and commercialized agriculture began to appear in some localities. The rise in the cotton prices offered in foreign markets led peasants to plant more land to cotton, not only in cotton-growing regions but also in areas where it had never before been cropped. By 1876 cotton covered eight-tenths of the cultivated land southeast of Shanghai; on the northern bank of the Yangzi it had spread from Nantong and Rugao as far as Suqian. It was on the increase in

Henan, Shanxi, and Shenxi. In 1884 cotton was the only crop of some districts in Hubei and Jiangxi.

For similar reasons silkworm culture also spread. Some parts of Zhejiang which were resettled after the Taiping rebellion were turned over to it entirely. Areas in Hubei, Anhui, Jiangxi, Guangxi, Guangdong, Zhili, Shanxi, and Henan concentrated on growing mulberry trees and silkworms.

In Hunan, North Jiangxi, and East Anhui tobacco was raised in increasingly large quantities for home consumption, which was rising, and for export. Opium growing, which had been introduced in Yunnan during the reign of the Daoguang Emperor, spread to Sichuan, from there to Gansu and Guizhou, then to Shenxi, the Northeast, and Shanxi. In 1882 it was the main crop in more than twenty districts of Shanxi, and it was grown in quantity in the rest, where it replaced food crops. In Jiangsu and Zhejiang the opium centers were Xuzhou and Taizhou, which no longer produced their own food. When all went well, trade between these regions and other provinces was brisk. But the peasants were highly vulnerable both to local natural disasters and to bad crops in the provinces which supplied them with grain.

The area planted to tea varied with fluctuations in the export market. Until 1880 the expansion of tea growing was rapid; then competition from India and Ceylon slowed down Chinese exports and led to a gradual reduction in the land devoted to tea. These changes can be traced clearly in the economic history of the Yangkou neighborhood in northwest Fujian. Between 1851 and 1880 prices were steady and 100 pounds of tea fetched over 20 taels. There was a rush to plant tea, until the hills were covered with it right up to their summits; peasants migrated there from as far away as Jiangxi and Guangdong. After 1881, however, prices fell. The best quality of tea sold for 7 to 9 taels less, the poorer quality for 3 to 5 taels less. It was no longer possible to live off tea. With varying degrees of success, craftsmen and peasants looked for other ways to supplement their resources. Grain became profitable once more; only peasants who produced enough grain to be self-sufficient continued to grow tea. After 1883 no more tea was planted, so that by 1887 eight-tenths of the hills lay fallow.

Owing to heavy taxation and archaic farming methods, Chinese tea was not in a favorable competitive position in world markets. Even so, over most of the period under consideration here the main phenomenon was the extension of the tea-growing areas in Fujian,

Hunan, Hubei, and Anhui. Moreover, vast plantations of a capitalist type appeared in some places. At Qimen in Anhui, a local landowner planted over 300 hectares to tea between 1851 and 1861. The slump in green tea sales in 1875 and 1876 led him to study methods for processing black tea. Then he raised 60,000 silver dollars, opened a processing factory, and converted the neighboring producers to the new technique. In this way he not only improved his own position but stimulated regional development.

The growth of specialized agriculture and the development of the open ports into urban centers encouraged the grain trade. An increasing number of regions were no longer self-sufficient in food production, so that domestic trade covered longer distances and involved larger quantities than before. Rice—more than 2 million tons a year—was sent from Hubei and Hunan to Jiangsu and Zhejiang, mainly via Hankou. Grain from Anhui and Henan was transported via Wuhu to Zhejiang, Fujian, and Guangdong.

In summary, the ups and down of the family handicraft industry, and the evolution of agriculture toward specialization and commercialization, gradually destroyed the balance of the traditional economy and turned the country districts toward a market economy. The Chinese peasant was no longer dependent on his local market alone, but also on the national and even the world market. These transformations resulted for the most part from foreign economic penetration. Thus the home market which was gradually forming was to a large extent a colonial market. Yet this market provided one of the main conditions necessary for the development of capitalist enterprises: cheap labor, supplied by the ruined peasants and craftsmen. There was now a possibility of amassing large amounts of money and concentrating wealth for capital investment.

Officials and merchants accumulate capital

A fraction of the bourgeoisie became rich on the spoils of war, misappropriations of military funds and the *lijin*, and speculation. Meanwhile the merchant class in general benefited from the increase in commerce at home. Traders in tea, silk, cotton, opium, wheat, and rice prospered, especially in the coastal and Yangzi valley provinces. Those who gained most of all were the compradors. They profited directly from the expansion of foreign trade after the restoration of peace, from the new privileges obtained by the foreigners in 1860, and from the rise of industry in the West. Between 1864 and 1875, the volume of this trade was 110 to 140 million customs taels a year; between 1876 and 1887, it was 140 to 190 million. Yet in 1865 legal commerce (excluding opium smuggling), which until then had shown a surplus, showed a deficit; from 1876 on, the deficit became permanent and increased. The wealth accumulated by the compradors therefore made a large hole in national resources.

Compradors generally invested in businesses with a high rate of interest: moneylending, real estate, banks, and traditional exchange offices. After 1860, attracted by high profits and apparent solidity, comprador money began flowing into Western enterprises in China. Between 1864 and 1871 five new foreign insurance companies were founded in Shanghai and Hong Kong. All (with the possible exception of one case where the documents are not explicit) had Chinese shareholders and Chinese directors. So did the Hong Kong and Shanghai Bank. All the directors of the Ewo Bank (1864–1867), founded by Jardine & Matheson, were Chinese. Many foreign banks opened after 1865, and all absorbed Chinese capital. The coastal navigation companies, wharves and warehouses, and shipyards also attracted Chinese shareholders.

Chinese money was invested in industry as well. In 1868 some Englishmen started an oil mill at Niuzhuang; a sugar refinery was opened in 1869 at Huangpu, and another in Hong Kong. Two years later, an American merchant founded a textile mill in Canton. Official opposition forced all these factories (except for the sugar refinery in Hong Kong) to close down fairly rapidly, but it is a significant fact that they were mainly financed by Chinese. In many foreign enterprises Chinese capital was now in the majority. The powers granted to the Chinese in the management of these firms encouraged more Chinese investments. By 1870, not only compradors but also merchants, senior officials, and even small shareholders invested their money in foreign businesses.

Criticism of the armaments industry

The contrast between the substantial profits earned by Western enterprises and the deficits run up by the mandarin-sponsored arsenals was striking. The management and even the usefulness of the arsenals came in for violent criticism, and in 1872 the Grand Council demanded that the Fuzhou and Jiangnan arsenals be closed down. The Western threat had shifted from the military to the economic field, now that the foreigners were opening mines and setting up firms in China outside the open ports.

The *ziqiang* movement was powerless against these new developments. Arms manufacture appeared less urgent once the great rebellions had been crushed, and with the foreign example before them, Li Hong-zhang, Zuo Zong-tang, and their friends realized how profitable nonmilitary enterprises could be. But since they wished to maintain the armaments industries which were the mainstay of their power, they decided to establish nonmilitary enterprises that could procure the raw materials and the funds necessary to operate their arsenals. To their goal of self-strengthening they added that of "enrichment" (*qiu fu*). They aimed to make China rise to "wealth and power" (*fuqiang*), as Li Hong-zhang wrote in 1872.

Thus the second phase of the *yangwu* movement was inaugurated. The mandarins intended to draw on the wealth and technical competence of the merchants to set up the new enterprises, though they planned to impose their own by no means disinterested control on the management. Actually, after 1872 the *yangwu* movement had wider support than the officials alone; it had won followers among the compradors, the merchants, and the scholar-landowners. Of course, it was the opening of new markets, the accumulation and concentration of wealth, and the foreign economic challenge— the same factors that had led to the reorientation of official policy —that also drove the merchants to look for new profits. They tried to free themselves of Western tutelage in order to create their own modern enterprises, and they were reticent when approached by the officials. The similarities—and the rivalry—between public and private enterprise left their mark on the entire second phase of the *yangwu* movement.

Fuqiang: The Appearance of Modern Enterprises (1872–1885)

The China Merchants' Steam Navigation Company

The second phase of the *yangwu* movement began with the founding of the China Merchants' Steam Navigation Company in

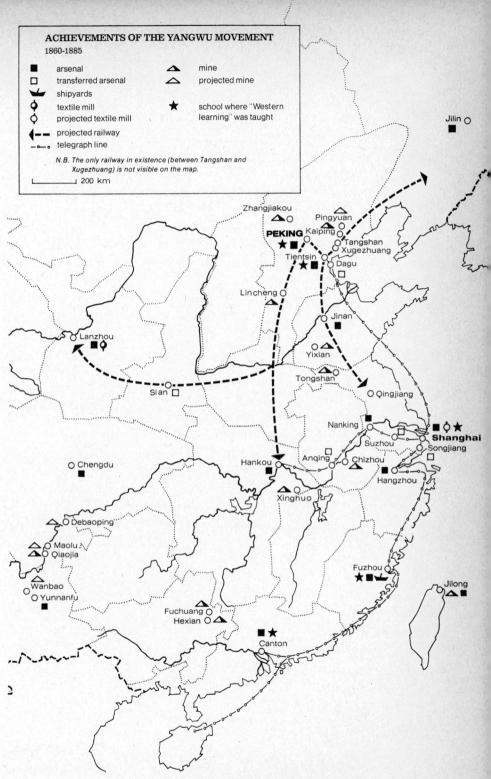

ACHIEVEMENTS OF THE YANGWU MOVEMENT
1860-1885

- ■ arsenal
- □ transferred arsenal
- ⛟ shipyards
- ⚲ textile mill
- ○ projected textile mill
- ◀--- projected railway
- –•–○ telegraph line

- △ mine
- △ projected mine

- ★ school where "Western learning" was taught

N.B. The only railway in existence (between Tangshan and
Xugezhuang) is not visible on the map.

⊢——————⊣ 200 km

Jilin

Zhangjiakou
Pingyuan
PEKING Kaiping
Tientsin Tangshan
Xugezhuang
Dagu

Lincheng

Lanzhou
Jinan

Yixian

Tongshan

Sian Qingjiang

Nanking Shanghai
Suzhou Songjiang
Chengdu Hankou Anqing Chizhou
Hangzhou

Xinghuo

Debaoping

Maolu
Qiaojia
Fuzhou

Wanbao Jilong
Yunnanfu

Fuchuang
Hexian

Canton

1872. Earlier, Feng Gui-fen had recommended in 1860 that a Chinese merchant navy of steamships be formed. During the following years the authorities became worried about the effects of foreign competition on the fleet of coastal junks, which shrank from 2,000 in the decade 1850–1860 to 400 in 1870. In 1867 Ding Ri-chang and Rong Hong submitted a draft of regulations for a Chinese steam navigation company. The Zongli Yamen gave its agreement, but nothing further happened. The following year, a junk owner proposed to Zeng Guo-fan that an association of merchants be formed to transport the grain tribute by steamship. Zeng refused.

To put an end to the attacks of a fraction of the bureaucracy on the Fuzhou and Jiangnan arsenals, the Zongli Yamen proposed in 1871 to encourage merchants to hire or buy the boats built there. Zuo Zong-tang did not commit himself, but Zeng Guo-fan and Li Hong-zhang approved of the idea. Li suggested that the merchants should be guaranteed a portion of the grain transport business as an inducement to take part in the operation. He got his assistants to draw up regulations for a navigation company, which was to take the form of an official office (*guanju*) established with the financial participation of the state as well as the merchants. It was to be granted a contract for 20 percent of the sea transport of the tribute. The technical responsibilities were to be delegated to the merchants, who would be supervised by appointed officials. In a letter written in December 1872, Li applied the term *guan du shang ban* (government supervision and merchant operation) to the system, which was inspired by the salt-tax administration. It became the model imitated by almost all enterprises later created by the authorities.

The original idea was to gather as many private contributions as possible and invest a minimum of public funds, but in fact, large official subsidies had to be granted before the enterprise was able to attract merchant capital. The power of decision lay with the officials, who delegated the day-to-day management to merchants. Until 1885 the officials retained control through the financial participation of the state, not through their personal investments.

At the end of 1872 Zhu Qi-ang, a junk owner who was also prefect and grain tribute commissioner of Zhejiang, was asked by Li Hong-zhang to launch the company and recruit shareholders among the merchants. The necessary capital was fixed at 130,000 taels. Zhu found investors, mostly among the traditional merchants, who subscribed a total of 120,000 taels, but they actually paid in only 10,000 taels. He appealed in vain to the big compradors like Hu Guang-yong, who had many connections in business circles linked with the foreigners. Li Hong-zhang had to give Zhu permission to borrow 135,000 taels at 7 percent interest from the Zhili military treasury. The company bought three ships as well as land and warehouses at Tientsin and Shanghai, and work began in January 1873. Its financial situation became stable six months later when Li Hong-zhang managed to persuade two rich compradors, Tang Ting-shu and Xu Run, to become director and assistant director. Tang was the comprador of the British firm Jardine & Matheson in Shanghai. Xu had once held the same post but for six years had been in business for himself, dealing in tea, silk, and real estate. Both men were natives of Guangdong and managed to attract investors from Cantonese business circles, which were the richest groups in China's merchant community.

Under their administration, which lasted until 1884, the company expanded rapidly. In 1876 it had twelve ships, and in 1877, after it purchased the Shanghai Steam Navigation Company (an American firm), it had thirty. Its contract for the transport of the tribute was extended to 40 and then to 60 percent. Ordinary freight and passengers eventually brought the company its biggest profits, particularly as in 1877 it obtained a monopoly over the transport of both government and duty-free cargoes. Its headquarters were in Shanghai, with branch offices in Tientsin, Hong Kong, Hankou, and Shantou. It carried traffic on the Yangzi as far as Yichang and along the coast from Macao to Tientsin, and a brief attempt was even made in 1880–1881 to establish a route to Europe and America.

By 1877 the China Merchants' had shares worth 750,000 taels. Two-thirds of them were held by Xu Run. Government funds invested in the company totaled 1,928,000 taels in the form of loans granted by the provinces under the influence of Li Hong-zhang. Li appointed all the senior staff members and maintained absolute control over them.[7] Together with the compradors Tang Ting-shu and Xu Run, who represented the "merchant" interests, Li appointed Zhu Qi-ang and Sheng Xuan-huai as assistant directors representing the bureaucracy. Zhu, who was in charge of organizing the tribute transport, on which he earned a percentage, did the job of an official rather than a merchant. Sheng Xuan-huai (1844–

---

[7] A practice criticized by Xue Fu-cheng. See document 4.

1916), who came from a family of scholar-officials in Jiangsu, had passed his district examinations but failed in the provincial examinations. In 1870 he entered the service of Li Hong-zhang to look after the army commissariat and quickly became Li's confidential agent in economic affairs. Sheng's rise to influence in the China Merchants' represented the interests of the bureaucracy and coincided with the decline in the power of the merchants. In 1884 he had Tang and Xu dismissed for misappropriation of funds; in August 1885 he was appointed general manager, a post which he held until 1902.

The China Merchants' brought in large revenues, and those who profited most were the small group of officials and merchants in direct control of the company. Shareholders were paid a fixed interest of 10 percent. The directors and administrators shared in the dividends but drew their largest profits from misappropriation of funds. This took the form either of shamelessly using company money as their own, or of investing company profits in other enterprises organized under the patronage of Li Hong-zhang, and then pocketing the interest.

The profits of the China Merchants' were not channeled into the Fuzhou and Jiangnan arsenals, because it quickly became obvious that their warships could not be used as trading vessels, and the arsenals made no attempt to build a merchant navy. The company did contribute to the upkeep of Li Hong-zhang's troops. Also, a very small part of the profits was reinvested in the enterprise. The China Merchants' paid twice what the American company, bought in 1877, was worth, financing the purchase through a loan which burdened the budget. The mandarins who controlled management were interested in immediate revenues and did not think in terms of building up the business. The China Merchants' was not vigorous enough to challenge the foreign domination of Chinese maritime trade. On the other hand, the foreign lines which until then had been rivals joined forces to obstruct the newcomer. They gained from a tariff agreement concluded with the China Merchants' in 1877, for the stability of prices enabled them to increase their business and their capital. The victims of the China Merchants' were more often the private companies of Chinese merchants.

Rather than overhauling its management, the China Merchants' boosted declining profits by extending its privileges in fields like the transport of state cargoes, where the competition was Chinese, not foreign. As document 4 describes, the company eventually had a kind of monopoly. When a rich merchant, Ye Cheng-zhong, asked permission in 1882 to found a large maritime transport firm, Li Hong-zhang refused it. Several similar plans were also turned down.

When it was founded, the China Merchants' fulfilled to a certain extent a need on the part of the merchants who wanted to create new enterprises. The role played by Zhu Qi-ang, and later by Tang Ting-shu and Xu Run, bears this out. But its usefulness in stimulating private enterprise grew less clear when, with the departure of Xu Run and Tang Ting-shu, most of the merchant capital was withdrawn from the company and it became totally dependent on the bureaucracy.

Mines

The mines were developed to meet the needs of the armaments industry and steam navigation, as well as to forestall the foreigners who were demanding the right to open mines on Chinese territory. In 1868 Zeng Guo-fan and Li Hong-zhang tried unsuccessfully to mine local coal for the Jiangnan arsenal. The creation of the China Merchants' gave fresh impetus to these attempts, not only because its ships needed fuel, but because coal from the North could provide a return cargo for ships carrying the grain tribute. In 1874 Li Hong-zhang engaged a British engineer and bought the necessary material for mining iron and coal at Cizhou in Zhili. The site was quickly abandoned because of technical difficulties.

In 1877 Li had the machinery transferred to Kaiping, where large deposits of coal and iron had been found. He put Tang Ting-shu in charge of organizing the operation, which he called the Kaiping Mining Company. The authorities had at first considered making it into a government enterprise combining the extraction of ore and the production of pig iron. But since public funds were lacking, the plans for a blast furnace were abandoned and Li turned to private capital. Out of the 800,000 taels which Tang Ting-shu was supposed to get together in 1878, only 270,000 taels were paid in, mostly by members of Li's entourage. Like the China Merchants', the enterprise was organized on the "government supervision and merchant operation" system. Production began in 1881 with an output of 500 to 600 tons of coal a day, which became 600 to 700 tons a day during the following year. The mine supplied the China Merchants' and the Tientsin arsenal first of all; the surplus was then put on the market. Imports of foreign coal in

Tientsin fell appreciably, and the Kaiping Mining Company brought in substantial profits.

In 1875 the Fuzhou arsenal engaged a British engineer to begin mining the Jilong coal deposits on the island of Taiwan. The mine was financed by the arsenal at 100,000 taels per year and was entirely government-controlled. In 1881 it employed over 1,000 workers and had an output of 54,000 tons per year, most of which was used by the arsenal and its ships.

About ten more coal mines were opened by the authorities between 1876 and 1885, all on the *guan du shang ban* system. With the exception of those at Tongshan, which had been founded by Zuo Zong-tang, and those in Guangxi, they were all under the control of Li Hong-zhang. The same was true of the lead mines in the neighborhood of Zhangjiakou (1877) and the lead and copper mines of Pingquan (1881), which supplied the Tientsin arsenal. Most of the operations were very small, used little or no machinery, and made scarcely any profit. Their novelty lay in the method of capitalization, since it was composed of shares subscribed mainly in Shanghai.

Private mines did develop, but they had great difficulty in getting beyond the stage of a handicraft industry. Archaic methods were used to extract coal in Anhui and Hubei, silver in Guangdong and Jehol, copper in Zhili, and lead in Fujian. The mines operated under the constant threat of having to close down from lack of the capital to finance the work that was necessary when a vein was exhausted.

The textile industry

Competition between official and private enterprise was still keen in the textile industry. In 1878 Zuo Zong-tang, taking advantage of the low price of wool in Gansu, bought machinery and engaged German technicians to set up a factory in Lanzhou to make the cloth needed to outfit his troops. All the funds came from the provincial treasury. The factory opened at the end of 1880 and produced 120 meters of cloth per day, using 1,080 spindles and 20 looms driven by two boilers. But the water was too salty in that locality, and there was not enough of it. One of the boilers was irreparably damaged by an accident; then the funds ran out. Furthermore, scarcely any market could be found for the cloth, either locally or elsewhere, because of the difficulties in communications.

When Zuo Zong-tang and the foreign technicians left Lanzhou in 1883, the factory closed down. It was later transformed into an arsenal.

In 1876 at the urging of the commissioner of customs in Tientsin, Li Hong-zhang assigned one of his assistants to collect capital in Shanghai to create a cotton cloth mill, with the idea that the industry would provide a source of wealth while limiting the imports of foreign cloth. The money could not be raised, however. Two years later Peng Ru-cong, who had the title of manager and was probably a comprador, undertook to find 500,000 taels for the project. He had the help of comprador friends (Zheng Guan-ying among them), and he suggested that they be appointed to direct the enterprise. The mill was to be run on the system of "government supervision and merchant operation." As it turned out, however, Peng quarreled with Zheng Guang-ying and the Cantonese merchants and was unable to raise the money.

Li appointed various officials in Peng's place, with no better results. Eventually he made Zheng Guan-ying manager and in 1882 obtained the imperial sanction, a ten-year monopoly of the industrial manufacture of cotton cloth and yarn, and exemption from the *lijin*. The necessary capital of 352,000 taels was raised—from officials, salt merchants, landowners, and compradors—more easily than it had been for the China Merchants'. The machinery was bought in England and arrived in 1883, but in that year an economic crisis linked with the Sino-French War bankrupted many merchants, so that considerable sums were withdrawn. Zheng Guanying was accused of embezzlement and retired in 1884. The Shanghai Cotton Cloth Mill did not start production until 1890.

Private enterprise

The Shanghai cotton industry, like the Lanzhou wool industry, was born of a bureaucratic project, but the officials were not the only ones to be interested in the textile industry. In the 1860s several textile companies were launched in Shanghai with the encouragement of a Chinese comprador who had the support of foreign firms. Official opposition led to their failure, however. In 1871 merchants belonging to the Thirteen Guilds of Canton financed a small mill set up by an American. Six months later the authorities had the plant closed down, and the Chinese merchants involved tried in vain to take it up again under their own names.

The first entirely Chinese textile factory was a silk-throwing factory opened in 1872 in the Nanhai district in Guangdong. The owner was a silk merchant, Chen Qi-yuan, who made use of the local handicraft traditions. The enterprise was a success; over the following years Chen created two more factories and his example was followed by others, so that the region soon had about ten silk factories. But the competition aroused protest from the artisans, who sacked one of Chen's factories. The local magistrate declared, "Only the public authorities have the right to use machines." Chen took refuge in Macao, but three years later he was back in Nanhai. Other silk mills were founded near Canton, and in 1882 Chinese merchants opened one in Shanghai.

Silk was the only sector of the textile industry where there was opportunity for private initiative. Seeing that the cotton industry was getting nowhere in Shanghai, the merchants concerned in it tried several times to found independent firms, but the officials managed to prevent them. And after 1882, the monopoly granted to Li Hong-zhang nipped all new attempts in the bud. As for the wool industry, it had neither a market nor raw materials in Eastern China, where all the capital was concentrated.

Private initiative then turned to fields which were neglected by the authorities, such as rice husking, flour milling, making cattle cake from soybeans, match manufacture, papermaking, and setting up machine-building and -repair shops. Most of the enterprises were small and only partially mechanized. Between the foreign competition and the hostility of artisans and local authorities, they found it difficult to survive.

Communications

The *fuqiang* policy led to two important innovations in the field of communications: railway lines and a telegraph and postal system. In 1863 Li Hong-zhang received a proposal from twenty-seven Western firms to build a railway line between Shanghai and Suzhou. Permission for that and many similar projects was refused. In 1877 the authorities purchased and destroyed a railway line 16 kilometers long that had been built illegally by foreign merchants between Shanghai and Wusong. The motive behind the government's resistance was not so much blind hostility to modernism as opposition to all new foreign encroachment. A climate of opinion favorable to the construction of railway lines was forming in official circles, however. Li Hong-zhang was its spokesman in a petition presented on December 31, 1880. His plan, which was later adopted, called for a network centered on Peking and radiating southward toward Hankou and Shanghai, westward toward Lanzhou, and northeastward toward Fengtian. Conservative opposition and financial difficulties prevented its immediate fulfillment. The first Chinese railway, put into service in 1881, was a line 11 kilometers long to haul coal from Tangshan to Xugezhuang for the Kaiping Mining Company.

Foreign companies installed telegraph lines linking Hong Kong, Shanghai, and Vladivostok in 1870–1871. In 1874 Shen Bao-zhen became the first Chinese to suggest the establishment of a telegraph, and five years later Li Hong-zhang built a line between Tientsin and Dagu. In 1881, urged on by Sheng Xuan-huai, he set up the telegraph administration primarily to serve the military, but with a secondary market of merchants and the general public. The system used was that of government supervision and merchant operation, with a monopoly over the development of commercial lines. The technical installations were entrusted to a Danish firm. The first line, opened in 1881, linked Tientsin and Shanghai. In 1882 service began between Nanking and Hankou, and between Shanghai and Canton, by way of the chief coastal towns. In 1885 another line was opened to Korea.

The establishment of a national postal service met opposition from three sources. The officials were opposed to the suppression of the official service (*yizhan*) which, under the authority of the Ministry of the Army, conveyed government dispatches. They were justifiably afraid that the political and financial power attached to the *yizhan* would fall into foreign hands. The banks and other companies which were transporting private mail over the most profitable routes did not want to lose the business. Lastly, the foreigners who had established their own service in the ports wanted to keep foreign mail in their own hands, and they demanded firm guarantees before entrusting their domestic mail to a Chinese service.

To protect the legations' mail from attacks by the Taiping and the Nian, the Zongli Yamen arranged for it to be sent under escort to Tientsin in summer and Jiujiang in winter. Responsibility for it was entrusted to the inspector general of the customs when he set up his office in Peking. Postal departments for foreign mail were attached to customs offices in towns in the North. In 1878 they formed a regular service under the supervision of Li Hong-zhang and Robert Hart. At that time the first stamps were issued, and China joined the International Postal Union. In December 1879 this service spread to the Yangzi ports and in 1882 to all the ports in north Fujian, while a "correspondence office" for Chinese mail gradually took shape. However, it was hampered by competition from both the official postal system and the private services, so that it expanded very little until 1885. Thus in spite of the insistence of the foreigners and the wishes of Li Hong-zhang, the project of setting up a nationwide postal system could not be completed.

The beginnings of modern education

With the development of industry, a few new schools opened that were designed to prepare a limited number of pupils for careers as technicians or officers. The Institute of Western Knowledge was founded in Canton in 1880. In Tientsin a telegraph school was created in 1880, a naval school and an army medical school in 1881, and a military academy in 1885.

One dramatic innovation was the program for sending Chinese boys to schools in the United States or Europe. Between 1872 and 1881 one hundred and twenty small boys, mainly from humble families in Canton, were taken to Hartford, Connecticut, to be given the complete fifteen-year cycle of American education. Rong Hong and a few scholars from the Hanlin Academy, who accompanied them, were to complement this with instruction in Chinese. The program was criticized for many reasons, among which were the horrified reports sent home by colleagues of Rong Hong describing the "Americanization" of their pupils. Chinese opposition reached a peak when the suspension of Chinese immigration to the United States was announced in 1880 and the American military acad-emies refused to admit young Chinese. The mission was sent home; the pupils were taken into the navy, the telegraph administration, the railways, the mines, and the diplomatic service.

A parallel mission to France was organized in 1876 under the auspices of the Fuzhou arsenal. In 1876 Giquel, one of the ar-senal's founders, himself traveled abroad with the group of thirty-odd young apprentices and pupils from the arsenal school who were destined to be either engineers or naval officers. They were assigned to various ships of the French fleet, factories at Le Creusot and Saint-Chamond, and marine and civil engineering schools. They went back to China after three or four years. Among them were Yan Fu and Ma Jian-zhong (1844–1900), an attaché from the diplomatic service and a former pupil of the Jesuits. Ma, who was admitted to the École Libre des Sciences Politiques in Paris, afterward worked as an assistant to Li Hong-zhang and played an important part in Chinese political and intellectual life at the end of the century.

During the same period a small number of young Chinese went abroad to study privately, often under the auspices of the missionaries. Their influence was possibly even greater than that of the holders of official scholarships: Sun Yat-sen is an example.

Effects of Modernization up to 1885

There is no doubt that among the Western-style enterprises founded by the Chinese between 1872 and 1885, those sponsored by the government were the most important. Provincial officials created about fifteen companies with a total capitalization of 5,700,000 taels, while barely 900,000 taels were invested in about a dozen private concerns. Historians agree that the state-sponsored enterprises illustrate the rise of modern capitalism in China. Where they disagree, and sharply, is on the meaning of this evolution in relation to the double context in which it took place: the persistence of the traditional society and the foreign penetration. Did the *yangwu* movement encourage the appearance of what Chinese historians call "national capitalism"? That is, were the *yangwu* companies favorable to the development of a modern economy that was independent of, and opposed to, foreign interests?

Origins of Capital

The first point of dispute in the controversy is the origin of the capital in the modern enterprises. The funds contributed by the compradors were an important element, and they were not entirely by-products of the exploitation of the Chinese market by the foreigners, as some historians claim. Part of the money came from income on land, houses, and traditional business activities in which the compradors had invested their fortunes. Thus it can be disputed whether most of the private investment in the China Merchants' was money made in the service of foreign employers. In fact the funds drawn directly from traditional revenues may represent the larger part.

Besides the private investments of merchants, landowners, and officials, which rose considerably after 1880, the government loans to the new enterprises represented traditional revenues in another form. And there seems to have been no difference, as regards the economic origins of the capital, between official and private enterprises.

These facts tend to prove, on one hand, that the modernization of China was not conditioned solely by the effects of foreign penetration, and on the other hand, that the government-sponsored enterprises, far from depending exclusively on the surplus wealth of imperialism, acted as a channel for the transformation of traditional revenue into capital for modern industry. The *yangwu* companies were not necessarily in a subordinate position relative to the foreigners; these enterprises consequently had the potential of becoming instruments of national development, capable of resisting Western penetration.

Role of the *guan du shang ban* system

Another much discussed question is whether the government supervision that was part of the *guan du shang ban* system furnished protection for infant industries or formed an obstacle to their evolution. State intervention in the Chinese economy had a long history, and it was skillfully used as a cover by the government when introducing innovations. Certainly official backing did enable modern enterprises to obtain large state loans. Without these they could not have survived long enough to train Chinese technicians and provide experience in modern management. And it was state support that eventually led the public to accept the new enterprises and develop new social attitudes that prepared the way for modern capitalism.

The privileges granted to the *yangwu* enterprises were intended to put them in a stronger position in relation to foreign competition. The ten-year monopoly granted to the Shanghai Cotton Cloth Mill, although it was an obstacle to the creation of private Chinese factories, did protect the interests of the investors and prevent the intrusion of a foreign cotton industry. Lastly, some of the profits made by the *yangwu* enterprises because of the special conditions they enjoyed were reinvested in private enterprises. The *guan du shang ban* system might be explained as a device to ensure the protection necessary for the development of a new industry.

But there are serious objections to this favorable view of the system. The state had to give generous subsidies to the *yangwu* industries precisely because the government control aroused the distrust of merchants and other investors. They were disinclined to fall victim to the usual incompetence and corruption of the bureaucracy. The difficulties experienced by Zhu Qi-ang with the China Merchants', Tang Ting-shu with the Kaiping Mining Company, and Peng Ru-cong with the Shanghai Cotton Mill all bear witness to this. Government control therefore prevented private capital from being properly mobilized. The private investments which the *guan du shang ban* enterprises absorbed did not receive their fair share of the profits and ultimately served to establish an industry which looked to the foreigners for support rather than resisting them. In fact, the officials in charge of the companies held all the power and seized all the profits. The shareholders received a meager 10 percent interest, which was just equal to that paid by traditional businesses. Merchants like Tang Ting-shu and Xu Run grew richer than the rest because they had been appointed to managerial posts, where they ranked as officials.

By maintaining the principle of the supremacy of officialdom, the *yangwu* enterprises protected the traditional social order. Furthermore, they were totally dependent on foreign countries for machinery and specialized personnel. In 1885 all the captains, boatswains, engineers, and shipbuilders employed by the China Merchants' Steam Navigation Company were British or American. The least important telegram sent by a Chinese official could be read by the foreign legations. The promoters of *yangwu* were so interested in immediate profits that they did not risk making the investments that would have created technical independence in Chinese industry. By preventing the development of competition in the most profitable sectors, the economic monopoly linked to the *guan du shang ban* system left private investors with a choice between putting their savings into traditional businesses, and investing in concerns founded by Westerners. In short, government control consisted essentially of giving a free hand to greedy officials. This was profitable both to the officials and to the foreigners, because it was a guarantee that Chinese industry would never be a threat to them. Therefore the *guan du shang ban* system, conceived by Li Hong-zhang to buttress his power with profits from modern industry, is branded by some authorities as having been an obstacle to national development.

Yangwu and regionalism

One of the characteristics that determined the role of the *yangwu* companies in the social and economic evolution of the years 1870 to 1885 was the provincial character of the government control over them. Apart from a few mines and the short-lived wool industry in Lanzhou, they were all dependent on Li Hong-zhang and were situated within his zone of influence. In these regions, particularly in Zhili and Jiangsu, they produced cooperation between a few compradors and mandarins that enriched both groups. Thus a pool of bureaucratic capital was gradually built up which sought to assure the supremacy of bureaucratic industry, not the elimination of private industry.

With this end in view, the official enterprises by degrees extended their privileges and their exemptions while slowly giving up their efforts to mobilize private investments. Since they were designed to uphold regional rather than national interests, their antagonism toward foreign imperialism was necessarily limited. Sometimes, depending on the momentary balance of power between rival factions, foreign support was very useful to them. Because of the links between the *yangwu* movement, the state, and the traditional society, the *yangwu* enterprises by their nature did not embody national capitalism.

In Zhili and Jiangsu the *guan du shang ban* firms preceded national capitalism, which did not begin until 1880 or thereabouts. Then it often took the form of private enterprises launched by or with the help of shareholders or former shareholders in official enterprises. But this does not mean that government-operated industries were an essential step in the development of national capitalism. In 1872, the same year that the China Merchants' steamship company was launched, Chen Qi-yuan's silk mill opened in Canton in a province to which the *yangwu* movement had not yet come. It was only in certain regions where the bureaucracy was particularly powerful that the *yangwu* movement prepared the way for creating industry.

Opposition to progress

From the beginning, the *yangwu* movement aroused the hostility of conservative circles led by Wo-ren (?–1871), a Mongol who was at various times Grand Secretary, tutor to the emperor, chairman of the Hanlin Academy, and the head of several of the six ministries. He was considered one of the greatest scholars of his time, and his moral authority went unchallenged.

Until about 1870 the antagonism between supporters and enemies of *yangwu* was based on political and intellectual motives. These crosscurrents were illustrated in the controversy in 1867 over the addition of science to the curriculum of the Tong Wen Guan. Using the orthodox interpretation of Confucianism of Zheng Zi and Zhu Xi to back his arguments (excerpted in document 3), Wo-ren showed that Western science and techniques were unable to cure the moral ills affecting the state. The risk, he declared, was that the ills would worsen if the door were opened wider to foreign influence. Prince Gong replied by pointing out that science led to superior weapons. He argued that the question was not one of replacing one culture by another, since only scholars who had received a classical education would be initiated in the new disciplines, and the *ziqiang* would be led by the traditional elite. To resolve the conflict, the court appointed Wo-ren as head of the mathematics department. He argued that his incompetence prevented him from accepting the post. But his attacks helped to turn most of the brilliant young scholars away from the Tong Wen Guan.

Above all, the conservatives were jealous of the influence that the *yangwu* faction was acquiring in the government. Ci-xi, the Empress Dowager, encouraged this rivalry in order to control both factions. As long as the *yangwu* movement was confined to making arms for suppressing rebellions, the controversy did not get beyond the stage of a power struggle within the bureaucracy.

In the 1870s, however, the conflict became sharper. Each project and each action of the supporters of *yangwu* came under heavy attack. The members of the *qingliu*, the purification clique, led the offensive. Their opposition was strengthened by popular resistance to mechanization and to the modern economic system. The mandarins used protests from merchants, boatmen, and artisans who were thrown out of work by foreign competition to prove that modern technology had disastrous effects. They pointed to the rioting over the Wusong railway in 1876 as evidence that the modern economic system endangered law and order. Sometimes, as when the Kaiping mines were opened in 1878, the local magistrates and gentry stirred up popular agitation themselves. Some aspects of the debate between the conservatives and the *yangwu* supporters reflected a struggle over the future of China in which one party merely sought to perpetuate the traditional state, while the other introduced a notion which was almost unknown to Chinese thought: the concept of progress.

It should be noted, however, that popular resistance was aimed mostly at private companies, both Chinese and foreign, rather than at *yangwu* firms. Popular opposition, although it was imbued with religious beliefs and superstitions, had economic motives; the artisans who burned factories were protesting against the machines which had destroyed their livelihood. While complaints were lodged against the China Merchants' and telegraph poles were torn up several times, there were no violent, spontaneous riots against the traditional enterprises. This fact suggests that the modernism of the *yangwu* companies was not strongly evident or widely felt.

Growth of the industrial proletariat

The development of factories and mines enlarged the industrial proletariat which had begun to form over the previous decades. In 1885 about 40,000 workers were employed by Chinese companies.

The Kaiping mines, for example, had 1,000 workers in 1884, though recruitment was extremely difficult. The miners included both men from Shantou and Canton, who were slightly better paid because they already had some technical experience, and peasants from the neighborhood, who were pleased to work in the mine during winter but refused to stay when the farming season began. In 1882 the local miners struck for the same salaries that their fellow workers from the South received. The average wage for a nonskilled worker was between 0.15 and 0.2 dollars for an eight-hour day. Workers were fined and beaten for the slightest mistake. The accident rate was high: twelve deaths occurred between 1878 and 1882, seven in 1883, and eleven in 1885. The company had a hospital, however, and paid a meager compensation to the families of the victims, which for that time was a considerable innovation.

Working conditions in private mines were far worse. The mines in Hunan literally practiced slavery. Their agents were posted in gambling dens, where they got peasants drunk and persuaded them to gamble. When a man was deeply enough in debt, the agent "bought" him and took him to the mine. There the wretched creature was shut up underground and driven until he died of exhaustion after a few weeks or months.

Taken as a whole, this proletariat made up of underemployed peasants rather than out-of-work agricultural laborers remained more or less part of the traditional society.

Emergence of a bourgeoisie

The most striking social development of the period between 1872 and 1885 was the emergence of a bourgeoisie. Its nucleus was the officials, compradors, merchants, gentry, and landowners with a financial interest in modern enterprises. In many ways it was a bureaucratic bourgeoisie, or a bourgeoisie assimilated by the bureaucracy. Not only were many of its members civil servants, but the ranks conferred by the Confucian state were the guarantee of its prestige and social authority, while the traditional economic activities brought it a large part of its wealth. A comprador like Tang Ting-shu, who never let slip an opportunity to belittle officials and their habits, managed to build up his fortune only by securing official rank himself and becoming the protégé of Li Hong-zhang.

These links with the world of officialdom were essential in a society still under the domination of the traditional gentry, where trade and manufacture were too weak to bring pressure to bear on the government. The mingling of the two groups also encouraged the old ruling class to "go middle class." Thus the antagonism between the new social class and the landowners of rural society was much less pronounced than in Japan, for example. Because there was no dividing line between the groups, it was often hard to determine exactly where an individual belonged with regard to social class. Certainly Li Hong-zhang cannot be considered a member of the bourgeoisie, but men like Hu Guang-yong (the banker of Zuo Zong-tang), Sheng Xuan-huai, Tang Ting-shu, Xu Run, and Zheng Guan-ying were a curious mixture of concerns appropriate to modern businessmen and interests characteristic of the scholar-gentry.

New intellectual tendencies

With the emergence of the bourgeoisie came new intellectual and literary tendencies which expressed bourgeois tastes and aspirations. In 1873 Wang Tao (1828–1898) founded one of the first Chinese daily papers, the *Tsun Wan Yat Pao* (*Natural Evolution Paper*), in Hong Kong. Its plain, elegant language appealed to a

larger public than scholars alone. Wang Tao had worked with the
London Mission Press in Shanghai, but after being accused of collaboration with the Taiping, he went into exile in Hong Kong and
assisted James Legge in his translation of the Classics. From 1867
to 1870 he accompanied Legge on a journey to France and England; there he abandoned his last preconceptions about Western
culture. On his return he wrote editorials advocating trade and
practical knowledge, praising Western political institutions and
national spirit, and criticizing the Qing government. In 1875 he
published *Remarks on Change* by Zheng Guan-ying, a short work
calling for the free development of trade and industry and denounc-
ing the harmful intervention of officials.

Spokesmen for these ideas were also to be found in official circles: men like Ma Jian-zhong, secretary to Li Hong-zhang, and
Guo Song-dao, who was ambassador to England. The most brilliant
was probably Xue Fu-cheng, who worked for Zeng Guo-fan and
then served Li Hong-zhang from 1874 to 1884. Among his many
essays his *Rough Discussion of the Management of Foreign Affairs*
(1879) was an argument in favor of national capitalism as an
institution for resisting imperialism.[8] Although none of these
thinkers really proposed political reform before 1885, they were
becoming increasingly aware that "Western knowledge," the secret
of the riches and power possessed by foreign countries, consisted of
more than pure technology.

Limits of the *yangwu* movement

What modernization the *yangwu* movement managed to accom-
plish in the years 1860 to 1885 had little effect on China as a
whole. The traditional economy and society resisted change, and
where change did occur (in the hinterlands of the open ports and
along the trade routes), it was due to foreign economic penetration.
The official policy of modernization, designed as it was to remedy
the failures of the traditional state, strengthened the bureaucracy's
power by extending its control over capital, technology, and the
market. In this way it prevented other social groups from gaining
enough strength through the resources of the industrial economy to
supplant the elite and set the state on new foundations. The *guan
du shang ban* system enabled the bureaucrats to control the mer-

[8] See the excerpts in document 4.

chants and compradors or to absorb them entirely. The *yangwu*
enterprises were pervaded by the traditional mentality and methods, because opposition from backward-looking circles slowed
down their progress and encouraged them to disguise their new
aspects. In this respect the *yangwu* movement was in line with the
conservatism of the Tongzhi Restoration. But this time the modernization contained too many contradictions to provide the country
with the economic dynamism it needed to stand up to the foreigners.

Certainly the fact that some officials and scholars took part in
modern activities began the transformation of the ruling class.
From ownership of landed property in an old-style agricultural system it moved on to industrial capitalism. But the phenomenon
affected a minority, which was too much a part of the established
order to be able to overthrow it. A real renovation of the state
could only come about outside the *yangwu* movement or by ac-
complishing a complete reshaping of its aims. Views such as these
began to emerge before 1884 among the merchants and even
among some supporters of the *yangwu* movement. The defeats of
the Sino-French War confirmed them by showing the ineffective-
ness of official modernization.

Summary: China in 1885

Regional contrasts

Throughout the period 1840 to 1885, the complexity of China's
evolution was accentuated by regional contrasts. Essentially, the
South, which had reached a much higher level of social and cultural
development and which was less firmly controlled by the Manchus,
opposed the North. The Taiping rebellion was itself a Southern
movement which did not manage to take root in the North. The
secret societies were also much more active in the South, and in the
Yangzi basin, than in the North. Provincial and regional particularism still weighed heavily on Chinese political life. The movements of dissent like the Nian, the Hui, and the Moslems of the
Southwest had only regional support. Provincial loyalties were also
important within the Taiping camp, particularly as regards the
special position of the people from Guangxi. The same was true of
the Hunan army and the Huai army, the forces suppressing the

popular movements. Regional tendencies were further encouraged by the *yangwu* movement, whose leaders carved out personal zones of influence in the provinces they administered.

The lack of balance between the regions was complicated still more by geographic differences in foreign penetration. The Westerners' chief zone of activity was on the Southeastern edge of the country, from Canton to Shanghai. Not until 1860 did Western power begin to extend to a few isolated places like Hankou or Tientsin. The vast regions of the North and the West were virtually untouched by the social and economic transformations which were beginning in the Southeast, particularly in Shanghai: enlargement of the market economy, expansion of production, and the emergence of the first elements of a proletariat, a modern bourgeoisie, and a new intelligentsia.

Two Chinas

Two Chinas were thus juxtaposed. There was the China of the open ports, which was becoming Westernized, and the China of the interior, where the gentry and the government mobilized their strength against the specter of the popular revolts, neglecting all other problems. This duality makes it difficult to evaluate the effects of foreign activity, for the answer varies depending on which China is under consideration. Some historians do not hesitate to speak of complete domination by Western imperialism from the 1870s onward, whereas others stress the "old, impenetrable China."

Certainly in 1885 China was not yet a country which the foreign powers were trying to dismember—not yet the "sick man of the Far East." By putting an end to the popular rebellions, the government had weathered a severe crisis. Moreover, the foreigners had virtually no hold over Peking; their political ascendancy extended only to the tributary states of the Chinese empire. Even their economic penetration of China was still essentially commercial. Although Western influence reached far beyond the open ports and disrupted the life of some regions, it mainly affected trade. The foreigners were not undermining the subsistence economy from which China still drew its main resources.

The only serious threat to the subsistence economy was demographic pressure, and this threat had withdrawn for the moment. In effect the Restoration during the reign of the Tongzhi Emperor had revitalized the traditional forces of the empire. The fact that the Sino-French War ended in a defeat which was much less catastrophic than the Opium Wars proved that the recovery was genuine, though limited. But the conclusion drawn from the war by Sun Yat-sen, Kang You-wei, and the reformists was that the traditional forces, their reserves now reduced by warfare, could go no further. Official modernization was merely an inefficient auxiliary to the traditional society; the renewal of Chinese power had to be based on other foundations.

In fact, the entire history of China after the first Opium War revealed the impotence of the Chinese ancient regime. The "barbarians" had imposed their conditions on the Middle Kingdom. Popular movements had all but overthrown the dynasty and made its weakness plain. The Restoration, in spite of real short-term successes, could not remedy the basic evils of the old China—and did not want to. The *Yangwu* movement sharpened the fundamental contradictions already in existence instead of resolving them. Power was still concentrated in the hands of a small minority. Though the elite were sometimes able and energetic, they remained preoccupied with their own privileges and profits, which were identified with public interest by means of Confucian principles. Hundreds of millions of peasants and poor people in the towns still had no control over their own fate.

ADDITIONAL BIBLIOGRAPHY

K. Biggerstaff, *The Earliest Modern Government Schools in China* (Ithaca, N.Y., Cornell University Press, 1961).

G. Chen, *Tseng Kuo-fan, Pioneer Promoter of the Steamship in China* (Peking, 1935).

G. Chen, *Tso Tsung-t'ang, Pioneer Promoter of the Modern Dockyard and Woolen Mill in China* (Peking, 1938).

A. Chih, *L'Occident "chrétien" vu par les Chinois vers la fin du XIXᵉ siècle, 1870–1900* (Paris, 1962).

A. Feuerwerker, *China's Early Industrialization: Sheng Hsuan-huai (1844–1916) and Mandarin Enterprise* (Cambridge, Mass., Harvard University Press, 1958).

J. L. Rawlinson, *China's Struggle for Naval Development, 1839–1895* (Cambridge, Mass., Harvard University Press, 1967).

DOCUMENTS

1. THE SELF-STRENGTHENING POLICY AS RECOMMENDED BY FENG GUI-FEN (1861)

SOURCE: Extract from Feng Gui-fen, "On the Manufacture of Foreign Weapons," *Personal Protests from the Study of Jiao-bin.* English version in Ssu-yu

Teng and John K. Fairbank, *China's Response to the West: A Documentary Survey, 1838–1923* (New York, Atheneum, 1967), pp. 52–53.

According to a general geography by an Englishman, the territory of our China is eight times larger than that of Russia, ten times that of America, one hundred times that of England. . . . Yet now we are shamefully humiliated by those four nations in recent treaties—not because our climate, soil, or resources are inferior to theirs, but because our people are really inferior. . . . Why are they small and yet strong? Why are we large and yet weak? We must try to discover some means to become their equal, and that also depends upon human effort. Regarding the present situation there are several major points: in making use of the ability of our manpower, with no one neglected, we are inferior to the barbarians; in securing the benefit of the soil, with nothing wasted, we are inferior to the barbarians; and in the necessary accord of word and deed, we are also inferior to the barbarians. The way to correct these points lies with ourselves, for they can be changed at once if only our Emperor would set the general policy right. There is no need for outside help in these matters. . . .

What we then have to learn from the barbarians is only the one thing, solid ships and effective guns. When Wei Yuan [who wrote *Atlas of the Countries Beyond the Seas*] discussed the control of the barbarians, he said that we should use barbarians to attack barbarians, and use barbarians to negotiate with barbarians. . . . In my opinion, if we cannot make ourselves strong (*ziqiang*) but merely presume on cunning and deceit, it will be just enough to incur failure. Only one sentence of Wei Yuan is correct: "Learn the strong techniques of the barbarians in order to control them."

Funds should be assigned to establish a shipyard and arsenal in each trading port. Several barbarians should be invited and Chinese who are good at using their minds should be summoned to receive their instructions so that they may in turn teach many artisans. . . . We are just now in an interval of peaceful and harmonious relations. This is probably an opportunity given by heaven for us to strengthen ourselves. If we do not at this point quickly rise to this opportunity but passively receive the destiny of heaven, our subsequent regret will come too late. . . . If we live in the present day and speak of rejecting the barbarians, we should raise the question as to what instruments we can reject them with. . . .

Some suggest purchasing ships and hiring foreign people, but the answer is that this is quite impossible. If we can manufacture, can repair, and can use them, then they are our weapons. If we cannot manufacture them, nor repair, nor use them, they are still the weapons of others. When these weapons are in the hands of others and are used for grain transportation, then one day they can make us starve; and if they are used for salt transportation, one day they can deprive us of salt. . . . Eventually we must consider manufacturing, repairing, and using weapons by ourselves. . . . Only thus will we be able to pacify the empire; only thus can we play a leading role on the globe; and only thus shall we restore our original strength, and redeem ourselves from former humiliations.

2. MILITARY INDUSTRIALIZATION: ZUO ZONG-TANG ADVOCATES THE CREATION OF A SHIPYARD AT FUZHOU (1866)

SOURCE: Extract from Zuo Zong-tang, *Complete Works* (memoirs, 18/1-3 passim).

Ever since foreign merchants have been given permission to transport goods from the North to be sold in the different ports, prices have risen rapidly in the North. The big Jiangsu and Zhejiang merchants in the junk trade who go and buy goods in the North have to pay more for them. When they come South again, the cost price is so high and the transport so slow that they cannot lower their retail price to compete with the foreign merchants. . . . After repeated losses, they show a deficit and even go bankrupt. . . . The customs and *lijin* revenues are falling, the rich merchants are growing poor, people of modest condition are reduced to servitude, and I am afraid that the seagoing junks will be abandoned. At the moment Jiangsu and Zhejiang lack sea transport, so that the shipment of the grain tribute is extremely uncertain. The only way to right the situation is to open a shipyard without delay. . . .

In an unusual undertaking, slander and criticism are frequent. To start with, people will be disappointed by the lack of results, then they will criticize the excessive expenditure or even mock at it and say that it is a total failure. All this is forseeable and will certainly happen. Japan recently sent men to England to learn the language and study mathematics as the basis of shipbuilding. In a few years, the foreigners from the Eastern Seas [the Japanese] will certainly be successful in building steamships. Only China, because of several years of widespread warfare [the war against the Taiping and the second Opium War], has not yet had time to attend to this. . . . China can judge the importance of the high seas just as well as Japan, but Japan has the means, whereas we have nothing. It is like crossing a river where others are rowing in a boat, while we are making a raft; it is like racing on a donkey against people who are riding thoroughbreds. Is it possible? We are all human beings whose intelligence and wisdom are similar by nature; but our habits inevitably make us different.* Chinese is active in abstract notions, whereas foreign intelligence concentrates on concrete things. For the Chinese, the principles of the Classics are the foundations, and technology is a practical detail. For the foreigners, technology is important, and principles are secondary to it. Each thinks he is right and neither can understand the other. . . . When steamships are built, the grain tribute administration will prosper, the military administration

---

* Paraphrase of a passage from Confucius: "Men are similar by nature, but differ in their habits."

will improve, the merchants' distress will cease, and the customs revenues will increase. The temporary expenditure will bring profits for several generations.

3. OPPOSITION TO THE MODERNIZATION POLICY: WO-REN'S INDICTMENT OF THE STUDY OF SCIENCE AT THE TONG WEN GUAN (1876)

SOURCE: Extract from *Collected Texts Concerning Barbarian Affairs* (*Chou-ban yiwu shimo*), 47/24–25. This is an essential work for everything to do with Chinese foreign relations under the reigns of the Daoguang, Xianfeng, and Tongshi Emperors. It contains a large number of important texts for each reign, collected and published during the following reign. It was finished in 1880. The English translation is taken from Ssu-yu Teng and John K. Fairbank, *China's Reponse to the West*, pp. 76–77.

Mathematics, one of the six arts,* should indeed be learned by scholars as indicated in the Imperial decree, and it should not be considered an unworthy subject. But according to the viewpoint of your slave,† astronomy and mathematics are of very little use. If these subjects are going to be taught by Westerners as regular studies, the damage will be great. . . . Your slave has learned that the way to establish a nation is to lay emphasis on propriety and righteousness, not on power and plotting. The fundamental effort lies in the minds of the people, not in techniques. Now, if we seek trifling arts and respect barbarians as teachers regardless of the possibility that the cunning barbarians may not teach us their essential techniques—even if the teachers sincerely teach and the students faithfully study them, all that can be accomplished is the training of mathematicians. From ancient down to modern times, your slave has never heard of anyone who could use mathematics to raise the nation from a state of decline or to strengthen it in time of weakness. The empire is so great that one should not worry lest there be any lack of abilities therein. If astronomy and mathematics have to be taught, an extensive search should find someone who has mastered the technique. Why is it limited to barbarians, and why is it necessary to learn from the barbarians?

Moreover, the barbarians are our enemies. In 1860 they took up arms and rebelled against us. Our capital and its suburb was invaded, our ancestral altar was shaken, our Imperial palace was burned, and our officials and people were killed or wounded. There have never been such insults during the last 200 years of our dynasty. All our scholars and officials have been stirred with heart-burning rage, and have retained their hatred until the present. Our court could not help making peace with the barbarians. How can we forget this enmity and this humiliation even for one single day? . . .

Now, the empire has already been harmed by [the barbarians]. Should we further spread their influence and fan the flame? Your slave

* In the classical tradition the six arts were the rites, music, archery, chariot driving, writing, and mathematics.
† Only Manchus and Mongols used this title when addressing the Emperor.

has heard that when the barbarians spread their religion, they hate Chinese scholars who are not willing to learn it. Now scholars from the regular channels are ordered to study under foreigners. Your slave fears that what the scholars are going to learn cannot be learnt well and yet will be perplexing, which would just fall in with [the foreigners'] plans. It is earnestly hoped that, in order to prevent the development of disaster, the Imperial mind will independently decide to abolish instantly the previous decisions to establish such studies in the language school.

4. THE IDEAS OF XUE FU-CHENG ON THE DEVELOPMENT OF TRADE (1879)

SOURCE: Extract from Xue Fu-cheng, "Foreign Trade," *Rough Discussion of the Management of Foreign Affairs*, pp. 14–15.
The author denounces the foreign stranglehold on Chinese foreign trade. He claims that it is responsible for a steady impoverishment of the nation, and continues:

As for China, since she cannot forbid international trade, she is left with only one alternative: organizing her trade herself. The prosperity of trade depends on three principles. The first is the profit earned from it.* Since our ports have been opened to international trade, it is the foreigners who convey Chinese goods with their steamships. Not only do they arrogate to themselves the profits from the exchanges between China and the West, they also seize the profits from home trade. Since China founded the China Merchants' Steam Navigation Company, the foreign merchants have been trying to get the upper hand. First of all they lowered their tariffs to try to win the market. Then, as they lost by this, they changed their tactics. Although they still seize four-tenths of our legitimate rights and profits, we have got back no less than three-fifths of them. Altogether, over seven or eight years, goods transport brought in nearly 20 million taels. Although the interest paid to the merchant shareholders of the China Merchants' has not yet been increased, it still means that 20 million taels have not fallen into foreign hands.

What is questionable is the policy of having only one official office,† directed by only a few people, exercising exclusive control over twenty-seven ports all far away from each other. The office is not dynamic enough to extend its activities everywhere. Now that it has absorbed the Shanghai Steam Navigation Company, the official capital involved is quite large.‡ Should there be even a slight weakening, it would be difficult to try to right the situation.

---

* In the rest of the text, which is too long to be quoted here, Xue Fu-cheng's second principle is the improvement of crops intended for export, and his third is industrial manufacture, which would allow China to do without foreign imports and would supplement the home trade.
† The China Merchants' was not a real commercial company. Its Chinese name included the word *ju* ("official bureau").
‡ To buy the Shanghai Steam Navigation Company in 1877 the China Merchants' had to borrow 1 million taels from the government. The official investments

The difficulties to be met when launching an enterprise are a question of rational organization, whereas people's concern for their own private interests is a question of mentality. At this moment, in markets and fairs, traveling merchants can always be found who sell at a loss. Yet they follow after each other, taking it for granted that they will grow rich. How does this happen? Each one wants to increase his own fortune. If each man wants to increase his own fortune, this cannot harm the public treasury, or so it seems to me. On the contrary, in the long run it brings profit for everyone in general.

To settle the present situation it is no doubt difficult to use the method of building many things with few resources and hastily disseminating official bureaus. If a suitable solution emerges at another time, it might be that of using the merchants who are in charge of matters within the official bureau, and as well as that, of calling on rich and competent people. The exploitation of a certain number of ports could be shared out among them according to their resources and their capital. Whether it was a gain or a deficit, a profit or a loss, the public authorities would take no part in it.

---

in the enterprise amounted to 1,928,000 taels, whereas the merchant capital was barely more than 750,000 taels. In 1873–1874 official funds had represented only 135,000 taels and the merchant capital 476,000.

Chapter Eight

Decline of the
Imperial System:
1885–1894

For the Chinese government the Sino-French War ended in 1885 in partial defeat, since China renounced all rights to the empire of Annam (the ancient name for Vietnam) and granted further privileges to the Westerners. This proof of weakness encouraged the foreign powers to continue dismantling Chinese sovereignty and leadership in East Asia. Contrary to the treaties negotiated after the Opium Wars, however, China was not forced to pay an indemnity or give up any territory in the strict sense. In reality, although the foreign powers were granted new concessions on paper, they were not in a position to make full use of them at the time.

The fact that the defeat was not worse can be explained partly by the strong forces of resistance to foreign encroachment then current within Chinese society. It can also be attributed to the foreigners' limited means, particularly their limited economic power, to fulfill their ambitions. But during the ten years between the Sino-French and the Sino-Japanese Wars, the Chinese lost strength and the foreigners gained it. The struggle became more and more unequal as the foreign powers improved their means of penetration and tightened the circle they were drawing around the empire. When China was defeated by Japan in 1895, the great powers were able to take immediate advantage of the opportunity.

At the end of the nineteenth century, China was indeed the "iron house without windows, totally indestructible, with many people sleeping soundly inside, about to be asphyxiated,"[1] of which the great Lu Xun wrote a little later, and which the revolutionaries attacked without hesitation during the period which followed.

A Partial Defeat

The peace treaty with the French (signed in Tientsin on June 9, 1885), a trade treaty of April 25, 1886, and a convention of June 26, 1887, increased the humiliating restraints which the foreign powers began to impose on China after 1840. The same was true of a convention concerning Korea, which Japan forced on the Chinese government April 18, 1885, during the confusion resulting from the conflict with France. All these agreements were part of the "unequal-treaties" system by means of which the foreigners were stripping China of sovereignty.

Territorial consequences of the Sino-French treaty

In the process of renouncing the duty to protect Vietnam and the right to receive Vietnamese tribute, China recognized all the treaties between France and the empire of Annam. In particular the Chinese acknowledged the Treaty of Hue of August 25, 1883, which made Annam a French protectorate.

Until then Vietnam had belonged to China's system of "tributary countries," along with Nepal, Burma, Siam, Laos, and Korea. The emperor of China made a purely nominal investiture to the sovereigns of these states and granted them protection which, by tacit agreement, did not involve interference in their home or foreign policy. In return the emperor received tribute from them in the form of presents sent at regular intervals in accordance with a highly elaborate ceremony. These special links with the tributary countries, all bordering on China and deeply influenced by Chinese culture, were a vital element in the territorial security of the empire. The zone formed by the buffer states protected China's frontiers where they were most vulnerable. The tribute system was very old and had fallen into disuse until it was revived during the eighteenth century to safeguard the conquests achieved by the Qing dynasty.

[1] Lu Xun in his preface to the selection of short stories *A Call to Arms* (Peking, 1922).

Although the French domination of Vietnam did not deprive China of territory, it transformed an ally on the southern frontier into a powerful neighbor determined to maintain and extend its influence by force, if necessary. And since this threat followed other losses of territory to the foreign powers, it opened the way for further encroachments.

The Portuguese occupation of the peninsula of Macao dated from 1557. In 1849 Portugal rejected Chinese sovereignty over the enclave. In 1842 Great Britain annexed the little island of Hong Kong and in 1860 the cape and bay of Jiulong (Kowloon) opposite it on the continent. These possessions quickly became a vital military and trade base for British power in the Far East. In 1858 Russia obtained the northern bank of the Heilongjiang (the Amur River) by the Treaty of Aigun, and in 1860 added the territory lying between the Ussuri River and the sea by the Treaty of Tientsin. The czar acquired the western part of the Ili region (Kouldja) on the Xinjiang border by a treaty signed in St. Petersburg on February 12, 1881. Both the Russians and the British had tried many times to get a foothold in Tibet. And in many of China's largest cities, the concessions, where foreigners were allowed to live according to the terms of the treaties, had become independent enclaves more or less beyond the jurisdiction of the Chinese state. In 1885 there were twelve concessions, some of them jointly held by several foreign powers, in nine different towns.

Moreover, the tribute system had begun to disintegrate even before the end of the Sino-French War. Peking had to renounce its rights to tribute from the Ryukyu Islands in 1875, when they were annexed by Japan. Great Britain had taken possession of lower Burma in 1852 and was trying to conquer the rest of the kingdom. A plot at the court of Seoul resulted in armed intervention by both China and Japan, after which a Sino-Japanese convention in 1885 deprived China of exclusive suzerainty over Korea.

Economic consequences of the Sino-French War

The erosion of Chinese territorial power was accompanied by increasing foreign economic penetration. As a result of the negotiations between France and China in the period 1885–1887, two places near the Tongking frontier, Longzhou and Mengzi, were opened to trade. France established a consulate at Mengzi, the Chinese created a customs office, and businessmen either of French nationality or under French protection were allowed to take up residence there. The hamlet of Manhao downstream from Mengzi was also theoretically open, and France had the right to send an agent to it from the consulate at Mengzi. In these places the customs dues on imports were reduced by three-tenths and the dues on exports by four-tenths relative to the usual tariff on maritime trade, which generally amounted to 5 percent of the value of the goods. The treaty of 1885 also stipulated that when China decided to build railways, the authorities would call on French industry, though this clause was not to be considered as creating an exclusive privilege for France.

Trade benefits like these helped consolidate the structure of judicial and *de facto* privileges which the foreigners had appropriated after the first Opium War. It was this structure, founded on the system of treaty ports, which formed the basis of foreign economic penetration.

Foreign autonomy in the treaty ports

The Treaty of Nanking in 1842 put an end to the "closed-door" policy of strict control over all Westerners on Chinese soil. After that, Great Britain—followed by France, the United States, Russia, Belgium, the Scandinavian countries, Italy, Spain, Portugal, Austria, Germany, and Japan—managed to establish direct official relations with the Chinese government. The foreigners' changed status in China was symbolized first by the installation of foreign consuls, and later by the exchange of diplomatic representatives.

Foreign trade in China was organized within the framework of the open ports, which numbered twenty-nine before the Sino-French treaty of 1885. A customs office was set up in each one, and foreigners had to pass through it when bringing goods in or taking them out. Citizens of the "treaty powers" were allowed to live and do business in these towns. They could travel but not settle in the interior of the country, and that only with a passport issued by the Chinese authorities. The personal and property rights of foreigners in the open ports were guaranteed by the principle of extraterritoriality, so that the foreigners were subject only to the jurisdiction of their own consuls. The local Chinese authorities generally entered into agreements with the consuls which stipulated the districts considered most suitable for foreign settlement. The choice fell on areas which were uninhabited or very sparsely settled, so that once the foreigners had moved in, Chinese magistrates had virtually no control over the districts because the foreigners were answerable only to their consuls. In fact, no matter which legal system governed the foreign settlement the Chinese were theoretically forbidden to live there unless they were employed as servants by the foreigners.

The system of granting foreigners a special residential area and the right to be judged by their own judges according to the laws of their own countries was invented by the Chinese for the Arab merchants who settled in Canton in the ninth century. It was then applied to oriental traders in the Middle Ages and later used in the Capitulations system. Chinese communities overseas were usually organized under the same plan of separate and extraterritorial residential areas. This pattern was based on the idea that differences in habits and customs made it simpler for the foreign communities to administer themselves, as long as their sphere of activities was delimited. But in nineteenth-century China, when the same pattern was applied to citizens of the countries which had reached the stage of industrial capitalism, it rapidly took on a completely different meaning. The most dramatic case was that of the concessions in Shanghai. In 1885 Shanghai contained an international concession and a French concession, both beyond the control of the Chinese authorities, each administered by a municipal council elected exclusively by foreign residents. The councils had been established unilaterally; the Chinese government was not consulted about matters within the concessions except on the subject of their boundaries. The vast majority of the concessions' population was Chinese: in 1885 there were 125,665 natives and 3,673 foreigners in the international concession, while there were about 25,000 Chinese and 300 foreigners in the French concession.[2] At first the concessions had tried to expel all Chinese, but they quickly realized that the Chinese could become a source of tax income, and soon the Chinese greatly outnumbered the Western residents in the concessions. The taxes paid by foreigners were very low compared with those collected from the natives, who had no rights whatever and were in the position of subjects of a colonial state.

The 451 foreign companies operating in the ports varied in size. Several of them, in particular the British firm Jardine & Matheson and the American firm Russell & Company, dominated the market

[2] Report by Charles Denby, U.S. Minister in Peking, July 28, 1890, U.S. State Department Archives, *Diplomatic Dispatches: China*, vol. 87, no. 1130.

in the ports where they were located and extended their economic influence far inland. The foreign businessmen found that their compradors, the Chinese whom they employed as managers in all their dealings with Chinese customers, were capable assistants who were ready to help enlarge the scope of the business. A foreign company would often use the comprador's name for transactions forbidden by the treaties: for example, to purchase warehouses or shops outside the prescribed area, to make investments in industrial enterprises, and above all, to invest in financial enterprises whose interests stretched well beyond the open ports. On the other hand, both foreign adventurers and well-known firms would more or less hire out their name to Chinese businessmen, who benefitted from the privileges and immunities granted to foreigners.

Western control of the customs

Besides the protection provided by extraterritoriality, foreign businessmen enjoyed many tax advantages. According to the general tariff of the maritime customs, import and export dues were fixed at only 5 percent of the value of the goods. The rate was higher for tea (20 percent) and opium (8 percent), but lower for silk. In overland trade with Russia, these dues were cut by one-third. The maritime tariff was applied only to goods conveyed on boats that had been built abroad—vessels possessed by few Chinese. The tariff levied on junk traffic, which was set by the Chinese authorities, generally ran higher than the maritime tariff. Thus in foreign trade the customs system encouraged a sort of monopoly in transport from which the Westerners benefited.

Moreover, the foreigners had taken the administration of the maritime customs service into their own hands. At the head of the service was an English inspector general, Sir Robert Hart, who had dictatorial powers over a staff made up of 500 Westerners and 2,000 Chinese. The Westerners were better paid and had authority over the Chinese. Hart's rigorous methods of collection secured large and regular revenues for Peking and eliminated fraud and smuggling. The efficiency of his organization was appreciated by Chinese and foreigners alike. However, foreign control over a branch of public administration represented a serious encroachment on the sovereignty of the state, particularly since the work of the customs service extended well beyond the collection of customs dues. It included the upkeep and improvement of harbors and rivers, aids to navigation, coastal geographic surveys, information on trade, health services, the supervision of emigration, and even the management of a postal service and the payment of China's foreign debts. Robert Hart was in charge of a large sector of Chinese economic life and had great influence in Peking. Acting on his own initiative, for example, he had opened the discussions with the French government which led to the settlement of the Sino-French War.

Foreign exemption from the *lijin*

Foreigners buying or selling goods not only had the advantages conferred by the customs system, but escaped the tax burdens imposed on Chinese inland trade. The heaviest tax was the *lijin*, a transport and sales tax which varied at the whim of officials. It was collected in an arbitrary fashion; sometimes as much as 10 percent of the value of the goods had to be paid every 20 kilometers.

In the territory of the concessions, however, trade involving goods (except opium) imported from abroad was exempt from all taxation besides customs duties. And outside the concessions, foreign merchants could usually take advantage of a system of transit permits. In return for a lump sum covering half of the customs duty to which the goods were liable, a Western trader was issued a certificate granting exemption from all inland taxation as far as his stated destination. In 1885 this system was in general use on the coastal routes between the open ports, although officials elsewhere fought it tenaciously. The *lijin* was the main income of local authorities, whereas the money paid for transit permits went to the imperial customs and therefore to the central treasury. Local officials often refused to honor the travel permits, complaining (justifiably) that foreigners lent their permits to Chinese merchants. Foreign diplomats were constantly protesting against the local authorities for violating the treaties in this respect. But even though foreign exemption from the *lijin* was not recognized everywhere, it was widespread enough to put foreign trade in a strong position.

Technological superiority of the West

Foreign economic penetration was facilitated by the material superiority that the West temporarily possessed because of its modern industrial technology. Mechanization lowered the cost of producing consumer goods such as cotton yarn and some woolen and cotton fabrics, so that Westerners could set prices below those of Chinese handicraft products. In addition, foreign industries could supply products that were beyond handicraft technology, such as machines, durable goods, modern weapons, and refined oil. The means of transportation available to foreigners were more rapid and less costly, and their cargoes could be insured. Wherever foreigners had a right to go in the areas between the treaty ports, they competed with Chinese water transport. Modern legal and management techniques enabled Western firms to obtain financial backing which none of their Chinese rivals could equal. In particular, foreign companies could carry out innumerable operations by telegraph without counting the cost.

In fact, as will be seen, Western companies did not have the economic base in China to exploit their technological superiority to the fullest. It was Western military power that enabled these companies to carry out their commercial penetration of China, just as it had permitted them to gain a foothold at the time of the Opium Wars. The foreign merchant traded in the shadow of the gunboats.

Political consequences of the Sino-French War

The defeat of 1885 was another blow to the traditional concept of the Chinese empire, which assumed that China was the center of the world and that Chinese civilization was supreme. According to this view, all nations were inevitably attracted to China's high culture and found it natural to submit to the Chinese emperor. That ruler, by virtue of his moral superiority, had been granted the Mandate of Heaven to govern the whole of humanity. Equality in international relations was obviously impossible. Through the tribute system the barbarians (meaning foreigners) acknowledged the unique position of the Son of Heaven, petitioned for his protection, and obeyed his decrees.

The treaties that were negotiated with the Westerners after 1842 punctured these Chinese pretensions. The fiction of Chinese supremacy was maintained, however, in China's relations with its immediate neighbors until 1885, when both the Sino-French treaty and the Sino-Japanese convention put an end to Chinese myths of grandeur.

In the nineteenth and twentieth centuries many other nations were victims of oppression and exploitation by the Western powers. Some suffered worse than China; but probably none felt, and indeed still feels, as strong a sense of humiliation. The intensity of Chinese resentment is largely due to the fact that when the Europeans arrived, China was a unified country with a civilization that assured national cohesion.

The defeat of 1885, which showed that China was still weak in spite of the modernization program begun in 1860, encouraged the imperialist drive of the foreign powers. It also convinced some Chinese that their leaders were incompetent, thereby creating a current of thought favorable to political change. The humiliation felt by the Chinese, however, was mostly expressed in a defensive reaction which drew no clear distinction between the cultural heritage of a certain social regime and the political and military policies that were imperative for national survival. This complex defensive reaction was disparaged by foreigners as arrogance and xenophobia of the Celestial ones.

The Sino-French War spread the Chinese resentment of foreigners into regions which until then had had little contact with the West (into western Guangdong, Guangxi, and Yunnan, for example) and accentuated it in regions where it already existed. All foreigners complained that after the war, negotiations with the Chinese became more difficult.[3] But the foreigners blamed the deteriorating relations on the inadequacies of the French victory, arguing that an unconditional surrender would have brought the Chinese to heel at last. Later on, Chinese reformists and revolutionaries also regretted that the defeat had not been total, though their reasons were entirely different. They believed that the concessions granted by France in the peace treaty disguised the failure of the old regime and created lasting ambiguities in the political and social content of Chinese nationalism.

The limited defeat of 1885

In the negotiations of 1885–1887 China lost no territory to France. It was stipulated that the French could not create extraterritorial concessions in the towns which were opened to trade in Yunnan and Guangxi. France was also obliged to renounce all claims to a war indemnity. The French expected to make up their losses through the trade benefits obtained, but they were in no state to do so. Their greatest hopes lay in the clause on the railroads, but that clause did not in any way oblige the Chinese to build them.

[3] Strained relations in Shandong are described by a German consul in document 1 at the chapter end.

China also retained rights to the exploitation of all the natural resources in the Southern provinces, rights which the Westerners, particularly France and Britain, had coveted for a long time.

The fact was that the material strength of the foreigners was not yet equal to their political and economic ambitions. The French in Tongking had been fighting more than 10,000 kilometers from home, with few troops and a low budget. The French government could increase its commitment in that territory only slowly, because it had to humor public opinion. The Chinese were fighting on their own frontier with an immense reserve of men close at hand, in a region which they knew well and where they had strong friendships. The level of industry and financial capitalism in Europe and the United States could not yet support vast undertakings in China.

Strengths and weaknesses of foreign imperialism

The total figure for Chinese foreign trade in 1885 was 153 million customs taels, or 4.5 percent of the gross national product. Opium accounted for 29 percent of all imports; next came cotton (26.5 percent), cotton yarn (9 percent), metal (5 percent), and paraffin (3.5 percent). The main exports were tea (50 percent of the total), silk (23.5 percent), silk fabrics (7 percent), and raw cotton (eighteen percent). The trade deficit had been permanent since 1877 and was counterbalanced by the money which the overseas Chinese sent home to their families.

Foreign trade in China had the same characteristics as colonial trade. Imports included a limited variety of manufactured goods and a large number of raw or semirefined materials. Exports comprised mainly raw materials and foodstuffs, which were processed in China. The silk exported from Canton, for example, was spun in about one hundred factories, which were entirely Chinese, used steam-powered machines, and employed between 300 and 1,000 workers. In spite of the numerous privileges which it enjoyed, foreign trade had a relatively low, and above all irregular, rate of growth, because it suffered from the monetary fluctuations of the world market. Most foreign firms did not have enough capital to enable them to take advantage of the instability of the currency. They preferred to trade in small quantities of a variety of articles as a safeguard against price fluctuations.

Besides foreign trade, other business activities such as the coastal trade, insurance, the banks, and some manufacturing brought in further profits for the foreigners, mainly for British businessmen, who greatly outnumbered the rest. (There were 2,070 British out of a total of 3,995 foreign residents in the treaty ports and 299 British firms out of a total of 451, and all the largest firms were British.) These newer enterprises were the beginning of new forms of economic penetration, and particularly of productive investments. For want of foreign capital, a large proportion of them were financed by Chinese money.

During the years before 1885 the European powers were preoccupied with the Balkan wars and colonial expansion in Africa. The United States still observed the policy of withdrawal from international affairs adopted at the end of the Civil War. (In 1885, however, the American historian John Fiske published *Manifest Destiny*, in which he declared that the Americans were destined to spread their economic influence and their political concepts throughout the world.) Japan had not then completed its internal political reorganization. Since the foreign powers were not strong enough for massive intervention in China, they followed a policy of support for the Qing government and modified their demands whenever these put too much strain on the imperial system. Their policy thus helped to perpetuate the traditional structure of the Middle Empire.

By 1885 the foreigners in China had further consolidated their influence. But they were still circumscribed by their own economic limitations, by the resistance of old Chinese institutions, and by vigorous Chinese patriotic feelings which were as yet unchanneled, though they were widespread in various sections of the population.

The reserves of power belonging to the traditional society were depleted during the Sino-French War beyond all possibility of renewal. The foreigners redoubled their efforts to break out of the limits imposed on them. The unequal aspect of the struggle became more obvious during the years between 1885 and 1894, while certain Chinese groups tried to find new ways of restoring their country's power.

Official Attempts to Offset the Defeat

Between 1885 and 1894 an effort was made in official Chinese circles to repair the damage arising from the defeat by the French. It was not a concerted effort, however, because the mandarinate was divided against itself.

Characteristics of the provincial officials

The most influential officials of the time were the leading governor-generals. Li Hong-zhang (1823–1901), governor-general of Zhili, superintendent of the Northern ports, and grand secretary, had considerable power and private wealth, which he worked hard to increase at the state's expense. As discussed in Chapter 5, he was in command of the strongest contingent of well-trained troops with modern equipment. Because of his intelligence, his resourcefulness, and his talent for acting, he was designated as plenipotentiary in all important negotiations. He was one of the officials who initiated the *yangwu* movement, seeing it as a way to defend the established order and silence his adversaries, who had accused him of capitulating to the foreigners. He gathered a huge team of brilliant secretaries and technicians. The network of his supporters spread throughout China. Although Li was better informed, more open-minded, and more realistic than most of his contemporaries, his conceit, ambition, and greed delivered him into the hands of the foreign ministers at decisive moments.

Zhang Zhi-dong (1837–1909), who was completely different in temperament, became Li's chief rival. Zhang was as thin, ascetic, and distant as Li was stout and fond of the pleasures of life. Zhang served as governor-general of Lianguang until 1889, when he was transferred to Huguang. There he stayed until 1907, with two interim periods in 1894–1896 and 1902 as governor-general of Liangjiang. Zhang Zhi-dong was considered the finest scholar in the empire, a model of Confucian principles, and a man who was irreproachable in his own morals. (His *yamen* and his administration, however, were scarcely less corrupt than the rest.) He was an extremely hard worker who wore out his assistants and won respect and fear. He had large ideas and great energy. Yet he lacked common sense, and he was afflicted with a sort of fundamental indecision which he hid under an authoritative bearing but which prevented him from carrying his projects through to the end.

It took the foreigners a long time to discover Zhang Zhi-dong's weaknesses. Until 1900 they considered him one of their worst enemies. Exasperated by his inflexibility and sarcastic irony, they did all they could to have him dismissed, but in vain. More than all the other mandarins, Zhang wanted to build up national power which no longer depended on foreign countries for capital, technicians, or raw materials.[4] But owing to his social background, his education, the responsibilities he exercised, and his conception of political power, in the last analysis he was a defender of the old regime.

The governor-general of Liangjiang, Zeng Guo-quan (1824-1890), and his successor Liu Kun-yi (1830-1902), were men similar to Zhang Zhi-dong but less forceful in personality. Both were natives of Hunan and derived their influence partly from the dedicated loyalty of the troops from their province, which provided the best soldiers in the empire.

The Empress Dowager

Although no leader in the years 1885-1894 dominated the decisions of Peking as had been the case in the preceding period, the Empress Dowager Ci-xi (1835-1908) was the ultimate arbiter of policy. She had come to power through crime and stayed there through guile. Her intelligence was above average for the imperial clan, but it was limited by boundless pride and an all-absorbing concern for her own interests. Her weak and timid nephew, the young Guangxu Emperor (1871-1908), remained a slave to Ci-xi all his life except for a few months in 1898.

How did such a greedy, mean, cruel woman retain so much authority right up to her death? For one reason, Ci-xi excelled in manipulating people. Although she herself violated dynastic laws and customs, she forced strict observance of them on the Manchus and inflicted severe punishments on anyone who transgressed them. On the Chinese she imposed respect for Confucian principles of loyalty to the prince. She was clear-sighted enough to perceive the degeneration of the Manchus, and consequently entrusted the most important posts to able Chinese. But while granting them high ranks and honors, she safeguarded her own position by secretly encouraging the reactionary opposition to attack them.

Leading figures in Peking

Ci-xi reigned like an autocrat at court after the war with France, which had enabled her to disgrace her chief rival, Prince Gong (1833-1898). He was called back to preside over the Zongli

---

[4] Document 2 gives Zhang's recommendations for constructing a railway from Peking to Hankou.

Yamen and the Grand Council in 1894 at the time of the Sino-Japanese War, but age and opium had made him a ghost of his former self. The emperor's father, Prince Chun (1840–1891), held a high post but had only mediocre abilities. He supported technical modernization by backing Li Hong-zhang, who wooed him with presents. Prince Qing, who was in charge of the Zongli Yamen, was a lazy man chiefly concerned with building up his personal fortune.

Like the imperial clan, the Chinese officials in the capital were split into cliques by rivalry and intrigue. Among the more outstanding men was a native of Jiangsu, Weng Tong-he (1830–1904), the emperor's tutor and president of the Ministry of Revenue from 1886 to 1898. He was a fine scholar whose circle included other distinguished intellectuals, all of them supporters of thorough government reform. On the reactionary side was Sun Yu-wen, a favorite of Ci-xi and one of the men chiefly responsible for corruption in the administration. Sun was a member of the Grand Council and of the Zongli Yamen, president of the Ministry of Punishments from 1889 to 1893, and president of the Ministry of War from 1893 to 1895.

Policies of resistance

The policy to be followed in the face of the challenge from the West was still a source of constant disagreement in official circles, as it had been since 1840. All factions were unanimous in their will to resist, but their methods differed.

Li Hong-zhang and the Zongli Yamen followed the old tactic of "using one barbarian to control another barbarian." They made legal quibbles over the interpretation of the treaties last as long as possible and thereby won small concessions. In 1886, for example, Li Hong-zhang induced the French to agree to destruction of the Beitang, a Roman Catholic cathedral which was in the same enclosure as the imperial palace and had towers overlooking parts of the palace, in defiance of the law. At a cost of 350,000 taels, the Chinese built a smaller church for the French on a neighboring plot of land.

In most cases, however, the diplomatic juggling obtained only the temporary postponement of a solution which eventually turned out to be prejudicial to Chinese interests. It meant making concessions to the foreign powers by turns in order to gain their support.

In Korea in 1885, China had to allow Russia to take Port Lazareff, while Britain took Port Hamilton. In the southwest, Britain obtained recognition of the annexation of Burma in 1886 and of the creation of a protectorate in Sikkim in 1890. Britain also secured facilities for the penetration of Yunnan and the opening of the Tibetan town of Yadong to foreign trade in 1893. The Russians received permission to conduct several "exploratory expeditions" in Xinjiang and Tibet. The Germans and the French obtained orders for military and industrial equipment.

Just after the Sino-French War, Zhang Zhi-dong introduced a new style of political resistance. The agreements with France only roughly defined the frontier between Tongking and China. They stipulated that committees should explore the region before marking out the borders. Zhang Zhi-dong took advantage of the slowness and ignorance of the French to send troops to occupy various areas of strategic importance. Some of these areas, in particular Cape Bailong, remained Chinese territory although they appeared on the registers of the empire of Annam.

Zhang also tried to use the Chinese communities living in European colonies to exert pressure on the European governments. In 1886 he sent a commission to visit the major Chinese settlements in Southeast Asia and Australia, where he requested permission to open consulates. In 1890 a Chinese frigate anchored off Saigon and asked for the abolition of the poll tax that was imposed on the Chinese in Indochina. A squadron was sent to Manila to demand the opening of a consulate. In the long conflict between China and the United States on the question of Chinese immigration, Zhang Zhi-dong manipulated public opinion in Canton, planting anti-American articles in the press and publishing scurrilous satires subsidized by his *yamen*, in order to intimidate the Americans through their fear of reprisals.

The tactics of Zhang Zhi-dong flattered the pride of the scholars. His policy was supported by the growing numbers of rich merchants who were interested in foreign trade, for they had discovered that trade follows the flag. And the governor-general achieved short-lived popularity among the humble people in Guangdong whose relations had been forced to emigrate as coolies and who were always the first victims of discrimination, looting, and massacres.

Zhang Zhi-dong, however, was a prisoner of the old structures; he lacked the material means for carrying his policy to the point where it brought substantial advantages to his country. At one time he favored a proposal that China forbid its people to emigrate to the United States in return for a promise from the Americans (especially missionaries) not to settle in China. But Zhang soon abandoned his support of this project because the resources of his provinces were not sufficiently developed to feed the annual population surplus. An alternative solution, to settle the Northeast, would have been an attack on Manchu privileges.

Zhang's policy of political resistance did educate public opinion on international problems, a result which was by no means negligible. With this exception, however, his methods were hardly more successful than those of Li Hong-zhang. The treaty of March 17, 1894, forbade the immigration of Chinese workers to the United States for ten years, with no compensation. And on the Yunnan frontier the French ruthlessly made up for the territory they had lost on the border of Guangxi.

Continuation of the *yangwu* movement

In spite of the failure they suffered in 1885, the supporters of *yangwu*, the policy of modernization, continued their activities and maintained their methods almost unchanged. The stress was still on the development of military and naval power. The idea of increasing the nation's wealth by developing civil enterprises was gaining favor, however, and more textile factories were founded on a larger scale than before. Li Hong-zhang was still the leading official, though his influence was threatened by the increasing power of Zhang Zhi-dong in Canton (and later in Wuhan) and of Liu Kun-yi in Nanking.

Development of military and naval power

The arsenals that had been founded during the previous period grew, and their production became more varied. The numbers of troops that were armed and trained in the European manner increased from 40,000 men in 1885 to 100,000 in 1894. The training of officers improved also because of the military academies. One had been founded by Li Hong-zhang in Tientsin in 1885, Zhang Zhi-dong had opened a naval school at Huangpu (Whampoa) near Canton in 1889, and other naval or technical schools had been established in Nanking, Shanghai, Fuzhou, Weihaiwei, and Lüshun (Port Arthur).

The growth of the navy impressed foreigners. Between 1884 and

1894 the number of modern warships increased from 42 to 67 and the total tonnage rose from 40,000 to 72,800. The fleet was divided into four squadrons: the Beiyang (northern seas) attached to Tientsin, Lüshun, and Weihaiwei; the Nanyang (southern seas) based on Wusong, Shanghai, Nanking, and Wuhu; the Fujian, spread out between Ningbo, Wenzhou, Fuzhou, Amoy, and Taiwan; and the Guangdong, centered in Canton. The strongest was the Beiyang squadron, headed by Li Hong-zhang; it had 29 vessels totaling 43,864 tons, including two cruisers of 7,430 tons that were each armed with four Krupp 30-cm. guns. Fortifications were also constructed on a large scale for the defense of the frontiers and the coast. The most important was the fortification of the harbor of Lüshun, which involved 13 forts, 330 guns, and a network of docks, warehouses, and modern repair shops designed by French engineers.

This strengthening of Chinese military power was heavily dependent on foreign goods and foreign personnel. In spite of remarkable growth in local production, a large share of Chinese arms was still supplied by foreigners. German and British instructors and engineers held the important posts, so that young Chinese with the necessary qualifications often had to be content with minor jobs which had nothing to do with their specialty.

Between 1885 and 1888, modernization in the military field absorbed a quarter of the central government's income. This cost was over and above the expenses of maintaining the traditional army, which themselves took half of that income. The funds were not always used wisely, however, and part of them were misappropriated by senior officials. After 1888 government spending on the military was severely cut back. The natural calamities which ravaged the country reduced the revenues from taxation and forced the state to increase the budget for hydraulic engineering. At the same time Ci-xi managed to lay hands on more than half of the navy's allowance, which she used to rebuild the summer palace. After 1888 China could no longer afford a single warship. Indulging a ridiculous whim, the Empress Dowager had a marble boat built on the lake of her new palace.

The efficiency of the military modernization program was limited because no overall leadership or coordination existed. An admiralty, created in 1885 and administered by incompetent and highly paid Manchu princes, was designed solely to defend Li Hong-zhang from the attacks of the censors and drain off all the navy's resources for the Beiyang fleet alone. Li's authority and interests were purely regional. The other governor-generals refused to co-operate with him; their sole ambition was to outrival him. The country's military potential was scattered, so that its real value in any national emergency was well below that implied by the total of men and matériel.

The rise of civil official enterprises

The modernization program also included civil enterprises. Some of them were directly linked with military projects, while the rest were intended to yield profits that would swell the defense budget.

One lesson of the Sino-French War was that China's entire system of communications must be improved. To defend Taiwan its governor, Liu Ming-chuan, built two short stretches of railroad track, from Taibei to Jilong in 1886–1891, and to Xinzhu in 1893. Under the auspices of the Chinese Railway Company created by Li Hong-zhang, the Tangshan railway was extended in 1886 as far as Lutai, and in 1888 as far as Tientsin. The line was also continued northward until in July 1894 it stretched 64 kilometers beyond Shanhaiguan. Between 1885 and 1894 the entire Chinese railway network was increased from 11 to 411 kilometers at a cost of about 2,500,000 taels, two-thirds of which was provided by foreign loans.

Meanwhile the telegraph system was extended to all the frontier regions, where it was linked with foreign lines. In addition, new mines were opened that utilized modern techniques: gold-bearing quartz mines at Pingdu in Shandong (1885), iron mines at Qingxi in Guizhou (1886), lead and iron mines at Zichuan in Shandong (1887), silver-bearing lead mines at Tucaozi and Bianshanxian in Rehe (1887), and gold mines at Mohe in Heilongjiang (1889). The copper and tin mines in Yunnan were also modernized (1887). The capital invested in all these mines, which employed about 8,500 workers, amounted to more than 1,500,000 taels.

Zhang Zhi-dong's iron- and steelworks

Another achievement of the *yangwu* movement was to establish foundries, the most important of which was the iron- and steelworks erected by Zhang Zhi-dong in Hubei. In 1885 when he was governor-general of Liangguang, he had issued regulations concerning the mines under his charge, to prevent direct or indirect exploitation by foreigners. In 1886 he had also created a general office for the administration of the mines in Guangdong, intended to encourage the development of the province's mining resources. Virtually nothing came of his efforts.

Zhang became more and more concerned over the rising imports of foreign iron and steel and increasingly anxious to obtain a regular, independent supply of raw materials for his arsenal in Canton and for the railways that he intended to build. In 1889 he ordered the equipment for an iron- and steelworks from Britain, and when he was appointed to Huguang at the end of that year, he had the machinery transferred with him. He built a huge plant at Hanyang that was first known as the Forges of Hubei or the Hanyang Iron and Steel Office and was later called the Hanyang Steelworks. It contained two blast furnaces with a capacity of 100 tons a day, eight boilers, four copper furnaces, one gun and rifle factory, and one tileworks. To supply the blast furnaces, Zhang began to mine the iron ore of the Tieshan (the iron mountain) on the south bank of the Yangzi about 100 kilometers downstream from Hanyang. Coal was to be furnished partly by privately owned mines in the region, whom Zhang promised a regular market, and partly by government-supported mining of the deposits at Wangsanshi. A narrow-gauge railway led from the mines to the Yangzi, where boats took coal and ore to Hanyang.

The Forges of Hubei were directed by a Belgian engineer. In 1894 they employed nearly 7,000 Chinese workers and about 40 foreigners, whose high salaries were a burden on the budget. Financial difficulties constantly threatened to close the enterprise. Its cost had been estimated at 2½ million taels, but at the beginning of 1893 over 4 million taels had been spent, with only the foundations to show for it. Zhang Zhi-dong had come to the end of his resources. He sought out some rich Cantonese merchants and proposed that they form a company to finance the forges, but they refused. In particular the merchants realized that the local coal was too low in quality for the blast furnaces and that coal would have to be imported. Zhang was forced to borrow 4 million taels from the Deutsche-Asiatische Bank to finish construction at Hanyang. The blast furnaces began working on June 28, 1894, with an annual production of 22,000 tons.

The textile industry

The development of the textile industry was intended to reduce foreign imports. Li Hong-zhang and Zhang Zhi-dong hoped above all to draw on its profits to supply their military budget. The Cotton Cloth Mill, launched by Li in 1876, began work in 1890 but burned down in 1893. It was replaced the following year by a larger mill, known as the Huasheng, which had 64,556 spindles and 750 looms. Four smaller cotton mills were also linked to the Huasheng and to the bureaucratic clique which administered it. In all, there were 135,000 Chinese spindles in Shanghai on the eve of the Treaty of Shimonoseki.

The other center of the cotton industry was Wuchang, to which Zhang Zhi-dong transferred a mill from Canton where it had originally opened in 1889. The Hubei Cotton Cloth Mill began production at the end of 1891 with 40,000 spindles and 1,000 looms. In 1893 construction was begun on a cotton-spinning mill and a silk-spinning mill, both of which went into operation four years later.

The official textile industry cost the government nearly 6 million taels after 1885. By 1894 it employed 10,000 workers.

Characteristics of the *yangwu* enterprises

During the ten-year period 1885 to 1895, the money invested in the nonmilitary official enterprises was hardly three-quarters of that spent every year on the modernization of the armed forces. The degree of industrialization achieved was not enough to halt foreign economic penetration. Even in the development of spinning mills, the new local output, which was half the imports of foreign yarns, did not prevent the latter from increasing.

Technologically the *yangwu* enterprises were largely dependent on foreigners, and to a certain extent they had to rely on foreign money as well. Alongside the "government operation" (*guan ban*) and the "government supervision and merchant operation" (*guan du shang ban*) systems that had been developed to finance the *yangwu* companies, there appeared a new system known as "co-operation between officials and merchants" (*guan shang heban*). This formula was simply a trick to attract merchant capital, but the merchants did not fall for it. They remembered all too well that in the concerns founded before 1885 under the *guan du shang ban* system, the bureaucrats had ousted the merchants from power, even to the point of buying back their shares with the help of foreign loans. Now the officials were obviously building into the new *yangwu* enterprises all the faults inherent in the public administration. Whether the financial system was that of *guan du shang ban* or *guan shang heban*, the merchant-partners were hardly merchants in the strict sense of the term. Such a company was more like a comprador bureaucracy—made up of officials who had grown rich on foreign trade and compradors who had acquired official titles or functions—which invested its private resources and managed the business for its own benefit, not that of the state. When money was lacking, it approached foreign banks, using public funds as a pledge.

Besides tax exemption, the official industries enjoyed other privileges. The most important was the ten-year monopoly granted to the Cotton Cloth Mill in Shanghai in 1882. This was replaced in 1893 by a scheme requiring new independent mills to pay the Huasheng mill a tax proportionate to their production. The special privileges granted to government industries put private initiative in an unfavorable position. As it happened, the nonmilitary *yangwu* enterprises, like the military ones, helped sustain the regional power of a few senior provincial officials and their coteries much more than the power of the nation as a whole.

Progress of Foreign Imperialism

While Chinese officials tried to offset the consequences of the defeat of 1885, the foreigners did their best to extend their gains. During the period 1885 to 1894, Western capitalism moved on to the stage of imperialism. Foreign penetration in China began to take new forms.

The encircling of the empire

The vise was tightening around the Chinese empire. Britain annexed Burma in 1886, made Sikkim a protectorate in 1890, and in 1893 obtained the opening of the Tibetan town of Yadong to foreign trade. France occupied Laos in 1893. Russia began to build the Trans-Siberian railway in 1891; by 1895 the line reached Lake Baikal and Siberia began to be populated at the rate of 100,000 immigrants per year. The foreign powers settled en masse in Korea.

Trade expansion

Within China, exploratory trade missions from abroad multiplied. The British consul Bourne led a mission to Yunnan and Guizhou in 1886; his colleague Hosie went to Sichuan; Macaulay went to Tibet in 1885. Fulford of the Indian Civil Service traveled to the North-east in 1886. The Frenchman Martin was sent by the Russian government to explore Tibet and Xinjiang in 1889. The German Schroeder went to Guangxi in 1885, and the French vice-consul Haas went to Sichuan in 1894.

The Zhifu Convention of 1876 stipulated that Chongqing would be opened to foreign trade when steamers managed to reach it. After several fruitless attempts, the British merchant Archibald Little managed in 1888 to get hold of a boat capable of surviving the rapids above Yichang. The Chinese managed to buy the vessel and put it into dry dock, but in 1890, the government gave in and granted foreign merchants the right to set up in Chongqing and trade there, using junks.

The consuls, the chambers of commerce, and the imperial customs undertook vast studies of trade routes, products, and markets. They hoped that foreign imports could develop markets among the mass of the people, not just the rich. The British and Americans made careful analyses of agricultural tools, handicraft equipment, and common local fabrics, to try to imitate them at lower prices.

Trade exchanges

	Value in current customs taels (1,000)				Index* of the real value of total trade†	Indices* of quantity	
	Net imports	Exports	Total exchanges	Trade balance		Imports	Exports
1885	88,200	65,006	153,206	− 23,194	23.1	40.5	47.6
1886	87,479	77,207	164,286	− 10,272	24.2	35.3	54.2
1887	102,264	85,860	188,124	− 16,404	28.4	41.6	41.2
1888	124,783	92,401	217,184	− 32,382	34.3	50.3	43.6
1889	110,884	94,948	207,832	− 13,936	31.4	44.0	45.2
1890	127,093	87,144	214,237	− 39,949	32.4	54.8	42.0
1891	134,004	100,948	234,952	− 33,056	35.5	60.8	47.9
1892	135,101	102,584	237,685	− 32,517	34.9	59.9	49.8
1893	151,363	116,632	267,995	− 34,731	38.8	59.4	57.2
1894	162,103	128,105	290,208	− 33,998	40.3	45.3	60.1

* In all indices, 1913 = 100.
† Total trade in current values divided by index of wholesale prices.
SOURCE: Albert Feuerwerker, *The Chinese Economy, ca. 1870–1911* (Michigan Papers in Chinese Studies, no. 5, Cambridge University Press, 1969), p. 48.

As the table demonstrates, the volume and the value of foreign trade increased. Trade was also becoming more varied. Among the imports, the proportion of opium fell in relative and even in absolute value (from 37 to 20 percent between 1883 and 1893). Cotton cloth remained stationary. On the other hand, the proportion of cotton yarn increased rapidly (5.8 to 14.6 percent between 1883 and 1893), as did that of paraffin, flour, sugar, and to a lesser extent, metals and coal.

Tea exports fell severely because of competition from the plantations in India and Ceylon and the heavy tax on the tea trade in China. In 1893 tea represented only 26.9 percent of the value of Chinese exports, compared with 46.2 percent in 1883. The proportion of silk exports rose in absolute but not in relative value, remaining at about 30 percent. New trade developed in oilseeds, leather, ginned cotton, matting, bamboo, hog bristles, and spices.

Transportation and industry

In 1891 more than thirty foreign companies were engaged in transporting goods between the treaty ports. These firms handled over 70 percent of the large-cargo traffic, which in that year reached the figure of 28 million tons, compared with 18 million in 1885.

Investment in industry increased. In 1894 there were at least 87 foreign industrial enterprises with a total of 34,000 employees and a total capital of 13 million taels (mainly subscribed by Chinese shareholders). They worked at shipbuilding and repairing, processing goods for export, and turning out products for sale in China, either to foreign residents or to prosperous Chinese.

One-third, or 28, of these firms were founded between 1885 and 1894. Although they were generally small, several important textile concerns, mainly silk-spinning mills, were created then. Foreign incursions into the cotton industry were forbidden; indeed, the Chinese government only tolerated the other factories. It claimed that the term *gong* used in the treaties authorized foreign handicraft production, not industry on a large scale. The foreign diplomatic corps made frequent but somewhat half-hearted attempts to break down the resistance of the authorities. Basically, foreign governments themselves had reservations about factories, even under foreign control, which could utilize cheap Chinese labor to undersell industry at home.

Foreign syndicates

On the other hand, foreign diplomats used all the means at their disposal to support the syndicates, a new instrument of economic penetration which appeared after 1885. The syndicates were groups of industrialists and bankers, all from the same country, formed with the intention of assembling the funds and orders for equipment which it was thought could not fail to bring about the modernization of China. Unlike the firms which had been doing business with China since 1840, these organizations had only one representative on the spot. All important decisions were made in foreign capitals. Similarly, the aim of the syndicates was not simply to sell the products of their own countries but to establish a financial and technical monopoly. For example, they did not merely sell railway lines on credit; they exported capital and engineers. The Mission de l'Industrie Française; which included the Comptoir d'Escompte de Paris and Fives-Lille; the German syndicate formed by the Diskonto-Gesellschaft, the Deutsche Bank, and Krupp; an American syndicate sponsored by Vanderbilt and another organized by Chicago industrial and financial concerns—all these harassed the Chinese government with their proposals. By 1894 the syndicates had not in fact obtained the concessions they were aiming at. But they had acquired the techniques and set up the structures which subsequently enabled them to put the economic clauses of the Treaty of Shimonoseki to full use on a vast scale.

Railways

Although the syndicates obtained large orders in China for constructing fortifications, performing hydraulic work, and arranging shipments of arms, the franchise to build the railways eluded them. In 1889 all classes of the Chinese population strongly opposed Li Hong-zhang's plans to construct a railway line between Peking and Tientsin with the help of foreign capital. As a result the court launched a great debate on the railway question, inviting all senior officials to give their opinions. The recommendations adopted for consideration were those of Zhang Zhi-dong. For the reasons given in document 2, he advocated a line between Peking and Hankou, to be built gradually using Chinese capital and Chinese materials that would be supplied by the developing iron and steel industry.

Foreign banks

On the other hand, the mere fact of the additional competition provided by the syndicates acted to lower the interest rate. In this way the syndicates increased the influence which foreigners already exercised on the Chinese financial market through the British banks in China. Between 1885 and 1894 the Chinese government borrowed 21 million taels (mostly in long-term loans) from foreigners —as much as had been borrowed over the twenty preceding years.

The foreign banking network embraced all the open ports. The old banks opened new agencies and increased their capital. The Hong Kong and Shanghai Banking Corporation, for example, had 45 agencies by 1894. In 1890 its capital rose from 5 to 10 million dollars and its deposits were worth 63,900,000 dollars, compared with 8,700,000 dollars in 1870. New banks opened—among them the Deutsche-Asiatische Bank (1890), the National Bank of China (1891), and the Yokohama Specie Bank (1892). These institutions controlled all foreign trade operations in the open ports, as well as the foreign exchange market. They attracted deposits from Chinese customers and consequently had ready money available for short-term loans to Chinese banks financing transactions in the Chinese interior. This system tended to bring the whole of the Chinese financial market under the influence of the Shanghai market which, since it was dominated by the foreign banks, linked Chinese banking to the world market.

Financial domination

One indication that the semicolonization of China was becoming more pronounced could be found in the growing influence of international monetary fluctuations on Chinese finance. Owing to the overproduction of silver and the abandonment of bimetallism by some countries, the world price of silver began to fall as early as 1873. It continued to drop between 1885 and 1894; the exchange rate of the customs tael, which had lost 16 percent of its value between 1873 and 1884, lost another 36 percent between 1884 and 1894. Since China was a silver-standard country, this decline favored Chinese sales abroad. The increase in the world price of gold, on the other hand, stimulated gold exports. The Chinese treated gold simply as a commodity which they exchanged for silver.

All these factors combined to produce a relative influx of silver into China. The outflow of money from which the economy had suffered since the early nineteenth century had apparently reversed. The consequence was slight inflation, which encouraged the growth of industry from 1895 on. The beneficial effects, however, were lessened by the fact that the general fall in the price of silver was irregular, subject to disastrous fluctuations and constant speculation. Similarly, the depreciation of silver, added to the increase in money transactions, brought a rise in the price of copper cash under conditions which were detrimental to the mass of the population.

Copper cash became rarer, while the copper coins in circulation depreciated and the volume of paper money grew. There was a tendency to reckon salaries and agricultural prices in silver, although they were paid in copper cash. Meanwhile the difference increased between the real rate of exchange determining payment for work, and the legal rate, fixed at a time when silver was expensive, governing the payment of land rent and taxes.

In a world system dominated by gold, the organization of foreign exchanges and the concomitant withdrawal of gold from the country, China was placed in a position of irremediable inferiority and forced to adopt the gold standard.

The network of economic exploitation

The development of foreign penetration was reflected in the growing number of foreign firms in China (396 in 1885, 580 in 1893) and foreigners living there (6,698 in 1885, 9,350 in 1894). The steady expansion of Western capitalism was due above all to the establishment of a network of economic exploitation based on Chinese intermediaries. This network was strong enough to survive an assortment of economic mishaps: the stagnation of trade on the Tongking frontier, the bankruptcy of the big American firm of Russell & Company in 1890, and the liquidation of the Mission de l'Industrie Française following the collapse of the Comptoir d'Escompte during the European financial crisis of 1891. (Among its other benefits, the existence of the network encouraged the formation of two new French syndicates to replace the Mission de l'Industrie Française.)

The networks were controlled from Shanghai, Hong Kong, and Tientsin. Most of the direct trading with foreign countries was carried out through Shanghai and Hong Kong. The banks, the warehouses, and the operations of the speculator, the gambler, and the criminal were centered in those cities. The life-style of the foreign colony, which was an extremely mixed community, was beginning to contaminate Chinese society. The open towns in Central and South China were satellites of Shanghai and Hong Kong. To the foreign residents, the high spots of their city were the racetrack, the bandstand, and the neo-Gothic cathedral, all of which they considered proof of the superiority of their civilization.

In contrast to Shanghai and Hong Kong, Tientsin owed its importance to the presence of Li Hong-zhang, who handled most of the orders from the Chinese government. The atmosphere of Tientsin was very different, pervaded by *yamen* intrigues. The foreign colony there consisted of only about one hundred people and was less varied.

Cultural penetration

Foreign cultural activities expanded along with foreign economic penetration. In the 1890s, for instance, about 200 Protestant missionaries, mainly Americans, most of them inspired with crusading zeal, were arriving in China each year. In all there were 1,500 Protestant missionaries in the country early in 1893. Following the example of the Roman Catholics, they moved further into the Chinese interior. Many of them were doctors and teachers, devoted to good works rather than preaching. In 1894 the number of their converts was still under 40,000, whereas the Catholics, with only 550 missionaries, had 530,000 followers. The Protestant missionaries opened hospitals (they had established 24 by 1892), dispensaries, and pharmacies. Like the Jesuits in the seventeenth century, they tried to reach the scholar class. The Methodist University of Peking was founded in 1891, the college which later became Lingnan University opened in 1885 in Canton, and the two colleges which later became Yanjing were organized in 1885 and 1893 in Peking. In the Protestant schools, where the teaching of English and science was given more emphasis than the catechism, the total number of pupils rose from 6,000 in 1877 to 16,836 in 1890.

The Protestant missions also undertook the translation of scientific works. In Shanghai two groups, which included laymen, were established to provide translations: the Educational Association of China, founded in 1890, and the Guangxuehui (Society for the Diffusion of Christian and General Knowledge Among the Chinese), founded in 1887. Under their supervision, over one hundred translations of books of general interest and many works of popularization were published by the missions' printshops. The Guangxuehui also published a monthly magazine in Chinese, *Wan Guo Gong Bao* (*The Globe Magazine*), with articles on politics, economics, science, and philosophy, for the scholarly circles in the open ports. As Chapter 6 has described, most of the outstanding missionaries who were active in education—men such as Timothy Richard, John Fryer, Young J. Allen, Joseph Edkins, and W. A. P. Martin—were associated with the mandarins behind the *yangwu* movement. Before becoming director of the Guangxuehui in 1891, Timothy Richard was editor of the Tientsin newspaper financed by Li Hong-zhang. W. A. P. Martin was president of the Ton Wen Guan, the official interpreters' school in Peking. Fryer was in charge of the translation department at the Jiangnan arsenal.

The Catholics devoted less of their effort to education. The Jesuits helped with a small French school for Chinese which the French municipality in Shanghai organized in 1886. But with the distinguished exception of the Observatory of Xujiahui (Zikawei), the Roman Catholic schools, although numerous, were directed toward an elementary level. Pupils recited the catechism instead of the Confucian Classics, and all the teaching was in Chinese, with a little Latin for future priests.

Problems arising from the missions

The development of the missions created endless difficulties. Although China had finally allowed the Catholics to recover the land that they had owned in the seventeenth and eighteenth centuries, the government would not acknowledge their right to acquire new property outside the treaty ports.[5] In the Chinese view, this was not a right but only a sometime concession contingent on the agreement of the authorities and the local population.

One way or another, the missionaries caused perpetual conflict. They used fraudulent means to enlarge their sphere of activities. They interfered constantly to protect their flock from the public authorities. They demanded enormous indemnities for the slightest incident. They complained that the punishments inflicted on their opponents were too mild, meanwhile railing against the "barbaric

---

[5] The conflict described in document 1 was based on such a quarrel.

cruelty" of the Chinese. The arrival of Protestant missionaries in the Chinese interior made things worse. Not only did they quarrel with the Catholics, but they knew nothing about the Chinese language and customs, and they showed such rash aggressiveness that they exasperated the diplomats who had to negotiate for their protection.

The missions made few converts, but they did attract Chinese hangers-on who had been uprooted from their normal surroundings and had broken with ancestral traditions. They were the people whom the missionaries recommended to the consuls to make up their network of informers. These informers, together with the compradors, the agents, the officials who sold *yamen* secrets to diplomats, and the servants of Westerners, all formed a sort of train of dependents who, whether they liked it or not, were instruments of foreign interests. Their activities, and the authorities' hostility to them, made the Chinese public aware of the political influence exercised by foreigners.

Political influence

The collusion between the Qing government and the imperialists during the period 1885–1894, denounced by present-day Chinese historians, was not the result of information which the foreigners managed to glean at court or in the *yamen*. The advance of Western capitalism resulted from objective circumstances that were independent of the intentions and preferences of those concerned. One illustration of this thesis is the fact that after more than fifty years of diplomatic relations with China, foreign ministers were still excluded from the imperial palace. Not one of them had ever seen Ci-xi. Seventeen years after the audience granted by the Tongzhi Emperor in 1874, they were admitted to the presence of the Guangxu Emperor to present their credentials or their letters of recall. The ceremony lasted about ten minutes; it was held in a hall outside the palace enclosure, so the French and Russian ministers refused to attend. It was only after the Sino-Japanese War that the diplomatic corps was received in a hall of the inner palace and obtained the right to enter by the central gate reserved for the emperor.

Diplomats in Peking were never invited into Chinese private houses. Jeng Ji-ze, who had once been Chinese minister to Britain, tried to break with this custom and was almost lynched by his countrymen when he returned to his own province. Foreign ministers saw only officials from the Zongli Yamen, which had no authority apart from the fact that its members held other offices in the government. The consuls had closer relations with the provincial administrative bodies, but as document 1 illustrates, these dealings were still marked by hostility and mistrust.

In spite of the lack of evidence, a growing number of Chinese were convinced that there was connivance between the government and the foreign powers. To them the proof lay in the steady progress of foreign penetration and in the fact that the official attempts to discourage it, such as the *yangwu* movement, seemed always to have the opposite effect.

Popular Resistance to Foreign Gains

Much of the popular unrest of this period was still aimed only at the mandarins and the gentry: the Mongol revolt in 1886, the disturbances in Hunan, Jiangsu, Fujian, and Zhejiang in 1887, the revolt of the aboriginal population of Hainan in 1886–1888, the rebellion of the Yunnan miners in 1889, and the endemic banditry in the Northeast. Dreadful natural calamities worsened the poverty due to the economic and social regime.[5] Zhili and Fengtian were flooded in 1886, 1890, and 1893. The Yellow River burst its dikes in 1887 and flowed south, laying waste the low-lying regions in Jiangsu and Anhui and leaving the higher ground ravaged by drought. Millions of people died or were left homeless. Epidemics of plague and cholera broke out every year in the Southern provinces from 1889 on.

More and more frequently, however, popular rebellions combined the theme of opposition to the government with a crusade against the foreigners. And the rebellions themselves created common ground between the invaders and the Chinese leaders, in spite of their antagonisms. When the foreigners negotiated with the government, the danger of a successful upheaval made them careful to stop short of impairing the authorities' ability to maintain order. And the government, since it could not fight on two fronts, often preferred to give in to the foreigners, who could provide material help.

---

[5] In document 3 Zhu De, the founder of the Red Army, recalls the terrible famine of 1893–1894 in Sichuan.

Hostility toward the missions

Popular opposition to foreign imperialism usually found expression in hostility toward the missions, because they were in direct contact with the Chinese people in all parts of the country. As happened during the preceding period, the missions' orphanages, their zealous protection of Chinese Christians, and their acquisition of landed property bred conflict and rioting. The peasant hostility was encouraged by the gentry, who saw Christian propaganda as a threat to their intellectual influence and their social position. When violence erupted, the local authorities usually adopted a wait-and-see policy. The growing number of Protestant missionaries made the clashes still more frequent, though now they were less likely to end in murder.

During this period the hostility toward the missions took on new characteristics in some places, where incidents of violence were numerous and organized. In the summer of 1886, for example, the mood of the peasants in Chongqing was ominous. The cost of rice was prohibitive; horrifying poverty was universal; the officials were prepared to do anything to placate the public. Newspapers arrived with reports of Chinese workers massacred in the United States. The scholars who had come to take the military examinations spread the rumor that the Protestant missionaries had built fortifications to bombard the town and occupy it. (In fact the missionaries had constructed a white wall surrounding their new buildings on a hill overlooking the city.) On July 1 the crowd, crying, "Burn the foreign devils, but don't kill them!" plundered and burned the American and British missions and the British consulate. Then they attacked the Catholic mission and destroyed the homes of Chinese Christians. The rioting spread to east Sichuan, where churches were burned and Christians beaten, particularly at Longshuizhen in the Dazu district. Afterwards the violence was repeated, becoming progressively more savage, almost every year in this little town and the neighboring villages. In 1890 ten Christians who were accused of having killed or wounded members of the public were cut into pieces and burned. The riots were led by a coal carrier, Yu Dongchen, who was head of a band connected with the secret societies and who worked in connivance with the gentry.

The uprising of 1886 in Sichuan impressed the peasants of Zunyi in Guizhou, who then expelled a Catholic missionary and a group of Christians and prevented their return for several years. In Shandong the German Roman Catholic mission and the American Presbyterians were subjected to similar harassment. (Document 1 describes an organized riot in that province.)

The riots of 1891

In the Yangzi valley in 1891 the movement of opposition to the missionaries acquired a wider scope and a new political dimension. A revival of anti-Christian propaganda had begun in 1889 with the appearance of posters, pamphlets, songs, and poems in the same vein as those which prefaced the Tientsin massacre of 1870. Rioting broke out here and there in Jinjiang, Hankou, and Jiujiang. In Canton a riot occurred early one morning when an outraged crowd stopped a servant from the Roman Catholic mission. He was carrying two baskets with the bodies of seven children who had died at the orphanage.

The coordination apparent behind all these developments led the foreigners to suspect that it was the work of the secret societies. Their impression was confirmed by a succession of thirty incidents between May and September of 1891 along the Grand Canal and in the Yangzi valley. The most serious were at Wuhu and Yichang. In these riots the plundering and burning were restricted to the missions; they did not spread to the homes of Chinese Christians. In one case the customs house, which was rented out to a mission, was attacked, along with the British consulate. Anti-Christian propaganda took on colossal proportions; pamphlets like *The Demoniacal Doctrines Must Perish (Gui Jiao Gai Si)* ran to 800,000 copies.

No exact explanation for these events has yet been found. Contemporaries were struck by the organization behind the rioting, which seemed to spread according to a plan—north to south along the Grand Canal, east to west along the Yangzi. Riots were preceded by the distribution of anti-Christian pamphlets, by rumors that there would be violence on a certain date, and by the arrival of many strangers in town. The rioters had instructions to spare the lives of foreigners (only two Europeans were killed, and that accidentally rather than deliberately), and they were closely supervised by leaders who maintained discipline. The overall direction of operations seems to have been taken by the Society of Brothers and Elders. This secret society, many of whose members were natives of Hunan, was assisted—indeed, sometimes guided—by the populist, anti-Christian propaganda of the scholars, especially those from Hunan. The peasants of the central provinces, exhausted by several

years of floods and famine, were particularly receptive to the agitation. The Chinese grievances against the foreigners and their missions were intensified by anxiety about the foreign merchants who
moved into Chongqing in March 1891. Boatmen and carriers especially were afraid that they would be thrown out of work by
steam navigation on the upper Yangzi. They, like the soldiers recently disbanded by the provincial officials to cut down on expenses, were often affiliated with the Gelaohui—the Brothers and
Elders.

Did the rioting have a political aim? The stated purpose of the
Society of Brothers and Elders was to overthrow the Qing and
restore the Chinese Ming dynasty, and most of the uprisings were
accompanied by anti-Manchu slogans and threats to the mandarins.
In June 1891 for the first time posters against the emperor himself
appeared on the gates of the imperial palace. It seemed that the
leaders of the movement believed that if the missions were destroyed, the foreign powers would have to declare war, and that the
Brothers and Elders could overthrow the Manchu government with
the help of the rebellious peasants. This interpretation of their rea-
soning was supported by a government seizure of arms and munitions that were being smuggled to the rebels by a British employee
of the customs, indicating that there was collusion between the
foreigners and the secret society. Moreover, the attitude of many
of the officials was ambiguous. Most of the anti-Christian propaganda which accompanied the rising reflected anti-Manchu sentiments and the scholars' attachment to the Confucian tradition; in
many places, on the other hand, the authorities were not troubled at
all. The riots appear to have arisen from several influences, which
produced different results depending on the place.

The disturbances spread

Agitation spread in Fujian, Guangdong, Guangxi, Yunnan,
Guizhou, Zhili, and the Northeast, without any serious incidents
involving Christians. In November 1891, however, a revolt broke
out in east Rehe, in the district of Chaoyang. It was led by two
sects, the Zaili (Temperance Society), of Taoist inspiration, and
the Jindan Dao (Gold Elixir Sect), whose numbers were expanded
by rebels from the South. The region had been sorely tried by
famine and by the exactions of the Mongol princes and Chinese
officials. The rebels, who quickly gained a following of nearly
20,000 fighters, carried banners inscribed "Annihilate the Qing;

death to the foreigners." During the revolt 1,500 Christians were massacred, and their belongings and those of the missions were plundered. The rebels then attacked the *yamen* and the houses of the rich, and ultimately proclaimed an emperor.

The foreigners' reaction

The spreading riots started a panic among foreign residents in China. It was obvious to them that the Chinese bore a grudge against foreigners in general, not simply against the missions. Foreigners everywhere felt that their lives and property were in danger. Even in Shanghai, the peasants from the surrounding countryside sabotaged bridges and roads. A wave of anguished petitions and atrocity stories broke over the European capitals. All available gunboats in the Far East were sent to China. In view of the danger, the foreign governments accepted the French suggestion to carry out combined action. Protests to the Chinese authorities, requests for indemnities, and demonstrations of sea power were made collectively. Plans for an international invasion of China and a division of its territory were drawn up in case the situation worsened.

This was the first time that China had had to face a coalition of foreign interests. Whereas the Zongli Yamen tried to break the coalition, the Qing government gave in. Caught between two fires, it tried to appease the barbarians and gain their support against the popular rebellion. On June 13, 1891, an imperial edict praised the Christians and their missions. Local authorities received orders to find the culprits responsible for anti-Christian violence, and disobedient officials were stripped of their office. The first indemnities were granted to the missions almost without question.

But the union of the foreign powers barely outlasted November 1891. Britain was afraid that its trade interests would be jeopardized if it opposed the imperial government. The United States did not want to be drawn into military operations in China. In 1892 the diplomatic corps managed to bring about the ruin of Zhou Han, a Hunanese official accused of being the author of an anti-Christian pamphlet, and in 1893 the corps exacted reparation for the murder of two Swedish missionaries in Hubei. But the Qing government was soon able to begin maneuvering again between foreign claims and popular demands. It refused to pay an indemnity to the Rehe missions, for example, on the grounds that according to international law, it could not be held responsible for damages caused by civil war.

Consequences of the riots of 1891

The events of 1891 were like a sort of general rehearsal for the Boxer Rising, and on both the Chinese and the foreign sides they had important consequences. The majority of the foreigners acquired the conviction that the only way to deal with the Chinese was through arms. As for the Chinese people, the executions and terrorism that followed the riots (20,000 died in Rehe), together with the heavy indemnities (370,000 taels to the Catholic missions alone), kindled hostility against governors and foreign invaders alike. The missions were frequently attacked in subsequent years.

Although the rebels' attempt at organized resistance to imperialism was a failure, it made plain the association between the Qing government and the foreign powers. The cowardly weakness shown by the government made it clearer than before to certain groups of scholars and officials that reform was needed. Although they had at first felt sympathy for the rioters, they attributed the movement's failure to violence and preferred not to be associated with it. As a result of the riots, however, they were more favorably disposed toward the new political ideas developed by a few thinkers after 1885.

The reformist current

In 1885 the Chinese defeat in the Sino-French War gave an impetus to the reformist ideas which had arisen during the preceding period. Zheng Guan-ying, Xue Fu-cheng, Ma Jian-zhong, and Wang Tao enlarged the scope of the criticism of *yangwu* and went into it more thoroughly. Basing their arguments on the example of the West, they advocated the encouragement of private enterprises, the development of trade, and the reform of education. They also inserted a new element: a demand for political reform.

This demand was published for the first time in March 1887 by He Qi (or Ho Kai, 1859–1917) in an article which caused a sensation in China. It took the form of a reply to a defense of the *yangwu* movement written by Zeng Ji-ze, the Chinese minister in London, which had appeared in several newspapers in China and abroad. He Qi was a brilliant young Hong Kong lawyer who had studied law and medicine in Britain. His article demonstrated that *yangwu* had led to disaster, denounced the government's corruption and exploitation of the people, and argued that political reform was essential for the development of the economic and military power which could enable China to resist the foreigners. The specific reforms that were necessary were detailed in writings published by He Qi in cooperation with Hu Li-yuan (1847–1916), a failed candidate in the imperial examinations who became a rich merchant in Hong Kong. Similar reforms were proposed by Zheng Guang-ying in the enlarged version of his book *On Change (Yiyan)*, written in 1875, which was reissued in 1893 under the title *Warnings to the Seemingly Prosperous Age (Sheng Shi Wei Yan)*. These ideas were also expounded by Tang Zhen (1857–1917) and Chen Chi (?–1899), both middle-ranking officials, and by Chen Qiu (1851–1903), a scholar and philanthropist from Zhejiang who refused to enter the civil service. They in turn influenced other writers, such as Xue Fu-cheng, Huang Zun-xian, Ma Jian-zhong, and Wang Tao. The entire group denounced absolutism and campaigned for some form of representative government, with legislative bodies elected from citizens who had reached a certain level of wealth or education. Their models were Britain, Germany, and above all Japan, which had adopted a new constitution in 1889. Chen Chi suggested that the system of representative government should be extended all the way down to the district level. He Qi advocated a real parliamentary system, with a responsible cabinet. Like Zheng Guan-ying, he believed that the people should have dominion over the sovereign.

This political program was by no means a doctrine of radical opposition to the traditional Confucian system or the *yangwu* ideology. The new reformers rejected liberty, equality, and democracy and conceived of political participation as being restricted to an elite. They denied that the traditional Chinese political system had any virtues, but they intended to maintain the Confucian morality. They had no plans for changing the agrarian system. Although they wanted to repulse foreign imperialism, they did not believe that the new institutions would be able to work without foreign advisers, and they were ready to accept foreign economic cooperation.

The audience for the reform doctrines

The ideas of the reformers spread among the senior officials—men like Zhang Zhi-dong, Liu Kun-yi, and Weng Tong-he. In 1894 Weng Tong-he went so far as to present the emperor with the writings of Tang Zhen and Chen Chi. In China at that period there were a growing number of newspapers, translations of foreign publications, and books giving information about the outside world. More Chinese were also traveling abroad; in 1889, for example, about twenty officials were sent on a study trip to Europe and the United States. This increased contact with the world created an intellectual climate which favored the adoption of new ideas, though among a very small public. It was a public which was growing larger, however, particularly after the riots of 1891, and it included industrialists and merchants who were striving to develop private companies in spite of the *yangwu* monopolies.

The growth of private enterprise

Modern private capitalism increased in size and variety between 1885 and 1894. The most rapid growth was in silk-spinning mills. In 1888 there were 120, equipped in European style, in the neighborhood of Canton. Statistics based on 68 of these recorded 28,000 workers in 1894. At the same date Shanghai had a dozen private mills employing nearly 5,000 workers, while the two main silk centers in Shandong contained 35 mills with 4,000 workers.

A partial census stated that 52 new factories opened in China between 1885 and 1894. It is known that half of these had a total capital of 4 million taels. In spite of the *yangwu* monopoly, some of them were plants for processing cotton. The largest groups, however, were match factories, paper mills, printshops, glassworks, sugar refineries, brick factories, tinworks, and shipyards. In addition, water and electric companies were founded in Shanghai and Canton.

Private capital was also attracted to mines that were utilizing modern techniques. Private companies, for example, were formed to extract and process silver at Danzhou and Taiyushan in Guangdong. But in the mining sector, which had always been under state control, private initiative was hampered by interference from the bureaucracy. The government seized the most productive deposits and mines, and private investors were discouraged by the cost of modern machinery and of the foreign experts who had to be hired to run it, as well as by the initial investment in time needed for preliminary work. Private mines, of which there were many in Yunnan and Guangxi, generally went on using traditional techniques. In this period they often began to employ a larger number of workers than before, however, and to modernize their administrative systems.

The handicraft industry went through a similar evolution. In regions where foreign imports arrived in large quantities, many individual and family enterprises lost out to the competition. In their place larger enterprises developed for weaving silk and cotton, some of them being set up as workshops while others were organized to job work out to individuals at home. These larger systems made it possible to introduce technical improvements. In Zhejiang, for example, the use of Japanese treadle looms increased productivity to over three times that of the traditional looms. The fact that the handicraft enterprises were concentrated geographically made it easier to commercialize their production. Thus in the space of ten years, sales of handicraft cotton fabrics from Jiangsu to the Northeast increased tenfold.

Big trading companies also grew bigger. And two Chinese steam navigation companies were organized, though they sailed under the British flag to get around the monopoly granted to the *yangwu* firm, the China Merchants' Steam Navigation Company founded in 1872. Large amounts of Chinese capital were also invested in foreign enterprises, many of which had to allow Chinese to become directors.

The new social mentality

Among the men who began to support private enterprise were merchants, scholars, and low-grade officials. These new capitalists did not form a large group, and they retained many links with the traditional society. But in the big towns of the Yangzi provinces and the south coast, they were slowly becoming a recognizable circle with its own political reactions. In 1886 the Chinese capitalists in Shanghai combined to attack the rule forbidding Chinese to enter the public gardens in the international concession. They called it insulting and illegal and demanded that the foreign municipality open the gardens "at least to well-dressed Chinese." Though their challenge was unsuccessful, it showed that a new spirit was developing which corresponded to the evolution of the Chinese press and the reformist current of thought. In fact, many of the modern private enterprises were formed with the avowed intention of transforming China and thereby repelling the foreign invasion.

This deliberate opposition to imperialism was still weak and highly vulnerable. It grew up in the shadow of foreign might, and its material means were more or less dependent on foreigners. At the same time it was constantly in danger of being stifled by the traditional structures and attitudes of ancient China.

The Sino-Japanese War

The war which broke out in July 1894 was a tragic revelation of Chinese impotence. Threatened by an insurrection, whose leaders blamed the government for having opened the country to foreign influence, the king of Korea appealed to China. Japan, under the terms of the 1885 convention, announced the intention of intervening as well. China sent 3,000 men, Japan 18,000. Japan presented the Korean government with a program of reforms to be executed with Japanese "aid," and forced the king to appoint a prime minister who was sympathetic to the Japanese proposals.

Demanding the withdrawal of the Chinese troops from Korea, the Japanese began to attack them. China declared war on August 1, 1894. Tokyo was ready, but in Peking there was panic, intrigue, and indecision. Though they were outnumbered at sea, the Japanese quickly gained the upper hand owing to the high quality of their command and equipment. Half of the Chinese navy, the pride of *yangwu*, was sunk. Crossing the Yalu, the Japanese landed at Lushan, Weihaiwei, and Taiwan and threatened Peking itself.

The Chinese government had asked the Western powers to act as mediators, but they were unable to agree among themselves. The imperial court sent Li Hong-zhang to Tokyo to negotiate an armistice, which was signed on March 30, 1895. Japan dictated the conditions, and they were ratified by the Treaty of Shimonoseki on April 17, 1895. China renounced suzerainty over Korea and ceded Taiwan, the Penghu Islands (Pescadores), and the Liaodong peninsula to Japan. The Chinese promised to pay a war indemnity of 200 million taels over eight years. The Japanese were to hold the port of Weihaiwei as security until the second installment of the indemnity was paid. China agreed to open Shashi, Chongqing, Suzhou, and Hangzhou; to allow access to them by steamer; and to permit the establishment of Japanese factories in all the open ports.

To be defeated by an Asian country which China had always considered its inferior was even more humiliating to the Chinese than their loss of the Sino-French War in 1885. It was the irrefutable proof of the failure of *yangwu*. It destroyed the people's confidence in their leaders and undermined their respect for the

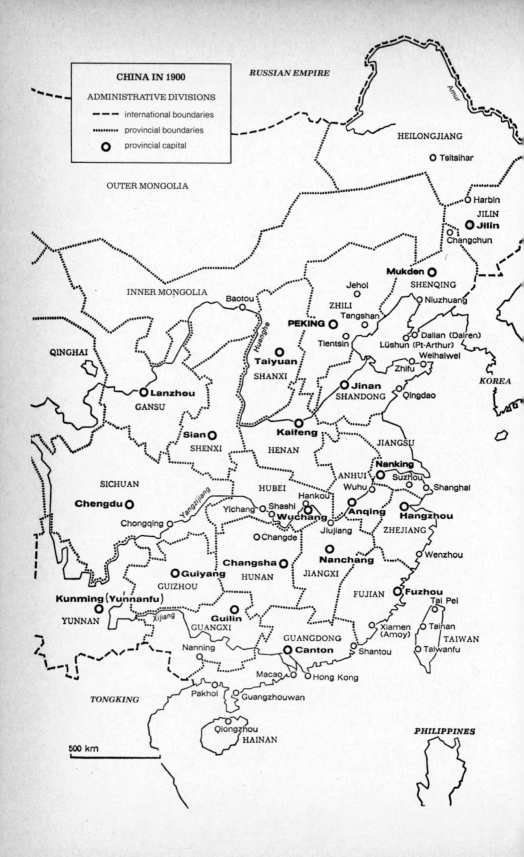

CHINA IN 1900

ADMINISTRATIVE DIVISIONS

- - - international boundaries
······ provincial boundaries
O provincial capital

RUSSIAN EMPIRE

Amur

HEILONGJIANG

O Tsitsihar

OUTER MONGOLIA

O Harbin
JILIN
O Jilin
O Changchun

INNER MONGOLIA

Baotou

Mukden O

SHENQING

Jehol
O
ZHILI
Tangshan

O Niuzhuang

PEKING O

Huanghe

Tientsin

Dalian (Dairen)
Lüshun (Pt-Arthur)
Weihaiwei

QINGHAI

Taiyuan O

SHANXI

Zhifu

KOREA

O Lanzhou

GANSU

Jinan O
SHANDONG

Qingdao

Sian O

SHENXI

Kaifeng O

HENAN

JIANGSU

Nanking O   Suzhou

ANHUI   Wuhu   O Shanghai

SICHUAN

HUBEI

Hankou

Chengdu O

Yangzijiang

Yichang   O Shashi
Wuchang O   Anqing O   Hangzhou O

Chongqing

Jiujiang   ZHEJIANG

Changde

Changsha O   Nanchang O

O Wenzhou

O Guiyang

GUIZHOU   HUNAN   JIANGXI

FUJIAN   O Fuzhou
Tai Pei

Kunming (Yunnanfu) O

YUNNAN   Xijiang

Guilin O

GUANGXI

Xiamen
(Amoy)   O Tainan

TAIWAN

Nanning

GUANGDONG   Shantou   Taiwanfu

O Canton

Macao O   O Hong Kong

TONGKING   Pakhoi   Guangzhouwan

Qiongzhou   HAINAN

PHILIPPINES

500 km

traditional institutions. It initiated a period of still more rapid progress by foreign imperialism, and stimulated a revival of political unrest and demands for reform at home.

ADDITIONAL BIBLIOGRAPHY

A. Feuerwerker, *China's Early Industrialization, Sheng Hsuan-huai (1844–1916] and Mandarin Enterprise* (Cambridge, Mass., Harvard University Press, 1958).

F. H. H. King, *Money and Monetary Policy in China, 1845–1895* (Cambridge, Mass., Harvard University Press, 1965).

J. L. Rawlinscn, *China's Struggle for Naval Development, 1839–1895* (Cambridge, Mass., Harvard University Press, 1967).

S. Spector, *Li Hung-chang and the Huai Army: A Study in Nineteenth Century Chinese Regionalism* (Seattle, University of Washington Press, 1964).

Tcheng Ki-Tong, *Les Chinois peints par eux-mêmes* (Paris, 1884).

E. S. Wehrle, *Britain, China and the Antimissionary Riots, 1891–1900* (Minneapolis, University of Minnesota Press, 1966).

DOCUMENTS

1. CHINESE RELATIONS WITH FOREIGNERS AT THE END OF THE NINETEENTH CENTURY (1891)

SOURCE: Extract from a letter from the Sinologist E. Chavannes, then attaché at the French legation in Peking, to P. Ristelhueber, the French Chargé d'Affaires in China. Archives du Ministère des Affaires Etrangères, *Correspondance politique des ambassades et légations*, Chine, vol. 77, fol. 119–121.

When traveling in Shandong, E. Chavannes met the German consul in Tientsin, von Seckendorff, who had come on behalf of the German Roman Catholic missions. They had previously been under French protection, but the Pope had just placed them under German authority. The missions wanted to settle in the neighborhood of Confucius's birthplace, and they were in constant conflict with the local officials and the public on this issue.

Jiningzhou, January 28, 1891

I found I was in the inn next door to the one where M. de Seckendorff is at the moment. I paid him a visit and learned from his own lips of the grave dangers which he has incurred during his mission.

This is what he told me: He went to Jinanfu [the capital of Shandong] first of all and asked to see the governor, Zhang Yao. That official twice refused to see him, referring him to the *daotai*. M. de Seckendorff then put on his uniform, mounted his horse and left for the governor's *yamen*, accompanied by three *tingchai* [official messengers]. When he saw the central gate of the *yamen* standing open, he spurred

his horse to a gallop and went in before anyone had time to shut it.*
He forced the governor's men to open the central gate of the inner
courtyard and so gained admittance to the presence of Zhang Yao, who
gave him an extremely cold welcome. He asked the governor for a
special pass,† which was brought to him the next day by a *kuli* [the
lowest-ranking messenger], without a visiting card or a letter. M. de
Seckendorff threw the pass on the ground, declaring that he would not
tolerate such lack of respect. The governor then sent the pass back
again with a *zhao hui*, or official message—which was an excessive
show of politeness. M. de Seckendorff obtained another audience, but
it was fixed for the fifth day of the Chinese lunar month (January 14),
which was a *ji zhen* day—the anniversary of an emperor's death. The
consul could only enter the *yamen* by the little door as a result,‡ but
the governor was suddenly extremely agreeable and gave his visitor
dinner, accompanied by champagne. M. de S. went from Jinanfu to
Taianzhou, where he stopped to climb Taishan [one of the five sacred
mountains of China]. He went on to Yanzhoufu, about sixty *li* [ap-
proximately 30 kilometers] northeast of the place from which I am
writing to you. As soon as he arrived, the walls were covered with
strips of red paper inciting the population to kill the foreigner. M. de
S. had some of these posters and showed them to me; they said: "The
people in the town and countryside must unite to put the foreigner to
death on the 15th."

M. de S. arrived in Yanzhoufu on the thirteenth day of the Chinese
lunar month (January 23); the rioting was planned for the second day
after that. He declared to the Chinese authorities that he was resolved
to confront the rioters. He found the *daotai* well disposed toward him
though not very firm, but he was thoroughly satisfied with the military
official, the *zhentai*. On the other hand, he is convinced that the other
officials and the scholars stirred up all the trouble. Whatever the case
may be, on the morning of the fifteenth, shouting was heard in the
town, and at midday the crowd gathered around the door of the inn
where he was staying. M. de S. was alone in the courtyard, revolver in
hand, while about forty soldiers guarded the door. In the afternoon,
the *zhixian* [the district administrator] entered the inn, and the noise
outside redoubled. M. de S. declared to the *zhixian* that he thought the
Chinese authorities were excessively weak. He said that if any armed
men entered the courtyard he would begin by killing six of them, and
would then be killed himself, but his death would bring severe reprisals
for the Chinese. The *xueguan*—highly respected officials who carry

---

* The entrance to official buildings consisted of a central gate flanked by two
lower side gates. The emperor alone had the right to go through the central door
in some halls of the imperial palace. Elsewhere, strict etiquette had to be observed
when entering by the central door or gate.
† When traveling outside the open ports and the capital, foreigners had to carry a
pass issued by the Chinese authorities. Depending on the type, it either did or did
not entitle a foreigner to receive official honors wherever he went.
‡ These days were considered ill-fated, and the central gate of every *yamen* was
closed.

out literary duties—were then called in to calm the crowd. Thanks to their intervention, the riot gradually ceased.

Next day M. de S. went to Qufu [Confucius's birthplace] to visit the temple of Confucius. He rode through Yanzhoufu again during the afternoon, followed at a respectful distance by a crowd shouting insults at him. He arrived here at Jiningzhou yesterday evening. In the morning a man called him *Yang Guizi* [Foreign Devil]; the consul had the man seized and got the *zhixian* to put him in the pillory. I saw him myself, at the door of the inn.

2. ZHANG ZHI-DONG RECOMMENDS CONSTRUCTION OF A RAILWAY LINE FROM PEKING TO HANKOU (1889)

SOURCE: Extract from the memorial of April 2, 1889, in the *Complete Works of Zhang Zhi-dong* [*Zhang Wenxiang gong quanji, zouyi*], Memorials, 25/12-17.

I consider that at the moment, the chief use of the railways is to stimulate the circulation of Chinese goods. In the conjuncture following the opening of trade relations with foreign countries, the standard of living of the Chinese population and the prosperity of its trade, both depend on abundant local production. The balance between Chinese exports and foreign imports is the deciding factor. For several years the value of foreign imported goods and opium has exceeded the value of Chinese exports by about 20 million taels each year. If this deficit is allowed to continue, it will never be made good. At the moment it is impossible to dry up the source of foreign goods and opium; the only solution is to find a way to export more Chinese goods, and to sell more Chinese goods, to make up for it. . . . Again, Chinese goods are rough in quality and not worth much. There must be more of them to bring in something, and to this end they must be made rapidly. Without machines and chemical means, a basic raw material cannot be transformed into a refined product of good quality, and useless things cannot be made useful. With railways, machines could be brought in and the raw materials transported. . . .

The opening of the market will benefit the merchants. An increase in production will benefit the workers. The products of cultivation and stock-rearing of farmers in the mountains and the plains, and the products of hard-working women, can be sold far away; the peasants will gain. The principal feature of the railways is that the people will gain from them. Now, what is in the interest of the people is in the national interest too. . . .

Along the proposed path of the Tientsin-Tongzhou line* there are about 60,000 carters, boatmen, innkeepers, and porters. Counting five people for each family, this makes a total of 300,000. It is hard to get accurate statistics concerning this category of society, but it can be

* The line suggested by Li Hong-zhang; Zhang Zhi-dong wanted to postpone building it for the benefit of his own project. Tongzhou is 25 kilometers east of Peking.

affirmed that the livelihood of at least 60,000 or 70,000 people depends on this traffic. . . . Suppose it were cut by half; over 30,000 people would be thrown out of work. . . . The distance between Tientsin and Tongzhou is only 200 li [about 100 kilometers], so the railway could not employ many people. If the British railways are taken as a reference —they employ 165,000 people for 40,000 li—the Tientsin-Tongzhou line could employ 800 people over its 200 li. If porters and servants are added, this would not exceed 3,000 people. . . .

If a line were built from Lugouqiao outside Peking, through Henan to Hankou . . . the advantages would be many. . . . The first advantage would be that in this region far from the ports, the railway would not arouse the envy of the enemy. The second advantage would be that over the 2,000 li from north to south there is plenty of space. It is not as densely inhabited as the neighborhood of Peking, and it would therefore be easy to avoid houses and tombs. The third advantage would be that factories would grow up along the line, and there would be many stations. The economy would become more active all along the way and the traffic on the transverse roads would grow, so that porters and shopkeepers could earn a better living. The old could be abandoned for the new, with no loss. The fourth advantage would be that if the main communication channels of eight or nine provinces were linked by one channel, men and goods would meet and trade would flourish. From Kaifeng to Luoyang, from Jingzhou to Xiang-zhou, from Jining to Donghu, from Huaian to Sizhou—in all directions the secondary roads of each province would communicate in a co-ordinated way. The consequence would be inexhaustible resources for the upkeep of the railway. The fifth advantage would be that if a bandit rebellion arose in the interior, the soldiers could arrive even before the need arose to give battle. The railroad is the most convenient way of transporting troops. The sixth advantage would be in the field of min-ing resources, where China's chief assets are iron and coal. They are most abundant north of the Taihang mountains, where they are of good quality and high grade. These deposits are the most difficult to reach. With the railway, machines could be conveyed there for ex-tracting them, and the minerals could be treated by Western methods. The yield of the mines would grow steadily, greatly increasing the re-sources of Shanxi, Henan, and southwest Zhili, filling in forever a breach through which China loses its riches.

3. Peasant poverty in Sichuan (1893–1894)

Source: Memories of Marshal Zhu De (1886–   )* reported by Agnes Smedley in The Great Road: The Life and Times of Chu Teh (London, John Calder, 1958), pp. 40–42.

There was no rain, and only a light flurry of snow that winter, so the winter crops were poor. The next spring rains failed. . . . In the hot

* Founder of the Red Army; now member of the Political Bureau of the Central Committee of the Chinese Communist Party.

summer months that followed, the grain bins of the Ting [a powerful landowning family of the neighborhood] remained full from previous harvests, but the peasants began to starve. Drums rolled in the villages as the people sacrificed to the Rain God. Long processions moved along the country roads, carrying the Rain God in an open litter to soften his heart by a sight of the suffering people. Yet the King of Hell [head of the Ting family] summoned his tenants as usual to transport his family to his cool mountain home.

Throughout the first year all members of the Zhu family carried water to their kaoliang [a grain] and vegetable patches, and Grandmother Zhu rationed food to two lean meals a day. . . . Merchants in the towns hoarded rice until people exchanged farm tools, cattle, clothing, household furniture, and, finally, their daughters, for it. . . . When winter came, the Zhu family still had enough money to pay tuition for their two sons. Peasants less fortunate than the hard-working, parsimonious Zhus wandered off to become contract labourers in the salt wells at Nanbu or coolies in Chongqing or other cities. The more desperate became soldiers or bandits. There were charity kitchens in the big cities where the starving could get one bowl of gruel a day, but in the villages there was nothing.

The Zhu men took turns standing guard over their crops at night and in the autumn harvested their kaoling, squash, and turnips and the children gathered wild greens and herbs from the mountains. The Ting family returned from their mountain home and their stewards brought back foreign-style rifles and ammunition from Chengdu against brewing trouble. . . . The family began to sell their few possessions, even their precious mats from their beds, but not their agricultural implements or their daughters.

In the second summer of the drought the people lost all faith in the Rain God, and haggard members of the ancient Gelaohui, or Elder Brother secret society, began whispering in the villages. Peasants arose from their beds at night to mutter against the merciless skies and the blank moon. One early summer day . . . a cloud of dust was rising along the Big Road. From the dust cloud there soon emerged a mass of human skeletons, the men armed with every kind of weapon, footbound women carrying babies on their backs, and naked children with enormous stomachs and cavernous red eyes plodding wearily behind. Through a vast confusion of muttering voices Old Three [Zhu De] heard the urgent clanging of cymbals and the roll of drums from the Ting mansion. The King of Hell was summoning his tenants to fight for him. The Zhu men heard the summons but did not move. The avalanche of starving people poured down the Big Road, hundreds of them eddying into the Zhu courtyard, saying: "Come and eat off the big houses!" Grandfather and Grandmother Zhu laid restraining hands on their sons. . . .

The next day the Zhu family heard that wild, weird yell of ruffian soldiers. "HUH-H-H-H-H-H-H-H!" it sounded savagely, and the family barred the doors of the house and fled to the mountains. . . . A few nights later desperate peasants took refuge in the Zhu home and talked in whispers of a wild battle in which hundreds of starving people had been killed, wounded or taken prisoner. They had fought fiercely, and had taken many soldiers with them back into the shadows. Before the soldiers caught up with them they had besieged the Ting estate and other big family homes, and though some had been killed they had entered and eaten.

How the Zhu family managed to live that last terrible summer General Zhu could not remember, but he could remember that now and then food was brought into the house by someone during the night; and that his father and one of his younger uncles sometimes disappeared and were gone for days. Many peasants turned bandit and went on raids of distant places. . . .

Blessed rain fell during the late summer and autumn that year. . . . By then many landowning peasants had sold everything and sunk into the ranks of tenants. Tenants had become coolies or soldiers or labourers on the landed estates. And all were in debt to moneylenders. . . . Though the Zhu family had taken no loan, they now had nothing left. One day a steward of the Tings appeared and informed them that since they had paid no rent during the famine, and since His Honour "had also suffered," henceforth their rent would be increased. Zhu the first pleaded on his knees, saying that his family had always been honourable in payment, hard-working and obedient, and that not one had joined the rice-rioters. He pleaded so hard that the steward agreed to speak to His Honour, and indeed later informed the family that they could keep half their land at the old rental, but would have to pay increased rent on the remainder.

After long conferences, the family decided to split, one branch retaining half the land at the old rental, the other renting elsewhere. It was decided that Zhu the First and Zhu the Fourth should move, leaving Grandmother and Grandfather Zhu with two of their sons and families behind.

Chapter Nine

Crisis, Reform, and Rebellion: *1895–1901*

The years following the Sino-Japanese War are among the most tragic and the most fertile in the history of modern China. As soon as the Treaty of Shimonoseki was signed, the foreign powers took advantage of the weakness of the Chinese government to satisfy their own ambitions. The result was the "breakup of China." In reaction to the imperialist expansion Chinese society and the economy went through a great change. Several sociopolitical movements, differing in their principles and methods, emerged from the national crisis. The most characteristic manifestations of these movements were the Hundred Days of 1898 and the Boxer Rising.

The "Breakup" of China

New international alignments in the Far East

During the last five years of the nineteenth century new elements modified the international configurations in the Far East. The main cause was that Japan, through the victory over China, had just proved itself a rival of the Western powers in their expansion in East Asia. Another factor was that Germany, a recent convert to colonial expansion, was correspondingly greedier and more aggressive in going about it. Generally speaking, the rapid rise of industrial and financial capitalism in Japan and the West gave imperialism a strength and dynamism which it had never had before. Each power tried to obtain "special privileges," and whenever it was checkmated, claimed that it was owed "compensations." In one area after another the Chinese government was stripped of sovereignty.

Russia began the new round of realignments. The Japanese occupation of Liaodong threatened Russia's Far Eastern possessions and denied the Trans-Siberian Railway access to a port in free waters. With the support of Germany and France, the Russian government exerted pressure on the Japanese government to give Liaodong back to China. The Japanese did not dare to resist and officially relinquished the territory in the convention of November 8, 1895, in return for a payment of 30 million taels. In the eyes of the powers which had intervened, this "service" naturally called for "pledges of gratitude" by China. This was the beginning, amid a tangle of diplomatic and financial intrigues, of the scramble for concessions, for government loans, for railway franchises, for "leased territories," and for recognition of "spheres of influence"— all of which were the new forms of foreign penetration in China from 1895 onward.

Franco-Russian interests and the first loan

To enable the Chinese to pay the first installment of their war indemnity to Japan, the Russian government negotiated a loan of 100 million taels from a syndicate of Russian and French banks, under its own guarantee. The agreement was concluded on July 6, 1895. The rate of purchase was fixed at 94.125 percent and the annual interest at 4 percent.

By a convention signed in June 1895 during the loan negotiations, France won an advantage of great strategic importance for the frontier of the French protectorate, Laos, when China abandoned most of the principality of Jianghong (Xieng Hong). Furthermore, China opened the towns of Hekou and Simao in Yunnan to French trade and promised to give preference to the French for developing the mines in Yunnan, Guangxi, and Guangdong. In September 1895 the French asked for the right to extend the railway built by the Fives-Lille Company between Hanoi and Langson into Chinese territory. In June 1896 the Chinese granted permission to extend the line as far as Longzhou, and a year later accepted an extension as far as Nanning. Meanwhile in April 1897 China agreed to the extension of the Hanoi-Laokay line as far as Kunming, the capital of Yunnan.

In return for its financial help and its part in recovering Liaodong for China, Russia expected to receive permission to complete the Trans-Siberian Railway by linking Chita and Vladivostok in a straight line through Manchuria. Otherwise the tracks would have to follow the frontier, which was 900 kilometers longer and lay in hilly terrain. The "Trans-Manchurian" would facilitate Russian penetration on the borders of the Chinese empire and Russian expansion as far as the sea. With this end in view, the Russo-Chinese Bank was founded in December 1895 with capital provided by seven French banks, and with a management composed of Russian senior officials. At first, however, the Chinese government refused to approve the proposal for the Trans-Manchurian, mainly because of protests from Britain.

British and German interests and the second loan

Britain was worried by the growing French influence in South China even though Britain and France signed an agreement in 1896 that the two countries would share any privileges acquired in Sichuan or Yunnan. The British seized on the pretext offered by the cession of Jianghong to France and demanded "in compensation" an extension of British territory on the Burmese frontier, the right to navigate on the Xijiang River, and the opening of the towns of Wuzhou and Sanshui to trade. In 1897 Li Hong-zhang eventually yielded to these demands.

Britain and Germany also agreed that the loan needed to pay the second installment of the indemnity to Japan would be supplied by their financiers. In 1896 the Chinese government signed a contract with the Hong Kong & Shanghai Bank and the Deutsche-Asiatische Bank for a loan of 1,600,000 pounds sterling (100 million taels). The terms were less favorable than those of the first loan: the rate of purchase was fixed at 94 percent and the annual interest at 5 percent. The loan was for a period of thirty-six years, with no possibility of advance repayment, and it was stipulated that the administration of the maritime customs, whose revenues served as the security, could not be modified before the entire loan had been repaid. This was a way of consolidating British protection of the customs.

The Russo-Chinese alliance and the
Trans-Manchurian Railway

The Russian offer of a defensive alliance against Japan, along with a "present" of 1½ million dollars for Li Hong-zhang, finally induced the Chinese government to accept the proposal for the Trans-Manchurian Railway. In the words of the treaty signed in Moscow on May 22, 1896, the railway would make it possible to speed Russian troops to any locality that was threatened with invasion. The contract, concluded on September 8, 1896, authorized the Russo-Chinese Bank to form a company known as the Chinese Eastern Railway Company, which was to build the railway in six years and operate it, with the exclusive right to fix the tariffs, for eighty years. At the end of that time the line would become the property of the Chinese government without payment of an indemnity, unless China wanted to buy back the railway before the appointed time, in which case it had to wait at least thirty-six years. The land needed for the line was to be given to the company free of charge where it belonged to the state, but the company had to purchase it where it was privately owned. All the land was then exempt from land tax in perpetuity.

The company also received the right to work mines existing in the "railway territory"—a territory which the contract did not define except to say that it would include the land needed for building the line, quarries and woods nearby which would be used to supply building materials, and the land essential for the "protection of the railway line," a formula which could be extended at will. The company had "absolute" rights of local jurisdiction and police power over the zone; it could employ an exclusively Russian staff and have a "protective guard." These exceptional privileges, which were still more favorable to Europeans than those of the concessions in the open ports, can partly be explained by the special situation of Manchuria. Not only was it isolated and sparsely populated, but the Russians had no rivals there. Subsequent renewals of this contract did not embody such extensive forfeits of Chinese sovereignty, but they were still sufficient to arouse the avarice of the other powers.

The Peking-Hankou line

The concession which encouraged the most rivalry between the foreign powers was the contract for a railway line between Peking and Hankou, across the heart of the empire. The project was launched by Zhang Zhi-dong in 1889 (document 2 in Chapter 8) but had to be discontinued the following year, because Li Hong-zhang managed to divert the funds to the Tientsin-Shanhaiguan line. In 1896 an imperial edict called on Chinese merchants to take charge of constructing the Peking-Hankou railway. However, their unfortunate experiences with the *guan du shang ban* system left the merchants with no enthusiasm for going into partnership with the government.

The only candidates for the task of organizing the project were bureaucrats and compradors, and the compradors were hand-in-glove with foreign business circles. In August 1896, acting on a proposal by one of them, Sheng Xuan-huai, Zhang Zhi-dong, and the governor-general of Zhili requested permission from Peking to borrow foreign capital and form a railway company with Sheng Xuan-huai as its general manager. All the foreign powers rushed to offer their services, but Zhang Zhi-dong ultimately decided to call on the banks and technicians of a "small European country," Belgium, to avoid being dominated by one of the giants. The contract was signed on July 27, 1897. In reality the group of bankers was Franco-Belgian, so that this important railway moved into the area of Franco-Russian interests. Britain reacted with an effort to extend its influence toward the Northeast, and as a result the Englishman Kinder was appointed chief engineer of the Shanhaiguan-Shenyang railway.

New concessions in the open ports and leased territories

Through the Treaty of Shimonoseki and various other agreements with the foreign powers, the number of open ports increased from thirty-four to forty-five between 1894 and 1899. The territory of the existing concessions in Shanghai, Tientsin, and Hankou was enlarged, and new concessions were created, particularly in Hankou, for the countries which until then had had none: Germany, Japan, and Russia. In 1899 the total number of concessions in China had increased to twenty-five, compared with twelve in 1885.

But the foreign powers had only begun to profit by China's weakness. The murder of two German Roman Catholic missionaries in Shandong in 1897 gave Germany the opportunity to achieve an ambition of several years' standing: a naval base in China to serve as a center for the German fleet in the Far East and as a bulwark for German economic interests in China. The location which Germany had first chosen was Shandong, with its large and varied resources, where German Catholic missions had been settled for some time. After sending several specialists to study sites, however, the German government finally decided on Jiaozhou, and consequently its expedition of reprisal for the two dead missionaries landed there. The Chinese, Russian, and French governments protested, but Peking gave in and Germany appeased the other two by pointing out that they could act in the same way when they desired.

The Sino-German treaty of March 6, 1898, gave Germany the two entrances and the islands in the bay of Jiaozhou for ninety-nine years, with the right to establish a fortified naval station there (the future port of Qingdao). Within the "leased territory," China renounced its rights of sovereignty. Germany was allowed military occupation of a zone within a radius of 50 kilometers around the territory, where China theoretically retained sovereignty but could take no action without the consent of the German government. Furthermore, Germany received the right to build three railway lines in Shandong forming a triangle between Jiaozhou, Jinan, and Yizhou. The railway company was managed by Germans, used German equipment, and fixed the tariffs itself. It was allowed to exploit the mines in a zone up to 15 kilometers wide on either side of the line. Here China maintained rights of jurisdiction, police power, and if necessary, protection. In all cases where Shandong needed foreign financial or technical assistance, the Germans were given priority. Germany did not try to disguise its goal: to obtain a "sphere of influence" in Shandong and the lower Yangzi valley.

The other powers quickly arrogated similar privileges. In December 1897 the Russian army occupied the road off Lüshun (Port Arthur). The convention of March 27, 1898, ceded the port, together with the port of Dalian, to Russia on a twenty-five-year lease which was renewable. There Russia had the right to construct a naval base, a trading port open to international trade, and a branch of the Trans-Manchurian, which would be called the South Manchurian Railway. Thus all the Northeast became a Russian sphere of influence.

Two weeks later the Chinese in effect recognized a French sphere of influence by promising France that they would not cede any territory in Yunnan, Guangdong, or Guangxi to another power. The next month France leased the territory of Guangzhou-wan in Guangdong for ninety-nine years, with the right to build a naval station, fortifications, and a garrison there.

Seeing that its once-predominant position in China was threatened by the partition movement, Great Britain made the loan of 1,600,000 pounds sterling which China needed to pay the third and last installment of the war indemnity to Japan. In return the British exacted a promise that none of the territories of the provinces bordering the Yangzi would be transferred to another power. The loan contract, signed in March 1898, fixed the rate of purchase at only 83 percent and the annual interest at 4.5 percent, and allowed 45 years for repayment. It also stipulated that during this period the inspector-general of customs would always be a British subject and would collect the *lijin* and the salt tax in a certain number of places. The revenue from these taxes, as well as from the customs, was security for the loan.

Under the pretext of counterbalancing French influence in Guangdong, the British also enlarged their possessions in Hong Kong. In June 1898 they obtained a ninety-nine-year lease on the north Jiulong peninsula and the neighboring islands, thus adding 376 square miles to the 29 square miles of the original Hong Kong colony. And to set a limit to Russian expansion in the gulf of Beizhili, the British obtained Weihaiwei in July as a military port for the duration of the Russian stay in Lüshun. These territorial annexations were accompanied by railway concessions: the Jiulong-Canton line, the Nanking-Xinyang line, the Suzhou-Ningbo line via Hangzhou, and the Shanghai-Nanking line.

Lastly, owing to British help, Japan obtained a promise from China to respect the territorial integrity of Fujian.

The American open-door policy

The European powers then drew up a series of agreements among themselves in which they recognized one another's privileges extorted from China and agreed to abide by the boundaries of their respective spheres of influence. This sharing of the spoils looked very like the prelude to a political partition. One of the Western Powers stayed outside the agreements, for when the European states were hewing out their shares the United States was too busy with the Spanish-American War to join the competition in China. Only one American company participated in the spoils by obtaining the Hankou-Canton railway concession.

American business circles soon became anxious, fearing that the Chinese market would be taken over by Europeans. Meanwhile the American annexation of Hawaii and the Philippines encouraged and facilitated the expansion of American interests in the Pacific. In September 1899 the secretary of state, John Hay, addressed a note to Britain, Germany, Russia, France, Italy, and Japan asking them to respect equal opportunity for trade in China, the status of the open ports, and the customs system. Hay also asked that the powers in possession of a sphere of influence, leased territories, or railway concessions refrain from setting preferential tariffs for citizens of their own countries. The countries concerned gave their agreement.

It has often been said that the open-door policy was proof of United States friendship for China and that it prevented China's territorial dismemberment. But in fact the American note, which had not been shown to the Chinese government, did not question the spheres of influence or the encroachments on Chinese sovereignty. It merely sought to limit the unfortunate consequences for the United States and claim a share in the benefits obtained by the other powers. And since no single one of the others felt strong enough to seize the whole of the Chinese empire, while each was afraid of being evicted by its rivals, they all concurred in the principles laid down by the United States note. These principles implied the recognition of the spheres of influence and amounted to a mutual guarantee of the foreigners' collective domination over China.

Financial domination by imperialism

In the space of four years, from 1895 to 1899, the take-over of China by the imperialist powers moved faster than it had throughout the fifty-five preceding years. For the Chinese it represented a series of unprecedented political humiliations, and it was accompanied by economic and social changes causing widespread confusion in the internal situation of the country.

Between 1894 and 1899 the Chinese government borrowed 370 million taels from the foreigners, whereas the annual income of the central treasury was only 80 million taels. Payments on debts every year amounted to a sum which was equivalent to the customs revenues, or in other words, a quarter of Peking's budget. Furthermore, the conditions of the loans deprived China of financial autonomy.

During the years 1895–1899 foreign investments spread over a considerably larger field than they had covered before. The banks that were already in China opened more branches, and sizable new ones started up, among them the Russo-Chinese Bank (1895) and the Bank of Indochina (1899). No longer did these institutions exist mainly to finance trade. With the support of their respective governments they became the basic instruments of the Western economic invasion. They took over the loans to the Chinese state and controlled its finances. They invested in the railways (over 113 million taels between 1898 and 1900), in industry (over 7 million taels between 1896 and 1900) and in the mines (over 10 million taels in the same period). They built up their capital at the expense of Chinese capital, draining off Chinese savings and issuing bank notes. During the preceding period they had already seized control of foreign exchange and of the Chinese monetary and financial market. Here as elsewhere, international financial capitalism was based on the fusion of banking and industrial capital. This synthesis tended to make international capitalism the sole arbiter of both economic development and politics in China.

Economic exploitation accelerates

Although China's exports of capital were already larger than its exports of goods, the treaty of Shimonoseki was the signal for a new foreign commercial offensive. Customs statistics recorded 552 foreign firms and 9,350 foreign residents in 1894, 1,006 and 16,881 in 1900. Businessmen and adventurers crowded into China. Huge trade missions arrived. One, organized by several French chambers of commerce for Lyons industrialists, conducted a detailed two-year study of commercial opportunities in Central and South China. Its example was immediately followed by British, German, and American chambers of commerce.

Between 1895 and 1899 the total value of Chinese foreign trade increased from 315 to 460 million customs taels, while the deficit in the balance of trade rose from 28 to 69 million taels. The rise in imports was fostered by the opening of new ports and the needs of the enterprises created by the foreigners, as well as by the new foreign privileges obtained from the Chinese government. In July 1898, submitting to pressure from Britain, China was forced to allow foreign ships on all inland waters and to exempt foreign goods from the *lijin* and other taxes.

Expansion of foreign industry

By virtue of the most-favored-nation clause, all the powers could benefit from the official permission to create manufacturing concerns which was granted to Japan by the Treaty of Shimonoseki. This privilege was exploited immediately, particularly as foreign goods produced in China enjoyed the same tax privileges as imported goods.

In 1895 four big foreign cotton-spinning mills were created in Shanghai and another was opened in 1896. Thus by 1897 there were 160,000 foreign spindles in Shanghai. In 1900 a group of German merchants opened a huge silk-spinning mill in Suzhou. Food industries flourished as well. At Hankou the Russians established new brick-tea factories and the Germans, Austrians, and French built five egg-processing factories. Foreigners also founded oil presses, soap factories, flour mills, tobacco and match factories, and a shipyard. Coal mines were opened in Zhili, Shandong, and Fengtian; mercury mines in Guizhou; and gold mines in Mongolia and Xinjiang.

The first wave of foreign industrial investments immediately after the Treaty of Shimonoseki produced 20 factories with a capital investment of over 100,000 taels, and 11 mining operations. According to available figures (which are incomplete), foreign investments of this kind between 1895 and 1900 represent about 20 million taels.

The rise of Chinese capitalism

By abolishing the monopoly of the official textile factories and the restrictions on the importing of machines by private individuals, the Treaty of Shimonoseki removed some of the obstacles to the development of private Chinese industry. The massive injection of foreign capital, combined with monetary inflation, acted as a momentary stimulus to national initiative. A business orientation formed in enlightened circles, with the watchword "Save the country by developing industry." The government did its best to encourage these tendencies. Edicts were issued urging the Chinese to build factories; industrialization offices were founded to organize the work and make it easier. The state no longer had the financial means or the authority to dominate industrial development; the new manufacturing companies were more like free-enterprise ventures, and the capitalist merchants played an important part in them.

According to incomplete records, 110 Chinese factories and mines were started up between 1895 and 1900, with a total capital of about 19 million taels. The major part of this investment was in the textile industry: 59 factories opened, and they were geographically more scattered than foreign capital. In 1900 Shanghai contained 47.8 percent of the total of 336,722 Chinese spindles, but large factories were also founded in the older centers of the textile industry: Suzhou, Wuxi, Nantong, Hangzhou, Shaoxing, and the Canton district. Also in 1900, 200 steam-powered silk-spinning mills were recorded in the neighborhood of Canton. New factories were created at Wuhan and Tientsin. Industrial activity spread as far as Shenxi and Sichuan in the form of oil presses, brickyards, cement works, and candle and match factories. The plants varied in size and sometimes had so few machines that it was difficult to tell them apart from the big workshops for handicraft production. Those handicraft enterprises were also springing up in every province to process foodstuffs for export or to produce consumer goods intended to supplant imported products.

Coal mining was another industry that took on considerable importance. Twelve large pits were opened between 1896 and 1899 in the Northeast, Anhui, Hubei, Hunan, Jiangxi, Jiangsu, Fujian, and Shandong.

The financial needs of the large industrial enterprises led to modifications in the traditional procedures for obtaining loans. The first modern-style Chinese bank, the Imperial Bank of China (*Zhongguo Tongshang Yinhang*), was established in 1896. Its founder was Sheng Xuan-huai, a former protégé of Li Hong-zhang and a director of many *yangwu* enterprises. Sheng was appointed general manager of the railways in 1896. The statutes of his bank were based on those of the Hong Kong and Shanghai Bank. The first task of the Imperial Bank of China was to finance the Peking-Hankou railway, but Sheng was quickly forced to give up the project for want of capital. He could not obtain the monopoly on the transfer of state funds, either. In view of the circumstances the institution had to become an ordinary private bank, even though it retained close business connections with the official world and with foreign finance. Thus the *guan du shang ban* system could no longer dominate national finance and industry, as it had during the previous period when the *yangwu* movement controlled the modernization of China.

The failure of *yangwu* and its sequels

The Sino-Japanese War marked the complete failure of the *yangwu* movement. By crushing the military "self-strengthening" which was at the heart of the undertaking, the total defeat of the Chinese army and navy sealed the fate of *yangwu*. The movement was discredited politically because its leaders, particularly Li Hongzhang, had not foreseen the war. Critics said that their compromises and their maneuvers failed to save anything and made the situation still worse. From an economic point of view, the invasion by foreign industry and finance following the Treaty of Shimonoseki eliminated all justification for *yangwu*'s dictatorship over the development of the economy.

The end of the *yangwu* era was not followed by the evolution of free-enterprise capitalism similar to that in Britain during the Industrial Revolution. Foreign penetration made a breach in the traditional structures and cleared the way for new economic forms. But the competition from foreign capital with its vast resources constantly threatened to suffocate Chinese initiative, while Chinese entrepreneurs also came up against the general resistance of the old regime to structural change. Chinese capitalists had to operate by two methods, singly or in combination: the Chinese formed an alliance with foreign interests, or they obtained support through the traditional channels of the Chinese economy and society.

The first large Chinese industrial enterprises that were created after 1860, when the *yangwu* movement began, were under close supervision by the bureaucracy and gave rise to a habit of constant interference in Chinese business by the official world. The habit continued, in spite of the weakening of the central government's power, for several reasons: because officials viewed economic profits as a way of asserting their personal influence, because they were one of the only groups with financial means, and because the exemptions and privileges which they could obtain seemed worth considering, at least for new enterprise. Chinese capitalism therefore maintained close links with the old social and economic regime even after the failure of *yangwu*, and Chinese entrepreneurs had great difficulty in throwing off these constraints.

Social evolution: The industrial proletariat and the bourgeoisie

The rapid development of the industrial economy was accompanied by social changes. Some of the repercussions among the lower classes will be discussed later in this chapter's section on the origins of the Boxer movement. To mention only one development, the industrial proletariat, which numbered barely 100,000 people in 1895, had grown by 1900 to a figure probably over 150,000. Industrial workers were fairly strongly concentrated in the large towns, where the jobless from the country districts also congregated even though few jobs were available. In 1897 Shanghai contained 25,000 cotton workers; the population of the town as a whole increased from 168,000 to 345,000 between 1890 and 1900. Workers were more militant there than anywhere else. The Shanghai proletariat led over half of all recorded strikes in the country during the years 1895 to 1900, and foreign capitalists considered the frequency of these strikes (seven in 1898–1899) a bad omen.

The Shanghai strikes were aimed at the atrocious living conditions of the workers. Adults and children alike in the textile factories there worked 72 hours a week for 300 to 320 days a year. They had one bowl of rice to eat a day. No compensation was paid in the case of injuries at work, and mines and industrial premises contained neither sanitation nor safety measures. The workers were often engaged by methods reminiscent of the slave trade. They had to submit to the tyranny of overseers and foremen, and corporal punishment was normal practice. Conditions in the foreign mines and factories were no better than in the Chinese.

A bourgeoisie, on which the old regime left its distinctive imprint, was also gradually forming. At the top were the men who had managed the civil *yangwu* enterprises in a semi-official capacity during the previous period. They formed a nascent upper bourgeoisie closely linked with the bureaucracy in which they originated or from which they bought titles and political privileges. They also had close links with foreign capitalists, with whom they tried to share the Chinese market. And they were beginning to assume individual characteristics which set them apart from the rest of the Chinese social elite.

For example, Sheng Xuan-huai (1844–1916) in 1894 was already at the head of the China Merchants, the telegraph, and the Shanghai cotton industry. Soon he took control of the Hanyang iron foundries and national railways and launched the Imperial

Bank of China. In these enterprises Sheng was no longer Li Hong-zhang's confidential agent for economic affairs, as he had been in the past. He acted on his own authority, using the support which he had in official circles as well as the credit he enjoyed in diplomatic and foreign banking circles. By freeing himself from the tutelage of the provincial bureaucratic apparatus and assuming personal own-ership of the companies, he became a power with which the gov-ernor-generals had to reckon.

The struggle of Chinese private capitalism against foreign com-petition also contributed to the formation of a bourgeoisie. The upper levels of this class grew fastest, as increasing numbers of officials, gentry, and merchants, whom it became customary to refer to as *shenshang* (gentry and merchants), invested in modern industry. They were simultaneously bureaucrats and businessmen, closely linked with the old regime. They formed a bourgeoisie which still halfway belonged to the traditional social hierarchy.

The evolution followed by the *shenshang* was significant, how-ever. The enterprises in which this group invested incurred the risk of being crushed eventually by imperialism. They often had different interests than the compradors. A case in point was that of Yang Zong-lian and his brother, the founder of the Yeqin spinning mill at Wuxi. Both were originally associates of Li Hong-zhang and share-holders in the Shanghai Cotton Cloth Mill, which Yang Zong-lian managed. They were simultaneously officials and businessmen. Yang Zong-lian was also a close friend of Weng Tong-he. After the fire which destroyed the factory in 1893, Li Hong-zhang reor-ganized the company and placed Sheng Xuan-huai in control. Hav-ing been ousted, the two brothers decided to start their own factory, and succeeded in opening it in 1896. Although conflicts arose between the brothers and Sheng's bureaucratic and comprador group, the Yangs managed to maintain close links with influential official circles.

The textile mills of Suzhou and Nantong were started on the initiative of the local authorities, who asked the gentry to recruit shareholders among the merchants. The form their organization took reflected the association of public and private capital. It was soon modified, however—replaced in some cases by a "delegation of powers to the merchants" and in others by purely private man-agement. Lu Run-xiang and Zhu Cheng-gui, who presided over the Sujing and Sulun mills at Suzhou, and Zhang Jian, who did the same at Nantong, were all eminent scholars.

In the lower Yangzi valley the new bourgeoisie remained closely linked to the leading class of the old regime—a characteristic which had a moderating influence on their political demands. In the Southern provinces the owners of modern enterprises were usually rich merchants, but there were fewer of them. In any case—and this was another reason for its weakness—the bourgeoisie as a whole was still only a tiny group. Modern capitalism was a small island in the ocean of the Chinese traditional economy. But its very existence was a symptom of the profound changes affecting the country, and it asserted itself with particular energy in the intellectual and political fields.

The Reformist Movement and the Hundred Days of 1898

In 1895 their defeat by Japan produced a wide variety of reactions among the Chinese. All were unanimous, however, in showing a determined desire for political change.

The first attempt by Sun Yat-sen

At the end of 1894 a Cantonese emigrant, Sun Yat-sen, founded a secret organization which he called the Revive China Society (Xingzhonghui). With the help of other secret societies in the Canton region, he organized a rebellion which was to begin on October 26, 1895. Its aim was to bring about the fall of the Qing, taking advantage of the discontent caused by the war among all sections of the population. The plot was betrayed, however, and Sun had to seek refuge in Japan.

Resistance in Taiwan

When the terms of the Treaty of Shimonoseki were learned in Taiwan, several thousand gentry sent a memorial to the throne protesting against the cession of the island. In view of the court's passive attitude, Qiu Feng-jia, the leader of the gentry, and a hundred of his friends proclaimed an autonomous republic on May 2, 1895—a fortnight before the territory was to be turned over to the Japanese authorities. Tang Jing-song, the governor of the island, was appointed president and Qiu Feng-jia became vice-president.

Two parliaments met, one in Taibei and the other in Tainan. Chen Ji-tong (Tcheng Ki-tong), a former student of Giquel at the Fuzhou arsenal who had spent several years as military attaché in Paris, suggested the form adopted for the organization of the new government. He became foreign minister and tried to secure recognition for the state, but with the exception of Russia, the foreign powers preferred to wait. Peking sent a plenipotentiary with instructions to hand the island over to Japan. Zhang Zhi-dong sent subsidies, but they were intercepted by Li Hong-zhang. On July 2 Japanese troops landed at Jilong, and two days later Tang Jing-song took refuge at Amoy, where he was shortly followed by the leading members of the gentry.

Popular resistance was led by Xu Xiang, a Taiwan farmer, and Liu Yong-fu, a hero of the Sino-French War who had commanded the Tainan garrison. The Tainan parliament went on passing laws in the name of the republic. The combatants, who had no help from the outside, fought bravely but could not repel the invader. On October 19, 1895, Liu Yong-fu fled to Amoy when the Japanese attacked Tainan. The resistance was crushed, but for several years Japanese troops did not dare venture away from the main roads for fear of ambush.

The republican experiment in Taiwan was brief. The association of political change and patriotic struggle, however, was in itself significant.

Divisions at court

From the beginning of the war against Japan, violent disagreements divided the court and the circles of powerful officials. The discord was extremely harmful to the Chinese armed forces, because its leaders were more concerned with the intrigues than with fighting. As one defeat followed another, a strong minority emerged among the high officials, led by Weng Tong-he and Zhang Zhi-dong, which wanted to fight to the end. The group was influenced by a German officer, von Hannecken, who compared the Japanese invasion to the Russian expeditions led by Charles XII and Napoleon. His theory was that the Japanese had to be swamped by the Chinese masses. The Chinese should not be discouraged by the first failures, because victory would be won by drawing out the war. The "war party," as it was then called, aroused strong sympathies among some of the provincial officials and among the scholars and merchants in the big towns. Poor scholars sold specimens of

their calligraphy in the streets of Jiangsu to get the money for a
coastal militia to drive back a possible Japanese landing. Cantonese
merchants formed a committee which included the 72 guilds and
corporations of the town to collect funds for the war.

The war party made strange bedfellows: survivors of the *qingliu*
(purification) clique, which had been active during the Sino-
French War; archconservatives for whom driving back the Japanese meant driving back change; and a new generation for whom
resistance represented the starting point for a new order. These
younger men were beginning to win over some of their elders,
among them Weng Tong-he. For several years Weng had been the
moving spirit of an "emperor's party," a group of officials and
scholars who wanted to oust Ci-xi so that the Guangxu Emperor
could lead the renovation of the country.

The memorials of Kang You-wei

It was against this background that 1,300 scholars, who were
gathered in Peking from the provinces to take the metropolitan
examinations, sent a memorial to the emperor on May 2, 1895. The
text was 10,000 characters long and had been written by Kang You-
wei, a scholar from Guangdong who had already written one
memorial in 1888 in an unsuccessful attempt to get a hearing at
court. This second memorial said that the Treaty of Shimonoseki
should not be ratified, that those responsible for it should be punished and replaced, that the Chinese capital should be transferred
from Peking to Sian, that the army should be reorganized, and that
numerous reforms should be made. These included reform of the
monetary, banking, and postal systems; government encouragement for private industry and commerce and for the study of
agronomy, modern science, and technical subjects; the construction
of more schools and libraries; changes in the examination system;
and the creation of councils, to be elected annually at the local and
national levels, that would deliberate on all important political and
financial matters.

The Guangxu Emperor did not see the text; it was intercepted by
the Board of Censors. But a month later he both read and approved
a third memorial by Kang You-wei. At that point the Treaty of
Shimonoseki had already been ratified, so that the memorial dealt
only with the reforms. A fourth memorial, in which Kang You-wei
openly advocated representative government, was stopped by conservative officials.

Study societies spread reformist ideas

The memorials of Kang You-wei were circulated in scholarly circles, and the emperor ordered the Grand Council to send a copy of the third memorial to all provincial governors. The 1,300 metropolitan candidates who had signed the original memorial became zealous propagandists. All the recent humiliations to national pride contributed to the emergence of "study societies," whose self-appointed task was to promote reform.

In July 1895 Wen Ting-shi, a disciple of Weng Tong-he, founded the Qiangxuehui (Society for the Study of Self-strengthening) in Peking. It immediately attracted Kang You-wei and other outstanding men. It organized lectures, commissioned the translation of foreign works, and published a daily paper running to 3,000 copies and distributed free of charge at the same time as the *Peking Gazette*, the official newspaper received by all civil servants. A branch was created in October 1895 in Shanghai under the aegis of Zhang Zhi-dong. In November of that year, accusations made by a close associate of Li Hong-zhang resulted in the closing of the Qiangxuehui in Peking on grounds that it was a hotbed of subversive agitation. Weng Tong-he managed to have the society transformed into an official translation office, which was enlarged and reorganized in 1898 to become the University of Peking.

The Qiangxuehui in Shanghai also closed down, but other associations flourished and new ones were created: the Society for the Study of the West, founded in 1897 in Zhili; the Agronomy Society (1897), the Medical Benevolence Society (1897), and the Society for Translating Books (1897), all three in Shanghai; the Southern Study Society (1897) in Hunan; the Essential Study Society (1897) in Hubei; the Society for the Study of the Sage (1897) in Guangxi; and the Society for Effort (1897) in Shenxi. A society opposing foot-binding and another campaigning for elementary education had branches in almost all provincial capitals.

The press publicizes the reform movement

Reformist ideas were also spread by the press, which expanded considerably in this period. Twenty-five important new journals began publishing between 1896 and 1898. Among the most influential was the *Shiwu Bao* (*Current Events Gazette*), created in Shanghai by some disciples of Kang You-wei after the shutdown of the local Qiangxuehui in August 1896. Within a few months, more than 10,000 copies of each issue were being printed—a figure unprecedented in the history of the Chinese press. In Tientsin the *Guowen Bao* (*National News*) was founded in 1897 by Yan Fu, a former student at the Fuzhou Arsenal. Yan's articles and translations for the journal had a lasting influence on modern Chinese thought. Both the *Shiwu Bao* and the *Guowen Bao* served to knit together the various groups of reformers scattered through the provinces.

Centers of reformism

A striking aspect of the reformist movement was the way it spread geographically. The most active centers were in the regions of the lower Yangzi, Guangdong, Hunan, and Zhili. Each had its own characteristics.

In the lower Yangzi provinces, where industrialization was moving ahead most rapidly and where reformist circles consisted mainly of scholars and officials who were involved in business, the chief concerns were economic and political. These people were relatively moderate and above all, realistic. On the other hand the group in Guangdong, which was closely connected with rich merchants overseas and had fewer members belonging to the bureaucracy, showed more radical leanings, as well as the turbulence typical of the South.

In contrast, Hunan became a center of reformism through its officials. The governor, Chen Bao-zhen, wanted to make the province a model for South China. Early in 1897 he founded the Southern Study Society with branches in all districts. The society acted as both a parliament and a cultural center and published a progressive newspaper, the *Xiangxue Xin Bao* (*New Hunan Study Journal*). In the same year Chen established the Current Affairs College (Shiwu Xuetang), in which Tan Si-tong, Huang Zun-xian, Tang Cai-chang, Xiong Xi-ling, and Liang Qi-chao taught the new doctrines to enthusiastic students. Many of them were to play a prominent part in the revolutionary movement at the beginning of the twentieth century.

The innovators in Hunan appear to have been interested in ideology above all, and they were the most radical of the reformists. This feature can be explained to a large extent by the sociology of the provinces. As was the case elsewhere, the reform-minded people in Hunan came from the upper crust of society, and in this particular province the upper crust consisted exclusively of *shenshi*. In

1895 it had not shared in the development which was already underway in Jiangsu and Zhejiang, for example, where certain members of the former elite had turned to modern activities. The Hunanese gentry—numerically an exceptionally large group in proportion to the population—had played a decisive part in the suppression of the popular rebellions in the middle of the nine-teenth century. Afterwards they had successfully opposed all influences likely to modify the established order. Local merchants and businessmen operated within the framework of the traditional economy, unable to defy the domination by the *shenshi*.

Many Hunanese *shenshi* supported reform for reasons which were essentially intellectual: it was the reaction of informed patri-ots who were alarmed by the national crisis rather than the re-sponse of a new bourgeoisie whose material interests were endangered by the old regime. This probably explains why most of the Hunanese reformers appeared to be ideologists. In addition, they met fierce and well-organized opposition to their ideas from the majority of their own class in Hunan. China's defeat by the Japanese in 1895, interpreted by most Hunanese *shenshi* as the result of the concessions made since 1840 to foreign methods and ideas, only intensified their conservatism. Realizing that no com-promise was possible, that determined opposition to the conserva-tives was their only course, the Hunanese reformers were led to adopt a radicalism which left its mark on the political life of their province for many years.

In Zhili the reformers came almost entirely from the *shenshi*, some of whom were involved in modern economic ventures. This group was much more moderate than that of Hunan because many of its members held offices in the central government. Experience had given them a firsthand knowledge of the countless political and administrative obstacles in the way of reform.

In addition to these four large centers of reform-minded people, there were smaller reformist circles in many areas. For example, active groups in Guangxi, Hubei, Sichuan, Shenxi, and Shandong had study societies and their own local presses.

Theorists of the reform movement: Kang You-wei

While the reform movement was spreading through the prov-inces, a few thinkers who later emerged as its leaders were molding its ideology. One of the most prominent was Kang You-wei

(1858–1927), whose memorials to the emperor were mentioned earlier. Kang was born in Nanhai, Guangdong, into an influential mandarin family. After receiving a traditional education from the best and most orthodox teachers, he studied Taoism and Buddhism. He also explored the ideas of the enlightened thinkers of the seventeenth century, who stressed the importance of "present-day affairs" (*jingshi*), history, geography, and contemporary politics, and criticized the official interpretation of Confucianism that had been inherited from Song scholasticism. He became acquainted with "Western learning" in a visit to Hong Kong in 1879. Passing through Shanghai in 1882 on his way home from Peking, where he had just failed the provincial examinations, he bought and pored over some translations of Western works published by the Guangxuehui and the Jiangnan arsenal. In 1888 Kang went back to Peking to sit for the examination again, and it was then that he wrote his first memorial. This document drew a lesson from the defeat of 1885 and asked in somewhat vague terms for reform of the laws and institutions and some degree of participation by the people in the government. The text never reached the emperor, but it was circulated among influential circles in the capital and earned sympathy and notoriety for its author. In 1891 Kang You-wei opened a school in Canton, where he taught Western ideas on the basis of a new interpretation of Confucianism.

He set forth this interpretation in two major works, *Xin Xue Wei Jing Kao (Study of the Classics Forged During the Hsin Period)*, published in 1891, and *Kong-zi Gai Zhi Kao (Confucius as a Reformer)*, which was almost finished in 1892 but did not appear until five years later. In them Kang proved, by systematizing the critical research of a long line of scholars known as the "new text" school, that the official version of the classics was not authentic. The "ancient texts," written in archaic characters and using archaic language, were fabricated to serve the interests of the usurper Wang Mang early in the first century A.D. The "new texts" (more recent in the style of writing and language used) that had been current under the Han during the second and first centuries B.C. were the only authentic ones. Although most of them had disappeared, their meaning could be deduced from the commentary by Gong-yang on the *Spring and Autumn Annals* (one of the Five Classics), written in the third century B.C. and attributed to Confucius himself.

The picture Kang You-wei drew from the interpretation of Gong-yang was one of Confucius as a fearless innovator who used the restoration of old traditions as a subterfuge to gain acceptance for radical reforms. Thus the real meaning of Confucianism was not to perpetuate an unchangeable tradition but quite the opposite: to make constant innovations that lead society toward a golden age. Kang combined the ideas in Gong-yang's commentary with the old equalitarian and utopian themes scattered through ancient literature to arrive at a view of human history as a progression composed of three ages. First comes the age of "disorder," second the age of "approaching peace," which is characterized by "small tranquillity," and third the age of "great peace" (*taiping*), in which "great unity" (*datong*) is achieved. In the last phase all inequalities are abolished, governments disappear, and men live in fellowship, happiness, and harmony. Kang developed the utopian vision of the great unity further in the *Datong Shu* (*Book of the Great Unity*). It was not published in its entirety until 1935, but the first draft dated from 1885, and in 1893 Kang made an almost complete manuscript available to his disciples.

The books of Kang You-wei had a considerable influence on the intellectual evolution of contemporary China. Mao Tsetung referred explicitly to Kang's utopia in describing the future communist society. Liang Qi-chao compared *Xin Xue Wei Jing Kao* to a typhoon (it was banned in 1894, after running through five editions and scandalizing the scholars, who read it avidly) and *Kongzi Gai Zhi Kao* to a volcano.

Kang's enduring contribution does not lie in the realm of scholarship. Although his analyses of the classics inspired a school of modern literary and historical criticism, in fact they were brilliant explanations of principles which many scholars had already discovered. His originality lay in his use of the principles to reinterpret Confucianism in such a way that it could be the theoretical basis for political reform.

Kang You-wei was a controversial figure both in his time and in ours. The central position that he gave to Confucianism, albeit in an up-to-date version, shows how dependent he remained on the old regime. Admittedly he could not have turned his back on tradition without becoming isolated and powerless. But the concessions which Kang made to Confucianism were not a mere subterfuge. He believed in certain Confucian values, and this conviction led him to appeal to the social elite alone and to approach political reform as an achievement that must be made from the top downward. Yet he realized that abolishing tradition, or overlaying it with a few elements introduced from outside, could not provide the foundation for national recovery. He assumed that a new culture must be created in which the heritage of the past would take its place, after reappraisal, as the mainstay of national identity. This was an undertaking which haunted the whole Chinese revolution.

Kang You-wei was neither the only figure behind the reform movement nor, perhaps, the one whose work had the most influence. However, he assumed nominal leadership of the movement from 1895 onward by appealing directly to the emperor and playing the chief role in all the political manifestations of reformism. He considered himself an eminent scholar and developed the arrogance allowed by ancient Chinese custom to outstanding masters. He was convinced that he had a mission to save China, if not humanity as a whole. Kang had a certain talent for publicity, and he found a few disciples, particularly Liang Qi-chao, who had a genius for it. Although during his lifetime he often damaged the cause he supported by his haughty pride, in official history he has remained the hero of the period 1895 to 1899.

Yan Fu: A cult of energy and struggle

Yan Fu (1853–1921) did more than Kang You-wei to introduce notions from Western thought into reformist theory. Born into a family of gentry in Fujian, Yan was left an orphan very young. The only way to continue his education was to attend the school at the Fujian arsenal, where students were paid. When he left there, he spent two years in England and then obtained second-grade posts in the service of Li Hong-zhang, who displayed the utmost contempt for Yan's talents and suggestions.

The events of 1895 gave Yan Fu the determination and the opportunity to express his ideas. In a series of essays written during the same year, he set forth his fundamental theory that the ultimate source of Western power, and therefore of the difference between East and West, was neither technology nor even political organization, but an entirely different vision of reality. Basing his arguments on Spencer and Darwin, Yan Fu described this vision as the cult of energy, struggle, and affirmation of all the vital forces. He said that it presented a biological picture of the social organism in which liberty, equality, and democracy made it possible for individual interest to become identified with the interests of the community.

In a further effort to transform the outlook of Chinese scholars, Yan Fu decided to translate what he considered to be the most significant European writings. He began with *Evolution and Ethics* by Thomas Huxley, published in 1897 in the *Guowen Bao*, which Yan now edited in Tientsin. Written in an admirable classical style, his translation caused a tremendous stir and appeared in book form the following year. The public was interested above all by social Darwinism, which Yan Fu stressed in his commentaries and notes. In 1897 he began to translate Adam Smith's *The Wealth of Nations* (published in 1900), and *A Study of Sociology* by Herbert Spencer.

Yan Fu had relatively little to do with the political activities of the reformists, and his proposals for concrete reforms went no further than theirs. But the influence of the concepts which he introduced was much wider than the reformist movement and affected Chinese thought throughout the twentieth century. Yan Fu denounced the whole moral and political system of Confucianism. As a replacement he was courageous enough to propose a Western philosophy and to label it plainly as Western.

Tan Si-tong: Progress toward political equality

Born of a great family in Hunan, Tan Si-tong (1865–1898) was both the bravest man of action and the most fearless thinker among the reformists.[1] In his youth he accompanied his father, an official whose duties involved traveling, on many journeys and acquired a knowledge of almost all the Chinese provinces. He not only received the traditional education of a scholar but also made an extensive study of science, Buddhism, and the dissenting Confucianist thinkers such as Gong Zi-zhen and Wei Yuan (discussed in Chapter 2).

In his *Ren Xue* (*A Study of Benevolence*), written in 1897, Tan Si-tong synthesized the elements of his education, treating them in a new and original way. At that time he and Chen Bao-zhen were directing the reformist innovations in Hunan. Through his association with Liang Qi-chao, a disciple of Kang You-wei, Tan was beginning to participate in the reformist movement at a national level.

The universe, as Tan describes it in his book, is a totally materi-

---

[1] A paragraph from his writings is given in document 1.

alistic one. All beings, all phenomena, including the human moral system and political institutions, are merely fractions of an eternal material reality. Although this reality grows neither larger nor smaller, it changes ceaselessly, advancing steadily, because it contains contradictory forces. Tan Si-tong used the word "benevolence" (*ren*) for the principles governing the metamorphoses of the prime reality. In Confucianism, *ren* is the name of the virtue supposed to govern relations between men. Tan saw it as a sort of cosmic love which brings all beings and phenomena into contact with each other and forms them into a whole in spite of their diversity.

Because the ruling principle of the objective world is evolution and constant progress, Tan Si-tong denounced the conservatism of the ruling class. This class, he said, denies that things change and refuses to change the moral system and the institutions. He attacked all rules and restrictions which hampered individual liberty: the Confucian moral code, the doctrine of the divine legitimacy of the monarch, the examination system, and Manchu domination over the Chinese. He dared to praise the Taiping and to argue for a republican regime. He viewed the ultimate aim of reform as the achievement of a peaceful, equalitarian world without frontiers of any kind. To reach that goal, reform measures must introduce liberty and equality into the relations between the upper and lower classes, between China and the rest of the world's nations, between men and women, and in fact between all individuals.

Liang Qi-chao and the disciples of Kang You-wei

The disciples of Kang You-wei spread and elaborated on the doctrines of their teacher through the study societies and the press. Liang Qi-chao (1873–1929) was closest of all to Kang, and like him, came from a family of scholars in Guangdong. He was a talented journalist, editor of the *Shiwu Bao*, and a participant in the Hunanese reformist experiments. In particular he set himself to expound foreign political theories and practices and to study the advantages and disadvantages involved in applying them to China.

The controversy with the conservatives

Although there were differences of opinion among the reformers, they were united in opposition to the conservatives and the supporters of *yangwu* on a number of points. The result was a common program of reform which slowly took shape through their writings and which embraced philosophy, politics, education, and economics.

The conservatives held that the established order was the will of heaven and, like heaven, unalterable. They maintained that it was useless to change the laws because it was not law but men, particularly the sovereign, who created good government. The reformers, however, introduced the notion of evolution and constant progress, ideas which were virtually unknown to Chinese thought. The reformist argument was that to improve men, the laws which keep men in a state of ignorance must be changed.

Whereas the conservatives defended absolute monarchy and the sacred power of the sovereign, the reformists did not really advocate democracy, because "The mind of the people has not yet been opened." They favored a constitutional monarchy in which an enlightened elite would share power by means of a national parliament and local assemblies.

To enlarge the elite and strengthen national power, the reformists aimed to encourage agriculture, industry, and trade, and to free private companies from the constraints which hampered them. They wanted schools where political and social doctrines would be taught, and where the sciences, not merely Western engineering techniques, would be given emphasis. They wanted to reform the examination system. Apart from Yan Fu and Tan Si-tong, the reformists did not intend to make "Western knowledge" the basis of Chinese education. They did not repudiate the *yangwu* formula described in 1898 by Zhang Zhi-dong in his *Exhortation to Study* (*Quan Xue Pian*): "*Zhongxue wei ti xixue wei yong*" ("Chinese learning for the essential principles, Western learning for the practical application").[2] They restricted themselves to changing the contents of the "Chinese learning" by emphasizing neglected aspects of the cultural heritage. For many Chinese this ambiguity in the reformers' position on *yangwu* obscured the difference in the principles behind reformism and *yangwu*. It enabled many *yangwu* supporters, particularly Zhang Zhi-dong, to cooperate with the reform movement for a time.

Kang You-wei summarized the difference between the supporters

[2] Translation by John K. Fairbank, Edwin O. Reischauer, and Albert M. Craig in *East Asia: The Modern Transformation* (Boston, Houghton Mifflin, 1964), p. 386.

of *yangwu* and the reformers by comparing them to the principles of *bianshi* (changing things) and *bianfa* (changing methods). The former stresses technical perfection; the latter emphasizes the political system. For Kang, "changing methods," or reforming, meant remaking the political system and adopting institutions imitated from the West, within a regenerated form of Confucianism. He and Tan Si-tong, however, were virtually alone in their insistence on priority for political reform.

Social foundations

The diversity of opinions grouped under the heading of reformism was also a reflection of its composite social makeup. The movement was born in a context of social changes. It began partly as the expression of the political aspirations of the people who were forming the new industrial and business bourgeoisie, but once launched, it greatly contributed to the growth of the bourgeoisie. Though businessmen and bankers supported the movement from the start, the majority of its members were scholars and officials. And as these men from the traditional elite assimilated reform ideas, many of them embarked on modern business projects and swelled the ranks of the *shenshang*. Zhang Jian, Lu Run-wiang, and Sun Jia-nai, all brilliant candidates in the metropolitan examinations, became factory owners after 1898.

The transformation of the traditional elite had begun. The merchant became involved in politics. The official began to invest in industry and trade as well as in land. The rural scholar started to become an urban intellectual. But the old regime still dominated Chinese life, for each individual was entangled in a network of family, personal, and professional relationships where traditional principles persisted alongside those belonging to the modern age.

Missionaries and reformism

British and American missionaries have often boasted that they instigated the reform movement and advised its leaders. Kang You-wei and Liang Qi-chao, for example, were associated with the Guangxuehui (Society for the Diffusion of Christian and General Knowledge). The missionary Timothy Richard was a member of the Qiangxuehui (Society for the Study of Self-strengthening). But in fact, although the reformers used the translations and the information made available to them by missionaries, they also had at their disposal the knowledge and reflections accumulated by a line of Chinese intellectuals who had been interested in the West since 1840. The reformers were thinking for themselves and had arrived at conclusions that were well beyond those the missionaries were urging on them.

The starting point of reformist theorizing was the determination to save China from foreign domination. It is true that the reformers nourished illusions on the nature of this domination; they believed, for instance, that the foreigners wanted the regeneration of China, and were waiting to treat the Chinese as equals as soon as they adopted Western concepts. The anti-imperialist feelings of the reformers gave them an audacity of which the Protestant zealots disapproved. In the firm conviction that the West was superior and enjoyed certain rights over China, the "enlightened" missionaries merely wanted to facilitate foreign penetration. Whereas the more conservative missionaries made the best of the traditional system, it seemed more profitable to the enlightened group to alter it in order to increase foreign control. And when the missionaries who were in favor of change recommended moderation, it was not because they were more acutely aware than the rest of the real state of Chinese affairs, but because they were afraid of seeing China shake off foreign domination.

The reformists gain power

At the end of 1897 and the beginning of 1898 the reformist drive for political power intensified because of the concessions Peking made to Germany and the series of foreign grabs for "spheres of influence" which followed. In December 1897 Kang You-wei addressed his fifth memorial to the emperor. In it he proclaimed the need for political reform, arguing that it was the only way to save the country and the dynasty from imminent disaster. In January 1898 Kang was received at the Zongli Yamen, where he submitted his plan to Li Hong-zhang, Rong-lu, and Weng Tong-he. Weng was enthusiastic and gave the emperor the fifth and a sixth memorial by Kang, as well as Kang's works on Peter the Great and the Meiji reform in Japan.

In April 1898 the Association for National Defense (Baoguohui) was founded at a meeting attended by 200 metropolitan examination candidates and officials from the capital. It rapidly spread to every province, forming the embryo of a political party. Prince Gong, who had always prevented the reformers from being received at court on the pretext that their rank was not high enough, died at this point.

On June 11, 1898, an edict from the Guangxu Emperor announced "decisions on national affairs." It marked the beginning of the attempt at reform known as the Hundred Days of 1898 (in fact it lasted 103 days, until September 16, 1898).

On June 16 Kang was received by the emperor, whom he assured that China would take three years to achieve what Japan had accomplished in thirty. Kang was appointed secretary to the Zongli Yamen, with the right to address memorials directly to the throne. Tan Si-tong, Huang Zun-xian, and Liang Qi-chao were summoned to Peking. High administrative posts were reshuffled and many were dealt out to reformers. The conservative faction led by Ci-xi did not lose power completely, however. It managed to oust Weng Tong-he, secure the appointment of Rong-lu as governor-general of Zhili and master of the armed forces, and retain its position in the Grand Council.

The Hundred Days of 1898

A flood of edicts between June and September dealt with the reform of the administration, education, and the economy. Large numbers of useless offices, sinecures, and posts were eliminated, such as the post of governor in provinces with a resident governor-general. The subsidies paid to all Manchus were abolished. The costly Army of the Green Standard, which had been useless since the formation of modern units, was disbanded. All officials and subjects were allowed to address suggestions directly to the emperor.

The old academies, as well as temples which had fallen into disuse, were to be transformed into schools. Peking University was founded. Science and politics were taught in schools and universities and were to be included in the examination subjects. The examinations themselves were reorganized and the eight-legged essay was eliminated. Rewards were introduced to encourage new works and inventions. Liang Qi-chao was placed in charge of a new translation bureau responsible for introducing foreign books. Permission was granted to found study societies and newspapers.

Plans were made for preparing a budget and publishing regular government financial statements. Two general offices were created that resembled ministries, one to supervise railways and mines and another to oversee agriculture, industry, and trade. Offices designed to regulate the economy were opened in the provinces, and towns were urged to form chambers of commerce. Industrial concerns were encouraged, while private individuals were given permission to found arsenals.

These measures did not overturn the power of the state; they did not even provide for a parliament. Yet they aroused determined opposition from traditionalist groups. Chen Bao-zhen, the governor of Hunan, was the only high-ranking official in the provinces who actively supported the new policy. Most of the edicts remained dead letters. Meanwhile, more and more people became discontented: officials who had lost their jobs or were afraid of losing them, scholars who had devoted their lives to preparing for the official examinations, Manchus who had been reduced to begging, and high-ranking members of the Grand Council whose authority had been supplanted by that of the young secretaries (Tan Si-tong and three of his associates) appointed as their assistants.

The reaction

So far during the Hundred Days, the Empress Ci-xi had given a free hand to the Guangxu Emperor in order to avoid an explosion of anti-Manchu feeling. She only fanned the growing discontent and watched for the moment to take back power. Peking was already tense when she had the eunuchs spread the rumor that the Guangxu Emperor wanted to kill her and that the foreign powers were ready to intervene. These reports shocked public morality and patriotism.

Ci-xi then suggested that the Guangxu Emperor accompany her to review the army at Tientsin. There, with the help of Rong-lu's troops, she intended to imprison him and force him to abdicate. The emperor learned of the plot and consulted Kang You-wei, who sent Tan Si-tong to ask for help from a subordinate of Rong-lu's, Yuan Shi-kai. Yuan had belonged to the Qiangxuehui in 1895 and was now in charge of training the new army. He agreed to enter Peking with his troops and keep a close watch on Ci-xi, but in the event, he betrayed the plan. Ci-xi immediately had the Guangxu Emperor held prisoner, took all power into her own hands under the pretext that he was ill, and on September 21, 1898, arrested the reformist leaders.

Kang You-wei and Liang Qi-chao managed to flee abroad. Tan Si-tong, who also had the opportunity to leave, refused to go. "In other countries," he said, "no reform has ever been accomplished without bloodshed. No one has yet shed any blood for it in China. . . . I shall be the first." He and five other reformers, among them the younger brother of Kang You-wei, were executed. Many supporters of the movement were imprisoned, exiled, or prosecuted. All the reform measures were revoked except for the edict founding the University of Peking. The suppression of reform and the persecution of the reformers aroused great indignation in the large towns of China, as well as self-interested protests from British, American, and Japanese diplomats. As a result Ci-xi did not dare assassinate the Guangxu Emperor, as she had intended, and was forced to tone down the prosecutions.

Failure of the Hundred Days

Although its failure aroused popular sympathy, the reform movement had very limited support within society. Its leaders had rashly reduced their backing still further by damaging the careers of numerous scholars through hasty and overly autocratic measures. In addition, the reformist program neglected agriculture almost entirely, although it was of fundamental importance to the country's future, and concentrated on the elite class. And the arrival of the reformers in power did nothing to end the encroachments of the foreigners; the scramble for concessions even intensified during the summer of 1898. The reformers' avowed resistance to foreign encroachment appeared to be contradicted by the Westernization which they advocated. For want of support elsewhere, they relied on the emperor to impose their reforms, whereas the real imperial power was in the hands of their worst enemies.

Although it was short-lived, the reformist attempt of the Hundred Days left a deep mark on the country, for it helped to familiarize educated people with political change and new ideas. Its failure affected the reformers themselves in different ways. Most of them adopted more gradual methods and turned to immediate, limited goals which depended on individual rather than government action: targets such as the establishment of modern businesses and schools, or the administration of local communities. But other reformers, concluding that peaceful change was doomed to failure, turned to revolution.

Popular Reactions: The Boxers

Among the Chinese masses, the imperialist expansion that followed the Sino-Japanese War provoked a violent reaction, which crystallized into a movement much further removed from the elite than had been the case during the preceding period. Also led by the secret societies, it was a peasant movement linked with the condition of Chinese agriculture. In addition it was a nationalist reaction. Most important, however, it was a campaign against the missions and the Chinese Christians.

Attacks multiply against the missions

In May 1895 rumors that the foreigners were about to invade Sichuan provoked a wave of violence in Chengdu and the neighboring districts. Seventy churches were burned. In August the Vegetarian Sect, affiliated with the White Lotus Society, massacred two children and nine foreign missionaries at Gutian in Fujian, after the sect had warned the authorities of the rebellion which it was preparing. In 1896 and 1897 there were similar incidents in Hunan, Hubei, Sichuan, Jiangxi, Jiangsu, and Shandong. Each time the foreign powers demanded heavy damages, backed up by gunboat policy. It was the murder of two missionaries in Shandong that provided the pretext for the German military expedition which resulted in the ceding of Chinese territories to the major foreign powers and the sharing out of China into "spheres of influence." Yu Dong-chen took up arms once more in Sichuan in the summer of 1898. In spite of his slogan "For the Qing; death to the foreigners," the authorities, worried to see his movement spreading to more than thirty districts, began to oppose him. Yu Dong-chen surrendered in January 1899. Disturbances continued, however, in Guizhou, Hunan, Hubei, and all the Southern provinces.

Continual agitation in rural China

The attacks on the missions were only one form of the constant violence in the country districts between 1895 and 1899. Banditry, famine riots, and riots against taxation and forced labor increased. They were direct results of the Sino-Japanese War: the devastation caused by battle and foraging armies, particularly in the Northern regions, and the tax increases in every province to pay for the war.

The perpetual uprisings also belonged to the context of an agricultural crisis which, though it had been severe for a long time, was growing still worse.

Demography and farm production

During the last years of the nineteenth century the population increase, which had been arrested by the great rebellions and the natural calamities of the years 1850 to 1877, seems to have resumed. According to one estimate, between 1873 and 1893 the population increased by 8 percent and the area of land under cultivation by only 1 percent.[3] The farmland in China still belonged mainly to peasant landowners, but the size both of their farms and of the farms worked by tenants grew smaller. Moreover, the tenant farmer's rent, which generally amounted to half and in some cases eight-tenths of his main harvest, deprived him of the means of keeping his family alive. Lack of capital prevented the introduction of technical improvements such as fertilizer, better tools, and better seed. Although there were a few attempts in these directions in the suburbs of large towns, they could do little to remedy the situation. The peasants went steadily deeper into debt, and the number of landless peasants, vagabonds, beggars, and emigrants grew.

Emigration, since it generally removed the strongest and most enterprising peasants, often contributed to the economic decline of a village. Not all villages became poor; some, in Zhejiang, Jiangsu, and Guangdong, appeared to be relatively prosperous. Prosperity was increasingly rare, however, and many regions which had been laid waste in the middle of the century had not recovered. This was the case in large areas of southern Zhili, Henan, Shanxi, Shandong, northern Shenxi, Guangxi, and Yunnan. They suffered from economic stagnation, or even worse, from a steady impoverishment which was not due to the demographic phenomenon alone. A succession of natural calamities devastated vast areas at regular intervals. Between 1886 and 1897 about sixty districts in Jiangsu and forty in Anhui were ravaged each year by floods, wind, drought, or insects. The worst damage occurred in the provinces on the Yellow River, where thousands of villages were blighted for several years running by floods and drought. Both time and the means to repair the dikes and canals were lacking. The abandonment of hydraulic

[3] Albert Feuerwerker, *The Chinese Economy, 1870–1911* (Ann Arbor, University of Michigan Press, 1969).

engineering work in many parts of China was caused not only by the inefficiency and corruption of the administration, but also by the depletion of local resources. In turn the deterioration of the flood-control system further impoverished local economies, thus magnifying the effect of the bad weather conditions.

Economic imperialism undermines the peasants

The farming community also felt the repercussions of the changes in commerce and industry that were caused by foreign imperialism. In some regions the rise in imports and in industrial production, particularly of cotton yarn and cotton fabric, contributed to the ruin of the home handicrafts which supplemented most farm incomes. In addition the development of steam navigation and the railways reduced countless numbers of porters, boatmen, and innkeepers to poverty.

A growing variety and quantity of Chinese agricultural products were now being exported. Their prices rose much more slowly than those of imported products, however, because the foreigners controlled the customs tariffs and the credit system which financed foreign trade. Moreover, the fact that the Chinese market was dependent on the world market in certain sectors meant that the peasants were the victims of international speculation and fluctuations. They were all the more vulnerable because their farms were small. During the years 1885 to 1900 the tea growers were the most seriously affected by world market events. Owing to the development of plantations in India, Ceylon, and Java, prices fell from 22.14 dollars for 50 kilograms of black tea in 1882 to 11.09 dollars in 1902. There was not much demand for ordinary Chinese tea outside the country.

Thus the rise of foreign trade, combined with industrialization and the growth of the large towns and the mining districts, impaired the traditional agrarian economy to some extent. In a few sectors it also encouraged the commercialization and specialization of agriculture. More farmland was turned over to cotton, sesame, and groundnuts, and in the process Chinese farming began to develop new economic patterns. Where land was good and communications were easy, the rich peasants began to play a more important economic role than the tenant farmer, for they became producers of commercial goods on a small scale. The trade network enabling foreigners to draw off agricultural products extended as far as the villages. Most of the landowners joined in too. In order to sell more, some of them abandoned the system of tenant farming and worked their land themselves with the help of laborers hired by the year. This method of farming, which greatly increased the yield, was a combination of economic exploitation from capitalism, the comprador system, and traditional Chinese agriculture.

Apart from commercial profits, many officials, merchants, and gentry also gained from the increase in taxes that was intended to pay off the foreign debt and support the *yangwu* enterprises. They made the peasants' burden even heavier by adding surtaxes and pocketing the profit, by moneylending, and by raising the land rent. The money they made enabled them to buy more land, particularly as many small farmers were ruined by this profiteering and had to sell out. Foreigners, whether missionaries or holders of railway concessions, also dispossessed the peasants of their farms. On newly acquired land the customs relating to long leases were no longer respected; new owners raised the rent or employed agricultural laborers at will. Absentee landlords also multiplied, especially in Jiangsu. The tendency toward the concentration of landowning grew stronger, as did that toward harsher exploitation of the peasants.

Since they contributed to the enrichment of the minority and the impoverishment of the majority, the disturbances affecting the Chinese economy crystallized social antagonism. They were one of the major causes of popular risings, including the Boxer movement.

Unrest in Shandong

During the last years of the century popular feeling in Shandong had reached the explosive stage. Since 1880 natural disasters had struck vast areas of the province every year: for example, 18,625 villages in 1895; 14,681 in 1896; 7,197 in 1897; 24,131 in 1898. During the Sino-Japanese War there were heavy military requisitions in Shandong for both men and equipment. In 1896 additional surtaxes amounted in some cases to a threefold increase in the land tax. In 1898 the central government decided that Shandong should provide 90,000 taels more each year for the defense of the frontiers. At the same time the authorities forced the population to subscribe to a domestic loan of 100 million taels to pay off the war indemnity. The demands for forced labor were particularly excessive, because mandarins and troops on their way to and from Peking constantly passed through the province. Wherever a relay of the imperial postal system did not exist, the local population had to provide escorts and crews. Similarly, the upkeep on the Grand Canal involved great expense to those living near it, although they no longer profited from the traffic because the canal was virtually unused.

Moreover, the province of Shandong was a target of foreign imperialism. Germany took Jiaozhou; Britain took Weihaiwei. Westerners opened factories and mines. For several years imported cotton yarn had ruined the market for domestic yarn and the livelihood of the women who spun at home. The Jiaozhou-Jinan railway eliminated the jobs of many workers in the traditional transportation system. Its construction was marked by violent incidents, in particular by a riot in which twenty peasants died.

In his province, the birthplace of Confucius, the activities of Protestant and Roman Catholic missions had angered the populace for a long time. The missionaries and their converts numbered 80,000. They were accused, justifiably, of land-grabbing, engaging in trade and moneylending, bringing pressure on the mandarins to favor Christians, maintaining gangs of armed toughs, protecting criminals, picking quarrels with non-Christians, and extorting scandalously large indemnities. For example, they demanded 24,000 taels for three churches and seven houses that were destroyed in 1897, 70,000 taels for damages in 1898, and 10,000 taels' indemnity in 1899. The public was particularly hostile to Chinese Christians, whom it regarded as traitors willing to become slaves to the foreigners in return for material advantages. All in all, the exasperated population of Shandong saw the missions as the cause of all the evils it was suffering.

Emergence of the Boxers

Between 1896 and 1898 numerous revolts, in which the secret societies played a leading part, broke out against the missions in south Shandong. Observers reported that the Big Sword Society seemed to be the ringleader, but that a new organization whose members practiced sacred boxing was also active in the disturbances. In the summer of 1898 groups of boxers formed rapidly in the Zhili and Henan border area, which had suffered most severely from the floods. They were known as Yihetuan (Righteous and Harmonious Militia) or Yiminhui (Righteousness Society).

The exact origins of the group are disputed. It seems certain, however, that its original name was Yihequan (Righteous and Harmonious Fists). It existed at the beginning of the nineteenth century and was doubtless connected with the White Lotus and the Eight Trigrams Societies; certainly it was banned along with those groups in 1808. It continued to develop, however, in Shandong and in the impoverished, underadministered area on the borders of Henan, Anhui, and Jiangsu.

Boxer rites and organization

The Boxers, as the foreigners soon called them, did not adopt the dogma and religious ritual of the White Lotus and the Eight Trigrams. They did not set out to be a religious sect, though like all secret societies they laid considerable stress on religious beliefs and magic. They attracted the public by the practice of boxing, and their adherents were let into the secret of amulets and incantations that made them invulnerable.[4]

The Boxers created a fairly strict organization. They were divided into two main sections, each named for one of the eight trigrams.[5] Members of the two sections wore different-colored turbans, belts, and standards—one yellow, the other red. The basic unit of each group was the *tan* (sacred area), which simultaneously denoted the altar, the headquarters of a unit, and the territory under its authority. Admittance to a *tan* followed an initiation period. Its leader, who was called Grand Master or Old Master-Father, generally commanded twenty-five to a hundred men. He was appointed by another, older *tan* which acted as patron to the new unit.

When in battle order, the Boxers were often divided into companies of ten men. Ten companies formed a large brigade (*da dui*). The *tan* leaders were given different ranks depending on their ability. The work of the commissariat, of liaison, of propaganda, and of combat with various weapons was carefully shared out. Discipline was strict, in contrast to discipline in the Chinese army. The Boxers were required to give total obedience to the leader and were forbidden to accept presents, plunder, steal, molest the populace, have relations with women, eat meat, and drink tea.

The coordination between the groups was fairly flexible. It was

---

[4] See the description of a Boxer ceremony in document 2.
[5] The eight trigrams, each composed of three parallel lines, either broken or unbroken, were handed down from ancient times. They were used for divination and for explaining the universal order.

carried out through the *tan* which were in the position of patron to others. Whether deliberately or not, the Boxers avoided the fixed hierarchy under a single leader which had divided and weakened the Taiping. Even so, various people in succession managed to set up a sort of overall regional leadership: for example, in Shandong there were Zhu Hong-deng, a seller of plasters, and the Taoist monk Ben-ming, both executed in December 1899; in Zhili there were Zhang De-cheng, a former boatman, and Cao Fu-tian, who had been a soldier.

The Boxer rank and file

According to a survey carried out among the survivors in 1960, 70 percent of the Boxers were of peasant origins. They were mainly agricultural laborers, generally very young—between twelve and eighteen. The movement also contained boatmen, porters, ruined craftsmen, small shopkeepers, peddlers, monks, a few schoolmasters and their pupils, and large numbers of soldiers. Officials, gentry, and their families also took part in the movement and became relatively numerous once the court at Peking took up the Boxers' cause. Vagabonds and dispossessed people also filtered into the *tan*, sometimes taking over the leadership and thereby damaging the Boxers' popularity.

Women were enrolled in special organizations: Red Lanterns for girls between twelve and eighteen, Blue Lanterns for middle-aged wives, Black Lanterns for older wives, and Green Lanterns for widows. The Red Lanterns, who were in the majority, owed allegiance to a single leader. Titled the Holy Mother of the Yellow Lotus, this woman was about twenty, the daughter-in-law of a boatman.

Rebellion and defeat

In June 1898 the governor of Shandong, Zhang Ru-mei, described the Boxers as bands organized for self-defense that were no particular threat to the state. He said that their hostility was directed solely toward the missions[6] and that they could easily be taken into the local militia (*tuan*) under the patronage of the gentry and the authorities. From then on the Boxers began to be

[6] Some Boxer complaints against the missions are given in document 3.

known as Yihetuan (Righteous and Harmonious Militia) instead of Yihequan (Righteous and Harmonious Fists). The movement grew, however, and threatened to become an antidynastic as well as antiforeign rebellion. The name of its leaders recalled the Ming dynasty, some of its slogans demanded the dynasty's return, and other slogans accused the authorities of coming to terms with the foreign invader.

In October 1898 eighteen bands of Boxers attacked the district of Guanxian on the Zhili frontier, and a large deployment of government troops was needed to suppress them. In March 1899 the German authorities in Jiaozhou seized on an incident involving three Germans and some villagers as a pretext to burn two villages and occupy the town of Yizhou. The new governor of Shandong, Yu-xian, a conservative Manchu who was a staunch upholder of the dynasty, was caught between the fear of a rebellion and the fear of harassment by foreign imperialists. He tried to take over the Boxers, eliminating the "bad," antidynastic elements and encouraging the "good" ones, particularly some bands whose slogan was "Support the Qing; exterminate the foreigner" (*Fu Qing mie yang*). At Pingyuan in October 1899, disturbances broke out during which the Boxers plundered Christian homes to avenge unjust arrests instigated by the Christians. The authorities then executed the most dangerous Boxer leaders, among them Zhu Hong-deng and Ben-ming. At the end of 1899 the slogan *Fu Qing mie yang* was used extensively by the Boxers; some of their banners even bore the name of Yu-xian. Foreign protests, however, forced the court to replace Yu-xian with Yuan Shi-kai, who used his modern army to carry out a brutal effective repression of the Boxers.

The extension of the movement to Zhili

Groups of Boxers appeared in south Zhili in 1897, and now the bands that had been driven out of Shandong swelled their numbers. By March 1900 the whole Baoding-Tientsin region was in the hands of the Boxers. At the end of May and the beginning of June they destroyed the railway line between Baoding and Tientsin, fighting off all the troops sent against them.

At the same time, the foreigners stirred up popular anger against themselves to a higher pitch than ever before. On June 4 twenty-four warships arrived at Dagu. On June 10 the British admiral Seymour left Tientsin with a force of 2,000 men of different nationalities to protect the legations in Peking. Sinister rumors immediately spread. On June 13 groups of Boxers entered Peking, joining other groups which had already formed in the city. That evening, provoked by American soldiers, they burned churches and massacred Christians. Peking became the center of the Boxer movement, which won control of Tientsin as well and spread throughout Henan, Shanxi, Inner Mongolia, and the Northeast. Secret societies became active in the Yangzi valley. Agrarian disturbances broke out again in the South. The whole country was in turmoil.

The Empress Ci-xi, terrified by the vast scale of the movement, begged the foreign diplomatic corps to halt Seymour's march. She promised them that the imperial troops would protect the legations against the Boxers, and she sent several faithful officials to persuade the Boxers to disperse peacefully. On June 16 the European admirals in charge of the warships at Dagu grew worried because they had had no news of Seymour since the telegraph had been cut two days before. Fearing that the Chinese military formations at Dagu would make it difficult to send reinforcements to him, they ordered the Chinese to surrender their forts within twenty-four hours. The Chinese refused, and the next day the allies attacked and took the forts. This operation was useless, because the allies could easily have landed their troops elsewhere, and it infuriated the Chinese. In spite of its orders, the Chinese army took arms against the foreigners. On the evening of the same day, the Tientsin garrison attacked the foreign concessions. Meanwhile the imperial troops barred Seymour's men, and he had to return to Tientsin.

When news of the capture of the forts reached Peking on June 19, antiforeign feeling intensified. At court the conservative Manchus, led by Prince Duan (whose son had just been proclaimed heir to the throne), assured Ci-xi that the foreigners wanted to oust her and restore power to the Guangxu Emperor. The officials whom she had assigned to negotiate with the Boxers persuaded her to put her trust in them. She consequently asked the foreign ministers to leave Peking within twenty-four hours and guaranteed their safe conduct as far as Tientsin. However, the German minister, von Ketteler, was murdered on the morning of June 20. That afternoon Chinese troops opened fire on the legations. The next day Ci-xi issued an edict declaring war on the foreign powers.

The siege of the legations

For two months the legation quarter in Peking, where 3,000 Chinese Christians had taken refuge with the 473 foreign civilians (including 149 women and 79 children) sheltering there, was defended by its 451 foreign guards. Several thousand Chinese Christians were also barricaded in the Beitang Cathedral, where there were only 400 men capable of fighting alongside the 43 French and Italian sailors delegated to protect them.

In spite of the constant shooting, their isolation from the rest of the world, the appalling sanitary conditions, and the shortage of food and ammunition, those besieged in Peking got off relatively lightly. Rong-lu, supreme commander of all the armed forces in North China, was convinced that the policy of the court would lead to disaster. Consequently he refused to allow the besiegers to use modern weapons, particularly artillery, which would have shattered all resistance. During the siege 76 foreign combatants, 6 foreign children, and several hundred Chinese Christians were killed; losses were far heavier among the besiegers. In the provinces of the Northeast, however, over 200 Roman Catholic and Protestant missionaries and 32,000 Chinese Christians died, often victims of terrible atrocities.

Throughout the siege the diplomats of the court in Peking reassured the foreign governments about the fate of the legations. They claimed that Ci-xi was held prisoner by the Boxers, and they gave great publicity to a present of watermelons which she had sent to the besieged.

"Mutual defense of the Southeast"

The hostilities were confined to North China. In Shandong, the Yangzi provinces, and the Southern provinces, the senior officials came to an agreement with the foreign consuls to organize the "mutual defense of the Southeast" (*dongnan hubao*). By this device they withdrew support from the government in Peking, openly treating the declaration of war and the edicts that followed it as "sham edicts." They were encouraged by the same section of society which had upheld the Hundred Days: gentry who were interested in modern activities and businessmen who saw the Boxers as an obscurantist and backward-looking movement, and who feared that the war would damage their business interests.

The international expedition sacks North China

The foreign governments were disturbed by the alarmist messages from North China, the pressure exerted by public opinion at home (which had been inflamed everywhere by the press and the religious communities), and the fear that the results achieved by half a century of political and commercial penetration might be swept away. These considerations led the foreigners to surmount their rivalries and unite as they had in 1891, except that this time their aim was military action.

"Peking should be razed to the ground," said William II, emperor of Germany. When the troops left for China, he declared: "Show no mercy! Take no prisoners! A thousand years ago, the Huns of King Attila made a name for themselves which is still considered formidable in history and legend. Thus may you impose the name of Germany in China for a thousand years, in such a way that no Chinese will ever dare look askance at a German again."[7]

At the beginning of August 1900, the international troops (16,000 men—Japanese, Russian, British, American, German, French, Austrian, and Italian) were concentrated in Tientsin. On August 14 the expeditionary force entered Peking and relieved the legations and the Beitang Cathedral. Ci-xi and her most trusted followers, disguised as peasants, fled to Xian, taking the Guangxu Emperor with them.

The systematic slaughter and plunder which then began far surpassed the worst excesses committed by the Boxers. In an orgy of cruelty the foreign troops massacred thousands of men in Peking; women and whole families committed suicide rather than survive the dishonor; the whole city was sacked. The imperial palace was occupied by the foreigners and stripped of most of its treasures. The same slaughter and looting were carried out in Tientsin and Baoding. Punitive expeditions were sent into regions of Zhili where missionaries had been attacked; the soldiers burned whole villages, sparing nothing.

In Manchuria, where the Russians undertook the "pacification," the atrocities were equally appalling. One of the worst massacres was perpetrated in reprisal for a few shots fired at the town of Slagovetchensk. The Russians slaughtered thousands of Chinese men, women, and children and threw their bodies into the Heilongjiang River.

---

[7] Quoted in P. Renouvin, *La Question d'Extrême-Orient* (Paris, 1945), p. 197.

The Protocol of 1901

While the foreign soldiers crushed the Boxers and massacred the population, Ci-xi appointed Li Hong-zhang as plenipotentiary. On January 16, 1901, he accepted the foreign demands, which were ratified in a protocol signed on September 7 by representatives of the eleven powers and by Prince Qing.

According to the terms of the agreement, the chief offenders were punished by death or exile. To penalize the scholars, the examinations were suspended for five years in forty-five districts where the Boxers had been active. Antiforeign societies were forbidden. The name of the Zongli Yamen was changed to Waiwubu (Ministry of Foreign Affairs), and in its new guise it took precedence over all the other ministries. China agreed to an indemnity of 450 million taels, payable in gold in thirty-nine annual installments and guaranteed by the revenues from the customs and the salt tax. When the interest and the substitution rates were taken into account, the real total amounted to well over 980 million taels. Several forts between Peking and the sea, including those at Dagu, were to be razed, and China forfeited the right to import arms for two years. The legation quarter in the heart of the capital was enlarged, and Chinese were forbidden to live there. It was protected by a permanent guard of foreign troops, as were twelve points on the routes leading from Peking to the sea.

Legacy of the Boxer wars and the Protocol

The Protocol clauses forbidding arms imports, ordering the destruction of forts, arranging to station foreign troops, and suspending the examinations were a flagrant interference in the domestic affairs of China. The indemnity's enormous drain on national finances removed all possibility of real economic development in the country. And the foreign diplomatic corps in Peking, now that it had its own armed force and the right to inspect finances and administration, became a sort of supergovernment which decided the fate of the empire regardless of the court's wishes.

The violence of the Boxers, exaggerated by sensational literature and illustrations in the tabloid press, resulted in a new atrocity folklore which reinforced the racial stereotypes already current in Western countries. The terror inspired by tales of the "yellow peril," whether conscious or unconscious, has affected American and European relations with China up to our own time.

Conversely, the humiliation inflicted by the foreigners and the atrocities committed by their troops left the Chinese people with memories which have not yet completely healed. Meanwhile the Chinese elite had their own complex reactions. Those who had supported the Boxers from motives of national pride now showed only servile fear of the foreigners. Those who disapproved of the Boxers' methods felt ashamed, and at the same time responsible, for the ignorant superstition of the masses. They also resented the masses for having given the foreigners the chance to take over China. And mixed with their shame, bitterness, and hostility toward the foreigners was a sneaking admiration for Western strength.

This emotional legacy of the events of 1900 and 1901 accentuated the consequences of the economic and political wrongs which China was suffering. Conflict, humiliations, and hatred mounted on the base of mistrust underlying the legacy which the relations between China and the West have not entirely shaken off today.

Boxer aims and achievements

Because they were crushed much more quickly than the Taiping, the Boxers did not have time to draw up a complete political and social program.[8] Although the Boxers fought above all against the foreigners, some groups connected with the White Lotus sect did aim at overthrowing the Manchus. This divergence of goals sometimes led to violent clashes between different groups of Boxers, but overthrowing the Manchu became the rallying cry of all those who continued their resistance, scattered in the countryside, after August 1900.

The social program of the Boxers apparently went little further than a rudimentary redistribution of the plunder seized from the rich and a watchword, "Protect the people," mainly intended to make it easier to obtain supplies from the peasants. The Boxers' alliance with the Qing certainly hampered the expression of social demands. The psychological process which led the Boxer leaders to adopt the watchword *Fu Qing mie yang*, and led their troops to agree to it, remains shrouded in mystery. Some Chinese historians contend that the crucial conflict of the time was between the Chinese nation and foreign imperialism, and that the Boxers formed a "united front" so as to concentrate all efforts against the foreign

---

[8] Document 3 suggests the skimpy state of Boxer ideology.

invasion. But this point of view leads on, logically, to the assertion that the conservative gentry who entered the ranks of the Boxers were more "progressive" than the Shanghai industrialists who supported the "mutual defense of the Southeast."

In fact, as established by the work of G. Dunstheimer in particular, the Boxer movement was on the dividing line between two historical eras: the Chinese Middle Ages—that is to say, pre-industrial society—and modern times. The mentality of the Boxers, steeped as they were in religion and magic, as well as their military training and their weapons, all belonged to the Middle Ages. Insofar as they embodied a defense against modernization, and in the process borrowed the general concepts of the traditional society, they obtained the approval of the privileged members of that society. But the modernization against which the Boxers rebelled was a modernization accomplished to serve the foreign enemy. In the world of the early twentieth century, the Boxers were above all the first great movement against modern colonialism. They demonstrated the existence and the strength of Chinese popular nationalism, and in the face of their intensity, the Western powers abandoned their intentions to divide up the territory of China.

Attempts at insurrection: Kang You-wei and Tang Cai-chang

Though Chinese reformists and revolutionaries condemned the Boxers, they made use of the government's confusion and the people's nationalism for their own revolutionary purposes. They launched several armed rebellions, trying to direct the nationalist feelings of the Chinese against the domestic evils afflicting China.

Early in 1899, in the name of secret instructions received from the Guangxu Emperor, Kang You-wei and Liang Qi-chao organized the Protect the Emperor Society (Baohuanghui). Its influence spread through all the Chinese communities overseas, so that it was able to attract large funds. During the spring and summer of 1900 the society assembled an armed force at Zhennanguan in Guangxi and negotiated with the secret societies in Guangdong to get control over both these provinces and from there to penetrate Hunan and Hubei.

Meanwhile in Shanghai a young Hunanese intellectual, Tang Cai-chang (1867–1900), suggested in July 1900 that a Chinese national assembly be created. He declared that he "no longer acknowledged the generalization of banditry and the sham edicts as

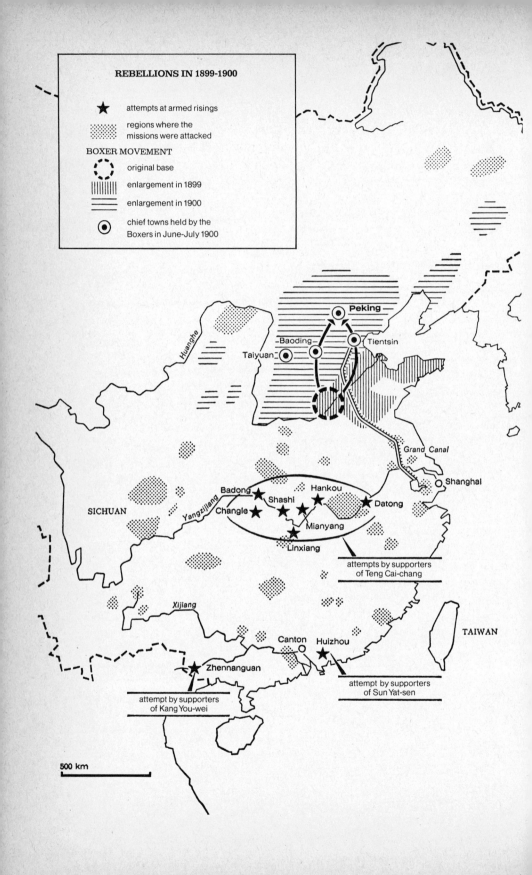

REBELLIONS IN 1899-1900

★ attempts at armed risings

regions where the missions were attacked

BOXER MOVEMENT

original base

enlargement in 1899

enlargement in 1900

⊙ chief towns held by the Boxers in June-July 1900

Huanghe

Peking

Baoding — Tientsin

Taiyuan

Grand Canal

Shanghai

Badong — Hankou

SICHUAN

Yangzijiang — Shashi

Changle — ★ — Datong

Mianyang

Linxiang

attempts by supporters of Teng Cai-chang

Xijiang

TAIWAN

Canton — Huizhou

Zhennanguan

attempt by supporters of Sun Yat-sen

attempt by supporters of Kang You-wei

500 km

government." Tang was associated with Kang You-wei, Sun Yat-sen, and the secret societies, and had the support of a few dozen friends, among them Yan Fu, Zheng Guan-ying, Rong Hong, and Wen Ting-shi. He organized an Independent Society and an Independent Army with the aim of overthrowing Ci-xi. He and Kang You-wei tried to win the governor-generals Zhang Zhi-dong and Liu Kun-yi to the cause. In August and September he launched rebellions in Anhui, Hunan, and Hubei, but they were suppressed by the authorities and he was executed.

Sun Yat-sen and the Huizhou rising

In the summer of 1900 Sun Yat-sen attempted vainly to organize a conspiracy with Li Hong-zhang and the governor of Hong Kong, and then with the governor of Indochina, to obtain the secession and the independence of the Southern provinces. At last he negotiated an agreement with the Japanese that they would support an armed rebellion in Guangdong with the aim of establishing a republic.

Sun's forces gathered near Huizhou at the beginning of October 1900. Composed of peasants and members of secret societies, and led by Christians and Hakka,[9] they numbered over twenty thousand after two weeks. They marched on Amoy, but the Japanese grew fearful of international complications and withdrew their support. The followers of Sun Yat-sen had to disperse for lack of arms and ammunition. The adventure did not go unnoticed, however; it attracted many young Chinese patriots to Sun Yat-sen.

Between 1895 and 1901, amid national humiliations and enslavement to foreign imperialists, currents of resistance and also of renovation emerged in China. They were scattered, contradictory, and still relatively weak. But the forces of resistance, embodied in popular patriotism, saved the empire from being divided, while the forces of renovation continued the process of developing a modern economy and an intellectual and political dynamism which the authorities could no longer ignore.

---

[9] Remember that the Hakka (Cantonese pronunciation of *kejia*, guest) are Chinese who emigrated to the Southern provinces, particularly Guangdong, from Central China at a fairly late date. They were generally relegated to the poorest land and were scorned by the other inhabitants, from whom they differed both in dialect and customs.

ADDITIONAL BIBLIOGRAPHY

G. Dunstheimer, "Le mouvement des Boxeurs," *Revue Historique*, no. 231, April–June 1964, pp. 387–416.

G. Dunstheimer, "Religion et magie dans le mouvement des Boxeurs d'après les textes chinois," *T'oung Pao*, vol. 47, nos. 3–5, 1960, pp. 323–367.

Jung-Pang Lo, *K'ang Yu-wei: A Biography and a Symposium* (Tucson, University of Arizona Press, 1967).

V. Purcell, *The Boxer Uprising: A Background Study* (Cambridge University Press, 1963).

B. Schwartz, *In Search of Wealth and Power: Yen Fu and the West* (Cambridge, Mass., Harvard University Press, 1964).

Chester Tan, *The Boxer Catastrophe* (1955; reprint ed., New York, Octagon Books, 1967).

——. "Tenure of Land in China and the Conditions of the Rural Population," *Journal of the China Branch of the Royal Asiatic Society*, New Series, vol. 23, 1888, pp. 59–174.

DOCUMENTS

1. TAN SI-TONG DENOUNCES THE TYRANNY OF THE OLD REGIME (1896)

SOURCE: Extract from *Ren xue* (*A Study of Benevolence*), 1/37b-38a

The sovereign has neither physical nor intellectual superiority over other men: what is his justification for oppressing 400 million people? His justification is the old formula of the three links and the five relationships,* by which he can be master of the bodies of men and also dominate their minds. As Zhuang Zi† said, "He who steals a hook is executed, he who steals a state becomes a prince." When Tian Cheng-zi‡ stole the state of Qi, he also stole the [Confucian] system of benevolence, wisdom and discernment. When the thieves were both Chinese and Confucianist, it was unfortunate. But how were we able to allow the vile tribes of Mongolia and Manchuria, who knew nothing of China nor of Confucianism, to steal China through their barbarity and cruelty? After stealing China, they dominated the Chinese thanks to the system they had stolen, and shamelessly used Confucianism, which until then had been unknown to them, to oppress China, which until then was foreign to them. Instead of burning the books to maintain the people in ignorance,§ they more skillfully used the books to maintain the people in ignorance. Compared with them, the first Qin emperor was a fool!

---

* The three links which in Confucian tradition implied the duties of the subject toward the sovereign, the son toward his father, and the wife toward her husband. The five relationships were between sovereign and subject, father and son, elder brother and younger brother, husband and wife, and friend and friend.

† Philosopher who lived at the end of the fourth century B.C.

‡ Tian Chang or Chen Heng, a noble of the state of Qi who in 481 B.C. dethroned his sovereign.

§ An allusion to the first Qin emperor (246–309 B.C.), the unifier of China, who

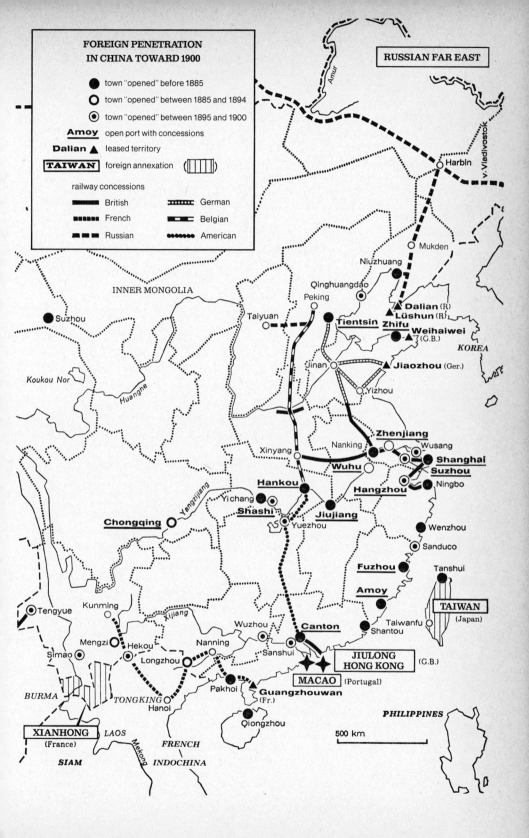

FOREIGN PENETRATION
IN CHINA TOWARD 1900

● town "opened" before 1885
○ town "opened" between 1885 and 1894
◉ town "opened" between 1895 and 1900

Amoy   open port with concessions
Dalian ▲ leased territory
TAIWAN foreign annexation

railway concessions
British
French
Russian
German
Belgian
American

RUSSIAN FAR EAST

INNER MONGOLIA

Koukou Nor

Huangne

v. Vladivostok

Harbin

Mukden

Niuzhuang

Qinghuangdao

Peking

Taiyuan

Suzhou

▲ Dalian (R)
Lüshun (R)
Tientsin Zhifu
Weihaiwei
(G.B.)

KOREA

Jinan

▲ Jiaozhou (Ger.)

Yizhou

Zhenjiang

Nanking   Wusang
Wuhu   **Shanghai**
            Suzhou
Xinyang   Ningbo

Hankou **Hangzhou**

Yichang   **Shashi**

Chongqing

Yangzijiang

Jiujiang

Yuezhou

Wenzhou

Sanduco

Fuzhou   Tanshui

Amoy

Kunming

Tengyue

Xijiang

Wuzhou

Mengzi   Hekou

Simao

Nanning

Longzhou

Canton

Wuzhou

Sanshui

Taiwanfu
Shantou

TAIWAN
(Japan)

**JIULONG
HONG KONG** (G.B.)

MACAO (Portugal)

BURMA

TONGKING

Hanoi

Pakhoi

Guangzhouwan
(Fr.)

Qiongzhou

PHILIPPINES

XIANHONG
(France)

LAOS

FRENCH
INDOCHINA

SIAM

Mekong

500 km

2. A DESCRIPTION OF THE BOXERS: A LETTER FROM A VICE-PREFECT ON A TOUR (MAY 1900)

SOURCE: French translation in G. Dunstheimer, "Religion et magie dans le mouvement des Boxeurs d'après les textes chinois," *T'oung Pao* (Leiden, E. J. Brill) vol. 47, nos. 3–5, pp. 344–345, 360–361. (Chinese text in *Yihotuan*, Shanghai, 1953, vol. 1, pp. 250–251.)

On the twenty-fourth day (May 22, 1900), when I arrived at Jingzhou [in Zhili], I learned that beyond there, to the north, there were difficulties between the Boxers and the Christian converts in all the prefectures and districts. Travelers were not molested, however. On the twenty-eighth day, I arrived at Renqiu and was there told that a few days earlier the Boxers had begun to fight the Christian converts in the region of Liangzhou, to the east of the Renqiu district. Over fifty Christian families had been massacred, making a total of over two hundred people. As to the burning of the houses, the curious thing was that the converts' houses were seen to catch fire immediately, while for those of the nonconverts, the fire went round them, moved away and they all remained intact. At that point I had not seen the Boxer bandits face to face. On the twenty-ninth day, when I arrived at Yongxian, they were to be seen all along the road, in groups of three or five, or eight or ten, sometimes forty or fifty, and so on, in varying numbers. They all had a red sash round their waists, and a red lining to their turbans; some had yellow sashes and turbans lined with yellow. Their flags were inscribed: "The Boxers enforce right principles on behalf of Heaven," "Support the Qing, exterminate the foreigners." On the flags of the group leaders there was the character *kan* or the character *qian*.* All the supporters were armed with knives and spears and advanced northwards by land and water. Those among them who are over thirty years old are very rare; the majority are under twenty, or twelve or thirteen years old. When I met them on my way, they did me no harm whatsoever. . . .

[A little farther on, the vice-prefect visited a boxing hall in a temple compound.]

I saw that they were all little boys of thirteen or fourteen; the smallest ones were not over eight years old. Three tablets stood on an altar. . . . After greeting the deities and taking their places respectfully on either side of the altar, the little boys suddenly began to look sickly, with red faces and staring eyes; they foamed at the mouth; they began to shout and laugh, and kicked and hit each other; even the seven or eight year olds jumped several feet into the air. They moved back and forth, got up, lay down, turned forwards or backwards in unison, as though led by a single man. Some old men who saw that I had come to watch asked me if similar things existed in the South. I asked them:

---

had the books burned and throughout history has been considered the archetype of the tyrant.

* *kan*, ditch; *qian*, sky: two of the eight trigrams.

"What sort of people teach the boxing?" They replied: "There are no teachers of boxing. There are only the gods who cling to the boys' bodies, enabling them to practice. It is called holy boxing. After ten days' practice, they reach perfection."

3. THE BOXER IDEOLOGY: PROCLAMATION BY A BOXER BAND IN A VILLAGE NEAR PEKING (1900)

SOURCE: English version in Ssu-yu Teng and John K. Fairbank, *China's Response to the West: A Documentary Survey, 1839–1923* (New York, Atheneum, 1967), p. 189. Chinese text in Yang Song, *Zhongguo Jindaishi Ziliao Xuanji*, pp. 507–508.

The Catholics since the Xianfeng period [1851–1861] have conspired with foreigners, have caused China trouble, wasted our national revenue, broken up our monasteries, destroyed Buddhist images, and seized our people's graveyards. All these myriad acts of evil should be bitterly resented. This has affected people's trees and plants so as to make them suffer from the catastrophes of locusts and drought almost every year. Our nation is deprived of peace and our people of security. This has angered the Court in Heaven.

Now by the grace of the great deity in Heaven, all the spirits have descended to set up an altar in the wall in order to teach our young men their magic boxing so they can support the Qing, extinguish the foreigners, and enforce right principles on behalf of Heaven. When we exert our energy for the nation in order to bring peace to the land, when we help the farmers and protect our villages, this is an omen that prosperity is coming after misfortune has reached its limit.

Nevertheless, we are afraid that some ignorant people and vagabonds may rely upon the foreigners' power in acting contrary to reason, and cling to the strong in order to oppress the weak. They should be reported to the village head and the chief of the society, who will handle public affairs justly and sentence them according to law, and who are not allowed to be influenced by selfish purposes. If they indulge in private favouritism, the eyes of our spirits like lightning will pierce through them without discrimination, and will not let them get away with any deviation from the just punishment. Because some people use foreign religion and tricky techniques to deceive the people, Heaven above is angered and is sending many sages to descend to earth and come to the divining altar to initiate our youths into the *Yihe* society. *Yi* means kindness, and *he* means politeness; kindness and politeness will make town and countryside peaceful and harmonious. Our people should take right principles and virtue as their foundation and should devote themselves to agriculture as their profession. They should follow and obey Buddhism. They are not permitted to resort to public accusations for avenging a personal grievance, to use poverty as a pretext for oppressing other poor people, to rely on strength to maltreat the weak, or to regard the right as wrong.

Chapter Ten

Advancing Toward
the Revolution:
1901–1911

The first decade of the twentieth century marked the end of an empire which was a thousand years old. The forces of opposition to that empire had emerged during the preceding century; now they developed and became organized. The imperial regime tried to disarm the opposition by taking over part of its program. The Manchu dynasty introduced reforms much more daring than those which had shocked the authorities when Kang You-wei suggested them a decade before. But the dynasty was too far gone;[1] instead of holding the revolution at bay, the reforms hastened it. Many of the features which, in ancient Chinese tradition, marked the end of dynastic cycles and the loss of the Mandate of Heaven were found during the years between 1901 and 1911: agrarian disturbances, the estrangement of the elite, and the weakening of the central power. The development of imperialism and of nationalism gave new meaning to all these phenomena, for in this momentous decade the fall of the dynasty became the fall of the imperial regime as well.

[1] The novel *The Travels of Lao Ts'an* gives an allegorical account of the declining regime. See the excerpt in document 1 at the end of the chapter.

Reforms by the Government

The vast program of reform now launched by the Manchu dynasty focused on three fields: education, the army, and administrative and institutional organization. The resulting upheavals in the political and social life of the country were as far-reaching as those which later emerged from the revolution of 1911.

The reforms were initiated by the court and by several senior officials, including Zhang Zhi-dong and Yuan Shi-kai. At the outset at least, they were not the result of pressure from the forces of opposition to the state. They were the expression of the government's determination to modernize for its own benefit. The failure of the Boxer rebellion and the defeat inflicted by the foreign troops left the imperial regime with no other choice. Far from revealing weakness in the dynasty, the reforms were its last show of strength as the court set out to restore imperial power by adapting the methods of government to the new necessities. Reform was intended to create a modern state by developing centralization, specialization, and information.[2]

Since its aim was conservative, a reform program such as this could not win over the progressive forces. Since its effects were revolutionary, it estranged the vested interests. Reform was therefore based entirely on the authority of the government, and when this began to waver after the death of the Empress Ci-xi in November 1908, the opposition forces turned openly against the regime. The reform which had been devised by the dynasty as a way to salvation became instrumental in its downfall.

The reform of education

Reform of the educational system was given first place among the reform measures announced by the edicts of January 1901. During the second half of the nineteenth century many scholars had called for changes in education, and Kang You-wei had begun making some of them in 1898. The moving spirit behind the rapid reforms achieved between 1901 and 1907 was Zhang Zhi-dong, whose book *Exhortation to Study* had appeared in 1898. In it Zhang criticized the extremely literary education given to Chinese

[2] The principles of reform are set forth in document 2.

intellectuals and the formalism of the examinations, arguing that this kind of training no longer met the needs of officials who had to run a modern state. Thus the reform of education, Zhang said, was a condition necessary to create a modern administration. The survival of the imperial government, and in the long run, the political and social innovations which a "new age" called for, depended on the quality of Chinese schooling.

Between 1901 and 1906 a series of imperial edicts remolded the system of education to follow the Japanese model. New examinations were based on the history of China and on information about foreign countries, and the eight-legged essay (*bagu*) was abolished (edict of August 29, 1901). The traditional academies (*shuyuan*) were transformed into schools organized on the pattern of those founded by Yuan Shi-kai in Shandong (edicts of September 16 and November 15, 1901).

The network of new schools was planned to cover the whole country, forming a hierarchy that corresponded to the government's administrative divisions: elementary schools in the districts, secondary schools in the prefectures, and a college for each province. The course of study was completed by the university; Peking University (Beijing daxue, generally abbreviated to Beida), was organized in 1902. The regulations establishing the new system, drawn up by Zhang Bai-xi in 1902 and altered and completed by Zhang Zhi-dong in 1904, outlined the hierarchy of the institutions, standardized the syllabus, and laid the foundations of the university administration. The abolition of the traditional examinations in September 1905 and the creation of a Ministry of Education in May 1906 confirmed the arrival of modern education in China.

The central government could not finance the new educational system alone, however; the entire program depended on the liberality of the provincial governors and the gentry. The provincial elite were in fact deeply interested in the new schools. They created education societies (506 were on record in 1908, with a total membership of 37,188) and in general cooperated with the government until about 1907. Their initiative, enthusiasm, and financial support varied from one province to another, as did the speed with which reforms were carried out. The most progressive areas were Shanxi, Hunan, and the coastal provinces of Zhili, Zhejiang, Guangdong, and Jiangsu. In the province of Jiangsu, for example, the number of modern schools approximately doubled every year:

1902	67
1903	140
1904	228
1905	564
1906	1,182

By 1909 China possessed over 100,000 modern schools. From the very beginning, however, there were severe shortages of textbooks and competent teachers. Foreigners, particularly the Japanese, furnished some help, but the quality of the teaching remained highly variable. In 1901 Zhang Zhi-dong encouraged Chinese students to go abroad for part or all of their education. Many chose Japan, which was nearer and less strange than the Western countries: 271 Chinese were there in 1902, 15,000 in 1907. Half of the students who went abroad were on scholarships, mostly provided by the provincial governments. In 1908, for example, the province of Hunan supplied scholarships for 475 students in Japan and 103 in Europe and the United States. The program of education abroad was overrun with problems concerning the choice of subjects and schools, the relations between the students and the host country, Chinese government control of the students' activities outside school, and the provision of suitable jobs for students returning to China. All the troubles which confront an underdeveloped country when it sends its best young people away to be educated were found in this first Chinese experiment.

Thus the central government, backed by the provincial elite, achieved a real, though incomplete, modernization of education. But its initial success concealed future dangers, because instead of contributing to the restoration of government power, the new intellectuals swelled the ranks of the opposition.

Military reforms

In 1901 China's military power was based on a conglomeration of troops whose origins and nature were extremely varied. The oldest were the Manchu Banners, who had conquered China in the seventeenth century. Their chief mission was to protect the dynasty and command respect for the conquerors. They were spread unevenly through the country, with the largest groups in Peking, Zhili, and Manchuria. The Army of the Green Standard, organized to act as an auxiliary to the Banners, was made up of 60,000 Chinese provincial soldiers and served as a police rather than a battle force.

These regular units were in the last stages of deterioration; corruption, collusion with bandits, gambling, and opium made them all but useless. Although officers were recruited through the traditional examinations based on a knowledge of the Classics, in practice their talents seemed to be confined to archery, swordplay, and shot-putting.

The other Chinese military forces had been organized in the nineteenth century. Among them were the regional armies recruited by Zeng Guo-fan, Li Hong-zhang, and Zuo Zong-tang to suppress the Taiping rebellion. These militia, composed of professional soldiers called the "braves" (*yong*), were paid out of provincial funds and given semimodern equipment. Even less under the authority of Peking than the regular troops, they were tied to their leader and dependent on his career. Thus Li Hong-zhang moved the Anhui army to Zhili when he was transferred there, and the Hunan army settled in the Yangzi valley under the command of Liu Kun-yi. The defeat of 1895 resulted in the formation of new armies, chief of which were the Self-strengthening army established by Zhang Zhi-dong, with European equipment and German officers in charge of its training, and the Pacification army or the Newly Created army (*Xinjianlujun*) organized by Yuan Shi-kai.

The defeats suffered during the Boxer rebellion revealed the weakness of the Chinese armies and the urgent need for military reform. The lines to be followed were laid down beginning in July 1901 by Liu Kun-yi and Zhang Zhi-dong: they stipulated that the Army of the Green Standard must be disbanded, modern arms adopted, Western methods used in training troops, an imperial general staff founded, and military academies created. The court approved most of these recommendations and published decrees. The traditional military examinations were abolished (August 29) and the governor-generals were required to found military academies in the provinces (September 1). New units were to be organized according to Western concepts of active and reserve troops: the active list was to form the foundations of the future modern army (*lujun*), and the reserve list was to provide a place for the traditional troops who were being disbanded (September 2).

None of these measures attempted to centralize military affairs. The power was still in the hands of the senior provincial officials, and whether or not reform was carried out depended on whether they were willing to execute it. After the death of Li Hong-zhang (1901), Liu Kun-yi (1902), and Rong-lu (1903), Yuan Shi-kai,

as governor-general of Zhili, played the main role in military reform between 1901 and 1907. With the help of support and subsidies from the central government, he created the Northern army
(known under the name of Beiyang) which in 1905 comprised six
divisions. They had modern equipment, Japanese instructors, and
officers of high quality, trained either abroad or in the new schools
opened in the provinces, in particular at Baoding. It was an army of
personal loyalties whose officers were devoted to Yuan Shi-kai and
threw in their lot with his. Later they became warlords, prime ministers, or presidents of the republic. The Beiyang clique grew out of
this army.

In Hubei, according to a French observer, Zhang Zhi-dong also
managed to create modern units which were comparable to the best
German troops. This force was smaller, less of a clique, and more
receptive to revolutionary ideas than Yuan's Northern army.

Impressive maneuvers in 1906, in which the Zhili and Hubei
units took part, bore witness to the progress accomplished in five
years. Military reform moved more slowly in the other provinces,
however; the plan for a modern Chinese army drawn up in 1904
by the military reorganization committee met resistance from local
bodies and local interests. Although a War Ministry was established
in 1906 which was more highly specialized than the old War Ministry, it was not able to impose centralization in the absence of any
central financial power.

Administrative and institutional reforms

The strong regionalism which slowed down educational and military reform was seen by the court as an obstacle to its policies and
its authority. The traditional balance between regional and Peking
officials had changed greatly over the preceding fifty years, to the
detriment of Peking. Now it was ill adapted to the needs of modernization, at least as they were understood by the government.
Peking was working to develop the branches of the central administration and to increase their efficiency. The process was often carried out by degrees; committees or offices were created within the
existing administrative structures and later raised to the rank of
ministries. The Foreign Ministry appeared in 1901, the Ministry of
Trade in 1903, and the Ministries of Police, Education, and War in
1906.

In November 1906 a regulation altered the allocation of functions among the ministries and increased their total number to ten owing to the recent additions. The rule stipulating that a numerical balance should be maintained between Manchus and Chinese in official appointments was abolished. The practice of serving in many posts, which had been common among senior officials, was also condemned. Thus Yuan Shi-kai, governor-general of Zhili, had to resign from seven other major offices he was occupying. The reform removed about 1,400 officials from office. Nominees to replace them were chosen according to traditional criteria, and scholars with a classical education were given preference. The elimination of a compulsory quota of posts to be allotted to Chinese officials worked in favor of the Manchus. All these changes generated a wave of discontent and reaction in 1907.

The program of reform also included measures to improve provincial administration. In 1907 an edict attempted to introduce specialization in administrative, economic, and legal duties at the different levels in the hierarchy. This administrative reform was not, however, accompanied by the tax and financial restructuring which would have made it effective. Taxes levied in the provinces were still applied directly to local needs; only a small proportion of the funds were turned over to the central government. The new sources of income, such as the *lijin* and customs revenues, eluded the central government entirely. In Peking each ministry still had its own budget, supplied by special revenues. This archaic structure inevitably weakened the measures taken for administrative centralization.

Like administrative reform, the reform of institutions aimed at uniting the nation behind the central power. Institutional reform, which developed between 1905 and 1911, introduced parliamentary features into the Chinese political system. An edict of September 1, 1906, proclaimed the throne's approval of the principle of constitutional government and stressed the need for closer links between the governors and those they governed. It declared that the central authority, without abandoning any of its prerogatives, expected to be informed on the opinion of the people and to associate the people in the work of renovation it had undertaken.

Here again the reformers had drawn their inspiration from the example set by Japan. For them, adopting a constitutional regime had seemed to be one among several ways to rally national energies around the empire and move forward along the road to wealth and power. Therefore the government had decided in 1905 to gather information about foreign political systems. Two enlightened Man-chus, Prince Zai-ze and Duan-fang, were put in charge of delega-tions which went to Europe, the United States, and Japan to study government institutions. On their return they submitted a report to a committee of twelve scholars presided over by Prince Chun, the younger brother of the Guangxu Emperor. The great edict of Sep-tember 1, 1906, ratified the conclusions of the committee and promised that constitutional government would be introduced after a period of preparation. Edicts issued a year later recommended the formation of a constitutional assembly (*zi zheng yuan*) and pro-vincial assemblies (*zi yi ju*), in which parliamentary debating could be learned. In August 1908 the constitutional principles were pub-lished. It was a hastily written document based on the Japanese constitution and reflecting the somewhat limited nature of democ-racy in that country. The parliament was to have a purely consulta-tive role with no power of decision, and there would be a nine-year interval of preparation before the constitutional regime was in-augurated. Provincial consultative assemblies were to be created in 1909 and a national assembly in 1910.

The death of the Empress Ci-xi in 1908, soon after that of the Guangxu Emperor, brought a complete change in government per-sonnel. The successor to the Empress was a child, her great-nephew Pu-yi, who reigned from 1909 to 1912 under the name of Xuan-tong. The emperor's father, Prince Chun, became regent. He sur-rounded himself with conservative Manchu princes and excluded Ci-xi's chief advisers, Yuan Shi-kai and Duan-fang. Zhang Zhi-dong died in 1909. The death of an empress whose authority was generally acknowledged although not always faithfully obeyed, together with the retirement or death of the statesmen who had influenced and supported her, left few chances of success for the policy of reform.

Nevertheless, the provincial assemblies met in October 1909, having been elected by limited suffrage consisting of scholars and rich landowners. In the province of Shandong, for example, 119,000 inhabitants voted out of a total population of 38 million; in Hubei 113,000 voted out of 34 million.

In spite of the carefully restricted suffrage and other precautions that went into their election, the assemblies immediately became centers of opposition to the imperial regime. The government lost the initiative in politics; the measures it took were merely clumsy and insincere replies to the pressures exerted by the provincial delegates. At a meeting in Peking in February 1910, the delegates asked that a parliament be called immediately. They obtained the convocation in October 1910 of a national consultative assembly, half of whose members were appointed by the government. The government promised that a proper parliament would be convened in 1913, and as an interim measure the regent formed a cabinet in April 1911. The cabinet members, however, were mainly princes of the imperial clan and Manchu nobles. Armed rebellion in the provinces in the autumn of 1911 led the regent to agree to turn the national assembly into a constituent assembly and to proclaim additional constitutional principles. But these were only the last convulsions before the abdication.

Economic and Social Upheaval

After 1908 both the weakening of imperial power and the return to a reactionary policy undermined the experiment in a Meiji type of reform that had been attempted by Ci-xi and the statesmen in her entourage. But in the long run the reasons for the failure of reform lie in China's historical circumstances at the time, and in the economic and social upheavals which nourished discontent and swelled the forces of opposition.

Foreign interests

China's economic evolution between 1901 and 1911 was closely linked with the development of international capitalism, for the growth of the modern sector in the Chinese economy went hand in hand with the progress of imperialist penetration. The latter was based on the privileges fixed by the international treaties of the preceding century. Extending these privileges were the clauses in the Peace Protocol of September 1901 revising the customs tariff, which was brought to an effective rate of 5 percent in 1903, and the provisions of the Russo-Japanese Portsmouth Treaty of 1905 for opening the Manchurian ports, which brought the total number of open ports to forty-eight. The Mackay Treaty, negotiated in 1902 with Great Britain, allowed for the revision of clauses on extraterritoriality under certain conditions, such as the adoption of taxation or monetary reforms. The treaty was not applied, however, and the questions it raised were not examined again until the conference of

Washington in 1922. The unequal-treaties system remained in force and provided the legal setting for the activities of the foreign economic groups. However, the numerous business contracts entered into by the Chinese with the foreigners, backed by their respective governments, had diplomatic implications. In economic practice, they tended to strengthen the position of the foreigners with regard to the Chinese state. For Peking had an international obligation to assume the responsibilities of an entrepreneur, which were normally subject to the hazards of circumstance.

Foreign investments in China grew rapidly, increasing from 788 million United States dollars in 1902 to 1,610 million in 1914. Two-thirds of these sums were directly invested by the foreigners; the rest represented funds lent to the government and, to a minor extent, lent to private Chinese enterprises. Great Britain was still the chief supplier of capital, followed at some distance by Russia, Germany, France, and Japan. From 1905 on, Japan invested more and more heavily in Manchuria. Foreign banks financed all these operations. The Hong Kong & Shanghai Banking Corporation controlled the market until 1908, but other financial groups were becoming active: for example, the Compagnie Générale des Chemins de Fer et des Tramways de Chine, backed up by the Banque Belge pour l'Etranger and the Banque de Paris et des Pays-Bas, and the Peking syndicate controlled by Lloyds Bank.

The money went into the modern sector of the Chinese economy. In 1911, 93 percent of the existing railways had been built by foreigners or with foreign loans. The railway network increased by about 500 kilometers a year and reached a length of 9,618 kilometers in 1911. The lines for which concessions had been obtained in 1897–1898 were completed: the Trans-Manchurian and the South Manchurian railway were finished in 1903, the German railway in Shandong in 1904, the Shanghai-Nanking and Shanghai-Ningbo lines in 1908 and 1912, and the French line in Yunnan in 1910. The Peking-Hankou line, built by a Franco-Belgian syndicate and bought by the Chinese government, was finished in 1906. After 1905 the Chinese government granted no further concessions. Instead it authorized loans, such as the British loan for construction of the Canton-Kowloon line (1907–1911) and the British and German loan for the Tientsin-Pukou line (1908–1911). Work was also begun on the Canton-Wuchang line and the Longhai line, but neither of them had progressed very far by 1911.

The railway network built by the foreigners was colonial in style

—fragmentary and laid out in accordance with the strategic and commercial concerns of the foreign powers. It sometimes accentuated the dissociation of the regional economies, as in the case of Yunnan, which had better transportation links with French Indochina than with the rest of China. The network strengthened the economic superiority of the lower Yangzi provinces, however; the hinterland of Shanghai stretched along the railway lines and a long way toward the Northern provinces. In this respect the railways contributed to the unification of the Chinese market. But progress was slow, irregular, and dictated by the needs of foreign trade, so that the integration of the national economy appeared to be a by-product of imperialist penetration.

Steam navigation also developed. In 1902 foreign ships representing a total tonnage of 44 million used Chinese ports; by 1907 the figure had increased to 63 million. Foreign ships accounted for 84 percent of the steamer traffic in Chinese ports. The chief companies were British (the China Navigation Company and the Indo-China Steam Navigation Company) and Japanese (Nishin Kisen Kaisha).

In the first decade of the twentieth century a number of modern mines were constructed and operated directly by foreigners or by companies jointly owned by Chinese and foreigners. As laid down by the agreements drawn up with the Chinese government in 1896, the Trans-Manchurian Railway Company began to work the Fushun coal mines in 1901. After the Russian defeat in 1905, the mines were handed over to the Japanese South Manchurian Company. Several coal and iron mines were opened by the Germans in Shandong. The Peking syndicate mined the coal in Henan; the Kailan Mining Administration, which was taken over by British interests after the Boxer rebellion, assured production in the Kaiping mines. Although relatively little of the total foreign investment was in mining enterprises (they accounted for about 3 percent of direct foreign investments in 1914), foreigners controlled 91 percent (4.7 million tons) of the coal production in the modern mines and the entire iron ore production (83,837 tons).

Foreign funds invested in industrial enterprises were spread over different sectors: dockyards in Shanghai, factories processing goods for export (tea, silk, soybeans), and factories making goods for the home market (cigarettes, cotton yarn, and cotton fabrics). The big foreign silk-spinning mills were established at the end of the nineteenth century; in 1897 they represented a total of 160,000 spindles. A few years later several Japanese companies were created, bringing the total of foreign spindles in 1913 up to 339,000, or 41 percent of the total equipment in China.

The development of modern transportation and industry supplied goods for foreign trade, the value of which rose from 437 million taels in 1901 to 848 million in 1911. Imports and exports increased together, but the balance of trade showed a constant deficit. Meanwhile the tendency in the terms in trade was reversed and the relation between the price of imports and that of exports, which had been fairly stable since 1867, became less and less favorable to China after 1908. The goods involved in foreign trade also changed. In exports, tea and silk became relatively less important, and new products like eggs, soybeans, and vegetable oils appeared. Among imports, cotton yarn and fabric became steadily more important and in 1905 amounted to 40 percent of the total value of imports. Foreigners still controlled all transportation, whether of funds or goods, between the Chinese open ports and the customer or supplier countries. Within China they made every effort to develop direct contacts with inland markets, thus encroaching on the activities of Chinese merchants.

National enterprises

The example and the challenge provided by foreign businessmen stimulated the growth of Chinese enterprises. Many semi-official companies (*guan du shang ban*) were created at the end of the nineteenth century, and after 1900 this bureaucratic capitalism continued to develop. The first modern banks—the Commercial Bank of China (1897), the Hubu Bank, which afterwards became the Da Qing, the Bank of Communications (1907)—were enterprises run on the *guan du shang ban* system. The same was true of the railway lines which the government either built (the Peking-Kalgan line) or bought back (the Peking-Hankou line), and of the few modern mines created by the provincial gentry and officials in Hunan, Zhili, and Sichuan.

Private enterprises (*shang ban*) also became more numerous. During the four years which followed the proclamation of the law on incorporated companies in 1904, 227 companies registered with the Ministry of Industry, Agriculture, and Commerce. Most of them possessed machinery but worked with very little capital and manpower. Only twenty or so were of any real economic importance. The effects of the Chinese contractors were concentrated on the textile industry; between 1905 and 1910 eleven spinning mills were established. The most important group was that of Zhang Jian; his two mills, one built in 1899 and the other in 1907, had a total of 66,000 spindles.

The Chinese private enterprises were financed by the *qianzhuang* banks, which replaced the old Shanxi banks. The *qianzhuang* banks were enterprises of a traditional type, operating in the modernized circles in the open ports. They acted as intermediaries between Chinese business circles and the big foreign financiers, who advanced the funds on which the entire system of credit was based.

The growth of the national modern sector was slow and uneven. It met numerous obstacles, such as the inadequacy of the institutional framework, rivalry and mistrust between officials and merchant-contractors, and the persistence of nepotism and corruption. It also came up against powerful foreign interests. Deprived of autonomy in the customs, China could not protect its market or its industries. Chinese manufacturers had to face competition from Western and Japanese rivals who were better prepared and who benefited from the tax system that exempted their goods from inland dues—from the *lijin*. The country had to hand over vast sums to pay off the Boxer indemnity: 224 million taels between 1902 and 1910, when it is estimated that the government's total annual budget did not exceed 90 million taels. After such a drain on national resources, where could the funds needed for industrialization be obtained except from foreign loans, which then worsened the financial situation still further?

The existence of a modern sector, no matter how weak, transformed the Chinese economy and made it assume the dual structure characteristic of a developing country. On one hand lay the vast inland expanse of rural and traditional China, whose prosperity depended on the harvest. This was the part which suffered most when natural disasters produced widespread famine in 1902, 1906–1907, and 1911. On the other hand lay the narrow coastal fringe of the treaty ports, whose activity was influenced by the rhythm of the international market, with the boom of 1905 and the crisis of 1906–1907.

In spite of the dualism of the economy, the modern and traditional sectors influenced each other, though no adequate studies of their interaction have yet been made. One example is the rural handicraft industry, which was both helped and harmed by the importing and the manufacture of industrial goods. It would be interesting to know how far the decline of spinning as a handicraft industry was compensated for by the increased prosperity of weaving which was made possible by low-priced industrial yarn.

The importance of economic modernization lay not in its achievements alone, but perhaps most of all in the conditions accompanying these achievements. Foreign imperialism stimulated the Chinese desire to modernize the economy, and to a certain extent, provided the Chinese with the example, the funds, and the technical knowledge to become a modern country. But at the same time, the state of dependence imposed on China and the exploitation suffered by the Chinese condemned the country to the condition of underdevelopment. A situation like this is heavy with consequences, which should be appraised in terms of social and political history.

New social groups

The partial transformation of the state and the economy resulted in the emergence of new social groups. In the treaty ports the business bourgeoisie was born of the fusion of various elements: businessmen and brokers engaged in foreign trade; bankers, whose numbers grew with the rise of the *qianzhuang* establishments; industrialists, who were fewer in number and generally combined financial and commercial activities; and of course, the compradors.

Compradors were found in all foreign enterprises acting as intermediaries between the Chinese public and the Western or Japanese businessmen. They often took considerable responsibility, choosing Chinese clients, guaranteeing the contracts made with them, and authenticating payments in local currency. These interpreters of old had become managing directors. At the beginning of the twentieth century the compradors' circle was influential and difficult to enter (because the post was lucrative, it tended to become hereditary). It provided the national bourgeoisie with some of its chief leaders: Chen Lian-bo in Canton, Yu Qia-qing and Zhu Bao-san in Shanghai.

Overseas businessmen formed another, somewhat marginal group of the bourgeoisie whose importance should not, however, be underestimated. As time went on the Chinese communities in Southeast Asia and the United States increasingly invested their money in China, particularly in the Southern provinces, from which most of the emigrants had come.

This bourgeoisie with its differing elements was grouped in traditional organizations: professional guilds, brotherhoods based on communities of provincial origins (*bang*), and chambers of commerce, created in 1904. Its numerical weakness was partially offset by its geographic concentration in the treaty ports.

Shanghai was the bastion and symbol of the new bourgeoisie, which prospered in the Westernized circles of the international concession. The low buildings of the first godowns along the Bund had disappeared, replaced by the tall blocks housing foreign banks and by the Shanghai Club building, its façade decorated with a Greek colonnade. In the main shopping street, Nanking Road, were the first big Chinese stores, belonging to the Sincere Company. Shanghai lived at the same rhythm as other modern cities. The streets of the concessions were filled with the clang of the newly installed tramways. The Shanghai-Nanking railway was completed. The first cars appeared. But the public gardens were still closed to Chinese, whose initiation into the modern world proceeded amid dependence and humiliation. The nationalistic feelings of the bourgeoisie and its resentment of the foreigners were expressed in the organization of boycotts in 1905 and 1907. Antiforeign sentiment was also transformed into hostility against the imperial authority and its inability to protect the interests of the bourgeoisie and those of China as a whole.

The officers of the modern armies and the students in the new schools, who were usually landowners' sons, were separated from their own class by their activities and their interests. However, they could not be said to form part of the embryonic bourgeoisie; they had few links with it. These two minority groups owed their originality and strength not to their economic functions, but to the special part they played in the introduction into China of new techniques and ideas.

In 1906 China had thirty-five modern military academies training 787 officers and 3,448 officer candidates. In addition, 691 officers were being trained abroad. These men, particularly the officers recruited by Zhang Zhi-dong, came from rich families. Many of them had degrees. Many students had "thrown away the pen to take up the sword" in the desire to serve their country better. The reform of the armies made it easier to choose a military career, and public opinion encouraged it, for China was in the grip of a military revival. Schoolchildren learned to handle rifles, merchants formed armed militia, and officers enjoyed new prestige and felt that they were entrusted with special responsibilities. The officers, however, were constantly reminded of China's backwardness and weakness. Their mission to defend the country implied that they were helping China move toward economic modernization and political and administrative reorganization. But the young officers were often commanded by higher officers from the old armies who were ignorant and corrupt; the new men felt frustrated both professionally and patriotically.

The frustration was shared by many students, even though the government was careful to find room in the administration for those who had studied abroad. Special examinations were organized to give them the corresponding Chinese academic rank and the necessary degrees. But with the growth in the number of students, particularly in the new schools, it became increasingly difficult to integrate them into the traditional society. The education they received estranged them from Confucian values and freed them from the network of duties weighing down the old scholars. The best of them did have a sense of duty, but not toward the real situation in China. They felt consecrated to a brilliantly imagined national future and thereby gave birth to revolutionary radicalism.

The social groups which emerged with the beginning of modernization were potential enemies of the established regime. Their opposition would probably have carried little weight had it not been combined with widespread discontent throughout Chinese society.

Rising Opposition

Discontent among peasants and gentry

Although no more large-scale peasant risings comparable to the Taiping or the Boxer rebellions occurred at the beginning of the twentieth century, disturbances were incessant in the rural districts. The Boxer movement was still threatening in Sichuan in 1902; Zhili was not completely pacified, and the Village League movement had a membership of some 160,000 peasants. Hundreds of thousands of soldiers were sent to suppress troubles in Guangxi in 1903. Rioting broke out in Leping in Jiangxi in July 1904 and spread to the neighboring province of Anhui. In 1909 the trouble increased; 113 risings were reported for that year, and 285 the next. The provinces which suffered most were in the lower and middle Yangzi region.

These were revolts due to poverty, or "primitive" revolts. The Yangzi and Han floods of 1909–1911 brought famine to thousands of people. Many extra taxes were created to finance the reforms, and the peasants bore the brunt of them. The census of the population undertaken by the imperial government upset the peasants, because they suspected that it was a tax maneuver. The rebels attacked the granaries of speculators, the tax collectors' offices, and the modern schools.

Was this agitation a symptom of the disintegration of the traditional rural society? Or was it a proof of the society's capacity to resist change? Or did it simply represent the peasants' permanent struggle for survival? The detailed economic studies needed to answer these questions are lacking. It is only possible to guess at the causes of the peasant risings. In our opinion bad weather, bringing with it harvest failure and famine, played a basic role; the effects of reform or foreign penetration were less of a burden than the chronic evil of overpopulation and the fundamental lack of balance in production.

The turbulence of the "primitive" social forces was reflected in the activities of the secret societies. Although they did not organize the agrarian rebellions, the secret societies were often associated with them. They were a traditional refuge for the discontented, taking in people from all social backgrounds.

> Officials and scholars, everyone is received into our ranks.
> Runners, servants, and soldiers, nobody is turned away.

Most of their members were vagabonds, smugglers, or deserters, but the societies were not organizations based on class distinctions. The renewal of their activities was as much a result of the gentry's growing dislike for the central government as of popular discontent.

The control of Chinese rural society was based on cooperation between the local elite and the public authorities, but at the beginning of the century the elite felt less and less loyal to Peking. The decline in loyalty went hand in hand with the decentralization which had begun in the nineteenth century. The gentry, the chief beneficiaries of the regionalization of power, defended their privileges at all costs. Even when they were in favor of reforms, they would not agree to the necessary strengthening of central power. When the economic imperialism of the foreign powers threatened their own economic interests, they were angry about the inadequate protection extended to them and reproached Peking with its power-lessness—which they themselves helped to perpetuate. Opportuni-ties for disagreement multiplied, particularly because at the end of the nineteenth century the provincial gentry included growing numbers of business managers coming from the ranks of the mer-chants, officials, and landowners. The leading elite referred to ear-lier as scholar-gentry (*shenshi*) became a merchant-gentry (*shenshang*) group.

The campaign for the return of the mining and railway conces-sions illustrated the *shenshang*'s determination to defend both their own enterprises against foreign competition and their political priv-ileges against the central authority. In 1905 Zhang Zhi-dong, with the support of the Hubei-Hunan and Guangdong gentry, managed to buy back the rights reserved by an American company to build the Hankou-Canton railway. Although the provincial companies which were organized to replace the foreign firm were unable to finance and supervise construction, the gentry were extremely hos-tile to the idea that the central government should take over railway policy. The proposal for nationalizing the railroads was sponsored by a highly unpopular minister, Sheng Xuan-huai. It was common knowledge that he had amassed a fortune from his management of various joint enterprises (*guan du shang ban*). It was also widely known that his ill-advised loans enabled Japan to gain control of the biggest Chinese coal and iron complex, the Hanyeping Company, after 1908. The general fear was that Sheng's negotiations with the foreigners to obtain loans to build the Sichuan-Hankou and Hankou-Canton lines would produce similar results. Unfortunately, the signing of a loan contract with a foreign banking syndicate coincided with a government decree transferring the control of all provincial railways to Peking. The gentry regarded it as an affront to their patriotism, their provincial liberties, and their economic interests. The discontent of the privileged classes corresponded to the agitation among the lower classes.

Chinese nationalism

The aspirations of the new social groups and the bitterness of the rural classes found joint expression in nationalist claims. Chinese nationalism developed at the beginning of the century and centered on two themes: hatred of the Manchu dynasty and hostility toward imperialism.

Anti-Manchu feeling pervaded Chinese society, but depending on the groups and the interests involved, it took on different meanings. In the secret societies it continued the tradition of racial hatred and condemnation of the usurpers. The alliance between the dynasty and the Boxers was merely a short-lived episode; the secret societies reverted to their former slogan of "Overthrow the Qing and restore the Ming." The anti-Manchu feelings of the mass of the people were born of loyalty for the former Chinese Ming dynasty. Among the provincial gentry, on the other hand, hatred for the Manchus was combined with hostility toward the central government. And among the intelligentsia and the radical bourgeoisie, it was identified with the condemnation of absolute power. Many historians have demonstrated the thesis that the rallying of new social groups to a traditional ideology of opposition renews the contents and the meaning of the ideology. A phenomenon which has received less attention is the distortions imposed on a modern revolutionary movement which borrows the style of thought and action belonging to a backward-looking society.

Opposition to the foreigners contained the same ambiguities. Xenophobia was still present in Chinese society, but an analysis of imperialism in political terms was also gradually emerging. Liang Qi-chao studied and denounced the economic penetration of the treaty powers in China. He compared the history of China with that of other countries like India and Egypt, placing them in the context of European colonial expansion.

Riots and attacks on buildings and people connected with the West gave way to more elaborate forms of action. In 1905 the bourgeoisie in the open ports organized a boycott of American goods to protest the new immigration laws in the United States which discriminated against Chinese. The students and the public joined the movement, and it extended to the nation as a whole. In 1908 a similar boycott was directed against Japan to express indignation over the *Tatsu-Maru* incident, in which Chinese seizure of a Japanese ship carrying smuggled arms had evoked angry protests from Tokyo. The campaign for the return of the mining and railway concessions, described in the previous section, also mobilized public opinion.

The economic effectiveness of these movements was doubtful, though at least they demonstrated a common determination to oppose foreign encroachments. Even so, Chinese hostility to imperialism was no longer the xenophobia of the nineteenth century, for the possibility of cooperation with the foreign powers was not excluded. Sun Yat-sen had already placed his trust in the West and sought its support. The pro-Western current of opinion that began with him was an important ingredient of Chinese nationalism during the following decades.

Countless contradictions existed between the loyalty to the Ming professed by the secret societies and the Western sympathies of Sun Yat-sen, and between the conservative anti-Manchu feeling among the provincial gentry and the anti-Manchu radicalism of the students. Chinese resentment of foreign intervention was expressed, paradoxically, in renewed hostility toward the Manchus—who for several centuries had been undergoing a process of assimilation into Chinese society and whose existence as a racial minority did not in any way threaten the country. Nationalism became, in a somewhat ambiguous way, the common factor in the discontent latent at all levels in Chinese society. The movements of opposition started and met there.

Reformists and revolutionaries

During this period the movements of reform or revolution were organized abroad (particularly in Japan) or in the concessions in the open ports. Their leaders were Chinese in exile, and their members were merchants overseas or students enrolled in foreign universities. The repression by the imperial police of the militants belonging to the opposition explains why they took refuge outside China. In doing so, however, they loosened their ties with their compatriots at home and reduced the chances that the movements they organized would become fully identified with the deep-seated forces at work in the country. On the other hand, their exile enabled them to obtain precious support, particularly from Japanese belonging to very different parties and sections of society. For example, there was Okuma, the former prime minister of Japan, and with him many Japanese who wanted to help China become free and achieve modernization (these included Inukai Takeshi and his agents, Miyazaki Torazo and Hirayama Shu). There were also Japanese nationalists, members of the Black Dragon Society, who saw the Chinese revolution as an opportunity to prepare for Japanese expansion on the continent.

The Chinese movements of opposition became polarized between reformists and revolutionaries—between Liang Qi-chao and

Sun Yat-sen. Liang, a reformist who advocated a constitutional monarchy for China, was born near Canton in 1873. He received a thorough education in the Classics from his family and became a provincial graduate at the age of sixteen. He took an active part in the reform movement as a disciple of Kang You-wei (Chapter 9). In September 1898 after the failure of the Hundred Days, he fled to Japan. He was briefly tempted to join forces with Sun Yat-sen, but eventually returned to Kang You-wei, who at that time was organizing the Protect the Emperor Society (Baohuanghui). In his journal *Public Opinion* (*Qing Yi Bao*, 1898–1899), Liang defended the cause of the Guangxu Emperor and attacked the conservatives in Peking.

However, Liang rapidly went beyond the themes of the movement of 1898. No longer satisfied by Kang's radical interpretation of tradition, he acquired new interests, among them Western history and philosophy, and became an admirer of Darwin, Martin Luther, Bacon, and Descartes. In a paper entitled *Renovation of the People (Xin Min Cong Bao)* he urged the Chinese to shake off their past and go forward, like "a ship leaving the shore." He supplemented his reading with trips to Hawaii (1900) and the United States and Canada (1903). He was a prolific journalist and essayist with a clear, brilliant, impassioned style which appealed to students. His influence eclipsed Kang You-wei's, for when he denounced the decline of Chinese institutions, the ignorance and poverty of the people, and the corruption of the officials, he became the spiritual guide for a whole generation.

Liang did not believe in the possibility of immediate and radical change. The Political Culture Association (Zhengwenshe), which he founded in 1907, advocated the adoption of a constitution, a parliament, a cabinet with real responsibilities, a separate and independent status for the judicial branch, the development of local autonomy, and acknowledgment of China's rights by other nations. Democracy was to take the form of a constitutional monarchy established voluntarily by the imperial government. Under this "enlightened despotism" the people would undergo preparation for exercising their rights.

Liang's relative moderation made him less popular than Sun Yat-sen in student circles, but he and Sun were appreciated equally by the bourgeoisie overseas. Chinese merchants in Yokohama financed Liang's paper *Public Opinion*; his lectures in Hawaii and the United States won many new members for the reformist organizations. He also had considerable influence within China; it is possible that his ideas may have guided Peking's attempt at institutional reform. He maintained contact with the court (especially with Duan-feng) in spite of the fact that he strongly criticized the slowness and timidity of the reform.

Though he did not organize it, Liang inspired the constitutionalist movement which mobilized the gentry against the government between 1906 and 1911. In its early stages the movement was sporadic, arising in scattered provincial organizations. The most active was the Society for Preparing the Establishment of Constitutional Government (Yubei Lixian Gonghui), created in 1906 by Zhang Jian in Jiangsu. The way these associations operated was to send out petitions; their aims were exactly the same as those of the Political Culture Association (which had numerous affiliated groups in China, consisting mainly of students, until it was forbidden by the government in 1908). The establishment of the provincial assemblies in 1909 and the national assembly in 1910 enabled the constitutionalist opposition to form new groups and develop on a national scale. The movement was directed by gentry who supported the ideas of Liang, which were given wide coverage in the Chinese press. The *Oriental Review* (*Dongfang Zazhi*), an influential publication, and the long-established *Shanghai Journal* (*Shen Bao*), sponsored by Zhang Jian, printed editorials by Liang. In practice, however, the movement grew away from Liang's ideas and to a certain extent, even betrayed them. Liang saw the parliamentary system as the means of progressing steadily toward democracy, national unity, and modernity. For the gentry who supported that system, however, its meaning was entirely different. They regarded it as an engine of war directed against the central power. Liang claimed liberties; the gentry defended privileges.

The other leader of the opposition—Liang's rival and ultimate enemy—was Sun Yat-sen (1866–1925). Probably the only thing the two men had in common was their Cantonese origins. Liang was a scholar and an aristocrat; Sun a professional revolutionary, educated first in Honolulu where his elder brother lived, and then in the British missionary circles of Hong Kong. From his peasant background and his family traditions he was at home in the world of secret societies and had a great admiration for the Taiping. Unlike Liang, he had never exercised power, even indirectly. In 1894 he attempted to utilize the regular political channels by submitting a petition to Li Hong-zhang, but he never received a reply.

Until 1900 Sun's career was that of an adventurer. He organized the secret Revive China Society (Xingzhonghui), refused to be discouraged by the failure of the rebellions he incited (the first was in Canton in 1895, the second in Huizhou in 1900), and lived in exile in Japan, taking trips to the United States and Europe. He was both victim and hero of an attempt to kidnap him at the Chinese legation in London in 1897. This incident established his reputation and confirmed his vocation. A man of great personal magnetism, he was capable of changing to suit the company he was in and thus moved at ease both among the secret societies, whose antidynastic policy and style of action he adopted, and among the bourgeoisie of the Chinese communities overseas, who were enthusiastic supporters of progress and already half Westernized. He had yet to win over the intellectual circles which were in ferment at that time, or to extend his influence from the foreign bases and the southern fringes of Guangdong toward the heart of the country, the Yangzi valley.

Sun could not lay claim to the leadership of the revolutionary movement unless he won the recognition of men like Zhang Binglin and Cai Yuan-pei. These two scholars with classical educations were behind a violent anti-Manchu campaign in Zhejiang and Jiangsu. Acting through the press, they enjoyed great popularity among students in China and abroad. The *Jiangsu Journal* (*Su Bao*), for which members of their group worked, published inflammatory pamphlets against the emperor, describing him as a "young clown." The journal was brought to trial in 1903 in a case which excited great interest.

Meanwhile, in the shelter of the Institute for Patriotic Studies (Aiguo Xueshe) created in Shanghai in 1902, preparations were being made for direct combat. Gong Bao-quan founded an Assassination Group (Ansha Tuan), and through Tao Cheng-zhang contact was made with the secret societies. The revolt was coordinated by the Restoration Society (Guangfuhui), organized in 1904. In Hunan, Huang Xing and the China Revival Society (Huaxinghui), which he created in 1903, led a similar revolt. Here again the chief activists were intellectuals and leaders of the secret societies (like Ma Fu-yi), with the addition of a few officers from the new armies. Huang Xing's revolt failed in Changsha in November 1904, however, and he had to flee to Japan. There, in July 1905, he met Sun Yat-sen.

From this meeting, which was arranged by Miyazaki Torazo, the

United League (Tongmenghui) was born. With Huang Xing to answer for him, Sun was accepted by the revolutionary intellectuals who until then had seen him merely as "an outlaw with no education," in the words of Zhang Bing-lin. The United League was formed by the fusion of the Revive China Society (Xingzhonghui), the China Revival Society (Huaxinghui), and the Restoration Society (Guangfuhui). It represented definite progress in the unification of the revolutionary movement and the formulation of an ideology.

The new party was republican. It supported the three people's principles (*sanminzhuyi*) which had recently been expounded by Sun: nationalism, democracy, and socialism, or "the people's livelihood." In *The People* (*Min Bao*), the intellectuals who formed the party leadership—Hu Han-min, Zhang Bing-lin, and Wang Jing-wei—gave detailed explanations of their program.

The first principle, nationalism, was aimed chiefly against the Manchus. The danger to which imperialist penetration exposed the country was subordinated to bitterness against a usurping dynasty. The second principle, democracy, called for the establishment of a republican constitution assuring equal rights for all citizens. It also demanded the separation of the executive, legislative, and judicial authorities, and of the authorities responsible for examination and control. As for the third principle, Sun's socialism was inspired by the theories of Henry George. It aimed at setting a limit on the effects of land speculation, which the industrialization and urbanization of China was bound to produce.

This astonishing program ignored all the basic problems facing the country: the agrarian question, peasant unrest, the threat from abroad, and the resistance put up by the traditional structures to all necessary change. But Sun Yat-sen's prestige and his authority in politics were not based on his intellectual superiority. The weaknesses in his ideology counted less than his optimism, his unshakable faith in the future of the country, and his conviction that the Chinese could make such rapid progress that they would establish a modern republic from one day to the next. Impatient young students were drawn to these magnificent visions rather than to the slow advance of the historical process stressed by Liang Qi-chao. The opposition between reformists and revolutionaries foreshadowed the recurring struggle between realists and voluntarists in twentieth-century China.

For ten years Sun Yat-sen tried to speed up the course of history.

The strategy of armed rebellion which he adopted was aimed at establishing revolutionary bases whose example would lead the provinces to throw off the Manchu yoke. For tactical reasons, most of the eight rebellions which took place between 1907 and 1911 broke out in the Southern provinces of Guangdong and Guangxi. In these regions the United League could count on the support of particularly active secret societies, with which it had many contacts. Furthermore, the geographical proximity of Hong Kong and the Indochinese frontier made it easier to smuggle in arms, funds, and reinforcements. The failure of the rebellions, in which many brave men died to no purpose, was due to faulty organization, especially to difficulties in coordination between the rebels at home and the militants overseas. It was also due to the violent suppression carried out by the imperial authorities. The last and most important of the unsuccessful rebellions was that of April 1911 in Canton. The massacre which followed is commemorated in the memorial built later to the seventy-two martyrs buried north of Canton at Huanghua-gang, "the Holy Land of the Chinese Republic."

It is true that the United League, the instrument which Sun had at his disposal to speed up the course of history, was ill suited to the purpose. The fusion of its different elements was incomplete, and the Restoration Society retained more autonomy than the rest. Disagreements arose among the leaders, and in 1907 Zhang Bing-lin came forward as a rival to Sun Yat-sen. The anarchism which developed just before the revolution in Chinese student circles in Paris and Tokyo attracted certain members of the League, such as Wang Jing-wei. The authority and the resources of both Sun and his party were worn out by a series of abortive plots.

Sun Yat-sen was neither a political thinker nor an administrative organizer, but a man of ideals with a temperament of an exceptional kind. He carried a heavy responsibility for the direction taken by the revolutionary movement before 1911. He discredited the concepts of Liang Qi-chao by his exaggerated support of anti-Manchu and pro-republican feelings. In encouraging the young militants to be satisfied with a radical utopia, he produced an enduring cleavage between the revolutionaries' ideas and the real situation in China, as well as a gulf between the revolutionaries and the revolution.

The End of the Imperial Regime

When the revolution did come at the end of the summer of 1911, it took Sun and the United League by surprise. The party had concentrated its work in the Southern provinces, whereas rebellions began in the Yangzi basin.

Protection of the Sichuan railways

The movement for the protection of the railways which shook Sichuan beginning in May 1911 was a prelude to the revolution. The decree of May 9 nationalizing the railways, which was accompanied by a foreign loan amounting to 6,000,000 pounds sterling, turned the provincial gentry against the central government. The Sichuan-Hankou provincial company, created in 1904 and reorganized in 1907 on a purely commercial basis, had already begun to build a section of the line. It was still only about 15 kilometers long, but the company had assembled 16 million taels from voluntary contributions and taxes, particularly from a surtax on the land tax. Many interests were involved in the management of the funds and the running of the company, which had a large staff. The central government offered compensations, but they were considered insufficient.

Public opinion was mobilized by people whose financial interests had been injured, patriots who felt outraged by the dependence on foreign funds, and provincialists who regarded intervention by the imperial government as a threat. A violent campaign was led by the gentry, whose interests were directly involved. With the backing of the provincial assembly and the shareholders in the railway company, they founded a Railway Protection League (Baolutong-zhihui) on June 21, circulated petitions, and organized demonstrations. When these measures produced no results, the shareholders met on August 24 in the provincial capital of Chengdu and decided to close shops and schools, refuse to pay taxes, and form local militia. On September 7 the governor-general, Zhao Er-feng, had the leaders of the League arrested. Several thousand people demonstrated for their release, and in the resulting turmoil the police killed about forty members of the crowd.

Until then, the protection movement had not gone beyond the law. Its leaders—Bu Dian-jun and Luo Lun, who were chairman and vice-chairman of the provincial assembly, and Deng Xiao-ke, who was chairman of the Railway Protection League—were constitutionalists, not revolutionaries. They were not trying to overthrow the government; they wanted merely to defend their interests and establish their privileges. The struggle for power occurred within one class, the gentry, which also included the local officials and the local elite. With the advent of violence, however, other social forces entered the conflict. At the end of August, peasant bands forming "armies of comrades" (*tongzhihui*) rebelled and obtained the support of the Society of Brothers and Elders (*Gelaohui*) as well as the support of two revolutionary students just returned from Japan, Long Ming-jian and Wu Yu-zhang. After the police killed the forty demonstrators in Chengdu in September, the rebels tried to march on that city. They did not arrive, but they scored some short-lived successes in about ten small towns in the province. Thus the Railway Protection League unexpectedly increased in scope.[3] Probably the railway movement provided a suitable opportunity for outbreaks of violence rather than actually causing them. After all, the peasants were the main victims of the gentry's railway policy, since they bore the burden of the additional taxes intended to finance the railway company. It is likely that by means of the secret societies, the gentry and the revolutionaries both tried to make use of the peasants. Certainly Luo Lun, the vice-chairman of the provincial assembly, and Wu Yu-zhang, a militant member of the United League, both belonged to the Society of Brothers and Elders. It does not seem probable, however, that these interventions alone could transform a rage for destruction, born of poverty and despair, into a political project.

The government was worried by events in Sichuan. Duan-fang received orders to advance on the province with units from the Hubei New Army. But instead of dying down, the disturbances increased, fanned by anger over the threat of troops from outside the province. Meanwhile a rebellion broke out on October 10 in Wuchang, where part of the garrison was absent.

The Wuchang rebellion

The "double ten" rising (the tenth day of the tenth month) is traditionally considered as the beginning of the revolution of 1911.

---

[3] In document 4 Wu Yu-zhang describes the internal politics of the movement.

Unlike the many attempts which preceded it, the Wuchang rebellion did not have the support of the secret societies or of the United League. Its main instigators were men from the New Army who had been members of the anti-Manchu opposition for several years. On the eve of the revolution, they belonged to the Literary Study Society (Wenxueshe), which had a membership of about 3,000 and was led by a young officer from Hunan, Jiang Yi-wu. The society was in contact with the revolutionary intellectuals belonging to the Common Advancement Association (Gongjinhui).

The association, founded in Tokyo in 1907, was a regional version of the United League. Its members were natives of Hubei, Hunan, and Sichuan who had returned to carry on their activities in Central China, maintaining only distant contacts with the leaders of the League. Under the direction of Jiao Da-feng, Liu Gong, and Sun Wu, the Common Advancement Association began to work closely with the Literary Study Society. The election of a bureau shared by both bodies sealed the alliance and facilitated the preparation of a revolt planned for October. It was an isolated undertaking, and Huang Xing, who was asked to assume the leadership, refused because he did not believe that it could succeed. The revolutionaries, however, continued their preparations.

On October 9 a bomb accidentally exploded at the headquarters of the Common Advancement Association, and when great numbers of police moved in, Sun Wu and Jiang Yi-wu were wounded or took flight. Many militant members were arrested, and some were executed. To forestall the police reign of terror which was beginning, the revolutionaries decided to act. Four battalions of the New Army mutinied on the evening of October 10. The rebels took the arsenal of Chu-Wang-tai and attacked the provincial government buildings. Panic-stricken, the governor-general, Rui-cheng, and the commander-in-chief, Zhang Biao, abandoned the town. By dawn on October 11 Wuchang was in the hands of the rebels.

They had no well-known revolutionaries among them; they were a group of soldiers led by a few sergeants and a major, Wu Zhao-lin. To consolidate their position and give their movement the prestige which they considered essential, they turned to a brigade commander, Li Yuan-hong, a model of respectability and conservatism. Pressed into accepting, Li became head of the provisory military government of the Chinese Republic, and the constitutionalist Tang Hua-long, chairman of the provincial assembly, was put in charge of the civil administration. Thus the revolt was prepared by revolutionaries, was carried out by the New Army, and gave power to gentry of moderate-to-conservative opinions. The task of imposing the revolution on the country, the court, and the treaty powers fell to them.

Independence of the provinces

The appeal from Tang Hua-long asking the provinces to declare their independence was widely followed, as the table shows. One after another, Hunan (October 22), Jiangxi (November 2), Jiangsu (November 3), and Zhejiang (November 4) repudiated the authority of Peking. The movement of dissent spread to the whole of the middle and lower Yangzi basin and to the Northern provinces; Shenxi joined it on October 22 and Shanxi on October 29. In the South, Guangdong and Yunnan aligned themselves with the rebels at the end of October and Guizhou and Guangxi at the beginning of November. Sichuan joined them a little later on November 27, so that the central government controlled only the three provinces of Manchuria together with Zhili, Henan, and Shandong near Peking.

EXTENSION OF THE MOVEMENT OF DISSENT IN THE PROVINCES, OCTOBER–NOVEMBER 1911

	Province	Independence proclaimed by
October	Hubei	Army
	Hunan	United League, army, constitutionalists
	Yunnan	Army, United League, imperial governor
	Shenxi	Army, secret societies
	Shanxi	Army
November	Jiangxi	United League
	Jiangsu	United League, army, imperial governor
	Zhejiang	United League, national bourgeoisie
	Fujian	(No details available)
	Sichuan	Constitutionalists, United League, secret societies
	Shandong*	Army, imperial governor (for a short time only)

* In Shandong the imperial governor remained in his post, and at the end of November reneged on his decision and annulled the proclamation of independence.
Source: J. Cheng and J. Chesneaux, "Chronologie politique de la Chine contemporaine (1911–1919)." Typescript. No date or place given, 296 pp.

The history of these provincial movements is little known at the present state of research. The social forces involved apparently varied enormously from one region to another. Both the secret societies and units from the New Army participated, but the situation was generally controlled by the provincial assemblies and the chambers of commerce. The officials rarely opposed their province's declaration of independence; they either fled or went over to the rebels. The speed with which the movement of dissent spread was largely due to the attitude of the governors. Sometimes they themselves announced the secession of the province, as Cheng De-quan did in Jiangxi and Zhang Ming-qi did in Guangdong. Moderation on the part of the gentry, and complicity or opportunism on the part of the local administrative bodies, made the movement on the whole a peaceful one.

Government reactions

But the Peking government was preparing to defend itself and on October 12 sent units from the Beiyang army south to suppress the revolt. The loyalty of the troops belonged to Yuan Shi-kai rather than the throne, however. The salvation of the dynasty depended on a difficult reconciliation with Yuan, who imposed his conditions from his place of retirement. Some of them were intended to win him the sympathy of the revolutionaries: the creation of a parliament, appointment of a responsible cabinet, and a general pardon for the rebels. Other more important demands were aimed at consolidating his own power by giving him control over all the imperial troops. Yuan preferred the role of the mediator to that of the savior.

The regent Zai-feng was in no position to resist Yuan's conditions. He had to face growing opposition from the constitutionalist members of the national assembly, who presented their "four demands" on October 27: abolition of the cabinet of princes of the imperial clan, preparation of a constitution, political amnesty, and the immediate convocation of a parliament. Meanwhile a few revolutionary officers of the Beiyang army, Zhao Shao-zeng and Wu Lu-zhen, were threatening to turn their troops against Peking. At the beginning of November the regent proclaimed a constitution of nineteen articles, and Yuan, who was already imperial commissar of the armed forces, became prime minister.

Yuan's return heartened the imperial troops and on October 27 they took Hankou in a victorious counteroffensive. They attacked once more on November 18, and after a week of fighting (the hardest and bloodiest of the revolution) occupied Hanyang. Wuchang, on the opposite bank of the Yangzi, seemed about to fall too, but the attack by the imperial troops suddenly stopped. This incident has often been cited to support the theory that Yuan Shi-kai wanted to keep one center of revolutionary activities going in order to keep the court in a state of fear which served his own ambitions. Although Yuan did have Machiavellian leanings, the revolutionary troops' capacity for resistance should not be underestimated. Moreover, there was a serious threat to the rear of the Beiyang army in the shape of the revolt of Shanxi and Shenxi and the defection of some of its officers, who had gone over to the revolution. (One of them, Wu Lu-zhen, was mysteriously assassinated on November 6, probably on orders from Yuan Shi-kai.) The comparative size and strength of the forces involved may have done just as much as the political maneuver of Yuan Shi-kai to encourage the search for a compromise. A truce signed on December 1 signaled the opening of negotiations in Hankou between Wu Ting-fang, formerly ambassador to Washington and plenipotentiary on the revolutionary side, and Tang Shao-yi, the representative of Yuan and the Peking government.

Reactions of the foreign powers

The success of the revolution depended not only on its acceptance by the country and the government, but also on the consent of the foreign powers in China. On October 13 the Wuchang government sent a note to the consular corps in Hankou promising that the future republican regime would recognize all the treaties and loans entered into by the Manchu dynasty. The revolutionaries also promised to protect foreigners and their possessions in China. These pledges were formally renewed in a manifesto to the foreign powers issued on November 17 by Wu Ting-fang.

From the beginning of the revolution the hostility toward imperialism, which had been a major theme of the opposition, gave way to a policy of reconciliation with the foreign powers. It was true that the comparative strength of the forces involved left the revolutionaries with no other choice. The powers themselves had scarcely more room to maneuver. Aware that the rebellion was country-wide, anxious to protect British interests in the Yangzi basin, and concerned to avoid offending the Chinese communities in Hong Kong and Singapore, the British minister in Peking, John

Jordan, spoke out against taking any action in favor of the dynasty. His attitude was decisive. The powers adopted a policy of neutrality, though some of them, particularly Japan, did it reluctantly.

In spite of the fact that sympathy for Yuan Shi-kai was fairly general in the diplomatic corps, no official foreign aid, not even in the form of a loan, was given to the Peking government during the last three months of 1911. On the other hand, the powers took advantage of the political confusion to tighten their control of the revenues from the maritime customs, which from then on were deposited in foreign banks. They also extended their jurisdiction over the Chinese population in the concessions by taking control of the courts which until then had been under the imperial administration, such as the mixed court of the international concession in Shanghai. Jordan's proclamation had removed the danger of intervention, but the foreign threat still existed. It weighed heavily on the revolution, for it created absolute necessities such as the maintenance of order and the protection of national unity.

The Chinese Republic is founded

The success of the revolution became apparent during the autumn of 1911. Was it really due to the revolutionaries, however? The leaders of the United League had refused to believe in the possibility of success for the Wuchang revolt; afterwards, Sun still considered it as "purely accidental." In October, when Wuchang was the center of the revolution, these leaders concentrated all their efforts upon it in an attempt to recover control of the situation. The officers of the Common Advancement Society returned to Wuchang on October 12, but Sun Wu was the only one to become a member of the military government. Huang Xing arrived from Hong Kong on October 20, too late to dislodge the president, Li Yuan-hong, who was displaying more authority and ambition than before. In spite of the protests of the militant revolutionaries, Huang Xing had to be content with the post of commander-in-chief of the people's army. His prestige suffered when the revolutionaries were routed by the imperial troops on November 27 at Hanyang, although he was probably not responsible for the defeat. Huang Xing then turned his back on the fighting, in which the fate of the revolution was being settled, and left for Shanghai and Nanking, which had been evacuated by government troops on December 2.

Having failed to gain control of the base at Wuchang, the revolutionaries decided to create a second center of action in the lower

Yangzi basin. There they had two advantages: the historical prestige of a capital, Nanking, and the support of the Shanghai bourgeoisie. As often happens in China, the struggle for power resulted in a geographic shift in the political center of gravity.

Bitter rivalry developed between the Wuchang group and the revolutionaries based in Shanghai and Nanking, the stake being the formation of a national government. On November 9 Li Yuanhong telegraphed the independent provinces and asked them to send representatives to Wuchang. On November 11 the military governors of the lower Yangzi valley took similar action. After meeting in Shanghai on November 15 and then at Wuchang (or to put it more accurately, in the shelter of the British concession in Hankou) between November 30 and December 4, the provincial delegates assembled in Nanking on December 14 to elect a President. Fourteen provinces were represented. Most of the delegates to the provincial council belonged to the United League and supported Huang Xing for President, but the generals from Zhejiang and Jiangsu, who had only just joined the revolutionaries, preferred Li Yuan-hong. The conflict paralyzed the council and prevented the organization of a national government until the return of Sun Yat-sen from the United States and Europe. After a lively debate, the council rejected a motion by Song Jiao-ren in favor of a cabinet regime. The Chinese Republic was to have a presidential government, and Sun Yat-sen was made its leader by an almost unanimous vote (16 to 1). He was inaugurated in Nanking on January 1, 1912, and a new era began. It was symbolized by the abandonment of the lunar calendar and the dynastic method of dating; 1912 became year 1 of the Chinese Republic.

After three months of revolution, the authority of the imperial government collapsed. In relation to the new decision-making centers at Wuchang and Nanking, Peking retained a degree of importance owing to the presence of Yuan Shi-kai, not to the prestige of the court. The overthrow of the Manchu dynasty was the end of a long decline which began in the nineteenth century and was accelerated by Western intervention in China. Many signs presaged it: failures in the military and diplomatic fields, agrarian revolts, and the declining loyalty of the gentry. During the decade preceding its disappearance, the regime gave proof of a certain capacity for adaptation by its attempts at reform, but it came up against growing opposition. The spread of violent anti-Manchu feelings strengthened the revolutionary current as well as the resistance on the part of the conservatives. The revolution of 1911 was born of the conjunction of all these trends. During the revolt, the weakening of the central government and the growing autonomy of the provinces established the power of the local elites. At the same time, however, the revolutionary movement had sufficiently strong roots to ensure that the fall of the dynasty resulted in the overthrow of the imperial regime. This was the regime which had for centuries given the gentry the ideological and political basis for their power, and which had provided the principle of unity and identity for China itself.

One characteristic of the revolt of 1911 was the ambiguity of the anti-Manchu slogan which ensured its success. However, it was the starting point of a long series of upheavals which gave birth to modern China, and the meaning and importance of the revolution of 1911 becomes clearer in the light of later developments.

ADDITIONAL BIBLIOGRAPHY

Marianne Bastid, *Aspects de la réforme de l'enseignement en Chine au début du XXe siecle* (Paris, 1971).

Marianne Bastid, "La diplomatie française et la révolution chinoise de 1911," *Revue d'histoire moderne et contemporaine*, vol. 16, April–June 1969.

Marie-Claire Bergère, *Une Crise financière a Shanghai à la fin de l'Ancien Régime* (Paris, 1964).

Marie-Claire Bergère, *La Bourgeoisie chinoise et la révolution de 1911* (Paris, 1968).

Marie-Claire Bergère, "La révolution de 1911," *Revue historique*, October–December 1963.

Martin Bernal, "Chinese Socialism Before 1913," in *Modern China's Search for a Political Form* (London, J. Gray, 1969).

Joseph R. Levenson, *Liang Ch'i-ch'ao and the Mind of Modern China* (Berkeley, University of California Press, 1967).

Mary B. Rankin, *Early Chinese Revolutionaries: Radical Intellectuals in Shanghai and Chekiang* (Cambridge, Mass., Harvard University Press, 1971).

Harold Z. Schiffrin, *Sun Yat-sen and the Origins of the Chinese Revolution* (Berkeley, University of California Press, 1968).

Mary C. Wright, *China in Revolution: The First Phase 1900–1913* (New Haven, Conn., Yale University Press, 1968).

DOCUMENTS

1. THE CRISIS WHICH SHOOK THE EMPIRE AT THE BEGINNING OF THE TWENTIETH CENTURY: PARABLE OF THE SINKING SHIP

SOURCE: Liu T'ieh-yün (Liu E), *The Travels of Lao Ts'an*, translated and annotated by Harold Shadick (Ithaca, N.Y., Cornell University Press, 1952), pp. 7–11.

This document is literary, not historical in the strict sense. The novel The Travels of Lao Ts'an is set in the last years of the Manchu empire. Its hero sees a shipwreck in which the ship represents the empire.

After about an hour the boat was so near that by looking closely through their telescopes the three men could see that it was a fairly large boat, about twenty-three or twenty-four chang long.* The captain was sitting on the poop, and below the poop were four men in charge of the helm.† There were six masts with old sails and two new masts, one with a completely new sail and the other with a rather worn one: in all, eight masts.‡ The ship was very heavily loaded; the hold must have contained many kinds of cargo. Countless people, men and women, were sitting on the deck without any awning or other covering to protect them from the weather—just like people in third-class cars on the railway from Tientsin to Peking. The north wind blew in their faces; foam splashed all over them; they were wet and cold, hungry and afraid. They all had the appearance of people with no means of livelihood. Beside each of the eight masts were two men to look after the rigging. At the prow and on the deck were a number of men dressed like sailors.

It was a great ship, twenty-three or twenty-four chang long, but there were many places in which it was damaged. On the east side was a gash about three chang long,§ into which the waves were pouring with nothing to stop them. Farther to the east was another bad place about a chang long through which the water was seeping more gradually.|| No part of the ship was free from scars. The eight men looking after the sails were doing their duty faithfully, but each one looked after his own sail as though each of the eight was on a separate boat: they were not working together at all. The other seamen were running about aimlessly among the groups of men and women; it was impossible at first to tell what they were trying to do. Looking carefully through the telescope, you discovered that they were searching the men and women for any food they might be carrying and also stripping them of the clothes that they wore.** . . .

Lao Ts'an answered, "As I see it the crew have not done wrong intentionally; there are two reasons why they have brought the ship to this intolerable pass. What two reasons? The first is that they are accustomed to sailing in the 'Pacific' Ocean and can only live through 'pacific' days. When the wind is still and the waves are quiet, the conditions of navigation make it possible to take things easy. But they

* The twenty-four provinces in existence just before the fall of the empire.
† The emperor and the four members of the Grand Council.
‡ The six traditional ministries, the Foreign Ministry, created in 1861, and the Board of Admiralty, created in 1890.
§ The three northeastern provinces (Manchuria), threatened by Japan.
|| Shandong, threatened by Germany and Japan.
** The sailors represented the officials: bureaucratic compartments and looting.

were not prepared for today's big wind and heavy sea* and therefore are bungling and botching everything. The second reason is that they do not have a compass. When the sky is clear, they can follow traditional methods, and when they can see the sun, moon, and stars they don't make serious mistakes in their course. This might be called 'depending on heaven for your food.' Who could have told that they would run into this overcast weather with the sun, moon, and stars covered up by clouds, leaving them nothing to steer by? It is not that in their hearts they do not want to do the right thing, but since they cannot distinguish north, south, east and west, the farther they go, the more mistakes they make." . . .

They were surprised to find that while the members of the crew were searching the passengers another man was making an impassioned speech in a loud voice.

They only heard him say, "You have all paid your fares to travel on this boat. In fact, the boat is your own inherited property which has now been brought to the verge of destruction by the crew. All in your families, young and old, are on this boat. Are you all going to wait to be killed? Are you not going to find a way of saving the situation? You deserve to be killed, you herd of slaves!"

The passengers at whom he was railing said nothing at first. Then a number of men got up and said, "What you have said is what we all in our hearts want to say but cannot. Today we have been awakened by you and are truly ashamed of ourselves and truly grateful to you. We only ask you: 'What are we to do?' "

The man then said,† "You must know that nowadays nothing can be done without money. If you will all contribute some money, we will give our energy and our lifeblood for you and will lay the foundations of a freedom which is eternal and secure. What do you say to this?" . . .

They saw the men on the boat collect quite a lot of money and hand it over to the speaker. Then they watched to see what he would do. Who could have known that when the speaker had taken the money he would seek out a place where the crowd could not touch him, stand there, and shout to them loudly, "You lot of spineless creatures! Cold-blooded animals! Are you still not going to attack those helmsmen?" And further, "Why don't you take those seamen and kill them one by one?"

Sure enough, some inexperienced young men, trusting his word, went to attack the helmsmen, while others went to upbraid the captain; they were all slaughtered by the sailors and thrown into the sea.‡

The speaker again began to shout at them, "Why don't you organize yourselves? If all you passengers on the boat act together, won't you get the better of them?"

* The "breakup" crisis.
† This man is a caricature of Sun Yat-sen, who was constantly looking for funds and inveighing against his countrymen's ignorance of politics.
‡ Liu E, the author of the novel, was a conservative reformist who disapproved of the premature revolts of the young republican militants between 1905 and 1910.

But an old and experienced man among the passengers cried out, "Good people! On no account act in this wild way! If you do this, the ship will sink while you are still struggling. I'm certain no good will come of it."

When Hui-sheng heard this he said to Chang-po, "After all, this hero was out to make money for himself while telling others to shed their blood!" Lao Ts'an said, "Fortunately there are still a few respectable and responsible men; otherwise the ship would founder even sooner."

2. THE IMPERIAL GOVERNMENT COMES AROUND TO A REFORM POLICY (1901)

SOURCE: Meribeth E. Cameron, *The Reform Movement in China, 1898–1912* (Stanford, Calif., Stanford University Press, 1931), pp. 57–58.

In the decree issued from Sian January 8, 1901, Empress Ci-xi, speaking in the name of the fallen emperor, announced that he had changed over to a reform policy, and set forth its principles.

We have today received Her Majesty's orders, and learn that she is now thoroughly bent on radical reform. Nevertheless, whilst we are convinced of the necessity of blending in one harmonious form of administration the best customs and traditions of Chinese and European governments, there is to be no talk of reaction or revolution. The chief defect in our system of administration is undoubtedly too close an adherence to obsolete methods, a too slavish devotion to the written word; the result is a surfeit of commonplace and inefficient officials, and a deplorable lack of men of real talent. . . . Our whole system of government has come to grief through corruption, and the first steps of progress in our Empire are clogged by the fatal word "Precedent."

Up to the present the study of European methods has gone no further than a superficial knowledge of the languages, literature and mechanical arts of the West, but it must be evident that these things are not the essentials upon which European civilization has been founded. The essential spirit of that civilization is to be looked for in the fact that real sympathy and understanding exist between rulers and people, that officials are required to be truthful in word and courageous in action. The teachings handed down to us by our sacred ancestors are really the same as those upon which the wealth and power of European countries have been based, but China has hitherto failed to realize this and has been content to acquire the rudiments of European languages or technicalities, while changing nothing of her ancient habits of inefficiency and deep-rooted corruption. Ignoring our real needs, we have so far taken from Europe nothing but externals; how can we possibly hope to advance on such lines? Any reforms to be effective and permanent must be made with a real desire for efficiency and honesty.

We therefore decree and command that the officials concerned shall now make close enquiry and comparison as to the various systems of government in force in European countries with special reference to those which obtain in China today, not only as regards the constitution of the Court and central government, but also concerning the things which make for the prosperity of our subjects, such as the system of examinations and education, the administration of the army and the regulation of finance. They will be required to report as to what changes are advisable and what institutions should be abolished; what methods we should adopt from abroad and what existing Chinese institutions should be retained. The things we chiefly need are a constant supply of men of talent, a sound basis of national finance, and an efficient army.

3. OPPOSITION TO THE DECREE NATIONALIZING THE RAILWAYS IN SICHUAN (1911)
SOURCE: Wu Yu-zhang, *The 1911 Revolution* (Peking, 1963), pp. 106–107.

Wu Yu-zhang, who became a member of the Central Committee of the Chinese Communist Party after 1949, recalls the rivalry between the constitutionalists, who wanted to limit the agitation, and the revolutionaries, who wanted to spread it.

For this reason, Pou Tien-tsiun [Bu Dian-jun] and others called on the people merely to defend the rights to the railway and not to stand up to the authorities, much less hold seditious gatherings. But could a revolutionary struggle, engaged upon by the masses, be restrained by a handful of constitutionalists, particularly when it was encouraged by revolutionaries? Although the League was not always at the head of the movement, which often evolved spontaneously, some of its members such as Long Ming-kien [Long Ming-jian] and Wang Tien-kié [Wang Tian-jie] played an important part in it, which contributed to some extent to the progress of the movement. Long Ming-kien and Wang Tien-kié both came from the same district as I did. Long studied in Japan and took part in the rebellion at Hokeou in Yunnan in 1908. After the movement failed, he had to stay and work in Yunnan for a time, and then returned to Setchouan, where he was elected member of the General Council. To create conditions which encouraged revolutionary activities he founded a Law Institute at Tchengtou. From the beginning of the campaign for the defense of the rights to the railway, Long Ming-kien, Wang Tien-kié, and other members of the League saw what Pou Tien-tsiun and his supporters were like, and how they had not got the courage to attack the Tsing reactionary regime; so they sided with them in the lawful struggle, and secretly joined various groups and societies which aimed at armed rebellion. Early in August Long Ming-kien and Wang Tien-kié conferred at Tsetcheou with Tsin Tsai-keng [Qin Zai-geng] and Louo Tse-tcheou [Lou Si-shou], two leaders of the Kehlao [Brothers and Elders] society, the largest secret society in Setchouan; and, keeping in line with the policy suggested by Long Ming-kien, which was to "remain united in public and struggle in secret," it was decided to create an "Army of Comrades," with the aim of launching a military struggle. When the tradesmen and the students went on strike in Tchengtou, Long Ming-kien hurried to the spot; to

Chronology

The half century between the first Opium War and the Sino-French War does not fall easily into "periods." Imperial policy developed within the traditional framework of reigns: those of the Daoguang (1821–1851), Xianfeng (1851–1861), Tongzhi (1861–1875), Guangxu (1875 onwards). As far as court politics were concerned, each reign can be seen as a separate unit. But the fate of the country no longer depended exclusively on internal factors; it was also affected by foreign intervention. The rhythm of these events was beyond Chinese control: the first Opium War and the Treaty of Nanking, the second Opium War and the Peking and Tientsin Treaties, the Zhifu convention and the Sino-French War. A third theme was the movements of popular opposition to the dynasty, the established order, and the presence of the foreigners: the Taiping rebellion (1850–1864), the Nian insurrections (1855–1868), Moslem risings in the Southwest (1855–1873), Moslem risings in the Northwest (1860–1877), and agitation against the missionaries (1860–1870).

Each of these three series of events—imperial politics, foreign intervention, and popular movements—had its own dynamics and its own historical unity. The Taiping movement, for example, overlapped the reigns of the Xianfeng and Daoguang Emperors and extended over two periods of Western intervention. Even so, the three themes cannot be reduced to a mere juxtaposition of autonomous phenomena, for the events reacted on each other. The treaties of 1860, for example, were the starting point not only for a great influx of Westerners, but also for the *yangwu* movement.

This chronology will help to clarify the sequence of events in Chinese history from 1839 to 1911 and to shed further light on their interactions.

1838–1839	The party favoring a hard line against the West gains the upper hand in Peking. A crisis in relations with Great Britain (the first Opium War).
1840–1850	The party advocating conciliation with the West

gains the upper hand.
End of the reign of the Daoguang Emperor.
The Westerners gain a foothold as five ports are
opened.

1850–1855   Beginning of the reign of the Xianfeng Emperor.
Victorious phase of the Taiping rebellion.
The conciliation party still dominates.

1855–1859   Taiping movement in crisis.
Progress of the Nian and the Moslem risings.
Increasing foreign pressure results in foreign con-
trol of the customs and leads to the second Opium
War.
Revival of the influence of the hard-line party.

1860–1872   Accession of the Tongzhi Emperor. Led by Prince
Gong, the supporters of a modernist policy of co-
operation with the West come to power.
The foreigners' sphere of activities is increased
(open ports, customs, missions, etc.).
First phase of the *yangwu* movement (*ziqiang*, or
military strengthening).
Agitation against foreign missions.
New upsurge and fall of the Taiping.
New upsurge and fall of the Nian.
Extension of the Moslem rebellions.

1873–1880   Second phase of the *yangwu* movement (*fuqiang*,
or modernization of the economy).
End of the reign of the Tongzhi Emperor; accession of the Guangxu Emperor; Ci-xi becomes
regent.
Suppression of Moslem rebellions.

1880–1885   Further increase in pressure from the foreigners
(Ili, Korea, Vietnam).
Conflict between supporters of *yangwu* and sup-
porters of the hard line (*qingliu*).
Sino-French War.

1885–1900   Sino-Japanese War.
Abortive "Hundred Days" ends short period of
reform.
Boxer Rebellion. Allied nations occupy Peking.

1900–1911   Russo-Japanese War.
Manchu dynasty overthrown.

Pronunciation Table

This is intended as a guide to the pronunciation of sounds in Pinyin

INITIALS

q = *ch*eer

x = *sh*ip

z = rea*ds*

c = tha*t's*

zh = lar*g*e

r = leisu*r*e

FINALS

o = s*aw*

e = French l*e*

i = mach*i*ne

u = r*u*de

ü = German ü

ai = I

ao = n*ow*

eng = close to s*ung*

ou = *o*ld

ia = *yah*

ian = *yen*

iang = *young*

uai = w*ife*

ui = w*ay*

uan = close to *one*

Other letters and groups of letters have approximately the same sound as in English.

The examples used here are listed in Fred Fangyu Wang in *Mandarin Chinese Dictionary, English-Chinese* (South Orange, N.J., Seton Hall University Press, 1971), pp. xi–xii.

The transcription is Pinyin, adopted in the People's Republic of China in 1958 and gradually coming into extensive use among Western scholars of Chinese and Western universities. The only exceptions are a few proper names such as Peking, Nanking, Sun Yat-sen, and Mao Tsetung.

Glossary of Chinese Terms and Names for Chapters 1-7

A aiguo huo 愛國貨

Aiguoxueshe 愛國學社

Anfu 安福

ansha tuan 暗殺団

B bagu 八股

bai lang 白狼

baihua 白話

Bailong 白龙

bang 帮

bao jing an min 保境安民

baoan 保安

baogong 包工

Baoguohui 保国会

Baohuanghui 保皇会

Baolutongzhihui 保路同志会

Beida 北大

Beijing daxue 北京大学

Beitang 北堂

Beiyang 北洋

Ben-ming 本明

bianfa 变法

Bianshanxian 遍山線

bianshi 变事

C Cai E 蔡锷

Cao Fu-tian 曹福田

Cao Ru-lin 曹汝霖

Changxindian 長辛店

Chaoyang 朝阳

Chen bao 晨报

Chen Chi 陈炽

Chen Ji-tong 陈季同

Chen Qiu 陈虬

Cheng De-quan 程德全

Chouanhui 筹安会

Chu ren zhi Chu 楚人治楚

Chu Wang-tai 楚望台

D da dui 大队

Da Qing 大清

Danzhou 儋州

datong 大同

Datong shu 大同书

Dazu 大足

Deng Xiao-ke 邓孝可

Ding Wen-jiang 丁文江

Dongfang zazhi 东方杂誌

dongnan hubao 东南互保

dudu	都督	
dujun	督軍	
dujuntuan	督軍團	
F	**fan Qing fu Ming**	反清復明
	Fang Wei	方維
	fu Qing mie yang	扶清灭洋
G	**Gelaohui**	哥老会
	gong	工
	Gong Bao-quan	龔宝銓
	Gong-yang	公羊
	Gong Zi-zhen	龔自珍
	Gongchandang	共产党
	Gonghedang	共和党
	Gonghe jianshe taolunhui	共和建设讨论会
	Gonghe tongyidang	共和統一党
	Gongjinhui	共进会
	guan ban	官办
	guan du shang ban	官督商办
	guan shang heban	官商合办
	Guangxuehui	广学会
	Guanxian	冠县
	Gui jiao gai si	鬼教該死
	Guomindang	国民党
	Guowen bao	国闻报
	Gutian	古田
H	**Han**	汉
	Hanyeping	汉冶萍

He Qi (Ho Kai)	何启	
Hongbang	紅帮	
Hongkou	虹口	
houdun	后盾	
hu fa	护法	
hu guo	护国	
Hu Li-yuan	胡礼垣	
Hu Ying	胡瑛	
Huanghuagang	黄花崗	
Huasheng	华盛	
Huaxinghui	华兴会	
Hubu	户部	
Huguang	湖广	
hui dang	会党	
Huizhou	惠州	
J	**Jiang Yi-wu**	蔣翊武
	Jianghong (Xieng Hong)	江洪
	Jiangnan	江南
	Jianshe	建设
	Jiao Da-feng	焦达峰
	jiao men	教門
	Jiefang yu gaizao	解放与改造
	Jilong	基隆
	Jinbudang	进步党
	jindai	近代
	Jindan dao	金丹道
	Jindehui	进德会

jingshi	經世	Long-hai	陇海
jingtian	井田	Long Ming-jian	龙鸣劍
jiu guo	救国	Longshuizhen	龙水鎮
Jiulong	九龙	Longzhou	龙州
junjichu	军机处	Lu Run-xiang	陆润庠
K Kong-zi gai zhi kao	孔子改制考	Lu Zong-yu	陆宗與
L Laodong jie	劳动界	*lujun*	陆军
laodong shensheng	劳动神聖	Luo Lun	罗綸
Laoxikai	老西开	Luo Pei-jin	罗佩金
Leping	乐平	Lutai	芦台
Li Lie-jun	李烈钧	*Lüying*	綠營
Li Shi-zeng	李石曾	M Ma Fu-yi	馬福益
Li Zhong	李中	Manhao	蠻耗
Liang-bi	良弼	Mao Ze-dong	毛泽东
Liang Shu-ming	梁漱溟	*Meizhou pinglun*	每周评论
Liangguang	兩广	*Min bao*	民报
Lianghu	兩湖	Ming	明
Liangjiang	兩江	*Minzhudang*	民主党
liansheng zizhi	联省自治	Mohe	漠河
Liao Zhong-kai	廖仲凱	Mu Ou-chu	穆藕初
lijin	厘金	N Nandao	南道
Lin Sen	林森	Nantong	南通
Liu Gong	刘公	Nanyang	南洋
Liu Si-fu	刘思復	*Nei chu guozei*	内除国賊
Liu Xiang	刘湘	*neige*	内阁
liushou	留守	Ni Si-chong	倪嗣冲

P	Pingdu	平度
	Pu Dian-jun	蒲殿俊
	Pudong	浦东
Q	Qiangxuehui	強学会
	qianzhuang	钱莊
	Qing	清
	Qing yi bao	清议报
	Qingbang	青帮
	qingliu	清流
	Qingxi	青溪
	Qiu Feng-jia	丘逢甲
	Quan xue pian	劝学篇
	quanguo	全国
R	Ren xue	仁学
	Rihua	日华
	Rong-lu	榮祿
	Rui-cheng	瑞澂
S	Sanminzhuyi	三民主义
	Shen bao	申报
	Sheng shi weiyan	盛世危言
	shenshang	紳商
	shenshi	紳士
	Shi Zhao-ji (A. Sze)	施肇基
	Shiwu bao	時务报
	Shiwu xuetang	時务学堂
	shuyuan	书院
	Simao	思茅

	Su bao	苏报
	Sujing	苏經
	Sulun	苏綸
	Sun Jia-nai	孫家鼐
	Sun Wu	孫武
	Sun Yu-wen	孫毓汶
	Sun Yuan-fang	孫圓方
T	taiping	太平
	Taiyushan	太嶼山
	tan	坛
	Tan Yan-kai	谭延闿
	Tang Hua-long	湯化龙
	Tang Jing-song	唐景崧
	Tang Shao-yi	唐紹仪
	Tang Zhen	湯震
	Tao Cheng-zhang	陶成章
	Tianyi bao	天义报
	Tieshan	铁山
	Tong wen guan	同文舘
	Tongmenghui	同盟会
	Tongyidang	統一党
	Tongzhihui	同志会
	tuan	团
	Tucaozi	土槽子
	tufei	土匪
W	Wai zheng guoquan	外争国权
	waiwubu	外务部

Wan guo gong bao	万国公报	
Wang Mang	王莽	
Wang Zhan-yuan	王占元	
Wang Zhi-xiang	王芝祥	
Wangsanshi	王三石	
Wen Ting-shi	文廷式	
Wenxuehui	文学会	
wenyan	文言	
Wu Lu-zhen	吴禄贞	
Wu Zhao-lin	吴兆麟	
X	xian	县
	xiandai	现代
	Xiang jiang pinglun	湘江评论
	Xiangxue xin bao	湘学新报
	Xiaoshadu	小沙渡
	xiaozu	小组
	Xin chao	新潮
	Xin min cong bao	新民丛报
	Xin qingnian	新青年
	Xin Shandong	新山东
	Xin she	新社
	Xin shiji	新世纪
	Xin xue wei jing kao	新学伪经考
	Xingzhonghui	兴中会
	Xinminxuehui	新民学会
	Xinyang	信阳
	Xinzhu	新竹

Xiong Ke-wu	熊克武	
Xiong Xi-ling	熊希龄	
Xu Shu-zheng	徐树铮	
Xu Xiang	徐骧	
Xuantong	宣统	
Xujiahuai (Zikawei)	徐家滙	
Y	Yadong	亞东
	yamen	衙門
	Yang Du	揚度
	Yang Zong-lian	揚宗濂
	Yangshupu	揚树浦
	yangwu	洋务
	Yeqin	业勤
	Yichang	宜昌
	Yihequan	义和拳
	Yihetuan	义和团
	Yimintuan	义民团
	Yiyan	易言
	Yizhou	沂州
	yong	勇
	Yu Dong-chen	余栋臣
	Yu Qia-qing	虞洽卿
	Yubeilixiangonghui	预備立宪公会
	Yue ren zhi Yue	粤人治粤
Z	Zai-feng	載泮
	Zai-ze	載泽
	Zaili	在理

Zeng Guo-quan	曾国荃	*Zhongguo tongshang yinhang*	中国通商银行
Zhang Bai-xi	張百熙	Zhonghua	中华
Zhang Biao	張彪	*Zhonghuagemingdang*	中华革命党
Zhang De-cheng	張德成	*zhongxue wei ti xixue wei yong*	
Zhang Ji	張继		中学为体西学为用
Zhang Jing-yao	張敬堯	Zhou Han	周汉
Zhang Ming-qi	張鳴岐	Zhu Bao-san	朱葆三
Zhang Ru-mei	張如梅	Zhu Cheng-gui	祝承桂
Zhang Shao-zeng	張紹曾	Zhu Rui	朱瑞
Zhang Zhen-wu	張振武	Zhu Zhi-xin	朱執信
Zhang Zong-xiang	章宗祥	*Zi yi ju*	谘议局
Zhao Er-feng	赵尔丰	*Zi zheng yuan*	谘政院
Zhengwenshe	政聞社	Zichuan	淄川
Zhennanguan	镇南关	*zongli geguo shiwu yamen*	
Zhili	直隸		总理各国事务衙門
Zhongguo	中国		

Glossary of Chinese Terms and Names
for Chapters 8-10

A *an min sheng gu min xin* 安民生固民心

Anping 安平

Anqing 安庆

B *bagu* 八股

bai shangdi hui 拜上帝会

bao 保

Baochi 宝坻

baojia 保甲

beitang 北堂

bendi 本地

bixie jishi 辟邪纪实

bianqu 边区

C Cao Zhen-yong 曹振镛

Cen Yu-ying 岑毓英

changmaofei 長毛匪

Chen Qi-yuan 陈啟沅

Chen Yu-cheng 陈玉成

Chizhou 池州

Chong-hou 崇厚

Chu jun 楚軍

Cizhou 磁州

D Dagu 大沽

Dali 大理

dao 道

Daoguang 道光

daotai 道台

datong 大同

Debaoping 得宝坪

Deng Ting-zhen 邓廷楨

Dinghai 定海

Du Wen-xiu 杜文秀

F *fan Qing fu Ming* 反清復明

Feng Yun-shan 馮云山

fengshui 凤水

Foshan 佛山

fu 府

fu qiang 富強

Fuchuan 富川

G Gaoyang 高阳

gelaohui 哥老会

geming 革命

Gong Zi-zhen 龚自珍

G *gonghang* (cohong) 公行

  gongsuo 公所

  gongyang 公羊

  Gulangyu 鼓浪屿

  Gu Yan-wu 顾炎武

  guan du shang ban 官督商办

  guan du shang xiao 官督商銷

  guanhua 官話

  guanju 官局

  guo ji min sheng 国計民生

  Guo Song-dao 郭嵩焘

H Han 汉

  hanjian 汉奸

  Hanxue 汉学

  Hanlin 翰林

  hang 行

  Hengzhou 衡州

  He-shen 和珅

  Hexian 贺县

  hong 行

  Hong Da-quan 洪大全

  Hong Liang-ji 洪亮吉

  Hongloumeng 红楼梦

  Hong Ren-gan 洪仁玕

  Hu Guang-yong 胡光墉

  Hua Heng-fang 华衡芳

  Huai jun 淮軍

H Huang Zong-xi 黄宗羲

  Hui 回

  hui dang 会党

J *jia* 甲

  Jiang Yi-li 蒋益澧

  Jiangnan 江南

  jiao men 教門

  Jiaqing 嘉庆

  jiazhang 甲長

  Jilong 基隆

  Jin Ping Mei 金瓶梅

  jindai 近代

  jing 經

  jingshi 經世

  Jingdezhen 景德鎮

  Jinjibu 金積堡

  Jintian 金田

  Jiujiang 九江

  junjichu 軍机处

K Kaiping 开平

  Kangxi 康熙

  koutou 叩头

L Lai Wen-guang 賴汶光

  Lanzhou 兰州

  Leshan 乐山

  li 里，礼

  Li Tang-jie 李棠階

L	Li Kai-fang	李开芳
	Li Ru-zhen	李汝珍
	Li Shan-lan	李善兰
	Li Shi-xian	李世贤
	Li Xiu-cheng	李秀成
	lianjun	練军
	Liang A-fa	梁阿发
	Liangguang	两广
	Lianghu	两湖
	Liangjiang	两江
	lijia	里甲
	lijin	厘金
	Lin Feng-xiang	林凤祥
	Lincheng	临城
	Liu Yong-fu	刘永福
	Luo Bing-zhang	骆秉章
M	Ma De-xin	馬德新
	Ma Hua-long	馬化潍
	Ma Ru-long	馬如龙
	Ma Xin-yi	馬新贻
	Mao Ze-dong	毛泽东
	Miao	苗
	Ming	明
	mu	亩
	Mu Zhang-a	穆彰阿
N	Nanchang	南昌
	Nanhai	南海

N	Nantong	南通
	neige	内阁
	Nian	捻
	Niuzhuang	牛莊
	nong	农
P	*pai*	牌
	Peng Ru-cong	彭汝琮
	Peng Yu-lin	彭王麟
	pingjun	平均
	Pingquan	平泉
	Pingyuan	平原
Q	Qi Jun-cao	祁寯藻
	Qi-shan	琦善
	Qi-ying	耆英
	Qianlong	乾隆
	Qimen	祁門
	Qing	清
	qingliu	清流
	qingyi	清议
	Qingjiang	清江
	qiu fu	求富
R	Rong Hong	容閎
	Rulin waishi	儒林外史
	Ruan Yuan	阮元
	Rugao	如皋
S	Sanshui	三水
	Sanyuanli	三元里

S	*shang*	商
	Shashi	沙市
	Shen Gui-fen	沈桂芬
	shenshi	紳士
	shi	士
	Shi Da-kai	石达开
	Shuihu	水浒
	Shunde	顺德
	sima	司马
	Song	宋
	Song Jing-shi	宋景詩
	Songjiang	松江
	Suqian	宿迁
	Suzhou	苏州
T	Taiping	太平
	Taiping Tianguo	太平天国
	taipan	大班
	Taiwanfu	台湾府
	Taizhou	太州
	Tang	唐
	Tangshan	唐山
	tiandewang	天德王
	tianmaiban	天买办
	tianming	天命
	tianxia	天下
	Tianjing	天京
	tong	桐

T	*Tong Wen Guan*	同文舘
	Tongzhi	同治
	tuanlian	团練
W	*wang*	王
	Wang Fu-zhi	王夫之
	Wang Shi-duo	汪士鐸
	Wang Ding	王鼎
	Wei Chang-hui	韦昌辉
	Wei Yuan	魏源
	wenyan	文言
	Wenzhou	溫州
	wu	吳
	Wu Lan-tai	烏兰泰
	wu lun	五伦
	wu wei	无为
	Wusong	吳淞
X	*xixue*	西学
	xian	县
	xiandai	現代
	Xianfeng	咸丰
	Xiang jun	湘軍
	Xiangtan	湘潭
	Xiao Chao-gui	萧朝貴
	Xingguo	兴国
	Xingning	兴宁
	Xingyi	兴义
	Xu Guang-qi	徐光啟

X	Xu Ji-yu	徐继畬	Y	Yunnanfu	雲南府
	Xu Shou	徐寿	Z	Zeng Guo-quan	曾国荃
	Xugezhuang	胥各庄		Zhang Luo-xing	張洛行
	Xujiahuai (Zikawei)	徐家滙		Zhang Xian-zhong	張献忠
	Xuzhou	徐州		Zhang Zong-yu	張总愚
Y	yamen	衙門		Zhangjiakou	張家口
	yang	阳		zheng	政
	yangwu yundong	洋务运动		Zheng Guan-ying	郑观应
	Yang Xiu-qing	揚秀清		zheng ming	正名
	Yangkou	洋口		Zhenjiang	鎮江
	Yangzhou	扬州		Zhifu	芝罘
	Yao	瑶		Zhihe	雉河
	Ye Cheng-zhong	叶澄衷		zhong nong bing shang	重农病商
	Yi	彝, 夷		zhongxing	中兴
	yi jun	毅軍		zhou	州
	Yi He (Ewo)	怡和		Zhoushan (Chusan)	舟山
	Yixian	嶧县		Zhu Xi	朱熹
	yizhan	驿站		zhuang	庄
	yin	阴		ziqiang	自強
	Yong'an	永安		zongli geguo shiwu yamen	总理各国事务衙門
	You He-chuan	游賀川		zu	族

Index

About the Authors

Marianne Bastid is maître de recherche at the Centre Nationale de la Recherche Scientifique and teaches Chinese contemporary history at the Ecole des Hautes Etudes en Sciences Sociales in Paris. She is the author of *Aspects de la réforme de l'enseignment en Chine au début du XXe siècle* and numerous articles on political and institutional developments in the People's Republic of China.

Marie-Claire Bergère is Professor of Chinese History at the Institut National des Langues et Civilisations Orientales. She is the author of *La Bourgeoisie chinoise et la révolution de 1911* and *Une crise financière à Shanghai à la fin de l'Ancien régime.*

Jean Chesneaux is a professor at the Sorbonne. He is the author of numerous works, including *The Chinese Labor Movement 1919–1927, Peasant Revolts in China, 1840–1949,* and *Secret Societies in China.*

Plant
Life

Plant Life

Growing a Garden
in the Pacific Northwest

Valerie Easton

Photographs by Richard Hartlage

SASQUATCH BOOKS
SEATTLE

Page vi: Hydrangeas, monkshood, and daylilies in a vase outside the front door.
Page vii: Top right: *Lilium* 'Copper King Clone.' Bottom left: English rose 'Sharifa Asma'.
Page viii: Top left: Chocolate cosmos *(Cosmos atrosanguineus)*. Bottom right: *Astrantia major*.
Page xi: Top left: *Aster novae-angliae* 'Alma Potschke'. Top right: Halloween pumpkins on the front porch. Bottom right: *Helleborus orientalis*.

Copyright ©2002 by Valerie Easton
Photographs ©2002 by Richard Hartlage

Published by Sasquatch Books
Printed in Hong Kong
Distributed in Canada by Raincoast Books, Ltd.
07 06 05 04 03 02   6 5 4 3 2 1

These essays appeared in slightly different form in the *Pacific Northwest* magazine
of the *Seattle Times*.

Book design: Karen Schober
Copy editor: Alice Copp Smith

Library of Congress Cataloging in Publication Data

Easton, Valerie.
          Plant Life: growing a garden in the Pacific Northwest / Valerie Easton;
photographs by Richard Hartlage.
          p.cm.
ISBN 1-57061-305-2 (alk. paper)
1. Gardening--Northwest, Pacific. 2. Easton, Valerie. I. Title.
SB453.2.N83 E28 2002
635'.09795--dc21

Sasquatch Books
615 Second Avenue
Seattle, Washington 98104
(206) 467-4300
www.SasquatchBooks.com
books@SasquatchBooks.com

To Greg, Katie, Spencer, Maggie, and Cooper,
each of whom, in their own unique way,
never fails to remind me of
what truly matters.
—Val

Contents

Preface

"In search of my mother's garden, I found my own."
ALICE WALKER

MY FIRST MEMORIES are of the garden where I grew up. When the salmon made their way up the creek to spawn, we kids squatted in the cold rushing water, hidden by ferns. Quietly we bore witness while the fat, shiny fish rested in the shallows of the creek bed. Their journey from the sea filled our imaginations as we feasted our eyes upon the luminous rainbows of their scales.

While it wasn't the plants themselves I concerned myself with, but the freedoms and the secrets of the garden, it turns out that the plants my mother grew in that wild garden are the ones I love most today. The multicolored bells of lungwort, tiger lilies, bleeding heart (whose flowers we tore open to find the princess inside), and flowering currant, whose rosy drips of bloom feed the earliest hummingbirds—all have a place in my grown-up garden, as they did in the garden of my childhood.

My ideas about scale and color, layering and patterning, were shaped during those long days outdoors by the drizzle, the tall trees, and the intense green. All the many shades of green still seem to me the most elegant of all palettes.

My mother had a huge garden to tend—a raspberry patch, lawns, woods, banks, and borders. There was no way she could be fussy or exacting, and I think it is that attitude that makes gardening a pleasure for me today. I don't care which bug is notched in the leaves of the rhododendron, and don't care to know how to kill it. I am interested in which rose is most fragrant and in all the shades of delphinium blues.

Growing up in an untamed garden made me tolerant of imperfections, and I welcome them as part of the nature of the garden. You can concentrate on ridding a garden of insects and blight, but you will, of course, fail. As artificial a construct as gardens are, they are created of living things that grow and change, are subject to wind, rain, frost, and baking sun.

Some rich East Coast garden-maker (perhaps a DuPont) said that we live in a house some of the time, but always in the garden. Maybe that is why gardens and plants, once truly noticed, tend to fill the mind. I wake up in the dark of winter nights thinking about which sweet peas to plant this year. I dream of wisteria and honeysuckle, not just their perfume, but how to prune and train them. This is the endless fascination of garden-making—to craft something uniquely beautiful out of dirt, plants, water, imagination, expertise, and toil. But gardening is ultimately a humbling experience—time and weather have their ways with gardens, foiling our best-laid plans, taking them beyond anything we conjured. Gardens grow, peak, and then decline, as do the seasons, as do we ourselves.

My family moved away from that wild garden when I was a teenager. I still drive slowly past sometimes, but it is diminished, the woods nothing but a strip of trees, the creek choked with mud. My mother lived long enough to work in more than one garden. My son, now taller than me, was not yet born when my mother died. I got a card last Christmas from a friend in our old neighborhood, inviting me to come over in the spring and dig some pieces of yellow primrose, a gift from my mother's garden, which still blooms in her garden every March.

Acknowledgments

IT WAS MY EDITORS at the *Pacific Northwest* magazine of the *Seattle Times*, Kathy Andrisevic and Ginny Merdes, who came up with the idea of my writing a weekly gardening column. Ginny said it would change my life, and I'm finally ready to admit that maybe she was right. It was also Ginny who handed back my first attempt at column writing and told me to try again, freeing me with such terse newspaper-speak as "it's our job to be arbitrary." Thank you both, along with editors Rick Zahler and Kathy Triesch, for your humor, your confidence in me, and the chance to write about what interests me most. Every writer should be so lucky as to have seven hundred words due each Monday.

The Northwest gardening community is unhesitatingly supportive, and I couldn't have written these columns, or pulled this book together, without the help of my friends. My thanks to Steve Lorton for his enthusiasm and advice, and for calling me up and singing to me over the phone. Dan Hinkley and David Lewis have never failed to encourage me with their generous words. The staff of the Miller Library is endlessly patient, and even pretend to be interested in whatever it is I'm working on. The late Stephanie Feeney taught me how to persevere. And I appreciate Richard Hartlage's friendship and artistry. The results of both are clear on the pages of this book. Special thanks to my mother-in-law, Laurel Easton, who tells me that she is proud of me.

I'm grateful to Gary Luke and Karen Schober at Sasquatch Books for their skill with words and photos, and to Alice Copp Smith for her insightful and consistent copyediting. I thank my agent, Betsy Amster, who thought this book was a good idea in the first place. Most of all, I'm in the debt of all the gardeners who read my column and have asked over the years for a collection of my work. It was a great satisfaction for me to pull these pieces together in one volume, and I would never have gotten it done without your questions and comments spurring me on.

LEFT: *The pitcher plant* (Sarracenia flava) *is a carnivorous plant that I grow in a pot so I can keep it very moist and in as warm a spot as possible, encouraging it to bloom and put out new bug-catching pitchers.*

Introduction

WHAT A PLEASURE IT IS to be able to write about what interests you most, every week of the year. I've been very lucky to have the opportunity to write a column about plants and gardens for the *Pacific Northwest* magazine of the *Seattle Times* for the past four years. This book is an updated and edited collection of those pieces, along with twelve months of photographs taken in my garden by my friend Richard Hartlage.

Now, it is true that all my garden writing comes directly from my own gardening experiences and, if the truth be told, most often from the mistakes I've made. I've had the opportunity to learn from many other gardeners' trials and tribulation as well from my work as a horticultural librarian. But having my own garden shown in these photos seems a bit self-revelatory, and I feel kind of shy about that. It is one thing to write about something, and quite another to have the results set before you in full color. I've often quoted Henry Beston, who said, "Gardens are a mirror of the mind." With my garden revealed in these pages, that concept is making me a little nervous.

All the photos in the book were taken between May 2000 and April 2001. Richard Hartlage came over just as the sun rose, at midday, and at dusk, in every month of the year. He obligingly plucked lists of plants off my door that I'd taped there for him, and photographed with patience and skill the plants I was excited about, while avoiding the parts of the garden that I was ripping apart or that embarrass me. Believe me, far more of the garden has been ripped apart since I've taken a good look at his photographs. There is nothing like the straightforward honesty of a camera to bring a gardener to her senses, or perhaps to his knees.

I garden on a hillside quarter acre (a lot and a half) overlooking Lake Washington. There is a steep bank in front and back, terracing in between, and lots of sun. There are also twenty-eight steps up from the street and no other access to the property, which makes gardening here an aerobic workout. I care for the garden myself, helped by a husband who has great patience and endurance but would rather be kayaking. I'm hindered, but amused, by two Wheaten Terriers.

What I love best about gardening is its changeability and unpredictability. If you plant a mix of perennials, deciduous trees and shrubs, groundcovers, and plenty of bulbs, something new is happening out there nearly every day. And, thank goodness, this isn't dependent on you, the gardener—you can tidy up, groom, and fertilize when you have the time, or let it go and catch up later. The fact is that it is all going to happen anyway. It is this parade of change, the variables of weather, light, and seasons, that keeps me gardening. Because I'm convinced that most gardeners revel, as I do, in the changing seasons, this book is arranged by month (with winter months grouped together in one chapter), rather than by topic. It is my hope that this will make it easy to dip into the book for inspiration on a spring morning, or for solace on a cold February afternoon. If you want to add color to the garden come April, it should be easy to find which plants are at their best that month, or, as the old year passes away, to compare your New Year's resolutions with mine.

The choice of the plants listed in the "Now in Bloom" sections, one for each week of the year, is arbitrary but thoughtful, based on my enthusiasms of the moment, or the fact that Richard's photos captured particularly well the best attributes of a given plant. Certainly most aren't especially unusual or rare— rather, they are the available, workhorse plants gardeners need to make an all-season garden. Dozens of other plants could have been chosen, but the point is that on every day of the year it is possible to step outside and find pleasure in the garden. One plant or another is ready and waiting to be cut for an arrangement, while others are perfuming the garden or just simply out there looking their best.

I write about plants and gardens to better see, understand, and appreciate them. I hope reading this book will bring you some of the pleasure I've found in writing it.

march

March Mulch Brings June Respite

MULCHING SEEMS TO BE GIVEN AS THE ANSWER to nearly every garden question these days, whether it be about plant health or garden maintenance. But "apply mulch" never seems like a thorough prescription to me, since there are so many variables from one garden to the next—soil, plants, routine, aesthetics—and so many different kinds of mulch.

I have, however, become a devoted mulcher in the past few years, nearly breaking my back as well as the bank account. Of course, I mulch because it conserves water and improves the soil. But the devotion part comes in because I so appreciate the rich and crumbly appearance mulch gives my heavy clay soil (miraculously, it has the same effect on sandy soil) even as, over time, it makes that appearance into reality.

Late winter and early spring are chilly and damp, if not soaked-through soggy. But the mush and mess of winter need to be cleaned up so that when narcissus and little *Iris reticulata* emerge from winter sleep they can be shown to best advantage against the warm brown of new mulch. As the days begin to imperceptibly lengthen and I get back out into my garden, it is not the swelling buds or bulbs breaking ground that I notice. What I see are hours and hours, days and days, of very hard work.

The last couple of years I've come up with a system of organizing all that early-spring garden labor, and it has paid off. Having a plan for bringing order out of the chaos (i.e., cut everything back to make room to spread mulch) helps keep my spirits up as I slog my way through it. My garden routines used to be as haphazard as the unfortunate results. Now all garden tasks fit neatly into pre- or post-mulching, early spring or late autumn. This twice-a-year mulching cycle lends a rhythm and discipline to garden chores that keeps even my packed-with-plants garden fairly tidy year-round.

PREVIOUS PAGE: *The smallest ornamentation, like this ceramic ball encased in metal swirls, shows up well when stuck in a pot with ornamental grasses.*

LEFT: *The snaky stems and buds of ornamental onion* (Allium giganteum) *rise above tulips and phormium in the spring garden. The colorful foliage of* Spirea japonica *'Magic Carpet' serves as a mounded backdrop to the other more vertical plantings alongside the back patio.*

In between February rain showers (is there anywhere else in the country where the weatherman touts "sun breaks"?), I go through the whole garden and cut back everything that won't suffer if a late frost should strike: asters, hydrangeas, iris. My garden has so many layers (this is a more agreeable description than "severely over-planted") that the old perennials and raggedy subshrubs need tidying before I can even see the ground. When I've finished all the cutting back toward the end of the month, it's time to prune the roses.

Next I divide the many overgrown clumps of perennials. Daylilies, hostas, ornamental grasses, penstemon, and especially crimson flag (*Schizostylis coccinea*), which seems to need dividing every year, get dug up, separated, and replanted. It is heavy, hard work and takes every minute I can spend in the garden. Of course, it's impossible to work outside without picking slugs off daffodils, watering plants under the eaves, and pulling a few weeds; gardening is not a single-track activity.

The next step is to fertilize. I used to concoct different mixes for different plants, consisting of bone meal, blood meal, manure, and greensand in varying proportions. It felt pleasantly witchlike: eye of newt, tail of salamander, with an unfortunately similar measure of expertise and precision. Lately I've streamlined the process, forgoing the witch's brew. My plants are subsisting on a simpler diet of organic rose and flower food, broadcast throughout the beds. It is always better to under- rather than overfertilize, and I'm in a hurry because by March I'm only on the third step. The fourth one is the killer, and the driving force behind all this activity. Despite all the weeks of work, the garden still looks messy, with dead leaves in the beds and the nasty clay soil showing all too clearly.

The satisfying finishing step is the addition of a feeding mulch. In my garden, this needs to be carried in buckets up twenty-eight front steps. In a flatter garden, a wheelbarrow would make the task much less punishing.

A dark, rich mix of composted manure and bark can be found at many nurseries and garden supply businesses. My favorite has the unsavory name of chicken-and-chips. A top-dressing of this mulch covers up a multitude of sins, leaving the beds smooth and tidy, as if blessed with fluffy soil. Over time it will sink into the ground and improve the soil; next autumn, when it is time to add mulch again, those many bucketsful will have disappeared.

When the garden (a quarter acre) was newer and sparser, we used six yards of feeding mulch, spring and fall. Now, half that amount, spread carefully around shrubs, trees, and the crowns of perennials, is enough to enrich the soil, feed the plants, and keep them from drying out too quickly later in the season. I pile it thickly around greedy plants like clematis, hydrangeas, roses, and hostas, and spread two inches or so over all exposed earth, making sure it is no more than a thin coating around plants with shallow feeding roots, such as rhododendrons. The yellows, pinks, and blues of spring flowers glow against the now uniformly dark brown earth; the tattered leaves I failed to rake from the beds are covered up; and, for the short time before the weeds work their way back to the surface, the garden looks beautifully groomed. After all this, I look forward to the late spring and summer garden, where the major tasks of watering and weeding seem nearly effortless after the mulching routine.

Clip with Care

IN EARLY MARCH garden chores beg for attention as relentlessly as a hungry baby bird begs for worms. Suddenly the reluctant gardener is plunged into the brief transition period between relaxed catalog browsing and the heavy-duty spade-and-clipper work necessary to get the garden ready for a new season.

There are two schools of thought on when to do cleanup chores. Some gardeners lean toward cutting back and raking up in the fall before bulb planting; others relish the untidiness of the winter garden. Leaves (except for diseased ones, which should be picked up right away) serve as nature's mulch, adding texture and color to the surface of the beds and protecting plants from cold. After a full spring and summer of sweeping, clipping, weeding, and edging, I welcome the garden's slide into decay, the inevitability of its dishevelment. And the respite of its dormancy.

Getting the bulbs into the ground and mulching are all the chores I'm up for as the weather cools and days grow too short to work outdoors in the evening. So in early spring my garden is in disarray. It conveniently provides its own motivation: the mush and mess of winter needs to be cleaned up so that hellebores can unfold and little *Iris reticulata* can emerge from winter sleep.

Common advice says that the best time to prune trees is whenever you get the chance. But cutting back perennials, shrubs, and semi-woodies is not that simple—a fact that I've learned the hard way. With perfectly hardy perennials such as coneflowers or asters, you can safely cut back whenever they become so ratty you can't stand the sight of them. However, I've lost or damaged a number of other plants by wielding an overeager pair of shears too early in the season.

Hardy fuchsias are a good example. With the first hard frost they turn into a clump of withered brown sticks. They are so ugly that I used to cut them to the ground in late fall, or as soon as I began tidying up. And I repeatedly killed them. It turns out that they need the protection of their aboveground parts until at least late April. So plant them in a spot where you won't see them during the winter, and cut them back only in spring, when it warms up; they will return more lush each year. This is true for artemisias too, although they never look as ratty as the hardy fuchsias. By late winter, their gray foliage is looking a little chewed, but resist the urge to tidy them up for another month or so, when you can safely clip them back by about half.

Unfortunately, the South African honeybush (*Melianthus major*), a favorite for its blue-green leaves and peanut-butter aroma, needs the exact opposite treatment. (A plant physiologist could no doubt explain why what works for hardy fuchsias kills *Melianthus*. I seem to need to learn by trial and error.) This large, exotic-looking plant reaches its peak in fall, flourishing until after Christmas. The first year I grew it, I left it standing, congratulating myself on having sited the plant so perfectly. My comeuppance was quickly provided: a hard freeze in February killed it to the ground, roots and all. I waited until June for it to sprout, finally facing the inevitable and buying a replacement. Now, right after Thanksgiving—when it is looking its very best—I reluctantly cut it to the ground, mulching it thickly with its own leaves. Given this treatment, it emerges reliably in May, and last summer it grew to six feet, filling an entire bed with its gorgeous foliage.

Cutting back greatly improves the form of some plants. *Eucalyptus archeri* would grow into a large, single-stemmed tree if left alone. Every other year, I cut it down to its base in late March, and it grows back into a bushy shrub that fits neatly into the border. Smokebushes (*Cotinus*) and catalpas also benefit from this treatment. A couple of years ago, a week of warm February weather inspired a burst of garden activity, and I cut the eucalyptus down a month or so earlier than usual. Then I panicked waiting for it to sprout. It did finally come back, but not until June, when it had gotten past the trauma of being exposed to such rude treatment.

The most useful advice I've ever read about the timing of cutting back was from Henry Mitchell, the longtime *Washington Post* garden columnist. He said to cut back butterfly bush (*Buddleia*) when the daffodils bloom. Most advice on when to prune is worthwhile only in direct proportion to how close to your home it originates. The genius of Mitchell's piece of wisdom, of course, is that the relationship between daffodils and butterfly bushes is the same wherever they occur geographically, whether the daffs bloom in March or not until May in colder climates. So if you have a butterfly bush you want to keep under control, watch for the daffodils to open, and hack it back to the ground.

If a tidy winter garden pleases you, go ahead and clean up in fall, but apply the clippers carefully. Many plants withstand the cold better when left intact through the winter months, coming back more quickly and dependably when the days lengthen and the soil warms up a bit. It isn't as though you won't be busy out there in the meantime.

Deep Green

GERTRUDE JEKYLL, THE EARLY ARBITER OF COLOR GARDENING, lamented that people often forget green is a color. This may be particularly true here in the Northwest, where we relax into the endless green. Taking for granted our back-drop of majestic evergreen trees, we too often overlook the myriad shades and possibilities of the color green in the garden.

Green unifies the garden, and I remember this most in early spring, while I wait impatiently for the green veil to spread itself about again. Only in winter, when the herbaceous level of the garden is mostly either missing or brown, do I understand the all-pervasiveness of green during the rest of the year. I wait eagerly for the noses of bulbs, the shoots of hostas and lilies and ferns, to push through the earth, for the green to emerge from the brown and animate the garden again. There is nothing more miraculous than that one week in spring when the trees are trans-formed from bare limbs to a film of hazy chartreuse as the new leaves come on all in a rush.

This fresh spring green speaks of the power of renewal, of life and fresh air and photosynthesis. By midsummer the leaves have changed to a deep emerald, and the gardener welcomes the shade they cast, their full leafiness. By autumn the greens turn to a blaze of color, or fade softly to yellows and rusts.

Along with changing through the seasons, garden greens vary according to their texture. Consider the filigreed leaves of corydalis or bleeding heart, which give lit-tle more than the suggestion of green, as opposed to the heft of a ridged *Rodgersia* leaf or the shiny slick of a broad fan of acanthus. And then the shades of green—all the way from the near-yellow of lady's mantle to the blue-green of 'Blue Moon' hostas to the gray-green of *Phlomis* to the deep dark green of yews. No other color holds such variety within it, or is such a reflection of its texture.

Japanese gardens have long taken full advantage of this range of green textures. A swath of fluffy moss, a needled pine, a pruned curve of azalea anchored by a stone, and you have a world of a garden, all in seasonless green. Used in the Japanese manner, green is the color of understated timelessness.

Green can also enliven a garden—think of the cheery lime-green bracts of *Euphorbia polychroma,* or the jazz of yellow-on-green variegation. Green is not a primary color, but a combination of yellow and blue. If yellow prevails, the effect is of sunlight and warmth; when blue predominates, it cools down the garden, creating distance. All tones of green work as a buffer for the brights.

Both in horticulture and in floristry, green flowers are excitingly new and sought after. And no wonder. Green flowers look good with every single other color in the garden—they are the ultimate mixer, the belle of the ball. Bells of Ireland (*Moluccella laevis)*, with their spires of soft green cups, and *Nicotiana alata* 'Lime Green' provide a visual rest from the hotter colors. Their effect is subtle yet sophisticated as they lure you in for a closer look, which is why green flowers are such a hit with flower arrangers.

A surprising number of flowers come in shades of green; in early spring look for 'Greenland' tulips, *Narcissus* 'St. Patrick's Day', or *Helleborus foetidus,* with its drooping green cups rimmed in burgundy. The spiny green bracts of *Eryngium giganteum* add texture to the garden during the summer, as do the yellow-green pokers of *Kniphofia* 'Percy's Pride'. Nearly all the euphorbias have green flowers. The chartreuse flowers of *E. characias* subsp. *wulfenii* contrast beautifully with the gray-green of its foliage; *E.* X *martinii* has flowers of a brighter green, each set off with a tiny red eye. There's even a rose, *Rosa* 'Greensleeves', that comes in a soft shade of true green.

Valuable Viburnums

REMEMBER THOSE GANGLY SNOWBALL BUSHES (*Viburnum opulus* 'Roseum') growing in so many old gardens? As a kid I marveled at how, in spring, a bunch of sticks
transformed itself into a green bush drooping with the weight of dozens of round
white balls that reminded me tantalizingly of those sticky, forbidden, coconut-
topped Hostess snowballs. I now grow its more compact, snowball-less relative,
V. opulus 'Nana', a three-foot dwarf as wide as it is tall, with the same maple-shaped
leaves and the added bonus of striking fall color.

More than a dozen different viburnums lend a framework to my garden year-
round, as well as sweet perfume and showy fruit. It is possible to have a viburnum
in flower nearly every month of the year. Some are compact, others imposing;
some are evergreen, most are deciduous. I still remember my first sight of the
metallic-blue berries on *Viburnum davidii*, which grew in a mass planting around the
Lake City library branch in north Seattle. I was shelving books there while in high
school. (It was one of the few jobs available for sixteen-year-olds unable to stay
awake late enough to work in a fast-food joint. Thus are careers chosen. Believe
me, a plant has to be pretty spectacular to catch the eye of a teenage girl. Despite
the scorn heaped upon this plant because of its overuse in municipal and roadside
plantings, I grow it in several spots in the garden, and I still admire the juxtaposition of glowing berries, pink buds, and dark, veined leaves. In summer, these low-
growing shrubs disappear amidst a haze of herbaceous plantings, but they emerge
undaunted to anchor the winter border.

Now that I've admitted to admiring two of the most common viburnums, we
can go on to the many more interesting possibilities. *Viburnum* x *bodnantense* begins
to bloom in late autumn and continues flowering off and on through spring. Its
upright, twiggy shape is awkward, so bury it amidst other plants—but plant it
where you will get frequent hits of its incredibly sweet perfume, especially welcome during the winter months. The cultivar 'Dawn' has bright pink flowers;
'Deben' has white flowers with a pink blush. An evergreen winter-bloomer is
V. tinus, which grows into a handsome, rounded shrub or small tree with dark

green leaves, red stems, and pink buds opening to fragrant white flower clusters from November through spring, followed by blue berries in summer. It is a bit tender and blooms most dependably in a protected spot. *V. tinus* 'Variegatum', which has showy, yellow-margined leaves, needs even more shelter from the cold.

Even in a genus known for its fragrance, the Korean spice viburnum (*V. carlesii*) stands out for its especially sweet, clove-tinged perfume—rather like that of a carnation, but more intense. It blooms in May, with pink buds opening to large (for a viburnum) white flowers in rounded clusters. The foliage is pale green and slightly felted, the shape rounded to about five feet.

Though you'd plant many viburnums for their flower and fragrance rather than their form, *V. plicatum* f. *tomentosum* 'Summer Snowflake', developed at the University of British Columbia, is an elegant, layered shrub, an ideal plant to anchor border plantings. Its gleamingly pure white blossoms, held in flat clusters, appear in abundance late in May and then on and off throughout the summer months. There are a number of different kinds of these doublefile viburnums, all useful in the garden for their leathery leaves and horizontal branching pattern. Nearly all viburnums want full sun but will tolerate some light shade, appreciate good drainage, have few disease or pest problems, and respond well to pruning.

Habits of Highly Effective Gardeners

I WAS SITTING AROUND RECENTLY with an expert gardener and a novice, talking about our favorite subject. The novice asked the accomplished gardener whether she considered herself to have a green thumb. There she sat, amongst more than an acre of beautifully designed and tended plantings, looking confused by such a question. Finally, she answered, "Well, I always kill houseplants."

Since that conversation I've been thinking about what makes a gardener successful, and it certainly isn't luck, happenstance, or a magical "green thumb." It seems to me that the attitudes or habits that result in successful garden-making can be described, and sometimes quantified, just as they can in any other field of endeavor. My list is no doubt as arbitrary—and perhaps as obvious—as the supposed insights in all those self-help books, but there the comparison ends. It isn't meant to be prescriptive, and there is no question it won't be as lucrative.

First, and probably most important, is the simple fact that a garden is successful if the garden-maker thinks it is. If a gardener takes pleasure in his or her handiwork, whether or not that garden appeals to anyone else, it is most certainly a success. If gardeners bask in their gardens, enjoying what they have created, what better measure of achievement can there be?

Good gardeners are happiest when fully engaged in the process of garden-making, accepting that a garden is never finished. The fact that change is the only constant is nowhere more obvious than in the garden, as plants vary with the seasons, the weather, and the years. Exterior decorating is very different from interior design. A sofa is selected, or a chair placed perfectly, and there it stays for years. Outdoors, the process of growth, maturation, and decay can be embraced or resisted, but it always needs to be dealt with, and happy and effective is the gardener who revels in it.

An active visual memory and imagination are as important garden-making tools as hoses and shovels. Most gardeners have a garden in their heads as well as one in the ground. We live in our imaginations, always thinking about next month and next season, new plants and new plans. Half the fun is aspiring, plotting, making lists, and dreaming. Your brain should be as well stocked with hopes and ideas as your toolshed is with gloves and clippers.

Of course, it is also vital to get out of your head and down to work. I've met a number of gardeners whose places are a mess because all they do is read and talk about gardening. Gardening is heavy, dirty, and timeconsuming; there's no way around it, and there are few shortcuts.

A trait I've noticed in the best gardeners is a spirit of experimentation. They think of the garden as a laboratory in which to mix ideas and plants. They try combinations of plants with no particular attachment to the outcome but with great anticipation. Unique and personal gardens don't happen because of detailed plans or superior plant knowledge (although both of these help) but through inspired messing around, observation, discarding, trying again and again.

Gardening is all about seeing: looking closely, paying attention to each plant, to other gardens, to works of art in a variety of media, the weather, the site. There is no way to learn, or appreciate, without patient and detailed observation.

Legendary English gardener Margery Fish, who made a world-famous garden and nursery at East Lambrook Manor in Somerset, had her own deceptively simple definition of a good gardener's essential achievement. For Mrs. Fish, a "real gardener" was someone who could go out into his or her garden on any day of the year and discover flowers or interesting foliage. Such a garden may be the pinnacle of gardening success—worth all that experimentation, observation, imagination, and hard work.

The New Front Garden

ANNE LAMOTT TELLS A STORY in her book *Bird by Bird* that goes something like this. A woman despairs over her husband, who comes home drunk every night and passes out on the front lawn. In the morning, the woman always gets up at first light and drags him inside so that the neighbors won't see him out there. An elderly woman passes the house early each morning on her way to the bus stop, witnessing the mortified wife's attempts to get her husband into the house. One morning she loses patience with the poor woman, and calls out, "Honey, just leave him lay where Jesus flang him!"

I'm reminded of this story when I see a street of typical front yards of grass and foundation shrubs. Flat, featureless, each indistinguishable from the next—all left lying just as the contractor flang them as he hurried off to build the next subdivision.

My neighborhood was built in the 1950s, the era of grass and junipers. Wide tree lawns (parking strips) border the sidewalks, devoid of trees. Most have been paved over; some are still planted in ratty lawn, the uniform dull green unrelieved by seasonal change. Unfortunately, this style, or lack of it, still seems to dominate in many newer neighborhoods. Drive through a new subdivision and try to differentiate among streets or houses on the basis of features such as a distinctive front pathway, a mature tree, or a flowering hedge. Good luck.

Our properties are too small to waste space so flagrantly—and wasted space it is. No privacy, no shade trees, no fragrant shrubbery, often not even a place to sit. The irony is that these spaces, which bring such little satisfaction, are so much work. Pruning those andromedas and rhododendrons to let light into the windows; fertilizing, edging, mowing, and watering the front lawn so that it looks as good as the lawn next door—all of these tasks take time and resources.

Garden writers have been deploring the vogue for open front lawns since early in the twentieth century. In 1909 Neltje Blanchan complained about the disappearance of "the hedge . . . without which the perfect freedom of home life is no more possible than if the family living-room were to be set on a public stage." In 1921

Grace Tabor wrote, "Boundary fences and walls have been sacrificed in the vain hope of creating an illusion of the spaciousness and splendor which the town or suburban place cannot possibly enjoy." And lots have grown still smaller in the succeeding decades.

The front yard can be turned into a garden that will provide comfort and privacy for the homeowner, while presenting a face of beauty and seasonal interest to the neighbors. The first step is to provide some kind of enclosure. Move those plantings that are engulfing the house out to form a perimeter hedge. Or, for a more open look, build a fence of lattice, ideal for lacing with flowering or fruiting vines. Add some bulbs, groundcovers, and ornamental grasses outside the hedge, or plant the parking strip, so that something is budding up, blooming, or declining all year long. Install an interesting gate, perhaps topped with an arbor or pergola, and you've created an entry that will stir the curiosity of those passing by and give a sense of seclusion to those within.

Inside the gate, the stage is set to make a garden you love, one that suits your own personal taste. You might lay a wide curving pathway up to the porch, bordered by generous planting beds. These can be filled with a low hedge of lavender, or an assortment of perennials, bulbs, and groundcovers. Go ahead and remove all the grass and create a front courtyard of paving or gravel, plantings, chairs, tables, and pots of flowers. Such a space captures warmth and encourages outdoor meals, relaxing, and entertaining.

If your front garden is the part of your yard that receives the most sun, it can be ideal for raised beds holding vegetables, or for dwarf fruit trees espaliered against the fence or the side of the garage. Rosalind Creasy, the author of several books on growing and cooking with vegetables, herbs, and edible flowers, began by sneaking these plants into the front flower bed. Finally, she dug up the whole front garden and devoted it to annual edibles. Her garden changes every four or five months as one crop follows another. For color and structure, she tucks in a few flowers or shrubs amongst the fruit and vegetables.

There's no need to be limited by what the builder, in his tightfisted haste, made of your front yard. And there's every reason to create a space that is individual, beautiful, and useful—a garden instead of just a yard.

They Were Here First

THERE IS NO QUESTION that native plants are politically correct—after all, they were here first. But gardeners too often use them in the quest for that mythical no-maintenance landscape, and almost always they are sorely disappointed. The ecology of the home garden can be hostile to natives. Stripped topsoil, heavy clay, and full sun are a far cry from such natural habitats as a rocky cliff or the dappled shade of a forest floor.

And exactly what is a native plant anyway? It is simply a plant that existed in an area before the arrival of Europeans. But not every plant growing in the wild is a native. Many introduced plants have escaped from cultivation, naturalizing and growing happily in the wild—and not just in sites that have been disturbed, such as clear-cuts. English ivy and English holly, two of our worst pests in the Northwest, have become all too well established in dense forests.

Many gardeners admire the pluckiness of natives: unlike more highly bred plants, they are able to grow and reproduce without help from humans. Most of the native plants available in reputable nurseries have been commercially propagated, but when you're buying large specimens it is always a good idea to ask where the plants came from: were they salvaged from construction sites, or were they dug in the wild?

Steve Lorton, Northwest Bureau Chief of *Sunset* magazine, suggests that the plants we see in nature have profoundly influenced the style of our gardens. "First, Northwest gardeners seem unafraid of big plants; secondly, we seem to love dense, mixed plantings (that look overgrown to outsiders); and finally, Northwesterners seem to have a special relationship with green," he writes.

Northwest native plants are wonderfully varied—evergreen and deciduous, from stately to shyly delicate. If you think of the variety of habitats in our region, you understand why; marshes, mountains, plains, and forests all have their typical flora.

Native groundcovers can effectively replace lawn or can fill in between larger plantings. Kinnikinnik (*Arctostaphylos uva-ursi*) thrives in dry, sunny conditions; its horizontal stems are thickly set with oval evergreen leaves, and it bears pinkish white flowers in springtime. The sand strawberry (*Fragaria chiloensis*) also likes sun and tolerates being stepped on, so it works between pavers or along walkways. It has glossy green leaves and the characteristic white strawberry flower.

Low-growing forest-floor plants, such as the delicate *Trillium ovatum* or the frothy foamflower (*Tiarella trifoliata*), thrive in shadier conditions. When I was a kid, we used to try to get rid of the stinky skunk cabbage (*Lysichiton americanus*) that grew along our creek. Now it is sold as an ornamental, and I have to admit it is a lovely perennial for boggy areas. (A more elegant white form from the Orient, *Lysichiton camtschatcensis*, likes the same mucky conditions.)

Native shrubs may not be as flashy as hydrangeas or lilacs, but there is a wide assortment, ranging from the reliably evergreen to the subtly showy. Two of the first plants I've put into any garden I've ever owned are red huckleberry (*Vaccinium parvifolium*) and red-flowering currant (*Ribes sanguineum*). David Douglas introduced the latter to England not long after it was discovered in the Puget Sound region in 1826, and it has been a favorite in Europe ever since. I love its month-long bright bloom in early spring, and I love to cut the huckleberry's delicately layered foliage for arrangements.

The evergreen huckleberry (*Vaccinium ovatum*) comes pretty close to being a perfect garden plant. Its black berries make delicious pies, jams, and jellies, and it stays at a manageable three to four feet high. It has white or pink bell-shaped flowers in spring along with bronzy new growth. More dramatic is *Garrya* x *issaquahensis* (to eight feet high), a cross named for the Seattle suburb where it was discovered in the garden of Pat Ballard. Its gray-green leaves look good year-round in sun or partial shade. I grow one in the front rockery, where its long catkins drip dramatically over the edge of the bank.

If we don't spend our time out botanizing, it is easy to forget that many familiar plants are natives. We may have seen vine maple, twinflower, Pacific coast iris, Oregon grape, sumac, and maidenhair fern only in cultivation, but all of them have their roots in the land outside our gardens.

In Praise of Pulmonaria

THE FIRST PLANT I REMEMBER NOTICING as a child was a lungwort, with its curious flowers that we called "soldiers and sailors." It grew thickly on the shady banks of the creek that ran through our lower garden. The steps leading to the creek were overhung with its speckled hairy leaves, and I remember marveling over how its bell-shaped flowers were rosy pink through lavender and pure blue, all on the same plant. We kids carried the little blossoms around in our pockets, fingering them and showing them off until they turned to a mushy pulp.

A plant so long loved has accumulated a variety of other colorful common names: "boys and girls together" (for the different-colored flowers on one plant), "cowslips," "spotted dogs," and "hundreds and thousands" (for the profusion of its vivid flowers).

Pulmonaria is the botanical name for these common plants, long grown in cottage gardens and passed about among friends, because they grow easily from bits of root. They are not fussy about soil and will grow into decent-size clumps even in the inhospitable, hard-to-fill spaces beneath rooty trees. Their agreeable, easygoing nature has no doubt worked against them in the rarefied air of horticulture, where the demanding and the obscure are most valued.

I'm sure I'm committing horticultural heresy when I say that pulmonarias are every bit as satisfying to grow as the far more popular hostas. While hostas suffer munched and tattered leaves, slugs leave pulmonarias alone. The small, bright flowers begin their long period of bloom as the daffodils open in March, providing sustenance for early bees and butterflies. Pulmonarias not only start up early but are useful bridge plants, providing color and foliage along with the bulbs until later perennials take over in May.

I grow pulmonarias in many spots around my garden, with a large colony of them beneath a buddleia at the front of a raised bed. I cut the buddleia back to a stub in March, just when the pulmonarias are showiest, giving them a chance to soak up the early sunlight. Later in the summer the buddleia grows up, its branches arching over the lush carpet of pulmonaria, whose dappled leaves not only shimmer in the shade but smother the weeds as well.

Pulmonarias are easy to care for. They prefer shade or semishade, but they will take sun in moist soil, with *P. officinalis* being the most sun tolerant. Though it may seem contrary to common sense, it is best to shear lungworts to the ground after they are through blooming in late spring. You'll rid the plant of fading flowers and tired foliage, and you'll be repaid with a flush of fresh, healthy leaves that will last, in mild winters, until the flowers appear the next spring.

In recent years, breeders have been producing a variety of flashy cultivars. *P. saccharata* 'Janet Fisk' has leaves so variegated as to appear nearly solid silver, and *P.* 'Spilled Milk' starts out with purple-tinged leaves that turn silvery green. The warm salmony coral flowers of *P. rubra* are stunning against the lime-green foliage of its cultivar 'Redstart' (one of the earliest-blooming lungworts) or the cream variegation of 'David Ward'.

I love the variability of flower and the speckled leaves, but I really grow pulmonaria for the pure and intense blueness *P. augustifolia* brings to the early spring garden. Beverley Nichols, writing in 1963, describes the color as "perhaps bluer than any flower in nature, bluer than gentians, with the luminous quality of a stained glass window when the sun shines through." Three of its cultivars are particularly notable: *P.* 'Benediction', with silver-spotted leaves and dark blue flowers, is named for Seattle gardener Loie Benedict; the dainty *P.* 'Munstead Blue' was selected by Gertrude Jekyll; and in *P.* 'Cambridge Blue' the flowers are much paler, echoing the watery blue of the sky in early spring.

There is no trick to placing pulmonarias in the garden. Massed, their bright patches of color please the eye amidst all the new greens of early spring. Any of the blues show off pink tulips and creamy narcissus. Or pair *P.* 'Sissinghurst White' or *P. officinalis* 'White Wings' with a snowy bleeding heart for a double hit of pale. One of my favorite mid-April garden combinations is *Daphne genkwa* underplanted with *P. saccharata* 'Mrs. Moon', whose classic combo of soft pink and lilac-blue flowers perfectly brackets the daphne's striking, intense shade of lavender.

In early medical lore, the appearance of leaf or flower was thought to offer up a clue as to how that plant could be used for people's benefit. Hence pulmonaria, so named because the shape of the splotched leaf suggested a human lung, was believed to be a remedy for lung disease. As winter ebbs and the lengthening days awaken our craving for color, it is true that lungwort serves as a tonic—not for the lungs, but for the human spirit. Its easy faithfulness, the dependability of its familiar leaf and blossom, offer a reassuring sign that the Earth is again spinning toward springtime.

Now in Bloom: March

1
Red-flowering winter currant
(Ribes sanguineum)

One of our showiest
Northwest native shrubs, this tough,
drought-tolerant beauty is both early
blooming and long lasting, providing
early nectar for hummingbirds and
honeybees as well as a jolt of hot
pink to the early spring landscape.
The pendant flower clusters are
two to four inches long, the leaves
are maplelike, and though the
shape of the shrub is a bit gangly,
it takes well to pruning.

1

2
Corkscrew hazelnut
(Corylus avellana 'Contorta')

The twisted and gnarled
branches of this large shrub or
small tree show best in winter when
the coarse leaves don't hide its
fantastical shape. By March, its yellow
catkins lengthen to several
inches, dripping down among the
distorted shoots for some late-winter
garden drama. You can discourage it
from its suckery ways by keeping it
in a pot, which I did for years
before I let this one loose in
the garden.

2

3
Buttercup winter hazel
(*Corylopsis pauciflora*)

This shrub is so graceful that it looks as
though it had been created for Japanese
flower arranging. Just as the witch
hazels cease their bloom, it carries on
the show with soft yellow, bell-shaped,
fragrant flowers on open, horizontal
branches. Eminently pruneable, in my
garden it's underplanted to form a delicate, spreading skirt beneath both
witch hazel and *Magnolia stellata*.

4

Lungwort
(Pulmonaria)

This plant is one of the earliest perennials to bloom each spring. The bright little blossoms—in shades of blue, rose pink, white, or a combination of all three—are shown off by leaves spotted or splashed with cream, silver, or white. Lungworts prefer shade and moist soil, and combine happily with tulips and narcissus, their leaves expanding obligingly to cover up the dying bulb foliage as spring progresses. *Pulmonaria rubra* is the first lungwort to show color, with lime-green leaves and salmon-coral flowers; *P. augustifolia* has flowers of intense gentian blue, while the flowers of *P.* 'Cambridge Blue' are a softer sky blue.

4

april

For the Love of Lilacs

EASTER AND LILACS ARE INTERTWINED IN MY MIND; when we have a mild spring and Easter falls late, lilac flowering may well coincide with the bunny's visit. And now, with the array of newer hybrids, it is possible to have lilacs in bloom for six fragrant weeks, bracketing the Easter holiday in cones of sweet, old-fashioned flowers.

Is any single plant, with the possible exception of the rose, so beloved and instantly recognizable? The common lilac (*Syringa vulgaris*) came to North America with the first Pilgrims, and followed the trail of westward expansion, proving a sturdy traveler able to withstand the worst cold and fend for itself once planted. In 1753 botanist John Bartram complained, "Lilacs are already too numerous, as roots brought by the early settlers have spread enormously." The oldest living lilacs in the New World are on Mackinac Island in Michigan. An ancient, gnarled clump of patriarchs believed to have been planted in the mid-seventeenth century by French Jesuit missionaries, they still bloom every spring.

No wonder lilacs have seized the imagination of authors and poets, who have used them to symbolize the essence of spring, the color of clouds, the scent of romance. In the novel *Silas Marner,* weddings are planned to coincide with lilac bloom. Robert Burns wrote, "Oh, were my love yon lilac fair." That oft-quoted line by T. S. Eliot, "April is the cruellest month," is followed by "breeding/Lilacs out of the dead land, mixing/Memory and desire, stirring/Dull roots with spring rain."

For modern gardeners, the lessons from all this may be that it is worth waiting for lilacs to bloom (sometimes as long as five years after planting) and that it pays to site lilacs thoughtfully, since they will no doubt outlive us all. Give lilacs lots of sun, good drainage, manure in springtime, and a dose of bone meal every three years. Lilacs will bloom for close to forever without any pruning, but they flower more abundantly if pruned right after

PREVIOUS PAGE: *Clematis montana 'Elizabeth' gilds a big old mugo pine with its baby-powder scented pale pink starry flowers.*

LEFT: *An assortment of pots filled with tulips, pansies, and wallflowers in tones of yellow and orange brighten the front terrace in early springtime.*

flowering each year, when dead, diseased, or crossing branches, along with any suckers and a quarter of the oldest wood, should be cut out.

Because lilac bloom is unfortunately brief and the plants themselves are no beauties, surround them with companions whose charms are longer-lived. Peonies, with their lasting foliage and similar cultural requirements, are ideal companions. Hostas plump up the scene, and daylilies add color in summer. A late-blooming clematis such as *C. tangutica* can be trained to use lilacs as a scaffold, providing a second season of flowers.

We grow lilacs for their exquisite color and heady perfume, so concentrate on these qualities when you are choosing which of the many to give garden room. For health, vigor, and less suckering, always buy lilacs grown on their own rootstocks. 'Ellen Wilmott' is one of the best whites, with large, double, fragrant, snowy flowers. 'President Lincoln' is the bluest lilac; 'Edith Cavell' has flowers of warm cream, sweetly scented. 'Primrose' has flowers of pale yellow; 'Sensation' has dark purple flowers trimmed in white.

For small gardens there is the lavender *S. meyeri* 'Palibin', which grows slowly to four feet; the ancient Chinese used it in pots in their walled patio gardens. The Korean lilac, *S. patula* 'Miss Kim', stays under five feet and has spicy-scented blue-lavender flowers.

To walk through acres of lilacs in bloom (more than seventy different cultivars), visit the Hulda Klager Lilac Gardens in Woodland, Washington (twenty miles north of Vancouver) during their Lilac Days festival, in late April and early May. The pioneer Victorian home and gardens of Hulda Klager, a lilac fancier and hybridizer who died in 1960 at age ninety-six, are open to the public during these weeks of peak bloom, with a variety of plants for sale, including some of those bred by Klager. Look especially for Klager's most famous lilac, 'My Favorite'—a dark purple, very fragrant triple.

Pest Control Is a State of Mind

EVERY FEW WINTERS we seem to get a dire warning that we're headed into a pest-infested summer season. Here in the Northwest, a mild winter (often courtesy of El Niño) just isn't harsh enough to kill off the bugs and diseases that lurk about, waiting for the chance to multiply, chomp, and disfigure.

As much as I do my best to ignore them, my garden is full of the worst of pests, though even after mild winters they seem no more troublesome than in the past. Aphids, indiscriminate feeders that suck sap from nearly every kind of plant, are at the top of most gardeners' list of insect pests. Fortunately, they are soft-bodied creatures and can easily be killed with a strong spray of water. I think I've had fewer problems with aphids than usual lately; a honeysuckle that often succumbs to them early in the season has woven its way through a clump of miscanthus, and bloomed happily into September. For the first time ever I did have rust on a couple of shrubby hypericums, but as soon as they looked so bad I couldn't stand them I cut them to the ground, and in a few weeks they came back bushy and healthy.

Nothing is more pesty than weeds, and gardeners too often resort to chemicals in an effort to reduce the repetitive chore of pulling. Bindweed, or morning glory, is on the top-ten list of the world's most troublesome weeds—earning its place by being as persistent as a teenager wheedling for a later curfew and as irritating as a dinnertime call from a siding salesman. Like that other most successful perennial weed, horsetail, it has a profuse and deep root system. Despite all my scruples, I could be tempted by some chemical that has proven successful, but it seems as though nothing is capable of eradicating these beasts. Theoretically, frequent pulling will starve the root system over time, but, particularly with bindweed, I seem to be losing the battle.

When I took the King County Master Gardeners training, we were told that about 70 percent of all plant problems are cultural. Plants most often fail to thrive because of problems with soil, water, nutrients, temperature, and amount of sun or shade, not because of some outside agent of destruction. If you are convinced that your particular garden problem is a bug or a disease, be sure you know exactly what hooligan you are dealing with, or your solution may well cause more harm than good.

Rejuvenate

"REJUVENATE" IS SUCH A HOPEFUL WORD: to restore to youthful vigor, to renew, refresh, and revive. "Renovation" is the term most often used in the context of garden remodeling, but it brings to mind choosing a new dishwasher or upgrading the wiring—all those boring and expensive projects with little visual impact. In gardening we are working mostly with living things, so "rejuvenation" it is . . . and our gardens usually need it as much as we do ourselves.

Human bodies are fragile, able to tolerate only a massage, or perhaps a nip here or a tuck there, in the way of renewal. You can't cut off our heads and expect a flush of fresh new growth, while vines and many woody plants, such as eucalyptus and shrubby dogwoods, benefit mightily from such pollarding.

Whether we ourselves planted those rhododendrons that have grown so leggy they cover the windows or whether we bought our overgrown garden ready-made, the challenges are the same. Trees grown out of proportion, no room for understory plants, a dearth of light and space. The first question is always "Where to start?"

Hold-your-hand kind of help is available in two particularly useful books, one of which is by a Northwest author. *Rejuvenating a Garden* by Stephen Anderton teeters successfully on that tightrope of offering advice both inspirational and realistic. Especially welcome are triptychs of color photos showing the out-of-control "before"; the bleak, stripped-down "in-progress" shot; and the gratification of the well-completed project. Such side-by-side photos provide a strong draught of encouragement laced with realism.

"Gardens are composed of many interlocking elements," writes Anderton, who goes on to explain that trees, shrubs, walls, and paving, let alone perennials and annuals, all have different cycles of decay. This is the dance of the ever-changing garden.

Assessing what you have is the first step in avoiding unrealistic plans and wasted work. Which existing plants give you pleasure? Which ones provide screening or desired shade? What areas work well? Caution, patience, taking it one step at a time, and then looking closely at the results before going on to the next project is

Anderton's message. Your plan of attack should include establishing realistic phases; perhaps starting close to the house and moving outward will maximize your enjoyment of the results as you go along.

Of course, a major element of any rejuvenation project is pruning, and who better to tell us how than Seattle author Cass Turnbull, the engaging and effective spokeswoman for the organization PlantAmnesty? It may seem odd to expect pruning advice from the founder of a group "dedicated to ending the senseless torture and mutilation of trees and shrubs." But even though Turnbull might dream of trees allowed to reach their full height and glory, she knows that pruning plays a vital role in garden maintenance, and she shares her expertise in *The Complete Guide to Landscape Design, Renovation, and Maintenance*. This book, originally published by Betterway Publications in 1991, is out of print, but a revised edition will appear in 2002.

Most pruning books show how to make elegant cuts on tidy little illustrated plants that exist all by themselves somewhere in garden la-la land. Such advice is pretty useless when you are up against a gnarled old wisteria weaving through a towering laurel. Turnbull wrote her book for everyone who is renovating a garden overgrown with previously malpruned trees and shrubs. Does that sound like an all-too-familiar scenario? Turnbull's advice is amusing, clear, and specific, with line drawings showing the right and wrong of pruning cuts, plus pithy words of advice such as "Your choice with each plant will be to get rid of it, move it, or prune it." She is always true to her mission, reminding the reader that the best pruning is invisible. And because rejuvenation is an ongoing project, Turnbull has organized a support group of like-minded enthusiasts in PlantAmnesty (906 NW 87th St., Seattle, WA 98117; 206-783-9813), whose membership benefits include a quarterly newsletter, pruning classes, and a referral service.

Red Hot

AUTUMN IS MY FAVORITE TIME OF THE YEAR in the garden, and the bright red of changing leaves is the pinnacle of its drama. But the show put on by maple and sumac is all too short. Is there a way to have such fireworks in the spring and summer garden too? Absolutely. Red-foliaged plants show off the power and energy of their hot coloration over a long season.

Red is brazen and bold, a pure primary color, and such a show-off that it can be tricky to mix with other plantings. Stick a scarlet daylily like *Hemerocallis* 'Aztec' or the shockingly colored red dahlia 'Arabian Night' into a pot, and you have a focal point. But such jolts of saturated color elbow out the more modest colors such as pink, blue, and yellow. A satisfyingly easy way to enjoy red's lively heat is with foliage plants. Leafy red is often shaded with other tones and spread over a larger surface, so it can serve as a warming backdrop to the less intense colors. Also, because foliage lasts much longer than flower, you can build whole color combinations around red-toned leaves.

Plants we prize for their dark foliage are often really the deeper shades of red, such as maroon and burgundy. Purple, when sunlight slants through the leaves, can shimmer to a glowing oxblood, as with the *Heuchera* 'Bressingham Bronze' or one of the dark smokebushes. And then there are plants with true ruby-colored foliage, like the castor oil bean, *Ricinus communis*, whose large, splayed leaves and sturdy stems glow a bright, glossy cordovan even without the touch of sunlight, as does the dissected red foliage of many of the cutleaf Japanese maples. A couple of escapees from the vegetable garden provide some of the flashiest red foliage around: the crimson stalks of ruby chard are an electric pinky-red, and the Chinese rhubarb, *Rheum palmatum* 'Atrosanguineum', has deeply lobed young leaves in vivid crimson.

There are some tricks to promoting red foliage in the garden. The strongest reds are usually produced in bright sunlight, so if you plant a crimson pygmy barberry (*Berberis thunbergii* 'Atropurpurea Nana') in the shade you'll end up with green leaves, but when it's sited out in the sun the little leaves are a bright purple-red. New springtime foliage is often the most colorful of the season, and for some plants, such as smokebush and *Prunus* x *cistena*, leaves are larger and more glowingly red if the plant is severely cut back in early spring.

In many plants, the new foliage just naturally comes on a coppery or bronze-red without the gardener doing a thing. The new shoots of peonies are a soft red, the fernlike foliage of many astilbes appears in a lovely coppery color, and the fresh foliage of *Pieris* 'Forest Flame' is appropriately named.

When you're glancing through catalogs or looking at plant tags, search for plants with the species names *atropurpurea, cupreus,* or *sanguineus* (meaning, respectively, "purple," "coppery," and "red"). Along with those mentioned above, here are some of the most effective red-foliage plants:

• Phormiums are sharp-bladed plants that flaunt assorted shades of reddish stripes along their leaves. *Phormium* 'Color Guard' has intense red-pink stripes set off by deep purple; *P. tenax* 'Dazzler' combines red, orange, bronze, and pink.

• Almost every coleus has some red on its leaves; look for 'Red Velvet' or 'Bronze Pagoda'.

• *Cercis canadensis* 'Forest Pansy' is a small tree whose heart-shaped leaves come on a glowing red-purple in spring and stay that color all summer.

• *Rodgersia podophylla* is a dramatic perennial with broad, crinkly leaves of rich bronze.

• *Berberis thunbergii* 'Red Pillar' has the reddest leaves of any of the barberries, accented by crimson berries.

• Japanese blood grass (*Imperata cylindrica* 'Rubra') is a clumping grass whose top half is a rich, strong red.

True Blue

AS THE EARTH TILTS US INTO SPRINGTIME, visions of colorful flowers dance in our heads. All tasteful talk about shape and form is forgotten—the thought of color at its most blatant is what gets us through until the days begin to lengthen.

Despite my best efforts to really understand terms like hue, shade, and tone, color in the garden remains a mystery to me. Color is the single most important element in garden design, yet it's surely the most changeable and subjective. How can you make any decisions when a purple that looks deep and liquid in some lights comes across early in the day as a muddy near-violet? Or when, having resolved never to put another chrome-yellow flower in your garden, you carefully choose a butter-colored trollius—only to find that, when you've planted it next to a bronze grass, it appears glaringly bright?

And then there are the season, the light, mood, and memory; all affect how we see color, and how we feel about it. Even the obvious yellow of forsythia looks great on a rainy February morning. How can someone say, "I hate pink," in that supercilious tone? There is a world of difference between months of that flat impatiens pink and the brief mid-March appearance of a pink-tinged narcissus.

Two colors are nearly mistake-proof, however: I have never seen white or blue look anything but wonderful. Each livens up the garden, and each cools it down.

Blue is rare in nature, too often tending toward lavender, violet, or plum. Clear, true blue has long represented both purity and wealth; it is the color of the Chinese transcendental path to immortality, of precious lapis lazuli, of the eyes of a newborn baby. Here in the Northwest, blue is the prized color of clean, fresh water and welcome clear skies.

Being a cooler color (absorbing less light than red or orange) blue recedes in the landscape, so it can be used to draw the eye toward a distant focal point, to create visual shadows, or to give a feeling of spaciousness.

Blue foliage can soothe jarring color contrasts, or it can stand out in a sea of other foliage plants. *Rosa glauca* has leaves of a bluish pewter; grown next to *Eucalyptus archeri*, with its rounded blue-green leaves, and underplanted with tufts of blue fescue grass (*Festuca cinerea* 'Elijah Blue'), it makes a symphony of shades that I accent with white, pink, or orange, depending on the season. Hostas such as *H. sieboldiana* 'Elegans' provide large glaucous leaves that cool down the garden all summer. For a double hit of blue, grow the Mediterranean self-seeding annual *Cerinthe major* 'Purpurescens', with its fleshy blue-silver foliage and curious turquoise-and-purple flowers.

Blue flowers not to garden without:

• *Corydalis flexuosa* 'Blue Panda' is a spring bloomer with ferny foliage and clear bluebird-blue spurred little flowers.

• Bog sage (*Salvia uliginosa*) blooms from late summer until frost, holding aloft spiky sky-blue flowers that accent all the golds and reds of autumn.

• Dwarf plumbago (*Ceratostigma plumbaginoides*), another late bloomer, is a low-growing mounding perennial with bronze foliage and intense gentian-blue flowers.

• Wild lilacs (*Ceanothus*) are shrubs or groundcovers from California, with shiny little evergreen leaves. *C.* 'Centennial' and *C.* 'Victoria' have dark blue flowers; Point Reyes ceanothus is a creeper with light blue flower clusters.

• Blue mist (*Caryopteris clandonensis*) is a small shrub with narrow silvery foliage and cool blue flowers from late July until frost.

• Monkshood (*Aconitum*) grows four to five feet tall, with velvety, deep blue, hooded flowers. It's as beautiful as delphinium but much easier to grow

• Love-in-a-mist (*Nigella damascena*) is a lacy self-seeding annual; 'Miss Jekyll' is cornflower blue.

• Look also for blue agapanthus, clematis, delphinium, muscari, hydrangeas, hardy geraniums, phlox, veronica, and lobelia.

The Great Crab Hunt

IT TOOK MY HUSBAND AND ME MOST OF ONE SUMMER to dig the pond in our back garden, so you can imagine that I had to find just the right tree to be reflected in its waters. The next spring I paid special attention to the parade of bloom as one kind of ornamental tree after another unfurled its flowers. Though the cherry's blowsy pink flower puffs are excitingly showy, I decided it was the open white flowers of the crabapple that would look best in my naturalistic garden. Those simple, familiar flowers seem to symbolize all the loveliness of springtime.

I love the way crabapple's bloom is shown off against the chartreuse of the new leaves, which come on quite early in March. (Many spring-flowering trees bloom on bare wood, to be followed by the foliage.) Add to that its sweet fragrance, its hot-pink balls of bud opening to snow-white flowers, and its bright autumn fruits to please the eye and the birds, and it seemed clear that a crabapple should overhang the new pond. But which one? Seattle tree expert Arthur Lee Jacobson says there are more than a hundred kinds of crabapples in commerce, and warns that "some have no business being for sale."

Though I admit that I look first at tree shape and flower, the most important consideration in choosing a crabapple should be disease resistance. In cool, moist climates like ours, crabs are notoriously subject to scab infection. The tree I ended up planting seven years ago, *Malus* 'Red Jade', which at that time was on the "recommended" lists, now shows up on the "to avoid" lists. I've had few problems with it, and its foliage stays fairly healthy into fall. However, if I were searching for a tree today I'd pay attention to current recommendations and find a different small weeper with white flowers, such as 'Sinai Fire', now considered the best white-flowered weeper.

Crabapples are reliably hardy, bloom for several weeks with flowers ranging from pure white through pink and purple, are not too fussy about soil, and come in a variety of shapes and sizes. They need good drainage and irrigation during drought periods. Crabapples cry out for underplanting—try a carpeting of small narcissus or crocus, followed by hostas, hardy fuchsias, or lady's mantle (*Alchemilla mollis*) for summer. And remember that these are not orchard apple trees, to be pruned hard for fruit production. They require only a gentle thinning to bring out their own graceful lines.

How to find the cultivars that perform best in our climate? Jacobson advises that responsible local nurseries carry only the relatively scab-resistant kinds. He warns that all too often the crabapples with the most glorious flowers follow up that display with the most disfiguring scab (which ruins the look of the leaves but usually doesn't hurt the tree's health). He appreciates crabs for their fruit rather than their flower anyway, particularly admiring *M*. 'Red Jewel', whose cherry-red fruit persists until the spring foliage unfurls; *M*. 'Professor Sprenger' for its "nearly walnut size and cheerful-looking" orange-red fruit; and the showy fruit of *M*. 'Golden Hornet'. He readily admits that these cultivars have less-than-exciting flowers, but their foliage stays healthy all summer.

We have a western native crabapple, *Malus fusca*, which makes up for what it lacks in showiness (small pink flowers and yellow or purplish red fruit) by tolerating wet feet, thriving along stream banks or in boggy areas.

Spring in a Vase

THE SUCCESS OF MOST ARTISTRY, visual as well as written, lies in the editing. A sculptor speaks of chipping away stone to reveal what exists inside. With flower arranging, the essence of springtime is captured with a single parrot tulip, the essential line of an azalea branch, or the tender unfurling of a fern frond. Such restraint and selectivity are especially difficult this time of year, when the garden explodes with possibilities for the vase.

I feel as though spring has really arrived—no matter what the temperature or how persistent the drizzle—when I can go outside, usually during the first week of April, and cut armfuls of flowers to bring in to fill a whole lineup of vases. For the first time since the asters faded in October I can have fresh flowers in every room. And in this surge of bloom lies the challenge—it is so tempting to create riotous, multicolored displays. Not that there is anything wrong with a great big mixed bouquet, and sometimes it is just the thing, but I'm afraid it too often looks as if it belongs in a hotel lobby rather than on the dining room table at home.

Try three white peonies in a glass vase, with their own fine foliage, for a stunningly simple arrangement. Or strip all the leaves off a single kind of rhododendron and arrange the flowers in a low bowl. What could look better than a blue jug brimming with pale daffodils? Or, if you want to use lots of different kinds of flowers, try sticking each in a little glass vase by itself, and then cluster the vases together; this creates impact but also lets you appreciate each exquisite blossom. What could be prettier and smell better than a tumbler full of lily-of-the-valley? Or you can dig up a clump and stick it, soil and all, in a shallow dish, where it will bloom happily indoors for weeks, spreading its sweet perfume through the house.

Don't overlook the small trees in your garden as vase material. Branches coated with cherry and crabapple flowers make fluffy bouquets, as pretty when they've strewn half their blossoms all over the table as when they are freshly cut. Then there are the flowering shrubs—you can't do without lilacs, daphne, mock orange, rhododendrons, exbury azaleas, Koreanspice viburnum.

Mix in plenty of foliage. Leaves are freshest as they first unfold, and they help to diffuse the clash of bright-colored blossoms. The gray felted leaves of lamb's ears find their way into many of my spring flower arrangements, as do darkly scalloped heuchera leaves, an array of euphorbias, and the little red-tipped yellow leaves of *Spiraea japonica* 'Magic Carpet'. I've planted these all over the garden, so I have plenty to cut from. As I write this on the last day of April, I'm looking at a stoneware vase stuffed with deep purple 'Queen of the Night' tulips, softened with silvered lamb's ears and an arch of white bleeding heart.

Vines, with their grasping tendrils, capture the buzz of springtime energy; no arrangement should be without their drape and curl. *Clematis armandii* lends perfumed white or pale pink flowers and pliable new foliage in bronze. I use it in every bouquet for at least a month, beginning when it opens its first flower in March. *Akebia quinata* has dramatic leaves and tiny, purple-brown flowers of great sweetness, and the little sky-blue bells of *Clematis alpina* are as beguiling dangling down the side of a vase as decorating a tree or an arbor.

Every garden and every vase depends upon the chorus girls of springtime—peonies, magnolias, fat cottage tulips, hyacinths, and camellias—blowsy and gorgeous, even when edited by the least self-indulgent of flower arrangers. The springtime garden offers an unsurpassed chaos of flowers and foliage to bring great enjoyment, on bedside tables or kitchen counters, from March through summer solstice.

Euphorbias

EUPHORBIAS LOOK AS IF THEY WERE MADE TO GROW beneath the waves rather than up in the fresh air. You can just picture an entire colony of the genus *Euphorbia* deep in the ocean, their green, gray, or maroon bracts swaying gracefully with each passing current. This underwater look may be why they're considered a bit of an oddity, an acquired taste. However, if you were to ask serious gardeners what kind of plant they would be most reluctant to give up, I bet euphorbias would often be the answer.

Even if your taste runs to flowering plants like rhododendrons and roses, euphorbias are easy to love for their sheer variety and easy-care usefulness. They mark a step in the evolution of a gardener; if we start out growing daffodils and dahlias and move on to clematis and daylilies, I guess euphorbias would fall right along with ornamental grasses as a benchmark in our appreciation of foliage over flowers. Not that euphorbias don't have interesting, colorful flowers, but bloom isn't really the point.

The virtues of euphorbias are many. They are dependably hardy and sometimes evergreen; no plant combines more easily with its neighbors; and they come in small, medium, and large, with textures varying from architecturally statuesque to fluffy to rockery-style dangling. One of the most familiar euphorbias is the donkey tail spurge *(E. myrsinites),* whose blue-gray stems trail down many an old rockery— and deserve to, with attractive leaves as fleshy and rounded as a succulent, and lime-yellow flowers in March and April. Donkey tails are drought tolerant, grow thickly enough to serve as a groundcover but aren't invasive, and make good companions for small early bulbs such as species tulips and *Iris reticulata.*

Euphorbia is the sixth-largest genus of flowering plants, with more than two thousand species, so there are plenty to choose from. Most are tropical, some growing as tall forest trees, many closely resembling cacti. Christmas poinsettias, native to Mexico, are *Euphorbia pulcherrima.* Various members of the genus are native to Pacific islands, to mountain peaks in India, or to Australian deserts. They also push their way up through the cracks in city sidewalks. Such adaptability, however, brings with it the tendency toward invasiveness in some of the species, so read up carefully before you plant.

Hardy garden euphorbias are usually leafy perennial herbs, but some develop woody bases. *E. amygdaloides* var. *robbiae* would be a good starter euphorbia for a less-than-convinced gardener, for it acts as a small, glossy evergreen shrub. It isn't fussy about soil, grows in either sun or shade, and, in early spring, holds its yellow flowers dramatically above the rosettes formed by its handsome dark-green leaves.

Another evergreen is *E. characias* subsp. *wulfenii*, whose four- to five-foot-high foliage is an arresting presence that pairs elegantly with grasses or hardy geraniums. The leaves are grayed and narrow, the head is rounded into a broad dome, and the flowers bloom early in a brilliant chartreuse. Even more colorful are *E. dulcis* 'Chameleon', a frothy mound of bronzed burgundy foliage and tiny yellow flowers; and *E. griffithii* 'Fireglow', which grows two to three feet high, with flower heads of bright orange-red over a long season.

Wear gloves and take care in planting or cutting euphorbia, as its milky sap is irritating and even poisonous. "Wolf's milk," "witch's milk," and "toad's milk" have been some of this plant's common names throughout its long history. Legend has it that the Numidian king Juba II discovered euphorbia atop Mount Atlas and named it after Middle Ages, resulting in the common name "spurge," which comes from the Latin word meaning "to purge." You get the idea. John Gerard was cautionary in his 1597 *Herball,* describing spurge sap as "a strong medicine to open the bellie," and advising against its use. Four centuries later, we still need to beware of its juice, but in the garden or cut for the vase, few plants can match euphorbia's beauty and diversity.

1

Crown imperial
(Fritillaria imperialis)

An imposing presence in the
spring garden, crown imperials
boast eye-catching hot orange
blossoms with prominent stamen.
Their cartoonishly exaggerated shape
of dripping bells and frilly topknot makes
themlook like long-stemmed burlesque
dancers rising up out of the soil. Plant
the large, fragile bulbs in very well-
drained soil; I've found they do
best in pots and window boxes.
Be sure to group them together
for the full impact
of a chorus line.

2

Akebia quinata

This exotic-looking vine is among the easiest to grow, climbing and
looping lustily in sun or partial shade. It has distinctive five-lobed leaves and
headily fragrant little cup-shaped flowers in cream or dusky purple. The flowers
are somewhat tucked beneath the leaves, and I'm often surprised in
early spring by a hit of strong vanilla fragrance wafting through the garden
before I've realized the vine is in bloom. Worth growing for its foliage alone,
A. quinata is semideciduous; it can be allowed to grow thickly or can be
pruned out to provide a tracery of leaves
against a wall or fence.

3

4

Flowering cherry
(Prunus X *yedoensis* 'Akebono',
sometimes called 'Daybreak')

Few things are more beautiful
than the spread of cherry trees, blooming pink and fading to white against the
dark skies of early spring, and just a
short week later scattering blossoms
along the sidewalk like pale, silky con-
fetti. These lovely year-round trees top
out under twenty-five feet, with textural
bark and a graceful line in winter, a
remarkable show of pink flowers in early
April, and healthy mid-green leaves all
summer. While flowering cherries are
plagued with disease in the Northwest,
this is one of the more disease-free kinds
for our climate; three of them grow
on my street, to the detriment
of the sidewalk.

3
Koreanspice viburnum
(Viburnum carlesii)

Named for both its place of
origin and its fantastic fragrance, this
bushy deciduous shrub grows to six feet
('Compactum' tops out at about three
and a half feet). It takes well to pruning
and has rounded mid-green leaves that
are handsome all summer. Garden
space is earned, however, by
the three weeks in April during
which it produces rosettes of bright
pink tubular buds that open to pink-
flushed-with-white flowers. Each
individual flower is large for a viburnum and arranged in neat clusters that
fill the garden with a sweet and
spicy perfume. There are three garden
fragrances I look forward to all
winter with keen longing: those
of lilac, mock orange, and
Koreanspice viburnum.

4

may

Artful Potting

WHOEVER INVENTED THE TERM "COLOR SPOTS" should be impaled on one of those pointy dracaenas planted dead center in nearly every pot I've seen lately, or perhaps left to contemplate the error of his ways surrounded by a sea of sticky petunias. Pot plantings need not be a mass of geraniums, impatiens, marigolds, and lobelia in competing colors; they have the potential to bring elegance and artistry to the garden. If the rhetoric of politics were applied to pot plantings, an appropriate slogan might be "It's the foliage, stupid." With the bright patterns of coleus, the luminous chartreuse of the felty-leafed licorice plant (*Helichrysum petiolare* 'Limelight'), or the richly dark blades of bronze flax (*Phormium*), you won't miss the flowers at all.

Heat-loving vegetables and herbs thrive in pots. Give a tomato plant a pot on the patio, plant some ruffly lettuces in another and basil in a third, and you have texture, color, and salad. In our chancy Northwest climate, eggplant (try the startlingly dark-leafed 'Slim Jim') and corn have a better chance to ripen if you plant them in pots—and if you don't get a crop you'll at least have spectacular foliage to enjoy all summer long.

I first started planting in pots when I owned a German shepherd who could behead a row of tulips with a wag of his tail and turn new annuals to mulch with a step of his huge, errant paw. To avoid pointless fury over his ruinous ways, I started thinking of the garden as divided into two distinct parts: permanent plantings in the ground, more delicate and seasonal plants in pots. Now I have pots filled with climbing roses, small trees, shrubs, annuals, bulbs, perennials—anything I want to feature, protect, or just look at more closely. Containers are the necklace, the shoes, the earrings—accessories

PREVIOUS PAGE: *Hydrangeas along the north side of the house are underplanted with poppies, hosta, and the tiny blue flowers and rounded leaves of* Brunnera macrophylla.

LEFT: *Aggregate pots on the front terrace change plantings with the seasons; here ranunculus, a lavender calla lily, and a colorful little abelia start the spring show. In mid-May, I'll move these hardy plants into the garden, and plant up the pot with summer annuals.*

that make the whole garden ensemble individual and eye-catching.

In most areas of the garden, considerations like expense and ease of maintenance force us to act grown-up and realistic, to make compromises. With containers, we can indulge both our plant lust and our creativity, without lasting repercussion to budget or landscape. Start with a pot you really love, one that is so fabulous it looks good even when empty. With the right container, simple is satisfying— think of fat terra-cotta rounds overflowing with a single kind of scented-leafed geranium, or a yellow water lily floating in a bright green pot. Just be sure to plant generously. Skimpy pots are pitiful, a wasted chance for beauty. Squeeze in as many little rootballs as you possibly can, and you'll be gratified with the look of overflowing abundance.

When using a mix of plants in a pot, make sure that each one looks as if it has a reason to be there, that each relates to its pot-mates. There is nothing more discouraging than a pot planted with marigolds, pink petunias, and red geraniums. What's the point? Combinations can be concocted to fit varied aesthetics, and for all kinds of reasons (food, fragrance, color, avant-garde pizzazz); just make sure that each component contributes to the purpose, or you'll end up with goulash. You can avoid this outcome altogether by using a single kind of plant per pot, and then group pots together for a look of uncomplicated sophistication. Think cherry tomatoes spilling down the sides of a cobalt-blue urn, or a nicely tarnished metal basin filled with sunny nasturtiums. The common becomes extraordinary when singled out in a container of complementary color and shape.

Perennials, vines, and shrubs make as good backbone plantings in pots as they do in the garden. On my back patio is a large terra-cotta pot, placed next to a pergola post, that for three years has held a clematis, some small-leafed variegated ivy, and a fluffy *Heuchera* 'Chocolate Ruffles'. In spring, crocuses and little yellow daffodils come up through the foliage; in July, three lilies add fragrance and flamboyance. In winter the heuchera and ivy, along with an edging of winter pansies, carry the show. In early spring I scratch in a bit of Whitney Farms organic rose and flower food and add compost, and several times during the summer I water with fish fertilizer.

Some plants are much easier to deal with when containerized. I love the groundcover *Houttuynia cordata* 'Chameleon' for its flashy cream, green, and watermelon-pink leaves, but not for its invasiveness, so I confine its creeping rhizomes in a pot. This technique works too for bamboo or other vigorous grasses. My contorted hazelnut hid its true nature while potted; once in the ground, it started suckering like crazy.

If you're ready for a break from the usual begonias and impatiens, try a few of these flamboyant annuals and tender perennials:

- *Petunia integrifolia*—This cascading petunia has little violet flowers.

- Dahlias—One of the prettiest pots I saw last summer held a purple-foliaged, bright-pink-flowered 'Fascination' dahlia surrounded by *Pennisetum setaceum* 'Purpureum', a dark ornamental grass.

- Coleus: 'Ullrich', 'Alabama Sunset', and the more subtle 'Inky Fingers' all have distinctive patterning that's perfect for mixing.

- Flowering maples (*Abutilon*): Orange or yellow bell-shaped flowers and strikingly variegated leaves can accent other annuals or carry a pot all by themselves.

- Fuchsia: 'Gardenmeister Bonstedt' has dark foliage and a free-flowering habit.

- Licorice plant (*Helichrysum petiolare*): Its spreading shape and felted leaves make this an ideal foliage plant for pots. 'Limelight' is chartreuse; 'Variegatum' is gray and cream.

- Heliotrope: The heads of little purple or white flowers and the dark crinkled leaves are modest in appearance, but heliotrope is worth adding to every pot for its strong, sweet, vanilla fragrance.

Annuals give their all in one season—they grow to maturity, bloom, and die with the first frost—so they need plenty of nutrition to help them reach their peak, especially when packed in tightly. They need great soil to encourage them all summer long. Try mixing together approximately five parts commercial potting soil, three parts composted manure, and, for good drainage, two parts perlite. Those popular time-release granular fertilizers don't kick in until the soil warms up, so it is more effective to foliar-feed your pot plantings every week or so with a diluted mixture, applied with a hose-end sprayer. Water daily, clip back spent blooms to keep the flowers coming, and enjoy a big dose of summer flamboyance contained.

Look for the Leaf—Green Foliage

IT MUST BE AN INTRACTABLE RULE OF HUMAN NATURE that what is generously provided is least appreciated. It took a garden fence painted a creamy mid-green for me to pay close attention to green as both animator and backdrop of the garden. This fence stretched around a cottage-style garden that was in riotous color during my midsummer visit. The color of the fence was what made it work. No other color, not even the traditional white, could have blended and softened those flower colors. Just as a green fence corralled all the colors into a whole, so does green foliage in the garden unify as well as enliven.

Though green flowers are a captivating oddity, it is the green of leaves and needles that counts every day of the year. We seem to concentrate on finding space for silver, yellow, purple, and variegated foliage, yet the funny thing is that all these lively and disparate foliages are knitted together and made beautiful by plain old solid green.

Of course, there is nothing plain—or often even solid—about green. Green can be steely cold, nearly blue or nearly yellow, two-toned, or soothingly deep and mellow. Maybe every gardener should set himself or herself the task of making an all-green garden, playing with nuances of texture and shading. Or at least study those elegant all-green French or Italian gardens. There is something to be said for learning the subtle arts before adding all the fireworks.

Green clothes the architecture of the garden, thus creating its shape and form. It could be said that all the other colors serve as nothing more than distractions from this original gemstone of a color, that they have little role in garden-making besides embellishing or distracting from the primary green.

Painter Robert Dash, in his book *Notes from Madoo,* says of his favorite garden color: ". . . my heart leans on green, for it is a world-class color, at once oasis and Eden." He describes his ideal garden as a great green house of grand green rooms roofed by the light of the sky. He also makes the point that green should be appreciated for more than its visual appeal. Green is the barometer of a garden's health. Rich, healthy green allows you to relax in a garden, knowing it is well cared for and thriving.

Green is the continuance between garden and borrowed landscape, so lift up your eyes from your own garden to the horizon and make full use of green's potential for connectivity. One way to do this is to pay close attention to green's lightness or darkness—it is possible to guide the eye from the dark green needles of pines and firs to the dense shadowy green of a yew hedge, which in turn makes a perfect foil for brighter or lighter flower colors.

Most of all, green provides an education in the use of texture. Green can be fluffy and feathery, as in fennel; so tough and leathery as to appear ominous in a broad splay of gunnera leaf; or neatly pleated, as in a spray of fern frond. Think of the silky droop of Solomon's seal, the rich luxuriance of cushiony moss or fat hosta leaves, the cunning of baby tears. Some of my favorite examples of green foliage are the absolutely easiest to grow, like lupines, spiny *Eryngium giganteum*, hellebores, and the cupped leaves of lady's mantle, shaped to hold a raindrop to reflect their chartreuse softness.

What I love most about green is that it is elegant yet supremely pure and simple. Green can be as formal as a clipped shrub in a terra-cotta pot or a series of tidy hedges, but it also means pastureland in the springtime, the curve of zucchini in the vegetable garden, or the moss, ferns, and imposing canopy of our rain forests. And all these shades and reverberations of greenness are available to us in the ornamental plants we use to shape our gardens.

A Puddle of Sunshine

YELLOW IS, HANDS DOWN, THE COLOR to throw into a mix of plants for instant warmth and spark. Orange or red flowers can generate that same heat, but they so often clash with other plantings. Yellow is a foolproof way to get the same effect. And yellow comes not only in flowers, but increasingly in foliage as well, making it a snap to plant a puddle of sunshine amongst plain green.

A friend recently lamented a failed experiment of mixing yellow into her usual color scheme of pink, mauve, and blue flowers. Her idea of using yellow to brighten up those tired pastels was inspired—but the shade of yellow in the marigolds and perennial tickweed (*Coreopsis verticillata*) that she chose was too brash. The paler cultivar *C. verticillata* 'Moonbeam' would have enlivened the pastels without jarring the nerves. And even the ubiquitous marigold now comes in a much-easier-on-the-eye warm vanilla.

We all know that pink isn't a single color but ranges from the softness of baby pink to hot fuchsia. Why, then, do we think of yellow as simply rain-slicker or school-bus yellow, as glaring as an overgrown forsythia in full bloom? Warm creams through buttery yellows bring luster, not competition, to other colors. Just skip those chrome yellows, and mix in plenty of sunflower and rudbeckia golds, set off by their own chocolate-brown centers. Both are clever enough to bloom along with the purples and deep reds of autumn with which they harmonize so beautifully.

You can use mass plantings of yellow for a sea of sunshine; *Potentilla recta pallida* and pale yarrows such as *Achillea* 'Moonshine', with its gray-green foliage, or *A. tomentosa* 'Primrose Beauty' are pleasing shades of yellow, and drought tolerant as well. My absolute favorites in the buttery yellow category are the tiered spires of Jerusalem sage (*Phlomis fruticosa*) and *Trollius* 'Cheddar'. The latter is a long-blooming perennial that sports a rounded flower in the most delicate yet warm tone of yellow imaginable. In my garden it blooms above a carpeting of blue star creeper (*Laurentia fluviatilis*) alongside the mounded foliage of the yellow-striped ornamental grass *Carex elata* 'Aurea'. The combination of yellow and sky blue livens the surrounding daphnes and witch hazels that have finished flowering months earlier.

Though these soft yellows are a fine addition to the spring and summer garden, yellow is never more welcome than when the Chinese witch hazels (*Hamamelis mollis*) bloom beneath dark winter skies at the beginning of the new year.

Some flowers that we might usually choose in pink, such as lupines, roses, and tulips, look particularly fine in yellow. 'West Point' tulips are pure yellow, and roses such as the pale, open 'Golden Wings' or the modern shrub rose 'Graham Thomas' are striking. For a surprising hit of yellow lace surrounding vivid pink flowers, plant *Dicentra spectabilis* 'Goldheart', the yellow-foliaged bleeding heart.

Colored leaves are the most effective way to have yellow in the garden over many months. Many yellow-foliaged plants positively glow, and it is possible to layer yellow into the garden from trees to groundcovers. The golden locust, *Robinia pseudoacacia* 'Frisia', has drooping leaves that stay the same sunny yellow from spring until frost; the elderberry *Sambucus racemosa* 'Sutherland Gold' is a midsized frothy filigree of finely dissected yellow foliage; the tiny yellow leaves of the shrubby honeysuckle *Lonicera nitida* 'Baggesen's Gold' are nearly evergreen in a mild winter; and even that dependable old groundcover dead nettle comes in a gloriously gleaming shade of pure yellow (*Lamium maculatum* 'Aureum').

Wherever a yellow flower, a leaf striped in yellow, or a plant with pure yellow foliage is planted, the effect is of a ray of sunshine illuminating that spot in the garden. And goodness knows that in our climate we can use all the warmth and sunshine we can get.

Self-Seeders

"What I like about gardening is that it makes a mockery of intentions."
—MIRABEL OSLER

PLANTS ARE NOT REPRODUCED SOLELY THROUGH HUMAN EFFORT—grafting, division, or collection and sowing of seed. They have babies, and spread themselves about. If we are not too enamored of our own intentions, we can accept nature's generosity—and often learn valuable lessons in how to arrange plants most naturally.

My garden holds many flowers that I never planted at all: rose campion (*Lychnis coronaria*), forget-me-nots, borage, fennel, feverfew. Then there are the ones that came from a single plant given by a friend and that I will now have forever, such as purple columbines, toadflax *(Linaria)*, and ruffled, double annual poppies.

It is amazing how often self-seeders seem to show up in just the perfect place, adding a spark to an otherwise dull color scheme or, in the case of feverfew, giving fluff to a bed of spindly plants. They fill in, sometimes crowd, adding a casual cottage-garden feel to even the most rigid of plantings. Self-seeders soften the edges. All you need to do is edit.

The gardener has more options than the two obvious ones, leaving a plant wherever it chooses to sprout or pulling it out. Wait until these uninvited guests have developed a bit of root and then move them to a better spot. My pots are full of *Verbena bonariensis* transplanted from where it popped up.

Along with pleasant surprises, self-seeders have provided me with plenty of humility. I tried to grow a certain hardy geranium at the top of my rockery, only to have it die. Geraniums are usually so easy to grow. I bought another one and tried again. I pampered it, watering and fertilizing and weeding. There was no sign of it this spring; however, an identical baby geranium grew out of a nearby crack in the cement of the stairway, the most inhospitable spot imaginable.

One year I planted several packets of Shirley poppies because one of my favorite authors, May Sarton, loved them and always found room for them in her garden (which I guess is as good a reason as any to try a new plant). The first summer I had an array of sherbet shades: white, pale pink, peach, and watermelon. I was thrilled when they came back the next year—until they opened. Red was the only color that had reseeded.

I grow a short variety of bamboo in raised planters alongside my front porch, and this spring a plant I didn't recognize came up in the midst of it. The large, cut leaves looked vaguely familiar; perhaps it was one of the newer exotics. I felt quite pleased that this unusual plant had volunteered in such a prominent spot. My brother, visiting from Alaska, asked what it was, and I spoke about the mystery of self-seeders, how exotic it looked there with the bamboo, and no doubt went on and on. He said it kind of looked like a potato to him. After he left, I pulled part of it up, and there was a tiny red new potato on the root.

Encouraging self-seeders and letting them do what they will can be a useful strategy for garden-making, rather like joining in a partnership with Mother Nature. Here are a few self-seeders that have been particularly welcome in my garden:

- *Verbena bonariensis:* The queen of the self-seeders. Tall, with a unique, spare branching habit that verges on goofiness, it will grow up happily between other plants; it bears small, single, purple flowers from midsummer to frost.

- *Linaria:* Tidy plants with soft pink, white, or violet flowers on narrow spikes softened with curiously uptilting blue-gray leaves.

- *Cerinthe major*: One of those plants you need to buy only once, with thick blue leaves and turquoise-and-dark-purple flowers; lovely with pink roses or in pots.

- *Nicotiana sylvestris*: Statuesque and fragrant, this tobacco plant grows four to five feet high with long, tubular white flowers.

- *Euphorbia dulcis* 'Chameleon': This dainty, dark-leaved euphorbia looks good with many other plants, retaining its distinct coloration all summer long.

Sowing Vitality

WE ARE INUNDATED WITH ADVICE on how to live long and healthy lives. Anyone who bothers to pay attention to all this information could come to only one conclusion: Take up gardening.

Gardeners need to band together to lobby insurance companies for lower premiums. A gardening discount would no doubt make as much sense for the insurance industry as do the price breaks for nonsmokers and good drivers. Our exercise comes hard and dirty, but with intense satisfactions; runners may cover the miles, but do they have a planting bed fresh with fluffy, nicely turned soil, or a border free of weeds, to show for their efforts?

If hallmarks of health are balance and connection, gardeners have both in spades. The ability to be absorbed by what you are doing, to sink into the kind of flow that gets going on a good day in the garden, is a gift of relaxation and rejuvenation. And has a gardener ever met a stranger? Rain, heat, wind, tall stories of giant zucchini and pumpkins, or the biggest slug or newest dahlia—all these provide endless topics for conversation.

A sense of wonder has been called the ultimate survival skill. No wonder I meet so many active gardeners who are well into their eighties and even nineties. Digging in the soil and noticing what goes on around us, we marvel at the bugs, appreciate the smell of earth, pay attention to each new leaf or bud. As we sow vitality, so do we reap it. And we are never, ever bored. There is always so much to learn, so many new plants to discover, so many problems to rectify, so many new ideas . . .

Garden historian Mac Griswold has described garden-making as the slowest of the performing arts. It certainly does teach patience, an antidote to hurry-sickness. There is no way to rush perennials; the first year they are going to just sit there, the second year they put down roots, and the third year they grow and bloom like crazy. Clematis will languish until it decides to explode; trees grow at their own pace. There is just no way to bend plants to your will, no matter how you may try to influence them with water, fertilizer, or cajoling. So we learn to relax, appreciate, and keep our blood pressure constant.

And gardeners certainly live in the real world; no virtual reality for us. A gardener knows exactly which day in June it was finally warm enough to leave basil out overnight—and not just this year, or last, but probably for the last decade. After a recent weekend away, I asked several neighbors how much it had rained. I got vague answers such as "I think it might have rained overnight." Then I asked a gardener, who gave me the exact measurement of precipitation for each day, plus the quality and the timing. Gardeners pay attention.

One of the most touching scenes in all of garden literature is the one E. B. White paints of his wife, Katharine S. White, in his introduction to her book *Onward and Upward in the Garden*. Despite age and infirmity, she struggled on to get bulbs into the ground each autumn. "As the years went by and age overtook her, there was something comical yet touching in her bedraggled appearance on this awesome occasion—the small, hunched-over figure, her studied absorption in the implausible notion that there would be yet another spring, oblivious to the ending of her own days, which she knew perfectly well was near at hand, sitting there with her detailed chart under those dark skies in the dying October, calmly plotting the resurrection."

Mrs. White wasn't worried about her own aches and pains—she was looking forward to glorious tulips next April. She was concerned with daffodils and hyacinths, next spring and then the next. She no doubt had dirt under her fingernails, and pictures in her mind of gardens past, present, and future. Bone meal, drainage, and all the different shades of pink busied her brain. What other human endeavor involves us in plotting the resurrection each and every autumn, not only of the garden, but of our own spirits, hopes, and schemes? It feels simply like hard and practical work, but of course it really is wild and happy optimism, over and over again in each season of every year.

Annual Climbers

ANNUAL VINES BRING TO MIND WEATHERED SHEDS smothered with sweet peas, morning glories, or climbing nasturtiums. The old-fashioned image seems at odds with the unpronounceable botanical names of most of these vines. Fortunately, length of name has absolutely nothing to do with ease of cultivation. Give annual vines sun, water, and nearly any kind of soil, and they happily climb, twist, and wind their way over whatever support is provided, reaching eight, ten, and even twenty feet in a single season. With a vine or two, you can cover a pergola to create a shaded bower, or screen out the neighbors for the summer. The very best thing about annual vines is that you don't need to worry when they shoot up at the pace of Jack's beanstalk. Control is not an issue here—just let them romp, and then, after the first frost, pull them out and toss them on the compost. It's easier to enjoy a vine's nearly unbelievable vigor when you know you won't be tearing your hair out over how to prune, train, and support it in future years.

You can grow most annual vines from seed, or you can get them off to a faster start by buying four-inch starts in nurseries. Most of them need sun and heat to perform their best. Last year I tried to grow a gourd vine up the sides of a pergola, the plan being that it would drip its lovely moonlike gourds down through the top. In late October, just before frost, one lone gourd hung forlornly through the cross-pieces. This year I planted a couple of nursery babies in a pot at one side of the pergola, set where it would capture all available sun. Thus encouraged, the vine reached the top of the structure by late July, with gourds ripening by August, so that we actually had a month or two to enjoy them before frost. So remember that annual vines hail from sunnier climes, and provide the warmest spot you can—no small trick in our sometimes cool and dampish summers.

One flashy vine to be sure to try is an unusual one from Mexico, *Rhodochiton astrosanguineum* 'Purple Bells', ideal for hanging baskets or for growing up trellises. Each richly purple, pendulous flower has a frill of rosy pink bells, and the foliage is broadly toothed and handsome. The vine grows to ten feet in full sun, its exotic look guaranteed to draw curious stares. Another eye-catcher is the corkscrew flower or snail bean (*Vigna caracalla*), which resembles no other flower I've ever seen. The vine grows to fifteen feet, and its two-inch flowers are creamy white and lavender, curling and coiling about like the shell of a snail. They'd be just a curiosity if each little flower weren't both delicately colored and highly fragrant.

The firecracker vine (*Mina lobata*), a must-have, works well in containers with a warm color scheme. This twining climber is a color crescendo all in one plant, with flowers starting out dark red, fading to orange and then to creamy yellow. The flowers of 'Revelation' begin scarlet and fade to cream; 'Citronella' has a paler palette, with flowers of lemon yellow, cream, and bright white. And the flowers are so appealing—bright amidst the lobed leaves and lined up along the vine like little trumpet-shaped soldiers. If you find a sheltered spot for cathedral bells (*Cobaea scandens*), it may well bloom and dispense its rich fragrance of honey right through Christmas. A shrubby climber that can be grown up through large shrubs or over pergolas or arches, it needs plenty of sun to reach its full twenty-foot height. Cup-shaped flowers, centered with flashy yellow stamens, bloom first in yellow-green, aging through violet to purple.

No wonder gardeners are scared of morning glories—we've spent far too much time locked in a losing battle with this maddeningly persistent perennial weed. You don't need to worry about—in fact, you'll only want to encourage—these annual vines (*Ipomoea*, sometimes confusingly sold as *Convolvulus*). The nasty perennial weed is really a *Convolvulus aruensis*. *Ipomoea* tricolor 'Flying Saucers' is noninvasive, with large, showy flowers marbled in white and purple-blue; the flowers of *I.* tricolor 'Heavenly Blue' are the color of the sky on a clear day.

As with many familiar annuals, everything old is new again, with a slight twist. *Tropaeolum majus* 'Jewel of Africa' is a climbing nasturtium with cream-marbled leaves and flowers of yellow, red, and peach-pink. You'd never guess that the canary bird vine (*T. peregrinum*) is a nasturtium at all, with its gray-green leaves and bright yellow flowers with fringed petals like tiny birds' wings raised in flight.

These annual vines are colorful, unusual, and often highly fragrant, but the truly delightful thing is that, when sited to receive plenty of sunshine, they grow and bloom like crazy, making you feel like a hugely successful gardener. Which you will be if you plant several of these beauties in early May, and then sit back to enjoy them all season long.

The New Petunias

HERDS OF GARDENERS MILL AROUND NURSERIES in late spring, feverishly choosing tiny starts to fill pots, baskets, and borders with summer color. After our relentlessly soggy winter, no wonder we crave color. When we use annuals only as color spots (or even color swaths), we limit ourselves to traditional "bedding-out" thinking—which is just so limited. New kinds of annuals and tender perennials, with their bold variegated leaves, dramatic blooms, or eye-catching structure, make it easy for us to move far beyond the familiar "blob" and "stripe" concepts of placing annuals. I used to think I was being practical to use mostly perennials because they return year after year—granted that they bloom only for short periods of time. Now I save more than half my gardening budget (the word "budget" is used loosely here, as I never dare to add up how much I spend on the garden) for plants that perform from May through October, the months when I am outside the most.

If you almost recognize some of these flashy new annuals, it's probably because you've seen them or their close relatives used as houseplants, or, if you travel in warmer climates, outdoors. I first saw bougainvillea smothering houses in San Diego; now I buy a plant or two each spring and train its bright blossoms to climb up and cover a bloomed-out wisteria vine. Angels' trumpets (*Brugmansia*) works beautifully as the centerpiece in a large pot, providing height and structure about which to group lower-growing annuals. The Gwyneth Paltrow of the plant world, angels' trumpets are eye-catchingly statuesque, with large, fragrant bells in purple, white, soft yellow, or pale pink. Every time I go to the nursery I seem to find more and different flowering maples (*Abutilon*), a smaller-scale plant with maple-leaf-shaped foliage. Some have foliage spotted or splashed with cream or yellow, others have plain green leaves, but all have flowers in shades of cherry, peach, plum, yellow, or tangerine that attract hummingbirds. Sweet-potato vines, with their large, bold leaves, make a fine change from lobelia or ivy if you want something that will droop down the sides of pots: *Ipomoea batatas* 'Blackie' has dramatically dark lobed leaves, and 'Margarita' has leaves of glowing chartreuse. These really don't work well as vines—they need much more heat than we have to grow well, so they're perfect for spilling over the sides of pots.

Low-growing, with appealing snapdragon-like flowers, *Nemesia fruticans* blooms all summer without deadheading. 'Bluebird' is semi-trailing, with purple-blue flowers; 'Compact Innocence' is white and fragrant. Nemesia blooms heavily all summer in full sun, doesn't need deadheading, and looks great mixed in with other annuals or filling a basket or pot by itself.

The new 'Temari' series of verbenas boast baseball-sized flowers in violet, burgundy, pink, and red. Vigorous and mildew-resistant, they thrive in full or partial sun, not only in containers but also as groundcovers, rooting as they spread about. The more familiar, nearly fluorescently purple *Verbena* 'Homestead Purple' remains one of my favorites, and I fill a large green pot with a mass of it every spring. It keeps going all summer long with just a little deadheading and, if grown in the ground, may well winter over in a mild year.

For scent, choose white heliotrope for its intense fragrance, and night-scented phlox (*Zaluzianskya capensis*), a homely little plant from South Africa, which releases its almond, honey, and vanilla perfume as the sun sets. I never tire of the many choices of starry pelargoniums with those fancy leaves, either. But my favorite new annual is the ruddy orange trailing *Bacopa*, with larger flowers than the more familiar white one.

Even petunias come in new and improved varieties. Pink 'Priscilla' is the only true trailing double-flowered petunia; there is also the single petunia 'Cascadia Yellow-Eye', which grows only nine inches high but spreads two to three feet. No other class of plants offers more bang for the buck, in such astounding variety, as annuals, and early May is the time to get them into the ground or into pots and growing in your garden.

The Great Pretenders

WHEN THE SPRING WARMS UP ENOUGH TO PLANT annuals in mid-May, many gardeners rush to the nursery for basil and tomatoes, but what I hunt for first and most eagerly is a group of plants with nondescript leaves and insignificant flowers. Like the shy child with thick glasses, scented geraniums may give a modest first impression, but their charms run deep. Their variously cut and textured leaves offer up a surprising potpourri of spicy and fruity fragrances. Suffering from a stuffy head? Rub a softly furred leaf of peppermint geranium, give it a good sniff, and your sinuses will clear right up. Drop a leaf of lemon geranium into a cup of hot tea, or enjoy the scent of roses wafting from the leaves of *Pelargonium* 'Little Gem'.

The mynah birds of the plant kingdom, scented geraniums mimic a variety of scents, releasing waves of apple, strawberry, ginger, nutmeg, coconut, apricot, cinnamon, or even chocolate (the warm brown blotch–centered leaves of this last one give a clue as to the scent). Hot sun, hard rain, rubbing fingers, or even the brush of a passing pants leg can waft their perfumes to an appreciative nose. The essential oils in the leaves are plentiful and close to the surface. On especially warm afternoons the aromas saturate the air, so intense as to seemingly soak in through one's pores—no need to even sniff. And the scent seems inexhaustible; there's no reason not to rub scented geranium leaves at every opportunity.

Scented geraniums, like their more familiar cousins that flaunt brightly colored globs of flowers, are in the genus *Pelargonium*. Their flowers are small, and the plants aren't hardy, although they'll overwinter on a sunny windowsill or in a greenhouse. I have to admit this technique has never worked for me, as they grow too leggy, or get whitefly, or both, and need to be tossed out in late fall. But that's okay, because then I get to choose a whole new kitchen shelf of aromas the next summer.

I've often wondered why these unassuming plants engage in such a sensual masquerade. Most are species, although some have been bred to create more unusual fragrances, such as that of after-dinner mints. Scented geraniums are native to South Africa, where they grow in an inhospitably dry and rocky environment and so have been forced to adapt to survive the harsh conditions. This adaptation has taken the form of tricking predators into believing that the plants aren't leafy snacks, but rather ripe strawberries, limes, or prickly roses. Most insects leave them alone, and one author claims that even her goats won't eat the scented ones. Because the leaves closest to the flowers are the most intensely fragrant, this charade plays double duty in also attracting pollinators to the plant.

Give scented geraniums plenty of sun and benign neglect. Adapted to desert conditions, they prefer under- to overwatering. They dislike wet soil, shade, and night temperatures below 40°F. Planted into garden beds or borders, they tend to disappear, outshone by flashier companions. Their perfumes and subtle beauty are best enjoyed when they're planted in pots and set around on outdoor tables or deck rails. Keep them in smallish pots—they bloom best when roots are cramped. It's fun to try out new fragrances each season, since different types vary widely in their potency, leaf texture, and flower color. But there are a few scenteds that I buy every year and grow in little pots lining the porch: *P. crispum* with its lemon scent and pale pink flowers, *P. tomentosum* for its sinus-clearing hit of peppermint, and *P. torento* for its gingery leaves and large lavender flowers.

Now in Bloom: May

1
Ornamental onions
(Allium spp.)

I can't think of any plant that creates such a spectacle in so little space as ornamental onions. They bloom dependably each year, adding height and flamboyance to the late-May garden. Hummingbirds and bees flock to them, while deer and squirrels leave them alone. Their cultural requirements are simple but essential: sun and good drainage. All you need worry about is finding the room to get those big bulbs into the ground, and in the spring they'll make their way up between perennials, shrubs, and groundcovers to bloom above the fray. Alliums are not only showstoppers during bloom, but dry to starry buff-colored spheres that give texture and structure to the garden all summer long. *A. christophii* has foot-high stalks and huge blooms packed with up to eighty star-shaped florets. *A. giganteum* grows nearly five feet high, topped with cantaloupe-sized blooms in rich purple-violet.

2
Euphorbia griffithii
'Fireglow'

Nearly three feet high, with showy flower heads of bright orange-red, this euphorbia provides an unexpectedly strong color in early May. Its brightness accents the pastels of springtime, such as chartreuse lady's mantle or creamy tulips, or the yellow variegated ornamental grass *Carex morrowii.* It is easy to grow, drought tolerant, and not fussy about soil. The vividness of its blossoms fades slowly to a dusky orange that blends well with the coppery pink of *Sedum* 'Autumn Joy' or the bronze leatherleaf sedge, *Carex buchananii.*

3
Solomon's seal
(*Polygonatum hybridum*)

Solomon's seal is a graceful harbinger of early summer, with arched stems (to three feet high) and dangling flowers that last a week in a vase and months in the garden. It disappears completely over the winter, and can spread about quite widely, but it's worth growing for its greenish white bells and shiny green foliage. It prefers moist, woodsy soil and consorts well with hostas and ferns. I grow a large cluster on a hillside beneath a Japanese maple, as a dramatic backdrop to pink tree peonies.

4
Daphne genkwa

For a full month from late April through May, this small shrub (to four feet) graces the spring garden with bloom. The intense lilac color of its numerous tubular flowers makes up for the faintness of its perfume, and the soft green leaves, gray stems, and graceful habit carry on through the summer months. Underplanted with orange ranunculus and yellow narcissus, it creates a vivid spring show; it pairs well with *Spiraea japonica* 'Magic Carpet' all season long, and looks especially good when grown against a dark green background of yew or other hedging plants.

3

4

june

No-Fuss Roses

ROSE FEVER GRIPS GARDENERS IN EARLY SPRING. I bet that even the most sophisticated gardeners, those who pride themselves on growing half-dead-looking tiny
brown-leafed plants, succumb to a craving for roses. I've rarely visited a garden
without a single rose (although I'm down to only about five). There is something
about the texture of the petals, the shape, and the fragrance that is so archetypal as
to render us helpless. How else to explain the fact that a piece of blatant sentimen-
tality like "God made memory so that we have roses in summer and mothers forever" strikes us a profound truth? Substitute "hostas" or "daylilies" for "roses" in that
sentence, and your lip will curl in disgust . . . but with roses, we fall for it.
Hermès, however, may have gone too far with its $645 rose clippers with red
leather handles.

Although we pride ourselves on gardening in a horticultural paradise here in the
Northwest, the sad truth is that our climate is not ideal for roses. Our summers are
short and mild, our winters wet. Roses too often develop black spot and mildew,
telling us clearly that these are not the conditions they relish. Most need a heavy
diet of water, fertilizer, and chemical sprays to look good. Are there roses that
flourish here without such interventions?

PREVIOUS PAGE: *The pond in the back garden
is 8 x 13 feet, providing an open space and focal
point amid the profusion of plantings. Later in
the summer, water lily leaf and flower cover the
surface of the pond so thickly that it is nearly
impossible to see the many goldfish, except when
they jump and play in the spray of the fountain.*

LEFT: *Glass Christmas tree balls serve double
duty floating in the pond. Come winter, before
the water freezes, I'll wash off the pond scum and
hang them on the tree.*

Even before my Scottie died, I was leaning toward organic gardening, eliminating
powders and sprays from my garden shed.
It was partly that nasty chemical smell, but
also because I could no longer make out
any of the instructions without my reading
glasses. I was impatient with all the careful
mixing, the wearing of special gloves, the
complicated rules for disposal.

After the little dog died a prolonged
death from eating rose systemic (he
always had his nose into everything, but

what a price to pay for greediness!), I got rid of all the chemicals. I felt guilty, of course, because I had dug in the rose systemic and then several days later had mindlessly strewn over the top a dog-attracting cocktail of manure, bone meal, and blood meal. Rain mixed the two, and proved lethal. I had no idea, until I helplessly watched the Scottie suffer convulsions and die, what it really was that I was putting on my plants.

Of all the fussy plants I no longer try to grow, the only kind I miss are roses. After one sprayless season of black spot and mildew, I tossed out all the hybrid teas. I have gradually added back some old-fashioned shrub roses, with mixed success. A recent spring was the true test—month after month of rainy weather, continuing into July, produced disease even on the most resistant of roses.

All I'm looking for are roses that will stay healthy and robust in our damp and variable climate without any spraying, will mix happily with other plantings (not too large and not too particular about crowding), and will thrive with only regular watering, yearly pruning, and plentiful manure. I don't expect any rose to be care-free, just chemical-free. And fragrant, of course.

A few years ago local gardeners were excited about David Austin roses, also known as English roses. Many combine old-fashioned fragrance and shape with fluffy flowers that bloom all summer long. Like a hybrid tea, but better. However, I've had to dig out and dispose of nearly every one I've tried because of leggy bareness and disease problems. They just don't seem to like our climate. I've been advised that there are several English roses worth trying to grow without spray, especially 'Moonbeam' (white), 'Peach Blossom', and the soft pink 'Lucetta'. Some of the less popular English roses seem most trouble free, such as 'Shropshire Lass' and 'Windflower'. But there's a reason these haven't proven popular—usually it's their smaller, single flowers or their trait of blooming only once each season.

The roses that meet my criterion of thriving sans spraying compose a much smaller palette, and they all belong to the less-glamorous categories. Rugosa roses are endlessly tough and accommodating; I particularly prize the intensely fragrant white 'Blanc Double de Coubert'. Rugosas have beautiful foliage and bright fruits in autumn, but they are large and spreading, so they're difficult to grow in borders. They work well as a hedge, or as a backdrop to perennials in larger borders. The 'Pavement' series of rugosas, introduced from Canada in the late 1990s, should be easier to mix into borders, since they grow only two and a half to four feet tall. Look for the lavender-pink 'Foxy' or the bold pink 'Showy Pavement'.

Rosa glauca, a species rose with soft-pink, single flowers, uniquely colored blue foliage, and bright red fruits, seems to be impervious to disease. So do the simple old alba roses such as *R.* 'Alba Semiplena' (white) and 'Great Maiden's Blush' (pink). A rose I particularly love, whose dark foliage not only looks healthy all summer but is nearly evergreen in my garden all winter, is R. 'Mutabilis', or the butterfly rose. Its flowers change from cream to butterscotch to watermelon, blooming repeatedly in different stages of coloration. It is said that nearly evergreen roses are most often not truly hardy, but I've seen many large and healthy specimens of *Rosa* 'Mutabilis.' I think it is worth a try.

'Town and Country' roses, a series from Denmark, are proving disease-free in our climate. They are small and spreading—almost groundcover roses. You might also try musk roses of all types, for disease resistance and a long bloom period. 'Cornelia' is a lovely soft apricot. I grow 'Penelope', which is peachy-buff, a dependable repeat bloomer, and quite fragrant. It had some black spot last summer, but the flowers were so spectacular that I'm giving it a second chance. I'm also giving my current terrier—who, like her predecessor loves nosing around the garden—a good chance to live to a ripe old age.

A Pattern Language for Gardeners

I'M ALWAYS TRYING TO FIGURE OUT what it is that makes a garden so beguiling I'm tempted to settle in, take a nap, and come back again soon. Why is it that some gardens both entice and satisfy, while others, no matter how lovely, don't lure you to linger? This level of comfort has little to do with plant choice, and nothing to do with the size of the garden or how much money went into its creation. I've come to believe that certain garden elements are archetypal, so deeply rooted in our natures that they make us feel instantly at home.

This pondering sent me back to a book I'd read years ago, a standard in design and architecture classes, called *A Pattern Language* by Christopher Alexander. In more than 1,200 pages Alexander expounds upon his thesis that people can and should design their own houses, streets, and communities. He believes that most of the wonderful places of the world have been made not by architects but by local citizens themselves. The core concept is that we rely on certain patterns to create coherent design, and these patterns function as a language that enables us to communicate and express design ideas. A few of the patterns that Alexander recommends for the home include deep windowsills, bedrooms facing east, alcoves, window seats, fireside corners, an open kitchen, and bay windows. He believes these patterns are based on human instincts and are the answer to all design problems.

Why wouldn't the concept of an archetypal pattern language hold true for gardens as well? There are certain specific elements we instinctively look for and treasure outside as well as indoors, and working with these patterns is the basis for all good garden design. Just as we love to curl up in a cushioned window seat or draw a chair up to a warm fireside, so do we enjoy passing beneath the dappled shade of a vine-draped arbor. Some garden patterns that seem to me to offer universal appeal are garden gates, white arbors covered in pink roses, mossy stones, private courtyards, curving pathways, pairs of Adirondack chairs, still ponds, and covered porches—we seek such elements in every garden we enter, and relax when we find them.

Successful gardens give a sense of enclosure and passage, shelter and solitude. The elements that provide these are the pattern language of gardens, a language that many gardeners speak instinctively. The archetypal nature of these elements transcends any specific style of design. You can have a sleek metal gate, or you can have a white wooden gate in a picket fence—the point is to make a clear transition between worlds, to both divide and enclose, while allowing a glimpse of what rests inside. The pleasure comes not from the style of gate, but from passing through it and hearing it click shut behind you.

The idea of passage provides many more kinds of opportunities in the form of pathways, pergolas, and bridges. These are potent linking elements that contribute to the mood and movement of a garden. Crossing over a bridge, even just a small arch from one side of a stream to the other, gives a sense of completing a journey. Alexander makes the point that people enjoy moving toward light; think of the satisfactions of walking through a shaded pergola to emerge into open sunlight at the far end.

Inspiration and ideas enough to shape an entire garden come from creating the reasons and places for these patterns. Although you may add such elements to your garden as poetic or symbolic gestures, they need to be substantive and sturdy design elements with a clear reason to exist. Fashioning a stream for a bridge to span, carving out a shady corner for a bench, or dividing the garden into rooms as an excuse to build gates or arbors results in a garden that pleases the eye as well as comforts the soul.

Pretty in Pink

DIANA VREELAND, LONGTIME EDITOR OF *VOGUE*, famously declared, "Pink is the navy blue of India." She was onto the fact that pink works as a neutral—and that's as true in the world of gardening as in fashion. Just as a pale pink mohair sweater outrageously flatters the complexion, so do soft shades of pink bring out the best in all the deep, dark shades of garden green, from yew to rhododendron leaves.

Paradoxically, though, after orange flowers, gardeners seem to dislike pink the most. "I try to avoid pink"—I've heard that a hundred times, and I've never understood why. Typical of easy-to-grow flowers like foxglove, bleeding heart, and carnations, pink perhaps seems too common to cultivate. Or maybe those who disdain pink have in mind searing shades of magenta or, worse yet, those fleshy pinks found in *Diascia* or some of the astrantias. It is easy to avoid these extremes and stick to the whole lovely range of pinks that fall in between. Think of baby pink, the palest stripes in a sunrise, the color of bubble gum or strawberry ice cream, the washy pink of sweet peas. What's to dislike?

Clear, soft pinks can be mixed with nearly anything in the garden—even with oranges in the apricot range and reds that veer toward ruby. Pink with gray-foliaged plants is a time-tested combination; pink roses underplanted with lacy silver artemisia is a classic. Lest pink appear old-fashioned, think about how artfully it plays off dark-foliaged plants like smokebush (*Cotinus*), or how it blends with burgundy in the variegated barberry *Berberis thunbergii* 'Rose Glow'. Pink associates easily with most any shade of blue. Right outside my front door, from midsummer until the first hard frost, I enjoy the intense combination of hot-pink *Gaura lindheimeri* 'Siskiyou Pink' tangling through willowy sky-blue *Salvia uliginosa*. The two positively glow beneath autumn skies, giving a jolt to the changing season that's far more arresting and unusual than the reds and purples so typical of the late garden.

The long-blooming pinks of *Rosa* 'Fairy' or 'Ballerina', or of *Lavatera* 'Barnsley', are vivid enough to hold their own with the chartreuse greens of late spring yet cool enough to soften the hotter golds and oranges of midsummer, and they will still please the eye as they play up the rich tints of autumn leaves.

If pale pinks seem too pallid, you might remember a couple of tricks to using the brighter pinks—worth trying, since nothing gives a garden a jolt like a real hit of hot pink. First, forgo the blue-tinged pinks (they always look a little off to me, as if they're a bit seasick). The warmer pinks blend better with other colors; the aster 'Alma Potschke' is an example of this warm, bright shade of watermelon, as is the pink trim on the variegated leaf of the groundcover *Houttuynia cordata* 'Chameleon'. Its little leaf swirled with buttery yellow, warm green and vivid watermelon enlivens and enhances just about any color it is put next to. (Nothing's perfect—*Houttuynia* can be invasive in wet soils.)

The second trick in selecting bright-pink flowers is to look for those whose own foliage accommodatingly provides a foil for their intense color. The magenta of *Lychnis coronaria* is softened by its silver foliage; the shocking pink of the dahlia 'Fantasy' is soothed by its deep, nearly black leaves. If dazzling rather than soothing is what you seek, go for plants with the built-in flamboyance of pink flowers combined with yellow foliage, such as *Spiraea japonica* 'Goldflame' or *Lamium maculatum* 'Aureum'. You might want to use these sparingly, perhaps as an accent to evergreens. The combination of yellow and hot pink in a single plant burns up Vreeland's dictum that pink is a neutral, while providing flamboyant color to animate all those soft, soothing, easily placed midrange pinks.

Cheap Thrills

PERENNIALS HAVE BEEN THE BIG DEAL IN GARDENING CIRCLES for nearly a decade, while annuals have been ignored, if not scorned. Perennials have character, but they bloom for such a short time, and they need lots of work, such as dividing and cutting back. Now the buzz is all about temp-perennials. It has become not only okay, but garden-forward, to grow petunias, impatiens, coleus, and geraniums.

"Temp-perennial" is a newly coined word, seen as a necessary step in ridding gardeners of their feelings of prejudice against boring old annuals. Years ago (and sometimes still today), lozenge-shaped beds of low-growing annuals were considered the height of fashionable bedding out. Such displays, most frequent in public gardens, are enough to curb anyone's enthusiasm for annuals.

Thank goodness most planting schemes have loosened up over the years. The name of the game is mixing everything, and it is fashionable to be garish. Planting beds now hold mixes of annuals, hardy perennials, vegetables, and foliage plants, some in the ground and some in pots. Many plants that we think of as houseplants can be put right into beds and borders, such as elephant ear (*Caladium*) and tropical gingers, their huge leaves effective from spring to first freeze. And don't forget to mix up the colors, too. Yellow, pink, purple, magenta, and orange; cosmos, nicotiana, marigolds—both the eye and the brain need to adjust to such aesthetic abandon. The abundant use of silver, chartreuse, and variegated foliage softens the profusion. Pom-pom dahlias mingle with perennials; petunias are planted en masse as groundcover; and vegetables and herbs thrive amidst the flowers.

Excitement is created by ignoring the old conventions—annuals in pots, houseplants indoors, and vegetables in a separate patch. But what is the difference between annuals and temp-perennials, or is one just a new term for the other? It turns out we in the Northwest weren't first with this idea—Pierre Benerrup of Sunny Border Nursery in Connecticut invented the term temp-perennial.

In contrast to perennials, which come back every year even though they may die to the ground in winter, true annuals are plants that are programmed to live just one season. A spiderflower (*Cleome*) dies at the end of the season whether you live in Alaska or Florida. No amount of digging it up and bringing it inside before frost will extend its lifetime; it is a true annual that flowers and then dies. Tender perennials, or temp-perennials, are defined as plants that would continue to thrive if grown in a warmer climate; they die only because they can't survive freezing temperatures. Our Northwest perennials are annuals to a Vermont gardener; our "annuals" are hardy in Hawaii. Confusion results because most plants sold here as annuals, such as geraniums, coleus, and begonias, are truly tender perennials.

Both annuals and tender perennials give cheap thrills in the garden. Fast-growing and long-blooming, they transform the garden dramatically in a short period of time. Our sense of seasonality is reinforced by plants that grow quickly, look spectacular, and bloom all summer, as opposed to the two-or-three-week flowering period of most perennials. The showy (some would say gaudy) patterns of coleus, the overblown leaves of canna lilies, the demanding yellow of marigolds—all would be too much if static. These are plants to play with. They bloom their heads off all summer long, and then you simply collect seed, take a cutting, overwinter them in the garage, or compost them and start over in spring.

Hosta Fever

A FRIEND ONCE TOLD ME ABOUT how, moving to a new house as a beginning gardener, she ripped out dozens of hostas, thinking them stodgy old-lady plants. In subsequent years, she has paid dearly in cash and labor by replanting them.

To some people, hostas resemble old-fashioned hoop skirts, and for others they bring to mind shady gardens surrounding old Southern mansions. Few plants, however, are so aggressively bred and marketed. The names of hosta cultivars are certainly up to date (or maybe just weird). How about 'Striptease', with violet flowers and white-striped leaves; 'Red Neck Heaven', whose white flowers are echoed in the white undersides of its leaves; or 'Abba Dabba Do', whose four-foot spread of yellow-trimmed foliage must have reminded someone of the Flintstones?

I lost my better judgment this spring and paid the expensive price typical of the newer cultivars for 'Guacamole'. I was seduced by its chartreuse leaves with deep green margins and by the promise of large, fragrant flowers. Its foliage is remaining unchewed—hostas with thick, ribbed leaves are the least attractive to slugs. I'm hoping it will fluff out to its promised two-foot width to fill a shady corner, where its bright leaves look as though they're illuminated by a ray of sunshine even on cloudy days.

Few genera of plants are so easy to recognize. Has anyone ever mistaken a hosta for something else? Despite this general uniformity of appearance, hostas range in size from the two-inch-high 'Tiny Tears' to the golden, Goliath-sized 'Sum and Substance'. To describe one of the giant hostas as showy is like saying a drowning person's skin is moist; each leaf can be two feet across, and a single clump can spread six feet wide.

Hosta foliage comes in scores of shades of green, gold, and blue, many with white and cream variegations, and in dozens of textures. Leaves can be slickly smooth, or rippled as if skimmed by a breeze, or they can resemble puckered seersucker or wide-wale corduroy.

Until my recent slide down the slippery slope of hosta cravings, I grew only a couple of kinds, including the hunky blue-leaved cultivar 'Krossa Regal', which creates a big puddle of cool in the midst of the border. My favorite of all hostas is the Chinese species *H. plantaginea,* which can take warmth and sun and has shiny green leaves. In form and color it is one of those quintessential yet unremarkable hostas—until it unfurls its spectacularly fragrant six-inch white flowers in August. Newer cultivars combine flashy foliage with sweet scent, as hosta breeders are currently emphasizing flowers and fragrance as well as foliage.

Most hostas do best in light-dappled shade cast by a pergola or a high tree canopy. Yellow-leafed hostas and those with yellow variegation take the most sun, while white-variegated cultivars need more shade. Blue-leafed plants will fade in bright sun. If you have more sunshine than shade, make sure your hostas have plenty of water. They like rich, moist soil, and a diet of compost and manure; the larger types are the greediest. Hostas do well in pots, and their leaves and flowers are ideal for flower arrangements. But wait until mid-June to cut hosta leaves—earlier in the season they'll just flop over in the vase.

There are few such welcome sights in spring as the plump points of hostas pushing up out of the earth. These tightly wrapped shoots are not just slug food—hostas are edible for humans as well. Young leaves, shoots, and flowers are delicious in salads and with dips, tasting like lettuce or asparagus.

To learn more about hostas, or to choose from more than two hundred different kinds, order a catalog from world-famous hosta fancier Tony Avent. Included are color photos, descriptions, and a chart organized by characteristics, such as gold edges or fragrant flowers. Plant Delights Nursery, Inc., 9241 Sauls Road, Raleigh, NC 27603; (919) 772-4794; www.plantdel.com. Catalog price is ten stamps or a box of chocolates (no kidding).

Sweet Scents and Stinky Essences

HAVE YOU EVER VISITED A FRIEND'S HOUSE for the first time and right away noticed some really interesting art on the walls, or a great overstuffed purple couch, so that on first glance you are drawn in? And then pretty quickly realized that there is no teakettle on the stove, and that the couch lacks extra pillows and an afghan? It is not the kind of house where you long to linger. That is exactly how I feel about a garden without fragrance. It may have great plants, but without the olfactory stimulation, why stick around? No number of elegant stone pavers or hot new cultivars makes up for the fact that when you draw in a deep breath there's no perfume from lily-of-the-valley or lilacs.

And just as a house in winter needs soup on the stove and lighted candles, and in summer needs open windows and bare floors, there are scents for every season in the garden. The fragrances of winter, such as sarcococca's strong scent of vanilla or the astringent sweetness of witch hazel, are perhaps the most welcome of all as they are borne on icy air. The scents of spring are more gentle—miniature narcissus and wisteria—appropriate to warm breezes. Of course, summer is the crescendo, with roses, lilies, sweet peas, and heliotrope, while in fall the lavish fragrances of tea olive (*Osmanthus* x *fortunei*) and the sweet autumn clematis compete with the brilliance of red and golden leaves. Fragrance is a year-round prospect in our encouraging gardening climate.

I always expect old-fashioned plants like lilacs and roses to be sweet-smelling, and it is true that they all used to be. Increasingly, as hybridizers have bred larger-flowered, newly colored, or especially long-blooming cultivars, fragrance has fallen by the wayside. These oversized, gaudy specimens may impress visually, but their essence has been left behind in the laboratory. Old-fashioned roses, with their scent of cold cream, and the antique varieties of sweet peas, such as 'Cupid' or 'Jet Set Mixed', are well worth searching out.

Why are some plants so fragrant? They are, of course, versatile chemical factories, producing a wide array of smells—only some of which are desirable in the garden, no matter how useful they may be to the plant. Odors either attract pollinators or repel predators, thus ensuring plant survival. During the course of evolution, the scents of flowering plants became geared to insects that evolved at the same time so as to enlist the insects' help with pollination. (How to lure the insects? Advertise the food available with an odor.) Whether you want to grow the plant in your garden depends on which kind of creature it evolved to attract.

Skunk cabbages are pollinated by flies, so they emit volatile substances that are evil-smelling to our noses but attractive to carrion-loving flies. Of great interest to small boys are carnivorous plants, which attract their prey with nasty smells. The American pitcher plant beckons to flies with its mousy scent, and then poisons them to make capture and digestion an easier process.

Particularly sweet-smelling flowers such as honeysuckle, stock, and flowering tobacco attract night-flying insects. Plant them by your open bedroom window, and enjoy their nighttime scents along with the moths. Fortunately, the odors attractive to most pollinators are the same odors agreeable to humans. As a matter of fact, the preferences of the honeybee are about the same as ours, as is the bee's threshold for detecting scent. The pungent, clear-out-your-sinuses aromatics of scented geraniums, lavender, and rosemary are due to the essential oils in the leaves, designed to deter leaf-eating predators—which is why herb gardens have so few pest problems.

Perhaps we too have evolved in tandem with the various scents of the plant world, and from this primitiveness stems the fact that smell is the most evocative of all the senses. People recall the smells of remembered childhood gardens, the scents of a warm summer's day, much more vividly than memories of specific plants. Whenever I smell the spicy sweetness of pinks, I feel again the helpless jealousy of a young child. My big sister's garden plot seemed always to be filled with delicately striped, exquisite pinks. How I coveted their clove-scented perfection, as I tried to weed between the stinky marigolds I'd hastily chosen early in the season. I still don't grow pinks; thirty-five years later, they remain tainted with envy.

Scent evokes strong emotion. Fragrance, in all its manifestations, is the quickest route to a sensuous garden. As you put on the teakettle and plump up the couch cushions, don't forget to pot up some heliotrope for the front porch and add a few Oriental lilies to the borders.

Celebrated Climbers

THE ONLY CONTROVERSY OVER CLEMATIS is its pronunciation. Gardeners fret about how to say its name, but my Webster's unabridged dictionary reassures with just one choice—"klem e tis," with the accent on the first syllable. The other pronunciation, which rhymes with "lattice," sounds pretentious to American ears anyway.

That settled, we can get on to the wonders of this diverse genus of woody climbers. Some have flowers nearly as big as a Frisbee (*C.* 'Nelly Moser'), others are vigorous enough to festoon a tall tree with their starry flowers (*C. montana*), still others are shrubby (*C. integrifolia*). The easiest, most versatile clematis have smaller flowers, often in the shape of delicate bells, followed by fluffy seed heads (*C. viticella, C. tangutica, C. macropetala*). You can find modestly sized hardy and disease-free clematis to bloom from spring through late autumn (*C. alpina* are some of the earliest; the soft yellow flowers of *C. rehderiana* linger late). Best of all, you can grow them up other plants to create surprising layers and new seasons of bloom (roses and clematis are a classic combo) without worrying about smothering the host. *C. integrifolia* 'Durandii' has indigo-blue flowers and a floppy enough habit to serve as a groundcover. *C. viticella* is great growing over winter-flowering heathers; when the heather flowers have faded, the vines take over the show.

The large-flowered varieties, gorgeous as they are, bring with them the heart-break of clematis wilt. It has happened too often; buds swell and stretch along the vines, raising my hopes. Then snow-white flowers (*C.* 'Wada's Primrose', for example) open to their full eight-inch span, revealing a fluff of yellow stamens. They are dazzling, and I go out to admire them several times a day. Overnight, buds and flowers collapse and shrivel to black ribbons. Thank goodness, small-flowered clematis, which are impervious to this fungal disease, are blooming their heads off elsewhere in the garden, or it would be too discouraging.

Clematis aren't difficult if their quite specific needs are met, and this is the only way to prevent wilt. It is best to plant them in spring, but they can be transplanted from containers at any time as long as you give them plenty of water. Before planting, cut the stem back to twelve inches (necessary to prevent breakage and promote branching) and soak the root ball in a bucket of water for a few minutes. Dig a nice big hole, mix rich organic matter with the original soil, and set the crown of the plant about three inches below the line of the soil. The most important thing to remember about clematis is that the roots want to stay cool and moist, while the vine and flowers need heat and sun. So plant in a nice, sunny spot, but keep the roots protected with a mulch of little stones or overplant with shallow-rooted groundcovers like artemisia or hardy geraniums. Provide support, manure in late winter, water weekly, and they will thrive beyond any reasonable expectations.

Pruning can be as intimidating as pronunciation, with whole chapters of some garden books devoted to a bewildering set of detailed instructions. It really is as easy as paying attention to when each plant flowers. Vines that bloom early should have all weak or dead stems cut out after flowering. The clematis that bloom in summer and fall should be cut back in late winter. Just clean them up; *C. montana* and *C. macropetala* don't need much pruning. Encourage branching by pinching back whenever you think of it. If your clematis is leggy or overgrown, as can happen with vines that flower each year on new wood, such as *C. tangutica* or *C. x jackmanii*, cut them back a foot or two from the ground. Because a couple of bird's nests were hidden in its snarls, I didn't cut back the yellow bells of my *C. tangutica* last year, and by autumn it had enshrouded three entire lilacs. This year it has already been chopped back to a few feet from the ground to remind it of its manners.

Fragrant Favorites with Humble Roots

SWEET PEAS PERSONIFY (flowerify?) the contradictions inherent in gardening. These most fragrant of flowers have a voracious appetite. Their silken pastel ruffles grow out of a trench dug in the mucky ground of late winter and filled with rich, stinky manure. Here in the Northwest, it is traditional to plant sweet peas (*Lathyrus odoratus*) on Washington's Birthday. I usually wait until early March, or even a little later, in hopes of drier weather. The seeds can, of course, be started indoors, but I never fuss with them that way.

If you get your sweet pea seeds into the ground before the equinox, you'll have flowers by mid-June. My sister and I, both June babies, have long marked our birthdays by when the sweet peas bloom. The best thing about sweet peas is that the more you pick, the longer they flower. If you keep filling your house with their brightly colored bouquets and heady fragrance, your plants will bloom through August.

There are three tricks to growing glorious sweet peas: choosing the right type of seed, preparing the soil, and providing support for the vines. The colors of sweet peas are as fresh as a new box of watercolor paints. From deep plum through red, pink, cream, and white (breeders are still working on yellow), each seems freshly washed. All the shades harmonize, so it makes sense to buy mixed seeds, but the single colors are hard to resist: 'Elizabeth Taylor' (the color of their namesake's eyes); 'Firecrest', a deep scarlet with a touch of orange; or midnight-blue 'Pluto'.

The large, floriferous Spencer type, also called modern sweet peas, were first found growing in the Earl of Spencer's garden at Althorp, Northamptonshire, at the turn of the twentieth century. (My son cringes at the thought that he was named after a flower. He wasn't—I wouldn't have dared.) The Spencers are popular for the size of their frilled blossoms and for their array of colors. But with showiness has come loss of fragrance; Spencers vary in their perfume. Old-fashioned sweet peas are reliably and profoundly fragrant, albeit with smaller flowers. Though many of the old-fashioned sweet peas have been lost over the years (300 varieties were available in the early 1900s), many seed catalogs now have a selection.

Pat Sherman, of Fragrant Garden Nursery in Canby, Oregon, offers a splendid assortment of English sweet peas, many available for the first time in the United States. She suggests planting one-third old-fashioned sweet peas, for their perfume, and two-thirds Spencers, for their long stems and big blooms. (Fragrant Garden Nursery puts out a free catalog: P.O. Box 627, Canby, OR 97013; fax 503-266-2804.)

Sweet peas like sun, air circulation, and deep, enriched soil. Dig soil two spades' worth deep, or to eighteen inches, adding generous amounts of manure. (To quote an old book on sweet pea culture, "It is said to be difficult to over-manure for sweet peas.") Like any other vining plant, sweet peas need support. Fences, trellises, or a wigwam of sticks at the back of the border all work. They can be grown through shrubs or twining with other vines. There are even dwarf types like 'Bijou' or 'Snoopea' that need no supports. Sweet peas grow happily in large pots; restrain yourself to four or five plants per pot to provide adequate room for greedy roots.

I bought one of those tall wrought-iron obelisks from a garden center, wound it with fine black (nearly invisible) netting, stuck it in the ground outside my study window, and planted sweet pea seeds around its base. In summer their perfume drifts through the open window, and I look out at my garden through a veil of sweet peas.

Now in Bloom: June

1

Spiraea japonica
'Magic Carpet'

The red-tipped yellow leaves of this ideal small mounding shrub come on early to accent spring bulbs and retain color until late autumn. The pinkish purple flower clusters open in early June and bloom all summer. Only two feet high by at least as wide, it can serve as a groundcover or a front-of-the-border plant, mixes beautifully with alliums or dark-leafed perennials, and seems to thrive just about anywhere but in serious shade. While all the books advise growing spiraea in well-drained soil, I have one planted in damp clay, and it is blooming its head off and spreading its leaves out to embrace the hot-pink *Gaura* growing up through it.

1

2

2

Japanese snowbell
(Styrax japonica)

In contrast to early-blooming crabapples and plums, Japanese snowbell flowers in June, when you are out in the garden to enjoy it. Be sure to plant this graceful little tree where you can walk beneath its spreading branches to fully appreciate the dangling, sweetly scented little white bells. A deciduous tree whose branches grow naturally into graceful horizontal layers, the Japanese snowbell needs summer irrigation and thrives in sun or partial shade. I grow it to further shade hydrangeas and hostas (both of which match its need for summer water nicely) on the north side of the house, with a mauvey-blue *Clematis macropetala* 'Blue Bird' threading through its branches.

3
Mock orange
(Philadelphus)

This beloved old-fashioned shrub remains a star of the June garden. Its clean white flowers last for nearly a month, wafting their intense perfume for long distances. Plant it at the back of a border, where, once out of bloom, it will provide a pleasant green backdrop for perennials. I grow *P.* 'Dame Blanche', a double-flowered, compact (to six feet) shrub, in my wild garden, where it is highlighted by the spiky shape and variegation of *Scrophularia auriculata* 'Variegata'.

4
Hosta
'Guacamole'

One of the newer, flashier hostas, 'Guacamole' boasts chartreuse leaves irregularly margined in deep green, and large, fragrant flowers. Like other hostas, it is attractive from the minute its fat pointed nose emerges from the ground in early spring until the leaves turn yellow in October. It grows to two feet in width, spreading wide leaves to illuminate a dark corner or enliven an all-green border. Its foliage is sufficiently ribbed to discourage all but the hungriest slugs, and the variegation and breadth of its leaves make a fine display in flower arrangements.

4

july

Casablancas and Golden Angels

"Lilies, comprising as they do some of the most stately and beautiful of garden flowers, are not nearly so much grown in gardens as their beauty deserves."

—GERTRUDE JEKYLL

THIS LAMENTATION IS EVERY BIT AS TRUE TODAY as it was when Jekyll, doyenne of English garden writers, first uttered it in 1901. Have you ever seen—or can you even imagine—a garden with too many lilies? Lilies are always a welcome sight: exotic as orchids, with exquisite color, shape, and scent. Best of all, lilies are the most rewarding and easiest of plants for the beginning gardener. Plant the bulb in November and feel like a wizard eight months later when a tall, glamorous trumpet flower graces your garden. The only time a lily will break your heart is when, on a drizzly morning, you find that a slug has slimed its way up the stem and eaten out the heart of the flower.

Many plants are pretenders to the mystique of the "lily" name: daylily (*Hemerocallis*), plantain lily (*Hosta*), calla lily (*Zantedeschia*), foxtail lily (*Eremus*), water lily, and lily-of-the-Nile (*Agapanthus*); there are more than thirty-five different false lilies. True lilies, native to Asia, Europe, and North America, are herbaceous perennials that grow from fat bulbs.

The formula for growing lilies is simple: plant the bulbs in deep, well-drained soil, with coolness and shade at the roots and sun or filtered shade for the flowers, and provide ample water year-round. Jekyll suggests planting lilies amidst shrubs, hostas, and ferns, to clothe the base of the stems and to provide support: "If they are tied up to stakes the variously

PREVIOUS PAGE: *The north side of the garden used to be a bleak expanse of ratty lawn and leggy rhododendrons. By midsummer it is nearly impossible to follow the pavers from front to back garden through the hydrangeas, asters, and Japanese anemones.*

LEFT: *I keep a wall vase by the front door filled with flowers in summer and foliage in winter. Cut hydrangeas, monkshood, daylilies, and Persian ivy stay fresh longer in cooler outdoor temperatures than when brought inside.*

and diversely graceful natural movements of lilies is necessarily lost . . . as is the naturally dignified and yet dainty poise of the whole plant." So, lest your lilies lose their dignity, try growing them through a clump of senecio or in amongst roses, and remember to plant at least three bulbs close together for a stand of lilies, rather than one spindly stem.

Asiatic hybrids bloom earliest and multiply rapidly, but unfortunately carry little or no fragrance. Many have appealing, up-facing flowers, with freckles or delicate shadings. 'Strawberry Vanilla Latte' is a double-flowered red swirled with creamy white; 'Sugar Bear' blooms in late May and early June, with ivory flowers and short stems ideal for growing in pots. The dramatic and sweetly fragrant trumpet and Aurelian lilies bloom in midsummer. Their names are almost as beguiling as the nodding trumpets themselves: 'Black Dragon', growing to eight feet in shades of pink, white, and maroon; multicolored 'Seventy-Six Trombones'; and the glowing 'Golden Angel'.

The spicy-scented Orientals are the Lexus of lilies, blooming later into July and August. They grow as high as six feet, bearing dinner-plate-sized flowers, in a fantasy of colors. Last summer I came home from vacation on Guemes Island, the southern-most of the San Juan Islands, to water my garden, and found that the 'Casablanca' lilies had burst into shimmery white bloom. I was going back up to the island that evening and couldn't bear to leave them all behind, so cut one ten-inch flower to take with me. The scent of the flower in the car was so intoxicating I feared I'd be pulled over for driving while on lily perfume. The old word "swoon" is the only one that describes what happened that evening, when the entire little cabin was heavy with the scent. If I wrote magic realism, I would tell you of the amazing dreams we all dreamt that night in an old cabin infused with the smell of a giant white lily flower.

Bringing Summer Indoors

SUMMER FLOWER ARRANGING IS AS EASY AS STEPPING OUTSIDE your back door and clipping whatever is at hand, or arranging prunings from the morning's gardening. The downside of such plenitude is that many midsummer flowers are so big and gaudy you can end up with a vase full of stars, unsupported by character actors or bit players. When each individual blossom is so distinctive, colors and forms too often clash—think of a dinner party where each guest is a self-satisfied celebrity intent on hogging the attention. You don't want to create such a disaster at your table, or in your vases.

Avoid mixed bouquets when arranging summer showboats like roses, lilies, sunflowers, dahlias, and hydrangeas—they look best by themselves. Think of a tall blue vase filled with golden sunflowers, a glass pitcher holding snowy 'Casablanca' lilies, or an open bowl filled with water on which a single waxy, lemon-scented *Magnolia grandiflora* blossom floats. Nothing could be less intimidating to put together, or more evocative of summer. And the roses! You don't need to grow classic, long-stemmed hybrid teas for cutting. A single multiheaded spray of *R.* 'Penelope' or 'Ballerina' is a bouquet all by itself, with roses in all stages of development from tightly curled bud to fully unfurled flower. My current favorite is the highly fragrant, ruffled, yellow-orange *R.* 'Westerland', which looks smashing arranged with the deep purple of monkshood or the glowing violet of *Verbena* 'Homestead Purple'.

Which brings us to those all-important bit players who complement the stars: the vines, foliage, and smaller flowers needed to plump up a bouquet with fluff and texture. They are what florists call "filler," although florists too often miss the chance to make a distinctive bouquet by making uninspiring choices such as baby's breath or salal. This layer is as important to the bouquet—and to the garden, for that matter—as the necklace worn with a plain black dress, or the red shoes that make the outfit. It is where the artistry of flower arranging comes into play.

Three things are necessary for such artistry, and they are all readily available in the summer garden. First, make sure you have plenty of small flowers, some with frothy texture. Plant meadow rue (*Thalictrum*) and love-in-a-mist (*Nigella*) for their airiness, *Knautia macedonica* for its ruby buds of flowers, and lots of *Astrantia* for long-lasting, neutral-colored interest. Yarrow, *Diascia*, snapdragons, astilbe, catmint, and ornamental grasses in both blade and bloom all provide different textures and tones in mixed bouquets. Vines look dramatic draped around and hanging down the sides of vases: little variegated ivies, akebia, small-flowered clematis, or honeysuckle belong in most arrangements.

Second, be sure to tuck some fragrant flowers into every bouquet—why do without the smell of summer when you have the look of it? Just a stem or two of sweet peas, phlox, flowering tobacco (*Nicotiana*), or roses can scent a room far longer and more sweetly than the most expensive aromatherapy candle.

The last ingredient, too often overlooked, is the foliage of summer, which supports and rounds out a bouquet, adding color and contrast. (Feel free to strip the foliage off the flowers you've chosen—there is nothing particularly pretty about hydrangea leaves.) Add the leaves of shrubby dogwoods, heavenly bamboo (*Nandina*), hostas, big glossy magnolia leaves, and leathery viburnum foliage. And don't forget small trees with interesting leaves—katsura and *Cercis canadensis* 'Forest Pansy' have heart-shaped leaves, in soft green and bronzy purple respectively. One of the loveliest midsummer arrangements I've seen was creamy flower spikes of *Hydrangea paniculata* combined in an old watering can with the foliage from black elderberry (*Sambucus nigra*), festooned with pink and orange honeysuckle blossoms. Simple, fragrant, and leafy—all the joys of the season brought indoors to give us the most intense hit of summer possible in these few short weeks.

Change of Habit

LAST TIME I RETURNED FROM A NURSERY TRIP with my car bulging with new plants, my husband made some supposedly witty comment about how I seem to be spending every bit as much time and money on plants as I used to devote to clothes, makeup, and shopping. I don't know where he has been for the last decade or so, but that has been true for some time now. And no wonder—nursery foraging is still a rewarding experience. It involves no mirrors, stretch fabrics, bright lights, or insincere saleswomen. I emerge from a nursery poorer, perhaps, but with ego unscathed. In fact, I usually feel quite clever about whatever plants I've tracked down, my head buzzing with ideas and plans for the garden.

It has been a long time since I got that kind of buzz from personal adornment, but it's true that I used to read fashion magazines with the same devotion I now lavish on garden literature. For many years, the part of my mind that obsessively observes color and design focused on clothes. I could tell you what my friends and I had worn to every important occasion since—and perhaps including—junior high school. I cruised fabric-store aisles the way I now hang out in nurseries—fingering the textures, comparing prices, considering the possibilities. I knew which shop was best for which item, just as I now try to keep up with the stock of every nursery within fifty miles. But somewhere along the line (and I'd rather not give a date), my power of imagination came up against the reality of middle age. It just wasn't fun anymore. Black pants, loafers, and a turtleneck work fine for nearly every occasion, can be put on quickly each morning on my way out the door, and take very little thought. I'd rather ponder the shape and size of leaves, the color of flowers, and how to combine them all into pleasing combinations out there in the garden. Far away from a three-way mirror.

Sure, a garden changes over time, just as we do ourselves. But I'd much rather think about shade and overgrown shrubs than about bags, sags, and gravity. Most important of all, a garden provides a fresh start every spring, with bare ground, emerging leaves, the promise of rejuvenation. Believe me, if I could wake up one spring morning with a twenty-five-inch waist and slim upper arms, I'd hightail it to Nordstrom. But things have come to the point where I need to rely on soil, sun, and seeds for my yearly dose of renewal. Maybe the humbling changes we experience as we age are nature's nudge toward our own personal evolution, forcing us to look at something besides ourselves. Focusing on anything for too long, even items as fascinating as nail polish or new coats, is as stultifying as planting petunias in the exact same spot each year.

Now, you may well be thinking that a broad and altruistic view of things should extend further than right outside your own front door. Not to sound defensive, but I truly believe that the act of tending a garden, of growing things beautifully and responsibly, contributes to the mental and physical well-being not just of the individual but of society and the earth. And it is certainly a whole easier to justify than a clothes habit.

I have to admit I've grown sorry for women with perfect manicures, sleek clothes, and those uncomfortable high heels. Don't they realize those spikes will sink right down into damp soil during an early-morning slug hunt? And how in the world do they weed with nails that long, let alone pull up carrots or turn the compost?

Or maybe there is no cosmic plan at all to get us to enlarge our interests, to grow up a bit—maybe Mother Nature is simply saving us from having more than one expensive preoccupation at a time.

Orange Aid

THE COLOR ORANGE BRINGS TO MIND such unfortunate associations. Hear the word "orange" and you picture the color of Howdy Doody's hair, those blaring highway construction signs, and the worst excesses of the '60s Carnaby Street look, such as neon orange striped with lime green. Add to that years of being told that pastels are the "correct" colors to use in our misty climate, and you end up with orange-phobia and a washed-out-looking garden.

Orange has been described as having the vitality of red as well as the light of yellow, but I think it brings a positive energy all its own to the garden. A single *Canna* 'Tropicana', its hot-orange flower set against huge pink-and-green-striped leaves, is a jump-start all by itself.

Like nearly every color, orange comes in a whole range of shades, presenting a smorgasbord of possibilities for perking up pastels. Think of the russet of fox fur, earthy umber, the saffron of monks' robes, the spicy hue of ripening pumpkins, the soft warmth of apricot, melon, and tangerine. Place any of these next to lipstick pink or sunshine yellow and you jolt the garden alive; use them against gray or deep-green foliage and they are a color scheme all to themselves; combine them with shades of purple and they create a symphony of eye-catching intensity. Orange is never a background color; it rarely fades, but that doesn't mean it can't mix easily with other colors.

As you dip your toe into the ocean of orangeness, start with plants whose flowers and foliage play off each other with a perfection rarely equaled by any combinations we devise ourselves. The clear orange flower of *Dahlia* 'David Howard' is made more congenial by its own bronzy foliage, and the lively green leaf and stalk of *Euphorbia griffithii* 'Fireglow' is a faultless foil for the intense orange-red of its long-lasting bloom. Many daffodils have orange cups softened by ivory petals, as in *Narcissus* 'Merlin', or by a primrose yellow surround, as in *N.* 'Grand Soleil d'Or'. The Alaska series of nasturtiums (*Tropaeolum majus*) ranges through all the shades of orange into mahogany, with leaves appealingly splotched and marbled in creamy white. I visited a garden last summer where the front porch was flanked with cobalt-blue pots overflowing with their gleaming blooms and fetching foliage; nothing could be simpler to grow yet a more effective evocation of high summer.

Of course it's easy to fill the autumn garden with orange—deciduous plants such as Japanese maples, katsura, and sumacs light a fire in the garden every October. The winter can be brightened by orange as well: plant the coppery witch hazel *Hamamelis* x *intermedia* 'Jelena', whose spidery blossoms bring surprising color to the frosty days of February. Orange glows beneath pale spring skies and against the chartreuse of new leaves; try the towering *Fritillaria imperialis* 'The Premier' and tulips such as 'Orange Favorite' or the hot-colored 'Orange Monarch.'

Then in June come the roses, with possibilities for orange ranging from brash to softly subtle. *Rosa* 'Westerland' is a rich tangerine highlighted by bright green foliage; the species rose *Rosa mutabilis* has blossoms that change color from deep pink through the melon shades before fading to cream. The fruit-scented, apricot English rose 'Abraham Darby' blooms all summer in my garden surrounded by a haze of blue catmint.

The midsummer garden burgeons with oranges. 'Tiger Baby' lilies add flashy splashes of speckled orange as well as sweet fragrance. A whole range of daylilies bloom in shades of orange as appealing as their names; look for *Hemerocallis* 'Real Wind', with salmon flowers streaked in orange, or 'Paper Butterfly', with its ruffled petals in warm peach. Mix in long-blooming perennials such as *Agastache* 'Firebird' (copper-orange) and the softer orange *A.* 'Apricot Sunrise', and plenty of the spicy, earth-toned yarrows (*Achillea* 'Paprika' and 'Terra Cotta') to keep the garden heated up until it is time for fall color to kick in yet again.

Mopheads and Lace Caps

HYDRANGEAS HAVE GONE IN AND OUT OF STYLE as regularly as capri pants, and for the last several decades they seem to have been replaced by rhododendrons in gardeners' affections. We think of hydrangeas as big, blue, and dependable, and we've always take them for granted. But nowadays it's safe, even in a gathering of horticulturists, to admit you love hydrangeas, and there are many unusual and newer kinds available.

The shady garden on the north side of my house is packed with hydrangeas, nearly every one purchased from Country Gardens in Fall City, Washington. You'll find the Howe brothers, Don and Keith, and their mother, Willa, at plant sales, selling and dispensing information about dozens of intriguing hydrangeas. "Years ago we were growing herbs, and a guy back East said he'd buy all the hydrangea flower heads we could grow," Don recalls. The family began looking closely at hydrangeas in Seattle's Washington Park Arboretum and then toured American and European gardens in search of unusual hydrangeas. They now stock several hundred different kinds, many from Belgium, Switzerland, France, and England, where hydrangeas have long been bred, named, and appreciated.

The books tell you that hydrangeas thrive in free-draining, moist soil, but they do perfectly well in my heavy clay soil, amended with compost and manure. Their name comes in part from the Greek word for water, and they are as greedy for both water and nutrients as clematis, roses, and hostas.

It is best to leave the old flowers on in the fall (except for those you can't resist cutting for bouquets) to protect the buds from harsh weather. New buds form beneath the old flower heads, so cut back carefully in March, which is also the time to cut out a quarter to a third of the older stems on mature plants.

There are several types of hydrangea flowers, or inflorescences. The term hortensia (which is what hydrangeas are called in French-, German-, and Dutch-speaking countries) refers to rounded flower heads composed mainly of large sterile florets. These are the familiar mopheads, or *H. macrophylla*. Lace caps are flatter and more spreading, with small, centrally placed fertile flowers and a crown of sterile florets around the outside. Then there are the hydrangeas with conical flower heads, white or ivory, known as peegees (*H. paniculata*); and there's even a climbing form, *H. anomala,* with clinging aerial rootlets and heart-shaped leaves.

Both oakleaf hydrangeas *(H. quercifolia)* and *H. aspera* are as noteworthy for their foliage as for their flowers. The handsome, deeply lobed, eight-inch leaves of the oakleaf hydrangea turn bronze and crimson in the fall, with clusters of creamy flowers; 'Snow Flake' has white, fluffy, very double flowers. You might not even recognize *H. aspera* as a hydrangea, for its large velvety leaves have a tropical look, but the pale-purple-to-white lace-cap flowers give it away.

Country Gardens (36735 SE David Powell Road, Fall City, WA 98024; 425-222-5616) carries a fine assortment of unusual yet dependable hydrangeas. *H. serrata* 'Blue Deckle' has vivid electric-blue flowers that age to violet, and *H. serrata* 'Beni-gaku', a graceful shrub with red-tinged flowers, is often seen in old Japanese paintings and prints. *H. arborescens* 'Annabelle' is the essence of old-fashioned hydrangea splendor, with showy snow-white flowers that bloom from June until frost.

When you pick hydrangeas for bouquets, dip the stems in boiling water for five seconds and they'll stay fresh in water for a couple of weeks. To dry them, wait until the flowers turn a bit leathery and dull slightly. Flowers picked too soon will wither no matter what drying technique you use. When they are picked at the right moment, all you need do is stand each stem separately (don't crush together in bouquets) in an empty vase or bottle to dry, and they should last, if handled gently, for several years.

Luscious Lavender

SEATTLE GARDENS FLAUNTED A MOST UNUSUAL HARBINGER of spring this year. Rabbit's-ear Spanish lavender (*Lavandula stoechas*) bloomed in two tones of purple above fat mounds of silvery foliage. Rarely hardy in our climate, this most appealing of lavenders was so encouraged by our mild winter that it burst into flower by mid-May and is still going strong.

Seattle gardeners tend to think of July and August as the peak months for lavender, and most years that's true. But a recent mild winter brought a most unusual harbinger of spring: rabbit's-ear Spanish lavender (*Lavandula stoechas*), rarely hardy in our climate, burst into flower in mid-May and was still going strong two months later. This most appealing of lavenders, blooming in two tones of purple above fat mounds of silvery foliage, encouraged me to add more lavender to my garden.

But which kinds to choose, from among more than two hundred species and cultivars? We think of lavender as that familiar aromatic herb that defines a color, whose pungent flower spikes scent soaps and sachets. Nowadays, however, lavender comes in deep purple to white, with shades of pink, cream, and red-violet. New lavenders seem to be introduced every year, each claiming longer bloom, brighter color, or lovelier foliage. While the nomenclature and even the history are gnarled, lavender's usefulness in healing and in the garden has never been in doubt.

Spanish lavender is the oldest of all the lavenders, grown by the Greeks and Romans, who used it as an antiseptic. The Phoenicians brought lavender to the British Isles, where it was later cultivated by Benedictine monks in their medicinal gardens and later still became an essential element of Tudor knot gardens. In France, lavender grows wild on the sunny, stony hillsides of Provence, where it has long been gathered for perfume and used to treat wounds. Commercial crops were planted there in the 1920s and are a thriving business today. In Australia, lavender farming was begun by the government at the end of the nineteenth century.

Gertrude Jekyll did much to popularize lavender in England; *L. angustifolia* 'Munstead', with dark violet buds opening to violet flowers on bushy plants ideal for hedging, is named for her garden at Munstead Wood in Surrey. Jekyll used sweeps of lavender in nearly every bed and border she created, illustrating its many uses beyond the herb garden.

Lavender is one of the few plants that are as effective in formal planting schemes as in the cottage garden. It looks stunning planted in a thick ribbon to flank a walkway, or can be interplanted with catmint, bachelor's buttons, Russian sage, and veronicas, above a white carpet of alyssum. Sited alongside rosemary, it will provide a one-two punch of fragrant foliage. It can trim a vegetable patch, serve as an edging to a perennial bed, or be pruned into a tidy hedge.

In our climate, lavender is more often killed by wet than by cold. Full sun and good drainage are the two essential elements for growing healthy lavender. My showiest swath of lavender is planted in slightly amended sand, right up against the house in full sun, and it has grown into a thriving mass of purple bloom. The hardiest lavenders are *L. angustifolia* and *L. x intermedia*, both of which will even tolerate snow if it doesn't stick around too long. I've killed lavender plants by overpruning— they look so ratty in winter that the temptation is to hack them way back. But they resent this, and do best when just the old flower spikes are trimmed off in autumn. It is best to leave shaping of the bushes until new leaves start to form in spring, when they can be cut back by a third at most. The trick is to prune them regularly enough to keep them in shape without cutting deeply into the woody part. Then let lavender plants alone, except to snip a few spikes to scent summer bouquets, and they'll bloom in waves of purple all summer long.

Garden Muscle

I USED TO EXERCISE TO STAY A CERTAIN SIZE (or in an attempt to reach a certain size) and as a social activity. That kept me running around Green Lake when I was younger, and paying for a gym membership. My current exercise program is more focused: I exercise so that I am able to garden.

I long for the days when I could go outside first thing in the morning and garden all day long. Now I put in a few hours of digging, transplanting, and pulling weeds and I am beat. My iced-tea breaks grow longer. I just have to rest. And nothing drives me more crazy than being unable to dig out a plant—sometimes I jump up and down on the shovel and just can't drive it deep enough. This may sound like a call for soil amendments (true), but it also indicates lack of strength.

Although I resent anything that takes me away from the garden this time of year, I do yoga every day and take a weekly yoga class for strength and flexibility. Yogis say you are only as young as your spine, and nowhere is this more important than out in the garden, with all the lifting and stooping. I've taken yoga for more than twenty years and credit it with the fact that I've never been injured by garden work. I also warm up for gardening by walking the dog up hills; warm muscles are resilient muscles. For endurance and for fun, I try to attend an exercise dance class twice a week. Great music and free movement always shake up brain cells. Many of my best ideas for the garden come while walking or dancing, rather than in the midst of the garden itself, where I get too focused to be creative. None of this activity, however, can match the exercise program of my friend Robyn, who rows with a team of women ages twenty-eight to sixty-five, early in the morning for an hour and a half, three times a week. She says this keeps her hands and wrists, and all the rest of her, strong for gardening. We had dinner last week, and she spoke cheerfully about her plans for the next morning—to dig a long ditch in heavy clay soil.

It turns out that gardening is now being touted as great exercise in and of itself. A University of Arkansas researcher found that women over age fifty who gardened at least once a week showed higher bone-density readings than those who engaged in jogging, swimming, walking, or aerobics. That makes perfect sense—it's weight-bearing activities that build strong bones, and in gardening we aren't just bearing our own weight, but that of soil, tools, and plants. Gardening is now seen as an effective way to prevent osteoporosis, a condition that threatens more than twenty-eight million people in the United States. An additional benefit of gardening is exposure to the sun, which boosts vitamin D production, which aids the body in calcium absorption, which in turn strengthens bones.

I got a kick out of a study by Melicia Witt at the University of Pennsylvania School of Medicine, which concluded that gardening could be as tough a workout as kayaking or weightlifting. The researcher sounded surprised—she must not spend too much time double-digging or spreading manure. What the studies miss is that gardeners are out there working for the sheer joy of it. What could be healthier? Gardening is transporting, one of those few activities in which we can lose ourselves while being fully engaged physically and mentally. How often have you looked up from a freshly weeded patch and been amazed at how much time had passed in happy, zoned-out activity? Most important, gardening provides its own motiva-tion— those plants are calling to us, there is work to be done—so people keep on gardening their whole lives. Which is why I keep exercising.

Dusky Leaves

GARDEN TRENDS COME AND GO, and just now plants with dark foliage are so hot they sizzle. Deep purple, chocolate, and near-black leaves are near-curiosities, and many of these plants can be hard to find or expensive—which, of course, makes them desirable. This kind of overwrought popularity can be off-putting, but when used well, dark leaves add great beauty and a new dimension to the usual foliage palette of green, gray, and variegated. What better way to add a bit of depth and mystery than with a filigree of maroon, a spread of chocolate-colored leaf?

These dark leaves, in all their various sizes, textures, and shades of duskiness, are so exciting that some gardeners have gotten carried away. Overdo it, and you end up with a Darth Vader landscape. Used too much or too boldly, dark foliage creates black holes that seem to suck all color into them, compounding the gloom of overcast days. When used gracefully and in moderation, nothing works better to contrast with brights or pastels, to create depth and mystery, than leaves of deep maroon or darkest purple.

A fine example of a startlingly black plant used effectively is the double lines of black mondo grass (*Ophiopogon planiscapus* 'Nigrescens') lining the pathway into the Japanese garden at the Bloedel Reserve on Bainbridge Island. If dark foliage seems hard to place in the garden, this is a good plant to start with, as it is dramatically black yet subtle in its size and shape. Despite the unfortunate resemblance of its curved blades to spiders' legs, it is really a most accommodating and useful plant. Its short, glossy black foliage lasts all winter, and looks wonderful dripping down the side of pots, growing between stepping-stones, or mulched with gravel. With black mondo grass, as with any other plant that seems a challenge to place, it's a good idea to use it first in a pot and become used to its color and habit before planting it out into the garden.

One of the loveliest of small trees comes in a dark-foliaged form: *Cercis canadensis* 'Forest Pansy' has large heart-shaped leaves of deepest, richest plum with an overlay of burgundy. Few trees are more dramatic than the weeping copper beech (*Fagus sylvatica* 'Purpurea Pendula'), whose foliage is so purple it is nearly black.

Such dark trees look splendid underplanted with silvery plants such as artemisia, lamb's ears, or senecio.

Shrubs with dark foliage abound; look for the Japanese barberry whose leaves are mottled in dark purple and pink (*Berberis thunbergii* 'Rose Glow'). There is an array of dark-leafed smokebushes (*Cotinus coggygria*) from which to choose; 'Royal Purple' is widely available, and holds its rounded purple leaves over a long season. Two other favorites, with lacy textures ideal for mingling with brighter companions, are black elderberry (*Sambucus* 'Nigra') and dark cow's parsley (*Anthriscus sylvestris* 'Ravenswing').

One of the easiest and flashiest ways to use dark foliage is as a carpet beneath plants with green or variegated foliage. The shrubby yellow honeysuckle, *Lonicera nitida* 'Baggesen's Gold', underplanted with a layer of bronze-purple bugleweed (*Ajuga reptans* 'Catlin's Giant') or one of the dark sedums, is a contrast of color and texture that lasts year-round. Or mix shiny black mondo grass with the soft, downy chartreuse leaves of lady's mantle for a combination you won't be able to resist reaching down and touching.

For dark-leafed drama, look to perennials and annuals: black-purple elephant ears (*Colocasia esculenta* 'Black Magic'); bronze flax (*Phormium*); the froth of maroon *Euphorbia dulcis* 'Chameleon'; castor bean (*Ricinus communis*); black bugbane (*Cimicifuga simplex* 'Brunette'), with its filigreed foliage and sweetly scented white flowers in autumn; dark loosestrife (*Lysimachia ciliata* 'Purpurea'), whose regrettable yellow flowers can be snipped off; paddle-leafed *Canna* 'Wyoming'; an array of dark-leafed coleus and begonias, ideal for pots; and perhaps the easiest of all to use, *Heuchera* 'Palace Purple' or *H.* 'Chocolate Ruffles', with evergreen foliage in deepest brown and purple-bronze.

Now in Bloom: July

1

Rosa '**Ballerina**'

Roses are a challenge to grow organically, so few have made the cut in my garden, despite my love for their fragrance and their beauty as cut flowers. *R.* 'Ballerina' is the exception, as it consorts well with other plants, and its foliage stays healthy all season long without spraying. A polyantha rose with a dense, spreading habit, it holds its little cup-shaped flowers aloft in mop-headed clusters that resemble the habit of a hydrangea, and blooms from early summer into autumn, with peak bloom in early July.

2

Lavatera '**Barnsley**'

You'd never expect such a lovely plant to be both dependably perennial and easy to grow. *L.* 'Barnsley' has soft pink, notched flowers that blend easily with other colors in the garden. Plant it anywhere you need some height and want bloom all summer long. This semideciduous beauty needs plenty of sunshine, moderate amounts of water, and severe cutting back in early springtime. Its pink flowers and lanky nature go well with silvery plants like lavenders or artemisia to skirt its base, stiffly upright plants such as rosemary, and architectural plants like the glaucous-leafed *Melianthus major*.

3
Lilium
'Copper King Clone'

Trumpet lilies are quintessentially lilylike—highly fragrant, tall and stately, with huge drooping bells in luscious colors. This one is as eye-catching in bud as in flower, with richly shaded elongated buds that appear along with the coppery orange flowers. Plant the huge purple bulbs in well-drained soil in plenty of sun, located close to a patio or a walkway so you can enjoy their sweet perfume on summer evenings. Lilies effectively fight their way up through groundcovers or small ornamental grasses (provided you protect them from slug predation); the brightly colored blossoms look smashing emerging from a frill of dark *Ajuga reptans* 'Catlin's Giant' or a fluff of gilded *Carex comans* 'Frosty Curls'.

3

4

4
Hydrangea macrophylla

Hydrangeas mean summertime, with colorful flower heads that manage
to look both traditional and modern. I cut them for every flower arrangement from
July through the holidays, since they are as striking dried as fresh. They can be
ungainly in the garden, so why not squeeze as many as possible in together to grow in
a symphony of blues, mauves, purples, pinks, and whites? Flower heads range from
cone-shaped (*H. paniculata* and *H. quercifolia*) to the familiar mopheads
(*H. macrophylla*), which work beautifully grown beneath the tall *H. aspera* with its
large, soft leaves and flat lace-cap flowers.

august

Edible Elegance

UNTIL RECENTLY, I HAD NEVER WANTED TO GIVE UP an inch of space in my too-small garden to grow vegetables. "No room for rutabagas" might have been my motto. I appreciated the Rosalind Creasey edible-gardening revolution of a decade or so ago, when she urged us all to grow vegetables in the front garden—but really, that looks messy most of the year.

I know there are all kinds of compelling reasons to grow your own produce—unusual varieties of fruits and vegetables that are fresh, flavorful, and free of chemicals. But because space is at a premium, and the tables at local farmers' markets overflow with lovely offerings, I've always stuck to simply growing a few tomatoes and herbs in pots. I admit that I thought of ornamental gardening as the peak of the pyramid, the aspiration of those who started out growing utilitarian things like potatoes and zucchini.

Several gardens I've seen in the last couple of years have convinced me how wrong I've been; gardeners are making beautiful vegetable gardens that are as visually exciting as any purely ornamental border. After a recent stay at Hedgebrook, a retreat for women writers on Whidbey Island, I began to better appreciate the appeal of vegetable gardens. Right up front on the property alongside the driveway is a huge deer-fenced garden of fruit trees and an array of vegetables that feed the writers in residence for many months of the year. Herbs and edible flowers are interplanted in pleasing patterns, presided over by a scarecrow with attitude, the Garden Goddess, complete with a sexy skirt and pink baseball cap.

France has set the standard since medieval times for the decorative kitchen gardens called *potagers*. From intricately hedged parterres to the simple walled kitchen gardens of the monasteries, the rest of the world has copied the inspired French mix of fruit, herbs, flowers, and vegetables. Even Versailles has a famous potager, ordered so the king could look down upon patterned plots from the terace above.

PREVIOUS PAGE: *Mildew-resistant* Verbena *'Homestead Purple' fills a sage green pot.*

LEFT: *Clematis, wisteria, and climbing roses grow at the base of the patio pergola.*

Contrary to my idea of evolution, the best ornamental gardeners seem to be growing into growing vegetables. Heronswood Nursery near Kingston is world-renowned for its gardens filled with unusual plants. Joining the woodland, bog, and trellised gardens is a huge and sunny vegetable garden of raised beds with bluestone walls and pathways. The rest of the garden houses rare treasures of plants collected around the globe, but the new vegetable garden is every bit as carefully designed and detailed. Acoustics are even provided, in the form of water music dripping from a morel-mushroom fountain created by Little and Lewis of Bainbridge Island. Dan Hinkley says he and his partner, Robert Jones (designer of the garden), are already enjoying salads from the new space, trying not to think of how much each lettuce leaf must have cost. But it surely looks fantastic.

Beautiful vegetable gardens need not be as elaborate as Heronswood's. A small vegetable plot alongside the road to our summer cabin on Guemes Island has had its simple wire fence charmingly and painstakingly woven with colorful sweet peas. I've seen a large, well-tended garden made exceptional by a row of leafy banana plants, lending the surprise of exotica amidst the cabbages. Dahlias, sunflowers, cosmos, nasturtiums, and marigolds are all traditional additions to the potager. And then, of course, there are the vegetables themselves: statuesque artichokes, yellow tomatoes, 'Bright Lights' chard with flashy stems, feathery fennel, beans growing up tepees of sticks—enough visual excitement to please even the most narrow-minded ornamental gardener.

Recent interest in the topic is captured in a couple of good books on the design and plant possibilities for beautiful vegetable gardens. *The Art of French Vegetable Gardening* by Louisa Jones includes fine photos, recipes, and quotes from Colette about the gardens of her youth; *The Art of the Kitchen Garden* by Jan and Michael Gertley takes a more practical approach, with plant lists and garden schematics.

And if aesthetics is a priority for a vegetable gardener, there are plenty of gorgeous vegetables to choose from. Seed catalogs offering edibles are getting to be even better reading than all the ornamentals catalogs that flood mailboxes early in the year. Territorial Seed Company's catalog (P.O. Box 158, Cottage Grove, OR 97424-0061; 514-942-9547) offers dozens of different kinds of tomatoes, ranging from early to late fruiting, from round and red to pear-shaped and glowingly golden. You can buy uncommon greens such as mizuna, tatsoi, and Niçoise lettuce from The Cook's Garden (P.O. Box 535, Londonderry, VT 05148; 800-457-9703) in colors and textures more exotic than their names. And catalogs like Shepherd's Garden Seeds (30 Irene Street, Torrington, CT 06790; 860-482-3638) offer edible flowers, beneficial insects, and trellis supports, as well as the seeds needed to plant a complete culinary herb garden, and a stunning array of new and heirloom vegetables in all their glossy glory.

White Wizardry

TO SIMPLIFY YOUR GARDENING LIFE, choose white. Flowers of pure white and foliage in gray-to-silver tones harmonize with all other colors, bringing unity and elegance to planting schemes. White is, hands down, the easiest color to use in the garden.

I must admit that the makers of garden rules don't agree with me on this. British colorist Gertrude Jekyll didn't approve of white and silver used alone, declaring that a bit of blue and lemon yellow was needed to bring out the beauty of white flowers. Her American counterpart, Louise Beebe Wilder, said, "White spotted all about the garden is simply a stirrer-up of factions, setting the flowers against one another instead of drawing them into happy relationships."

How, then, to explain the continued appeal of the celebrated white garden created by Vita Sackville-West at Sissinghurst, which, fifty years after its creation, remains one of the world's most visited gardens? Planted in white flowers, silver foliage, and the dark green of boxwood hedging, its effect depends as much on the varying shades of foliage as it does on flower color. Without the distraction of color, all the subtleties and interplay of foliage colors become apparent, the form and textures of the plants becoming clearly visible.

White is especially welcome for its luminescence under overcast skies, in fog or mist, and at twilight, for it gives back more light than it receives, with its ability to bend invisible ultraviolet and infrared light into the visible spectrum. Our black-and-white vision is a thousand times more sensitive than our color vision, which explains the dichotomy of white both as an absence of color and as a powerful presence in the garden.

As if their beauty weren't enough, white flowers carry the most potent and memorable of garden fragrances. White lilacs, such as the double 'Mme. Lemoine', epitomize the sweetness of springtime. A single flower of the trumpet-shaped *Lilium regale* fills an entire room with its scent. Mock orange (*Philadelphus*), sweet box (*Sarcococca*), osmanthus, stock, spicy little white carnations—all exude exceptional perfumes.

White can play the starring role, as with flamboyant Casablanca lilies, or serve as a bit player. Smaller white flowers (*Geranium incanum* 'Album', for instance) can weave in and out of plantings, perking up other colors. Think of the white eye in the center of a purple delphinium—therein lies the buzz, the energy. Plants whose bloom is a haze of tiny white flowers, such as gypsophila and *Crambe cordifolia*, create a softening scrim for bolder, brasher colors.

Have you ever tried to match a white paint chip? There are seemingly hundreds of tints, hues, and shades of warm or cool, gray, yellow, pink. In the garden, I try to avoid the cooler, muddier tones of white and look for pure, glowing whites such as the ones found in 'Iceberg' roses or the blossoms of the potato vine (*Solanum jasminoides*).

You might start the year with pearly white snowdrops, followed by the creamy double tulip 'Mt. Tacoma'. In March, the fragrant evergreen vine *Clematis armandii* opens pale star-shaped flowers, and nothing is more charming than the white form of the bleeding heart, *Dicentra spectabilis* 'Alba'. For summer, plant daisies, Matilija poppies (*Romneya coulteri*), and white forms of foxglove, delphinium, and rugosa roses. Pot up white annuals such as impatiens, bacopa, and tuberous begonias. White single Japanese anemones, *Gaura,* and white hydrangeas set off red and gold autumn leaves. And don't forget all the silver and white foliage plants, which range from the groundcover *Lamium maculatum* "White Nancy', through lamb's ears, white-trimmed ivies, and a wide variety of silvery artemisias, to stunning architectural plants such as cardoons and *Melianthus major.*

Vita Sackville-West best evoked the romance that white brings to the garden when she wrote in the *London Observer* in the early 1950s: "I cannot help hoping that the great ghostly barn-owl will sweep silently across a pale garden next summer, in the twilight—the pale garden that I am now planting under the first flakes of snow."

Fronds and Fiddleheads

AS I GROW MORE INTERESTED in foliage plants and pay less attention to flowers (a natural progression for gardeners, it seems), I've been searching nurseries and books for reasonably sized plants with unusual, long-lasting leaves. And I've just figured out that what I've been hunting for is that most familiar of plants—ferns.

Check out any book on perennials, and you'll find scarce if any mention of ferns. These plants have, perhaps, a couple of strikes against them. First, we Northwesterners all think first of bracken and sword fern, so common as to be boring, and we forget about the many other gardenworthy ferns. Second, the Latin names for ferns are as confusing as those of ornamental grasses—with many genera, all unpronounceable. *Cryptogramma, Selaginella, Matteuccia,* and *Polystichum* are in part made up for by the charmingly descriptive common names: ostrich fern, sensitive fern, shaggy shield, and—who could resist?—the robust hybrid male fern.

Ferns have a feel of mystery about them, in part because they are some of the oldest plants on earth, their fronds etched as fossils alongside the footprints of the dinosaurs. How to reconcile this ancient hardiness with their frou-frou air of British Victoriana, let alone their ignominious appearance in the fern bars of the 1970s?

Given their long and checkered history, you might expect ferns to be persnickety, but in fact they are easy to grow and nearly foolproof. Clip back the old fronds in the spring, to let the new ones uncurl unfettered by tattered foliage. Water until they're well established, and top-dress with compost or well-rotted manure, and that's all there is to it.

I'm embarrassed to admit that the main reason I haven't grown ferns is that I thought of them only as moisture-loving woodlanders, unfit for a sunny garden. The little bit of shade I have is packed with hydrangeas and hostas—no room for ferns. The only type I've grown up to now has been the autumn fern (*Dryopteris erythrosora*), which I bought despite myself, beguiled by its coppery pink fiddleheads and russet fronds.

The Japanese painted fern (*Athyrium nipponicum* 'Pictum') is another irresistible small fern, mainly because it carries a complete and lovely color scheme on its small fronds. By late spring, it has opened its delicate foliage of soft gray-green, white, and burgundy. This small fern needs rich soil, moisture, and light shade, rewarding the gardener with its tricolored foliage until the first frost.

Judith Jones, world-renowned fern expert and proprietor of Fancy Fronds nursery in Gold Bar, Washington (P.O. Box 1090, Gold Bar, WA 98251; 360-793-1472; www.fancyfronds.com; catalog $2; open by appointment only), says that the golden scale and common male ferns of the genus *Dryopteris* are the workhorses of the garden. "They come in an amazing range of size, shape, and texture, from dwarfs to huge hybrids," says Jones, "with a single set of growing instructions."

The Fancy Fronds catalog lists more than forty different species of *Dryopteris*. The dwarf-crested golden-scale male fern has a name bigger than itself—the fern, shaped like an upcurved bowl, reaches a scant six inches after several years. A Victorian favorite known as 'Cristata the King' grows to four feet, symmetrical and crested. And lest you think of ferns as plain green, there is the limelight shield fern (*D. formosana*), whose eighteen-inch fronds are an intense, glowing yellow-green.

Jones explains that ferns are known as "pioneer colonizers"; native ferns were some of the first plants to sprout after Mount St. Helens blew in 1980, just as they no doubt were first on the scene after whatever cataclysm destroyed the dinosaurs. Ferns flourish in bright sun, anchoring the soil, and continue to thrive even after the trees grow up to shade them. Jones suggests that, next time you marvel over the age of a huge tree, you notice the ferns at its base, which may well be older than the tree. You can't count their rings, but old ferns have been known to have hundred-pound root balls.

Coping with Summer

EVERY YEAR IN MIDSUMMER I HIT THE WALL on taking care of my garden. Spring plant lust has subsided, and I'm scrambling to keep everything watered, weeded, and deadheaded. I'll love the garden again come September—I always do—but right now it's a drag.

I'm often asked how much time I spend working in my garden. My answer is that I spend every minute I can possibly squeeze in, as there is nothing I'd rather do. This is an honest answer—except in late July and August, when I need a break from dragging hoses about and cutting off withered roses.

I sought inspiration and advice from garden books on how to deal with this malaise but found little help there. The authors are all too perky about summer maintenance, and the elaborate perfection shown in the photos is depressing when my garden is looking its overgrown worst. So I returned to three thoughts, from three quite disparate people, that have helped me cope during those few weeks when my garden feels like more trouble than it's worth.

I have to admit that none of these quotes has anything to do with the subject at hand, but I see garden metaphors everywhere. It is like that "Six Degrees of Kevin Bacon" game—all things lead back to the garden. Years ago I read that Disney CEO Michael Eisner said that Disneyland concentrates its resources on what it wants people to notice and skimps on everything else. He said anybody would go broke (or exhaust themselves) trying to keep all aspects of any operation at full-tilt perfection. How is that for an excuse for summer slacking? Turn your attention to weeding and watering around the patio where you most often sit, or your vegetable patch, or whatever is most important to you. Then don't worry about the rest. This one concept helped me to let go of my garden's back border, planting it thickly with wildlife-friendly species that have successfully outcompeted the weeds. It is wonderfully luxuriant, self-sufficient, and filled with birdsong. It's also a bit of a tangled mess, but I don't look too closely.

Poet and diarist May Sarton was a gardener herself, so she may have had her garden at least partly in mind when she wrote, "The quality of life depends on small

amounts of fully experienced or 'taken-in' material for the senses and the mind."
And she wrote this years ago, before the Internet, pagers, and cell phones were so
ubiquitous as to barrage us with information and interruption. The point is to limit
the scope of our efforts to what we most enjoy, and not spend all our time skim-
ming through the garden, fretting and tidying up. Slowing down and looking closely
are what makes all the work worthwhile. Maybe Sarton was talking about nothing
more than taking the time to smell the roses, but she said it more eloquently.

Speaking of eloquent, as Harvard University's 1978 commencement speaker,
author Alexander Solzhenitsyn, said, "Hastiness and superficiality are the psychic
diseases of the Western world." I think he meant the same thing as May Sarton, and
if we are ever to heal such insults to our psyches (which have only grown worse in
the years since his speech), the garden seems an ideal place to start. There is nothing
superficial or hasty about sitting back in an Adirondack chair, lemonade and novel at
hand, and simply soaking up the smells and sights of the garden that surrounds you.

These may seem like pretty highfalutin justifications for midsummer indolence,
but they work for me. This is the time to step back, acknowledge what you've created outside your windows, and revel in the fact that there is so much more to the
garden than all the work involved. And hope for a burst of energy come autumn.

Splashes, Stripes, and Splotches

IF WE AREN'T ALREADY CONVINCED THAT GOOD GARDENS are made by leaf more than by flower, the stripes, splatters, splotches, and splashes of variegated foliage will convince us. Although there's an ephemeral quality to the shimmer and surprise of variegation, it endures over the months, with the long life span of the foliage forming the basis for entire color schemes.

Gardeners can be so snobbish about variegated plants. Some allow leaves trimmed in snow white into their garden but permit nothing as vulgar as yellow freckles. Others appreciate delicate spring stripings but would never think of using golden splashings beneath the summer sun. I admit that some variegations appeal to me tremendously—in fact, compel me to take them home and squeeze them in—while others appear garish or bland. But we miss so many possibilities if we fail to take advantage of variegations to light up and diversify our gardens.

Variegated plants are often less robust than their solid-leafed counterparts, and sometimes have fewer flowers. But this isn't always true; *Daphne odora* 'Aureomarginata' is hardier than the species, with the added bonus that its waxy leaves are trimmed in a cream that sets off the little pink flowers. It's true that many variegated plants need more shelter from hot sun, extreme cold, or wind than all-green plants do. Yellow-variegated leaves color up best in sunshine, while some of the cream-and-white-trimmed plants need more shade. And watch out for reversion: if an all-green shoot appears, cut it out completely so that the rest of the plant doesn't follow suit.

The science of variegation is complex. Oddly, even variegations so lovely as to look expertly painted on first appear randomly as mutant variegated shoots on otherwise plain-leafed plants. Some variegations are induced by harmless viruses, such as the streaked colors of 'Bizarre' tulips, or the mottling on the leaves of *Abutilon pictum* 'Thompsonii'. The green pigment chlorophyll in the leaves of certain plants is masked by other pigments, or is imperfect or absent in parts of the leaves, and this is what causes the wide range of colors and patterning that makes variegated plants so appealing. It always amazes me that a scientific phenomenon can result in something as fetching as the yellow-spotted leaves of the leopard plant (*Farfugium japonicum* 'Aureomaculatum'). Despite its feline name, its rounded leaves and nearly bulbous splotches remind me of nothing more than a fat, lumpy toad. And to think it began as a random mutant.

In pot plantings I feature patterned foliages in all their glory, such as a drape of marbled nasturtium leaves (*Tropaeolom majus* 'Alaska') or a billow of the shimmery yellow-and-green-striped grass *Hakonechloa macra* 'Aureola'. But in the ground, to create flow and avoid choppiness, I try to use variegated plants not as star players, but to emphasize, by contrast, the solid-color leaves or flowers of other plants. In midwinter, my front terrace is edged with a mass of silvery leafed *Lamium maculatum* 'White Nancy', which froths beneath the plain green foliage and little white flowers of fragrant sweet box. An effective pairing is to use the hotly patterned leaves of *Euonymus fortunei* 'Emerald 'n Gold' as a beacon to lead the eye to the more delicate yellow flowers of a nearby witch hazel.

An easy way to integrate more variegation into the garden is to use dependable old favorites in their newer, variegated forms. The familiar carpet bugle, *Ajuga reptans*, now comes in a metallic-sheened cream-and-lavender cultivar named 'Multicolor', and the ungainly weigela gains new life when its pale green leaves are margined in creamy white (*Weigela praecox* 'Variegata). Wallflowers come with leaves striped in bright cream (*Erysimum linifolium* 'Variegatum'); old-fashioned pink phlox has striking ivory and green leaves (*Phlox paniculata* 'Norah Leigh'); and the tolerant-of-nearly-all-conditions elderberry (*Sambucus*) can be found in golden or white shades of variegation.

Wet and Dry

THERE IS SO MUCH TALK THESE DAYS about naturalistic gardening and sustainable gardening that such good ideas are starting to sound—unfortunately—preachy. It seems to me that the basic principle of environmentally sound gardening is simply common sense—to put the right plant in the right place. If you read up on where a plant originates, its habits and preferences, and then site it accordingly, you won't need to use chemicals to keep it healthy. It will grow and thrive all by itself, making you feel like a clever and successful gardener. You contribute to the health of the earth while saving your own back, and end up with a lovely garden as well.

We may pretend that we are designing our gardens, but what it often comes down to is simply observing closely and then moving plants about until they are happy. I was given a red lace-leaf Japanese maple, and planted it at the top of a rockery to show off its graceful drape, but it needed constant watering. Ever since I moved it down the hillside to where it can slurp up the runoff from the slope, it has flourished with no supplemental watering.

Rather than cursing the soil conditions in your garden, try to work with what you have (and, for many Northwesterners, that is damp-to-outright-soggy soil for much of the year). Our hillside garden is constantly moist with water draining toward Lake Washington. Some spots, no matter how much drainage we put in, stay mucky all the time. Now that I've accepted the fact that I can't grow lavender or other silverlings in what is essentially a bog, I've planted those wet parts of the garden with moisture lovers. The good news is that many plants that prefer shade, such as hostas, can tolerate sun when they receive plenty of moisture. Often gardeners expand their plant repertoire by stretching liners beneath a section of soil to create bogs to enable them to grow plants that want wet feet. And many of the exotic-looking plants that are now so popular crave plenty of moisture to look their best.

"Moisture-retentive soil" is the nicest description of what many of us deal with, and the trick is to select plants that prefer wet to dry, mucky to well-drained. Groundcovers that grow lush in moist conditions include carpet bugle (*Ajuga reptans*), with bronze leaves and purple flower spikes. Its cultivar 'Burgundy Glow' has cream-trimmed leaves suffused with magenta and rose, with light-blue flowers; 'Catlin's Giant' has foliage much larger than usually found in carpet bugle; and 'Metallica Crispa' has little crinkled dark leaves. Wood anemone (*Anemone nemorosa*), creeping jenny (*Lysimachia nummularia*) and its pretty yellow form 'Aurea', Bowles' golden grass (*Milium effusum* 'Aureum'), shamrock plant (*Oxalis*), and lungwort (*Pulmonaria*) all happily carpet damp soil.

There's a wide choice of perennials that prefer wet feet, including beauties like *Salvia uliginosa*, which has sky-blue flower spikes from midsummer to frost; *Lobelia cardinalis,* with scarlet flowers; and *Trollius* 'Cheddar', whose globes of flowers are the color of butter. Japanese anemones, miscanthus, phormium, primulas, and astilbes all prefer damp soil. Then there are all those bold plants that make a garden interesting: *Ligularia dentata, Rodgersia podophylla, Rheum palmatium,* and *Gunnera scabra* all have leaves as hefty as their names, effectively adding a touch of the jungle to any temperate garden. Many trees besides weeping willow enjoy the damp, including birch, sweetgum, aspen, hawthorn, and hornbeam. A wet spot in your garden allows you to grow shrubs such as red-osier dogwood (*Cornus stolonifera*), flowering quince, bog laurel (*Kalmia polifolia),* and spiraea.

For extensive lists of moisture lovers, take a look at *The Pacific Northwest Gardener's Book of Lists* by Ray and Jan McNeilan. Beth Chatto's book *The Damp Garden* (J. M. Dent and Sons, 1982) is a literate and thorough exploration of the many possibilities for gardening in wet soil.

But what about all those areas of the garden that turn to dust in midsummer? Many of us face extremes of both wet and dry in a single garden. Although I seem to remember many damp Labor Day weekends, it is usually late in the summer that plants suffer from drought. Our mid-July-through-September stretch of dry weather includes plenty of misty mornings, but we need hours of good, steady rain to soak the soil and restore the plants. Gardeners clever enough to emphasize drought-tolerant plantings have borders that look fresh and colorful into autumn. As water bills go up, all gardeners would be wise to increase their proportion of plants naturally adapted to stretches of droughtiness. And by this point in the summer, aren't we all sick and tired of dragging hoses about?

Xeriscaping, the environmentally friendly technique of gardening with less-thirsty plants, sounds so Texan or New Mexican that Northwest gardeners may think its principles don't apply here. But many Northwest native plants thrive in the rooty shade beneath large conifers, or on rocky and exposed hillsides. Our native Pacific madrone (*Arbutus menziesii*) suffers (and can even die) if it receives any irrigation. Several of our native groundcovers, such as bunchberry (*Cornus canadensis*), salal (*Gaultheria shallon*), and sand strawberry (*Fragaria chiloensis*), once established, will spread to cover the ground with little or no supplemental watering.

"Once established" is the key phrase. All too often plants that would do beautifully if well watered in the first couple of years expire because gardeners expect instant self-sufficiency. As with puppies, there is no such thing. Every plant needs supplementary watering for the first couple of years until it is well established. This is why it's so important to water less frequently, for longer periods of time, so that roots will be forced to penetrate deeply into the earth for moisture. A strong, extensive root system makes any plant more drought tolerant. Frequent, shallow waterings produce H_2O junkies, which learn to depend on more of the same. (None of this applies to plants in pots, which need watering at least once a day in the summer—with such a limited root run, they need all the help they can get.)

Drought-tolerant plantings are ideal on hillsides, beneath trees, and in areas with naturally dry soil. Gravel gardens sound bleak, but in truth they are easy-care—and newly fashionable. Designed with drifts of drought-tolerant plants and thickly mulched with gravel, they are handsome and tidy. The gravel forms paths and patios between the plantings, retains soil moisture, and keeps down the weeds. A recent book, *Beth Chatto's Gravel Garden: Drought-Resistant Planting Through the Year*, outlines the steps Chatto went through to transform a compacted, sun-baked parking lot into a lushly planted, much-admired garden. I was surprised to learn that kniphofia, bergenia, and even lilies can be drought tolerant in properly prepared soil.

Some of the best plants for dry gardens include the silver-foliaged ones native to the Mediterranean, such as lavender, santolina, senecio, catmint (*Nepeta*), and all the artemisias. *Perovskia* 'Blue Spire' forms a haze of blue flower spikes from mid- to late summer. Sunroses (*Helianthemum*) sprawl over gravel or down rockeries in shades of red, pink, apricot, yellow, and white. Rosemary, various kinds of euphorbia, verbascum, and the whole gamut of sedums thrive in dry soil. For height, bush anemone (*Carpenteria californica*) has sweet-scented white flowers in late spring. Rockrose (*Cistus*), wild lilac (*Ceanothus*), and barberries all have year-round presence. Carpeters like thyme and Corsican mint add fragrance as well as texture. Xeriscaping brings to mind cracked earth and skimpy cactus, but in fact gardening with nature's patterns in mind, paying close attention to the conditions that exist in our own gardens, allows all kinds of lovely and pleasing plants to thrive in the conditions that suit them best. And that makes the gardener's job a whole lot easier.

Now in Bloom: August

1

Inula magnifica

Inula is a bold perennial with bright yellow daisylike flowers held atop branched stems that reach six feet tall by August. What makes it such a show-stopper, in addition to its gargantuan size, is the unexpected combination of numerous frilly flowers and large, soft leaves. Because inulas tend to die down unattractively (those great-looking leaves turn black and shrivel but refuse to drop off the plant), plant them toward the back of the border, where they'll happily tower over the late summer garden.

1

2
Ornamental oregano *'Kent Beauty'*

This little perennial blooms all summer long with curious
layered bracts and flowers ideal to drip down the sides of containers or retaining
walls. Oreganos perfer full sun and very well-drained conditions, and if provided dry
enough soil to make it through the winter, will spread beautifully and retain their
subtle coloration when brought indoors.

3
South African honeybush
(*Melianthus major*)

This spreading shrub is
prized for its exotic toothed
foliage in an ethereal shade of
blue-gray. Though the leaves look
tropical, they carry the familiar
scent of peanut butter. Our summers
are usually too cool and short to
produce the dark red chenille-like
flowers, but the foliage is far
lovelier than the
bloom anyway.

4
Hardy fuchsias
(Fuchsia **spp.)**

Blooming profusely until frost, hardy
fuchsias are one of the best shrubs for
late summer. Not as overblown, greedy,
or frilly as their annual cousins, they
tolerate shade or partial afternoon sun
and droughty conditions. The trick to
making sure they survive winter cold is
to leave them untouched through the
winter. Don't cut back the dead top
growth (it's ugly, so you might not want
to plant them near walkways) until the
soil begins to warm in the springtime,
and you'll have a large and healthy plant
growing up from the roots.

4

september

Autumn Edge

BY SEPTEMBER I FEEL DESPERATE for some clarity in the garden. Just when I should relax and enjoy the lush fullness of the garden, I want to see edges, stems, each individual rather than an overgrown mush of plants. Put it down to the basic perversity of my nature, but at the end of the season I long for the clean-edged look I worked so hard to obliterate in the spring. I know, I know, there will be months of bare dirt and all the structure I could ever want to see, all too clearly revealed during the winter, but now I am tired of the fullness of summer, the billowing of plants past their peak.

I try to temper my frustration by reminding myself that, after all, the garden is doing just what I planted it to do. I blur my eyes a bit so that I don't see the buddleia and the lavatera toppling over with the weight of their own luxuriant foliage. It is the time to sip a cup of tea, sit in the garden, and enjoy the last of the warm days. Or so I tell myself—but to no avail.

Maybe it's that autumn light, misty in the mornings and so bright and clear by afternoon that it makes the garden appear dusty, dull, just too much. So I go out with my clippers on a mission to discover the corners of steps, pavers, and patios buried in foliage since early June.

First I pull out all the skeletons of summer, such as the ghostly remains of the lychnis and nigella. I cut back the spent blooms on the senecio, the daisies, the dried heads of the buddleia. Then I attack the lamium and thyme groundcovers that I nurtured along all spring, now sprawling out over pathways in an irritating manner. I prune up small trees, strip the leaves off the bamboo up to a bit above eye level to reveal the glossy canes, and cut back all

PREVIOUS PAGE: *Cardoons (Cynara cardunculus) tower over the garden in summer with bigtoothed silvery-gray leaves and flowers that look like artichokes topped with a purple buzz cut. The drama continues into autumn when the foliage yellows and the flower heads begin to droop.*

LEFT: *This favorite front porch pot holds a different combination of flowers and foliage each season. By late summer, the tender* Fuchsia triphylla *'Gartenmeister Bonstedt', the ruffled leaves of* Coleus *'Inky Fingers', and an abutilon have peaked, and I'm thinking about what to add to the bronze grass for autumn interest.*

those leggy hardy geraniums whose wandering habits were so charming a few months ago. In the same way that my eye adjusts to new skirt lengths, leaving last season's popular style looking silly or dowdy, so do plants that pleased the eye in July look all wrong by October.

This year, what I most enjoyed when I had finally reduced the garden's biomass to reasonable levels were all the white flowers still blooming into autumn. I guess I had grown weary of the oranges, yellows, and purples so appealing in July and August. White glows in the slanting autumn sun and lights up the evenings that close in so surprisingly early. Single white Japanese anemones, white mophead and peegee hydrangeas, *Gaura*, the last of the iceberg roses, snowy, late-blooming phlox, and the cream-splashed-with-pink-and-green *Persicaria virginiana* 'Painter's Palette' are all a welcome relief from the intensity of fall color. Their paleness appears luminous against the red of the turning maples and burning bush (*Euonymus alata*). White provides a bit of simplicity, a restfulness, before we head into all the richness of the holidays.

The bonus to cleaning up the garden is the space found for bulbs. At the base of trees and shrubs and along pathways I find pockets of soil to stuff with daffodils and tulips, crocus and hyacinth: all the ingredients to color and spark the garden again next spring.

A wonderful book of collected letters between two of England's most famous living gardeners is *Dear Friend and Gardener: Letters on Life and Gardening* by Beth Chatto and Christopher Lloyd. In a letter dated mid-September, Chatto writes to Lloyd from her garden in East Anglia, "With colour coming in fast all around it is such an exciting time of year building up to the great climax when Michaelmas daisies, dahlias and all will stand in defiance against the threat of frost, until the trees and shrubs take over with the final burst of colour—and then the carnival is ended. Winter will bring other stories. . . ."

The Midas Touch

THINK HOW WE ADMIRE THE GOLDEN AUTUMN FOLIAGE of birch trees and witch hazel. The flame red of maples is stunning, but it is the burnished yellows that I covet for my own garden. We don't have to wait for autumn to work its magic—it's possible to warm up the garden all year round with yellow and golden foliage, in solids or patterns of variegation.

The predominant color in any garden, no matter how flowery, is always green. This must be why yellow is endlessly useful—it is such a perfect contrast to green. How better to brighten and lighten the deep richness of yew, fir, camellia, rhododendron, and hemlock than with vivid yellow and gold? Even on the grayest days, these warm colors create the welcome illusion of reflecting the sun's radiance, almost as if the colors themselves are capable of plucking the sunshine from the sky and drawing it down into the garden.

As yellow-leafed trees and shrubs mature, they create the mirage of large pools of sunshine nestled in amongst the green of grass or shrubbery. An old area of my garden, planted in rhododendrons and a big pine, looked heavy and dull in its evergreen sameness. So beneath the pine, to stretch above the rhodies, I planted a golden locust (*Robinia pseudoacacia* 'Frisia'), a fluffy burst of gold foliage that lights up that whole corner of the garden from April through October. In front, a group of burgundy barberries (*Berberis thunbergii* 'Rose Glow') are underplanted with a puddle of golden creeping Jenny (*Lysimachia nummularia* 'Aurea'). Now this area of the garden shines even from a distance, the dark stolidness of the rhodies a fine foil for the gaudiness of locust and barberry.

Two of my favorite variegated plants have tricolored leaves that feature the color of butter, along with watermelon pink and green. *Houttuynia cordata* 'Chameleon' should be contained in a pot for its spreading ways, but its gorgeous foliage sparks every flower arrangement from May through the first hard frost. This same flashy pattern of colors decorates the fancy-leaved pelargonium 'Miss Burdett-Coutts', so colorful it is best grown alone in a pot, its red flowers nipped off.

Yellow's virtues are especially well displayed when splashed onto leaves as if from a careless shake of a paintbrush, as in nasturtiums (*Tropaeolum majus* 'Alaska') and flowering maples such as *Abutilon pictum* 'Thompsonii'. It also seems well suited to bladed plants, such as the striped golden flag (*Iris pseudacorus* 'Variegata') and all the spectacular yellow ornamental grasses, from the statuesque *Cortaderia selloana* 'Sun Stripe' to the flowing *Hakonechloa macra* 'Aureola'. And for warmth where you need it most, plant a couple of gold-toned conifers, such as the little Hinoki cypress 'Goldilocks' or the Japanese cedar 'Aurea' to brighten the winter landscape.

Ideal for hedging, in pots, or as a single specimen is *Lonicera nitida* 'Baggesen's Gold', with tiny yellow leaves crowding along the drooping branches. The golden elderberry (*Sambucus racemosa* 'Aurea') has leaves as dissected as gold filigree, and is especially lovely planted with dark phormium or smokebush. Such purples and bronzes look their best with their duskiness offset and emphasized by yellow.

Speaking of combining colors, I've heard talk lately about how we should avoid using yellow-variegated plants in the same beds with—or even in the same garden with—white-variegated ones. Those gardeners must have a far more refined eye than mine. Though I see the need for avoiding a checkerboard effect of white/yellow/white/yellow, I have no problem with throwing together all the shades from icy white through deep butterscotch. It's true that we need to consider variations in a color's warmth and coolness when putting together plant combinations. But such rules limit our options to play around with color, which is such an endlessly intriguing and gratifying game.

Mossy Charms

THE BIG-NAME CHEMICAL COMPANY whose billboard pictures a bag of moss killer with the caption "It's green. Better kill it," just doesn't get it. Not only is that an ugly sentiment, but these days gardeners are trying to encourage moss rather than eradicate it. Nothing gives a garden an air of permanence, of venerability, more than moss, its plush texture and hushed green bestowing a subtle grace upon the hard edges of the landscape.

Moss has so much going for it, not the least being that it appears all on its own. Where conditions are too shady for lawn to thrive, moss begins to take over; smart gardeners are removing the grass and letting the moss fill in. It may not end up smooth as a golf course, but moss doesn't soak up extra water, time, energy, and chemicals, either. Moss gardens have a softly aged, emerald charm all their own, particularly when crossed by stepping stones and trimmed in ferns.

Moss looks so thick and lush you'd expect it to absorb water like a sponge—and it does, which is why, paradoxically, it requires far less supplemental water than other groundcovers. Instead of relying on roots as most plants do, moss is anchored to tree trunks, stones, or earth (and unfortunately sometimes to roofs) by primitive little structures called rhizoids. The job of taking in water is shared by all the surfaces of the moss—hence it's efficient at making use of any droplet that comes its way.

There are more than 14,000 different species of moss, and most will grow in spots where not much else will thrive. Hairycap moss (*Polytrichum commune*) is a good lawn substitute because it spreads to cover large areas, is dark green, and is of uniform height. The common fern moss (*Thuidium delicatulum*) is lighter green and more featherlike, and cord moss (*Funaria hygrometrica*) fills in readily in rooty, shady areas where little else will thrive. The survival tactics that have kept moss around for so many centuries are a gardener's friend. During severe heat, cold, or drought, moss will go dormant, and when conditions improve it greens right back up.

If you've visited Bloedel Reserve on Bainbridge Island anytime in the last twenty years, you've had the pleasure of walking through the green cocoon of the moss garden, which looks as if it had emerged from the primeval ooze along with the first amphibian. Surely, no humans created this place—let alone within recent memory? Actually, in the early 1980s a busy staff set out thousands of half-dollar-sized rounds of Irish moss. The well-prepared ground encouraged the arrival of a variety of true mosses, which joined with the planted moss and crept over the trees and swampy ground to form one of the most beautiful gardens in the Reserve.

If mosses haven't already found a foothold in your garden, you can easily get them going, whether as a sweep of groundcover or to soften logs or rocks. Moss likes moist soils, summer shade, and acidic soil. Start by removing any plants that would interfere with its progress, such as grass, pachysandra, and ivy. You can buy moss starts, or transplant them from other parts of the garden, being careful to get enough soil along with the rhizoids to keep them from drying out. Provide ample moisture until established, and keep weeded. A number of elixirs are said to encourage moss to grow on rocks; the simplest are egg whites beaten with water, beer, and unsalted buttermilk. For a more potent potion you might try a slurry of manure.

"The idea of growing mosses most often comes to gardeners, I would think, as it came to me, on meeting these plants rain-fresh in woods and fields," says George Schenk in his book *Moss Gardening: Including Lichens, Liverworts, and Other Miniatures*. It is a book worth seeking out for the well-told story of an accomplished gardener's love of moss and its relatives.

Good Faders

WHEN WE'RE TEMPTED BY ALL THOSE FRESH BABY PLANTS at the nursery, we don't pause to wonder how they'll look in their waning days. We try to picture flower color and eventual size, but rarely do we consider the visual impact of a plant's death throes. But plants have a life span in which they leaf out, flower, reach their peak, and then fade away. And, just like humans, some plants progress through this cycle far more gracefully than others. How plants look as they fade is every bit as important as their appearance when budded up.

We live in a climate where summer and autumn gardens can be as lovely as springtime ones, if we remember to site plants with consideration of how they look throughout the year. I have a towering *Inula magnifica* front and center in the rockery, where its yellow daisylike flowers and soft, broad leaves are magnificent in midsummer. Then I, and everyone who passes by, can't avoid the less-than-elegant look of its huge, withering carcass for the next several months. I should have sited the *Inula* at the back of a border, where it could shine during the glory of its bloom and where its slow and messy decline would be shielded by other plants.

Unless you are out there with clippers for hours every day, destroying all evidence of death and decline, you probably don't want the ugly faders in prominent spots. Constant trimming back results in cute little bumps of plants, which is boring. Only as plants live out their yearly cycle do they take on height, shape, and character. A garden is far richer visually for seed heads and the mellowing colors of plants past their prime; and besides, over-the-hill plants serve as a buffet for the birds.

White-flowered plants, such as jasmine and the pale roses, are notoriously bad faders. As white flowers turn brown, they dangle limply on the plant like soiled handkerchiefs. Because white flowers at their prime are so lovely, we put up with this from them; but we might consider threading a jasmine with another kind of vine, or surrounding white roses with plenty of colorful perennials to distract from their less-than-attractive stages. And what about sweet peas? Nothing is more appealing in flower, or less appealing when the ratty pods hang limply on the mildewed vines. Not a pretty picture. Nor are poppies, whose luscious bloom is quickly followed by ugly withering. I've never seen a plant go from beautiful to gross as quickly as a bearded iris. Hardy fuchsias have a great many virtues (long bloom, drought tolerance), but they're nothing but a pile of dead sticks once frost hits them. And you need to leave their aboveground parts intact until April, so be sure to tuck them into a part of the garden where you won't have to look at them all winter.

Plenty of flowers that perform well in all life stages are available to fill in front-of-the-border spots. *Knautia macedonica* is a fine example, with its ruby button flowers that look as charming after they've bloomed as when in bud. So do the flowers of chocolate cosmos. I leave the heads of alliums in place to dry in the garden, where they lend a strong presence and intriguing texture long after their color has bleached to buff. Hydrangea blossoms are more interesting as the weather cools and they take on tinges of mauve, plum, and bronze. The tall sedums change from pink to bronze over many months, and *Stipa gigantea*'s tall, corn-colored flower spikes grace the garden from June through late winter. Other good faders include verbenas, eryngiums, *Gaura*, bee balm (*Monarda*), *Phlomis, Rudbeckia*, meadow rue (*Thalictrum*), and yarrow (*Achillea*).

A Look Back at the Best of Summer

LATE IN THE SEASON I try to take a few minutes to walk around the garden with pencil and paper, concentrating on which plants have performed well and which have been disappointments. Gardeners always get a second (and third, and fourth), chance with the turnings of the season, and a thoughtful look back is the best way to take advantage of those opportunities.

Usually I lose my notes by the next spring, or forget to look at them, but at least I've gone through the exercise. When I am in the nurseries, I hope I'll be less tempted by the newest or showiest and will instead buy more of the plants that do best in my garden. You know how when your kids are little, the way to look like a wonderful parent is to leave a gathering before they get tired and fussy? Same idea in the garden—avoid problems by using more of the plants that do best and you'll look like a great gardener.

Some gardeners choose plants for flash and dash, while others prize a long, dependable season of gardenworthiness. My plant heroes are the ones that needed a bare minimum of care in my garden last season and had showy flowers or foliage over several months. A maximum of beauty with a minimum of fuss: great criteria, but hard to figure out until the plant has been in the ground in your own garden for a year or two.

For outstanding color over a long season of bloom, nothing beats bog sage (*Salvia uliginosa*). Despite its name, it is a beautiful plant, with sky-blue flowers from midsummer to frost, held spikily aloft on a plant that can tower to five or six feet. I killed this plant several years in a row, trying to grow it on a slope where it didn't get enough moisture. This year I finally figured it out and planted it in an area with damp, heavy soil (easy enough to find in my garden), and it has repaid me with spectacular bloom over many months. Nothing could be so striking as that clear blue flower color against an autumn sky, mixed in with the yellows and reds of fall. This salvia is borderline hardy, so mulch it well; if you lose it, it is worth growing again as an annual.

Another color I loved this year was the jewel-like red of *Penstemon* 'Ruby'. It has narrow leaves and is tall, skinny, and a little too floppy, but the intense color of its tubular foxglove-like flowers is compelling when mixed with white or any shade of green. It bloomed early, I cut it back, and then it flowered again continually from July until October, glowing against a backdrop of rosemary, 'Iceberg' roses, and variegated thyme.

A sturdy, long-blooming plant I used over and over in the garden this year, from rockery to flower beds and in pots, is *Sedum telephium* 'Matrona'. It is a tall, flat-headed sedum similar to the more familiar *Sedum* 'Autumn Joy', but its flowers are larger and a lovely pale pink, drying to soft copper. 'Matrona' has large, slightly scalloped, fleshy green leaves (it looks much prettier than it sounds) with purple veining and purple stems. This foliage provides interest from the time it emerges in the spring, and the dried flower heads lend structure and color until you cut them back in winter.

The fringe flower (*Loropetalum chinense* 'Razzleberri') is a New Year's Eve party of a plant, with bronze-burgundy foliage and shocking-pink flowers. A relative of the witch hazel, this rounded, slow-growing shrub bears blooms with that same spider-like, wiry fluffiness. Its dazzling foliage looks great with pale daffodils early in the year, and with asters late in the season—the flowers of the magenta aster 'Winston Churchill' nearly match its leaves. Plant it in full sun and in a spot sheltered from the worst of winter weather. It hasn't even lost its leaves during a couple of our mild winters, but it's best to mulch it heavily in case one of those oft-predicted cold winters actually comes along.

Far more unusual and deserving of garden space than the familiar St. John's wort *Hypericum androsaemum,* the cultivar 'Albury Purple' is noteworthy for foliage color, fruit, and flower. This shrubby hypericum is evergreen in milder winters—just cut it back to within a few buds of old wood in early spring to prevent legginess. Though it's worth growing for the rich plumminess of its foliage alone, 'Albury Purple' has small golden flowers with a sunburst of stamens in summer, and upright oval fruits late in the season, when it is ideal for flower arrangements. Its cultural requirements are few and straightforward: sun or partial shade, and well-drained soil. Rust can be a problem, but I've only had rust on my plants one partic-ularly wet spring; I cut them to the ground, and they grew back in a few weeks, bushy and healthy. 'Albury Purple' looks well in a wild garden, mixed into borders, as an informal hedge, or massed as a tall groundcover. I grow it along the edge of a patio, next to a rosemary bush, backed by the pale-pink flowers of *Lavatera* 'Barnsley' and festooned with the yellow leaves and intensely magenta flowers of the wandering hardy geranium 'Ann Folkard'.

I grow many different kinds of ornamental grasses, but giant feather grass was particularly satisfying this past season. *Stipa gigantea* is stately, distinguished, and oversized. Unlike many of the bulkier large grasses, though, it fits easily into borders and rockeries, and it's effective grown as a single specimen to add color, movement, and structure to other plantings. With a tidy clump of narrow, arching foliage that grows to only about eighteen inches, *S. gigantea* unfurls its golden sheaves of shimmery flowers early in June. Most ornamental grasses don't bloom until autumn, so the six-foot-high, open, airy inflorescences of this feather grass are exceptionally useful for height and as scrim from late spring until frost. The wheat-colored flowers are the largest on any ornamental grass; held aloft early in the season, they are spectacular. As the rest of the garden catches up later in summer, the flower stalks remain strong and erect, mixing beautifully with buddleia, sunflowers, and shrubby variegated dogwoods (*Cornus alba* 'Aurea' or 'Elegantissima').

S. gigantea does best in full sun and likes well-drained soil. Water generously until established, after which it can tolerate drought, and divide every three or four years. It's native to the mountainous regions of Portugal and Spain, and a clump feels right at home on a dry, rarely tended hillside in my garden, where it adds seasonal interest to a backdrop of darker pines, yews, and osmanthus. The florets rustle in the slightest breeze and reflect the glow of the sun or the moon, their soft wheat color standing out yet not overshadowing other plantings.

Lawn Be Gone

THE DUCHESS OF WINDSOR is said to have declared that a woman can never be too thin or too rich, and I'd say the equivalent landscaping truism is that a garden's beds and borders can never be of too generous a size. Plants need room to weave, and to grow to their full potential. And you don't need a grand garden; many a small garden has been made to appear more spacious by borders with real width.

In a slim strip of soil, all you can do is arrange a line of plants, a row of little soldiers. Even in just four feet of width it is possible to plant a small crabapple, skirted by spiraea or hostas. Beneath that, bulbs for spring and asters for fall can be tucked in among groundcovers planted in an overlapping tapestry carpet. Anything less is static, one-dimensional.

As plants grow larger, and after each successful trip to nursery or plant sale, it is impossible not to cast covetous glances at all that flat, boring space taken up by grass. Many gardeners have removed all the lawn, virtually making it into one large garden area filled with paths, patios, pavers, ponds, and plantings. If that seems a bit much, there is a method of slowly whittling away at the lawn, of gradually transforming turf into planting beds. The no-dig method is easy and foolproof, and makes great dirt, while sparing hands, back, and shovel. Gardeners with heavy clay soil will be particularly grateful for this technique; it not only cuts way down on moving that heavy muck but greatly improves the composition of the soil.

I learned the no-dig method from a landscaper friend who has used it many times in her clients' gardens, either to create new planting beds or to widen or change the shape of existing borders. Autumn is the perfect time to begin the process, and by spring, when plant lust is upon you, beds full of fluffy soil will be ready and waiting. A supply of newspapers, a shovel, mulch, and four to six months are all that is needed to transform turf grass into ready-to-plant soil. The joy of this method is that time and nature do most of the work.

Five easy steps:

1. Begin by digging a shallow ditch about four inches wide and four inches deep outlining the edges of the future border. Throw the dirt and grass dug from this moat onto the lawn you plan to ger rid of—it becomes part of the mulch.

2. Cover all the grass you want to eliminate with a layer of newspapers half an inch thick, overlapping each stack of open sheets by four to six inches, and let the edges fall down into the little ditch.

3. Now it's time for the mulch: leaves, grass clippings, or purchased mulch, or a combination of all three. Cover the newspapers with a foot-deep layer of the mulch.

4. Ignore the resulting mound until spring, letting it all rot down for four to six months. No air or light will penetrate to the turf grass, so it will die, roots and all. The mass will shrink by more than half on its way to becoming great planting soil.

5. In spring, top off the new planting areas with four to six inches of a feeding mulch (a mixture of bark and manure, available in bulk or bags from a nursery or garden center), and you are ready to plant into the rich soil of your new border.

The Pick of the Grasses

GRASSES HAVE BEEN CALLED THE HAIR OF THE EARTH, and a variety of New Zealand sedge is known as 'Frosty Curls'. Although ornamental grasses don't require a trim every six weeks, most types do need an annual haircut. In the last few years, so many fabulous ornamental grasses have become available that it's easy to be overwhelmed by their charms. Which are worthy of garden space? Just as it's a challenge to navigate the nearly impenetrable botany of grasses, it is also difficult to distinguish among their great variety of habit, bloom, and coloration. Lurking in the back of our minds, worrying us, is the image of huge clumps of pampas grass—few of us want such size or girth, let alone cliches, in our gardens. The problem is that the lovely, reasonably sized, easy-to-grow alternatives all look so similar as babies, innocently lined up in little nursery pots.

I've found the sedges to be the most useful of all the grasses in my garden. When you grow lots of perennials, the garden is always in a state of flux. These small, sturdy grasses provide continuity in their fluid forms, perfect for trimming out the edges of steps and patios, for containers, or for the front of the border. They look soft, natural, and flowing, and only need to be cut back every year (or two or three) in early March. That's it for care, except for some summer watering. Because I love variegation, particularly next to the gray of stone or concrete, I grow several golden variegated Japanese sedges (*Carex morrowii* 'Aureovariegata') along the front walkway. Only about a foot high and as wide, they keep their good looks year-round. I plant bronze sedge (*Carex comans* 'Bronze') everywhere I don't have any other ideas because it makes all other plants look good, as does the gilded little beauty *Carex comans* 'Frosty Curls'. Just this fall I discovered the short ground-cover *Carex siderosticha* 'Island Brocade', which has creamy stripes on its wide blades and likes part shade and moist soil.

The little feather grass *Stipa tenuissima* is a billowy all-summer bloomer; its finely cut, fluffed-up flowers are white at first, fading to wheaten-tipped silver as the summer goes on. Grow it with pale yarrow and burgundy *Euphorbia dulcis* 'Chameleon' for an all-season-long stunner of a combination that takes up very little space.

Another grass with a delicate, hazy appearance is purple moor grass, *Molinia caerulea* var. *arundinacea* 'Skyracer' (who makes up these names, anyway?). It sends flower spikes more than seven feet into the air; at first tinged with purple, they turn a rich gold in autumn. It shimmers like the sun when planted among a grouping of evergreens, or seems to draw all available light into a planting of perennials.

Who can resists the fat, furry foxtail flowers of the purple-bladed fountain grass (*Pennisetum setaceum* 'Rubrum')? Not hardy in our climate, it's worth growing as an annual; or you could choose its slightly less flashy but still handsome cousin *Pennisetum alopecuroides,* which is reliably hardy. A tiny form of this grass is easy to squeeze in just about anywhere; *P. alopecuroides* 'Little Bunny' has fluffy cream flowers and grows only eighteen inches high.

Few plants have such dramatically colored foliage as the grasses. Blue wheat grass (*Agropyron magellanicum)* is truly, iridescently blue, while the deepest ebony of all plants is a grass look-alike, black mondo grass (*Ophiopogon planiscapus* 'Nigrescens'), a short creeper of surprising darkness. Bowles' golden grass (*Milium effusum* 'Aureum') brings bright chartreuse to the spring garden, and my favorite of all the autumn red grasses is the glowing switch grass *Panicum virgatum* 'Haense Herms', a tidy specimen that grows to four feet in flower.

Grasses are fine plants for beginning gardeners because they are rarely bothered by pests or diseases, they are easy to maintain (give them sun and good drainage, avoid fertilizers), and most are fairly drought resistant. I grow grasses for none of these practical reasons. I appreciate that most grasses bloom late and look their best all through the autumn. I love their bold foliage colors, and use their inflorescences as long-lasting additions to flower arrangements. Whenever a grouping of plants seems dull, the addition of an ornamental grass or two often provides just the spark that is needed. One of the giant feather grasses used for vertical punctuation, a short mondo grass as an edging, or the addition of colored blades, such as in blue oat grass (*Helictotrichon sempervirens*), can tie the planting together, making all the other plants look their best. (And if that still doesn't do it, I mix in a plant with great big leaves.)

The botany of grasses is confusing, and as a group their scientific names are among the toughest to pronounce in the horticultural lexicon. Strictly speaking, true grasses belong to the grass family (Gramineae). Mondo grass, lily turf, rushes, and bulbs with grasslike foliage, such as fairy wand (*Dierama*) and Pacific Coast iris, look like grasses, but are not. Most, but not all, of the ornamental grasses you see in nurseries and catalogs are in one of the following genera: *Miscanthus* (maiden grass), *Panicum* (switch grass), *Pennisetum* (fountain grass), *Stipa* (feather grass), *Festuca* (fescues), or *Carex* (sedges).

You can try to ignore the names, but before you select grasses, be sure you find out the answers to two important questions: Are they invasive (spreading runners, too-generous seeding)? Are they hardy?

For the purposes of care, it's convenient to think of grasses as falling into two categories, warm-season and cool-season. The warm-season grasses go dormant in winter and don't begin growing again until the soil warms up in spring. Cool-season grasses (sedges are an example) thrive in our climate, are often evergreen or semievergreen, and grow best in fall, winter, and spring. The most important maintenance task for growing healthy grasses is to cut back the foliage once a year. The easy answer on timing is to cut them all back in early March shortly before the new shoots appear. The dead foliage and flowers of the warm-season, deciduous grasses are looking bleached and tattered by then, so they should be cut back clear to the ground. They will grow to their full height during the coming growing season. (They can be cut down earlier if they look so bad you can't stand them, but cutting late in the winter leaves a bare spot for the shortest possible time.)

The cool-season, evergreen grasses resent being cut back too hard. If the older foliage looks messy, or if the tips have been burned by winter cold, trim them back by no more than a third. The clumps of golden variegated Japanese sedge along my front walkway look great all season long with no care except some summer water and an occasional light trim.

Succulent Sedums

YOU COULD PLANT AN ENTIRE GARDEN OF SEDUMS, and no one would ever guess you were using just one kind of plant. What other single genus contains such a variety of size, habit, and coloration, yet is so adaptable and easy to care for? Sedums define drought tolerance, never flagging or wilting down in the heat. Every time we have a dry summer, a garden full of these succulent beauties sounds like a fine idea.

This is just a partial list of sedum's attributes; they grow tall and stately, carpet the ground, or dangle down a rockery. They maintain their good looks year-round in pots. Sedums are spectacular foliage plants, with leaves of distinct coloration and shapes varying from broad to rosette. And they have lovely clusters of flowers that bloom over a long period of time, often retaining color until the first frost. They spread just as much as you'd like them to but never push out or strangle their neighbors.

Sedums may be the one group of plants that defy the oxymoron "low-maintenance garden." Truly adaptable, they shine in a wide variety of situations with no pampering. Though sedums love dry soil, I grow *S. telephium* 'Matrona' in a pot with a climbing rose that needs daily watering. Despite getting much more water than it would prefer, it looks just as healthy as other 'Matrona's in the garden that receive no water at all. The red stems and chalky green leaves grow up to disguise the legginess of the rose, and the sedum's soft pink flowers start blooming when the rose goes out of flower.

I'm trying to think of some criticism of sedums, but I can only come up with the fact that if you eat them they'll probably upset your stomach, and some people get mild rashes from their sap. Both of these problems should be easy to avoid.

It is worth growing all the tall kinds just to cut them for bouquets, as they last for weeks in the house, adding height, heft, and unexpected texture to any arrangement. And sedums exaggerate the quality I love best about perennials, without all the dividing and staking most perennials require: they change throughout the season. Though sedum leaves may start out green, they flush with russet, lavender, or copper over time, and the flowers only look better as their colors deepen and soften with age.

Gardeners would, of course, be unable to limit themselves to sedums because they'd miss all the fun of combining them with other plants. Sedums pair beautifully with perennials and ornamental grasses, their fleshy leaves a pleasant surprise in temperate gardens and a welcome counterpoint to the fluff and droop of other plants.

And the colors of the leaves! I just planted a big aggregate pot with a thick bunch of *Sedum kamtschaticum* 'Variegatum', whose mottled foliage nearly matches the grays, roses, and tawny colors of the stones. The spoon-shaped leaves are gray-green, tinted in pink and trimmed in warm cream, with yellow flowers that age to crimson. Now that is a whole garden in a pot, achieved with a single kind of tough, weather-resistant plant.

Here are a few other favorite sedums:

- *S. alboroseum* 'Frosty Morn', an upright plant whose pale foliage is margined in white to accent its white-tinged-with-pink flowers.

- *S. sieboldii*, a delicate, drooping sedum with exquisitely colored blue-green leaves trimmed in lavender and star-shaped pink flowers.

- *S.* 'Vera Jameson', a low-growing plant with bronzy purple foliage and rose-pink flowers.

- *S. spurium* 'Dragon's Blood', a spreading groundcover with maroon rosettelike foliage.

- *S. spectabile* 'Brilliant', a tall sedum with hot-pink autumn flowers beloved by bees and butterflies.

1

Aster novae-angliae
'Alma Potschke'

I've rarely seen an aster I didn't covet, and if you plant a variety
of different kinds they fill the garden with color from mid-August through late
October. The shocking pink of 'Alma Potschke' is stunning up against the reds
and golds of autumn foliage, as useful in the vase as in the garden. It grows in a
healthy, wiry clump to four feet high in a sunny, moist spot in my garden, in
front of an old fence and across from hydrangeas, whose mauve flower heads
accent its brilliant color. 'Alma Potschke' needs staking, but its height
can be controlled by pinching it back severely in late spring, and its
vigor encouraged by dividing it every two or three years.

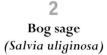

Bog sage
(Salvia uliginosa)

Its common name gives an important clue to siting this unusual salvia.
It prefers moist soil and full sun, where it grows luxuriantly to six feet, with
spires of sky-blue flowers from late summer through first frost. Somewhat
tender, it should be mulched in winter. The spectacular blue of its flowers is
emphasized, and its legginess disguised, when surrounded by red-toned
ornamental grasses such as Japanese blood grass or the vivid
switch grass *Panicum virgatum* 'Haense Herms'.

4
Autumn-blooming crocus
(Colchicum autumnale)

A surprise in the late-September garden, this crocus seems to invoke spring more than shortening days. Grown from corms planted in summer, the delicate-appearing yet sturdy little flowers bloom for weeks when sited in sun and well-drained soil. In my garden they are planted along an east-facing terrace, where they liven up a grouping of spotted deadnettle (*Lamium maculatum* 'White Nancy'), the little evergreen shrub *Sarcococca humulis,* and the wispy *Carex comans* 'Frosty Curls'.

3
Variegated Elderberry
(Sambucus nigra **'Aureomarginata')**

This cream-trimmed elderberry is a large, deciduous shrub that grows lustily to eight or nine feet, but can be kept in bounds by cutting it nearly down to the ground in early spring. I let it go on my back bank, where its patterned leaves are a welcome contrast to all the greens, and its flat, white flower clusters are lovely in summer flower arrangements. It is filled with birds, nesting in summer and flocking to the shiny black berries in autumn.

october

Leap of Faith

A CONSIDERABLE LEAP OF FAITH takes place when we put bulbs into the ground in late autumn. It is hard to even imagine the splendor that, next spring, will grow from the holes we dig on chill, wet October days and the unprepossessing lumps we put into them.

Bulbs come in a variety of choices so numerous as to put Baskin-Robbins to shame, from delicate checkered fritillaria (*F. meleagris*) to three-foot-tall 'Hocus Pocus', a skyscraper tulip of sulfur yellow flamed with jasper red. I've come up with a few guidelines to keep from getting overwhelmed by all those pretty pictures displayed in the catalogs and at the nurseries. First, I try to limit myself to bulbs that bloom early. On dank February days no sight could be more welcome than a lavender crocus or a pearly white snowdrop (*Galanthus*). The later tulips, lovely as they are, just don't seem as special in May when so much else is blooming. That said, I can't resist the ruffly roselike pink tulip 'Angelique', which blooms quite late but is worth waiting for.

Somehow we always expect tulips to be perennial, but most either disappear or decline dramatically after their first season. You can encourage them to bloom again by planting deeply (eight to ten inches) in light, fluffy soil with perfect drainage and by withholding summer water. Or you can relax and enjoy them as annuals. The most dependably perennial tulips are the shorter, less showy ones (*Tulipa greigii* and *T. kaufmanniana*), which work wonders to brighten up a rockery in early spring.

PREVIOUS PAGE: *The yoshino cherries along the street have formed a canopy of fall color for several weeks, but now are beginning to drop their leaves. Maggie, my constant gardening companion, is a soft-coated Wheaten Terrier.*

LEFT: *A staghorn sumac's filigreed foliage is set off by the large, soft leaves of* Inula magnifica, *with a backdrop of the large ornamental grass,* Miscanthus sinensis.

Why give garden room to bulbs without fragrance, when so many are sweetly scented? The rich perfume of hyacinths is heady by the front door or beneath a bedroom window. Many of the little narcissus are surprisingly aromatic; try 'Ice Wings' for its ivory white flowers and fruity fragrance, or 'Baby Moon', a lushly scented, multiflowered golden yellow.

I look for bulbs that bloom in more

163

intriguing colors than the usual pinks and yellows. Scillas come in shades of blue from sky to violet, and are small enough to be easily tucked in front of other plants. Even the large daffodils come in subtle colors, like the creamy white 'Ice Follies', or 'Kissproof' in buff with a copper-tinged cup. My current favorite tulip is the stately 'Queen of the Night', irresistible not only for its name but because of its deep, silky cup of blackish maroon. I grow it set off by variegated vinca, along with the darkly matching *Heuchera* 'Chocolate Ruffles'.

Surrounding plants can either accent or harmonize with the colors of the bulbs, and once the show is past, they will grow up to cover the withering remains. Tulips or daffs growing beneath spring-flowering trees is a classic look. I grow the daffodil 'Pink Charm' beneath my three Yoshino flowering cherries (*Prunus* x *yedoensis* 'Akebono') along the sidewalk, for a match of creamy pink beginning at the end of March. Lady's mantle, ferns, bleeding heart, daylilies, and hosta are all traditional companions, growing in to fill the gaps left when bulbs fade.

Perhaps most important, when you are planting bulbs, remember that real estate motto: Location, location, location. Bulbs need plenty of sun, and they will perform poorly or rot away in heavy, slow-draining soil. So think ahead about where you have space on a slope, or where you can build up some raised beds with good soil.

And it takes a fair amount of energy to plant bulbs correctly—that is, with their tops at a depth equal to three times their height—which is no mean feat with some of those hunky daffodil or allium bulbs. Soil amendments help, as do strong muscles and a sharp shovel.

Potting Up Springtime

I'M ALWAYS TRYING TO FIGURE OUT ways to keep the containers on the back patio and front steps looking good year-round with as little refurbishment as possible. Considering that a pot is stuffed full of plants raised above ground level, competing for nutrients and water in a meager amount of soil, it can be quite a trick.

Bulbs are ideal for pot culture, as they themselves contain all they need in their own small, tidy package. They can be shipped, stored, or even left in paper bags, and most will still sprout come springtime. A bit of an evolutionary miracle, bulbs shut down in the fall, storing an embryonic flower and enough food to last until warmer temperatures awaken them.

You can take advantage of these sleeping beauties by layering them in pots this fall, then enjoying waves of bloom from February through June. It is best to use a large pot—one with an interior diameter of at least twenty-four inches is ideal, although I've used smaller pots and still had a fine springtime show.

Just when summer flowers are getting so ratty you can't stand to look at them a minute more, it's time to plant bulbs. Assembling what you need for winter pots is like gathering the ingredients to bake a cake, except less exacting. What you need is one woody plant for height and structure, low-growing plants to group around its trunk, and several different kinds of bulbs to layer into the soil.

Start with the woody plant—most small trees and shrubs can stay in a pot for several years before being put into the ground. I kept a corkscrew hazel (*Corylus avellana* 'Contorta') in a pot for years before I let it loose to grow happily in the border. Dwarf Hinoki cypresses are evergreen and slow growing; dogwoods and Japanese maples have a lovely line in winter and decorative foliage in summer. I have a yellow variegated false holly (*Osmanthus heterophyllus* 'Goshiki') in a pot on the front porch that I string with Christmas lights in December and surround with bacopa in summer, and in springtime purple crocuses bloom around its trunk. This is easy gardening.

Place the tree or shrub in the pot first, with plenty of fresh, well-draining potting soil beneath it. Place the bulbs that bloom latest on the bottom layer, about halfway down inside the pot. These could be late tulips, like the ruffled pink 'Angelique' or deeper pink 'May Wonder', or the darkly elegant 'Queen of the Night'. Use at least seven or nine bulbs—as many as you can squeeze in without touching each other or the sides of the pot (they need plenty of soil for insulation from the cold). Fill in around them, sprinkling in a little bulb food, and cover with a few inches of soil. Then nestle in a layer of midseason bulbs, perhaps hyacinths for fragrance (these are fat bulbs, so you won't be able to use as many) or narcissus. Fill in with soil again, and add a top layer of early-blooming crocus, grape hyacinth, or little *Iris reticulata.*. Water in, patting down the soil until it settles between all the layers of bulbs. At this point you should still have about six inches left at the top of the pot, which you can stuff with groundcovers, little ornamental grasses, winter pansies, or perennials. I often use the dark-leafed heucheras, which keep their foliage all winter, a few colorful pansies, and one of the small sedges, such as bronze *Carex comans*, to droop down the side of the pot. It's best to keep the pot in a protected spot over the winter, moving it to a more exposed place in early spring to bask in any available sunshine. The warmth will encourage the bulbs to push through the soil and bloom, one kind after another, until it is time to garnish the pot again with summer flowers.

Oh, Deer!

DEER DRIVE GARDENERS CRAZY. Used to battling only slugs and a predatory heron, I had no idea how crazy, until I was a guest on a live radio show about gardening. Every other call was a lament for lost plants, a litany of munched flowers, a plea for help in thwarting the four-footed, doe-eyed menace.

One gardener, writing in *Pacific Horticulture* magazine, tells how the deer that visited her garden had at first avoided walking on paved surfaces. But her nightly visitors became emboldened, their hooves on her patio sounding like a troop of ladies in high-heeled shoes. Come morning, she now finds her plants (especially the rare or expensive ones) decimated; the ladies come not only for tea, but breakfast, lunch, and dinner as well.

My sister gardens on thirty-six acres in Clatskanie, Oregon, and I've always been impressed by her cheerful intrepidness as she ekes out space for flowers, fruit, and vegetables on a rough hillside, competing with cows, cats, dogs, rabbits, chickens, and geese (at any rate, she does have a steady supply of manure). But when I visited in the autumn, she had clearly lost her patience (and perhaps her mind), as shown by a hand-printed sign stuck out into the garden: "Keep Out Of My Pumpkins! You already ate my strawberries and my roses. Thanksgiving dinner doesn't have to be turkey you know!" The deer lifted the chicken-wire fence and ate the pumpkins. The medium *was* the message—they ate the sign, too. I traveled to the farm again for Thanksgiving dinner, and the deer's bravado was proved correct: roasted bird, not venison, was served, accompanied by brussel sprouts from Safeway.

My sister's neighbor has a large Rottweiler that sleeps outside to guard against trespass. He has proved somewhat effective, but big dogs do their own damage to the garden, plus they become accustomed to deer. And, as my sister points out, deer do their damage mostly in spring and fall. You have the Rottweiler year-round.

Short of employing a dog the size of a truck, or building a very tall fence (deer are rumored to be able to jump eight to ten feet with a running start), how does a gardener coexist with deer? Chicken wire looks like heck, but it's easy to bend into cages around your most precious plants. If the deer are really hungry, though, they've been known to pull up even staked-down chicken wire, especially to get at strawberries.

My sister has for years planted a sacrificial rose near the spot where the deer enter her garden, hoping they'll go for the fast-food snack and leave her favorite roses alone. Some years it works; some years they nibble *all* the roses. And don't think deer will be reasonable or easily pacified—she has tried leaving fallen apples on the ground for them, but they stand up on their hind legs and pick the best apples right off the tree. I'd like to see that.

Nancy Goodwin, famous North Carolina gardener, divulged the recipe for her secret deer deterrent when she spoke in Seattle. Put 1 tablespoon Tabasco sauce, 1 egg, and 1 cup water into a blender, mix well, and then strain into a gallon jug (the straining is important, she says). Fill up the jug with water. As the last step, add 1 tablespoon liquid dish detergent. Mist onto plants. Goodwin swears by this stuff, saying that it saves hostas, roses, and all kinds of choice plants from deer decimation. I wonder if it rains as much in North Carolina as it does here? Does she spray it on daily?

Deer are unpredictable, and some have more adventurous palates than others. I've sifted through more than a dozen lists of deer-resistant ("deerproof" would be an untruth) plants, and found little agreement. Only generalities are safe—deer tend to dislike strong-tasting plants (eucalyptus, rosemary), plants with milky sap (euphorbia, poppies), twiggy plants with tiny leaves, and thorny plants like barberries (although they love roses). They rarely eat ferns, and they pass up poisonous plants such as daffodils and senecio. My sister says she is trying to learn to love iris and dahlias—two plants not found on the official lists but (so far, anyway) not a menu preference of Clatskanie deer.

The Silverlings

IT HAS BEEN SAID that the mark of an expert gardener is the favoring of foliage over flower. For those of us who aim to make a garden with year-round good looks, this is largely true. But "foliage" should not be viewed as a single category—it runs the gamut from spindly and nondescript to big and bold to wildly variegated. And the most useful foliage of all is gray or silver.

To make certain that such a decisive statement is demonstrably true, I just walked around my garden (early October) and counted thirty-seven plants of silvery hue, many still looking their best despite the droughty summer and last night's temperature of 35°F. Despite my love for yellow leaves and yellow variegation, I find that I've planted far more plants in the cooler tones of silver and gray. My new favorite, just found this summer, is little *Helichrysum* 'Icicles', a groundcover that grows to only about a foot high. It likes full sun and dry soil, and has narrow leaves of intense silver. It looks as if it would be right at home growing beneath the water, tendrils waving about in the tides. If those beguilingly slender leaves were green, it would be boring. Now I'm waiting to see whether it will make it through the winter—supposedly it withstands temperatures down to 15°F. There are other wonderfully silvery helichrysums, such as the curry plant (*H. serotinum*), dependably hardy with aromatic foliage, and the annual licorice plant, *H. petiolare*. All are slightly hairy, giving them a velvety sheen and making them the kind of tactile plants that are hard to keep from stroking as you walk by.

A plant that's impossible to pass without rubbing it between your fingers is the easy-to-grow lambs' ears (*Stachys bzyantina*), which spreads to carpet the ground with its appealing woolly whiteness. Few plants are more useful in more places than this humble herb. Like many of its fellow silverlings, such as lavender and santolina, it hails from Mediterranean climates, so is naturally adapted to dry conditions and prefers soil that is not too rich. This means that most thrive on neglect, saving the gardener time and water.

Another plus is that it's nearly impossible to create color clashes with silver and gray foliage plants. Combined with white, they provide a duet of paleness that is especially welcome at twilight (which is why gardens devoted to these plants are called moon gardens). Silver softens bright colors, sparks yellow, cools the garish, and blends with pastels. I even like magenta (almost) if it is surrounded by enough silver. Nature provides its own clues for such pairings—think of how the silver foliage of *Lychnis coronaria* soothes the difficult pink of its flower.

But silverlings don't always need to play a supporting role—they can be the showboats. Silver-leafed weeping pear (*Pyrus salicifolia* 'Pendula') is a focal point of sparkling silver so soft as to appear ethereal. Also on the grander scale are statuesque cardoons, with huge, gray, toothed leaves, and tall gilded verbascums, with felted flower stalks that mimic the majestic shape of candelabra. Smaller silvery gray plants with a presence include *Euphorbia characias* subsp. *wulfenii* and donkeytail spurge (*Euphorbia myrsinites),* both striking when combined with the lacy froth of near-white *Artemisia* 'Powis Castle'.

There are plenty of gray and silver perennials to choose from, often with aromatic foliage, mostly sun-loving, wanting to grow on slopes or other well-drained areas. Catmints (*Nepeta*) are a classic underplanting for roses, while Russian sage (*Perovskia atriplicifolia)* has blue spires of flowers atop a haze of soft gray foliage. The gray shrublet *Hebe pimeleoides* 'Quick Silver' is lovely edging beds of brighter colors, as is dwarf lavender cotton (*Santolina chamaecyparissus* 'Corsica'), which can be trimmed into a dense, pale low hedge.

If foliage plants are truly the backbone of the garden, then the silverlings are the elegant icing. They bring an old-fashioned tactile herbiness (as with catmint and lambs' ears) as well as the poetry of the moon's reflection brought to earth.

Autumn's Lushness Brought Indoors

LUXURIANT SUMMER BOUQUETS START TO LOOK ALL WRONG once the mornings become chilly enough to see your breath. My perceptions change with the slant of autumn sunlight, and now I love weedy arrangements that look as if I've spent a day in the country, gathering whatever was at hand. To this end, I collect tall stoneware or glazed pitchers (you can never, ever have enough vases) in shades of buff, blue, olive, and caramel, and stuff them full of the blooms from ornamental grasses, or fill them with sunflowers, coneflowers, or rudbeckia. It can be just that easy in autumn.

Autumn is a time to come indoors and enjoy the pleasures of the fireplace, warm lamplight, and hot soup. The mellow colors of autumn foliage and flowers add to this atmosphere of drawing in. The burnished, slightly faded autumn colors all go together so beautifully that there's no need to worry about matches or clashes. Think of the soft mauves of dried hydrangea heads, the wheat and creamy whites of ornamental grass inflorescences, the rich purple-bronze of smokebush foliage. Combined and brought indoors they glow softly, as if they themselves carry the scent of wood smoke and crunchy apples. Add the surprise of a few fat rugosa rose hips, and a branch of those renegade blackberries that poke through the fence, letting the berries drip down the side of the vase. You've created the essence of autumn in the center of your dining room table.

The color scheme starts to veer toward autumn when the *Crocosmia* bloom. By late August, the sweet peas and lavender fade, and I begin to make bouquets grouped around the bright oranges and golds of the crocosmia, accented with *Aster* x *frikartii* 'Mönch'. This soft purple aster has yellow centers, and such a long bloom season that it can work as the backbone of arrangements from Labor Day through Thanksgiving. Ornamental grass blades and flowers give that hazy, roadside look, as do clumps of papery orange Chinese lanterns (*Physalis alkekengi*). The bouquet is completed with a spray of hypericum fruits or the curious red-orange berry spikes of *Arum italicum*, along with a cluster of sneezeweed (*Helenium autumnale*) in shades of yellows, rusts, and coppers for depth of color.

To spark these mellow autumn tones, be sure to plant some vivid blues and crisp whites that bloom late in the season. *Boltonia asteroides* 'Snowbank' has bright white flowers that persist through October. Single white Japanese anemones lend a graceful line to any arrangement, or look lovely paired with darkly red Japanese blood grass (*Imperata cylindrica* 'Rubra'). Dwarf plumbago (*Ceratostigma plumbaginoides*) is a low-growing perennial with plum-colored leaves and little gentian-blue flowers, which look great cascading down the side of a vase.

By autumn, the garden has usually grown up enough to supply big, bold hunks of foliage to fill jugs and pitchers. Cut whole branches of Japanese maple, sourwood (*Oxydendrum arboreum*), with its brilliant scarlet leaves, or flame-red burning bush (*Euonymus alata*) to stick in a basket on the hearth (lined with a water-filled jar). The berry-laden branches of hawthorns, pyracantha, and crabapples provide both line and color. For a more traditional bouquet, dahlias or chrysanthemums look lovely with maroon Virginia creeper vines, or with bunches of herbs clipped just before frost.

Lest you think you don't have garden room for all these selections, remember that all are hard-working landscape plants (except that marauding blackberry vine) that provide foliage or flower in more than one season. None need be grown in special cutting gardens—who has space or time for that? The trick, and the fun, is to look at every single plant in your garden with an eye to its potential in the vase, and to celebrate this season of ripening by bringing the garden indoors.

Pumpkins and Gourds

PUMPKINS GET A BAD RAP, carved up and filled with a candle or used as decorations for the Thanksgiving table. To some people they're a symbol of haunted nights, to others just an orange mush that comes out of a can to make delectable pies for end-of-the-year holidays. We forget that pumpkins are easy-to-grow vining fruits that come in a wide assortment of shapes, sizes, and shades, providing garden pleasures over a long season.

A pumpkin is a winter squash that is usually orange to yellow, with the exception of the pale ghost pumpkins. Some ornamental gourds look very pumpkin-ish, and they share the same family name (Cucurbitaceae), but gourds are distinguished by their durable shells, some so hard they can last for thousands of years. Other vine crops, such as cucumbers and melons, originated in Asia and Africa, while pumpkins are New World fruits—hence their association with early settlers and Thanksgiving.

Then there is the whole pumpkin frenzy that has nothing to do with holidays but everything to do with machismo. And lest you think that a sexist remark, every photo in the book *How-To-Grow World Class Giant Pumpkins* by Don Langevin features a guy, usually wearing a cap, standing proudly next to a swollen orange orb weighing hundreds of pounds. You wouldn't catch a woman spending her time, or giving up garden space (giant pumpkin vines cover eight hundred to twelve hundred square feet), to grow such grotesques.

The chapter entitled "The Heavy Hitters" profiles dozens of men devoted to the quest of coaxing along the world's first thousand-pound pumpkin, competitors in the sport of pumpkin growing as regulated by the World Pumpkin Confederation. There are lists of the thirty heaviest pumpkins ever grown, and photos of little boys sitting atop the bloated prizewinners, their legs dangling off into space. Life's a competition. So be sure to start out right: pumpkins grown from the seed of Dill's Atlantic Giant have won all recent world records. A surprising number of champions have been grown here in the Northwest, including the nine-hundred-seventy-four-pound giant that won a major competition for Fife, Washington, resident J. Lincoln Mettler.

Conditions for growing healthy pumpkins, giant or not, are pretty straightforward. Pumpkin patches need full sun, plenty of water, and good soil enriched with compost and manure. It is tough, if not impossible, to overfeed a pumpkin vine. It takes anywhere from eighty to one hundred twenty days for a crop to ripen and develop color.

I remember as a kid pushing pumpkin seeds into damp dirt in a paper cup, transplanting the prickly vine into the garden, and being amazed at the results. I'm sure kids still plant pumpkins as science projects. Every part of growing them is so satisfying: leaves like rough lily pads, fruits that seem to double in size each day. And then there is the carving, the toasting and eating of pumpkin seeds. This year, a neighbor grew a pumpkin vine in a raised bed along the sidewalk, and it slows down all the kids on their way to the bus stop (even the so-cool middle-schoolers) as they stop to count the little pumpkins coloring up.

While pumpkins might not come to mind as we search out the most delicious, sophisticated, or showy plants for our gardens, I'd argue that pumpkins are all of the above. Consider these varieties: 'Baby Boo Mini' is a white three-incher ideal for growing up an arbor; each vine of 'Jack-Be-Little' bears dozens of deep orange, perfectly proportioned miniatures; 'Lumina' is a plump, satiny cream-colored twelve-pounder with sweet golden flesh for pies and soups. Or what about 'Cinderella', an antique French variety whose flattened, deeply lobed shape served as the original model for Cinderella's fairy-tale coach? Plant an assortment for a flashy pumpkin patch guaranteed to bring out the kid in us all.

Spooky Plants

HALLOWEEN HAS LONG BEEN MY FAVORITE HOLIDAY. I liked it even better before Martha Stewart jumped on the bandwagon, but she hasn't ruined it for me yet. There are so few expectations—no big meals to cook, no gifts to buy, no eggs to hide—just a deliciously scary celebration of the turning of the season, the last of the leaves, the plunge into winter.

In recent years I have expanded my decorating, beyond a twisted, bare-twig wreath and a pumpkin-headed stuffed man to greet trick-or-treaters by the front door and out into the garden itself. The texture of tree bark on bare branches etched against the early darkness of the sky, thorns, berries, gnarled vines bare now of foliage—all are ominous once you get into the Halloween mood.

I found inspiration for this celebration of nature's less obvious charms in a display at one of the early Seattle Flower and Garden Shows, held in February, which was designed by Dan Borroff, with plants supplied by Peter Ray (of Puget Garden Resources on Vashon Island) and Dan Hinkley (of Heronswood Nursery in Kingston). Entitled "It Was a Dark and Stormy Night," this murder-mystery set of a garden was filled with thorns, dark leaves, and gnarled branches, all creating a creepy graveyard ambience.

All this atmospheric creativity sprang from practicality. "We had forced plants for the show two years previously and had a technical breakdown," said Borroff. Half the plants perished, and the team wasn't eager to repeat the uncertainties of forcing. "We decided to use what looks good in the winter and make the most of it." Good advice not only for a five-day display garden, but for an entire season in our home gardens. Borroff deems the usual garden-show themes, such as an idyllic summer setting complete with hammock, tea table, and Victorian novel, "far too 'pretty' for winter. I'd rather curl up with a mystery on the sofa, branches and vines knocking against the house in the rain. It's a far better fit with the mood of the season, don't you think?"

Perhaps the most obvious way to create a feel of foreboding is to use a carnivorous plant or two. While the native habitats for these open-mouthed exotics are steamy swamps, pitcher plants (*Sarracenia*) can survive outdoors as far north as Vancouver, British Columbia, and the better-known Venus's flytrap tolerates light freezes. Flies, ants, and wasps fall drunk to their deaths after following a trail of intoxicating nectar down into the pitcher plant's darkly veined throat; skinny teeth line the margin of the flytrap's clamshell-shaped halves and snap shut once an insect enters, holding it captive until drowned in the plant's digestive juices. If you are interested in creating a Little Shop of Horrors in your own garden, take a look at the book *The Savage Garden* by Peter D'Amato.

It was with an anticipation of the dark windy days of autumn that I planted a 'Little Prince' *Corokia* (*Corokia cotoneaster* 'Little Prince') in my rockery this September. It is drought tolerant and likes bright sun, so it's ideal for this exposed slope, but I really chose it for its bizarre appearance: growing three to four feet high, it resembles nothing more than a wild snarl of snaky gray witch's hair. I surrounded it with arching brown clumps of leatherleaf sedge (*Carex buchananii*), and I'm hoping to create a little Halloween apprehension as the two grow up and mingle in an eerie tangle.

Miss Wilmott's ghost (*Eryngium giganteum*) is a biennial with white, spiny flower heads, uncannily pale and jagged in the moonlight. But if we were choosing spooky plants on name alone there is a gardenful of candidates: witch hazel, devil's comb, creeping toadflax, stinking hellebore, blood sedge, pig's squeak, and dead nettle are just a few plants that arouse cautious curiosity about the derivation of their common names.

Some of the following plants are seriously creepy; others reveal their most dramatic characteristics beneath gloomy skies or the golden shine of the harvest moon:

• Dragon arum *(Dracunculus vulgaris)* smells and looks like something that has pushed its way up through the earth all the way from the underworld. Black-red hooded flowers and a long black tongue (is it forked?) complete the disgusting picture.

• Ghost bramble (*Rubus biflorus)* has ghostly canes arching to six feet. After the leaves drop off in fall, the tangle of stems glow snow-white through the winter.

• *Rosa sericea pteracantha* has thorns every bit as intimidating as the thought of trying to pronounce its name. Winged thorns of deep and glowing red line the stems, abruptly and sharply pointed as a vampire's fingernails. Oh, and it has creamy single flowers in early summer, too.

• *Solanum pyracanthum* has aggressively sharp orange thorns thickly lining the stems, toothed foliage, and pretty purple flowers. Its air of spiky malevolence makes it hard to believe it is a member of the humble potato family.

1

Cortaderia stelloana
'Sun Stripe'

The two fat clumps on my steep front hillside hold their good looks year-round with very little supplemental water. A small pampas grass, 'Sun Stripe' has bright yellow and green blades that grow into an arching clump about four feet high and as wide. It throws up fluffy white plumes in late summer that last until a snowstorm knocks them down. One of my favorite sights in late winter is small birds clinging to the stalks of bloom, picking off the remaining fuzz for their nests.

3
Staghorn sumac
(Rhus typhina)

One of the best small trees for late color, staghorn sumac keeps its vivid yellow, orange, and red leaves into November. Accented by velvety red shoots and, on female plants, erect clusters of deep crimson fruit, its spreading shape and deeply dissected foliage are stunning. It suckers freely, so it's best grown on a neglected bank or in a wild area. In winter, the widely spreading branches are coated in soft brown velvet and topped by the fruit clusters. Perhaps the only criticism of this plant (besides its suckering habit) is that it leafs out late in the springtime. But the autumn color is worth it.

2
Mountain ash
(Sorbus hupehensis)

A flashy small tree that grows fairly slowly to twenty-five feet, mountain ash has bluish green leaves that turn a strong orange-red in late fall. It shares the graceful, finely cut, fernlike foliage of its more common relatives, but is notable for its prolific white-blushed-with-pink fruits, which show up beautifully against autumn foliage and persist through the winter if the birds don't finish them off.

4
Harlequin glorybower
(Clerodendrum trichotomum var. *fargesii)*

The attractions of this small deciduous tree are as showy as its common name. The variety *fargesii* (eight to ten feet) has bronze young leaves, hails from China, and is the hardiest type. It has large (to five-inch) leaves that smell strongly of peanut butter, with small, more conventionally fragrant white flowers in late summer. But the main justification for giving it garden space becomes clear in late September and October, when brilliant pink calyxes surround metallic turquoise fruit for an inspired and surprising combination of colors for the autumn garden.

3

winter

A Time for Reflection

I SAW THIS QUOTE IN THE SAN FRANCISCO AIRPORT a couple of years ago. No matter that it was part of a surfboard exhibit—for me, the words seemed to capture the allure and addiction of gardening. If ever there is a time to reflect on how we've become inextricably hooked on a pursuit so dirty, expensive, and time consuming as gardening, it must be now, I thought—at this darkest time of year, at the dawn of a new millennium.

Printed out in huge letters, amidst a display of shiny surfboards, were these words: "There are uncounted millions of people right now who are going through life without any sort of real, vibrant kick. The legions of the unjazzed. But surfers have found one way." And so, I do believe, have gardeners. (The quote is from noted surfer Phil Edwards, writing about his sport in 1967.)

Gardening provides its own jazz; as it exhausts, so does it rejuvenate. Soil, worms, and compost are real; torn and dirty fingernails and mud-coated tools are real; flowers, foliage, birds, and bees are vibrant. All of it is one big creative kick.

I bet that most gardeners will still venture outdoors as the winter solstice and the year's shortest day approach, to clip a last rose or push some soggy leaves aside for a glimpse of a fat hellebore bud. We feel the turn of the year, the push toward new life and bloom. There is always so much to do, to look at, and to learn that it is impossible to be bored or complacent, and I'd suggest that whatever being jazzed means, it must be the opposite of being bored or complacent.

So what is it that will jazz up gardeners in the coming years? What trends and ideas will excite us, give us the juice we need to get outside to rake and dig, divide and plant?

Scientists tell us that our weather will continue its shift toward warmer, wetter

PREVIOUS PAGE: *The entire front rockery used to be covered with a monolithic juniper. Now the dwarf pampas grass 'Sun Stripe' is lit by the winter sun, its snowy flower spikes shown off by the burgandy fruits lingering on the bare branches of the staghorn sumac.*

LEFT: *The pleasures of the winter garden are more subtle but nonetheless dramatic. The spent flowers of* Miscanthus sinensis *nearly engulf the furry stems and burgundy fruits of the staghorn sumac.*

winters and drier summers. As watering becomes more expensive and less ecologically sound, the adage "Right plant, right place" becomes a litany. The flip-flop
sprinkler will be history, along with the lawn mower (maybe that will take a few
more years), as gardeners eliminate grass, learn the beauty of drought-tolerant
plants, use mulch, bury soaker hoses, and invest in drip systems.

Our garden aesthetics will change; in fact, they are already changing. To garden
ecologically means to garden organically, to consider how each action affects all the
life in the garden. When we recognize that perfection is not the goal (whew—why
frustrate ourselves by aiming for the impossible, anyway?), we learn to tolerate some
damage from caterpillars, because those same caterpillars will turn into beautiful
butterflies. Slightly munched leaves become the sign of a garden brimming with life
and health rather than a source of shame.

The garden as sanctuary seems to be the subject of every second book published
about gardening these days. I think we'll move past altars in the garden to the
larger meaning of "sanctuary"—gardens as personal space, whatever that means
to the individual gardener. Rather than displaying the uniform look of lawn dotted
with shrubs, each garden will be unique, a reflection of the person who lives there.
Picture a street filled with front-yard vegetable gardens, spreading street trees,
lushly planted parking strips, and mysterious gates shielding interior courtyards.
I'd like to take a walk on that street.

Best of all, plant breeders and explorers will introduce a great number of new
and exciting plants with forms and colors not yet imagined, early and late bloom,
exceptional patterns of variegation. Just think about a spring-blooming hydrangea
or a double white hellebore for a rush far jazzier than any triple shot of java.

The Zen of Path Perfect

STANDARD WISDOM TELLS US that the "bones" of the garden (walls, fences, evergreens) are the fundamentals of garden design. True, at this time of year, when the herbaceous level of the garden has all but disappeared, it is these that dominate. It seems to me, however, that clear, clean, and dry pathways are the single most important element in any rainy-climate garden.

How better to lure a gardener outside than by providing easy access to every part of the garden? If you can't reach that early-blooming viburnum without crossing a soggy lawn, you won't be near enough to get a hit of its perfume on a cold January day when you need it most. Many winter pleasures are small in stature; snowdrops, hellebores, early crocus, and *Iris reticulata* are ideal for edging pathways, giving you good reason to venture out despite the weather.

Pathways are far more than just their materials, length, or shape. You have only to navigate the stepping stones and wander the atmospheric paths of the Japanese Garden in Seattle's Washington Park Arboretum to appreciate the full effect of artful walkways. When designing your garden's circulation system, you can't go wrong if you keep three concepts in mind.

Mixing materials is fine—in fact, it makes passing through the garden much more interesting. I have gravel pathways leading around my garden, some with pavers set into the gravel and some not. Other paths consist of stones laid stepping distance apart, surrounded by groundcovers. These widen to aggregate steps and patios, which in turn nudge up against wooden decking. I'm able to go outside first thing in the morning or just before bed in whatever shoes I'm wearing (not hipwaders) to cut a branch of witch hazel or to wreak havoc on slugs. It is possible to walk to the farthest corner of my garden on an unmucky surface on any day of the year—except in late summer, when you'd need a machete to fight your way through the foliage.

Which brings me to my second point: Be sure to make paths nice and wide. Gardeners never, ever do this, despite the fact that we know better. The problem is that before the plants grow in, an adequately sized path can look as wide open as a

German autobahn. It's charming to have ornamental grasses and groundcovers tumble over the path and soften its edges—but only if you can still walk past, which is the whole point, after all. The space needed for two people to walk side by side is a good minimum width, except where you want the path to wind a bit, to narrow, to draw the garden visitor along. And that leads us to the essential conundrum.

The discrepancy at the heart of pathway design is as contradictory as human nature: we want a path that gets us where we're going as quickly and in as straightforward a manner as possible, yet at the same time we don't really want to see the end of the path when we first put foot to paver. Though we may say that efficient passage is the goal, in our hearts we prefer a puzzle, the mystery of a garden obscured. Because the function of a path is to lead us from here to there, curves, obstructions, and surprising destinations must appear uncontrived, integral to the design. So wind a pathway around a tree, hide a tea table and chair at the furthest point of a dead end, train trees or vines to meet overhead, or place scrim plants to obscure a bend in the road—but never, ever forget where you are going. And if this dictum seems confusing, you might try reading some books on Zen, and then try again. I'm still working at it myself.

Perhaps the very best thing about pathways is that they have two edges, both of which need planting. As you carve pathways into your garden, you'll have places for more plants—and isn't that always the goal?

Nose Against the Windowpane

THIS TIME OF YEAR we most often see our gardens through a pane of glass. Darkness, cold, wet, wind, or the likely combo of all four keep us stranded inside more often than we'd like. There is a lot of talk about how lucky we are to be able to garden year-round in our climate. Sure, plants will grow and maybe even bloom during the winter, but the problem is how to catch a glimpse of what is happening out there.

I'm afraid that our architecture hasn't encouraged the integration of house and garden. We've been too often influenced by tall, stately English-style houses with those lovely paned (small) windows. They make great fortresses but don't provide much access to the garden. In our climate, it makes more sense to emulate Japanese architecture, with its broad overhangs, wooden verandas, wide window walls, and courtyards. This comfortable scale and near-transparency of the house facilitates garden viewing in all seasons. Nature has long been venerated in Japan, considered something to contemplate at all times of the year, so houses there are designed to invite the garden in—and invite the viewer out.

When we remodeled a few years ago, we pushed a new addition all the way to the property line in order to wrap a bedroom, bath, and study around a small courtyard. Now this garden, a mere eight feet wide, is ringed by two glass doors and a wall of glass block; three rooms open out to its mossy stones. It was well worth the cost of a little extra foundation.

A simple way to make the garden more accessible is to light it up, placing stubby lights along pathways, and using spotlights to showcase garden art or distinctive tree trunks. Lighting gives back the parts of your garden that you choose to dramatize, so that you don't look out at a black hole every evening after five p.m.

Cutting flowers or foliage to bring indoors is a most satisfying way of getting enjoyment from the winter garden. To this end, it is worth putting in paths and stepping-stones to the farthest reaches of the garden so that you'll have a dry and paved route to get out there and forage. Believe me, you won't take the time to pull on hip waders to seek out that last rose, but if you can get outside to clip wearing your street shoes, you just might really do it.

One clever trick is to prune up trees and shrubs that grow close to the house. This not only lets in more light (we need all we can get for the next few months) but also affords a view of the garden from the house, put into perspective by a foreground of curving tree trunk or leafy branch. Rhododendron, vine maple, and other multitrunked small trees adapt well to this strategy. Such thoughtful planting and pruning help to ground the house as part of the garden, melding the line between structure and plant, between indoor and outdoor rooms.

Even on the soggiest days, we venture out along our customary routes to the mailbox or to and from the car. This is where to plant those fragrant or colorful winter bloomers such as sarcococca, with its strong scent of vanilla, witch hazel, winter-blooming iris, and daphne. Give yourself a reason to pause on your mad dash through the rain. Plant up pots of winter-flowering pansies and kale, centered with interestingly shaped deciduous trees or small evergreens, and group them on decks, porches, and steps, where you'll have the most chance of seeing them often. It doesn't take much in the winter to remind us of why we have a garden—a pot of pansies placed just outside a windowpane might be just what we need.

It's Bleak Out There

AS THE YEAR DRAWS TO A CLOSE, it is almost scary to look out the window and see the garden revealed in all its winter nakedness. The last leaves are down, and the herbaceous layer of the garden has been turned to mush by rain and frost. During the three warmer seasons of the year, the bones of the garden are disguised by the ephemeral fluff of perennials, grasses, and annuals. Now any and all design flaws stand out all too clearly. It is bleak out there.

But it doesn't need to be. Much of our native flora is evergreen, and although most of us don't have space in our garden for a stand of Douglas fir, we can take advantage of a climate that encourages plants with year-round foliage. The variety is surprising—broadleaf evergreens, variegated foliage, and needled conifers all add texture and color, provide privacy, and screen out the view of the neighbor's garbage cans all through the winter.

The small but statuesque *Magnolia grandiflora* 'Victoria' is worth planting just for its broad, glossy green leaves, backed with copper fuzz, that are ideal for use in wreaths and vases. Sweetly perfumed *Daphne odora* 'Marginata'; leather-leaved, blue-fruited *Viburnum davidii*; the little running bamboo *Sasa veitchii,* with its tawny trim; spiny *Osmanthus heterophyllus* 'Goshiki', with its gold-splotched leaves; and all the various mahonias are sturdy evergreens that help fill in that mid-layer of the garden so recently vacated by more ephemeral plantings. Add beautyberry (*Callicarpa*) for the unreal flash of its metallic lavender berries; *Pernettya mucronata*, a small evergreen with winter fruits in shades of pink, red, and white; witch hazels; and the winter-flowering cherry (*Prunus subhirtella* 'Autumnalis') for fragrant flowers, and you have yourself a winter garden of complexity and variety.

Too often, when the leaves fall, holes appear in our privacy screen, letting passersby see in or exposing unwanted views. Start at the perimeter to define the garden; more interesting than the ubiquitous row of Leyland cypresses are plantings of deciduous trees and shrubs mixed with evergreens to form a year-round tapestry of bark, leaves, flower, and fruit. Such hedgerows provide shelter and food for birds, and they're a fine place to include lanky or briefly blooming plants such as forsythia, mock orange, and lilac.

If you lack room for a thick, mixed hedgerow, consider carefully contained bamboo. A tall cedar fence with a row of black bamboo in front, pruned up to reveal the notched black canes, is a stunning, year-round screen that provides plenty of verticality, takes up very little space on the ground, and enlivens the garden with its lovely sway and rustle.

Deciduous trees that have striking bark and form can be especially effective close to the house or near walkways, to be viewed close up, or placed as a scrim so that the garden is viewed by looking past their trunks. The Japanese snowbell (*Styrax japonica*) and Japanese maples have spreading, tiered branches that create a striking silhouette, as do the multiple trunks of vine maple and *Parrotia persica*. There is nothing subtle or subdued about the cinnamon-colored, peeling bark of paperbark maple (*Acer griseum*) or the intense red of coral bark maple (*Acer palmatum* 'Sango Kaku').

Since we most often see our winter garden only on the way to or from the car, or when looking out the windows, it makes sense to concentrate our efforts on these areas. Plant fragrant little treasures along pathways or in pots by the front door; winter-blooming iris (*I. unguicularis*), hellebores, vanilla-scented sarcococca, all add the surprise of flowers and scent on bleak days. I have a sasanqua camellia espaliered by the front door that begins to open shell-pink flowers in mid-November and is often still in bloom at Christmas.

Hollies Past and Present

COME DECEMBER, I APPRECIATE A FRIEND WHO GIVES GARDEN ROOM to one of those big green holly trees. She lets me come by to cut branches for wreaths and swags, so I get the seasonal benefit without the mess, girth, and prickliness such a dense plant brings to the garden. It turns out there are less-imposing hollies that still have plenty of spiny attitude yet make fine additions to the garden, as well as supplying festive greenery for decking the halls.

The fat little hedgehog holly, also called porcupine holly (*Ilex aquifolium* 'Ferox Argentea'), is a year-round looker, perfect for anchoring the corner of a border. It is a berryless male, and slow growing—mine is only three feet tall and as wide after seven years. Each leaf is margined in warm cream, with a crinkly twirl that makes it appear as if perpetually caught in a high wind blowing in different directions. The leaves of *Ilex aquifolium* 'Golden Milkboy' have bright golden yellow centers and edges of dark green; *I. aquifolium* 'Silver Milkmaid' is stunning, with silvery white and green leaves plus an abundance of scarlet berries. Some hollies are really tiny; *Ilex* 'Rock Garden' is perfect for containers because it grows to only about a foot high.

When you choose a holly for your garden, think about its natural shape, habit, and eventual size. Hollies are, however, the most prunable of plants—except for the fact that you'd better wear thick gloves for the task—and make handsome hedges. One of the finest I've seen is an old one, where the gardener has encouraged rogue seedlings to settle in and mix with the holly to create a thick tapestry reminiscent of a tidily trimmed hedgerow. Hollies can be pruned into topiary or into bonsai, kept a tidy size in containers, or pruned in the Japanese style into rounded curves that resemble boulders. Some are deciduous, most are evergreen, some form low cushions, others grow naturally into tall, slender cones—hollies come in every plant form except for vining. And if you want berries, remember that hollies are dioecious, meaning that they come in male and female, and only the females bear fruit. You'll need one male of the same species for one or more females. The same-species part isn't a strict rule, as sometimes bees pollinate different holly species if they flower at the same time, but to be sure your hollies bear fruit, plant a same-species male nearby.

Rich in symbolism and superstition, holly has served as medicine and legend in diverse cultures for thousands of years. The pre-Christian Druids in England and Gaul brought holly boughs indoors so that woodland spirits could safely shelter from the winter cold—hence the first holiday decorations. Holly has long been associated with Christmas; an old legend claims that all holly berries were yellow until Christ's blood spilled upon them, staining them red forever. Not all holly associations are so grim—in Rome, holly wreaths were sent to newlyweds as a token of good wishes, and holly has been used as a cure for coughs, rickets, and tuberculosis. Many holly traditions have to do with decorating, no doubt because early peoples appreciated its glossy leaves and bright berries in the dark of winter, just as we do today. But beware—in early England it was thought that if you decorated with smooth holly, the wife would command the household during the coming year; if prickly holly was used, the husband would be in charge.

I found these tales of hollies past in Fred Galle's encyclopedic book *Hollies: The Genus* Ilex. If you prefer to stretch your legs while you learn, the holly collection at Washington Park Arboretum serves as a fine excuse for a winter walk. One of the oldest collections at the Arboretum, it has such a diversity of plantings that you'll never again be able to think of hollies as simply shapeless, prickly green bushes with red berries.

New Year's Resolutions

BEVERLEY NICHOLS WAS A WICKEDLY HUMOROUS ENGLISHMAN who wrote about travel, religion, cats, plants, and politics as well as publishing plays and detective mysteries. I recently reread my favorite of his books, *Merry Hall*, the saga of how Nichols rescued a forsaken country estate and garden in post–World War II England.

It being the end of one year and the beginning of the next, I was particularly struck by these words: ". . . it seems to express an important truth about the gardener's life as opposed to the lives of other people—the fact that each new year is, *ipso facto*, more startling and more rich in beauty than the one that preceded it."

If this is true, and I believe that it is, why don't we gardeners revel in our immense good fortune at choosing an enthusiasm that gives us such opportunity? Why do we so often ruin this fresh start with the same old worries?

It is so easy that it isn't even sport to list all the things gardeners worry about— aphids, black spot, rust, rot, drought, too much rain, cold, wind, apple maggots. As we start a new year, here's a list of what *not* to worry about.

First of all, color. Don't rack your brain working out waves of color, symphonies of color, color echoes, gradations of cool to warm, or any other Jekyllian or Hobhousian formula. You have multiple shades of green, silver, and golden foliage, let alone all the splashy variegated leaves available, to blend and balance out bright colors or perk up dull ones. Use them. Color, more truly than just about anything else, is in the eye of the beholder. (How else to explain what people choose to wear with what?)

Don't worry about your garden looking any certain way, or like anyone else's garden. Remember that control-freak grade-school teacher who used art class to demonstrate his or her authority? It was excruciating to try to cut, color, or paste the snowman or bat to look exactly like the sample tacked up on the blackboard. It seemed so important to get it just right. We aren't in grade school anymore, and that teacher isn't grading our work. Your garden can look however you want it to. If a garden is truly the mirror of the mind, each should be as individual and personal as our fingerprint.

Don't worry about your plants looking good all the time, because they won't. Evergreens are used as reliable, backbone plants, but even they change throughout the year. Expect needles to yellow, leaves to brown and fall off. Sure, they have most of their leaves or needles most of the time—but in the same way that, despite shedding, a dog always has fur.

Don't worry about planning a garden as you go. Dan Hinkley said it best in his Heronswood Nursery catalog back in 1998: "Never feel guilty about standing in, and staring into, your garden with a plant under your arm ready to plant. It will be the most productive time you will ever spend." And another emancipating Hinkleyism: "Follow directions, then improvise."

Perhaps most of all, don't expect to get it right the first time. There are just too many variables—soil, weather, season, plant growth. Gardening isn't fascinating because it is easy, but quite the opposite. Whether you work from plans or wander around the garden with nursery finds in hand, you will make mistakes—and you'll also stumble onto wonderful serendipitous combinations.

For the new year, I wish you copious time in the garden, and inspiring new plant finds—but most of all, a relaxed attitude, along with four new seasons of satisfaction and delight.

Warming Up Winter

RED IN THE GARDEN NEVER LOOKS BETTER THAN RIGHT NOW, in the middle of winter, when we need a little more passion in our landscape. It isn't just the perversity of human nature in most desiring the color that is scarcest, either; it's the fact that gray and brown have been the predominant garden colors for several months, and we crave the warmth and vitality of red.

There is nothing ambivalent about red; it's the color of stoplights, Christmas sweaters, valentine hearts, and fire engines. Even the names of its shades are sumptuous: crimson, carmine, scarlet, vermilion. Red is drama—think of the deep red velvet of theater curtains, Chanel lipstick, a swirl of a dark cape lined in red satin. These associations carry over to the garden, where saturated red has the longest wavelength of any color, bringing a commanding, eye-catching intensity to any mix of plantings. Unfortunately, there aren't many red flowers blooming this time of year.

How to inject red into the late-winter and early-spring landscape where its warmth is most needed? Early reds can help offset the insipidity of pastels, adding the richness and depth lacking in pretty pinks, sky blues, and all the narcissus yellows. The broad leaves of bergenia have a reddish tinge, and the new foliage of pieris and photinia comes on bright scarlet. *Camellia japonica* 'Glen 40' has double flowers of a strong, clear red; even earlier, *C. sasanqua* 'Yuletide' has rich, red blossoms accented with yellow stamens. Wallflowers (*Erysimum cheiri* 'Carmine King' and 'Vulcan') bloom early in shades of bronze and crimson, and there are a number of early red tulips ('Red Wing', 'Prominence', and 'Red Shine') from which to choose. A little later, the blood-red oriental poppy 'Beauty of Livermere' and red peonies command attention until all the reds of summer take over the garden.

As with most colors, reds tend either toward the blue tones or toward the warmer, orangey ones. Cherry and magenta, the cool reds, are more difficult to use than the hotter scarlet and sunset colors. The blue-reds always look somber, weighty, and dull to me, while the warmer reds spark the paler colors and the green around them.

Because green is the predominant summer color, and directly opposite red on the color wheel, it is easy to create eye-catching vibrancy by combining the two. It is trickier to soften reds, to blend them harmoniously into beds and borders. Think of the pleasing contrast created by twirling a spoonful of sour cream into a pot of borscht. The same cooling effect can be had by pairing red flowers with the silvers of summer—artemisia, lamb's ears, curry plant, and senecio.

To appreciate reds even under the glare of summer sunshine, choose the darker maroon or wine tones. Chocolate cosmos (*C. atrosanguineus*) are softly, deeply red; the little button flowers of *Knautia macedonica* glow like rubies over six to eight weeks of bloom time. The bright scarlet of the famous 'Bishop of Llandaff' dahlia is mellowed by its own dusky foliage. Even brazen red can be subtle. By using plants with a number of small blossoms, such as *Potentilla* 'Gibson's Scarlet' and *Crocosmia* 'Lucifer', you can create a haze of red, an impression of red. If your sensibilities are as bold as red itself, you can celebrate all the fire that red brings to a garden by growing dahlias such as 'Summer Night' or 'Arabian Night', red cannas, velvety red snapdragons, and classic red roses such as 'Dusky Maiden' and 'Mr. Lincoln', or the shrubby red rugosas.

However clever we are in our choices and combinations, by the time most red flowers bloom in midsummer, we're satiated with all the hot colors. Despite our best efforts, red can seem bossy and obvious. But red comes into its own again in autumn, glinting in the slanted light, glowing beneath darkening skies. That is when the vibrant reds of maples, burning bush (*Euonymus alata*), rose hips, and Japanese blood grass are once again welcome garden sights.

Now in Bloom: November

1
Crimson flag
(Schizostylis coccinea)

The genus name of this South African native sounds like a sneeze. It is nearly evergreen, and very easy to grow, tolerating drought or damp soil, full sun or light shade. The foliage is grasslike, growing about a foot high, and the plant needs dividing every year or two in early spring. I use the long-lasting flowers in arrangements from late September through the end of the year. But it is in November when very little else is left in bloom that crimson flag is most welcome, as its open, pale pink, white, or rosy pink flowers belie their delicate look to continue to bloom until almost Christmas.

3
Dwarf burning bush
(Euonymus alatus 'Compacta')

Although 'Compacta' is
the dwarf form, it still grows as
tall as ten feet. Burning bush is so
hardy and dependable that you'll
see it used in median strips and other
municipal plantings. This is no reason
to slight it, for its corky bark and
spreading, twiggy shape have presence
in the landscape year-round. Tolerant
of dry soil, preferring sun but
tolerating light shade, this garden
workhorse moves center stage in
November for a searing display of
blazingly red autumn color.

2
Beautyberry
(Callicarpa bodonieri var.
giraldii 'Profusion')

In summer this bushy
deciduous shrub, with its
tapered bronze-green leaves
and pale pink flowers, disappears
into the border; but when
the leaves start to fall in autumn,
glowing bunches of fruit
line the branches, looking like
tiny, intensely lavender
beads glossed with a
metallic sheen.

Nerine bowdenii

The recurved, wavy-edged pink blossoms of this very late bloomer
resemble finely cut lilies. Nerines are bulbous perennials that like heat and
well-drained soil and should be well mulched in winter. They start to flower
just as the weather cools and the days shorten, reminding us of summer
and looking impossibly exotic in the November garden.

4

Now in Bloom: December

1

Sweet box
(Sarcococca humilis)

Sweet box gets its common name from the overwhelmingly sweet, vanilla-like fragrance that its tiny flowers waft through the winter garden. Tapered, glossy evergreen leaves nearly hide the white flowers, but you'll know when they start to open in mid- to late December by the outpouring of perfume. Plant this dwarf (eighteen inches to two feet) shrub near the front porch or walkway to take full advantage not only of its scent but also of its handsome evergreen foliage and shiny blue-black berries.

2

Strawberry tree
(Arbutus unedo)

Although you'd never know it to look at its graceful curves and flashy fruits, this is a workhorse of a small tree. Strawberry tree puts on its best display at the darkest time of the year, right when the garden most needs some fireworks. An evergreen with good-looking, rusty, rough bark (it is related to the madrone), it requires sun and does best in a somewhat sheltered site. Late in the year, the little white flowers start to bloom, and at the same time the plump, warty fruits that earn it its common name start to color up to a rich red. Startlingly, on one branch you'll find both flowers and fruits in shades from yellow through orange to brilliant scarlet. Cut a branch, stick it into a vase with a metallic glaze, and you'll have an entire arrangement of fruits, leaves, and flowers.

3
False holly
(*Osmanthus heterophyllus* 'Goshiki')

Like the true hollies,
false holly bears the classic
sharp-toothed, spiny leaves. But this
plant is small (to three and a half feet),
tidy, rounded, and easy to grow in a
pot or in the landscape, where its
splashed-with-yellow glossy leaves
look good year-round, and are
especially flashy in the spring when
the new foliage comes on a bright
salmon color. I've grown mine
in a big terra-cotta pot for years,
strung with white Christmas
lights in winter and underplanted
with annuals in summer.

4
Senecio greyi

This shrub (which has the
unwieldy new name of *Brachyglottis*
Dunedin Group 'Sunshine' but is still
sold under the old, more familiar name)
is one of the most useful plants in my
garden. It keeps its looks outdoors year-
round, and in indoor arrangements it
lasts for weeks. Its stiff, curving stems
grow into a four-feet-high, six-feet-wide
mound. The gray-green leaves trimmed
in silver light up the winter garden and
serve as a great backdrop to the brighter
colors of spring and summer. The flowers are little bright yellow daisies, which
I always cut off, as they seem to take
away from the elegance of the
rest of the shrub.

4

2

Now in Bloom: January

1
Black mondo grass
(Ophiopogon planiscapus '*Nigrescens')*

This dramatic little plant creeps very, very slowly, which is why it is expensive to buy. But it is well worth the price for its sleek, glossy, year-round good looks; its diminutive size (to eight inches high); and the deep ebony color of its blades. Although the newer foliage is a dark green, it quickly turns the closest to a true black of any of the foliage plants. Black mondo grass is very effective in containers, edging walkways, or alongside stone or water.

2
Witch hazel
(Hamamelis spp.)

Witch hazels are the pride of the winter garden, with their spidery blossoms and sweetly astringent fragrance just when we need it most during the dark days of January. I grow *Hamamelis* x *intermedia* 'Pallida' because it is one of the earliest-flowering of the witch hazels, its bright yellow blossoms opening soon after Christmas and perfuming the chilly air for nearly a month. 'Arnold's Promise' has larger yellow flowers but blooms a month later, 'Jelena' has copper-colored flowers, and 'Diane' has dark red blooms that age to an orangey red. The leaves that clothe the widely spreading branches are unremarkable in summertime, but they look their best in autumn as they take on bold tints of gold, orange, and scarlet.

3

3
Viburnum davidii

Many gardeners scorn this shrub because of its overuse in municipal plantings, but there is a good reason it shows up so often in tough locations. Its ribbed, leathery leaves are handsome in all seasons, it thrives in sun or partial shade and nearly any kind of soil, and its low (to three feet), mounded habit is useful in many garden situations. Though the spring flowers—pink buds opening to white clusters—aren't particularly showy, they are followed by glowingly blue metallic berries set off by red stems, which look smashing all fall and winter set against the green of the leaves.

4
Garrya × *issaquahensis* **'Pat Ballard'**

This is my favorite evergreen shrub. Just as the garden becomes its midwinter drabbest, the *Garrya* unfurls long, dangling catkins of pearly purple-gray that dazzle against the leathery green leaves and red stems. I've planted mine near the top of a hillside rockery, where I can admire the jewel-like catkins that bedeck the plant all through the winter. It thrives in full sun or partial shade and needs well-drained soil. Female plants have purple-brown berries but shorter catkins, so it is worth searching out a male plant for catkins that can drip twelve dramatic inches long.

4

Now in Bloom: February

1
Lenten rose
(*Helleborus orientalis*)

2
Donkey tail spurge
(*Euphorbia myrsinites*)

This hellebore is a sturdy perennial that blooms from January into March, with freckled flowers in shades from cream through yellow, and pink to dark purple. Handsome, splayed leaves follow the blooms, lasting until the flower buds emerge from the ground the following winter. Moist, well-drained soil and partial shade assure that these winter-blooming evergreens will persist to form larger colonies each year.

I use this old-fashioned plant in several locations: sprawling between yellow daffodils, where its lime-green flowers are shown off to perfection, and dangling down the rockery, over retaining walls, and down the sides of pots. The bright new green of its flowers contrasts beautifully with springtime pastels, as well as with its own pale blue-green foliage, which persists through the seasons. Its semi-succulent look (it appears to be more sedum than euphorbia) makes it clear that this spurge prefers sun and dry conditions.

4

3
Iris reticulata

Gardeners know spring will
return when they see *Iris reticulata,* one
of the earliest bulbs, blooming with the
crocuses. Only about six inches high,
these charmers resemble the larger
Dutch irises, with narrow blue-green
spears of foliage and the sweet scent of
violets. Planting them in bunches adds
impact to their diminutive size. They
are ideal for pots, among groundcovers
(where they need protection from
slugs), or in the rock garden.
'Harmony' has purple-blue falls marked
in yellow; 'Cantab' is pale blue; and
'J.S. Dijt' is a deep reddish purple.
Plant the tiny bulbs in autumn in full
sun and well-drained soil.

4
Crocus spp.

Tiny species crocuses open
their cup-shaped flowers to the
winter sunshine, blooming dependably
early no matter what the weather. Plant
handfuls of little crocus bulbs in the
autumn, and you'll be rewarded with
larger and larger colonies of crocus over
the years. Tuck crocuses and
Iris reticulata into a swath of the
groundcover *Lamium maculatum*
'White Nancy', which will
grow up and hide the dying
bulb foliage later
in the spring.

Recommended Reading

The titles below, many mentioned or quoted in these pages, are the books that have most influenced my thoughts about gardens, that I return to most often for instruction or for inspiration. Mostly I just remain appreciative that they exist.

Alexander, Christopher, with Sara Ishikawa and Murray Silverstein. *A Pattern Language*. Oxford: Oxford University Press, 1977.

Allen, Christine. *Roses for the Pacific Northwest*. Hatfield: Steller Press, 1999.

Anderton, Stephan. *Rejuvenating a Garden*. San Francisco: Soma Books, 1999.

Bickell, Christopher. *The American Horticulture Society A–Z Encyclopedia of Garden Plants*. New York: DK Publishing, Inc., 1997.

Chatto, Beth. *Beth Chatto's Gravel Garden: Drought Resistant Planting Through the Year*. New York: Viking Press, 2000.

Chatto, Beth, and Lloyd Chatto. *Dear Friend and Gardener: Letters on Life and Gardening*. London: Frances Lincoln Ltd., 1998.

Chatto, Beth, et al. *The Damp Garden*. London: J.M. Dent and Sons, 1983.

Conran, Terence and Dan Pearson. *The Essential Garden Book: Getting Back to Basics*. Minn.: 3 Rivers Press, 1998.

Heronswood Nursery Catalog. Kingston, Wash.

Link, Russell. *Landscaping for Wildlife in the Pacific Northwest*. Seattle: University of Washington Press, 1999.

McNeilan, Jan and Ray McNeilan. *The Pacific Northwest Gardener's Book of Lists*. Dallas: Taylor Publishing, 1997.

Mitchell, Henry. *The Essential Earthman: Henry Mitchell on Gardening.* Bloomington: Indiana University Press, 1981.

Nichols, Beverly. *Merry Hall.* Portland, Ore.: Timber Press, 1998.

Sarton, May. *The House by the Sea.* W.W. New York: Norton & Co., 1977.

————. *Journal of Solitude.* W.W. New York: Norton & Co., 1973.

————. *Plant Dreaming Deep.* W.W. New York: Norton & Co., 1968.

Brenzel, Kathleen N. *Sunset Western Garden Book.* Menlo Park: Sunset Pub. Corp., 2001.

White, Katharine S. *Onward and Upward in the Garden.* New York: Farrar, Straus, Giroux, 1979.

Also mentioned in the pages of this book:

D'Amato, Peter. *The Savage Garden.* Berkeley: Ten Speed Press, 1998.

Galle, Fred. *Hollies: The Genus Ilex.* Portland, Ore.: Timber Press, 1997.

Gertley, Jan, and Michael Gertley. *The Art of the Kitchen Garden.* Newton, Conn.: Taunton Press, 1999.

Langevin, Don. *World Class Pumpkins.* New York: Annedawn Publishing, 1993.

Schenk, George. *Moss Gardening: Including Lichens, Liverworts and other Miniatures.* Portland, Ore.: Timber Press, 1997.

Jones, Louisa. *The Art of French Vegetable Gardening.* New York: Artisan Press, 1995.

Turnball, Cass. *The Complete Guide to Landscape Design, Renovation and Maintenance.* Cincinnati: F & W Publications, 1991

Index

R-S

About the Author

Valerie Easton has managed the Miller Library at the Center for Urban Horticulture at the University of Washington since 1985. She has contributed articles to *Gardens Illustrated*, *Horticulture*, *The Gardener*, *Fine Gardening*, and *Pacific Horticulture*, among others, and is co-author of *Artists in Their Gardens* (Sasquatch Books, 2000). Her own garden has been featured in print in *Better Homes and Gardens* and *Fine Gardening* and on television on *The Victory Garden* and *Grow It!* Since 1997 she has written the weekly column "Plant Life" in the *Pacific Northwest* magazine of the *Seattle Times*. A lifelong Seattle resident, she retreats to Guemes Island as often as she can during the summer.